ENCYCLOPEDIA OF The Animal Kingdom

ENCYCLOPEDIA OF The

Animal Kingdom

MAURICE AND ROBERT
BURTON

CRESCENT
BOOKS

Contents

Copyright ©1968, 1969, 1970, 1976 Phoebus Publishing
Company/BPC Publishing Ltd
Copyright ©1988 Macdonald & Co (Publishers) Ltd

This compilation first published 1976.
Reprinted 1977, 1984
Reprinted 1988 by Macdonald & Co (Publishers) Ltd
under the Black Cat imprint
Macdonald & Co (Publishers) Ltd,
3rd Floor, Greater London House,
Hampstead Road, London NW1 7QX

a member of Maxwell Pergamon Publishing Corporation plc

This book is adapted from Purnell's 'Encyclopedia of
Animal Life'.
This 1988 edition published by
Crescent Books, distributed by
Crown Publishers, Inc.,
225 Park Avenue South
New York, New York 10003

ISBN 0–517–44801–7

h g f e d c b

Printed in Czechoslovakia

Introduction

The word 'animal' is often equated with mammals in everyday usage, but the Animal Kingdom includes a wide range of organisms from the single-celled protozoans to human beings. This being so, it is worth re-stating the characteristics that distinguish animals from plants: animals cannot manufacture their own food, they have a sensitivity that is usually operative through special sense organs (or organelles, i.e. parts of a cell), are capable of locomotion and have no cellulose cell-walls.

It is usually stated that there are a million species of animals. More correctly, this should be at least a million known species. By 'known' is meant species that have been given a scientific name and of which a description has been published in a recognized scientific journal. It is important to make this distinction because the truth is that there are not enough zoologists classifying animals to keep pace with the collection of new forms. In addition there must be large numbers of species yet to be discovered, and estimates of the true number of animal species living today vary between three and ten million.

The great majority of the million usually referred to are insects, of which there are at least 750,000. If we ever reach the point where all the species of insects have been described and named the total will probably be nearer three million.

There must be few, if any, large animals yet to be discovered. Among mammals, small species are occasionally discovered, especially mice, shrews and bats. An interesting example from the last of these is Brandt's bat (*Myotis brandtii*), a species that was masked by another species. The whiskered bat (*Myotis mystacinus*) has been

known for a long time but in the last few years it has been realized that many bats we have been calling whiskered bats really belong to a different species and have been named Brandt's bat. The distinguishing feature of Brandt's bat lies in the shape and size of the premolar teeth.

Most of the species yet to be discovered, apart from insects, must comprise those of microscopic size, particularly Protozoa, as well as the parasitic species, such as the various kinds of so-called worms, like the threadworms and flatworms. There must also be a very large number of mites yet to be identified and described. Thus we have the anomaly that the most familiar animals, including those of large bulk and those upon which the human economy is based because they represent food, beasts of burden or sources of supply of raw materials, represent only a small minority in terms of numbers of species and populations.

The classification of the Animal Kingdom is based on an evolutionary principle. The first animals to appear on earth must have been single-celled and therefore of minute size. They are grouped in the phylum Protozoa (Greek *Protos*=first, *zoon*=animal) and this phylum is usually taken to represent a subkingdom.

How the Protozoa gave rise to the rest of the Animal Kingdom is still a matter for speculation. The only reasonable assumption is that in the course of evolution some protozoans came to live together in colonies and that in time a differentiation of the constituent cells into tissues came about, which gave rise to the main bulk of the Animal Kingdom – namely the multicellular animals, regarded as forming the subkingdom Metazoa (Greek *meta*=after).

There is, however, an aberrant offshoot represented by the sponges and for convenience these are placed in a third subkingdom, the Parazoa (Greek *para*=beside). The course of events that led from the early Protozoa to the Parazoa is as much an unresolved problem as that which led from the Protozoa to the Metazoa. Earlier in the century it was thought that certain simple animals might help bridge the second of these gaps and they were named the Mesozoa (Greek *mesos*=middle) but there is now the strong suspicion that these are merely degenerate flatworms.

As well as being unresolved problems, the genesis of the Parazoa and Metazoa from the Protozoa belongs more to the field of academic zoology. The practical result is that we have the three subkingdoms of which the largest and most important is the Metazoa, and this is divided into a large number of phyla (Greek *phylon*=race or tribe), grouped according to one outstanding feature of their anatomy into the invertebrates and the vertebrates, according to whether they lack or possess a backbone.

To an extent this last subdivision is the result of history rather than logic. In the early 19th century it became apparent that some animals had a backbone, others lacked this supporting axis of bones, and the names 'invertebrates' and 'vertebrates' came into general use. Apart from this very obvious difference, the two groups showed other fairly consistent differences. Thus, in the invertebrates the main nerve cord is ventral, in the vertebrates it is dorsal, and the main blood vessel is dorsal and ventral respectively. In effect, therefore, a vertebrate is an invertebrate turned upside-

down, and for many years there was much fruitless discussion about how the vertebrates evolved from the invertebrates. Then, in the closing years of the 19th century and the early years of the present century, what are apparently missing links between the two were discovered. These will be discussed later.

The most conspicuous thing about the division of the Animal Kingdom into invertebrates and vertebrates is that this division is hopelessly illogical. First, both the subkingdom Protozoa and the subkingdom Parazoa are normally embraced in the general term 'invertebrates'. Secondly, whereas the vertebrates include only one phylum, the Chordata, the invertebrates comprise nearly a score of phyla of most diverse characteristics. Paradoxically, this illogical subdivision has proved to be a great convenience for everyday purposes. Moreover, it is a convenience to speak of lower invertebrates and higher invertebrates, although where the line between these two should be drawn defies definition. Usually it denotes invertebrates lower in the scale than the phylum Arthropoda (insects, crustaceans and spiders).

The present-day classification of animals emerged after a series of tentative attempts on the part of a number of authors to arrange animals in orderly groups, but the real breakthrough came with the accept-ance of Darwin's theory of natural selection and involved an arrangement along evolutionary lines. The theory of evolution itself had been mooted long before Darwin's days, but his theory of how species arose gave the maximum publicity to an idea that previously had interested only a select few scholars.

Arrangement on an evolutionary basis meant that the classification was based mainly on the study of comparative anatomy. In practice, this meant putting the simplest, least organized animals at the bottom of the scale and the most highly organized at the top. The rest were arranged intermediately according to the degree of organization of their bodily structures.

While these events were proceeding, from the mid-eighteenth to the mid-nineteenth century approximately, the study of palaeontology was born and was developing. One upshot of this was that in time it became possible to arrange the sequence of rocks composing the earth's crust and their contained fossils according to their age. It was then seen that the times when the various groups of animals came into being corresponded closely with their order in the classification table. Thus, the earliest fossils were of simple, lowly animals, while the latest were of birds and mammals which include the most highly organized. The others arose intermediately where one would expect them to be, judging by study of their anatomy.

The word 'palaeontology' is from the Greek meaning 'ancient discourse', but anyone with only a slight knowledge of the language might be forgiven for translating it as 'ancient bones', because that is the main contribution of this science. In other words, the fossils it deals with are mainly the hard parts of animal bodies, the soft tissues having almost invariably been lost. At best, they leave impressions only. The marvel is that anything at all survives burial for millions, even hundreds of millions, of years. Perhaps even more astonishing is the way, by comparing ancient remains with living animals, the palaeontologist has so often been able to deduce and reconstruct the soft parts.

Nevertheless, it is this virtual lack of knowledge of soft tissues that has almost certainly left us with the major gaps in our knowledge of the evolution of the Animal Kingdom as a whole. Thus, the Protozoa are for the most part without hard skeletons, and our knowledge of their past history rests upon the preserved remains of the few that possessed a skeleton. If those Protozoa that combined to live in groups and formed the ancestors of Metazoa had no skeletons – and this is the most likely course of events – it is not surprising there should be the unbridgeable gap between the two groups. Similarly, the animals now living which appear to represent the ancestral vertebrates, such as the acorn worms, sea-squirts and lancelet, are all without hard parts. So there are no satisfactory fossils to guide us and the bridge between invertebrates and vertebrates becomes a matter for speculation, or, to be honest about it, no more than guesswork, however inspired this guesswork may be.

What palaeontology does contribute, which the study of living animals never could, is the knowledge that whole groups of animals have come into being and have died out leaving no surviving representatives. The trilobites, relatives of present-day crustaceans (crabs, lobsters), are a good example. These were like large woodlice, lived in the sea, and 500 million years ago were the most numerous, most varied, the dominant and most highly-organized animals. In another hundred million years they had died out. Palaeontology has also revealed that among species, genera and families there can be detected something approaching a life-span. Some groups appear, rapidly proliferate, become highly successful, diversify and as rapidly die out. 'Rapidly', in this context, means in the course of no more than tens of millions of years. At the other extreme are the plodders, groups that are markedly uniform in structure, not numerous, yet continue on from an early age, with survivors today, over a period of time measured in hundreds of millions of years. These are the groups that supply the living fossils.

There is, perhaps, a tendency at times to envisage animal evolution as a slow, steady progression in an orderly sequence. This is largely because of the vast periods of time involved that almost baffle the imagination. Were it possible to compress the 3–4 thousand million years that have elapsed since life appeared on earth, and present it as a moving picture, the appearance would be very different. It would be more like a stream with here a slow current, there a fast one, with stagnant backwaters in some places, whirlpools that arise and die out, eddies that go backwards and other diversities that make a moving, natural body of water so dynamic.

Like a river, also, the stream of life would be three-dimensional, something virtually impossible to portray adequately in pictorial or book form. There is another obstacle to presenting in adequate form a full picture of the progression of animal life through the vast ages and that is the immense number of animal species that have appeared on the scene, to play their part, die out and be replaced by others, or be transmuted by slow degrees into other species. Merely to enumerate those living today, variously estimated at anything up to ten million species, of which only something like a million have been named and described, would require a massive volume on its own. If it were possible to add to these the species that have existed in the past and have died out the total would be even more formidable.

The most that can be done, and this is the purpose of this volume, is to give a scanty skeleton in pictorial and textual form of the living members of this vast assemblage of organisms we refer to when we speak of The Animal Kingdom.

In the following pages, a selection of the known animals living today are set forth, arranged in sections, representing the lower

invertebrates, the higher invertebrates and the vertebrates, the latter comprising four sections, the fishes, the amphibians and reptiles, the birds and the mammals. All the phyla are illustrated with rare exceptions, which include some small, numerically inferior invertebrate phyla of obscure

relationships, difficult to illustrate adequately, that add little to the general story. When we come to the phylum Chordata, which comprises mainly the subphylum Vertebrata, representing the more advanced and, generally, the more familiar animals, it is possible to include representatives of classes and orders.

This alone is something of an achievement, and the effect is to provide within two covers a brief outline of the scope of the Animal Kingdom, its components arranged in their evolutionary sequence, so far as we know it.

Before treating each of our six sections in turn, there is another point that should be made. In the pages that follow there will be seen a spectacular array of colours as well as a wide diversity of form. The Animal Kingdom, no less than the plant world, sparkles with colour and has even greater diversity than all the plants put together.

By contrast, the world of fossils appears drab, except where a succession of artists, under the guidance of experts, but also using their imagination, have portrayed extinct animals in colour. Sometimes a fossil is discovered showing traces of original coloration, though this is rare. Even those artists who are courageous enough to add colour to their reconstructions do so hesitantly for fear they may be wrong and therefore misleading people.

It is a reasonable guess that brilliant colours always have occurred in animals, almost from the beginning of time. It is not the same with plants because they were green or brown until flowering plants evolved, which was about a hundred million years ago. It is impossible to conceive how much colour there has been in the world during the countless years in which the animal kingdom, as we know it today in its living form, was evolving.

The Lower Invertebrates

The invertebrates, or animals without backbones, include 21 phyla, all but one of which can be reasonably referred to as lower invertebrates, the exception being the phylum Arthropoda. The number of living species of lower invertebrates so far named and described is nearly a quarter of a million, but the actual number yet to be described must far exceed this. For example, the lower invertebrates include many small to minute parasitic worms and these have by no means been exhaustively studied. Probably every species in the animal kingdom is parasitized by several different kinds, and if this surmise is correct, it would mean that species of parasitic worms alone are numbered by the million instead of the 10,000 or so described to date.

The lower invertebrates are more diverse in form and structure than any other section of the animal kingdom. Their remains give us the earliest fossils known. These two facts taken together suggest that these animals represent early 'experimentation' in evolution, before the main pattern had emerged that would lead to the production of the higher animals. Looking at the various types they comprise it is as if attempts had been made to try this or that shape, this or that way of life, this or that type of nervous system and so forth.

Animal feeding and digestion is of various types, but in the main the digestive apparatus must follow fairly orthodox lines. The main differences between the various lower invertebrates lie in their shapes and in the development of the nervous system and the sense organs.

In the Protozoa, the single-celled animals, all the life processes take place within the confines of a single cell. The animals are sensitive but have no nerves, therefore no brain, and the special sense-organs do not go much beyond an eye-spot, a granule of pigment reacting to light, the simplest forerunner of an eye. In the next group, the Parazoa or sponges, there is a slight sensitivity but at best only scattered and very simple nerve-cells, and no sense-organs. In the Cnidaria, the anemones, jellyfishes and corals, the body is controlled by a simple network of nerve-cells and there may be, in rare instances, eye-spots and organs of balance, known as statocysts, although these are found only in those Cnidaria, for example jellyfishes, that move about.

The remaining lower invertebrates have nerves. In some there is even a ganglion, a knot of nerve-cells foreshadowing the brain, and more or less of special sense-organs. In a few, such as the squid and octopuses, the brain is of a fairly high order and the eyes are well developed, quite unlike anything found in other molluscs. Taken as a whole, however, the lower invertebrates are somewhat senseless animals – in more than one meaning of the term.

Most animals are what is know as bilaterally symmetrical. That is, if a line is drawn down the long axis of the body the half on one side is the mirror image of the other half. Many of the lower invertebrates are radially symmetrical, the body plan being apparently based on the spokes of a wheel, as in sea-anemones, jellyfishes and starfishes. The bilateral symmetry is the only shape permitting the segmentation leading to a higher organisation of structure. Segmentation can readily be seen in the earthworm. Its body is divided into rings, or segments. This permits the elaboration of an efficient muscle system, and thus more controlled and co-ordinated movements, especially for locomotion.

The classification of the lower invertebrates is as follows:

Phylum Protozoa	50,000 species
Phylum Mesozoa (possibly degenerate flatworms)	50 species
Phylum Parazoa (sponges)	2,500 species
Phylum Cnidaria (sea-anemones, corals, jellyfishes)	9,600 species
Phylum Ctenophora (comb-jellies)	80 species
Phylum Platyhelminthes (flatworms)	13,000 species
Phylum Nemertina (ribbonworms)	750 species
Phylum Aschelminthes (rotifers, small worms)	12,500 species
Phylum Acanthocephala (thorny-headed worms)	650 species
Phylum Entoprocta	60 species
Phylum Bryozoa or Polyzoa (moss animals)	4,000 species
Phylum Phoronida (horseshoe worms)	15 species
Phylum Brachiopoda (lampshells)	260 species
Phylum Mollusca (snails, bivalves, octopus, etc.)	128,000 species
Phylum Sipunculoidea (peanut worms)	250 species
Phylum Echiuroidea (echiuroid worms)	150 species
Phylum Annelida (ringed worms)	8,700 species
Phylum Chaetognatha (arrow-worms)	50 species
Phylum Pogonophora	100 species
Phylum Echinodermata (starfish, sea-urchin, etc.)	44,066 species

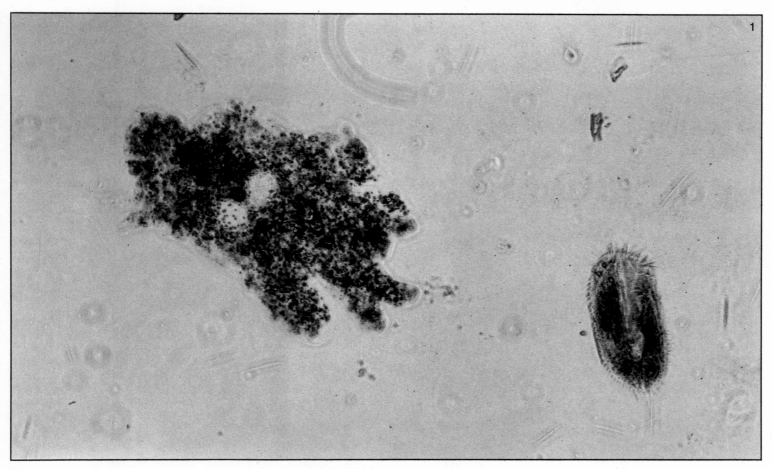

Amoeba

Amoebae form a group of the single-celled organisms called Protozoa. Protozoa means 'first animals'. These organisms have affinities with plants – some of them photosynthesise.

Like any cell the amoeba consists basically of an envelope containing the substance protoplasm. In the middle of the cell, surrounded by the protoplasm, is the nucleus, a body which can be thought of as a blueprint for the organisation of the cell's activities. If an amoeba is cut in two the half with the nucleus may survive and reproduce; the other moves around for a while but cannot digest its food, and when its reserves are gone it dies.

The protoplasm is not, as was once thought, a jelly; it has a very complicated structure, and consists of a cytoplasm divided into a granular endoplasm and at the ends of the pseudopodia, and elsewhere under the surface, a clearer layer known as ectoplasm.

Many amoebae

The name amoeba is applied not only to members of the genus *Amoeba* but to a range of different types of Protozoa with pseudopodia (see below) living in the sea, in fresh water, in damp soil and in the bodies of larger animals. They include some with shells, like *Arcella*, and also the half-dozen species that live in the human mouth and digestive system, one of which is the cause of amoebic dysentery *(Entamoeba)*. Some

amoebae contain many nuclei, among them the giant *Chaos carolinensis*, which may measure up to $\frac{1}{5}$ in.

Amoeba proteus, the textbook amoeba, measuring about $\frac{1}{50}$ in., is just visible to the naked eye and may be found in fairly still fresh water. It moves about by extending a finger of protoplasm, called a pseudopodium ('false foot'). As the pseudopodium enlarges, the cell contents – protoplasm and nucleus – flow into it, while the rest of the cell contracts behind. Though it has no definite shape, the amoeba is not a shapeless sac of protoplasm, for it has a permanent hind end and forms its pseudopodium in a characteristic pattern according to the species.

Feeding

The amoeba feeds mainly on other Protozoa and also small rotifers. It does so by 'flowing' around them, the protoplasm completely surrounding the food to enclose it in a 'food vacuole' containing fluid in which the prey was swimming. Digestion is a similar process to that occurring in many other organisms: digestive juices are secreted into the food vacuole and the digestible parts are broken down and absorbed. The rest is merely left behind as the amoeba moves along.

This process is known as phagocytosis, from the Greek 'eating by cells'. In a similar process called pinocytosis, or 'drinking by cells', channels are formed from the cell surface, leading into the cell. Fluid is drawn into the channels and from their tips vacuoles are pinched off. The fluid is then absorbed into the protoplasm in the same way as the digested contents of the food vacuoles. This is a method of absorbing fluids in bulk into the cell.

1 *The well known one-celled animal, amoeba, showing large water excreting vacuoles. This picture includes a Stylonychian which belongs to another, ciliated, group of protozoans. (Magnified 150 times.)*

Water is continually passing in through the cell membrane as well as being brought in by phagocytosis and pinocytosis. Excess is pumped out by contractile vacuoles which fill with water and then collapse, discharging the water to the outside.

Reproduction

The amoeba reproduces itself by dividing into two equal parts, a process known as binary fission and taking less than an hour. It begins with the amoeba becoming spherical. The nucleus divides into two. The two halves move apart and the cell then splits down the middle.

Some species of amoebae can reproduce in a different manner. The nucleus divides into hundreds of small ones and each becomes surrounded by a little cytoplasm and a tough wall – all within the original cell. The resulting 'cysts' can survive if the water dries up and can be dispersed to found new populations. Larger cysts may be formed without reproduction taking place, when the whole cell surrounds itself with a thick wall. Though some amoebae reproduce sexually, *Amoeba proteus* has never been seen to do so.

Pushing or pulling?

The story of the amoeba illustrates not only the advances made in the last few decades in the techniques of microscopy but also

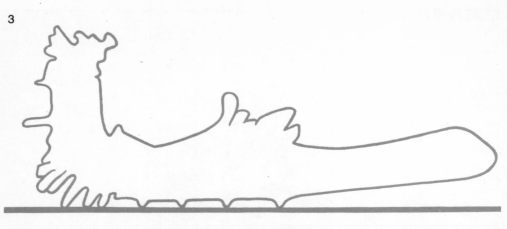

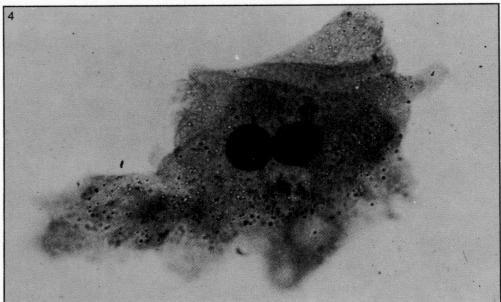

2 *Amoeboid movement – showing pseudopodia in action, from above.*
3 *Diagram of modern microscope's side view of amoeba moving to the right on small protoplasmic pegs with pseudopodium, or false-foot, extended.*
4 *Amoeba with nucleus, which controls cell, divided, prior to cell splitting into two.*
5 *Special light phase contrast microscope gives this beautiful view of amoeba showing food in vacuoles.*

the difficulties involved in research.

Years ago microscopists could watch amoeba only from above in the usual manner of looking at very small objects. From this angle one could see the pseudopodia advancing over the surface of the microscope slide and apparently in contact with it. In recent times a technique has been devised for watching it from the side and a new detail has come to light. In fact, when each pseudopodium moves forward it is supported by an extremely small peg of protoplasm which remains attached to the ground at one spot while the rest of the animal, raised just above the ground, advances over it. Finally, the pseudopodium is withdrawn and reincorporated into the body of the amoeba.

A number of theories of 'amoeboid movement' have been proposed over the last 20 years but its mechanism is still not thoroughly understood. One can see, under the higher powers of the microscope, the protoplasm streaming forwards along the centre of the pseudopodium and moving out to the sides at the tip in what has been descriptively named the 'fountain zone', and there acquiring a firmer consistency. At the same time the reverse change occurs at the 'tail', where the protoplasm resumes its forward flow.

What is still in doubt is whether the advancing protoplasm is being pushed forward from behind, like toothpaste in its tube, or pulled by changes in the proteins in the fountain zone. The problem is by no means trivial, for some of our own cells move in an amoeboid manner and its solution in terms of the behaviour of protein molecules could cast light on one of the basic properties of protoplasm.

phylum	**Protozoa**
class	**Sarcodina**
order	**Amoebida**

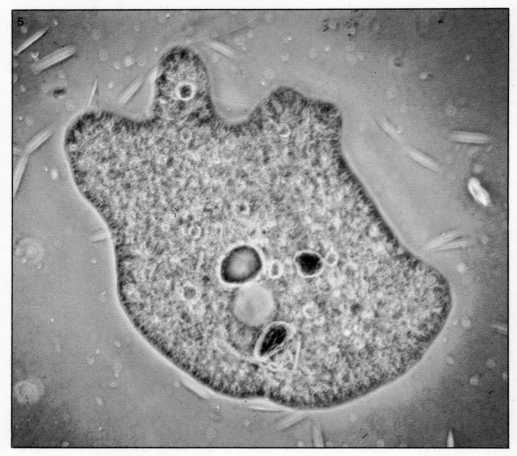

Bath sponge

The sponge seen in the bathroom is the fibrous skeleton of one of the lower forms of animal life. In life the gaps in the skeleton are filled with a yellowish flesh, the whole being covered with a dark purple skin. A sponge has no sense-organs and few specialized organs apart from chambers containing collared cells. At best there are a few scattered muscle cells and very simple nerve cells.

Although there are nearly 3,000 species of sponges, the most familiar is the group of half a dozen species of horny sponges known scientifically as

Spongia. On the market, bath sponges are given common names, such as fine turkey, brown turkey, honeycomb for Mediterranean sponges, and wool, velvet, reef, yellow and grass for Bahamas sponges. These names express mainly the varying textures of the fibres. There are many other names, but the fine turkey and the honeycomb are those most often seen for sale. They are found in warm seas only, at depths down to 600 ft. They are most numerous in the Mediterranean, particularly the eastern half, and in the Bahamas and Florida. Elsewhere, in tropical and sub-tropical waters, sponges are found of similar type but less durable or

pleasing texture, although in places, as in south-east Asia, there may be limited fisheries supplying a local market.

Sedentary habit

A sponge normally draws all it needs from the sea without departing from the spot on which the larva settled. The beating of the protoplasmic whips, or flagella, of its collared cells, which are grouped in rounded chambers in the network of canals running through the body, draws in currents of water. These enter through many minute pores in the skin. Having passed through these chambers the water is driven towards the surface and expelled with moderate force, through crater-like vents. In its course

▽ *Bath sponge growing in natural surroundings. They are found only in warm seas at depths down to 600 ft.*

and, when ripe, they burst from their capsule into the water canals and escape by the vents into the sea. They swim around until near another sponge and are drawn in by the water current entering through its pores. Inside, they travel through the canals until they meet an ovum, which one of them fertilises.

The ovum, once fertilised, begins to divide repeatedly to form an oval mass of cells, the embryo. Some of these put out flagella, and as they beat together, they cause the embryo to rotate. This breaks its capsule, and the embryo, now a free-swimming larva, swims out through one of the vents. For the next 24 hours it continues swimming in a spiral motion, with its flagella. Then the flagella begin to weaken, the larva sinks to the sea-bed, and is transformed into a small platelet of tissue, the size of a pin head. This is a new sponge.

Enemies
Sponges are virtually without enemies and subject to only one known disease. This is a fungal disease which was unknown until 1938, when it attacked sponges in the Bahamas and adjacent seas, almost wiping them out.

Sponge farming by cuttings
From the moment that the larva changes into the pinhead-sized sponge to the time this has grown large enough to be put on the market, 7 years must elapse. Then the pinhead would have grown to a purple-skinned sponge the size of a man's two fists. This gives us an idea of how long a sponge could live assuming no diver comes down to cut it from the rock and take it to the surface to be cured for market. Bath sponges 20 in. in diameter have been brought up. These were probably 20 or more years old.

You can cut a bath sponge into two and each half will heal the cut and grow into a new sponge. The same will happen if you cut it into 4, 6, 12, or even more pieces. A century ago Oscar Schmidt, the Austrian zoologist, suggested that sponges might be grown as one does plants, from cuttings. Fifty years later the idea was adopted by the British Colonial Office. Experiments were carried out in the Bahamas and elsewhere in the Gulf of Mexico, in growing sponges by cuttings, each fastened to a concrete disc, and all laid out in rows on the sea-bed. One misfortune after another dogged the experiments. But by 1938, sponge-farming was seen to be a practical proposition when some 600,000 tons of sponges were harvested from the Gulf of Mexico alone. That was the year the fungal disease struck, causing 90% mortality among bath sponges in the Bahamas and Florida.

△ *Curing sponges on Kalimnos, Greece. Greek islands are the centre of the sponge industry.*

▽ *The finished article which gives good service on bath night. Largely replaced by synthetic ones.*

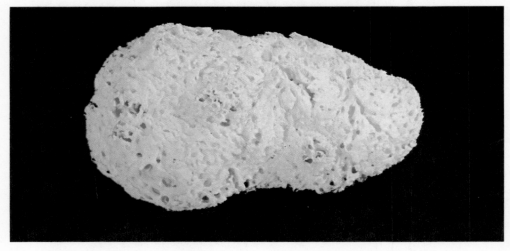

through the sponge the water yields food-particles and oxygen and it leaves bearing waste products of digestion and respiration.

Sponges are almost completely still once the free-swimming larva has settled on a solid substratum—usually a rock or a large stone. There is, however, some evidence of limited movement, particularly in the young sponges, their speed being 1 in. in a fortnight. Some movement may be in response to adverse conditions.

Particulate feeders
We know more by inference than direct observation that sponges feed on bacteria and minute particles from the breakdown of plant and animal bodies. They are therefore particulate feeders, and scavengers.

Having no separate digestive system, food particles are taken into the collared cells which digest them and reject any inedible scraps. The food is then passed into the body by specialised migrating amoeba-like cells.

Ciliated larva
There are no males and females, ova and sperm being found in the same individual, but not in specialized reproductive organs. At various points in the body of the bath sponge, one of the body cells will be fed by neighbouring cells so that it grows noticeably large. Of the many thousands that do this, some are destined to become egg cells or ova. The others have a different fate. They subdivide repeatedly until masses of tiny cells are formed. These are the sperms,

phylum	**Parazoa**
class	**Gelatinosa**
order	**Keratosa**
family	**Spongidae**
genus & species	***Spongia officinalis** bath sponge others*

Anemone

'Anemone', from the Greek for wind, was first used for a flower in 1551. At first the marine animals that look like flowers were called plant-animals. The name 'sea-anemone' was not used until 1773. Today, marine zoologists almost invariably speak of the animals as anemones. That they are truly animals is no longer in doubt although the order to which they were assigned is still called the Anthozoa, that is, plant-animals. The basic differences between plants and animals are:

1 A plant manufactures its own food, by photosynthesis, using the green chlorophyll in its leaves; an animal takes solid food.

2 A plant is incapable of locomotion; an animal can move about.

3 A plant has no obvious sensitivity; an animal usually has recognisable sense-organs

There are exceptions to all three principles, especially among the lower plants and the lower animals, but these are good working guides.

A sea-anemone has simple sense-organs, takes solid food and, surprisingly, is capable of locomotion.

The most outstanding feature of sea-anemones is the variety of their colours and, in many species, the beauty of the patterns these make. Colours and patterns in higher animals are known to serve as camouflage, warning coloration, recognition marks and other utilitarian purposes. Sea-anemones neither need nor could use any of these; their colours and patterns consequently appear as pure art-form.

Long-lived and motile

Anemones are found only in the seas but there they are world-wide, from between tide-marks to the great depths of the ocean. They are most abundant in warm seas where they can reach up to 3 ft across. The smallest are little more than a pin's head, but this requires some explanation. Voracious feeders, anemones will eat any animal flesh they can catch and swallow, and they may swallow prey of large size relative to their own bulk. It is not unknown for one anemone to swallow another and they are not immune to each other's poison. They can, however, survive for a long time without food, gradually dwindling in size until quite minute. This may be one of the secrets of their long life—anemones have been kept in aquaria for as much as 100 years.

Sea-anemones are by no means 'rooted to the spot'. There are even burrowing anemones. Those that are normally seen fixed to a rock move by gliding on their base. Others somersault, bending over to take hold of the substratum with their tentacles, then letting go by the base and slipping this over to take hold beyond. A few species lie on their side to glide along, or blow themselves up, let go with their foot, and float away.

Stinging tentacle feeders

An anemone is a cylindrical bag with a ring

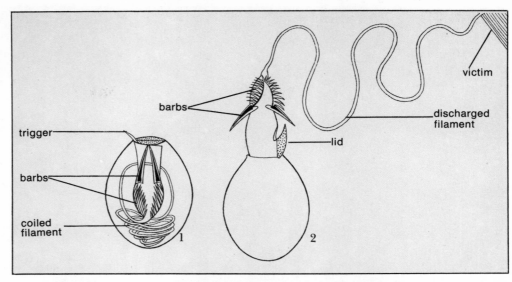

1. Bag-like stinging cell of cnidarian full of paralysing poison and with coiled filament inside.
2. When the cell is activated by having its trigger touched or by food chemicals, the lid flies open and the coiled contents turn inside out, shooting the poison-filled filament into the body of its victim, which is also retained by the barbs.

Plumose anemone, **Metridium senile**, can be quite large, up to 9 in. high and 6 in. across the head.

of tentacles surrounding the mouth on the upper surface. The opposite end is flattened and forms a basal disc, or foot, by which the animal sticks to a solid support. The interior of the bag is one large stomach, subdivided by curtains of tissue, or mesenteries, which hang down, partially dividing the stomach into eight compartments. Food is caught by the tentacles, which are armed with stinging cells. When a small animal, such as a shrimp or a fish, touches a tentacle the stinging cells come into action, paralysing and holding it. Adjacent tentacles also bend over to continue the stinging and holding until all begin to move towards the mouth, where the prey is engulfed. Indigestible remains from a meal are later voided through the mouth.

Stinging cells are a characteristic of the phylum Cnidaria to which sea-anemones belong, and included in the phylum are jellyfishes, the stinging cells of which are more familiar to most people. The Cnidaria are accordingly spoken of as stinging animals or, better still, nettle animals. Sting-cells, or nematocysts, are double-walled capsules, filled with poison, set in the outer surface of the tentacles. Each contains a coiled hollow thread, sometimes barbed at the base. At the outer end of the capsule is a thorn-like trigger. When this is touched the coiled thread is shot out. It turns inside-out as it is ejected, its fine point pierces the skin of the prey, and the paralysing poison flows down the hollow thread. Some kinds of nematocysts stick to the prey instead of piercing the skin, and in a third type the thread wraps itself around the victim. In addition to being triggered off by touch some nematocysts come into action as a result of

*Left: Anemones can have little use for warning coloration or camouflage, so their colours appear as nature's art. This red anemone is **Tealia crassicornis**.
Right: **Anthopleura xanthogrammica**, the giant green anemone, is one of the few anemones to live in direct sunlight. Its green colour is due to minute one-celled green algae living in its cells and photosynthesising.*

the presence of certain chemicals.

The body-wall of an anemone is made up of two layers of cells. There is, however, a good series of muscles. One set is longitudinal, running from the foot to the bases of the tentacles. The other is circular, running round the body. By the lengthening and contraction of these muscles the body can be drawn out or pulled in. There is also a series of retractor muscles which assist in the sudden withdrawal of body and tentacles. There are only very simple sense-organs and there is only a simple nerve system, a mere network of nerve-cells.

The action of the nematocysts is automatic, the result of the trigger being touched—it is a reflex action. A nerve strand also runs to the base of each nematocyst and it is these nerve strands that control the concerted action of the tentacles once a nematocyst has been discharged. The nerve network comes into action to cause the contraction of an anemone when it is touched. It can be made to expand again by adding a nutrient solution to the water. The slime from a mussel, for example, in the proportions of one part in a million, will make the body expand, and the tentacles extend, very slowly, perhaps taking an hour to come full out. Then the body sways slightly and the tentacles wave as if groping for food.

Sexual and asexual reproduction

Most anemones are either male or female, but some are hermaphrodite. In some, eggs and sperm are shed into the surrounding water, in others the larvae develop inside the parent body. The eggs vary in size, the largest, only $\frac{1}{25}$ in. wide, being a thousand times larger than the smallest. The fertilised eggs sink to the bottom and divide, or segment, to form oval larvae. These move about the seabed but finally each comes to rest, fastens itself to the bottom of the seabed,

grows tentacles and begins to feed.

An anemone can reproduce in other ways. It may split longitudinally to form separate individuals, or grow a ring of tentacles halfway down the body, after which the top half breaks away to give two anemones where there was one before. Young anemones may be formed, in some species, by fragmentation, or laceration. In fragmentation small anemones, complete with tentacles, arise from the base of a parent, become separated and move away. Laceration occurs in some species with a roving disposition. As the anemone glides over the rocks pieces of the base are ripped away and, being left behind, regenerate to form very minute but otherwise perfect anemones.

Enemies

Enemies are large sea-slugs, sea-spiders, fishes and sometimes starfishes and crabs.

Restless anemones

Aside from their diverse methods of locomotion, which are used but sparingly, anemones are always on the move, in a kind of slow-motion ballet. This led to an important discovery, the subject of which was the plumose anemone, 3–4 in. high, with a feathery crown of numerous small tentacles. When several scores of these are living in a large aquarium they are seen, at any given moment, to be in different attitudes. The body of some may be stretched up, others shortened and thickened; perhaps it is shortened and slender, its surface thrown into wrinkles, or it may be bent over to one side. The tentacles also will be in various stages of extension and retraction. Sometimes one or more anemones will be dilated and their tentacles withdrawn, so that they look like balloons anchored to the rock. Others may be so withdrawn that they look like buttons on

the rock. They may be watched for some minutes and no movement seen; but when anemones are watched closely and continuously against a black background, and their shapes drawn at intervals, they can be seen to be in continuous movement. This has been confirmed by other experimental methods, including a speeded-up film. Even when anemones are kept under conditions of constant temperature, in water free of food or undisturbed by vibrations the rhythm of activity continues. It can be interrupted by the presence of food or other disturbing factors, when the anemones react by more purposeful movements. One effect of this inherent rhythm of activity is to keep the animal in a state of constant preparedness for feeding, defence and other activities essential to the maintenance of life.

This movement is called the inherent rhythm of activity because it is self-starting and self-maintaining. It is common to all living organisms, as we now know. Obvious manifestations of it are seen in such processes as the beating of the heart, as well as in less obvious ways. When we sleep, for example, we do not simply lie still. Our bodies are in constant, if slow movement, in much the same way as the bodies of plumose anemones were shown to be.

phylum	**Cnidaria**
class	**Anthozoa**
order	**Actiniaria**
genera	*Actinia* *Anemonia* *Metridium* *and others*

Coral

Corals are polyps similar to anemones (see page 17) except that they are supported by a hard chalky skeleton. This, often white when dead, is covered in life with a continuous layer of flesh from which the polyps spring, and the whole is often beautifully coloured. The true corals, or stony corals as they are often called, may be either solitary or colonial. In the first a single polyp lives on its own, seated in a chalky cup or on a mush-room-shaped chalky skeleton. The colonial corals are made up of a sheet of tissue, formed by hundreds or thousands of polyps, covering the chalky skeleton. They may be tree-, cup- or dome-shaped, made up of flattened plates or branching like stag's horns.

There are also soft corals, some of which are precious. They are not true corals. One important difference is that their tentacles, instead of being simple as in the true corals and sea-anemones, are fringed, and each polyp has eight tentacles instead of, as in true corals, six or some multiple of six. Soft corals are usually tree-like and the centres of the stems and branches are strengthened by a chalky material, coloured red or black, and this, stripped of its flesh, gives the precious corals of commerce. Related to the precious corals are the sea-fans, the stems and branches of which are strengthened by a flexible horny material. Another relative is the beautiful organ-pipe coral, a mass of vertical tubes joined at intervals throughout their length by thin horizontal plates. The skeleton is reddish-purple and the polyps a pale lilac. When expanded these look like delicate flowers.

Tropical reef builders

Corals live in all seas, but few are found in temperate and polar regions compared with those found in the tropics—and in particular the reef-builders. Thousands of miles of tropical shores, especially in the Indian Ocean, are edged with reefs. In places, barrier reefs are formed, many miles off-shore, like the Great Barrier Reef, which runs for 1 200 miles parallel with the northeast coast of Australia. In mid-ocean, especially in the Pacific, are ring-shaped atolls made of living coral, topping accumulations of dead coral skeletons, which in places go down to about a mile deep.

Birth of a reef

Reef-building corals are found north and south of the equator about as far as the 25th line of latitude, where the temperature of the sea does not fall much below 18°C/65°F. Each begins as a larva which, after swimming about for a while, settles on the bottom and changes into a polyp. A small lump appears on its side. This is a bud. It gets bigger, a mouth appears at its free end and a crown of tentacles grows around the mouth. The bud then continues to grow until it is the same size and shape as the

parent, but without becoming separated from it. By repeated budding of the parent stock, and of the new growths formed from it, a colony numbering sometimes hundreds of thousands is formed. Between them they build a common skeleton, which in the end may be several feet high and the same across. Since all the polyps are in close connection with each other they are fed communally by their many mouths and stomachs.

Living animal traps

Corals, whether solitary, reef or soft, feed like sea-anemones. The tentacles are armed with stinging cells by which small swimming animals are paralysed and then pushed into the mouth at the centre of the ring of tentacles. In reef corals the polyps are with-drawn during the day, so the surface of each coral mass is more or less smooth. As night falls and the plankton animals rise into the surface waters, the polyps and their tentacles become swollen with water drawn in through the mouth by currents set up by cilia on the skin. The polyps now stand out on the surface, their delicate tentacles forming a semi-transparent pile in which are many mouths waiting to receive prey. The seemingly inert coral has been con-verted into a huge trap for any small animals which pass nearby—underlining the rela-tionship with anemones.

The polyps of some corals have short tentacles, which do not carry food to the mouth. Instead, it is passed to the mouth by the cilia coating the tentacles.

There has always been some doubt, how-ever, whether this was their only method of feeding. In coral tissues live microscopic single-celled plants known as zooxanthellae. It has been supposed that these two, the polyps and the zooxanthellae, were living in symbiosis: that the zooxanthellae received shelter and used the waste products from the coral, while the coral benefited from oxygen given off by its plant guests. Some scientists maintained that in addition the coral fed on the surplus populations of the plants.

This has been disputed, and one reason why it was hard to reach the truth is that digestion is very rapid. Consequently no animal food is found in the coral stomachs by day, therefore it has been assumed that they must be feeding on something else and, so it was argued, they must be eating the zooxanthellae. On the other hand, the tentacles react to animal food only, suggest-ing that corals are wholly carnivorous. More-over, if coral polyps are deprived of animal food they soon shrink, showing signs of malnutrition. These are only a few of the arguments and they are enough to indicate the causes of disagreement.

From investigations carried out about 1960 by TF Goreau in the West Indies it seems that the zooxanthellae help the corals to grow by removing carbon dioxide from their tissues. Corals grow best in bright light, less well in dull light when zooxanthellae are fewer, and least of all in darkness when their zooxanthellae have been killed off by lack of sunlight. This alone suggests that there is a close link between the rate of growth of the coral and the presence of tiny plants in its tissues.

Walking corals

The majority of corals are sedentary. The original meaning of this word is 'to sit for long periods', but in zoology it is used more to indicate animals that are permanently fixed to the substratum. There is, however, at least one coral that moves about, but it does not travel under its own steam. It represents a very picturesque example of symbiosis, or living together for mutual benefit.

In October 1967, TF Goreau and Sir Maurice Yonge were exploring the Great Barrier Reef of Australia when they dis-covered on the lee side of the reef, on a muddy bottom, small corals, less than an inch across, which moved about over the mud. They were able to take some to the laboratory and watch them in an aquarium.

The coral *Heteropsammia michelinii* is solitary, with usually one polyp seated on the limy base, although sometimes there may be two or even three polyps on the same base. This coral belongs to the same kind as those that form the reefs, but its limy skeleton contains a cavity and in the cavity lives a marine worm. The worm drives its head into the mud to extract edible par-ticles from it, in the usual manner of a worm, but as it feeds it travels along drag-ging the coral with it.

phylum	**Coelenterata**
class	**Anthozoa**
order	**Scleractinia**
genera	*Fungia, Porites,* *Heteropsammia* others

▽ *Diagram of the basic colony of the* **Heliopora** *blue coral shows the shape of the hard, chalky skeleton (in red) and the polyps which grow from it (top).*

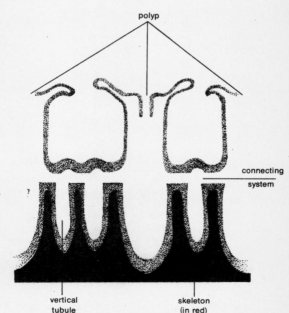

polyp

connecting system

vertical tubule

skeleton (in red)

◁ *This assortment gives a good idea of the different types of coral which will grow side by side to form a coral reef.*

△ *All systems 'go': the polyps of a coral, fully extended while feeding at night.*

◁ *A closer view of feeding polyps of a hard coral show the fine, whiskery tentacles that sweep the surrounding water for food.*

▷ Living polyps protrude from branches of staghorn coral off Mauritius.

▷▷ Unidentified shallow-water coral in the Seychelles has a squat, bunched structure.

▷ Fish swarm around a coral reef precipice in the Red Sea.

Hydra

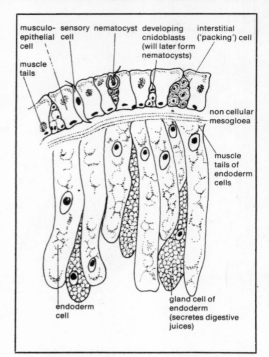

musculo-epithelial cell

muscle tails

sensory cell

nematocyst

developing cnidoblasts (will later form nematocysts)

interstitial ('packing') cell

non cellular mesogloea

muscle tails of endoderm cells

endoderm cell

gland cell of endoderm (secretes digestive juices)

△ Cross-section through body wall of hydra. It has only two layers of cells. The inner (endoderm) cells are for food breakdown. The outer (ectoderm) cells perform all other functions.

The hydra's simple tubular body with its crown of tentacles has earned it a place in every elementary textbook of zoology and made it the object of many detailed studies. It is one of the few freshwater cnidarians, the bulk of which are marine. The body of a hydra is a bag whose wall is made up of two layers of cells separated only by a very thin layer of non-cellular material. The tentacles, which usually number 5 or 6 but may be as few as 4 or as many as 12, are hollow. They surround the mouth, while the other end of the body is a basal disc which normally anchors the hydra by a sticky secretion. Though often abundant in ponds, hydras frequently escape notice because of their habit of retracting into a tiny blob when disturbed.

Both tentacles and body are very extensible, for the bases of many of the cells are drawn out as muscle fibres—those of the outer layer of cells running lengthwise and those of the inner layer running around the body. The nervous system co-ordinating the movements is extremely simple, consisting of only a network of nerve cells. There is no brain of any sort.

There are three species of hydra in Britain. The green hydra **Chlorohydra viridissima**, which used to be called **Hydra viridis**, has short tentacles that are never as long as the body. The brown hydra, **Hydra (Pelmatohydra) oligactis**, has tentacles 4—5 times the length of the body, which is usually clearly divided into a stomach region and a narrower stalk. These two species are found throughout the world and their colours are caused by single-celled algae living within their cells. When animal prey is scarce the hydra draws nourishment from these algae. In both species the body may be as much as $1\frac{1}{5}$ in. long but it is usually much shorter. The third species found in Britain is the slender hydra **Hydra attenuata**. Its body is never much more than $\frac{1}{2}$ in. in length when fully extended, it lacks a stalk, and its tentacles never measure any more than 3 times the length of the body.

▽ Stuck to a water plant by special cells in their basal discs, five brown hydras hang in wait for the touch or taste of prey (7 × life size).

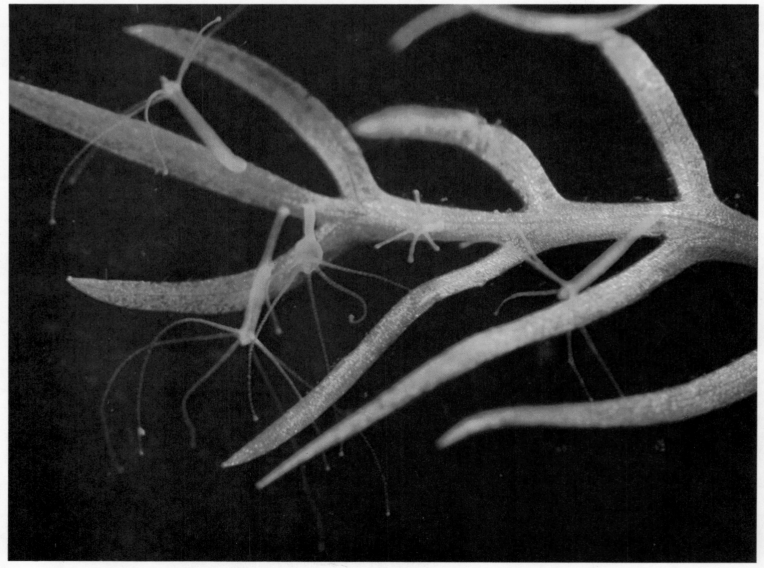

The stinging cells

Hydras, like their relatives the sea anemones and jellyfishes, have stinging cells with which they capture their prey. Each stinging cell or nematocyst is a rounded cell with a hollow coiled thread inside that can be shot out at great speed (see anemone, page 17). Hydra has four kinds. In one kind the thread is shot into the prey, injecting a poison. In a second kind the thread coils after it is shot out, and if the prey has bristles of any kind these tend to become entangled in it. The third type of nematocyst is probably truly defensive. It is shot out at animals not normally eaten by the hydra. The fourth kind of nematocyst is used to fasten the tentacles when the hydra is walking. This is not strictly a stinging cell, and is best referred to as a thread capsule. Some people prefer to use the term 'thread capsule' for all of them, because some do not sting.

When a nematocyst is discharged, its thread is forced inside out like a stocking, except that forces inside the thread itself are responsible for driving it out. The nematocysts used in capturing prey are discharged when the prey touches a little trigger on the side of the cell. Touch, however, is not enough, for the stinging cell must also be stimulated by chemicals in the water that are given out by the prey.

In all types, the stinging cells cannot be used again but are replaced by new ones migrating in from other parts of the body.

Progressing by somersaults

Although normally anchored, hydra can move about by creeping slowly on its basal disc in a sort of sliding movement. It can move more rapidly by a looping movement or a series of somersaults. To do this, a hydra bends over and gets a grip with special thread capsules on the tentacles. It lets go with its basal disc and brings this over in turn, very much like somebody doing 'cartwheels'. Hydras can also float at the surface of the water buoyed up by gas bubbles given out by the basal disc. The characteristic feature of the behaviour of hydras is that they suddenly contract into a tight ball every 5 or 10 minutes, for no obvious reason. This happens less often at night than by day.

Snagging its prey

The diet includes insect larvae, water fleas, worms, even newly-hatched fishes and tadpoles. Between meals the tentacles are held outstretched and more or less still, but at the approach of prey they start to writhe and later they bend in towards the open mouth. They will do these things if offered only extracts from other animals without

△ *Murder in miniature: after paralysing a water flea with stinging cells and drawing it in with sticky threads and tentacles, a hydra stretches its mouth round an outsize victim.*

▽ *Coelenterate mealtime: the green hydra at left is stinging a water flea into submission, the one at right is swollen with similar repast (9 × life size).*

23

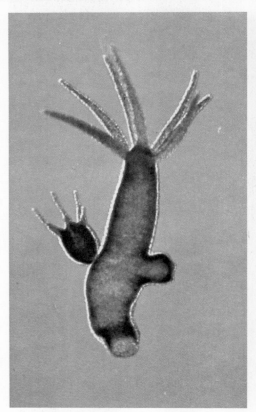

△ *Chips off the old block: a parent hydra with two buds, one advanced, one very very young.*

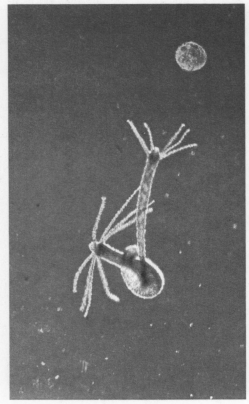

△ *Budded hydra almost ready to break free while a* **Volvox**-*like 'plant animal' just escapes.*

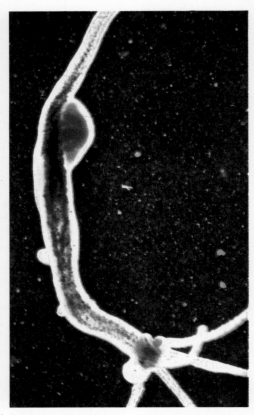

△ *Hydra forming an ovary for sexual reproduction. It does this in harsh conditions.*

any solids. For example, the juice from crushed water fleas alone will make a hydra go through the motions of putting food into its mouth. In fact a single chemical—glutathione—is responsible. If, however, the prey touches the tentacle the threads of the nematocysts are shot out, it is caught, held and paralysed, then carried to the mouth and swallowed. The mouth can open wide enough to take in animals that are themselves wider than the body of the hydra, which will stretch to accommodate them. Once inside the baglike body of the hydra, the prey is partially digested by enzymes given out by the inner layer of cells. Small particles breaking off are engulfed by individual cells for the final stages of digestion and indigestible particles are rejected through the mouth.

While food is in the body whiplike flagella on the cells of the inner layer are stirring the food around the inside of the body, a churning which aids digestion.

Multiplying in two ways

Hydra reproduce both sexually and by budding. Most species of hydra reproduce sexually in autumn or early winter although some do so in spring or early summer. One thing that can cause sexual reproduction, even out of season, is an accumulation of carbon dioxide in the water—as happens when a number of hydras are overcrowded. There are no special reproductive organs but small cells appear as bulges on the body in the upper half. Ovaries which are borne on different individuals in most species appear lower down on the body, also as bulges, each containing a single large egg-cell, or ovum. The ripe ovum pushes through the outer layer of the hydra's body and the cells around it form a little cup or

cushion for the ovum. The male cells or sperms are shed into the water where they swim about and eventually reach the ova and fertilise them. The embryo which results from the division of the fertilised ovum secretes around itself a hard, sticky yellow shell $\frac{1}{50}$ to $\frac{1}{25}$ in. across. The shell may be smooth on the outside or spiny, according to the species. Thus enclosed, the embryo can survive drying and freezing. After lying dormant for 3–10 weeks it breaks out of its capsule, grows tentacles and becomes a new hydra, a perfect miniature of the adult.

Budding technique

New hydras can also be formed by buds. Each bud begins as a little bump on the side of the body. This grows out, and an opening appears at its free end. Tentacles are pushed out all round the mouth and finally the bud breaks away from the parent, settles down and grows into a new hydra, the whole process occupying 2 days, and a single hydra may bear several buds at once.

Inside-out hydras

In Greek mythology Hercules found himself trying to kill a monster called Hydra which had many heads. As fast as Hercules cut off one head another grew in its place. In 1744, Abraham Trembley, Swiss tutor to the children of the Comte de Bentinck, published his story of another hydra—the animal we are concerned with here. Trembley had found that a complete hydra would be regenerated from only ⅛th of the parent body. He also succeeded in turning these animals inside out, a remarkably delicate operation which he performed by threading them on horse hairs. Trembley showed that the hydras would survive even this drastic operation. These experiments caught on

and for a while became very popular among certain scientists. More recently, they have been pursued in much greater detail. We now know that even tinier pieces of hydra, even a piece only $\frac{6}{1000}$ in. long, will grow into a new hydra provided that cells from both layers of the wall of the parent body are present. Even if the cells are separated into a mush of independent cells, these will come together to form a new hydra. The experiments are called 'Dissociation and Regeneration'.

We also know now that when a hydra is turned inside out it gets back to normal because the cells of the two layers migrate past each other to get into their proper positions. In fact, hydras are continually remodelling themselves and replacing old cells with new. If the tissues just below the tentacles of a hydra are marked with dye, they can be seen to move gradually down to the basal disc, eventually being lost and replaced by growth of new cells in the region from which they started.

phylum	**Cnidaria**
class	**Hydrozoa**
order	**Hydrida**
family	**Hydridae**
genera & species	*Chlorohydra viridissima green hydra*
	Hydra attenuata slender hydra
	H. oligactis brown hydra
	others

Jellyfish

Jellyfish are free-swimming relatives of sea anemones, corals and hydroids, all belonging to the phylum Cnidaria. In the life cycles of many cnidarians there are two distinct phases. One is a free-living jellyfish, or medusa, that reproduces sexually, while the other develops from an embryo and is an anchored, or sessile, polyp, or colony of polyps, that in turn buds off jellyfish. One or other phase may be dominant and the other less important or even non-existent. The large jellyfishes make up one class, the Scyphozoa (or Scyphomedusae), in which the polyp stage is very small. Attention will be concentrated here on this group.

Upside-down hydra

The typical jellyfish is umbrella-shaped, globular or conical with 4 or 8 tentacles around the margin, or many tentacles may form a ring around the margin. Under the umbrella, and like a handle to it, is the mouth, leading into the digestive cavity. The mouth is drawn out at the corners into four long lips. The basic form of the body of the jellyfish can best be understood by comparison with that of hydra. The body of hydra consists essentially of two layers of cells forming a sac and separated by a very thin layer of non-cellular material, mesogloea. In the jellyfish the mesogloea is very thick. Although the body of a jellyfish is more elaborate than that of hydra it still has the same two-layered structure and ring of tentacles around the mouth.

Some common jellyfish

A jellyfish found in seas throughout the world and which is common off the coasts of Europe is *Aurelia aurita*. It grows to nearly 1½ ft across, with many very short tentacles. The blue, yellowish, reddish or brown jellyfish *Cyanea*, also known as sea blubber, can reach 6 ft across in Arctic waters but is usually less than half that. The jellyfish *Chrysaora* has 24 tentacles, and these may be 20 yd long in one species. Around the centre of its white or yellowish disc there is often a brownish ring from which streaks of the same colour radiate. Another common jellyfish is *Rhizostoma*, or 'the rootmouthed', named for the shape of its lips. It is a whitish dome, about a foot across, with a deep purple rim. It has no tentacles but is easily recognized by the cauliflower-like oral lips. In the United States it is called 'cabbage blebs'. Some jellyfish are luminescent and one of the most intense, which is occasionally found in north European waters, is *Pelagia noctiluca*.

Different ways of feeding

Jellyfish swim by rhythmic pulsations of the umbrella or bell. The movement is very like an umbrella being opened and shut slowly. It is co-ordinated by a very simple nervous system and by sense organs around the·edge that are sensitive to light, gravity and chemicals in the water. Jellyfish are carnivorous and many of them capture fish, shrimps and other animals on their trailing

*The polyp generation of **Aurelia aurita**, like all other jellyfish, is a small sedentary phase passing the winter hanging from a rock. In spring the polyp becomes divided by transverse grooves, a process known as strobilisation, until it looks like a pile of saucers.*

tentacles, paralyse them with their stinging cells and transfer them to the mouth. *Aurelia* catches fish when young, but once grown to about 1 in. across feeds in quite a different way on small planktonic animals. These are trapped in sticky mucus all over the surface of the body and are driven by cilia to the rim. There the accumulating blobs are licked off by the 4 long oral lips. Further cilia propel the food in currents of water into the digestive cavity, from which a system of branching, cilia-lined canals radiate out to the rim, carrying food to all parts of the body. *Rhizostoma* feeds in the manner of a sponge, drawing in small planktonic animals by means of ciliary currents through thousands of separate mouths on the greatly elaborated oral lips. It is these mouths and the many little sensory palps on the oral lips that give the

jellyfish its characteristic cauliflower appearance. Another plankton feeder is a tropical jellyfish *Cassiopeia* which lies mouth upwards on the sea bottom in shallow water, pulsating its bell gently and capturing plankton with its lips as it is wafted by. It has symbiotic algae in its oral lips which benefit from the sunlight falling on them (see also anemone *Anthopleura*, page 18).

Piles of saucers

The common *Aurelia* is readily recognised by the four nearly oval purple or lilac reproductive organs, ovaries in the females, testes in the males. These lie in pouches in the digestive cavity but show through the transparent bell. The male sheds his sperm into the sea and these are wafted to the female and taken in along with her food. The eggs are fertilised and develop for a

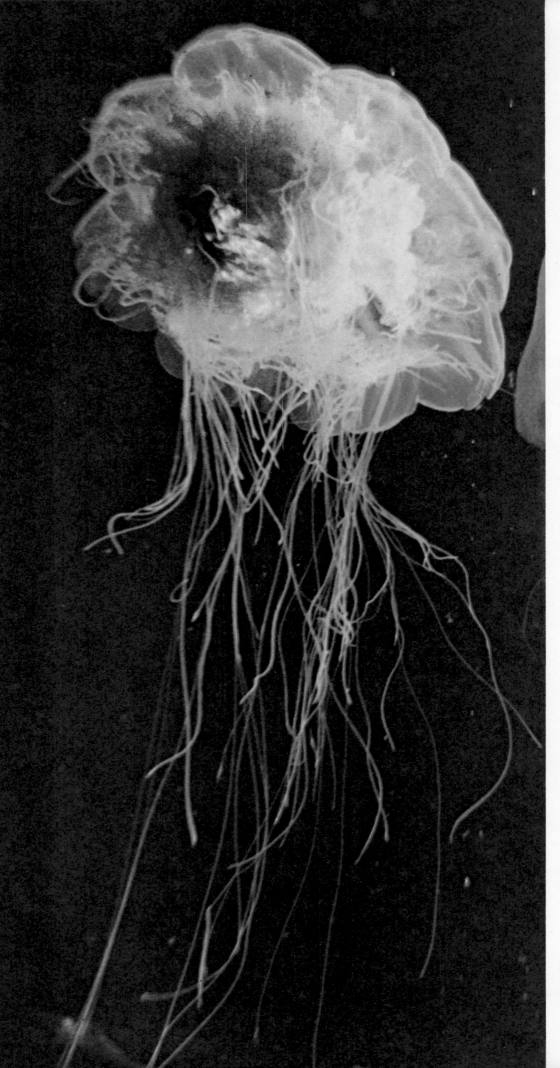

while in pouches on the oral lips. They are eventually set free as tiny planula larvae which soon attach themselves to seaweed or stone and develop into small polyps, known as scyphistomas or hydratubas, each with 16 tentacles. From the base of each, stolons, like runners of strawberry plants, grow out and new polyps develop on them. Each polyp eventually gives rise in the following winter to a number of young jellyfish called ephyra larvae, not round like the adult, but with the edge of the bell drawn out into 8 arms, notched at the tips. To do this, the polyp becomes pinched off into segments so it resembles a pile of lobed saucers. Then the tissue connecting these saucers contracts and snaps and each one swims off as a little ephyra. The growing ephyras transform gradually into adults by filling in the spaces between the arms.

An alternation of forms like this is typical of these jellyfish, though, in *Pelagia*, the egg develops directly into ephyras.

Sea wasps

Jellyfishes are practically all water. A jellyfish stranded on the shore will soon vanish under the hot rays of the sun leaving little more than a patch of water in the sand. Their bodies are nearly 99% jelly and the whole body contains less than 5% organic matter. Yet jellyfishes can be extremely venomous as anyone knows who has hauled on a rope covered in long trailing tentacles. The stings of jellyfishes come from the many stinging cells or nematocysts which shoot out a poisonous thread when touched. The severity of the sting depends very much on the number of nematocysts discharged and also on the type of jellyfish. The most venomous jellyfishes are those living in the coral seas and the least troublesome are those in temperate seas, but even these, if enough tentacles are allowed to touch our bodies, can sometimes lead to a loss of consciousness and, in the case of one bather, to drowning. This kind of accident is happily very rare. The most venomous jellyfishes belong to what are known as the Cubomedusae, so called because of their somewhat squarish shape. They range in size from as small as grapes to as large as pears and have four tentacles or four groups of tentacles. Some of these, like bathers, seem to prefer quiet shallow waters in the warmer seas, and are particularly troublesome around the northern Australian coasts, the Philippines and Japan. They have been called sea wasps and they can kill in as short a time as half a minute, usually in a quarter of an hour, the victim dying in excruciating pain.

phylum	**Cnidaria**
class	**Scyphozoa**

◁ *Young* **Cyanea** *or sea blubber. This is the giant among jellyfish, sometimes 6 ft across with trailing tentacles 200 ft long.*

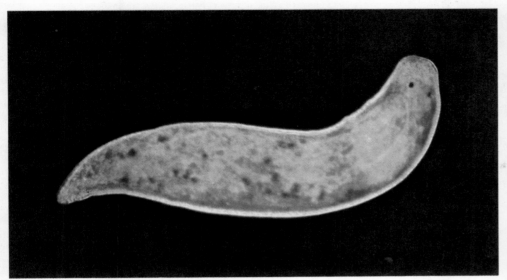

△ Not a sliced unripe banana but a freshwater flatworm rejoicing in the name of **Dalyellia**, enlarged 110 × natural size. These flatworms normally get about by crawling on a track of slime.

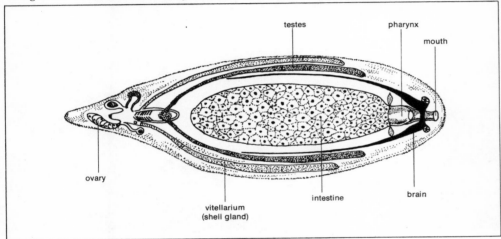

△ Diagram of the 'working parts' of a similar flatworm (after von Graff). The nervous system is simple and very primitive; a flatworm does not die if it loses its brain in an injury.

△ Land planarian on a Malayan forest floor. These tropical land-living species grow large.

Flatworm

Free-living flatworms are of great interest to scientists because of the light they shed on animal behaviour at a low level. There are three classes of flatworms: a variety of free-living forms and also the parasitic flukes and the tapeworms. Only the free-living Turbellaria will be considered here. They are soft-bodied, unsegmented and generally flattened worms. The planarians of our rivers and ponds are the best known. They range in size from microscopic to, exceptionally, well over a foot long in the case of certain terrestrial species in humid tropical forests.

Living without a brain

Turbellarians live mainly in fresh or salt water. Those living on land are restricted to moist places and are mainly tropical, although there is one, *Rhynchodermus terrestris*, like a small slug, ¼ in. long, sometimes as much as 1 in., dark slate grey, found under the bark of decaying trees in Britain. Turbellarians usually move about in two ways. Most of the time they crawl on a track of slime laid down by their undersurface, movement being due to cilia beating against the track. At other times they move more rapidly, by means of muscular contractions. Certain freshwater species move about over the surfaces of such animals as crustaceans and snails by alternately attaching themselves by a sucker at the hind end and by tentacles at the other.

The nervous system is primitive and extremely simple, and ill-defined. There is a simple 'brain' at the front end where the eyes, if any, and other sense organs are located. The brain is in some respects relatively unimportant. For example, the animal can feed almost normally even when the brain has been lost by injury. Nevertheless, turbellarians do show well-defined reactions to light, gravity, water currents and chemical stimuli, and these reactions have interested biologists because of the lowly state of the nervous system which produces them. Moreover, flatworms also show an ability to learn, for example, to turn right or left in particular laboratory situations. They have attracted special attention because of experiments carried out in the hope of showing that 'memory' can be transferred from one animal to another in chemical form. As we shall see later, a flatworm can be cut into several pieces and each will reform to make a new, very small flatworm. In an experiment a flatworm was 'trained'. Then it was cut up, the separate pieces regenerated and each new flatworm was tested to see if it 'remembered' the training. The scientists carrying out the experiment claimed that each new flatworm remembered. Were this so it would mean that memory, contrary to what we normally suppose, could have a chemical basis independent of the nervous system. There is, however, some doubt about the validity of these experiments.

Secondhand defence

The digestive system has only one opening, the mouth, and the form of the mouth serves to distinguish the four different kinds of flatworms. In the Rhabdocoelida the intestine is straight and the mouth is at the front of the body. In the Tricladida, or planarians, the mouth with a protrusible proboscis is near the centre of the body and the digestive system has three main branches, each of which branches extensively through the body. In the marine Polyclads, there are many branches of the gut leading from a mouth at the posterior end of the animal and in the Acoela there is a simple gut that is not even hollow. This last is less mystifying than it appears when we realise

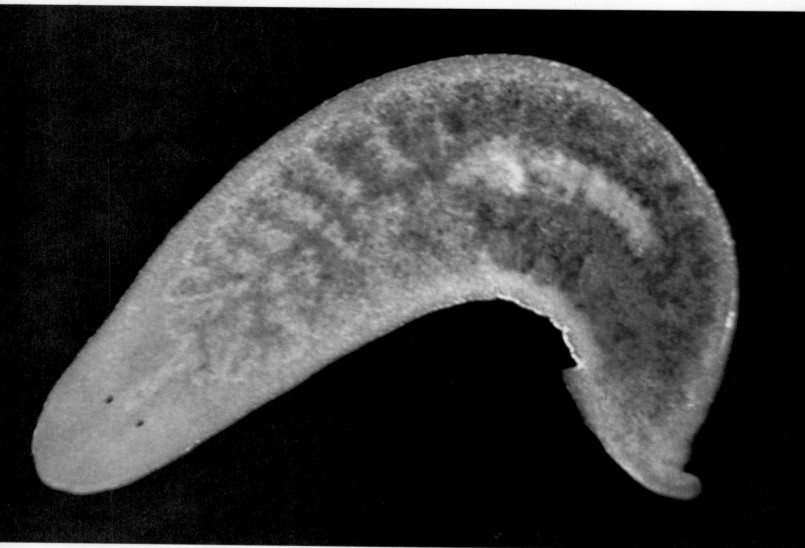

△ *Planarian flatworm* **Dendrocoelum lacteum.** *The mouth with a protrusible proboscis is near the centre of the body.*

that digestion in all these animals is largely carried on, not inside the intestine but in the cells of the wall of the intestine.

The turbellarians are carnivorous, feeding on a variety of small animals. Some of them can be caught by lowering a piece of meat on a string into a pond. The typical planarian catches its prey with the help of sticky secretions from glands in the head region. When the prey gets caught in these the planarian wraps its body around it. The proboscis is then protruded from the mouth and small particles of the prey are sucked up. One of the Rhabdocoelida *Microstomum* has the remarkable habit of feeding on hydra, a freshwater relative of anemones. It eats portions of the hydra, including its stinging-cells and these find their way into the skin of the *Microstomum* and are used in defence by their new owner. In fact, *Microstomum* is believed to eat only hydra when it needs to replenish its armoury.

On the sandy shores of Normandy and Brittany live two species of flatworm Acoela that may be so abundant as to colour the sand green. The colour is due not to the worm itself but to single-celled algae living in its tissues. One of them, *Convoluta roscoffensis*, gets all its food from these plant cells once it is mature, but the other, *C. paradoxa*, like the young of *C. roscoffensis*,

takes in solid food as well.

Cannibalism is common in Turbellaria. Even *Convoluta* when kept in the dark will eat their fellows. By contrast not many other things eat them.

If starved, flatworms get smaller and smaller, their internal organs disappearing in an orderly sequence, the reproductive organs first and the nervous system last.

Elaborate reproductive organs

The reproductive organs of Turbellaria are most complicated. Each individual has elaborate sets of both male and female organs. Propagation is, however, not always sexual. A number of freshwater planarians reproduce by tearing themselves in half, the front end of the body advancing while the rear attaches itself firmly to the substratum by sticky secretions. The body gives way along a predetermined line of weakness. The two halves subsequently reconstitute themselves as whole worms. The common American *Dugesia tigrina* does this, and in some localities there is, apparently, no sexual reproduction at all. In some rhabdocoels a chain of individuals is formed, each with its own brain and other organs, and after that they separate. Other turbellarians propagate by fragmentation. An interesting example is provided by the large *Bipalium kewense*,

discovered in 1878 in the greenhouses of Kew Gardens and now occasionally turning up in others elsewhere. It is also established in gardens in the West Indies and the warmer parts of North America although its relatives are mainly native to the forests of southeast Asia. It sometimes reaches 1 ft long and has five dark stripes on a lighter background. This species cannot reproduce sexually in temperate regions so for its survival there it depends on multiplication by fragmentation.

Regeneration

Turbellarians also have very good powers of regeneration following injury. Indeed, they have been favourite animals for studies on this subject and zoology textbooks often contain pictures of monstrous flatworms with several heads or with a head at each end. In some species, new individuals may be regenerated from as little as a thousandth part of the whole.

phylum	**Platyhelminthes**
class	**Turbellaria**

Ribbon worm

'Ribbon worm' aptly describes many of these long, thin, often flattened animals. Many are gaily coloured, especially on the upper surface, in various shades of orange, red, green or brown, often with contrasting stripes or bands. A few are transparent and one Japanese species is luminescent. There are nearly 600 named species—and probably many more yet to be discovered—varying in length from a fraction of an inch to yards. About 60 yd is the extreme, although the majority are less than 8 in. A characteristic feature of all ribbon worms is a long muscular proboscis which can be shot out at prey from its sheath down the middle of the body, becoming turned inside out in the process. The proboscis may be two or more times the body length, sticky or armed with one or more stylets. In **Gorgonorhynchus** *it is divided into as many as 32 branches and looks like a bunch of writhing worms when shot out. At the front end of the unsegmented body there may be a lobe bearing from two to several hundred eyes and other sense organs, but this area is not called the head since the brain may be further back. The pore by which the proboscis emerges is just below the tip of the body, or just behind that, on the lower surface. The digestive tract may share this opening, but usually there is a separate mouth farther back. The body sometimes ends in a short slender tail.*

Ribbon worms are known also as nemertines or nemerteans—after Nemertes, one of the sea-nymph daughters of Nereus and Doris. Nemertine worms are not to be confused with nematode worms (Nema= thread), for example the hookworm and the threadworm.

Mainly in shallow seas

Most ribbon worms live in the sea, mainly on temperate coasts among seaweed or in mud or sand. Some inhabit mucus-lined cavities or parchment-like tubes while a few live in association with other animals, like *Carcinonemertes* on the gills and egg masses of crabs. Nemertines living in deep water are usually either swimmers, with fins on the sides or at the hindend, or more gelatinous floating forms. There are some freshwater ribbon worms, especially in the northern hemisphere, and also a genus of terrestrial worms, *Geonemertes*, found along shores, under logs or in soil in warm regions such as Bermuda, New Zealand, Australia and many of the islands of the Pacific. One species lives, often high off the ground, in the leaf bases of screw pines which grow in the Seychelle islands in the Indian Ocean.

Ribbon worms typically glide along on a trail of mucus using the cilia that cover their bodies, but sometimes the muscles are brought into play. The proboscis is sometimes used as an aid to locomotion, the worm throwing it out and pulling itself along, and also in burrowing, but it is more important in feeding. Ribbon worms feed mainly at night, principally on annelid worms, but also on crustaceans, molluscs and fish. These are caught by the proboscis as it is shot violently out and wrapped around them. The prey may be swallowed whole or, if large, its tissues sucked out of its body. Prolonged starvation is tolerated by ribbon worms in captivity but with great reduction in size. In an extreme case of starvation, lasting more than 2 years, some regenerating pieces of ribbon worm ended up as masses of large round cells.

Three kinds of larvae

Though some species are hermaphrodite, particularly among those living on land or in freshwater, the sexes are usually separate and look alike, although the male of one swimming species *Nectonemertes mirabilis* differs from the female in having a tentacle on each side in the position of arms. The reproductive organs are generally arranged in a row on each side of the body and each discharges by a separate hole. In *Carcinonemertes*, they all discharge into the rear end of the intestine. Males and females may spawn without touching or a male may crawl over a female releasing his sperm; or two or more worms may spawn enclosed together in a sheath of mucus. Fertilisation can be internal or external and the eggs may be laid in strings or in masses of jelly, or, less often, develop into young worms while still inside the mother.

Some ribbon worms leave their eggs as small worms, while others hatch as ciliated pilidium larvae, usually described as 'helmet-shaped' because of the two lobes directed downwards like ear-pieces either side of the mouth. The pilidium larvae swim around, feeding on minute plants and animals, and eventually a worm emerges from each one, casting aside the outer skin. In addition to these distinct types of development, there is a third involving the so-called Desor's larva. This is an oval ciliated larva named after E Desor who observed

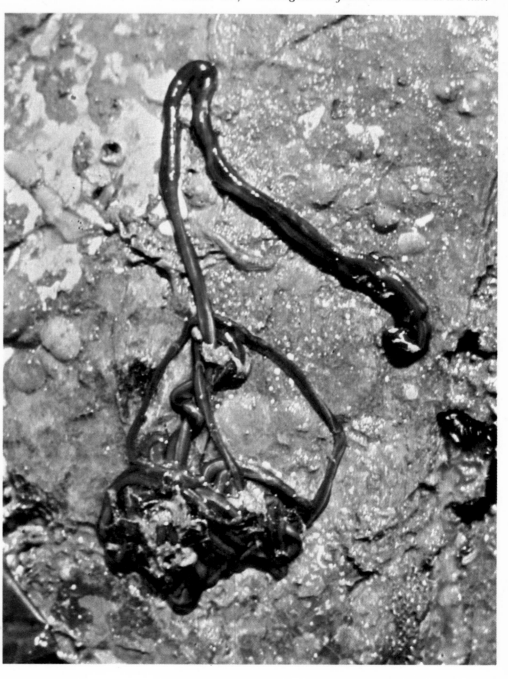

▽ *Turning over stones often reveals the unexpected such as this 'boot-lace worm'* **L. longissimus** *found on the shore at low tide.*

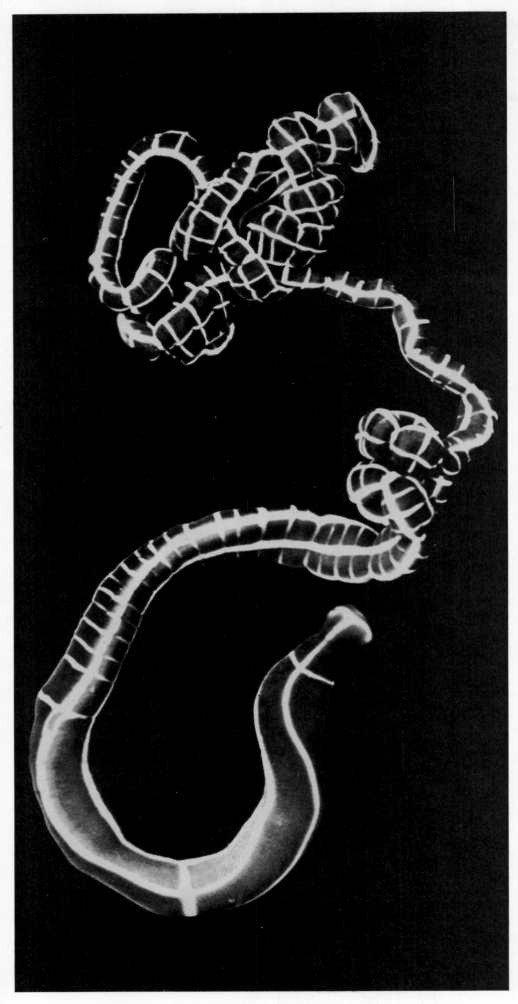

it in the eggs of *Lineus* in 1848. It develops in much the same way as a pilidium larva but remains inside its egg membranes. This larva is thought to be an adaptation to shallow water where conditions are more variable than those in the open sea.

Some ribbon worms, such as *Lineus,* propagate asexually by fragmentation. The hind end of the body breaks up by strong muscular contractions into a number of pieces, perhaps 20 or more, and each one grows into a new worm. Longer fragments may in turn break up into shorter lengths before becoming fully regenerated. Worms that can reproduce in this way are also those with good general powers of regeneration and, in some, even tiny pieces suffice to produce new worms provided they contain part of the nerve cord. Ribbon worms are apt to break up when handled or otherwise disturbed and the proboscis may be thrown out with such force as to tear itself loose from the body.

Yards of ribbon
The maximum length of a ribbon worm is given above as 'about 60 yd' and it is perhaps as well to reassure the reader now that this is no misprint. Some books quote a more hesitant 'several yards', but there is little need for such scepticism. It was Professor WC McIntosh who described, in a monograph on these worms, a giant specimen of the bootlace worm *Lineus longissimus* he had found at St Andrews after a severe storm in 1864. It half filled a jar 8 in. wide and 5 in. deep and McIntosh was able to measure 30 yd of it before it ruptured. Apparently he gave up at that point, 'yet the mass was not half uncoiled'. Just how long it was we will never know, but in any case an individual worm can vary its length very considerably, perhaps contracting from a length of several yards to several inches. An even more extreme shrinkage can occur on contact with alcohol with one part of the body becoming turned inside out on another and it has been known for specimens of *Lineus gesserensis* to turn completely inside out as a result of the influence of certain irritants in the water.

phylum	**Nemertina**
class	**Anopla**
order	**Palaeonemertina**
order	**Heteronemertina**
family	**Lineidae**
genera	*Lineus* *Gorgonorhynchus*
class	**Enopla**
order	**Bdellonemertina**
order	**Hoplonemertina**
family	**Prosorhochmidae**
genus	*Geonemertes*
family	**Emplectonematidae**
genus	*Carcinonemertes*

◁ *Its body thrown into coils,* **Tubulanus annulatus** *is a strikingly marked ribbon worm.*

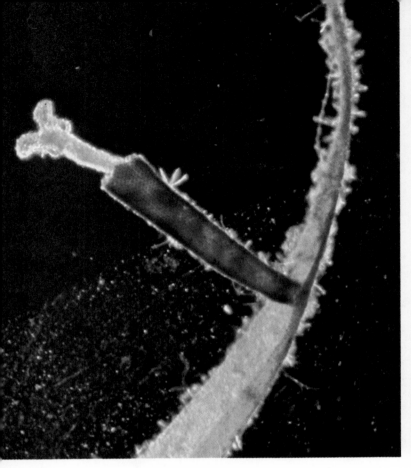
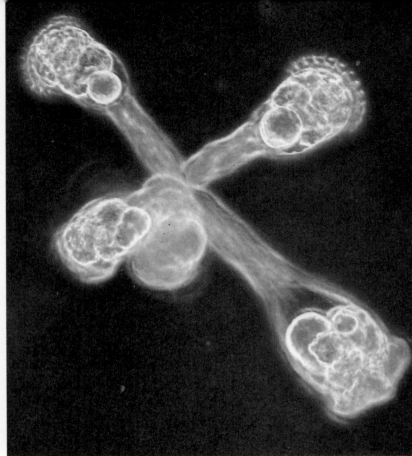

Rotifer

*Rotifers have long been a delight to microscopists. They are very numerous, easily obtained from almost any pond and are of endless variety. Wheel animalcules, as they are also called, are among the most abundant of freshwater animals. Only a few live in the sea. In the British Isles alone, there are more than 500 species. They range in length from 0·04 to 2 mm., and most are shorter than ½ mm. They are therefore about the size of Protozoa and were once confused with them, but they are nevertheless multicellular. They are unusual in that, within a species, every individual and each of its organs is made up of a definite number of cells. The adult female of **Epiphanes senta**, for instance, is made up of 959 cells. There is even a parasitic rotifer with all its minute organ systems living within the confines of a single protozoan. This is **Proales latrunculus**, which lives in a heliozoan **Acanthocystis**. Rotifers are named for the arrangement of cilia on the front end which often look like rotating wheels for which they were mistaken by some early microscopists, including Leeuwenhoek, the inventor of the microscope.*

Endless variety
The body of a rotifer may be worm-like, flattened, bag-like or spherical, symmetrical or skewed, soft-skinned or armoured. It is generally divisible into what may be called for convenience a head, a trunk and a 'foot' ending usually in one to four 'toes'. Covering the body is a yellowish cuticle, often ringed so it looks as if the body is segmented. This cuticle is thickened, especially on the trunk, to form one or more hard, and sometimes ornamented, plates. It is usually transparent enough for all the internal organs to be seen. There are endless variations on the basic body plan: there are species with dumpy trunks and feet like the stems of wineglasses, species with long thin bodies and even longer feet and a spherical species *Trochosphaera* with no feet. The trunk may have projections of various kinds including long fixed spines and moveable spines which enable the rotifer to skip through the water. The head bears a mouth, a variety of projections, often sensory, single or paired eyes seen as red flecks, and the cilia of the wheel organ or corona. The latter varies greatly in form and function.

Several ways of feeding
When we say rotifers occur mainly in fresh water, this includes even the thin films and drops of water in such places as the surface layers of the soil and the moss on walls. Some propel themselves through the water by the cilia of their wheel organs or by special appendages. Those of the order Bdelloidea are typically bottom dwellers and loop about like leeches (*bdella* = leech), alternately attaching the toe and head ends to the substrate. Yet other rotifers live anchored by their often elongated feet, and secrete around themselves tubes or cases of jelly. The 'floscule' *Floscularia* — formerly known to thousands of microscopists as *Melicerta* — is famed for its tube of neatly arranged little pellets. These are made by concentrating particles in a special ciliated pit on the head before being cemented to the rim of the

*◁△ The 'floscule' **Floscularia ringens** a freshwater, sessile rotifer which makes a case of neatly arranged little pellets from particles in the water and its own excrement (× 60).*
*△ **Conochilus hippocrepis** a colonial rotifer (× 800), individuals attached in a common ball of mucus. The wheel organ is the crown of cilia.*
▽ Rotifer of the order Monogononta (× 500).

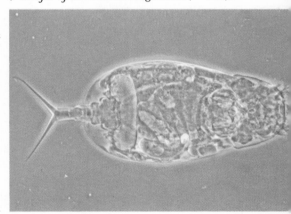

tube. If particles of carmine dye are added to the water, this rotifer will use these producing a gay red tube. The wheel organ of *Floscularia* has four large ciliated lobes which set up currents of water bringing in food particles. Rotifers feed in one of three ways: by extracting small organisms and particles from water currents set up by the wheel organs, grasping large prey, and trapping it. Rotifers are peculiar in having a masticating pharynx, called the mastax. This is muscular with several hard pieces. It takes several forms and may be used in chewing, sucking or grasping prey. Among the trapping carnivores are species of *Collotheca* that catch their victims with a widely spread funnel on top of the body. This bears long

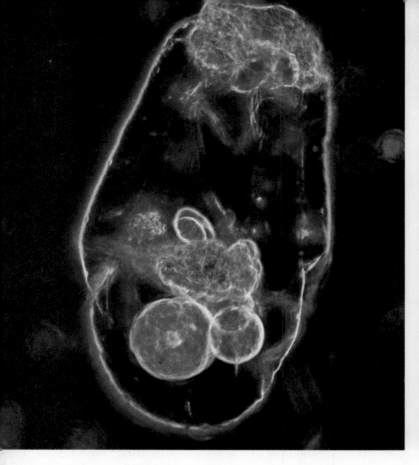

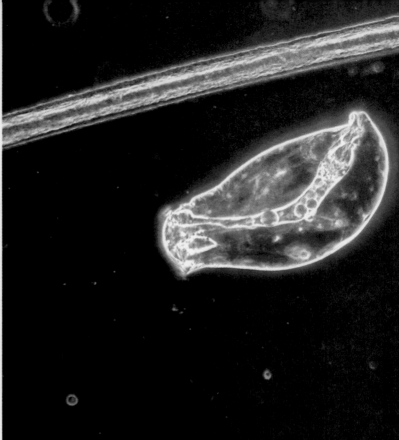

△ *Asplanchna priodonta — predatory rotifer able to swallow whole crustaceans and other rotifers as well as colonial algae after chewing them in its masticating pharynx, called the mastax. The less frequent male (right) with human hair to show size is much smaller than the female (left) (× 625).*

▽ *Fimbriatus stephanoceros on plant (× 75).*

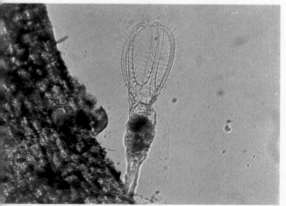

motionless bristles instead of the usual cilia and, should a small animal blunder into it, the lobes or arms bearing the bristles close over it and the mastax is soon at work.

Males adult at birth

What has been said so far applies particularly to the females, for in most species the males are much smaller, being perhaps only one half or a tenth the size of the females. The males sometimes have a degenerate gut. In any case, females are more often seen, since the males usually appear only at certain times of the year, though they may then be very abundant. The small size of the typical male is due to the fact that he hatches from a smaller egg and does not subsequently grow. He is often sexually mature at birth and so large numbers of mature males can be produced in a short time. In the order Bdelloidea, there are no males and the eggs develop without fertilisation. In some other rotifers males deposit their sperm in the cloacas of the females, but it is more usual for them to inject it through the cuticles and into their general body cavities.

Each female can produce only as many eggs as she has nuclei in her ovary to begin with—less than fifty, and often only ten in some species. The oval eggs are laid on the bottom or stuck to the body of either the mother or another animal. They have shells and in some cases these have gelatinous envelopes or thin membranes which enable them to float. In some species the egg has no shell, but develops inside the mother.

Females of free-swimming species usually hatch with the adult form and are mature in a few days, but in sessile species the females emerge as free-swimming juveniles. These eventually attach themselves and undergo changes necessary for their sedentary mode of life such as loss of eyes, elongation of the foot into a stalk and changes in the wheel organ.

Three kinds of egg

In most rotifers, three kinds of egg are laid, though not by the same individual: thin-shelled eggs that produce females without being fertilised; smaller thin-shelled eggs that can be fertilised but produce males if they are not; and thick-shelled eggs that are always fertilised and always give rise to females. These thick-shelled eggs often bear spines, bristles or other ornaments. While the first two kinds hatch in a day or so, the last may remain dormant for months and survive drying and low temperature. When they do hatch, the females that emerge soon start to lay eggs of the first kind and the population is built up by successive generations of females. Eventually a new kind of female appears, laying only the second, smaller, kind of egg. These are necessarily unfertilised at first and give rise to males. Then, to complete the cycle, thick-shelled, resting, fertilised eggs are produced again and the population perhaps dies off.

The thick-shelled dormant egg is clearly most helpful for the survival of the species, but most of the rotifers of soil and moss belong to the Bdelloidea which do not lay them. The bdelloids, the types most subject to drying, can, however, survive extreme desiccation lasting for periods even up to 4 years, during which time they may be blown about by the wind to seed new habitats. The longest dormancy on record is of one recovered from moss kept 59 years in an herbarium but it cannot be ruled out that dust from other specimens may have contaminated it. While dry, some have withstood temperatures up to 200°C/392°F for 5 minutes in an electric oven, and down to minus 272°C/457°F. In Antarctic lakes some rotifers are inevitably frozen in ice for most of the year but can make do with occasional periods of activity of a few days or weeks. At the other extreme, some bdelloids spend their lives in springs at 46°C/115°F.

phylum	**Aschelminthes**
class	**Rotifera**
orders	**Bdelloidea**
	Monogononta
	Seisonidea

Moss animal

There are 4 000 living species of moss animals. Most of them live in the sea, but a few live in freshwater. In the sea they coat almost every solid object, from the surfaces of rocks and seaweeds to the hulls of ships and shipwrecks lying on the seabed. In spite of their numbers, moss animals are unknown to most people. As a rule they form colonies, encrusting stones, shells and seaweeds, but some of them grow up into branching or fan-shaped colonies, looking like corals or millepores. Many are white or pale in colour and those encrusting pebbles and seaweeds are usually small and lacelike, although some-times they cover several square feet of rock surfaces. Some moss animals are often mistaken for seaweeds, such as the seamat **Flustra**. It can often be seen on the shore when the tide is out or cast up with sea-weed along the driftline.

In Britain moss animals are usually called Polyzoa, which means many animals, but in other parts of the world they are given the collective name of Bryozoa, meaning moss animals. Moss animals are colony builders; each colony is made up of a number of tiny chambers like boxes, in each of which lives a polypide, a sort of polyp. Small colonies are made up of scores of polypides, large ones of hundreds or even thousands of polypides, and sometimes a single colony may contain millions of polypides. At first sight the polypides look like the polyps of corals, except that they are much smaller, but they differ considerably in structure, which is why they are called polypides, to distinguish them from the true polyps. Each has a crown of 8 — 100 or more ciliated tentacles around the mouth for capturing the microscopic plants and animals on which the polypides feed. The anatomy of each polypide is very simple because there are no special organs for breathing and excretion and there are no blood vessels. The mouth leads into a simple U-shaped digestive tube. There are a few simple muscles and a simple nervous system.

Until the last few years all moss animals were put into one phylum divided into two distinct classes, the Ectoprocta and the Entoprocta (often mis-spelt Endoprocta). Although superficially alike, the two groups are now thought not to be related and are no longer classed together. As a result, the ectoprocts, or true moss animals, are generally regarded as constituting a phylum of their own. The long-lasting and unresolved controversy as to whether they should be called Polyzoa or Bryozoa is also coming to an end as the phylum is now called Ectoprocta.

◁ Freshwater moss animal **Plumatella** (×25)

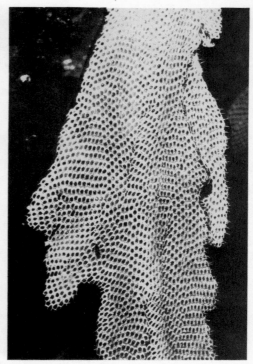

*Rose coral **Pentapora foliacea**. This brittle moss animal, about 3 — 4 in. across, is found in the Mediterranean living on underwater rocks. The small crabs are **Porcellana longicornis**.*

Flustra, seamat, is often mistaken for the seaweeds it encrusts (about × 3).

From the depths to freshwater

The walls of the chambers of some of the marine moss animals are decorated along the sides or around the opening, with long or short spines. The chamber or box is rarely more than $\frac{1}{50}$ in. across and it may be tubular, oval, squarish or even vase-shaped. The walls of the chamber are generally horny, but they often have a thick inner layer of calcium carbonate. At one end of each chamber is an opening through which the tentacles and the front part of the body can be pushed out. In one group, the opening has a hinged lid worked by muscles. Variations occur between the species and between individuals in the same colony who may do different work, as in a colony of termites. Some polypides are reduced to nothing more than the body wall and a few strands of tissue inside the chamber. These degenerate individuals make up the stalks, roots, stolons and attachment plates, or the margins of the colony.

Moss animals live in all seas and fresh waters, both warm and cold. Some live at great depths in the sea, but most live in shallow water or on the shore and they are among the most important fouling organisms on ships' hulls. Only a few species inhabit freshwater, and most of these, about fifty, belong to a distinct class in which, except in one genus, the crown of tentacles has a horseshoe arrangement. These freshwater forms sometimes block water pipes, as some of them such as *Pectinatella magnifica* form gelatinous masses which are occasionally up to several feet across. One of the gelatinous forms *Cristatella* moves by forming elongated colonies up to several inches long, which creep about on their flat undersurfaces at rates of up to 1 in. a day. Other freshwater species form branching or bushy colonies.

On the surface of the colony in some species are what look like very tiny birds' heads continually swaying to and fro and snapping their beaks. These 'avicularia', as they are called, are highly modified individuals in which the operculum, or lid, has become the 'lower jaw'. The avicularia may be either stalked or immobile, sometimes both types occurring in the same colony. The function of these structures seems to be much the same as the little jawed 'pedicellariae' of echinoderms—that is, capturing small organisms as they roam over the surface and, more important, preventing larvae of other encrusting animals from settling. Related to avicularia, and having probably a similar function, are the 'vibracula' in which the operculum is changed, not into a jaw, but into a long bristle that sweeps back and forth over the colony, keeping the surface clean.

Brooding the young

Some moss animals shed their eggs directly into the sea but the majority brood them. In freshwater species the embryos are nourished, until their release as ciliated larvae or juvenile colonies, in sacs attached to the body wall of the parent. In the marine species there is great variety in the method of brooding, which may be internal or external. Thus, the embryos may be sheltered outside in a space roofed over with arched spines or in a hood-like brood chamber, or they may be retained inside the body cavity, either free or in special sacs. Often each individual only nurtures a single embryo. The ciliated larvae vary in shape, some having a bivalve shell.

The freshwater moss animals also reproduce by an asexual method. They produce what are called statoblasts that can survive being dried up as well as extremes of temperature. Each statoblast, less than $\frac{1}{20}$ in., consists of a mass of cells enclosed in a pair of shells. Some kinds sink or are cemented to the parent colony but others have a ring of air-filled cells around them which act as a float. Other statoblasts have circlets of hooked spines by which they cling to a support. In due course a new polypide is formed from the cells in a statoblast, and hence a new colony is formed.

The shell of the statoblast breaks in two to release a mass of cells inside. These half shells are extremely small and they float. Quite astonishingly, drifts 1 — 4 ft across of millions of statoblast shells were reported along lake shores in Michigan, USA.

Moss animals' vital clue

Moss animals are relatively insignificant, and apart from the fact that they foul the bottoms of ships or choke water pipes they really have little value or interest to anybody but a scientist. People sometimes ask why is it necessary to spend so much time studying animals of this kind? Perhaps an incident that took place during the First World War may show how the unexpected can happen. A piece of metal from a sunken submarine was fished up by the Royal Navy and it was important to know how long it had lain on the sea bottom. The only possible clue lay in the marine animals such as the barnacles, the worm tubes and above all the moss animals encrusting it. The piece of metal was handed to a marine zoologist who was able, because of his knowledge of the moss animals, to say to within a few days how long the metal had been there. This represents the yardstick one must always use in assessing the value of a piece of research: you never know when it may be of use.

phylum	**Ectoprocta**
class	**Gymnolaemata**
genera	***Bugula, Flustra, Membranipora***
class	**Phylactolaemata**
genera	***Cristatella, Fredericella, Pectinatella, Plumatella***

Lampshell

Lampshells, which are all marine, look like clams and until the middle of last century were classified as molluscs. They are all small, at most 2 in. long, although some extinct forms were nearly a foot long. The shell is made up of two unequal parts or valves, which may be circular, oval or triangular. Sometimes it is made of carbonate of lime, sometimes of calcium phosphate with a horny covering. The shell is usually a dull grey or yellow, but it may be red or orange. Although so like a bivalve mollusc there is a basic difference between it and a lampshell. In the bivalve the valves can be regarded as left and right even though one lies uppermost. In a lampshell one shell is dorsal, or uppermost, and the other is ventral.

Lampshells are divided into two kinds depending on whether the two valves are hinged on each other or not. Usually a short fleshy stalk sticks out at the rear of the shell, anchoring the animal permanently to a solid surface, such as a rock or a branching coral, but in one kind it is used in burrowing in mud. The stalk may come out between the valves or through a special notch or hole. It is the presence of such a hole at the end of a sort of beak at the hind end of the larger ventral valve that makes some of the lampshells look like a Roman oil lamp, and so suggested the common name of these animals.

Inside the shell the greater part of the animal's body lies in the rear third, leaving a large space between the valves and the mantle or layer of tissue lining them. Within this mantle cavity lies a complex feeding organ known as the lophophore. It is covered with cilia and although its shape varies, most commonly it consists of coiled arms looking like huge moustachios on either side of the mouth. Along the arms are grooves and one or two rows of tentacles. The lophophore is stiffened by a skeleton of chalky rods.

There are about 260 living species, in almost all latitudes and at most depths although lampshells are most common in warm seas and the majority live on the continental slope. In some parts of the world they may occasionally be found on the shore.

Living food-pumps

Most lampshells remain permanently fixed after the larval stage. They can, however, move up and down and from side to side on the stalk. In a few species only, lacking a stalk, the shell itself is cemented to the rock. They have little need to move about since they feed on tiny particles, especially diatoms, that abound in the water around them. These are drawn in between the edges of the gaping valves in water currents set up by the concerted thrashing of the cilia on the lophophore. Edible particles are caught on the lophophore and driven along the grooves to the mouth. Unsuitable particles such as sand grains are rejected and carried out again in the outgoing current. If too much silt is accumulating within the shell, some species can reverse the flow of the current to flush out the mantle cavity.

Mud-burrowing lampshells

One group of lampshells of the genus *Lingula* have a muscular stalk which can be shortened or lengthened and used for burrowing. There are a dozen species of these in the Indo-Pacific region, especially off Japan, southern Australia and New Zealand. In some places they are used for food. Their burrows, in the black and smelly mudflats, are vertical, 2—10 in. deep and with a slit-like opening at the top to match the animal's flattened shell. The advantage *Lingula* gains in such a habitat is that few other animals can live there. *Lingula* lies with its shell near the top of the burrow, filtering water in the usual way. Bristles around the edges of its mantle can be bent over the opening as the shell gapes, to keep out the larger grains of mud and sand. The tip of the long stalk reaches to the bottom of the burrow. When the animal is disturbed the stalk contracts, drawing it down into the safety of the burrow.

Simple life history

Lampshells are usually male or female, although there is no obvious difference between the sexes, but a few species are hermaphrodite. The eggs, heavily charged with yolk, and the sperm are passed out through the kidneys and shed into the sea where fertilisation takes place. The fertilised eggs develop into tiny larvae that swim around for a day before settling on the seabed and becoming fixed. In some species the larvae look like miniature lampshells with a pair of valves and a stalk, which is coiled in the back of the mantle cavity. The larval lophophore is simple; its cilia are used not for feeding but for driving the larva through the water. A few lampshells brood their eggs in the mantle cavity and some of these have a special pouch, or they may brood them actually in the kidneys.

Few enemies

The living lampshells number fewer than 300 species compared with 30 000 known species of lampshell fossils. In past ages they must have been as numerous as molluscs are today and in some parts of the world whole layers of rock are made up of little else than fossil lampshells. The earliest known animal fossil is a lampshell, and the group as a whole reached its peak during the Ordovician period, which lasted from 500 million to 440 million years ago. *Lingula* was one of the earliest and it has persisted virtually unchanged throughout this long period of time. Other groups of animals have come and gone, flourished and died out, but *Lingula* has gone steadily on. Apart from its simple way of life one reason for this is that it can live in foul water that few other animals can tolerate. So it has few competitors for the available food and very few enemies.

There has been more change in those lampshells that look more like cockles and

△ Opened lampshell shows feathery lophophore, which sorts sand from food particles.
▽ *Lingula* lampshells showing attachment stalks.

other clams. Their shells mainly have altered, some being ribbed or folded or ornamented with spines. Such changes are largely superficial but they have their uses. One of the main interests in lampshells is that they are especially useful in helping the geologist to identify and date the rocks in which he finds them.

phylum	**Brachiopoda**
class	**Articulata**
order	**Atremata**
genera	*Lingula, Crania*
class	**Inarticulata**
genera	*Terebratulina, Terebratella*

Neopilina

In the eyes of a non-scientist neopilina is a somewhat uninteresting animal—just another limpet. To the scientist it is one of the most exciting discoveries of the mid-20th century. Apart from the fact that it is yet another living fossil, the whole circumstances of its discovery are astonishing.

*In 1952, when the Danish research ship **Galathea** was nearing the end of her cruise in the Pacific, her dredge was hauled up from a depth of 11 878 ft off the coast of Costa Rica. In it were 10 living limpet-like animals and 3 empty shells. They belonged to a new species, of a group of molluscs known as the Monoplacophora, which seemed to have died out 350 million years ago. Each empty shell was spoon-shaped, thin, fragile and semi-transparent, coloured pale yellowish white. The largest was 1½ in. long, 1¼ in. wide and ½ in. high. The top of the shell rose to a peak the apex of which tilted over at one end. The inside was a lustrous mother-of-pearl.*

The body of the living neopilina was like that of an ordinary limpet at first sight. When the shell it was in was laid on its back there was the usual fleshy foot, not so large as in the common limpet and it was bluish round the edges and pink in the centre. Either side of the foot was a row of 5 gills, and the mouth was at the centre of a fleshy triangle situated at one end.

Which way up?

Nothing quite like neopilina had been seen before the mid-20th century, and because it had been brought up from the deep ocean bed, it was not possible to do more than speculate about neopilina's way of life. The stomach was filled with radiolaria, tiny single-celled animals with jewel-like siliceous skeletons. The floor of the ocean where it had been living was dark muddy clay. Dr Henning Lemche who examined these first specimens formed the idea that they normally rested on the clay with the foot uppermost and collected the radiolaria that drifted down onto them. Sir Maurice Yonge, the leading British marine zoologist, takes the view that it could not feed this way. He agrees the foot is smaller than one would expect to carry a limpet-like animal over the soft clay bed. But he believes it moves the 'right way up', gathers its food from the seabed as it moves along helped by the gills which act not only for breathing but for locomotion. There is a pair of fleshy tentacles just behind the mouth, and these may perhaps help in gathering food into the mouth. Yonge's view is supported by the fact that each of 4 specimens caught off the coast of Peru, in 1958, had a layer of mucus on the foot, as if neopilina laid down a track of slime on which to crawl, like a garden snail.

Four species discovered

The importance of the discovery of neopilina lies in two things. The first is that it should have been followed so quickly by the findings of other species in other parts of the world. The second is that it vindicated forecasts made by scientists about the relationships of the mollusca to other phyla of invertebrates. Concerning the first of these it is surprising, in view of what happened later, that neopilina remained undiscovered for so long. Since about 1850, when ocean dredgings began in preparation for the epic voyage of HMS *Challenger*, there have been dozens of voyages by ocean-going research vessels, some covering small areas with intensive dredging, others covering much wider areas of the ocean but not so intensively. Nothing like this remarkable mollusc was brought to the surface in that century of searching. Yet 6 years after neopilina had been found off the coast of Costa Rica, another species was caught in 19 200 ft off the coast of Peru, and 4 years later 4 specimens of a third species, each ⅔ in. long, were brought up from 8 250 ft off the coast of California. Then, in 1967, only 9 years later, a single specimen of a fourth species was caught in the Gulf of Aden in 9 000—11 850 ft. From these figures it seems a fair assumption that these animals have a much wider distribution than is represented by these finds.

Missing link found

It has long been supposed that the ancestors of molluscs must have been some kind of ringed worm, like the marine bristleworms such as the fanworms. Yet if we put the two animals side by side they look very different. Moreover, when we look at their anatomy we find two very marked differences. A worm has a segmented body. It is also bilaterally symmetrical. That is, if we cut a worm through the middle lengthwise, the right hand half will be the mirror image of the left hand half. By contrast, a mollusc is not segmented and its body is not bilaterally symmetrical or only slightly so. Instead, it has become twisted, and this is especially true of its internal organs. So altogether molluscs and ringed worms seem to be very different kinds of animals and yet there are some things about them that suggest they must be related. Scientists studying this took the view that if ringed worms and molluscs had a common ancestor, then somewhere along the line there must have been a mollusc with a bilaterally symmetrical body, gills in pairs and a shell like a limpet. They made drawings of what this 'missing link' mollusc ought to look like. When neopilina was found it turned out to be almost identical with these drawings.

phylum	**Mollusca**
class	**Monoplacophora**
order	**Tryblidioidea**
family	**Neopilinidae**
genus & species	*Neopilina adenensis* *N. ewingi* *N. galathea* *N. valeronis*

Neopilina galathea. The top of the shell rises to a peak which tilts over.

*Diagram of underside of **Neopilina galathea** shows the five pairs of gills, mouth and anus.*

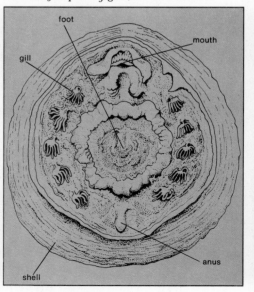

foot

mouth

gill

anus

shell

*On its back—the fleshy foot of **Neopilina galathea** is smaller than the common limpet's.*

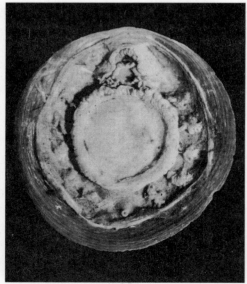

Abalone

A genus of single-shelled molluscs related to the limpets. Also known as ormer, sea ear, or earshell, the abalone (four syllables, the final e being sounded) somewhat resembles a snail, the body being little more than a muscular foot with a head at one end, bearing a pair of eyes and sensory tentacles. The body is also fringed with tentacles.

Over the top of the shell lies a line of holes, through which water is exhaled after it has been drawn in under the shell and over the gills to extract oxygen. New holes are formed as the shell grows forward, while the old holes become covered over, so that only a few younger holes are open at any one time, the rest appearing as a line of bumps.

*Some abalones are among the largest shellfish: they range in size from the 1 in. long and very rare **Haliotis pourtalese** to the red abalone of California, which is a foot across.*

Abalone showing edge of foot and its frill of tentacles which seek out its seaweed food.

Distribution, habitat and habits

Abalones are to be found in many parts of the world: along the coasts of the Mediterranean, Africa, Australia, New Zealand, the Pacific islands, and the western coast of North America. In the Atlantic they are found as far north as St. Malo and the Channel Islands. The rare species *Haliotis pourtalese* is found off Florida. It is known mainly from specimens washed up on the shore, as it lives at depths of 350–1 200 ft. It is thus the deepest-living of all abalones; the rest live between the extreme low-water mark and a depth of about 60 ft along rocky shores where there is no sand to clog the gills or in rocky pools large enough not to be heated too quickly by the sun. The only other exception is the black abalone, which lives in the splash zone where waves breaking against rocks alternately cover and expose it.

Unlike their limpet relatives, abalones have no 'home', no spot on a rock where they always return after feeding. They simply hide up in a crevice or under a rock, avoiding the light and coming out at night. When disturbed an abalone grips the rock face, using its foot as a suction pad: the two main muscles of the body exert a tremendous force—up to 400 lb in a 4 in. specimen. Unlike the limpet, the abalone cannot bring its shell down over the whole of its body: the edge of the foot, with its frill of tentacles, is left sticking out.

Abalones move in the same way as limpets and snails. Waves of muscular contraction pass along the foot, pushing it forward. As each part expands it is fixed to the ground by slimy mucus: the part in front, expanding in turn, is pressed forward and then itself stuck down. Abalones differ from limpets and snails in having a sort of bipedal movement. Alternate waves of movement pass down either side of the foot, so that as a part of one side is moving the corresponding part on the other side stays fixed.

△ *Left: Mother of pearl, used in making jewellery, lines the inside of the abalone shells. Right: A black abalone without encrusting seaweeds which grow on most other species.*

▽ *The starfish is one of the abalone's main enemies. It uses its hundreds of sucker feet to prize the abalone away from its rock. The starfish then turns its stomach inside out and pushes it beneath the abalone's shell to dissolve away its flesh.*

△ *The abalone breathes through the line of holes in the top of its shell. As it grows, new ones form and others are covered over.*

▽ *The remarkable teeth of a radula, the mollusc tongue, magnified 1,450 times by using a deep field scanning electron microscope.*

The rate of travel is very rapid for a shellfish: a speed of 5—6 yd/min has been recorded—although no abalone would cover this distance in one dash.

Many-toothed tongue for feeding

Abalones are vegetarians, crawling over rock faces and browsing on seaweeds that they seek out with their sensitive tentacles. Their favourite foods are the delicate red weeds and green sea lettuces, although they also scrape tissue off fragments of kelp that have been torn away by waves. Young abalones eat the forms of life that encrust rocks, such as the coral-like plant *Corallina*.

Food is scraped up and chewed into small pieces by the rasp-like action of the radula, a tongue made up of large numbers of small, chalky teeth.

100,000 eggs laid

Some molluscs are hermaphrodite but all individual abalones are of one sex or the other. They reach sexual maturity at six years. The germ cells, or gametes, are shed directly into the sea, causing great wastage. Thus a female will liberate 100,000 or more eggs, and the sea around a male turns milky over a radius of 3 ft when he sheds his spawn. To reduce wastage, however, the female does not shed eggs until induced by the presence of sperms around her.

The fertilised eggs are covered by a gelatinous coat and float freely in the sea until they hatch a few hours later as minute trochophore larvae. These trochophore larvae are top-shaped and swim around by means of a band of hair-like cilia around the thickest part. Within a day the trochophore develops into a veliger—a miniature version of the adult complete with shell but still with the band of cilia. Two days later it loses the cilia, sinks to the bottom and starts to develop into an adult, a process that takes several weeks.

The free-swimming larvae have advant-

ages in that they are the means by which the otherwise rather sedentary abalones can spread, but they are very vulnerable and are eaten in their millions by plankton-eating fish like anchovies and herrings.

Enemies everywhere

Although mortality is heaviest during the free-swimming stage, adult abalones also have several enemies. Fish, sea birds, sea otters, crabs and starfish dislodge the abalones or chew bits off them. Their only protection lies in their tenacity in clinging to rocks and the protective camouflage of the shell and foot. This camouflage is improved by the seaweeds and sedentary animals that settle on the shell. Also, it has been found that when young abalones feed on red weeds their shells become red.

On the other hand abalones are more vulnerable due to the boring sponge *Cliona lobata,* which erodes holes in their shells and so opens them up to other predators. In the Channel Islands as many as 95% of a sample of abalones have been found to be infected with boring sponges.

Dark pearls, called blister pearls, are sometimes found in abalones. Like the real pearls of oysters, these are formed by the animal to cover up a source of irritation— in this case a minute parasitic clam, *Pholadidea parva,* that bores through the abalone's shell and into its tissues.

Prized for shell and meat

The shells of abalones are prized because, although they are superficially rough and dull, cleaning reveals the gleam of mother of pearl. This and the large size of the shell make abalones popular with shell collectors, and they are also used for making costume jewellery. The body itself is much esteemed as food. The large foot is cut into strips, beaten with a mallet to make it soft, and then fried. The edge of the foot is trimmed off to make chowder.

The popularity of abalones and the ease with which they can be collected from the shore has led to stocks being severely depleted. In California, which is the centre of the abalone industry, only strict laws have prevented its extinction. As abalones do not breed until they are six years old and perhaps 4 in. long, there is a minimum length at which they can be taken: for the common red abalone this is 7 in., corresponding to about 12 years of age. There is a close season—though it now seems that abalones breed all the year round—and catches are limited to five a day and can only be taken by a licence-holder.

Finally, abalone meat cannot be exported from the State of California. This does not mean, however, that it cannot be obtained outside California, as tinned abalone meat is exported from Mexico and Japan.

phylum	**Mollusca**
class	**Gastropoda**
order	**Prosobranchiata**
genera	***Haliotis rufescens*** (*red abalone*) ***H. fulgens*** (*green abalone*) ***H. cracherodii*** (*black abalone*) *others*

Cone shell

There are 500 to 600 species of cone shells—sea snails named for the shape of their shells. As in an ordinary snail, the shell consists of a tube wrapped round a central column. In the cones the tube is flattened making a long, tapering shell. The cone is formed by the large outside whorl of the tube, with its narrow, slit-like opening extending to the tip of the cone. The base of this cone is formed by the short, and sometimes almost flat, spire formed by the exposed parts of the inner whorls. The surface of the shell is generally smooth with a dotted or lacy pattern of brown on white.

The cones range up to about 9 in. long, the majority being much smaller. Attached to the foot of the mollusc is an elongated operculum, the horny lid or door that seals the aperture of the shell when its owner retires inside. When the snail is active, a pair of sensory tentacles and a long siphon protrude from the front of the body. Water is drawn in through the siphon by the cilia and passed over the gills in the cavity within the shell.

Habits

The cones are found in tropical and subtropical waters, mainly in the western Atlantic and around the Philippines and the Malay Archipelago across the Indian Ocean to East Africa, up the Red Sea and in the Mediterranean. They live in shallow water to a depth of several hundred feet. Some live in coral reefs, others in coral sand or rubble. They are active mainly by night, coming out to feed after lying up in crevices or under stones during the day, or burying themselves in the sand with only the siphon showing.

Hunts with a poison harpoon

The cones are carnivorous, feeding on worms, other molluscs or even live fish such as blennies or gobies, each species having its own preferred prey, which it first paralyses and then swallows whole. Capture of the prey is accomplished by means of a snout-like proboscis armed with long poisonous teeth. The teeth are basically the same structures as those on the tongue or radula of other snails, like the abalone (see page 37) or banded snail. In most snails there are many small teeth forming a file for scraping off particles of food, but in the cones there are only a few teeth, each as much as ⅜ in. long. Each tooth is a long, barbed, hollow

harpoon mounted on a mobile stalk. Associated with these teeth is a poison gland, connected by a long tube to the teeth. The viscous, milky white poison is squeezed out by the contraction of muscles around the poison gland.

Cone shells detect scent particles secreted by their prey with a sense organ called the osphradium, which 'tastes' the water as it is drawn through the siphon. A fish-eating cone shell will respond if water from a tank containing fish is put in its own tank.

The cone will either track down its prey, if it is another slow-moving animal such as a worm or mollusc, or lie in wait. The final stages of attack are controlled by touch. The proboscis is brought out of its sheath and held poised, then brought rapidly down onto the prey. At the same time a single tooth is everted and thrust into the victim's body. In seconds it is paralysed by the poison and the cone shell can eat it at leisure. The mouth at the end of the proboscis dilates and engulfs the victim's body, rapid muscular contractions forcing it down the gullet with the help of a lubricating secretion. Swallowing and digestion may take several hours, and during this time the snail cannot retreat into the shell.

The tooth usually breaks off when it has been used and another is brought forward

The marble cone, **Conus marmoreus**, a common inhabitant of coral reefs of the Indo-Pacific, is up to 4 in. long. It feeds on other cones.

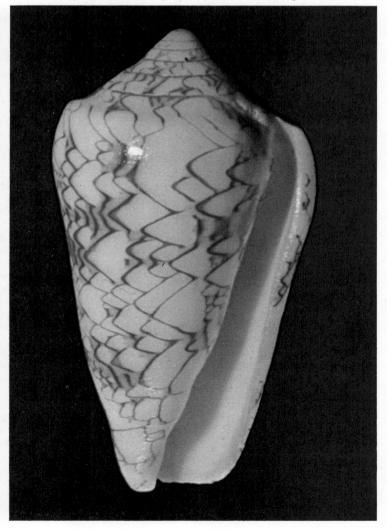

The poison teeth of the striated cone, **Conus striatus**, are used as miniature harpoons to kill small fishes, such as blennies and gobies.

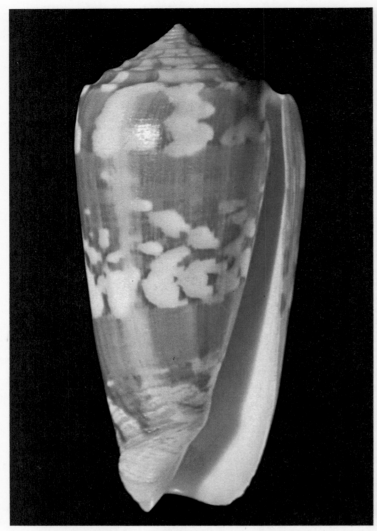

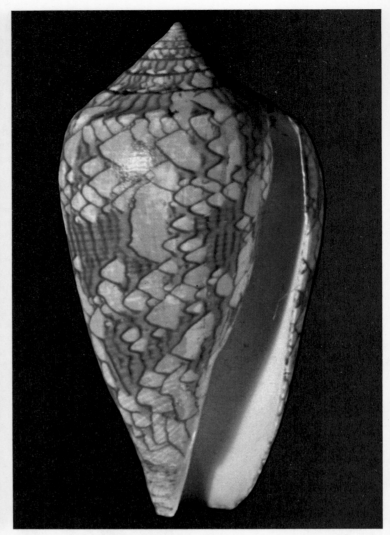

Conus textile, one of several sea snails of tropical seas, known as cone shells. These molluscs are carnivorous, and have poison glands associated with their radula teeth, for killing prey.

Another example of *Conus textile* which, when compared with the first, shows how patterns vary from one individual to another within the same species. *Textile* is Latin for a piece of cloth.

for the next victim. The poison is related to curare (the famous arrow poison of American Indians) and paralyses the victim's muscles. If the prey is another mollusc the paralysis makes it lose its grip on its shell so the cone can draw it out.

Breeding
The eggs are laid in vase-shaped capsules of a hard, parchment-like material. The capsules are attached by their bases in lines or groups to the coral or rock. They hatch in about 10 days.

The Glory of the Sea
Their beauty has resulted in cones being used for money, in the manner of cowries, and Rembrandt was sufficiently impressed by the marbled cone *Conus marmoreus* to depict it in his etching of 1650, 'The Little Horn'. Careful as ever to etch his signature in mirror image, he neglected to do the same for the shell which therefore twists the wrong way in the print.

The shells are also highly esteemed by collectors and of all shells the one that has been held most precious is the rare Glory of the Sea, *Conus gloriamaris*. Its shell has a fine network pattern of pink-brown on a light background. Although a most beautiful

shell, it was its rarity that once tempted an American collector to pay $2 000 for a specimen, and others regularly change hands for several hundred dollars. The earliest record of the Glory of the Sea is in a catalogue of 1757 when a specimen was sold at the Zoological Museum of Copenhagen. A few other specimens were found later, but towards the end of the 19th century the species was considered by some people to have become extinct as a result of the destruction of the reef which was its only known home. In fact, specimens had been found elsewhere before this, but many years passed before the next came to light in 1957, when one was found in the Philippines. Since then a number of others have been found off Indonesia, the Philippines and in the sea east of New Guinea, so that by 1966 over 50 had been found and the Glory of the Sea was no longer the most prized of shells.

The poisonous teeth with which the cones despatch their prey present a great danger to the collector who must pick up the living animals with extreme caution. Some, like the Mediterranean species *C. mediterraneus* are too puny to be troublesome and others may sting no more severely than a bee, but in other cases the pain may be excruciating and even fatal, death ensuing in 4 or 5

hours. One survey gives the death rate as 20% of all people stung, higher than that due to cobra or rattlesnake. When the cone stings it does so very rapidly and the victim may at first be unaware of the attack. Pain comes later, together with numbness, blurred vision and difficulty in breathing. A Japanese collector who was stung by the geographer cone *C. geographus* was able to walk just over a mile before collapsing, and dying of heart and breathing failure. The Glory of the Sea and many others are also very poisonous, and with the increase in the number of people collecting shells with aqua-lung apparatus, the number of deaths is sure to rise.

phylum	**Mollusca**
class	**Gastropoda**
sub-class	**Prosobranchia**
order	**Neogastropoda**
family	**Conidae**
genus	***Conus***

Giant snail

A pest in many parts of the world,
Achatina fulica *is a large land-living
snail, native to East Africa. With its
pointed shell, 5 or even 8 in. long, it
weighs about ½ lb. This species deserves
the title of giant snail, although there are
other large terrestrial snails in many of the
warmer countries, because of its notoriety
and economic importance. The fact that
even larger snails live in the sea seems
somehow less remarkable.*

*In other respects, there is little of
note in the appearance of the giant snail
as compared with the snails of our gardens.*

Dusk feeder

The giant snail feeds mainly by night or
at dusk, usually returning after its forays
to a regular 'home'. However, it will also
come out by day if there is rain or if the sky
is overcast. For continued activity, dampness
and a temperature above about 24°C/75°F
are needed. On the other hand, during dry
or cold periods it remains inactive, often
deep in some hollow log or under a rock
and withdrawn into its shell, the aperture
closed off with a thin membrane. This state
of inactivity, or aestivation as it is called,
has been known to last for as long as a year
—a long enough time, but not to be compared with the 6 years recorded for an
individual of another species of snail. When
so much time can be spent in suspended
animation, records of longevity have little
meaning, but one specimen is recorded as
having lived 9 years in captivity.

Voracious feeders

To a large extent the giant snail feeds on
rotten plant matter and dead animals but
it will also feed voraciously on the leaves,
fruit, bark and flowers of a great variety of
plants—including, unfortunately, crops
like beans, breadfruit, cabbage, cacao,
citrus trees, melons, yam plants and rubber.
Needing calcium to form its shell, it may
even climb walls of houses to ravage the
whitewash on them for its lime content.

Pea-sized eggs

These giant snails begin breeding when
about a year old and, like their smaller
relatives, are hermaphrodite. They lay eggs
the size of small peas, like miniature bird's
eggs with lemon-yellow shells. These they
deposit, 40—500 at a time, in or on the
soil, doing so every 2 or 3 months. The
young hatch in 1—10 days. A single snail
can apparently lay eggs without mating
after months of isolation, for evidently
sperm can be stored for this time before
being used. One result is that a single snail
can suffice to found a new colony if it was
fertilised before being transported.

Growth of a pest

In its East African home, the giant snail
is hardly a pest, but it has spread from
there to many of the warmer parts of the
world, becoming in most of them a considerable pest. Like the rabbit in Australia,
it is one of too many examples of animals
or plants, originally fairly innocuous,
that have become pests outside their native
lands. Everything about this snail, such as
its ability to eat almost any plant material
and its high rate of reproduction, combined
with its hardiness and a scarcity of natural
enemies, favour its chances of colonising
new areas, provided that the climate is
suitable. Just a few individuals need be
introduced—even one is enough.

The spread of the giant snail started in
about 1800 when some were taken to
Mauritius by the wife of the governor on
doctor's orders (medicinal properties have
been ascribed to these snails as to others).
There they multiplied and became a pest.
Some were taken to the island of Réunion
and to the Seychelles and, in 1847, some
were released in Calcutta. From then on the
snail has appeared in more and more countries—particularly in the Indo-Pacific area,
including Malaya, Indonesia, the Philippines, Thailand, Vietnam, and China.

Sometimes introductions have been accidental, the snails being transported while
aestivating in bananas, in soil, or in motor
vehicles. Sometimes they have been deliberately introduced. In 1928, for instance,
they were introduced to Sarawak to be used
as poultry feed and in 1936 to the Hawaiian
islands by a lady wishing to keep two in her
garden as pets. The Japanese forces took
them as food for themselves into New
Guinea and elsewhere and, before the
Second World War, they were eaten by
Malays and by Chinese in various places.
Other related giant snails are important as
food in parts of West Africa. In Ghana
they are the greatest single source of animal
protein. The value of snails as food, however, even to those willing to eat them, is
more than offset by the damage they can
inflict on crops and gardens, for they can
occur in huge numbers, like apples under
an apple tree.

The nuisance does not end there, for in
places the ground may become slippery
with slime, excreta and dead snails, and
roads in Sri Lanka and Saipan have been turned into 'stinking nightmares' as more
and more snails are attracted to their crushed
fellows. Worse still, the slimy mess provides
breeding grounds for disease-bearing flies.
With others dying in drinking wells, devouring with impunity the warfarin bait
and springing the traps put out for rats,
it is hardly surprising that much effort is
devoted to their control. Poisons have been
used as well as various predators—including
other carnivorous snails—but always there
is the danger in these methods of upsetting
the balance of nature in yet other ways,
such as the controlling predators attacking innocuous species, and so becoming
pests themselves. The best method of all,
if it can be used in time, is a rigorous system of control to prevent the spread of the
snail. It is encouraging that, in some areas,
after an initial heavy infestation, the population diminishes to a steady level at which
they are not such serious pests.

phylum	**Mollusca**
class	**Gastropoda**
order	**Stylommatophora**
family	**Achatinidae**
genus & species	***Achatina fulica*** *East Africa* *A. achatina* *West Africa*

*This West African giant snail has a pointed shell 5—8 in. long and weighs about ½ lb. Introduction
into many parts of the world mainly for its food value has resulted in it becoming a pest.*

Limpet

'Limpet' is a term applied to various kinds of snails which, while not necessarily closely related, have two features in common. They cling tightly to rocks or other surfaces and they have a shell that is more or less tent-shaped. The best-known is the common limpet, flither or papshell, and related to it is the pretty little blue-rayed limpet or peacock's feathers, found on some of the large brown seaweeds at low tide, and the tortoiseshell limpet **Acmaea tessulata**. The keyhole limpet **Fissurella costaria** is named for the hole in the top of its conical shell and the slit limpet **Emarginula elongata** for the slit at the front. The Chinaman's hat **Calyptraea chinensis**, which retains a trace of its spire, is classified in the separate order Mesogastropoda. The limpet form has also been evolved independently in certain relatives of the pond snails. This repeated emergence of the limpet form in the evolution of snails is due to the advantage it gives in withstanding the action of fast-moving or turbulent water. It is particularly advantageous on rocky, wave-battered shores and it is on these that the common limpet, the main subject of this article, is so successful and abundant.

Under the protection of its ribbed, conical shell, which may reach nearly 3 in. in length, the common limpet has a grey-green oval foot with a large flat adhesive surface. At the front is the head with its big ear-like tentacles, each bearing an eye near its base. Lining the shell around its margin is the thin layer of tissue that secretes it and all around this skirt and lying in the space between it and the foot are many small ciliated gills and short tentacles.

Limpets are not suckers

The common limpet may occur in great numbers on rocky shores, from low water even to above the highest tide levels, provided the rocks are well splashed and shaded. As well as being resistant to wide temperature fluctuations limpets may flourish where the sea is greatly diluted with fresh water. Shells high up on the shore tend to be taller and thicker, especially near the apex, than those living lower down or in rock pools. Limpets are very difficult to dislodge, unless taken by surprise, and Reaumur found that a weight of 28 lb could be supported when attached to the shell.

Carving itself a niche

As well as giving resistance to wave action the ability to cling serves to protect limpets from predators. They are, however, a favourite food of oystercatchers and rats may take them in large numbers, dislodging them by a sudden movement of the jaws. It has been known for the tables to be

△ *Chain of slipper limpets (with shore crabs). The slipper limpet forms chains of eight or nine, one on top of the other.*
▽ *Flattened delicate tortoiseshell limpet.*
▷▽ *The blue-rayed limpet with its rows of vivid blue spots.*
▷ *Village of common limpets.*

turned and for a rat to become trapped with its lip under the shell, and birds have been caught by their toes. That man at one time ate them in large numbers is evident from the shells in his old kitchen middens.

A further advantage is that the limpet can seal a little water amongst its gills and so avoid drying up when the tide is out and in this, as well as in its clinging, it is helped by the close fit of shell to rock. This comes about in the first place from the choice of a suitable resting place, but it is improved both by the growth of the shell to fit the rock and by the abrasion of the rock to fit the shell. Each limpet has a definite 'home' to which it returns after each feeding excursion. Often the rock becomes so worn the limpet comes to lie in a shallow scar of just the right size and shape.

How limpets get home

Limpets leave their 'home' when the tide is in and the water not too rough, also when the tide is out at night or if they are sheltered by seaweeds. They feed by rasping at the small green algae on rocks, moving around with head and tentacles protruding and swinging from side to side. Large seaweeds are not often eaten but these may be prevented from colonising areas of rock through being devoured when small. On the return journey, the limpet tends to retrace its outward track at least in part. It seems to have some kind of directional

memory for feeling its way about like a blind man as it can still return even if its tentacles are removed and its outward track is obliterated by scrubbing with detergent or chipping away stone placed in its path. The journey may cover 2 or 3 ft and limpets moved farther away rarely return home.

Cold-weather larvae

The common limpet breeds during the colder months—September to April—shedding its eggs freely into the sea. The tiny trochophore larvae hatch out about 24 hours after fertilisation. Each is $\frac{1}{120}$ in. across, with a belt of long cilia around its middle, a tuft of them on top and short cilia covering the surface between the two. A day later, the larvae become veligers with little shells. These settle and grow to about an inch long in a year. Limpets may live as long as 15 years.

Changeable sexes

Most limpets start life as males and remain this way until they are 1 in. long. As they get older, however, the proportion of females increases as the limpets reverse their sex. This has gone much further in the slipper limpet *Crepidula fornicata*, a native of North American seas which was accidentally introduced into British waters in a cargo of oysters and has since made its way round the English coast. It is not related to the common limpet, and its shell resembles a rounded slipper when laid on its back. The slipper limpet forms chains of up to eight or nine, one on top of another. It is a serious pest of oyster beds and its arrival was first noted in Britain in the 1880's and since then it has become very well established on some parts of the coast and it has spread from there to other parts of Europe. In a chain of slipper limpets, the bottom ones are females and the upper, younger ones, males: those in between are of intermediate sex. It is believed that the females release a substance into the water that causes young limpets to stay in the vicinity and to develop male characters. Young males may later move off, however, and become females, and immature individuals that settle on rock and not on females may themselves become females with only a short male phase, or none at all. Slipper limpets do not move about in search of food, but strain it from the water.

phylum	**Mollusca**
class	**Gastropoda**
subclass	**Prosobranchia**
order	**Archaeogastropoda**
family	**Patellidae**
genera & species	*Patella vulgata* common limpet *Patina pellucida* *blue-rayed limpet, others*

Slug

Broadly speaking a slug is a snail without a shell. This is, however, not strictly correct because it may have a vestigial shell, usually hidden within the body. Slugs belong to the Pulmonata, a large group of land and freshwater molluscs that breathe by means of a lung. There are three types: keelback slugs, roundback slugs and shelled slugs, forming the families Limacidae, Arionidae and Testacellidae respectively. The first are named for the ridge or keel on the upper surface of the body towards the hind end. Behind the head with its four tentacles the back is covered by a roughly elliptical mantle-shield perforated by the respiratory pore on its right margin. In the keelback slugs this opening lies behind the middle of the mantle shield. In the roundback slugs the pore is farther forward. The tiny shell is a flattened oval, horny and with little lime in it, hidden under the mantle shield in the keelback slugs, but usually reduced to a number of separate chalky granules in the roundback slugs. An exception is seen in the North American roundback slug **Binneya** in which there is an external spiral shell. The largest of these slugs may be 8 in. long, as in **Agriolimax columbianus** of North America.

In the third group, the shelled slugs, there is a small shell visible on the surface towards the rear of the animal. A shelled slug may be anything up to 5 in. in length. Its mantle, heart and kidney lie under the shell towards the broad rear, instead of towards the front as in the other two families and a groove runs forward from the mantle on either side of the body, giving off branches to the back and flanks.

Tree climbers

Through having such a useless, almost nonexistent shell a slug is more vulnerable to predators and, more important, perhaps, to drying up. However, the animal's load is lightened, its need for calcium is much less and it can creep through much smaller holes than a snail. So slugs live in damp places and some species spend most of their lives underground. They are most active at night, or by day when it is wet, and some regularly return to the same 'home' after feeding. Though most feed near ground level, some are good climbers and regularly ascend trees to heights of 30 ft or more; the tree slug, Lehmannia marginata, formerly known as Limax arboreum, and field slug, Agriolimax agrestis, are two such climbers. The silver trails of slime running up and down some tree trunks attest to these activities, but the slug may take a more rapid route for the descent and lower itself many feet through the air on a string of slime. Such slugs spend the day in knotholes, coming down to the ground at dusk and climbing up again about dawn.

△ Month-long incubation nearly over, **Limax flavius** eggs with embryos visible (approx ×5).

▷ A roundback, **Arion ater**. Although called the large black slug, its colour is very variable.

Other food than seedlings

Although hated by the gardener slugs may be vastly more numerous in his garden than even he is aware and, taking them as a group, very little of their food consists of the plants he has cultivated, except where there are few alternatives. Some slugs feed almost entirely on fungi, eating little or no green food and then only when it is dying or rotting. Many slugs are omnivorous and are attracted by fungi, greenstuff, tubers, carrion, dung, kitchen refuse or the metaldehyde-baited bran put out to kill them. They are drawn to such foods over distances of several feet by the odour, a slug's organs of smell being in its tentacles. In confinement, slugs may turn upon each other, but the shelled slugs are particularly notable for their predacious habits. They are most common in well-manured gardens and live underground most of the time. They feed by night on earthworms and to a lesser extent on centipedes and other slugs, seizing them with their needle-like teeth and swallowing them whole.

Aerial courtship

Slugs are hermaphrodite and although self-fertilisation can occur a two-way exchange of sperm between mating pairs is usual. In the first stages of mating, roundback and keelback slugs typically trail around each other in a circle, constantly licking each other and devouring each other's slime until they come to lie side by side. The great grey slug Limax maximus, up to 4 in. long, concludes this circling in a particularly spectacular manner. Climbing first up a tree or wall, the two slugs circle for a period of $\frac{1}{2}-2\frac{1}{2}$ hours, flapping their mantles and eating each other's slime. Then suddenly they wind spirally around each other before launching themselves heads downward into the air on a thick cord of slime perhaps 18 in. long. Now the penis of each is unrolled to a length of 2 in. and entwined with the other into a whorled knot. Sperm masses are exchanged after which the slugs either fall to the ground or re-ascend their lifeline, eating it as they go. The eggs are laid soon afterwards in some damp recess such as under a stone or among roots. The soft amber eggs hatch in about a month.

Many enemies

Despite their unpleasant slime, slugs are eaten by a variety of predators, including frogs, toads, hedgehogs, ducks, blackbirds, thrushes and other birds. Ducks are especially good for controlling the numbers of slugs. Slow-worms and various insects also take their toll. Though sheep are not deliberate predators of slugs, they do eat them accidentally and in doing so may become infected with lungworm, a parasitic nematode, whose larvae have formed cysts in the foot of the slug.

Universal panacea

For many centuries slugs have been regarded in folk lore as a sovereign remedy for a variety of ailments, eaten alive or boiled in milk for the cure of tuberculosis, for example, or in the form of ashes to relieve such diverse ills as ulcers, dysentery or hydrocephalus. The internal shell, or the little chalky grains representing it, were often regarded as particularly efficacious and, as Pliny recorded, quick relief could be obtained if the granules were placed in a hollow tooth. Warts even now are the target of various odd forms of treatment and one in recent use, at least until the turn of the century, if not later, involved the use of slugs. The method was to rub the wart with the slug and then to impale the mollusc on a thorn. As it died and withered away, so did the wart. One may doubt the value of these old remedies, but there are many people today who seek 'solace in a slug'.

phylum	**Mollusca**
class	**Gastropoda**
subclass	**Pulmonata**
order	**Stylommatophora**
family	**Limacidae**
genera	**Limax, Agriolimax, Lehmannia, Milax**
family	**Arionidae**
genera	**Geomalacus, Arion**
family	**Testacellidae**
genus	**Testacella**

Cockle

Of the various cockles the commonest by far is the edible cockle. Although its scientific name is now **Cerastoderma edule**, it is referred to in many books by the older name of **Cardium edule**, a name that reflects the heart-shaped appearance of the pair of shells viewed end-on, as well as the tastiness of their contents. The cockle is an unusually globular bivalve mollusc and the two 'valves', or shells, are similar in shape, unlike those of the scallop which, however, they resemble in being radially ribbed.

There are ten other British species of cockle in the superfamily Cardiacea. The largest, growing to a length of 4 in., is the spiny cockle, or red-nose, **Acanthocardia aculeata (Cardium aculeatum)** found mainly on the South Devon coast. It is named for the spines along the ribs on its shell and for its cardinal-red foot. Another spined species, smaller and more widely distributed, is the prickly cockle **A. echinata**. There are other bivalves that are known as cockles, but belong to other groups of molluscs, including the large heart cockle, **Glossus humanus**, **Cyprina islandica**, **Isocardia cor** and others.

The 200 or so species of cockles in the Cardiacea have a world-wide distribution and 11 occur around the coasts of Britain. The edible cockle is found from high-

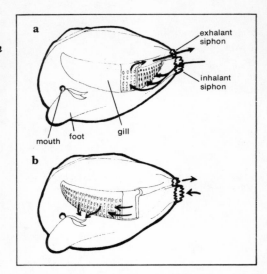

Above right: Cockle's siphon mechanism. **a**: Water is sucked in by one siphon and expelled by another, after passing through the gill. **b**: Trapped food drawn in with water is passed to the mouth by cilia. *Below*: Spiny cockle with siphon on right and pink foot showing between edges of mantle.

tide level down to 8 000 ft deep, lying obliquely not more than 2 in. below the surface of clean sand especially but also in mud or muddy gravel. Generally the average size increases from high to low water. It is particularly common in the sheltered waters of bays and the mouths of estuaries, as many as 10 000 having been recorded to a square metre. Although cockles do live in estuaries, the largest, about 2 in. long, are found far from fresh water. Dilution of the salt water with fresh has the curious effect of producing a less regularly shaped shell which is thinner and has fewer ribs than usual.

Digging with its foot

A cockle, in a most remarkable piece of behaviour for a mollusc, may sometimes skip upwards, bending in the middle, its orange, tongue-like foot protruded between the two valves and pressing the tip into the sand before suddenly straightening it. Usually, however, this merely rolls the cockle over a few times. More often if the cockle has been dislodged and has to move it will creep along with its foot and re-bury itself.

It has been suggested that the 20—24 ribs that radiate out from the hinge region help to hold the cockle firmly in the mud or sand in which it is usually just buried, and that the globular shape helps to protect the animal should it be dislodged and rolled about by wave action.

At the back of the body is a pair of short tubes, or siphons, joined at the base like the legs of a pair of trousers. Water containing oxygen and the plankton and organic matter which are the food of the cockle, is drawn in through the lower one, that farthest from the hinge. Through the upper sweeps an outgoing jet, carrying wastes. The siphons are the only parts of the buried animal to project above the sand, and so they are an appropriate site for the eyes. These are small but surprisingly complex, with retinas and lenses, and are mounted on sensory tentacles. They enable the tentacles to be withdrawn if a shadow falls on them, so protecting them from predators, but presumably eyes can have little other use in such a sedentary, filter feeding animal.

To see what drives water through the siphons, one must open the valves which can be done when the cockle is clamped shut, by cutting through the two muscles, the adductors—one on each end and on either side of the hinge—that pull the valves together. If the cockle is dead, the valves may have already been forced partly open by the elastic ligament associated with the hinge which opposes the action of the muscles. The shell opened, the gills are revealed as a pair of flaps of tissue on each side of the foot, covered with countless tiny cilia whose beating sets up currents of water and propels the particles of food towards the mouth.

Usually a cockle stays in one place, and a tuft of algae may grow on it as if it were a stone. When the tide goes out the siphons are withdrawn but the site where the cockle is buried just below the sand may be revealed by the tuft of algae.

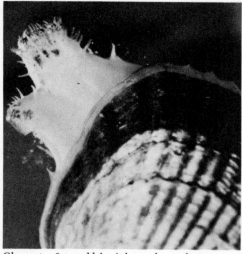

Close-up of a cockle's siphons shows the eye-bearing tentacles at their tips.

Conveyor belt digestion

Cockles feed on the small plant particles that abound in the water: single-celled plants such as diatoms and the spores and fragments of larger algae. There is little selection of what is eaten, however, and the stomach usually contains much sand and mud as well. The water bearing these particles enters through the lower end of one of the siphons and out by the other after passing through the fine latticework of the sieve-like gills. The cilia, as well as creating this current, also act to propel the trapped food towards the mouth, itself flanked by a pair of cilia-covered lips. In the stomach is a curious structure found in molluscs only, a rotating coiled rod 20—26 mm long called a 'crystalline style', turned by cilia lining the pocket which secretes it. The crystalline style, made up of digestive enzymes, gradually wears away and dissolves at the tip. Its rotation serves to draw along the food particles trapped in strings of mucus, as on a windlass, and at the same time its enzymes help to digest the food.

Chancy breeding

Though some related species are hermaphrodite, the sexes are separate in the edible cockle. Spawning begins at the end of February or early in March and continues till June or July, the eggs and milt being released freely into the water. Such eggs as become fertilised by this uncertain means develop into minute, free-swimming 'veliger' larvae, propelled by the beating of cilia. Eventually each develops a shell and foot, if it has not been eaten, and the resulting young cockles, still less than 1 mm long, settle on the sea bottom, some falling on stony ground and others on the sand or mud in which they can grow to maturity. The success of spawning varies from year to year and populations tend to be kept up by particularly good 'spat falls' perhaps once in 3 or 4 years.

As the shells grow, fine concentric grooves appear, marking former positions of the shell edge and providing a guide to age. The groove reflects the slower growth of the shell in winter when lack of sunshine means there is less plankton food available. A full-grown cockle has some 3—6 grooves and is about that many years old.

Cockle graveyard. Cockleshells are distinguished by their 20—24 radiating ribs.

Many enemies

For those cockles that escape man, life is still precarious, for they may be attacked by various parasites from within and by other creatures from without: snails that bore holes through their shells, starfish that pull open the valves by sheer persistence and push out their stomachs between them (see abalone, page 37), gulls that attack when the tide is out and flatfish, like plaice and dab, when the tide is in. In addition, cockles can be stranded above high tide level by storms or carried away to other unsuitable areas. They may be killed, like other shore creatures, by excessive heat or cold as in the winter of 1904—5 when the Lancashire coasts were covered with ice floes and hundreds of tons of dead cockles were washed up the beach.

Athletic cockles

It has often been said that cockles can leap across the sand. A naturalist in the early years of this century used to entertain his friends with a story about cockles hitting him in the back. As he was walking up the beach he felt something, perhaps a stone, hit him in the small of the back. He turned about, to find nobody in sight. Continuing up the beach he was again hit in the back. Again he turned and could see nobody. This time, however, he saw one of the cockles leap, and realized what was happening. He did not say what kind of cockles they were, however.

Admittedly, this naturalist was not a tall man, but his story may have made up for his own lack of inches. From what we now know, the spiny cockle does leap, but to nothing like that extent. It has a very long red foot, much longer than most other cockles. When the tube-feet of a starfish, the cockle's hereditary enemy, touch its shell the spiny cockle leaps—for a distance of 8 in.

phylum	Mollusca
class	Bivalvia
subclass	Lamellibranchia
order	Heterodonta
family	Cardiidae
genus & species	*Cerastoderma edule* others

47

Mussel

Various kinds of bivalve molluscs are known as mussels, including horse mussel **Modiolus modiolus**, fan mussel **Pinna fragilis** and the freshwater swan mussels **Anodonta spp**. The best known, however, is the common or edible mussel **Mytilus edulis**, a species widely distributed over most of the temperate and subtropical coasts of the northern hemisphere, where it is found in very large numbers on the shores and down to about 30 ft. There are closely related species in other parts of the world. Both 'mussel' and 'muscle' derive from Latin **musculus**, a small mouse.

The adult edible mussel is 2–5 in. long but may be much smaller in some localities or, exceptionally, nearly 9 in. Typically blue or purple, or sometimes brown or with radial dark brown or purple markings, each of the two valves making up the shell is broad at the hind end and narrow at the front. Near the front end is the hinge and the elastic ligament that pushes the shell open when the muscles inside relax. There is one of these 'adductor' muscles at each end, running from one valve to the other, that at the hind end being largest and strongest. Their points of attachment can be seen as 'scars' inside empty shells, together with those of other muscles that withdraw the foot. When the mussel is submerged, this long brownish foot may be seen protruding from between the valves. Not only is it used for moving about, but also for making the tough protein threads, forming the byssus or beard, with which the mussel is normally anchored.

Millions of mussels

Secured by their byssus threads as by guy ropes, edible mussels are found from high on the shore to a depth of a few fathoms, principally near low tide mark, on rocks, pier piles or stones lying in mud or gravel. Few molluscs can rival them in abundance. Exceptionally, concentrations of 16 000 to a square foot have been seen and in some parts of the coast there may be 20 million in a mile stretch. In the northern hemisphere they range from the Kara Sea to the Mediterranean, on both coasts of North America and around Japan, as well as in a few other localities outside these areas, but not in the high arctic. The other species, such as the California mussel, *M. californianus* and the Australian mussel, *M. obscurus*, are so like the common mussel of the northern hemisphere that only an expert can tell them apart. Mussels can live in sea water considerably diluted with fresh water and can tolerate even further dilution for a while by clamping their shells. The adults rarely move about but the young do so fairly often, sometimes freely by means of their long extensible foot and sometimes by throwing out fresh byssus threads to pull themselves along with and then cutting loose the old byssus threads.

△ A series of attachments. Mussels, themselves now covered by small organisms, coat the mooring chain of a ship in the Mediterranean.

▽ Permanent fixtures. Once anchored, adult mussels rarely move about although the young often do so for short periods.

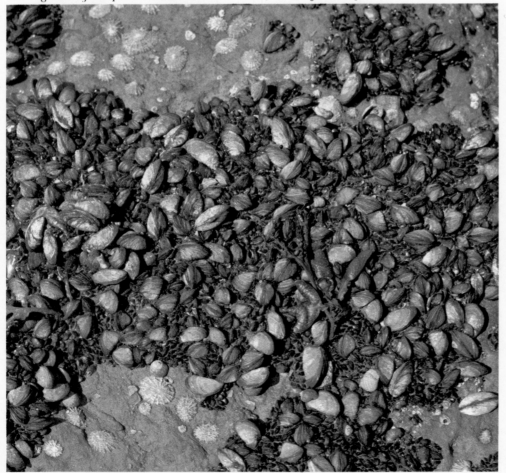

Water purifiers

Mussels feed by straining fine particles from the water together with small floating organisms like diatoms. On each side of the foot is a large gill, each double so there are actually four similar 'gill plates'. Each bears countless cilia beating in such a way as to draw water in at the hind end of the body, through the gill plates and out through a special opening at the rear. The inhalant and exhalant currents do not pass through siphons as well-developed as those of the cockle (page 46). As the food particles hit the gills they are caught up in mucus given out by the gills and are driven with it by cilia to the edges. Here the mucus enters special ciliated channels and moves forwards towards the mouth. On either side of the mouth are two much smaller gill-like flaps that sort the particles, directing the indigestible matter out along special rejection paths and the digestible into the mouth. All this requires the coordinated action of several different kinds of cilia with different functions. Some indication of what happens may be obtained by opening a mussel (cutting the adductor muscles), scattering powder on the gills and watching how it is carried along by the cilia.

Mussels and other animals feeding on microscopic particles are ultimate scavengers in the sea. Some idea of the effect they have can be gauged from an incident that took place at the Millport Marine Biological Station, in Scotland. There was a tank containing a number of common mussels and although there were other animals in it the mussels kept the water so clean that anyone looking down on it from above was unaware that there was any water in the tank. One day a visitor to the Station leaned over this tank and to get a closer look at the animals on the bottom of it, he lowered his face — right into the water!

Only one month's freedom

The breeding season varies with the locality, and also with the temperature of the water. Each egg is only about $\frac{1}{800}$ in. across but a single female may release $5-12$ or even 25 million of them. The eggs are grouped together in short pink rods when they are shed, but these break up on sinking to the bottom. They are fertilised by sperm also released into the water and give rise to free-swimming ciliated embryos after about 5 hours. Towards the end of the second day, the shell appears, at first horn yellow and without a hinge. At this stage, the larvae feed and propel themselves by means of ciliated lobes projecting from their shells. Later the young mussels lose these lobes and improve their buoyancy by giving out a bubble of gas between their valves. Later, this is released, the larvae sink to the bottom, settle and give up their floating life. The free larval stage lasts about a month and by the time of settling, the larvae measure about $\frac{1}{50}-\frac{1}{25}$ in. Having settled, the young mussels may glide about rapidly on their ciliated feet or they may simply anchor themselves with the byssus threads. Until they are about $\frac{1}{8}$ in. long, they have the choice to do either of these, and they sometimes do them even at the surface of the sea, presumably held there by surface tension.

Mussels **Mytilus edulis**, *barnacles and a colony of tunicates grow side by side but independently.*

The world is against them

Mussels have many enemies, including dog whelks, herring gulls, oystercatchers, ducks and walruses as well as fish such as flounders and plaice. Starfish are often their chief predator, however, apart from man. Mussels are considered large enough to eat when just over 2 in. long and two or more years old. They are generally collected by dredging or raking, but in France they are farmed by a method said to have been invented in 1235 by a shipwrecked Irishman whose original intention was to construct a trap for sea birds. In this, tall hurdles are planted in the mud on the foreshore and on these the mussels are hung in bags of netting which eventually rot away after the molluscs have fastened themselves to the hurdles. For commercial purposes mussels are carefully washed and care must be taken by anyone collecting mussels for themselves, since their method of feeding is ideal for concentrating the bacteria in sewage, including those of typhoid. Sometimes, too, mussels produce an alkaloid that can cause death by stopping the breathing. As well as being sold as food, mussels are useful as bait in long-line fishing, as fertilisers, as chicken feed and sometimes for stabilizing the foreshore. At St Anne's-on-Sea, in Lancashire, mussels settle every 2 years on a gravel bed. During the next 2 years they form a mass of mussels and mud 2 ft deep. Then heavy seas roll the whole mass up like a carpet and smash it to pieces, after which the gravel is repopulated with mussels and the process starts all over again. Even so,

the mussel carpet protects the foreshore from violent erosion.

Cloth of gold

The byssus threads are so strong that they can be woven into cloth. There are in various museums objects made from the beards of common fan mussels, for example gloves. The cloth woven from the larger bivalves was extensively used centuries ago to make some garments that had a golden sheen, and were used by the aristocracy especially those of southern Europe. The Field of the Cloth of Gold was an historic meeting between Henry VIII and the King of France. It was so called because so many of the nobles assembled there wore tunics made from the beards of bivalves. It had nothing to do with gold thread. Some other bivalves themselves make unusual use of their own beards. One *Modiolaria* lives embedded in a nest of its own byssus threads. The file shell *Lima* a relative of the scallop, builds a similar nest up to 10 in. across by darning bits of sea-bed debris together.

phylum	**Mollusca**
class	**Bivalvia**
sub-class	**Lamellibranchia**
order	**Anisomyaria**
family	**Mytilidae**
genus & species	*Mytilus edulis*

Oyster

The true oyster of the family Ostreidae is the European flat oyster, **Ostrea edulis**. Its well-known shells are untidy and irregular in outline (often made more so by a variety of encrusting animals and plants growing on them) and there are such big local differences in appearance that with experience one can sometimes tell in which bed a particular oyster lived. The two valves are unlike, the right one being flat and the left convex. They are hinged in the pointed region of the 'beaks', held together by the triangular elastic ligament. There are no hinge teeth such as are found in many bivalves. On each valve a series of wavy ridges centres around the beak, marking former positions of the margin. Ill-defined ridges radiate from the beak of the left valve, while the other valve bears horny scales, which are less rigid than the rest of the shell, allowing the valves to make good contact around the edges when pulled together. Oysters are unusual for the soft porous chalky masses laid down within the substance of the shell. Often, also, in the convex valves of older oysters, there are chambers filled with sea water smelling of hydrogen sulphide. These chambers are the result of the mantle surface shrinking during life, and they get their smell from the putrefaction of organic matter.

Looking between the valves when they are agape, one sees just the edges of the mantle—the tissue that lines, and secretes, the inside of the shell. This thickened mantle edge has short sensory tentacles and a muscular fold that controls the flow of water. Opening the shell farther with a knife, one sees the large central adductor muscle that closes the valves against the pull of the hinge ligament. Arranged more than halfway around this and the general body mass are two double crescentic gills.

The oyster family includes two other genera, **Pycnodonte** and **Crassostrea** (formerly **Gryphaea**). Amongst the latter are the American, Portuguese and Japanese oysters more of which are eaten than of the sweeter European flat oyster. The Portuguese oyster, **C. angulata**, introduced into France in 1868, has been relayed, during the last few years, to beds on the east coast of Britain, but it seldom breeds there. **Crassostrea** is easily distinguished from **Ostrea** since its shell is elongated rather than round, its left valve is more deeply convex and the muscle scars inside are deep purple. Apart from these true oysters, there are other bivalves bearing the name of 'oyster'. These include the tropical pearl oysters **Pinctada** which are closer to the mussels and are, like them, attached by byssus threads, the thorny oysters **Spondylus**, and the saddle oysters **Anomia** which live attached to rocks by thick calcified byssuses which pass straight through a notch in the lower valve.

△ Gourmet's delight, an oyster lies in its larger left valve, pinky white and glistening.

▽ The highly convoluted shell with a fan-shaped base is the home of **Ostrea gigas**.

Several ways of feeding

The European flat oyster occurs down the Atlantic coast of Europe from Norway (latitude 65°) to Morocco and also in the Mediterranean and Black Sea. When it first settles as spat, it becomes attached by its convex left valve, but later it may become detached and turned over. The adult oyster then stays in one place, feeding by filtering small particles from the water. By beating the cilia on its complex, lattice-like gills, it draws a current of water in at a rate of perhaps 2 or 3 gallons an hour. The food particles, caught in mucous strings on these ciliated sieves, are wafted either to the bases or to the free edges of the gills and thence forwards to the mouth via the palps which sit either side of it and have a sorting function. Once in the digestive tract, the particles continue to be propelled by cilia to the elaborate ciliated stomach. It is in the stomachs of bivalves and of a few snails that there occurs perhaps the only truly rotating structure in the whole animal kingdom. This is the crystalline style, a rod of solid digestive enzymes, rotated by cilia in the sac that secretes it, dissolving at the tip where it rubs against a piece of cuticle, the gastric shield, and helping to wind in the strings of mucus in the manner of a windlass.

Not only does digestion take place in the cavity of the gut, but cells lining it also take in particles and digest them in their cytoplasm. Furthermore, some of the particles are engulfed by amoeba-like blood cells that come out into the gut cavity through the stomach walls and then migrate back with the food particles trapped in them.

At times the oyster is in danger of becoming clogged with sediment in its mantle cavity and at such times the valves are clapped shut which suddenly expels the water and sediment. This sudden 'cough' contrasts with the sustained closure of the shell in response to dangers from outside. The adductor muscle is in two parts, different to the naked eye as well as in microscopic structure. One part can contract rapidly; the other is able to remain contracted for long periods without tiring.

Male or female

An oyster may change sex many times during its lifetime. This is not unusual amongst bivalves and the reproductive systems are so simple that the change involves little reorganisation. Maturing first as a male, the oyster takes some weeks to become a functional female but recovers his virility within a few days of discharging her eggs. In the cold waters off Norway, an oyster may change sex once a year, but in warmer waters, many times. Spawning occurs in summer when the temperature of the water exceeds about 15°C/60°F. The eggs pass through the gills against the water current and are fertilised in the mantle cavity by sperms carried in by the feeding current. They are not freed for about another 8 days. Then the shell is opened wide and closed violently at intervals, each time expelling clouds of larvae. Up to a million larvae may be incubated at a time, a large enough number, but small compared with the American oyster, *Crassostrea virginica*, which does not incubate its eggs but can release over a 100 million eggs at a time.

△ *All valves shut tight, a bed of European flat oysters lies exposed on rocks at low tide.*

The eggs of the European flat oyster are about $\frac{1}{200}$ in. across and as they develop within the shell of the parent they change from white to black. At one time, 'whitesick' and 'blacksick' oysters were thought to be males and females respectively.

Explosive spawning

When released, the young, then known as a veliger larva, has a tiny shell with two adductor muscles, a ciliated tuft, or velum, for swimming and feeding, and a foot. For between 1 and 2½ weeks the larva swims in the plankton, but when ready to settle, it protrudes its foot and grips any solid object it should touch. It then starts to crawl, but if the area is unsuitable, it can swim off again. Eventually, however, if it survives, the larva sticks itself down by its left valve using a drop of cement from the glands that in other bivalves secrete the byssus threads. At this stage, the oysters, about $\frac{1}{25}$ in. across, are known as spat. Now the shell grows rapidly and the body changes dramatically; foot, velum and eyes are lost, together with the anterior adductor muscles, the gill is increased and the mouth moves around through a right angle to the adult position.

It is important that males and females should spawn at the same time and to some extent this is aided by the dependence of spawning on temperature. In *Crassostrea* at least, however, chemical stimulation is also important. The sperms carry a hormone-like substance that stimulates spawning in both sexes and the males are also stimulated to spawn by the presence of eggs and by various organic compounds, including one present in seaweed. Thus one spawning individual can cause the whole population to release their eggs and spawn.

Downfall of the oyster

Great mounds of shells in coastal regions all over the world testify to the importance of oysters in the diets of many prehistoric communities. In Brittany there are banks 15 yds high, 700 yds long and 300 yds wide, containing shells of oysters, scallops and mussels. The Romans delighted in oyster orgies and were sufficiently impressed by English oysters to export them to Rome. Pliny records that the first person to establish artificial beds was Sergius Orata. During much of the 18th and 19th centuries, British beds were the most productive in Europe and vast quantities of this poor man's food were eaten. Today that huge harvest has dwindled so much that few can afford the price of a dozen oysters.

phylum	**Mollusca**
class	**Bivalvia**
subclass	**Lamellibranchia**
order	**Eulamellibranchia**
family	**Ostreidae**
genus & species	*Ostrea edulis* *European flat oyster, others*

Octopus

The name 'octopus' means literally 'eight feet' and the animal, indeed, has eight arms, joined at their bases by a web, and surrounding a beaked mouth. Octopuses differ most obviously from squids and cuttlefishes, the other well known members of the Cephalopoda, in lacking the extra pair of long tentacles. Moreover, their suckers, which run right along the arms, are not strengthened by the horny rings seen in the suckers of squids. Other differences are that octopuses have no trace of an internal shell and their body is short and rounded instead of being streamlined.

The 150 species of octopuses are distributed throughout the seas of the world, but are especially numerous in warm seas. The smallest is **Octopus arborescens**, less than 2 in. across. The largest is the Pacific octopus, **O. hongkongensis** which reaches 32 ft across the arms although its thimble-shaped body is only 18 in. long. Another giant is **O. apollyon**, of the North Pacific, 28 ft across. The Octopoda also include species that are very different in form. One is the argonaut. Another is the blind deep-sea **Cirrothauma** of the North Atlantic, which has two large fins on its body. The web between its arms reaches almost to their tips and it swims by opening and closing this umbrella. Besides the suckers on the undersides of its arms, it has rows of filaments which are believed to be used for catching food particles. Its body has the texture of a jellyfish and it is said to be so transparent one can read newsprint through it. The common octopus, the species mainly dealt with here, lives off the coasts of tropical and subtropical Africa and Atlantic America, is especially numerous in the Mediterranean, and reaches the southern coasts of the British Isles. It may, exceptionally, reach a span of 10 ft but is usually much smaller. The lesser octopus, ranges from Norway to the Mediterranean. It is rarely more than 2½ ft across the widest span of its arms and can be readily recognized by the single row of suckers on its arms, instead of the double row in the common octopus.

Master of disguise

The common octopus lives among rocks in shallow water, spending much of the time in a hole in the rocks or in a 'villa' built of stones. When outside, it creeps about on its arms most of the time, using its suckers to grip, though it can also swim. It usually swims backwards with its arms trailing, by blowing water out through its siphon. As in cuttlefish and squid, this water is blown out from the mantle cavity which houses the gills and the openings of the kidneys, rectum, reproductive organs and ink sac. Like cuttlefish and squid it can send out a cloud of ink to baffle pursuers.

There is no evidence that octopuses react to sound. However, the arms are very sensitive to touch and taste, and the eyes are well developed. The importance of vision is reflected in their outstanding ability to change colour. This is done with two kinds of chromatophores, or pigment cells, in the skin that vary in colour according to how much they are expanded or contracted. One kind varies from black to red-brown and the other from red to pale orange-yellow. Beneath these chromatophores is a layer of small bodies known as iridocytes that reflect white light or give a blue or green by refraction. The variation in appearance is not, however, just a matter of colour patterns but also of posture and of general texture. The arms may be extended, tucked underneath or curled stiffly back over the body as armour and the suckers may be out of sight or protruded to give the arms a wavy outline. By suitable adjustments in colour, posture and texture an octopus can merge completely with its background so it is extremely difficult to see. Octopuses also have a conspicuous display that often gives them away to fishermen searching for them. This is the so-called dymantic display, given when octopuses are frightened by large objects. The animal flattens out, coiling its arms in beside the body and extending the web between them. The body grows pale but dark rings develop around the eyes and the edge of the web also becomes dark. Presumably the purpose of this display is to deter predators, at least long enough for the octopus to change colour, blow ink and shoot away. With their large brains and adaptable behaviour, octopuses have been the object of a number of revealing studies on learning and brain function in lower animals. In captivity they rapidly settle down and become used to their captors.

Octopus attack

An octopus usually attacks only moving objects. It glides smoothly to within a few inches of its prey, collects itself together and then jumps forwards at it with a sudden backwards spurt from the jet. Small prey, mainly fish and crustaceans, is trapped beneath the expanded web between the arms, and then seized with the parrot-like horny beak around its mouth. At the same time a poison is given out that paralyses the prey. An average-sized octopus eats perhaps two dozen small crabs in a day. There are many reports of people being seized and held by octopuses and there is little doubt this does happen, perhaps rarely, and especially in warm seas. It seems, however, that these are not deliberate attacks but more a matter of investigating a moving object, and people have found that if they keep still, the octopuses will 'feel' them for a short while, then let go.

Coldblooded courtship

In mating, which may take several hours, male and female sit apart. There is almost no courtship display, although the male may expose certain particularly large suckers near the base of the second pair of arms, as if 'making a pass' at the female. The only contact he has with her is through a single arm which he extends to caress her. This arm is always the third arm on the right side which is specially modified for the purpose and has a spoon-shaped tip. It is called the hectocotylus arm. The tip of this arm is placed in the female's gill cavity

▽ *Smoke screen: an octopus ejects a cloud of ink to deter a predator and to escape behind.*

▷▽ *Tiny suction pads to grip the rock cover the tentacles which surround a central mouth.*

▷ *A cruel but beautiful animal, an octopus glides effortlessly through the deeps.*

△ Blue-ringed octopus **Hapalochlaena maculosa** swimming backwards, its arms trailing.

◁▽ An all-seeing eye of an octopus. The siphon blows out water from the mantle.

△ Sea-spider: blue-ringed octopus. It usually attacks only moving objects.

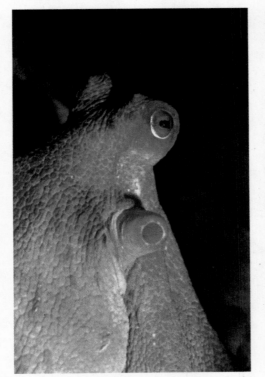

▽ The ever-changing octopus camouflages itself as coral, altering both its shape and colour.
▷▽ The focal point. The well-developed eyes of the octopus have a large cornea which gives them a range of vision of 180 degrees.

and the sperms are deposited near the opening of her oviduct in elaborate packages called spermatophores.

A female lays about 150 000 eggs in about a week, each in an oval capsule slightly smaller than a grain of rice. They are attached by short stalks to long strands that festoon the mother's lair. The mother broods over the eggs for several weeks, often cleaning them with her arms or blowing water over them with her funnel. During this time, she eats little. Indeed, she may fast completely for weeks, or for as much as 4 months in one species, and a brooding female in an aquarium has been seen to remove food placed near her and drop it well away from her. The short-armed young hatch at about $\frac{1}{8}$ in. long and drift around for a while before they start their own life on the bottom, by which time they may be $\frac{1}{2}$ in. long and several weeks old. The common octopus rarely, if ever, breeds on the coasts of the British Isles although, year after year, larvae migrate across the Channel from Brittany. Sometimes after a mild winter, the numbers of octopus may reach plague proportions, to the detriment of the crabs and lobsters.

True or false?

It is sometimes said that octopuses can feed on bivalve shellfish by jamming stones between the valves to stop them closing. Pliny, the Roman naturalist, recorded this

and in 1857 Jeannette Power, the French naturalist, wrote of an octopus, failing to force open a large mussel, picking up a stone and inserting it when the shell next opened.

This is a very pretty tale and not to be discounted out of hand, but several zoologists have watched in vain for this behaviour, and some have experimented with octopuses in aquaria but without result. Moreover, it is unlikely that the octopus, for all its relatively capable brain and sensitive arms, can ever perform such skilled manipulations. The trouble is that the shape of the body is just too variable, so the nervous system would need to be very complex to take into account all the bends and twists in the arms, and at the same time monitor and control such an intelligent action.

phylum	**Mollusca**
class	**Cephalopoda**
order	**Dibranchiata**
suborder	**Octopoda**
family	**Octopodidae**
genera & species	**Eledone cirrosa** lesser octopus **Octopus vulgaris** common octopus, others

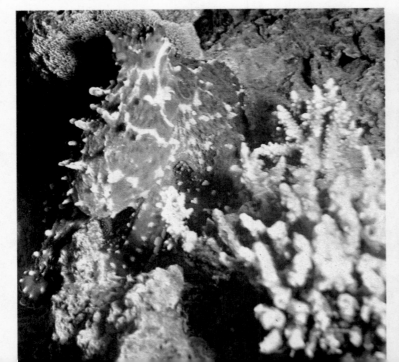

Earthworm

The earthworm, so familiar to gardeners, has many varieties, and the two dozen British earthworms are not all easily recognised at a glance. The brandling **Eisenia foetida** has alternating bands of red-brown and yellow and a strong smell, and has always been sought by anglers as a potent worm bait. It lives in dung and compost heaps, as does the gilt-tail **Dendrobaena rubida**. Another distinguished by its colour is the green worm **Allolobophora chlorotica**. The species usually referred to as the earthworm is, however, the large **Lumbricus terrestris**, up to 10 in. long (rather short by comparison with the 11ft earthworms of Australia). The reddish tinge of this and other earthworms is due to the oxygen-carrying pigment haemoglobin in the blood. The long body is divided into ring-like segments (150 of them in **L. terrestris**) and some of the internal organs, those for excretion for example, are duplicated in most of these segments. At the tapering front end is the mouth with its overhanging prehensile lip, but with no teeth or jaws. Around the body, like a cigar band (segments 32-37 in **L. terrestris**) is what is sometimes taken for a scar, where the worm has been cut in two and healed again. It is in fact a special gland, the saddle or clitellum, which secretes the cocoon.

How the earthworm burrows

An earthworm moves along by waves of muscular contraction travelling back along the body. Each body segment acts as a unit lengthening as it becomes narrower under the action of circular muscles, becoming broader as it shortens, pulled in by longitudinal muscles. When a group of the segments are pushing out sideways into the wall of a burrow, holding the worm firm at that point, elongation of the foremost segment of the group pushes forwards the segments in front. At the same time another segment, in the group at the rear, becomes shorter and fatter. This continues until the whole worm has moved forwards.

Extra grip is given during crawling, especially on the surface of the ground, by short, backwardly-directed bristles, which can be pushed out as required. There are four pairs on each segment except the first and last. These can be felt on the underside, more easily than seen, by drawing a worm backwards through the fingers.

Tree-climbing earthworms

Although a worm burrows partly by pushing soil aside, it also eats much of it. In some species, swallowed soil is voided at the surface in the familiar worm casts, though this is not true of *L. terrestris* which seldom makes casts. Some earthworms, like the gilt-tail, climb trees and may sometimes be found under the bark. The brandling, too, often scales trees and fences. After heavy rain in India, earthworms have been seen

migrating uphill and even up trees, presumably to avoid immersion. They were, however, probably in no danger of drowning, since earthworms can be kept under water for months and still survive. Those found dead in puddles have probably died from other causes. Getting too dry is more dangerous for a worm than getting too wet. In dry weather and in winter, worms may burrow as much as 8 ft below the surface. At such times, they may pass into a state of inactivity in mucus-lined chambers in the ground.

Fleeing from moles

Earthworms have no ears or eyes but their surfaces – especially the upper – are sensitive, even to light. A worm can detect the vibrations from a mole digging, and large numbers of earthworms will come to the surface, as if in panic, when a mole is working nearby. Pushing a stick into the ground and wriggling it about also brings worms to the surface. Should an earthworm fall foul of a predator, it may lose only part of itself, torn or cast off by reflex action (autotomy). The remaining portion of worm can often regrow the lost part. The amount of this regrowth varies from one species to another, but it is usually limited to a few segments at the front end and slightly more at the hind end.

Rudimentary intelligence?

The chief food of earthworms is decaying plant matter although they sometimes eat small dead animals, such as other worms, and droppings. Some food is taken in with soil swallowed in burrowing, but vegetation lying on the ground near the mouth of the burrow is also important. This is pulled into the burrow and to some extent pre-digested by digestive juices from the mouth before being eaten. Charles Darwin in *The formation of vegetable mould through the action of worms,* a book published in 1881 just before his death, showed that leaves, pine needles and even paper would be drawn in and used to line the upper parts of the burrows. In spite of the fact that worms are blind, the leaves and paper triangles with which he experimented were usually drawn in by their pointed ends. Clearly it is easier to

draw in a leaf by the tip than by the edge, and Darwin reasoned that this behaviour showed rudimentary intelligence. Several biologists have since looked into this and it seems clear now that leaves are pulled down in the way which is mechanically most efficient, that is, by the tips. The worms reach from their burrows, grasp leaves at random, and pull. If the leaves meet with resistance they let go and try again. Success comes when they happen to grasp the tip of the leaf, and so they do this largely by simple trial-and-error and not by intelligent action. There is, however, more to it than this, for worms respond to some of the chemicals in the vegetable matter, showing a preference for the chemicals of the leaf tips rather than those of the bases and stalks.

A worm's castle

It is not unusual to find heaps of pebbles on gravel paths, as if torrential rains had washed the gravel uneven. This is probably the normal interpretation. But if one takes a closer look it is possible to see that around each hillock there is bare earth, and in this are impressions of the outlines of pebbles on the heap nearby, showing that something has lifted the pebbles up carefully and placed them on the heap. If one of these heaps is carefully taken apart we find a worm-cast at the centre and beneath it a small mound of earth forming the core of the heap. The heap will consist of up to 200 pebbles of a total weight of about 22 oz, the pebbles ranging from pea-sized to $1\frac{1}{2}$ in. across and weighing $1\frac{1}{2}$ oz.

The best way to see what is making these heaps is to go out after dark after a light shower of rain with a red lamp, walking carefully so as not to cause vibrations in the ground. From each heap a worm will be seen stretching out, anchored by its tail in the centre of the heap, and with luck one may see a worm pressing its mouth against the surface of a pebble to form a sucker. It is not easy to catch the worm actually in the act of moving the pebble but one can hear, as one stands silent, the occasional chink of a pebble being moved, and there is the impression in the surface of the soil, already mentioned, showing the outline of a pebble now lying on top of the

heap, to give evidence that it has been moved gently.

We know that worms will pull leaves into the burrow, and they will also drag in small sticks, feathers, even pieces of wool lying on the ground. We can only surmise that it is necessary for the worm to clear part of the earth's surface to feed. On a piece of ground without pebbles it is possible with care to watch earthworms feeding by stretching out from the entrance to the burrow and running the mouth over the surface of the earth rather like the nozzle of a vacuum cleaner while swallowing movements can be seen, as if the worm were sucking in minute particles of soil or food material as part of a meal.

Economical breeding

A visit to a lawn on a warm, still night that is not too dry will show worms joined in pairs, each with its hind end in its burrow. Some species pair below ground. Each worm is hermaphrodite and sperms are exchanged during the three or four hours in which the pairs are united, held together by slime from the clitellum and by certain of the bristles.

Egg-laying begins about a day after mating, and this may continue for several months without further pairing (belying the view of Gilbert White, the 18th-century English clergyman and naturalist, that the earthworms are 'much addicted to venery'). As they are laid, the eggs become enclosed in a cocoon secreted by the clitellum and are fertilised by sperm stored in it—not, as one might expect, from inside the body. The cocoon of *Lumbricus terrestris* is pea-sized and dark brown. Although several eggs are laid in each cocoon, together with a thickish albumen, only one embryo usually survives. The young worm emerges after 1—5 months and is ready to reproduce after another 6—18 months. How long worms usually survive is uncertain but *L. terrestris* has been kept 6 years in captivity and *Allolobophora longa* $10\frac{1}{4}$ years.

Churning up the soil

Estimates of earthworms to the acre have been as high as 3 million, or 15 cwt. Without their continual action in aerating and drain-

An earthworm's main nerve (centre) branches off into each segment of its body. Septal branches run next to each dividing wall; interseptal branches run into the middle of each segment. The 'brain' (not shown here) consists of 2 knots of nerve cells above the gullet.

Two blood vessels run the length of a worm, one above, one below. Connecting these like the hoops of a barrel are circular vessels; 5 pairs of these (in segments 7—11) are dilated and pulse rhythmically forming the 'pseudo hearts' (ringed in the horizontal section below).

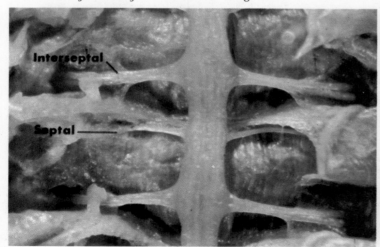

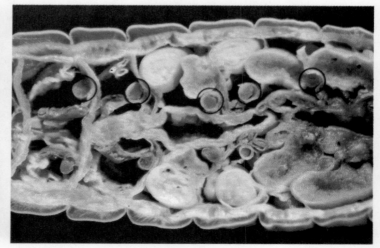

△ *Earthworms mating; the process takes 3–4 hours, during which the couple both keep their hind ends in their respective burrows.*

▽ *Sweating it out; to conserve moisture in a dry spell, an earthworm coils itself in a small chamber which it lines with its own mucus.*

ing, pulling down leaves and throwing up worm casts, the earth, or at least uncultivated land 'would soon become cold, hardbound, and void of fermentation; and consequently sterile', as Gilbert White wrote in 1777, a time when 'gardeners and farmers express(ed) their detestation of worms'.

Darwin pointed out, however, that the action of earthworms may be harmful on sloping ground and assist in denudation, the soil brought up from below the surface being washed or blown downhill.

Worms occur in the highest numbers in grassland, where there is plenty of food and no disturbance, and the population declines drastically if the ground is dug or ploughed. There is a limit to the earthworm's toleration of soil acidity and, if this is exceeded, vegetation accumulates on the surface as a mat which eventually becomes peat.

From the weights of daily collections of worm casts, Darwin estimated that $7\frac{1}{2}$ to 18 tons of soil can be thrown up per acre each year, equivalent to $1-1\frac{1}{2}$ in. over 10 years. One result is a very fine surface layer of soil and, at the same time, large stones tend not only to be buried under the collection of casts but also to be undermined. This is why some of the outer stones of Stonehenge have started to disappear—the present rate of covering there is estimated at about 7 in. per century, a rate considerably exceeded in some of Darwin's experiments. This also explains why so many Roman remains are now buried. In a ditch at Verulamium (St Alban's) which had been sealed over by the floors of successive buildings during the first 4 centuries AD—with no apparent way in or out – have been found certain 'mud worms' *Eophila oculata*. These require very little oxygen and had plenty of food.

phylum	**Annelida**
class	**Oligochaeta**
order	**Prospora**
family	**Lumbricidae**
genus & species	***Lumbricus terrestris*** *others*

To add to the worm's grip while tunnelling and crawling, pairs of bristles (setae) grow through the skin (top left). The central gut is buckled, increasing the surface area.

An earthworm strains liquid waste through tubes (nephridia) inside the body wall, one pair per segment. Also shown below is the ventral nerve cord below the central gut.

In the worm's 13th segment the ovaries flank the ventral nerve cord (centre, with one of the two main blood vessels above it). Eggs are laid in a cocoon already containing sperm.

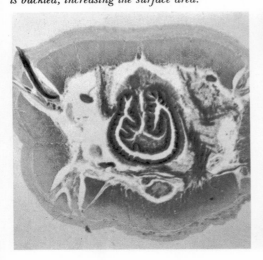

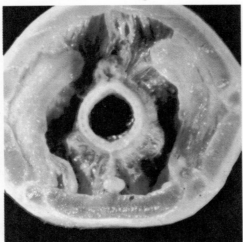

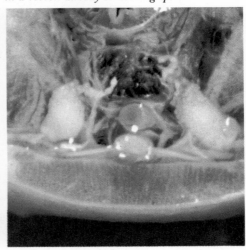

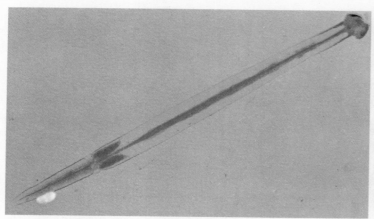

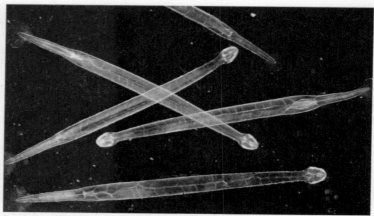

Arrow worm's body is divided into head, long trunk and tail. A jaw-hook and spines can be seen on the head; and two ovaries, full of eggs.

Sagitta elegans × 3½. *The silvery network in the trunk is the nervous system. Millions drift passively with the currents in the sea's plankton.*

Arrow worm

Among the myriads of tiny animals that float in the sea and are known as plankton, there are some with narrow, transparent bodies ¾ in. — 4 in. long. These are the arrow worms. At certain times of the year a tow net will catch vast quantities of them, but, when one looks down into the water, they will be very difficult to see. Their bodies are transparent, save for a pair of minute black eyes on the head, and can be seen readily only with food inside them.

When taken into the laboratory and coloured with special dyes, an arrow worm's body can be seen to have three sections: a short head, a long trunk comprising most of the body and a short tail. Arrow worms swim by up-and-down movements of the trunk and tail, aided by fins on the side of the body. **Sagitta**, *the common arrow worm around the British Isles, has two pairs of fins on the trunk and a single, paddle-like fin on the tail.*

The mouth is surrounded by a thin hood covering two sickle-shaped hooks that serve as jaws. On the hooks and around the mouth there are sharp spines which are used for capturing food when the hood is drawn back to expose them.

Throughout the oceans

Almost any bucketful of sea water will contain arrow worms. Most species live near the surface of the open seas but others live around the shores or at great depths, where they may be a beautiful golden-orange. They can swim by flexing their bodies but they cannot travel far on their own accord. Usually they hang passively in the water drifting with the currents.

Although the ocean appears to be the same in any part of the world, parts of it are as different as jungles and deserts on land. Throughout the ocean, the temperature and salt concentrations vary, and the distribution of the different animals varies with them, each animal being restricted to areas where conditions suit it. This is not strictly true for all marine animals, as the common mauve jellyfish *Aurelia* is worldwide, but it is true for arrow worms.

Arrow worms often migrate vertically, from the surface layers to deeper water and back. This is a habit of many planktonic animals and it is thought that many of them swim down to get away from too bright a light during the day. Arrow worms sink during the day and night, coming to the surface at dawn and dusk so that they are always in the most suitable dim light intensity.

Voracious feeders

Arrow worms are voracious creatures. They hang motionless in the water and dart at their prey, propelled by rapid flicks of the body. In a flash, they cover distances several times their own length, an unusual turn of speed for a planktonic animal, many of whom can barely swim at all but merely drift about. The prey is grappled by the bristle-covered jaws and hauled into the mouth where a sticky secretion, from special cells in the lining of the mouth, at once immobilizes it by gumming up its legs. It also acts as a lubricant to ease the passage down the gut.

Any small animal is taken, including other arrow worms, while herring larvae larger than the arrow worm itself are eaten in large numbers, especially in January and February when just hatched.

Not all arrow worms chase their prey. *Spadella* from the shores of south-west England lives in pools, attached to rocks or seaweed by special suckers on its tail. As a small crustacean swims past its head the arrow worm strikes at it with its jaw, without releasing its hold on the rock. The prey is worked round by the spines until head or tail can be dragged into the mouth.

Breeding

Like many invertebrate animals, arrow worms are hermaphrodite, that is, each individual has both male and female reproductive organs. In arrow worms the ovaries lie in the trunk and the testes in the tail. Eggs of one individual are usually fertilised by sperms from another, but self-fertilisation occurs in some species. The eggs are released into the sea where they develop into larvae, that later change into adults. Correct water temperature during the breeding season appears to be important to many arrow worms. If the sea currents carry them too far north, into colder waters, they fail to breed and, instead, grow to twice their normal size.

Guide to ocean currents

If a plankton net is towed up the English Channel from the open Atlantic Ocean the arrow worm *Sagitta elegans* will be caught in large numbers, but, just as the ship nears Plymouth, it disappears, to be replaced by another species *Sagitta setosa*. The change is so abrupt that on one occasion a marine biologist was able to catch *elegans* from the bows of his ship and *setosa* from the stern. The two look very much alike but can easily be told apart because if dropped into weak formalin preservative *setosa* remains transparent while *elegans* becomes opaque. This is a great convenience to the biologists of the Marine Laboratories at Plymouth because they can instantly distinguish between water from the channel, called *setosa* water for convenience, and water upwelling from the Atlantic, *elegans* water.

To the man in the street it may appear a matter of little importance whether one kind of arrow worm is found in one part of the Channel and not another, but in fact this knowledge helped to account for an otherwise baffling problem. During the first part of this century, fishermen used to put out from Plymouth to catch herring that appeared in the Channel off Cornwall every winter. During the 1920's the herring gradually ceased coming up the Channel and in a short while no more herring boats were to be seen. The fishermen, deprived of a means of livelihood, were unable to say where the herring had gone. For some years at the Plymouth Marine Laboratory routine tow-nettings were made and samples of plankton were brought back to the laboratory and analysed. These showed that *Sagitta elegans* was gradually moving further up the Channel. This could mean only one thing: that oceanic water was coming in from the Atlantic across the fishing grounds. Herring are very sensitive to changes of temperature. It became clear that the loss of the herring fishery off the south coast of England was due to the herring being driven away by the shift in the water currents.

phylum	**Chaetognatha**
genus & species	*Sagitta setosa* *S. elegans*

Pogonophore

The name of these marine animals means literally 'beard-bearers', and if the name sounds mildly ridiculous, this is in keeping with the whole history of the group. The pogonophores represent a branch of the animal kingdom that was completely unknown until 1914, and which attracted little attention even among marine zoologists until about 25 years ago. Yet they seem now to be the most widespread and abundant sea animals.

The 100 or more known species of pogonophores are worm-like and extremely slender; a 5in. individual being $\frac{1}{20}$in. thick. Most are a few inches long; the largest is just over a foot. Each lives in a transparent horny tube little wider than itself, but five times as long, which has ring-like markings at intervals along its length. The animal itself is made of different sections, each having a slightly different shape. In front is a long tentacle or tentacles—there may be as many as 200 or more in some species—fringed with pinnules. At the rear end are spines, or short bristles, like those on the bodies of earthworms and marine bristleworms. They probably help the animal to move up and down inside its tube. No mouth or other special organs have yet been identified.

These animals have now been found in all oceans, mainly at great depths, down to 25 000 ft, but in recent years some have been discovered in shallower water.

Mystery tube-dwellers

Dredged up and kept alive for only a few hours, living pogonophores are difficult to observe. Their way of life has to be deduced from what can be seen in the dead animal. They live only where the seabed is fine mud, and seem to spend most of their time inside semi-permeable tubes, through which water can pass. This may be important to the animal inside the tube because incoming water would bring oxygen for breathing. Studies at very high magnification with electron microscopes have shown a complicated body structure, including a nerve network and blood vessels containing red blood with haemoglobin. No digestive organs have been seen. The nearest thing they have to a brain is a group of nerve cells, the ganglionic mass. Tests made with living pogonophores showed that they reacted only slightly to being touched.

A question of feeding

There has been much speculation about the way pogonophores feed, as to whether they take particles of food from the water by gripping them with the pinnules on the tentacles or whether the pinnules give out a sticky secretion to which the particles adhere. Another suggestion has been that the tentacles may sweep the surface of the mud for particles. Where there are many tentacles they form tubes or complicated spirals, and it is believed food may be caught and digested in these, as in a sort of external stomach. These tentacles may also secrete fluids which digest the food externally, the nutrients being absorbed through the skin. The most favoured view is that these animals absorb nutrients dissolved in the seawater through their skin, but all these suggestions are no more than inspired guesses.

*Overleaf: The single tentacle of **Siboglinum** often coils up into this shape. Along its length is a double row of fine unicellular pinnules.*

▽ *A rare photograph of the pogonophore **Oligobrachia ivanovi** from the north east Atlantic. This large pogonophore is seen partly removed from its tube, its seven tentacles coiled up into an orange mass (× 10).*

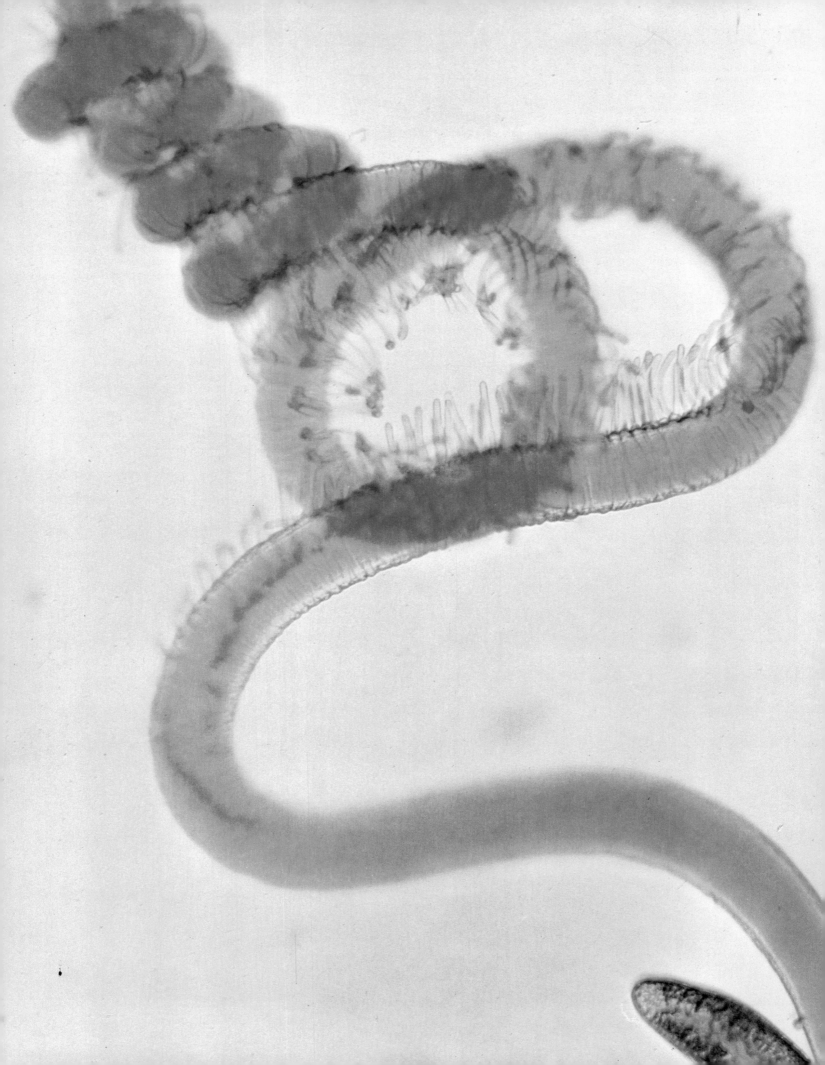

Unknown breeding habits

Some pogonophores that have been examined have contained large yolky eggs, others have had sperms enclosed in capsules, or spermatophores. There is nothing to show whether the sperms are merely liberated into the sea to find their way to ova in other individuals, or whether pogonophores join together in some simple form of mating. Estimates have been made of how densely they live. These vary from 50 to 500 per sq yd, but even the more densely crowded would have difficulty in contacting each other. The most reasonable assumption seems to be that the sperms are liberated into the sea, yet the fact that they are in a capsule, would suggest that the male places them on the female, or in her tube. Embryos and larvae have been found in some of the tubes. The embryos are rounded, with two girdles of cilia around the front and the rear ends. As the cilia beat in a wave-like action the embryo slowly revolves on its axis. Later, the embryo grows longer, into what may be called a larva, in which the future hair-like adult pogonophore is foreshadowed.

*Ancestral pogonophore—the tapering tube of the fossil **Hyolithellus**, buried over 500 million years ago in Cambrian rocks in Greenland. The indentation above the tube probably marks the position of the animal when feeding (× 8).*

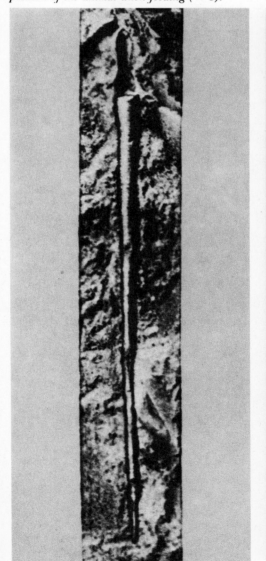

The youngest phylum

The very existence of the phylum Pogonophore was entirely unknown and wholly unsuspected until 1914, when specimens were examined by the French zoologist Professor M Caullery. These had been collected by the Dutch research ship *Siboga* dredging in the seas of the Malay Archipelago. He worked on them from 1914 to 1944 but was unable to find any relationship between them and other animals. He named them *Siboglinum* after the Dutch ship, *linum* being Latin for flax or linen thread. Then, in 1933, more were dredged up in the Pacific, and the view began to be taken that they were degenerate bristleworms. Soviet research ships began to find large numbers of pogonophores in the Sea of Okhotsk and later in the Indian Ocean, Antarctic and Atlantic Oceans. The Russian zoologist AV Ivanov decided, in 1955, that they represented a new phylum, which he named the Pogonophora. In plain terms an entirely new section of the animal world had been discovered.

The pogonophores have been described as looking like threads, like bits of string, or like trawl twine—or even contemptuously as

*A developing ciliated embryo of **Siboglinum** removed from its mother's tube. There is a broad ciliated band on the protosoma below the apical cone, and another smaller band at the end of the body on the metasoma (arrowed) (× 160).*

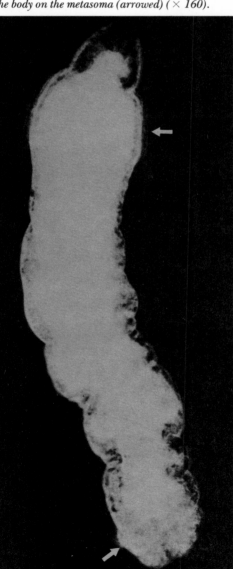

looking like chewed string! We know now that research ships at sea had been finding masses of these tangled threads in their dredges. They cluttered the decks when the dredges were emptied onto them and on a British research ship they were given the name of the Gubbinidae—and shovelled back into the sea ('gubbins' is a slang name, often used by scientists, for unidentifiable 'insignificant' rubbish!). This alone shows how abundant they are on the ocean bed. It also shows why nobody took any notice of them; they looked like fibrous rubbish.

There is a great deal yet to be learned about the pogonophores. Some of it may shed light on the evolutionary history of the vertebrates. The current opinion is that they are most closely related to the supposed forerunners of the vertebrates, such as the **acorn worm**.

phylum	**Pogonophora**
order	**Athecanephria**
order	**Thecanephria**

*Tree-like tube of **Polybrachia**, this middle section has membranous frills. Like many small pogonophores it has ring markings and is divided into segments. The rigid tube is composed of chitin and proteins (× 5).*

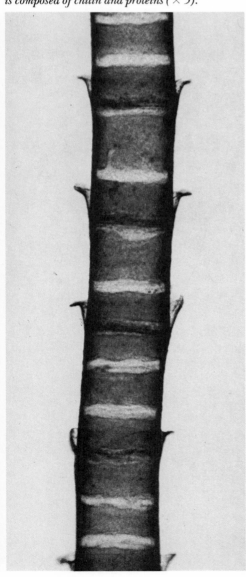

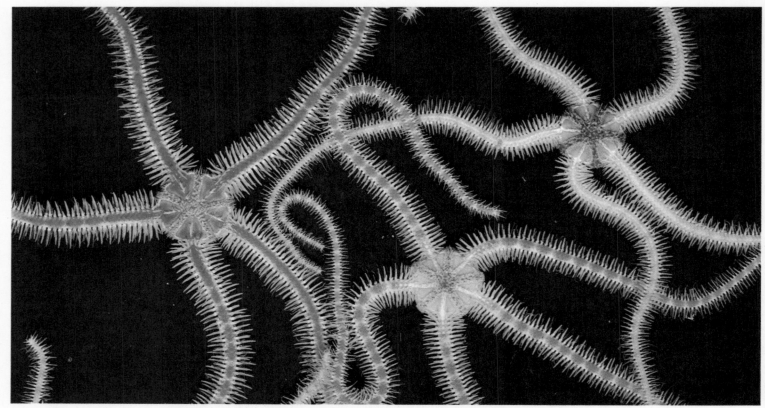

*In some places, the floor of the English Channel is carpeted with masses of common brittlestars, **Ophiothrix fragilis**. These are shown here at about the size of the largest specimens, but they are usually half this size. The name refers to the ease with which the arms fall off when handled.*

Brittlestar

*These are echinoderms closely related to the basket stars and somewhat more distantly related to the starfish. Like the latter, they have five arms joined to a central body, although some species may have more arms. The body, or disc as it is known, is button-shaped, and the arms are snake-like, hence the scientific name of its class, Ophiuroidea, from the Greek **ophis**, serpent. The English name alludes to the ease with which the arms fall off. Any that do come off are regrown.*

Some brittlestars are a light grey in colour but many are delicately coloured. The largest brittlestars have discs of 4 in. diameter with a spread of 2 ft across the arms. Another has a disc only ½ mm across.

The arms are covered with rows of hard plates and spines, while running down their centres are 'vertebrae' forming a flexible structure very much like our backbone. Muscles controlling movement are attached to these vertebrae. Along the underside of the arms are rows of tube-feet, or podia. These are badly named as they are used for feeding. Similar structures in starfish are used for walking.

Widely distributed

Brittlestars are found in seas all over the world from the tideline to deep water. One species is almost cosmopolitan, being found off the shores of Europe and New Zealand and on both east and west coasts of America.

Many species of brittlestar live on the seabed, burrowing into it if it is muddy.

Others live amongst seaweeds and corals, climbing around the fronds by grasping them with their flexible arms rather like a monkey swings through the trees. On the seabed they move by waving the arms in a rowing action. Either two or four arms work together in pairs. The fifth is held out in front or trails behind, sometimes assisting in the motion by a beating action. By this means brittlestars can travel at speeds of as much as 2 yd/min, which is quite fast compared with the slow crawls of other echinoderms such as starfish or urchins which drift along on their tube-feet.

Two ways of feeding

Brittlestars have two basic feeding methods. They capture small particles on the arms, which are then passed to the mouth that lies on the underside of the disc, or they tear off lumps of dead flesh or seaweed with the tube-feet and teeth around the mouth.

Collecting small particles is a passive method of feeding. The brittlestar rests on the seabed or burrows down into the mud, leaving only the arms from which long sticky mucous threads wave about in the water. Organic debris in the mud or floating in suspension, as well as minute planktonic animals and plants, are trapped in the mucus.

The skin around the arms is covered with cilia (protoplasmic hairs) which sweep the mucus and the entrapped particles in towards the tube-feet on the underside of the arms. The tube-feet also help in this movement by 'licking' around the parts of the arm within reach. In this way they become covered in a mixture of mucus and particles. This is then wiped off against a spine near each one and the resulting mass transferred on the tip of the tube-foot to another nearer

the mouth. As the mass is moved inwards more is added and it is patted by the tube-feet to form a compact ball. Eventually it is brought to the root of the arm, where it is transferred to tube-feet around the mouth. These taste the ball and, if it is acceptable, they force it into the mouth. If unpalatable, they reject it, pushing it back onto the arm. It is then passed back down the arm and released to drift away.

Brittlestars also feed on larger animals or carrion. Large lumps of food, up to 1 in. across are caught, wrapped in an arm and held by the tube-feet. The arm then curves over to carry the food to the mouth. Smaller lumps are grasped by the arm then transferred along it by the tube-feet in the same way as the mucous ball. Lumps of food still smaller are merely grasped by the tube-feet without the arms flexing over to hold them.

Brittlestars can detect the presence of food, provided it is upstream of them, presumably by 'tasting' chemicals liberated from the food. The arms wave about. Then having found out in which direction the food lies, the brittlestar moves towards it.

Simple sexual organs

In most species, eggs and sperms are merely shed into the sea, where fertilisation takes place. The sexual organs are, therefore very simple. There are genital openings at the base of each arm through which the sex cells are discharged. There may, however, be a bag, or bursa, just inside the slit, into which the cells are discharged from the gonads.

The fertilised eggs develop into delicate larvae with long arms, stiffened with fine rods, and covered with cilia whose beating keeps the larva from sinking. The larva is called an *ophiopluteus, pluteus* meaning easel-like, an apt description. After floating about for some time, the larva develops into the adult form and settles on the seabed.

A few brittlestars do not have free-swimming larvae but retain their eggs in the bursae or in the ovaries, where they develop into small adults before crawling out through the genital slits. These species are often hermaphrodite, having both male and female sex organs, but they avoid self fertilisation by the cells of one sex ripening before the other.

Lost arms replaced

Brittlestars fall a prey to fish such as plaice and dab, that feed on the sea bottom. The species that burrow into the mud avoid predation to some extent, apart from having their arms bitten off which is of no great importance as the arms are readily regrown.

Some brittlestars have light-producing cells on the spines of the arms and when one arm is bitten off, the others produce a flash of light as the brittlestar withdraws. This, presumably, deters the predator from following up the attack (and may even put it off attacking any more brittlestars).

Brittlestars cling together

Around the shores of the eastern coast of the United States there is a brittlestar that normally lives amongst the stems of eelgrass, hanging onto them by its arms. In winter the eelgrass dies back and the brittlestars twine their arms around each other to form a tight bunch. This habit has been examined in the laboratory. Whenever they are deprived of eelgrass the brittlestars bunch together, but it has been found that if vertical glass rods are placed in the aquarium, the brittlestars treat them as substitute eelgrass and twine their arms around them.

It seems, then, that the brittlestars have some need to twine around something and when there is no eelgrass or artificial substitute they will cling to each other. This contrasts with the usual gatherings of animals which are normally only for breeding or feeding.

The bunches form by random movements of the individuals, the more active ones clinging to the inactive ones, reacting to them as if they were a piece of glass or eelgrass. When gathered together, the bunch is drawn tighter and tighter. Brittlestars in bunches live longer than isolated ones and they are less likely to shed their arms. When curled around an object a brittlestar is exerting tension and the rate at which its body functions work goes up. For some reason that is not properly understood, this enables them to live longer. Therefore it is an advantage to cling to any object, so, without the normal solid supports, they cling to each other.

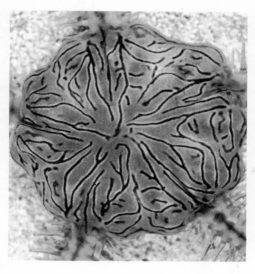

△ Central disc of brittlestar magnified 12 times.
▽ The star-shaped mouth is on the underside.

△ Closeup of mouth, armed with spines serving as teeth, which leads directly into the stomach.

phylum	Echinodermata
class	Ophiuroidea
order	Ophiurae
genera	Ophiura, Ophiothrix, Amphiura, others

Sea urchin

Sea urchins—or sea hedgehogs—are the spiniest of the Echinodermata or 'spiny-skins', the group that includes starfishes, brittlestars, sea lilies and sea cucumbers. Their internal organs are enclosed in a test which typically takes the form of a more or less rounded and rigid box made up of chalky plates fitting neatly together. There are, however, sea urchins with leathery, flexible tests. In sea urchins with the rigid box the shape may be nearly spherical, rounded and somewhat flattened, heartshaped, or like a flattened disc, as in the sand dollar. In most sea urchins the test is covered with spines, which may be short and sharp, long and slender or thick and few in number. When the spines are removed knobs can be seen on some of the plates. These form part of the ball-and-socket joints on which the spines move. Also seen when the spines are removed are the double rows of pinholes arranged in a series of five, forming a star in the heart urchin or running from the bottom to the top of the test when this is spherical. In the living sea urchin the tubefeet project through these pinholes. Among the spines are small jointed rods with two or three jaws at the top, which act like tiny pincers. These are known as pedicellariae, and each moves like the spines on a ball-and-socket joint. Sea urchins are not only attractive in appearance when living, but their tests, cleaned of their spines, are collected because of the beauty of their design. In life they are attractively coloured from greens to yellow, red, orange and purple. The smallest sea urchins are barely ½ in. across, while the largest are up to 1½ ft across, including the spines.

The 800 species have a worldwide distribution, mainly in shallow waters, usually at less than 600 ft although some live down to 1 500 ft.

Burrowing through steel

In addition to the spines and the pedicelliariae, the teeth of a sea urchin play an important part in its life. These too are objects of beauty. Over 2 000 years ago Aristotle wrote of the teeth as resembling a horn lantern with the panes of horn left out. There are five vertical teeth supported on a framework of rods and bars, and the whole structure, teeth and supporting skeleton, is now called Aristotle's lantern. Some sea urchins move freely over the seabed using their tubefeet to pull themselves along. When walking the tubefeet are pushed out, their suckers take hold and then the tubefeet shorten, pulling the body along. Its course is usually an erratic one, as first the

△▷ Pink pin cushion: an edible sea urchin **Echinus esculentus** on **Laminaria**. Only the ripe ovaries are eaten, raw like caviare, or cooked.
▷ Sea mine: small spines surround the bases of the larger primary spines of a **Cidaris cidaris**.

tubefeet on one side are pushed out, then the neighbouring tubefeet, each side pulling the sea urchin in a slightly different direction. Other sea urchins use their tubefeet, assisted by the spines, while yet others walk on the spines in a deliberate way, pursuing a steady course, and when viewed from the side the animal appears to be walking on many stilts. There are also sea urchins, including the heart urchins, so named from their shape, that plough through sand and burrow into it, using their spines. *Echinocardium* sinks vertically into the sand, to a depth of 8 in.—twice its own length or more. It lines its vertical shaft with mucus and pushes several very extensible tubefeet up the shaft to the surface of the sand to breathe. It also keeps a horizontal shaft open behind it with other tubefeet, to receive its excrement, while tubefeet in front are picking up particles of food and passing them to the mouth. As the *Echinocardium* moves forward it abandons the vertical shaft by withdrawing its tubefeet, then pushes them up through the sand, making a new vertical shaft to the surface.

There are sea urchins that burrow into soft rock, using their spines to scrape away the surface, some using their teeth as well. *Echinostrephus molaris* of the Indo-Pacific makes cylindrical burrows several inches deep. When feeding it comes up to the mouth of the burrow. Should anything disturb it, it merely drops into the burrow and wedges itself in with its spines. On the Californian coast steel pier piles put in position in the late 1920s were completely perforated by the sea urchin *Strongylocentrotus* in 20 years, the steel being ⅜ in. thick. In other places the anti-corrosive surface layer of the steel piles was abraded and polished by the sea urchins' spines.

Surface cleaning pincers

Sea urchins are mainly vegetarian, chewing seaweeds with the teeth of their Aristotle's lantern. Burrowing forms eat fragments of dead plants in the sand, but probably also take animal food. All get some food as a result of cleaning their tests. The pincers of the pedicellariae are constantly moving about picking up grains of sand that fall on the skin covering the test and also any tiny animals that settle, such as barnacle larvae. These are passed from one pedicellaria to another to the mouth.

Free-swimming larvae

Male and female sea urchins shed their sperms and eggs respectively into the sea where fertilisation takes place. The larva, known as an echinopluteus, is like that of other members of the Echinodermata, with slender arms covered with bands of cilia. Before it settles on the seabed it already has a mouth surrounded by a few tubefeet and spines and the arms are shorter. It is when the arms are too short for swimming that the tiny sea urchin, barely half-formed, settles on the bottom.

Protected from predators

Sea urchins are eaten, especially when small, by bottom feeding fishes but have relatively few other enemies when fully grown. The roes of *Echinus esculentus* have long been eaten in Mediterranean countries and other species have been fished in the Caribbean, South America, Malaya and Japan. Off Barbados they are fished by naked divers with handnets. Most echinoderms have unusual powers of regeneration which sea urchins lack. They can re-grow tubefeet and pedicellariae and if one of the plates in the test is cracked it will be cemented and healed. If a part of the test becomes pushed in, however, the damaged plates will be merely cemented together but will not be pushed out into their normal position. Nevertheless, what sea urchins lack in healing powers they make up for in armaments. In many species the spines are sharp, hollow and brittle, and readily break off. Bathers getting such spines into their feet can sustain painful wounds, and in some places sea urchins are so numerous on the seabed it is practically impossible to put a foot between them. We can be fairly sure that most animal predators treat them with as much respect as the human bather or diver. Many, as we have seen, burrow in sand or rock. Others hide by day under rocks coming out at night to feed. This is purely a reaction away from the light but the practical effect is to keep the animals hidden. Those that do not hide from the light, including the European *Psammechinus miliaris*, hide by holding pieces of seaweed over themselves with their tubefeet. *Diadema* of the Caribbean has light-sensitive cells scattered all over its test. It also has long needlelike spines. Any shadow falling on its body makes the spines in the shaded area point towards the object causing the shadow, thus presenting a formidable array of weapons to a potential attacker.

phylum	**Echinodermata**
class	**Echinoidea**

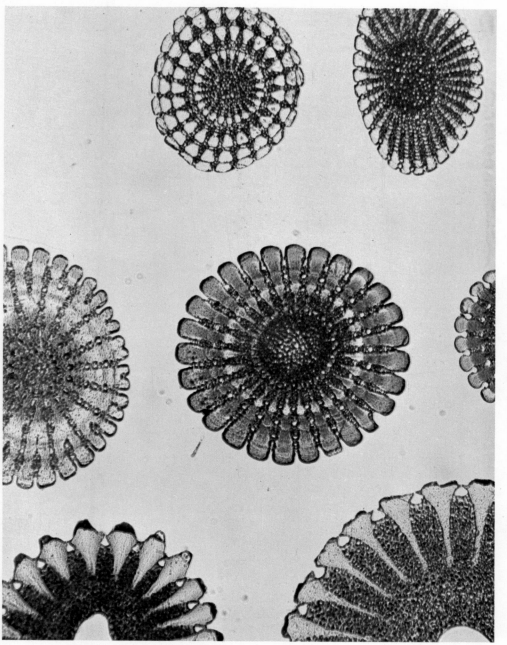

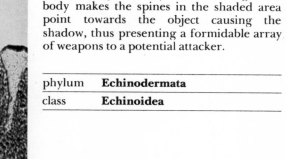

◁ *Natural radial symmetry—a section through the spines of various sea urchins (approx × 20).*

The Higher Invertebrates

The single phylum referred to on page 10 as containing all the higher invertebrates is known as the Arthropoda or 'jointed-legged' animals. Since we normally expect a leg to be jointed it should be explained that in these animals, which include insects, crustaceans, millipedes, centipedes, spiders and a few others, the legs are typically many jointed. The phylum is enormous, both as to species and populations, comprising nearly a million known species.

The progression towards bilateral symmetry, a segmented body and a well-defined nervous system with special sense-organs, noted in the introduction to the previous chapter, takes an important stride forward in the Arthropoda. The members of this phylum also have in common a chitinous exoskeleton. That is, instead of an internal skeleton of a hard material, such as bone, the body is encased in an outer covering of chitin, a nitrogenous carbohydrate similar in consistency to horn. This not only supports and contains the body as a whole but affords attachment on its inner surface for the muscles.

It is very clear from the structure, particularly of some of its members, that the arthropods must have evolved from worm-like ancestors. Millipedes and centipedes, for example, are elongated with obviously segmented bodies that recall the form of an earthworm. This is reinforced by the shape of peripatus, the unusual and primitive arthropod, as well as by some of the more

primitive insects. In most arthropods, however, the segments tend to be reduced in number, as in familiar insects, such as beetles and bees, and even more so in spiders, ticks and mites.

Fossils of the earliest arthropods are found in the rocks of the Cambrian period laid down over 500 million years ago. They included mainly small crustaceans and the trilobites. These were all aquatic. Some 150 million years later, in the Devonian period, there were land-living arthropods, including millipedes, mites, spiders and wingless insects. Winged insects, in the form of dragonflies, have been found in deposits of the Carboniferous period, 50 million years later.

The lower invertebrates are all aquatic, living in the sea or in freshwater, or in damp situations on land. Among the arthropods, crustaceans are also typically aquatic, most numerous in the sea, and generally require a damp environment in those instances in which they have become land-living. Insects and spiders, by contrast, can tolerate a dry environment and, having thrown off the shackles of a life spent totally in a fluid medium, have been able to extend the range of their activities. The whirligig beetle, for example, can survive in air, can fly or live on the surface of water or even dive and remain submerged, taking its air supply down with it, like a scuba-diver.

In the main introduction reference was made to the proliferations of animal forms.

The arthropods are a good example of such proliferation. They have produced species numerically almost without end, for almost every kind of habitat and diet, to almost every kind of parasitism and symbiosis. More than that, they give us examples of how a small increase in the proportion of nervous tissue in the body can lead to an integrated social structure, as in termites, bees, ants and wasps and to an appearance of intelligence which, although illusory, is none the less remarkable. Perhaps the most remarkable discovery in biology of this century is that concerning the methods of communication used by honeybees and their almost incredible ability to navigate by the sun.

The classification of the Arthropoda, showing the classes, is as follows:

Class Onychophora (peripatus)	100 species
Class Merostoma (horseshoe crabs)	4 species
Class Pycnogonida (sea spiders)	600 species
Class Symphyla	120 species
Class Pauropoda	400 species
Class Diplopoda (millipedes)	8,000 species
Class Chilopoda (centipedes)	2,750 species
Class Crustacea (crabs, lobsters)	30,500 species
Class Insecta (insects)	750,000 species
Class Arachnida (spiders, ticks, mites)	66,000 species

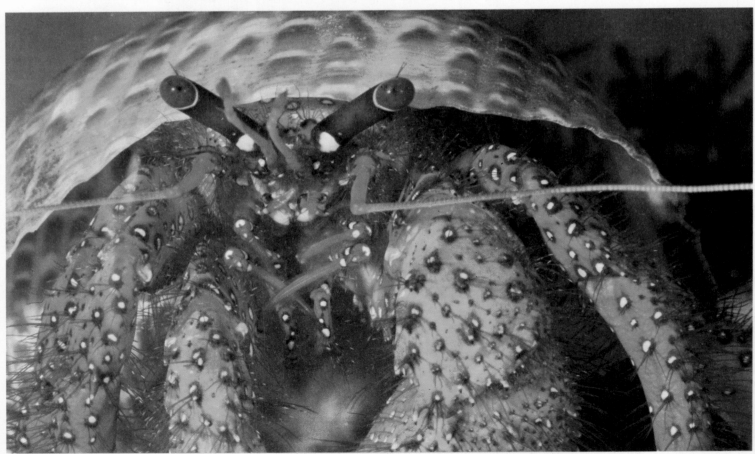

Peripatus

Peripatus is one of the most extraordinary animals living today. A relic from the past, it was once thought of as a link between the soft-bodied ringed worms, such as the earthworm, and the hard-bodied arthropods, which include insects, spiders and crustaceans.

Its body is rather worm-like, tapering towards the hind end. It is 1—3 in. long but can be extended or contracted, and is sinuous in movement. The colour of peripatus is very variable, ranging from dark slate to reddish-brown in the various species, and there is usually a dark stripe down the back. The skin is dry and velvety to the touch and there are 20 or so pairs of short baggy legs each ending in a pair of hooks and ringed like the body. There is a pair of flexible antennae on the head with an eye at the base of each. The eyes are simple although each has a lens. They are directed outwards and upwards and probably do no more than distinguish between light and darkness. The sensory hairs clothing the antennae and most of the body are organs of touch and taste.

Must live in damp places

Peripatus is dependent on moist conditions, being found only in damp forests in South Africa, Australasia and South America. It lives under stones, rotting wood, the bark of fallen trees and similar damp places, being unable to withstand drying. In a dry atmosphere it will lose a third of its weight in less than 4 hours and will dry up twice as fast as an earthworm, and 40 times as fast as a smooth-skinned caterpillar its own size. The cause lies in its breathing system. An insect breathes through branching tubes or tracheae. Because the openings are few there is little loss of water and, moreover, there is an efficient mechanism for closing the openings when necessary. Peripatus has unbranched breathing tubes so it needs far more of them, with an opening to each tube, which means a rapid loss of water from the body when the surroundings are dry. As a result peripatus is found in 'islands', damp localities separated from other colonies by dry country.

Sticky threads for defence

The moment peripatus is disturbed it throws out one or two jets of a milky-white fluid from little nozzles or oral papillae, on the head, one either side of the mouth. On contact with the air the fluid solidifies immediately into sticky beaded threads of slime 3—12 in. long. The fluid is in reservoirs, one each side of the head, shaped like the rubber teat of an eye-dropper. Although the threads stick to one's fingers they do not stick to the velvety skin of peripatus itself, but insects and other small animals become entangled in them.

This entangling seems to be accidental because the threads serve more as a defence. Their food is mainly small insects such as termites and they also eat other small animals such as woodlice.

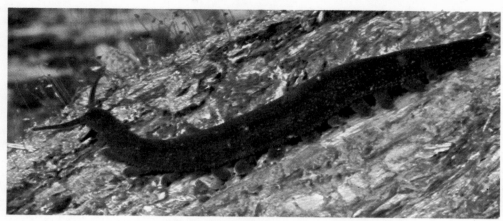

Going for a stroll: a peripatus from New Zealand **Peripatoides novaezealandiae.**

Haphazard mating

The mating of peripatus can only be described as casual. The male places capsules containing sperms on the female, apparently at random since he will place them even on her legs. He may place them at times on another male. For a long time it was not known how the sperms reached the ova. Then it was found that white blood corpuscles in the female body migrate to the skin immediately beneath a capsule and break through it by digesting the cells of the skin. At the same time the lower wall of the capsule breaks and the sperms enter the female's blood stream and find their way to an ovary. There in large numbers they force their way through the wall of the ovary. If an immature female receives sperms the young egg cells feed on them and grow for a year before they are ready to be fertilised by a second mating. Except in a few species which lay eggs the embryos develop in the uterus taking in nourishment from the mother through its walls. In one South American species special tissues are formed, making a kind of placenta, to pass food from the mother's body to the growing embryos. Development takes 13 months and as young are born each year there is one month in each year when a female is carrying two sets of embryos, one just beginning to develop, the other nearly ready to be born.

Evolutionary bridge?

The theory of evolution, in which it is assumed life began in water, requires two main invasions of the land. One, by the vertebrates, meant a change from gill-breathing to lung-breathing and indications of how this may have taken place are seen, for example, in the lungfishes, the coelacanth (page 228) and the various newts and salamanders. Among the fossils, also, there is an almost complete series showing how this came about. The other invasion is that which brought the invertebrates on land, and the most important change was that from the aquatic ringed worms, such as the fanworm, and the crustaceans, leading to insects and spiders. If one were asked to draw a hypothetical animal to bridge the gap between the ringed worms and the insects, one could not fail to draw something very like peripatus. Moreover, in its internal structure as well as its outward appearance, this animal looks like the forerunner of both millipedes and centipedes, and they in turn look like forerunners of modern insects. We know from fossils that insects, millipedes and centipedes, in the form we know them today, were already in existence 400 million years ago, so any ancestors linking the two must have been in existence even earlier. It is of interest therefore to find there is a fossil *Xenusion* in the rocks of over 500 million years ago that looks almost the same as peripatus. It is little more than a rusty coloured stain in a piece of limestone rock, yet its shape and the structure of its body and legs can be seen clearly enough to leave little doubt that the peripatus living today and the *Xenusion* of 500 million or more years ago could be closely related. From it or from animals very like *Xenusion* began the line which, through numerous changes, led to the millipedes, centipedes and insects, while another line of descent was continued, almost unchanged, in peripatus.

Theory devastated

This represents the views held a few years ago. It reads almost like a scientist's dream, for everything falls so neatly into place. Then two things happened. First, fresh fossils have come to light from Australia, southwest Africa and England, which are clearly related to *Xenusion* but are much more complete. Together, this fresh evidence leaves little doubt that this supposed missing link between worms and insects was, in fact, a near relative of the sea pens, of the phylum Cnidaria, that are related to corals and jellyfishes.

The second event was hardly less devastating to the cherished idea that peripatus is a worm-insect, a bridge between the Annelida, and the Arthropoda (insects, spiders, crustaceans, millipedes and centipedes). Dr. Sidney Manton, the leading authority on the Onychophora, leaves us in no doubt that in its structure, mode of development from egg to adult and in its movements, peripatus is wholly arthropodan. Although it is undoubtedly primitive in many of its features, such as the simple head, the long series of similar limbs and, in certain features of its internal anatomy, peripatus is utterly unconnected with the ringed worms.

phylum	**Arthropoda**
class	**Onychophora**
genus & species	*Peripatus capensis* *P. moseleyi, others*

Bird-eating spider

Among the largest of living spiders are the so-called bird-eating spiders of the family Theraphosidae. The largest, from the Amazon basin, can attain a length of $3\frac{1}{2}$ in. with a leg span of 10 in. The body and legs are hairy and the hairs have an irritant effect on the human skin. The theraphosids, which belong to the order **Orthognatha**, differ from the more numerous and generally smaller **Labidognatha** in having four lungs instead of two, four spinnerets instead of six, and jaws that work vertically instead of sideways.

There are over 600 species, all living in the tropics. A number of other spiders, in related families, have also been called bird-eaters, and there are others, only distantly related, that are referred to by this name.

The bird-eating spiders are sometimes referred to as tarantulas, especially by American writers. The true tarantula, however, is a wolf spider, **Lycosa tarentula**, found in Southern Europe. Some trapdoor spiders, for example, will kill small birds and there are a number of spiders of the genus **Nephila** that spin such a stout web that small birds are trapped and accidentally eaten.

Hairy night-hunter

During the day the bird-eating spider hides in a rock crevice or a hole in a tree and comes out into the Amazon jungle at night to hunt. With its legs spreading $7\frac{1}{2}$ in. or more (as wide as the span of a man's hand) it does not spin a web but runs down its prey or seizes it by a sudden silent dash, to catch small mammals or drag hummingbirds from their nests. In spite of its size and the revulsion most people feel on seeing this spider, it is not especially dangerous to humans. It is not easily provoked into attack and its venom is usually no more troublesome than a bee sting. On the other hand the whole body and legs are covered with fine hairs which can be very irritant. A curator of the insect house at London Zoo was once injured so badly by handling one of these spiders that his hand was red, swollen and painful for several days and one of his fingers remained permanently crooked.

Fangs for stabbing prey

Once the prey is captured it is instantly stabbed by the sharply-pointed hollow fangs and a fluid injected. It is not clear whether this fluid is a venom or merely the first of a series of injections of digestive juices. It is said to be very mild as a poison, neither killing nor paralysing the prey and yet it can cause a painful local reaction in man, which suggests that it could be a protein-splitting digestive enzyme. Most spiders digest their prey by injecting powerful digestive juices which liquefy the victim's body and then they suck out the contents. Early stories of bird-eating spiders tell of them chewing their food as well as liquefying it, but it is now known that movements once mistaken for chewing are really repeated insertions of the fangs to liquefy more of the victim's body during the lengthened feeding process.

Female spider guards her babies

The bird-eating spider's instinct to attack and eat any moving thing it can manage is so strong that the male has to approach the female very cautiously during the brief courtship. To avoid being eaten he grasps her fangs with his front legs and after mating he eases himself away from her, then hastily retreats. It is not known whether he finds his mate by smell or touch but his sight is poor.

Each female lays 500 – 1 000 eggs in sum-

△ The fangs of the bird-eating spider are sharply pointed and hollow. As soon as the prey has been caught and quickly stabbed, a fluid is passed down the hollow fang. It is not clear whether this fluid is a venom or merely the first of a series of injections of digestive juices.

mer, in a loose cocoon, which she guards by resting with her front feet on it or sitting on it as a hen broods her eggs. If disturbed, she spreads her fangs in a threatening posture. After three weeks white baby spiders hatch from the eggs but stay in the cocoon for up to five weeks. When they leave the cocoon, they are brown with a black spot on the abdomen. They stay near the cocoon for a further 3 – 12 days, then they scatter.

Baby bird-eating spiders feed at first on very small, slow-moving insects, and grow from 4 mm to 16 mm in the first three years, and increase in weight from 0·0052 gm at birth to 0·8 gm. When adult these large spiders have been known to fast for nearly two years; and they can live for 30 years. They moult about 4 times in each of the first

Bird-eating spider
(family Theraphosidae)

three years, twice in each of the fourth and fifth years, and after that once a year. During the moult the senses of sight, hearing and touch are suspended, and the spider remains motionless for several hours.

Enemies

The bird-eating spider has few enemies, largely, it is claimed, because of the irritant nature of its hairs, which it is said to scrape from its abdomen with its hind legs so releasing a cloud of fine hairs which blind and stifle its pursuer. Its main, and probably the only effective, enemies are the hunting wasps, against the paralysing sting of which it is defenceless. The most the spider can do is to rise high on its legs and spread its fangs, in a threat display, which the wasp ignores.

In spite of the parental care enjoyed during the first weeks of life, it has been estimated that not more than 0·2% of bird-eating spiders reach adulthood.

An artist vindicated

The first person to record the carnivorous habits of the bird-eating spiders was Maria Sibilla Merian who, in 1705, published in Amsterdam, a large book called *Metamorphosis Insectorum Surinamensium*. She was an artist and worked in what was then Dutch Guiana. In her book, which was mainly devoted to insects, was a picture showing a large spider dragging a hummingbird from its nest. Beside it was an account of how these spiders take small birds from their nests and suck their blood. No one believed her and in 1834 WS Macleay, an Australian zoologist, made a vitriolic attack on Madame Merian's book, and it was not until 1863, when HW Bates watched spiders killing finches in the Amazon Valley, that Merian's account was fully accepted.

phylum	**Arthropoda**
class	**Arachnida**
subclass	**Araneae**
order	**Orthognatha**
family	**Theraphosidae**
genus	*Theraphosa*, others

△ ▷ *The bird-eating spider has few enemies, largely it is assumed, because of the irritant nature of its hairs. The main and probably only effective enemy of this spider is the hunting wasp whose sting paralyses it.*
▷ *Mother with baby bird-eating spider hatched at the London Zoo in October, 1966. The parents were brought back from Guyana earlier in the year. The female laid over 50 eggs in cocoons she had woven and hidden amongst the vegetation in her cage. On hatching, because of the danger of cannibalism between the young, they were each put in a separate glass tube where they were fed on fruit flies (life size).*

Black widow

*This name is given to a number of species of spiders widely distributed over the warmer parts of the world. The North American species **Latrodectus mactans** is especially noted for its powerful venom, a reputation which is not fully justified. The female is about ½ in. long, a shiny velvety black with a red hour-glass mark on the underside of her almost spherical abdomen. The male is much smaller. The size and colour of the female has led to the alternative names which include shoe button spider, red mark, red back, jockey and also hour-glass spider. The more familiar name of black widow is based on her colour and on the reputation she has for eating her mate as soon as he has fertilised her. It seems possible that the strength of the venom varies with the species and the one inhabiting the southern United States seems to be the worst.*

△ *Black widow, sitting on its web with the feet touching the silken strands, waits for a victim (× 6).*

▽ *The spider begins to wrap and secure its victim by using quantities of silk from spinnerets (× 18).*

▽ *Often it is only at this stage that the victim is stabbed with the fangs and paralysed, then the back legs are skilfully used to enshroud almost completely the ant victim in the viscid silk (× 6).*

Painful but not fatal

The black widow spins a coarse irregularly designed web which often has a short funnel of silk, usually in the more elevated area. The male spins a similarly textured web but much smaller. Cool dark places are chosen, in cellars, outbuildings, ruined or abandoned houses, under doorsteps and porches, beneath floorboards or in piles of rubbish. Among the outbuildings must be included the primitive latrine where, it seems, most human victims have been attacked. Proportionately with the large numbers in which it exists the number of people who fall victim is surprisingly small. The known cases of injury or death in the United States for the 217 years between 1726 and 1943 are 1 291, only 55 of which are known to have been fatal. That is, one death in every 4 years and half a dozen injuries per year. Moreover, the evidence suggests that a high percentage of injuries have been sustained in rural areas where the plumbing is primitive, and even there the victims are mainly children or elderly or unwell people. Above all there seems a strong suggestion that when death does occur shock is a contributory factor if not the sole cause. Nevertheless, the non-fatal consequences are unpleasant enough. The poison is a neurotoxin which attacks the nerves to cause severe pain, muscular cramp, paralysis and hypertension. Fortunately the spider itself is retiring and more concerned with avoiding people than with attacking them. And only the females are troublesome as the male is too small to have enough venom to have any significant effect on humans.

With the exception of one family all spiders have poison glands. These lie in the cephalothorax, the smaller and front portion of the two parts that make up a spider's body, and the poison passes through slender ducts to the fangs. In all but a few spiders, the black widow being one, the venom is effective only against small animals such as insects. It is introduced into their bodies by a stabbing action rather than a bite since no jaw mechanism is involved, the mouthparts of a spider being capable only of sucking.

Paralysed victim enshrouded in silk

As with other web-weaving spiders the black widow sits on the web with her feet touching the silken strands. When an insect flies into the web and starts to struggle the vibrations are detected through the feet of the spider who immediately runs out, and by skilfully using her rear legs and quantities of the viscid silk from the spinnerets, quickly binds and secures it. Often it is only at this stage that the victim is stabbed with the fangs and paralysed, subsequently to be almost completely enshrouded in silk. Meanwhile a drop or two of saliva containing a protein-splitting ferment is exuded from the spider's mouthparts into the insect's body, the contents of which are therefore digested externally. This takes an hour or two, at the end of which the spider, by using its muscular stomach as a pump, sucks out the 'soup', leaving behind only the husk of its prey. This the spider finally cuts away and lets fall to the ground.

Pedipalp sperm reservoir

When adult, the male seeks a mate but before doing so he spins a very tiny web, rubs his abdomen against this and ejects on to it a drop of seminal fluid. This he then takes up in his pedipalps, a pair of specially adapted appendages situated near the mouth and resembling short legs. In mating the male merely transfers the sperm from the reservoir in the pedipalp to the female's body, only one mating being necessary for several bouts of egg-laying, since the female stores the sperm and uses it over a period, often of months. The eggs are laid in silken cocoons and the spiderlings hatching from them are, apart from colour, more or less replicas of the parents and independent from the start.

Self imposed widowhood

Almost everyone believes that the female spider invariably eats her spouse after mating. Even some of those who study spiders join in the chorus possibly after having occasionally seen this happen. This, it is said, is the reason for naming this most venomous spider the black widow. Certainly few people have ever sat down and watched hundreds of spiders mating to see whether the male is invariably eaten. Therefore this idea that the female always eats her spouse is based on this act of cannibalism being occasionally seen. There is, however, a more reasonable explanation. For example, we are told by one expert after another that when the male spider has transferred his sperm to a female he replenishes the reservoir in his pedipalps and will do so several times. This is consistent with the accepted and oft-repeated statement, that male spiders are polygamous—a polygamous male obviously cannot meet his death at each mating. The more likely explanation, and one consistent with the facts, is that after several matings the male becomes enfeebled, is indeed moribund, and then it is that the female devours him, as she would any similar small animal that came her way.

It is a fact that in the insect house at the London Zoo where black widows have been bred in large numbers for many years, individual male spiders have often been mated many times.

phylum	**Arthropoda**
class	**Arachnida**
subclass	**Araneae**
order	**Labidognatha**
family	**Theridiidae**
genus & species	***Latrodectus mactans***

Black widow with her completed cocoon. On hatching the spiderlings, apart from colours, are more or less replicas of the parents and independent from the start. The name widow comes from the belief that the female eats the male after mating. This does happen, but only occasionally.

Crab spider

*Crab spiders are so called because of the length and curvature of their legs and the way they scuttle rapidly sideways, like the true crabs of the sea shore. Crab spiders are all much alike wherever they are found. Many are found in flowers, the colours of which they often match to perfection. They make no web but lie in wait for their prey. They are represented in Britain by 41 species, many rare or of local distribution, and they range from very tiny to not much more than ¼ in. All but one of these belong to the family Thomisidae, there being a single representative of the family Sparassidae, the beautiful, green **Micrommata virescens** which is comparatively large, the female being ½ in. long, the male ⅓ in.*

Beauty lies hidden

Crab spiders' colours or marks blend with their surroundings and this helps in capturing prey. Some spend most of their time in flowers, others lurk among leaf litter or low vegetation, and some lie along the stems or leaves of plants, head-downwards with the legs on each side held together in the same plane as the piece of foliage. Many combine effective camouflage with considerable beauty. *Thomisus onustus,* for example, is often a bright pink, blending perfectly with the flowers of the bell heath or certain orchids. Another, *Misumena vatia,* sometimes called the 'white death', occurs only in white or yellow plants, the white forms being found in flowers like the butterfly orchis, yellow varieties in mullein and gorse. If one of these spiders is transferred to a flower of a different colour, it quickly leaves it and seeks out another flower to match its own hue.

Danger in a flower

As the crab spider seizes its prey it pumps a poison into the victim's body along ducts in its sharp-pointed jaws. This quickly affects the insect's nervous system or its blood, or both at once. The paralysed prey is then drained of its body fluids through the cuts made by the jaws. The husk is discarded. A wide variety of small insects and other invertebrates is taken.

Those crab spiders which lurk in flower heads often take insects like hover-flies, bees and butterflies which visit the flowers for nectar. Sometimes the prey is bitten in a non-fatal part, such as the abdomen, in which case the spider manipulates it until it is able to administer the *coup de grâce* in the head or thorax where the central nervous system can be more directly reached.

Captive courtship

A few days before the male undergoes his final moult he builds a small band of web on which to discharge a drop of seminal fluid. This he takes up into each of his two palps and then goes in search of a mate. There is little preliminary courtship, only tentative caressings with the legs which enable the two partners to recognise each other and which stimulate the female to

An example of crab spider technique on a flower in the Transvaal veld: sudden death for a honey bee. In this case the spider has selected a flower in which its own colour will not be noticed by the victim until too late. Crab spiders kill by striking at the victim's head and thorax.

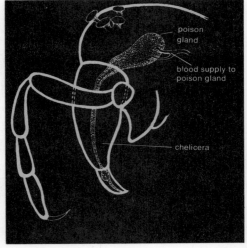

poison gland

blood supply to poison gland

chelicera

▷ *The crab spider's hypodermic. The venom is held in the sac-like gland, which is covered with secretory cells. Muscle fibres encircle the gland; when they are contracted, venom is forced down the long duct running through the chelicera (fang).*

△ *The face of an assassin: head-on view of a crab spider showing groups of eyes and pedipalps hiding the chelicerae or poison fangs.*
▽ *Female crab spider, with male. Like other spiders, mating is fraught with peril for the male crab spider, for the female will often seize and kill the male. In one species the male ties down the female until mating is completed and he can make good his escape.*

accept the male. Grasping the female by a leg the male inserts the sperm into her genital aperture. If she has already mated she will not allow the male to approach but menaces him by raising her front legs and jerking her body. If he persists she may well seize and kill him. Mating may last for less than a minute or go on for several hours.

In one species *Xysticus cristatus* the male employs a device to prevent the female from seizing him. He binds her legs to the ground with threads of silk, after caressing her into accepting his initial advances. When mating is over the female is delayed just long enough in freeing herself from her bonds to allow the male to make good his escape.

Most crab spiders lay their eggs in early summer. The female makes a silken saucer into which to lay her eggs. This she then covers with another silken layer, forming a cocoon. It may be built between leaves lying on the ground or among foliage. Sometimes the female makes a silken tent within which she sits guarding the eggs. Many females eat nothing during the period of incubation, becoming extremely emaciated. Others capture prey as usual, though never straying far from their eggs. Young crab spiders are hatched as miniatures of their parents, though often differing considerably in colour. As in other spiders they grow by shedding their skins at regular intervals.

Many enemies

Spiders have many enemies. Small mammals, birds, reptiles and amphibians eat them, as do beetles, ants, and centipedes. Certain species of wasps and ichneumon flies lay their eggs in living crab spiders. Not least, considerable spider mortality is caused by different species of spider killing and eating one another. Indeed, it is likely that spiders indirectly play a major part in controlling their own numbers.

WS Bristowe, distinguished student of spiders, once estimated that the spider population of England and Wales alone was probably of the order of $2\frac{1}{5}$ billions (2 200 000 000 000) at any one moment—or some 40—50 thousand times the human population of Britain! If each spider eats only 100 insects a year, a conservative estimate, then the value of the service spiders render us in keeping insects down to a reasonable level is obvious. On a world scale it is incalculable.

△ *The crab spider's sharp-pointed jaws inject paralysing venom. It then drains the helpless victim of its body fluids.*

▽ *Crab spiders specialise in camouflage; this species is a perfectionist, even matching the flower's yellow-pointed stamens.*

phylum	**Arthropoda**
class	**Arachnida**
subclass	**Araneae**
order	**Labidognatha**
family	**Sparassidae**
genus & species	*Micrommata virescens*
family	**Thomisidae**
genera & species	*Thomisus onustus* *Misumena vatia* others

Scorpion

Scorpions are notorious for their stings, the venom of which, in some species, is fatal to man. They range in length from $\frac{1}{4}$ in. to as much as 8 in. in **Scorpio viatoris** of Africa. The body is segmented and bears a pair of powerful chelicerae or pincerlike claws similar to those of a lobster. The thorax has four segments each with a pair of walking legs on the under-surface and the abdomen has six segments tapering to a single sharp sting at the end with a small opening supplied by two relatively large venom glands. Such animals as the 8in. African scorpions have a very large sting and venom dangerous to humans.

The lobster-scorpion of Sumatra is even larger but as it lives in dense forest it is not often encountered by man. Although the United States has about 40 species, only two, the 2–3in. **Centruroides sculpturatus** and **C. gertschi**, have venom which can be fatal.

The 650 species are found in all the warm regions of the world. They are particularly abundant in deserts but are found only sparsely in the temperate zones. In America they are found as far north as British Columbia, and they also live in southern Europe. They are extremely adaptable and can stand fierce heat.

Dangerous in the house

One of the main dangers from a scorpion is its habit of living in human dwellings, crawling into beds, furniture, under carpets and into shoes. Away from houses they hide by day under logs or rocks, or in holes in the sand which they dig with their middle legs. Scorpions lead solitary lives, being very hostile to other scorpions, the females may even devour the males after mating.

Tearing their victims to pieces

Scorpions hunt by night. Their prey consists almost entirely of insects and spiders. They seize a victim with their large claws and tear it to pieces or crush it, extracting its body juices. If it offers any resistance the scorpion may then, and only then, use its sting by bringing its abdomen forward over the body and thrusting the poison-bearing tip into its prey. The prey is then slowly eaten, an hour or more sometimes being spent in consuming a single beetle. Scorpions can survive long periods without eating and it is said that they never drink, getting all the moisture they need from their food or from dew. This is not true. In captivity they will readily take water. The usual method of supplying a scorpion with water is to put a wad of wet cotton-wool in its cage, which it will visit regularly to drink.

▷△ *The sting, with its poison-bearing tip, is stabbed into any victim which puts up a fight.*
▷ *Young scorpions ride on their mother's back for nearly a week. These miniature adults are born alive over a period of several weeks.*

Some species of scorpions stridulate, or 'sing', by rubbing the bases of their clawed limbs against the bases of the first pair of walking legs. In some there is what is known as a rasp at the base of each claw with a 'keyboard' on the walking legs. In others the 'keyboard' is on the claw. Scorpions do not stridulate for the same reason as grasshoppers do. Their 'song' is used as a preliminary to attack or as a defensive warning. It is interesting that the positions of the claws differ: in the attack posture they are held wide apart with the claws open and pointing upwards, while in the defensive position the claws are held low and in front of the head. Only the pseudoscorpions have similarly enlarged pedipalps or claws.

Courtship 'dance'

Like spiders, scorpions indulge in a form of courtship before mating. Normally when the female is responsive the male first grasps her with his claws and then manoeuvres to face her, gripping her claws with his own. Sometimes when the female is not submissive and tries to pull away, the male raises his sting almost straight above his claws and the female does the same. It happens very rarely and then only for a few seconds. Having grasped the female the male drags or pushes her to a suitable place where he scrapes away the soil with his feet and deposits his spermatophore. Then, still holding her by her claws, he manoeuvres her over it so she can take up the sperma-

tophore with her cloaca. The two animals remain together for about 5 or 6 minutes before breaking away.

Development in scorpions is especially interesting because the entire order is either ovoviviparous or truly viviparous. The young scorpions are born alive, one or two at a time, over a period of some weeks. In some species a placenta-like tissue is formed in the mother's body through which food is passed to the growing embryo and waste products removed. After birth the baby scorpions ride around on their mother's back. Only after their first moult do they leave the mother and become independent. Some scorpions are known to live for as long as 5 years.

Danger when provoked

The ferocity of scorpions has probably been much exaggerated although there is no doubt that some species are very dangerous. They will not, however, use their sting against humans unless considerably provoked. The danger lies in their coming into houses and, where they are common, this can make living hazardous unless special precautions are taken. In the United States and Mexico it is estimated that more people are killed by scorpions than by snakes. In a town in Brazil, with a population of only 200 000, in 1954 alone nearly 200 people needed emergency hospital treatment for scorpion stings. It is much the same story in other tropical parts of the world and in some places the number of scorpions is amazingly high as shown by a report from Bombay in India. There, what was described as a casual hunt revealed nearly 15 000 scorpions in an area inhabited by only 13 000 people, and the writer of the report suggested that a closer search might have revealed even more.

A sting from one of the more dangerous species is often followed by collapse, profuse perspiring and vomiting, and the skin becoming cold and clammy. Even when drugs and oxygen are administered the patient has difficulty in breathing, with a profuse frothy fluid coming out of the mouth and nostrils. Even with modern medicines this usually ends in death.

phylum	**Arthropoda**
class	**Arachnida**
order	**Scorpiones**
genera	*Ospistobuthus* *Buthus* *Scorpio* *Tityus*

▽ *Battle in the sand. The triumphant victor of these two* **Centrurus** *grasps its overturned opponent's claw. The last two sections of the large pedipalps are modified and enlarged to form claw-like pincers. The overturned scorpion displays its segmented abdomen and the arrangement of legs on the thorax.*

Tarantula

Although everyone knows that the tarantula is a spider, few people are sure of its exact type; great confusion exists over the name. Originally, it referred to a small spider, belonging to the family of wolf spiders living in southern Italy. Its name was derived from the town of Taranto where legend stated that its bite was fatal unless the patient danced until exhausted, and the poison had been sweated from the system. The dance became known as the tarantella. All this happened in the Dark Ages, possibly earlier, and long before Columbus discovered America. Soon after that discovery the large bird-eating spiders of South America were called tarantulas. Their large size and, to most people, repulsive hairiness epitomized the popular horror of spiders and the image in many people's minds of the dreaded spider of southern Italy. Setting the seal on the confusion, certain harmless whip-scorpions that are not even spiders have been placed in a family named the Tarantulidae.

There are nearly a dozen species of the genus **Tarentula**, including the one that started all the fuss. This used to be known as **Tarantula inquilina**, then **Lycosa narbonensis** and now it is named **Tarentula narbonensis**. Its long, somewhat narrow, grey body is just over 1 in. in length, with dark spots, and its legs are hairy and about the same length as the body. Other European species are similar but only just over ½ in. long, or less, and one, **T. fabrilis**, has a dark, dagger-shaped mark on its abdomen. The tarantula of southern Europe is **Lycosa tarentula**.

Poison investigated

Tarantulas are found in different habitats according to the species, from lowlands to mountains up to and above 2 000 ft, on open country such as moors, heaths and grass-land, and also in woodlands. They live in short burrows in the ground and spin no web but, like wolves, run down their prey which is mainly small insects. They kill these by injecting a poison. Henri Fabre, the famous French entomologist, found this was instantly fatal to insects, but he went further to investigate the potency of the poison in relation to the legend. He found the tarantula would bite a sparrow but that a young sparrow took 3 days to die, and a mole died in 36 hours. From this he concluded that the bite could be troublesome to people and that measures to counteract the poison should be taken.

Male tarantula dances

As in all spiders the courtship is elaborate, and, fittingly, in these species the male does a dance. WS Bristowe, in his Comity of

A tarantula attacking a grasshopper. Tarantulas kill insects by injecting them with a poison.

Spiders, has given a detailed description of what happens in some of them. In two species the male moves his palps up and down, slowly at first, then more quickly, and he begins to pulsate his abdomen. Then he walks around the female with jerky steps, with his front legs bunched up and pulsating both his palps and his abdomen, the latter making a tapping sound on the ground. In a third species the male paws the ground in front of him with his front legs, in the manner of a horse, and then starts to circle the female, getting slowly closer and closer to her. He rears up with his palps pointed upwards and his first pair of legs raised in a curve. He then jerks them upwards before lowering them, trembling, to the ground. The female eventually becomes receptive and the male transfers the packets of semen first from one palp, then from the other, to the female.

So far as we can see, these strange convolutions eventually bring the female into a mood to mate, and it is not without profit to recall that the human victim of the tarantula's bite, dancing to cure himself, infected those who watched. In his case, however, he produced a kind of mass hysteria, which has been called tarantism.

The female, like other wolf spiders, carries her eggs in a silken cocoon attached to the tip of her abdomen. When the 40 or so spiderlings hatch they ride in a crowd on the back of the mother's abdomen.

Disease and remedy

The bite of the tarantula was supposed to bring on a general melancholy which in the end proved fatal. The only thing for the victim to do was to call for one or more musicians who, with their pipes and fiddles, would play a succession of tunes until they hit upon one that set the patient dancing,

slowly at first but with more and more speed and vigour—rather like the male tarantula's wooing—until the patient finally fell sweating profusely, exhausted but cured. By that time all of his neighbours might be affected and they would take up the dance, and this might spread to other communities.

It sometimes happened that mass hysteria would break out and spread across Europe. The tarantula was blamed for this. By contrast we find Robert Burton, in his Anatomy of Melancholy (1621), recommending hanging the spider in a nutshell around the neck as a cure for the ague (malaria). He says he got this cure from his mother but seems to have been doubtful of its value until he found it had been recommended by Dioscorides, Matthiolus, Aldrovandus and other authors of high standing from the days of the Ancient Greeks onwards.

▷ Tarantula: the spider that started all the fuss. **T. narbonensis**, poised menacingly above its burrow. Its long, hairy legs and body and beady stare make it easy to see why many people find it so repulsive.

phylum	**Arthropoda**
class	**Arachnida**
subclass	**Araneae**
order	**Labidognatha**
family	**Lycosidæ**
genus & species	**Tarentula barbipes** **T. cuneata** **T. pulverulenta** others

△ *Cracking the eggs. Millipedes hatching.*
▷ *Changing outline. A millipede of the order* **Spirobolida** *nibbles at an orange leaf.*
▽ *A pill millipede,* **Sphaerotherium**.

Millipede

Millipedes range from being soft-bodied and less than ¹⁄₁₀ in. long, to heavily armoured forms exceeding 8 in. Many are poisonous. One of the most obvious ways in which they differ from centipedes, with which they used to be classified under the name 'Myriapoda', is in having two pairs of legs on most of their body segments—the first 4 segments have only single pairs—and in the variable number of segments. The head has short antennae, and some species have no eyes. The general body surface may, however, be sensitive to light.

Millipedes are typically light-shy, nocturnal animals living in moist soil, leaf mould and crevices. They feed on vegetable matter and though valuable in breaking this down, some cause much damage by attacking crops especially in wet weather. The ½ in. spotted snake millipede **Baniulus guttulatus**, *for instance, eats potatoes. The potatoes are probably attacked only when the tough skin has already been broken, for the jaws of these and other millipedes are not powerful. They then burrow inside, making them unfit for human consumption.*

Chemical warfare

In contrast with the fast-running centipedes, millipedes are built not for speed but for pushing their way powerfully through soil or vegetation. When walking, each leg is a little out of step with the one in front, so waves appear to sweep back along each side of the body. When attacked, some make a rapid escape without using their legs, writhing and wriggling their bodies through the vegetation, while others have a protective reflex of coiling up like a watch spring as soon as they are disturbed. The pill-millipedes curl into small balls, and in warmer parts of the world there are millipedes that roll into golf ball size. The usual defence of millipedes is, however, a row of poison glands down each side of the body. The secretion may be red, yellow, white or clear, but typically it is brown or yellow-brown and smelling of excrement, chlorine or prussic acid. The latter two are probably present, as well as iodine or quinine, so it is not surprising that some species are unpleasant to handle. Indeed, in central Mexico one species is ground up with various plants as an arrow poison. Usually the venom simply oozes from the glands, but some larger tropical millipedes discharge it as a fine spray, even to distances of up to a yard. Such millipedes may blind the incautious chicken molesting it, or it may discharge onto human skin, making it blacken and peel. Some of the large tropical

millipedes sport contrasting, bright warning colours. There are even a few luminous species. One, sometimes conspicuous at night in the Sequoia forests of California and aptly named *Luminodesmus sequoiae*, is blind and its light shines continuously from the time of hatching. The light is probably a warning signal to potential predators rather than a recognition sign for its fellow millipedes. That the warning is no mere bluff was shown by the death, from cyanide poisoning, of a bee accidentally imprisoned with one of these millipedes in a test tube.

Tents and mud huts

In mating, which may last for several hours, the male embraces the female, lower surface to lower surface. The genital openings are in pairs on the third body segment and fertilisation takes place inside the female. According to species, 10–300 eggs may be laid. Some millipedes simply coat each egg with soil and excrement, so disguising it, and leave it in a crevice in the earth, while the females of other species make elaborate nests and may remain coiled tightly around them for a few days. The nest can take various forms: a hollow sphere of soil and saliva, lined with excrement or a thin-walled dome of excrement, anchored to the substratum with a narrow tubular chimney, and covered with bits of leaf. The mother will replace these if they are removed. Some-

times the nest is a tent spun from silk. Some millipedes conceal themselves in such silken chambers or tents when they moult, for having cast their skins, they are temporarily very vulnerable to attack. Usually a millipede eats its cast skin, and also the silk tent. The young millipede starts life without the full number of legs, perhaps only three pairs, and acquires more at successive moults.

Millipedes by the million

In 1878, a train was brought to a halt in Hungary by a black mass of millipedes that carpeted the ground and made the wheels slip on the rails. Trains were again stopped in this way in northern France in 1900 and mass migrations of millipedes of various species have been recorded periodically in various countries, including once in Britain, in 1885, when a large number were seen crossing a road. More than a score of such phenomena have been recorded in the United States as, for instance, when 75 acres of West Virginia farmland were covered by these animals in 1918. Cattle would not graze and men hoeing in the fields became nauseated and dizzy from the smell. In the end, most of the millipedes, about 65 million, were killed when they were halted at a cliff bottom and were parched by the sun.

Such plagues are rare, but sudden attacks on crops in lesser numbers are familiar, and tend to occur in times of drought following damp weather. The size of millipede populations does not seem to be governed by predators and parasites, though there are plenty of these, including spiders, toads and birds, particularly starlings. The main controlling factors seem to be physical conditions. The best conditions for the buildup of a population occur when there is plenty of moisture and organic matter in the soil, as for example when farmyard manure has been spread. If the soil then becomes dry, the millipedes move to a more congenial environment. What then could be better than a damp cavity in a sugar beet? Sometimes the migrating masses of millipedes have been accompanied by centipedes and woodlice, for reasons far from clear. Conversely, it is not unknown for millipedes to accompany the marching columns of army ants. Again it is not known why, but millipedes are among the 'guests' to be found in the nests of ants and termites.

phylum	**Arthropoda**
class	**Diplopoda**

△ *Cylindroiulus. Walking is a serious business with so many legs—two pairs to a segment.*

▽ *A long embrace. Millipedes, entwined around each other head to head and lower surface to lower surface, may take several hours over mating. These millipedes belong to the order Iuliformia.*

Centipede

There are many different kinds of centipedes but as they are little noticed and even less liked they do not have common names individually—to most people one centipede is much the same as any other. Scientists, however, have divided them into four orders, the Scolopendromorpha (millipede-like forms), Lithobiomorpha (living-under-stone forms), Geophilomorpha (earth-liking forms), and Scutigeromorpha (shield-covered forms). The first two include the active, elongate but not very slender animals having respectively 21 pairs and 15 pairs of legs. The Geophilomorphs are slender, worm-like centipedes with the pairs of legs varying in number from 31—177, so that some of them more than justify the name 'centipede' or 'hundred-legs'.

The Scutigeromorphs are very distinct and curious. The body is cigar-shaped, not sinuous, and the 15 pairs of legs are very long and slender, enabling the animals to run with remarkable speed and agility. Their respiratory system and the oxygen-carrying capacity of their blood is more efficient than in other centipedes, a feature related to their high rate of activity. Although their appearance is so distinctive, the Scutigeromorphs are allied to the Lithobiomorphs, both orders having 15 pairs of legs.

As there are no common names the scientific (Latin) names must be used. The most familiar British species is **Lithobius forficatus**, the dark-brown centipede that scuttles away when a log or a rock is lifted. Another common species, **Lithobius variegatus**, with speckled legs, is unusual in being apparently confined to the British Isles. The long, slender Geophilomorph centipedes are also common in Britain and are most often found when digging the garden. Most of them are only 1 or 2 in. long, but the North African species **Oryza barbarica** may measure up to 7 in. Many of the Geophilomorph centipedes exude a strongly luminous fluid when molested or injured.

There are only three small Scolopendromorph centipedes in Britain but in the tropics they are very numerous and varied and include giant forms. The tropical American **Scolopendra gigantea** may be 1 ft long and the common Asian species **Scolopendra morsitans** reaches 8 in.

The long-legged Scutigeromorphs occur in southern Europe, the United States and throughout the tropics.

Unwelcome visitors

The body covering of centipedes is not waterproof and they easily die of desiccation. They are confined, therefore, to humid surroundings and are commonly found in leaf mould, compost heaps, under logs and stones, beneath the bark of trees

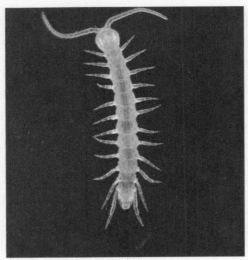

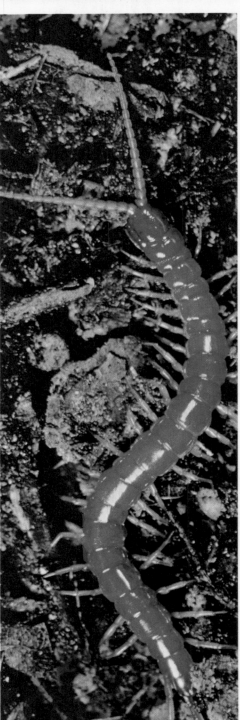

and in the soil; they come into the open only at night when the air is moist and cool. One British Geophilomorph *Scoliophanes maritimus* lives on the seashore under stones that are covered at high tide. Centipedes often enter houses and a long-legged centipede *Scutigera forceps* found in dwellings in the warm parts of the world, is regarded as beneficial as it preys on insects. In tropical Asia the large and venomous *Scolopendra morsitans* is often found in houses, but is by no means a welcome visitor. Many caves in hot countries harbour centipedes, especially the long-legged Scutigeromorphs, which look quite remarkable in the light of lamps or torches, racing about on the floor and up the walls.

Active hunters

Centipedes are active predators, hunting insects, spiders, worms and other small prey. The common *Lithobius forficatus* readily accepts flies in captivity and a large tropical *Scolopendra* kept for over a year in the London Zoo fed mainly on small mice. In the wild state these large centipedes prey on big insects such as locusts and cockroaches and also on geckos and other nocturnal lizards. The marine centipede *Scoliophanes maritimus* has been seen eating barnacles. Some of the worm-like Geophilomorpha feed partly on plant tissues.

Poisonous legs

The poison bite of centipedes is used to paralyse and kill prey. All centipedes have a venomous bite that is inflicted not by the jaws but by the front pair of legs, which are specially modified as 'poison claws', being hollow and connected to poison glands. The bite of the large tropical Scolopendras is excessively painful and occasionally dangerous, though very few fatalities have been recorded.

Breeding

The sexes are very similar and can usually be distinguished only by microscopic examination. All centipedes lay eggs and in the Lithobiomorpha and Scutigeromorpha when the young hatch they have fewer legs than the adult (7 pairs in *Lithobius*) and they reach the full number in the course of development.

Most centipedes merely lay their eggs in the soil and leave them, but the big Scolopendras brood and guard their eggs and young, fiercely fighting any enemy which attacks, and also protecting them from fungal infection by mouthing and licking them. If seriously disturbed they will often eat the eggs or young, or may desert them, and, unattended, the eggs always go mouldy and die.

Centipedes are long-lived creatures and even the little *Lithobius forficatus* may live for 5 or 6 years. The big tropical species probably take at least 4 years to reach full size and may live for considerably longer.

Well protected from enemies

Small centipedes are readily eaten by birds when exposed by spade or plough but they are well protected from enemies of their own size by their poisonous bite. One Malayan monitor lizard, after dissection, was found to have a stomach almost full of

large *Scolopendra* centipedes. Very few animals, however, have an appetite as robust as this, and these big centipedes must have few enemies. In staged combats they are almost always more than a match for spiders or scorpions of their own size.

Rapid movers

In the earlier days of zoology, the rapid movements of centipedes made the details of their locomotion something of a puzzle and the only conclusion reached was that if the animal stopped to think about how it should move its legs it would make poor progress. This situation has been celebrated in rhyme:

A centipede was happy, quite
Until a toad in fun
Said, 'Pray which leg goes after which?'
This raised her doubts to such a pitch,
She fell exhausted in the ditch,
Not knowing how to run.

The problem has been resolved by high-speed photography. In most centipedes the legs move rhythmically in waves which alternate on either side of the body, so that in any part, at a given moment, the feet will be bunched on one side and spread on the opposite side. When the legs bunch the tips often cross, but the centipede seems to be immune to the hazard of falling over its own feet. In the long worm-like Geophilomorph centipedes this pattern of movement is not seen; each leg seems to move on its own, picking its way independently of the others. Much of the movement of these centipedes consists of burrowing rather than running, and this sort of leg action is more suitable for such deliberate pushing along of the body.

phylum	**Arthropoda**
class	**Chilopoda**
orders	**Geophilomorpha**
	Lithobiomorpha
	Scolopendromorpha
	Scutigeromorpha

Centipedes paralyse and kill their prey with a venom from poison claws which are developed from the first pair of legs. The giant Malayan centipede (bottom right) may grow to 8 in. long and can inflict a very painful bite which has occasionally killed a human. The tropical American species of **Scolopendra**, *bottom left, may grow to 1 ft long. The young* **Lithobius** *centipede (top left) hatched from its egg with only seven pairs of legs. When fully grown it will have 15 pairs. This type is common in Britain and grows to only 1 or 2 in. long but it may live for 5 or 6 years. Centipedes are often confused with millipedes but they may easily be told apart as these pictures show: each segment of a millipede* **Polydesmus** *(top right) has two pairs of legs; centipedes have only one pair to each segment.*
These pictures of different centipedes show how they walk with rhythmic waves of leg movements alternating on either side of the body. At any one part of the body the feet are bunched on one side and spread on the other.

Kitchen nightmare: a common cockroach has a wash and brush-up after a meal of bread. These household pests have the depressing habit of fouling far more than they actually eat.

Newly-moulted cockroach larvae. They may moult 6—12 times before they are fully grown.

Cockroach

Cockroaches used to be classified together with the grasshoppers, crickets, stick-insects and others in one large order, the Orthoptera. This has now been split up into several separate orders of which one, the Dictyoptera, comprises the praying mantises and the cockroaches.

These are fairly large insects, flattened in shape, with two pairs of wings, the fore-wings being more or less thickened and leathery, serving as a protective cover for the delicate hindwings, just as the hard-ened forewings or elytra of beetles do. The hindwings of cockroaches are pleated like a fan when not in use; when expanded for flight they have a very large surface area. In the commonest European species, the black beetle as it is called, the male has very small wings, the female has

mere vestiges, and neither can fly. The female has reduced wings and is flightless in some of the other species also.

The most familiar of the 3 500 species of cockroaches are those tropical and sub-tropical forms which have taken advantage of the warmth and the opportunities for scavenging afforded by homes and premises in which food is made or stored. By this means they have ex-tended their range into temperate and cold regions, and some of them have been artificially distributed all over the world. In the wild state, the great majority of species are tropical. In the outdoor fauna of Britain they are represented by 3 small species only, belonging to one genus, **Ectobius**.

Three of the most common cockroaches are: Common cockroach, or black beetle **Blatta orientalis** *length variable, averaging about 1 in., dark brown*

(females almost black) wings not reaching the tip of the body in the male, vestigial in the female; both sexes flightless. A common pest in house. Now cosmopolitan in distribution, the region of its origin is unknown.

German cockroach, steamfly or shiner **Blatella germanica** *about ½ in. long, yellowish-brown with two dark brown stripes on the prothorax, or fore-part, of the body. Wings fully developed. Almost as abundant as the common cockroach and certainly not of German origin; probably a native of North Africa.*

American cockroach **Periplaneta americana** *males nearly 1½ in. long, reddish-brown, with fully developed wings. Found mostly in sea port towns and on ships. In tropical countries it is the chief house-living cockroach. It is not an American insect and probably also originated in North Africa.*

The young of the common cockroach are white on hatching, gradually becoming brown.

A brace of American cockroaches. Unlike the common cockroach, the American version has fully-developed wings. Despite its name it is not an American insect: it probably originated in North Africa.

They come out at night

In the wild, most cockroaches live on the ground among decaying vegetation or behind dead bark, and are coloured brown to match their surroundings. The 'domestic' species probably all lived in this way once. Some cockroaches are found among growing plants and are patterned in brown, yellow or green. The ground-living cockroaches are nocturnal, hiding away by day and coming out at night, just as the house-living ones do. Some of the large tropical species fly freely at night and are attracted to artificial light.

Their flattened bodies allow them to creep into cracks and crevices; in houses, cockroaches hide in inaccessible places and are not easy to get rid of.

Poisoned baits may be effective if used persistently, and insecticidal powders and sprays kill them if introduced well into their hiding places. Bad infestations, however, are best dealt with by professional pest controllers.

Unwelcome scavengers

In the wild, most cockroaches are scavengers on dead insect and other animal remains, fallen fruit and fungi; the transition to scavenging in human habitations is easy and obvious. Some of the wild species feed on wood, which they are able to digest with the help of protozoans, microscopical one-celled animals, in their intestine. Termites, which are closely allied to cockroaches, eat and digest wood by the same means.

In houses, cockroaches will eat any kind of human food that they can get at. They will also eat a variety of substances not generally regarded as edible, such as book-bindings, boot-blacking, ink and whitewash. Frank Buckland, in his *Curiosities of Natural History*, tells of a gentleman on his way home from India by ship who was much annoyed by cockroaches. At night, when he was asleep they 'came and devoured the little rims of white skin at the roots of the finger nails'. The harm they do is greatly increased by their habit of fouling, with their droppings, far more than they actually eat. The only good that can be said of them is that so far as is known they do not convey any disease.

Breeding

The eggs are enclosed in a purse-like capsule called the ootheca. In the common cockroach this is carried for a day or two, protruding from the body of the female, and then dropped, or sometimes stuck in a crevice, after which the insect takes no further notice of it. It is white when it first appears at the tip of her abdomen, but darkens later and, when deposited, is almost black and rather less than ½ in. long. Normally an ootheca contains 16 eggs in 2 neat rows of 8, but there may be more or less than this. The eggs hatch 2—3 months after the formation of the ootheca, which splits to allow the young to emerge. The young of the common cockroach are about ⅕ in. long on hatching, and white, gradually becoming brown as they grow. They resemble their parents in form, except that the wings are lacking, and take 10 months —1 year to reach maturity. Moulting of the skin, or ecdysis, takes place anything from 6—12 times in the course of growth. The breeding habits of the American cockroach are similar.

In the German cockroach the ootheca is carried by the female until a day or less before hatching, and the eggs may even hatch while it is still attached to her. It is chestnut brown and, a few days before hatching, a green band appears along each side of it. Hatching usually takes place 4—6 weeks after the ootheca is formed and it normally contains 35—45 eggs.

Hated and loathed as a household pest because of its habit of defiling food, the cockroach is nevertheless one of the best examples of success in surviving; and it has an important role in the teaching of entomology.
This close-up shows the organs of special sense: the eyes, which are compound, consisting of many small elements; the palps and antennae, which are organs of touch. On the highly mobile antennae are structures which are used for smelling. Above the front of the 'shell' are the semi-transparent elytra, or wing cases.

Living fossils

In a manner of speaking the world went wild with delight when the coelacanth, a living fossil, first came to light. The same intense interest would be shown if another living fossil were to be discovered. There is something in the psychology of these events which recalls the parable of the pieces of silver that were thought lost and were found again. Nobody but the most devoted scientist, however, would think of rolling out the red carpet for the roaches. Yet they are extremely interesting and primitive insects.

Many fossils have been found, showing that there were already many species and abundant populations of roaches at the time when coal measures were being deposited, 300 million years ago. These cockroaches of the Carboniferous period look similar to many of the present day ones and the family as a whole must be regarded as insects which, by adopting a simple and secure way of life at an early period of the earth's history, and never departing from it, have inherited the earth by their very meekness. As an example of success in survival they have few equals, but because they

intrude themselves on our notice in such an unpleasant manner, few people find themselves able to regard them highly. Nevertheless, there are a few people whose sole purpose in life is to rear cockroaches.

Partly because they are so easy to obtain and partly because their structure and anatomy is so simple and generalised, cockroaches are widely used to introduce students to the science of entomology, and breeding them for this purpose is one of the less well-known human occupations.

phylum	**Arthropoda**
class	**Insecta**
order	**Dictyoptera**
family	**Blattidae**

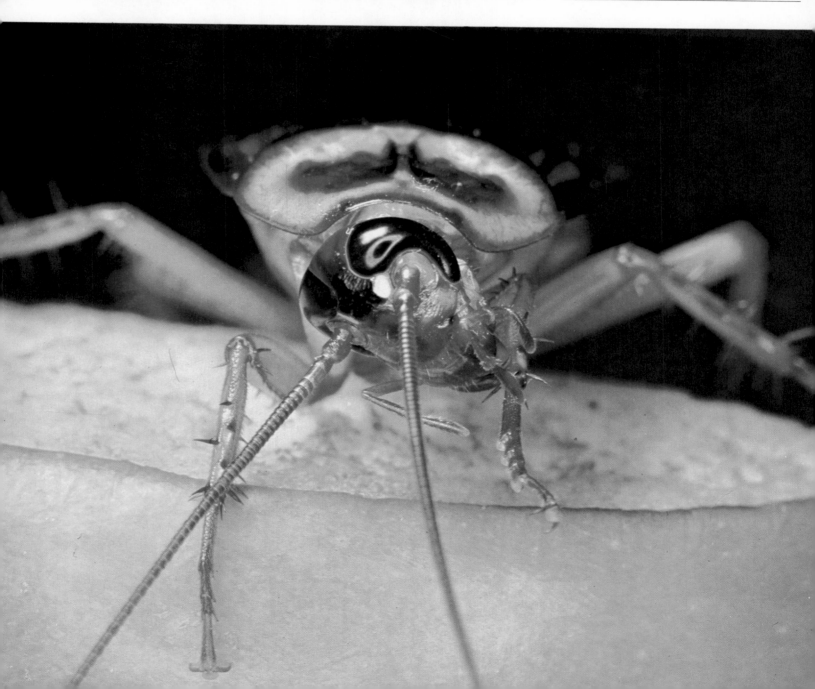

Grasshopper

As their name suggests, most grasshoppers live among grass and herbage on the ground. They are variously coloured—mostly green and brown—and are protected as long as they keep still by blending with their surroundings. Grasshoppers are active by day and if disturbed jump suddenly and powerfully, using their greatly-enlarged hindlegs. They can also crawl slowly by means of the other two pairs of legs.

Nowadays the term 'grasshopper' is applied to the short-horned Acrididae, while the long-horned Tettigoniidae are called 'bush-crickets' because they are more closely allied to the other main family of the order Orthoptera (the Gryllidae or true crickets) than to the Acrididae. In all Orthoptera the forewings are leathery and serve as coverings for the folded, membranous hindwings which, in the flying species, are the sole organs of flight.

Grasshoppers are mainly ground-living insects, while most bush-crickets live in the foliage of trees and bushes. Locusts, which are in fact swarming grasshoppers, will be dealt with under a separate heading (page 90).

Fiddlers in the grass

The familiar chirping chorus in the fields and hedgerows of the countryside is the result of grasshoppers' stridulation. A row of evenly spaced, minute pegs on the largest joint of the hindlegs is rubbed over the more prominent veins or ribs of the forewings. Usually, but not always, only males can sing. Each species has its own song, and these may be learned, like the songs of birds, and used in identifying the species. The colours of species of grasshoppers vary so much that their song is a better means of recognizing them than their appearance.

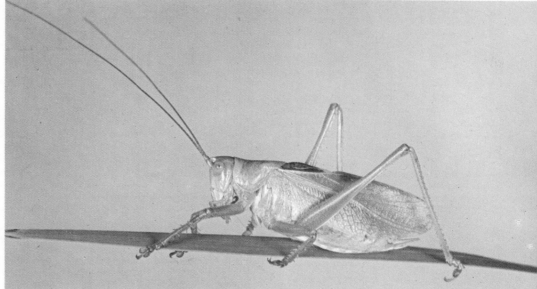

Apart from stridulation, both pairs of wings serve their usual function. In most of the common species the hindwings are fully developed in both sexes and the insects can fly. One exception is the meadow grasshopper *Chorthippus parallelus* in which the hindwings are vestigial; even in this species there are occasional individuals in which the wings are fully developed and functional. Among Orthoptera it is not uncommon for species to occur in two forms, winged (macropterous) or wings much reduced (brachypterous). The most usual cases are like the one described, in which occasional winged individuals occur in a normally brachypterous population.

Top right: Bush-crickets mating. Male (right) is placing the spermatophore – package of sperm – at the base of the female's ovipositor. The blade-like structure of this organ is typical of bush-crickets. Centre: Bush-cricket **Tettigonia cantans**. *Bottom right: Short-horned grasshopper* **Chorthippus parallelus**.

Openings to the hearing organs on the foreleg of a bush-cricket—sensitive enough to pick out the calls of different species.

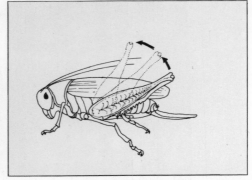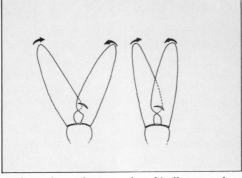

Stridulation—the voice of the grasshoppers. Left: Long-horned grasshopper rubs a hindleg over the ribs of the forewing. Right: Bush-crickets have one of the left wing ribs adapted to form a row of teeth, which is rubbed against the trailing edge of the right forewing to produce the sound.

Bush-cricket crawlers

Although some species live on the ground, most bush-crickets are at home in the foliage of trees and bushes. These tend to be mainly green while the ground-dwelling ones are brown or blackish. Unlike grasshoppers bush-crickets are not lovers of the sun, but become active in the late afternoon, or may be wholly nocturnal. Their hindlegs are adapted for jumping, but they have not the prodigious leaping powers of grasshoppers, moving mainly by climbing and crawling.

Singing a different song

They are also noisy and call by stridulating, but the mechanism is very different from that of grasshoppers. In the left forewing a rib, formed by one of the veins, has a row of minute teeth and this is rubbed against the hind edge of the right forewing. The arrangement is the same as in crickets except that the roles of the left and right forewings are reversed. Here again the species all have distinct songs, and there is good reason for this. In both bush-crickets and grasshoppers the song is mainly a courtship invitation addressed to the female, and it is important that the females should be able to recognise the call of males of their own species.

The great green bush-cricket *Tettigonia viridissima* ranges across Europe, Asia and North Africa. The female is 2 in. long, including the straight, blade-like ovipositor, and is bright green in colour. The male is a little smaller and his song is very loud and sustained, and uttered at night. In the late summer and autumn the speckled bush-cricket *Leptophyes punctatissima* is common in gardens and hedges. It is a plump, soft-looking insect, green with the wings reduced to small vestiges; the female ovipositor is broad and curved.

Two ways of laying eggs

Both grasshoppers and bush-crickets lay eggs. In the former they are enclosed in a tough case called the egg-pod, which the female buries in the ground. Each pod has from 5 to 6 or up to 14 eggs, more or less according to the species. Bush-crickets lay their eggs without any covering and usually singly, some putting them in the ground or crevices of bark, others inserting them in stems or leaves by cutting slits with the ovi-

Standing room only: a crowd of **Phymateus** grasshopper nymphs. Wings show after moulting.

positor. In both, the young hatch in the form of tiny worm-like larvae which moult immediately after hatching. They then resemble their parents except that they have no wings. With each moult (ecdysis) their size increases. The wings also appear and grow larger at each moult, becoming fully formed and functional, in the species that fly, at the last moult. Most of the common species have one generation a year.

Mainly vegetarian

Grasshoppers are entirely herbivorous and can be fed in captivity on bunches of grass tied with string and lowered into their home. The floor of the receptacle should be covered with 1½ in. of slightly damp sand, and in these conditions they will breed readily.

Bush-crickets are at least partly predatory and one species, the oak bush-cricket *Meconema thalassinum*, is entirely carnivorous and hunts caterpillars and other insects in oak trees. The others feed partly on grass and leaves and partly on insects. In captivity they must be given plenty of room; if they are crowded cannibalism will occur. Lettuce leaves seem to suit most of them, but they should have some animal food as well. Small looper caterpillars can usually be found by shaking bushes and branches into an open umbrella held underneath them.

Colour means nothing

Some grasshoppers show an extraordinary range of variation in the colour and markings on both legs and body. In the stripe-winged and common green grasshoppers *Stenobothrus lineatus* and *Omocestus viridulus* there is a small number of well defined colour varieties, but in the common field and mottled grasshoppers *Chorthippus brunneus* and *Myrmeleotettix maculatus* there is almost every shade of colour: green, brown, yellow and red are the main colours and to these must be added extremely varied patterns of stripes, spots and mottling. As a result it is hopeless to try to tell a grasshopper by its colour.

class	**Insecta**
order	**Orthoptera**
family	**Acrididae**
genera	**Chorthippus, Omocestus, Stenobothrus, Myrmelotettix, Tetrix**
family	**Tettigoniidae**
genera	**Tettigonia, Leptophyes, Meconema**

Rhapsody in purple: an inch-long South African grasshopper of the family Eumastacidáe.

Locust

Although the term 'locust' is loosely applied to any large tropical or subtropical grasshopper, it is better restricted to those whose numbers occasionally build up to form enormous migrating swarms which may do catastrophic damage to vegetation, notably cultivated crops and plantations.

Africa suffers most seriously from locust swarms and three species are of special importance. These are the desert locust, the red locust and the African subspecies of the migratory locust.

Both the red locust and the African migratory locust have their own regional control organisations which effectively prevent plague outbreaks. The desert locust, however, presents a real international problem which has yet to be solved and is the main subject of study of the Anti-Locust Research Centre in London. It will therefore be the main subject of this entry.

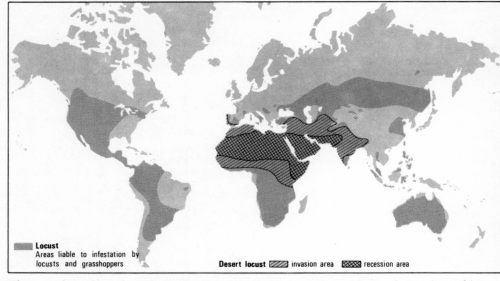

Locust
Areas liable to infestation by locusts and grasshoppers

Desert locust ▨ invasion area ▧ recession area

The map above shows the wide distribution of locusts. In some places, like North America, cultivation of their breeding grounds has reduced their numbers. In Africa, however, the desert locust is public enemy number one. Other locusts are easier to control, because after their migrations they recede to small areas; the desert locusts' outbreak area is very wide, as indicated.

Locust or gregarious grasshopper

The vast plagues of locusts which periodically create such havoc in many regions of the underdeveloped world are really nothing more nor less than hordes of gregarious grasshoppers. For locusts can exist in two phases: a solitary, grasshopper phase, or a swarming locust phase. When the grasshoppers are crowded together they change their behaviour, and, if kept like this for a generation or more, also change their shape and colour to that of the swarming form.

Solitary locusts come together only for mating and then behave very much as other grasshoppers do. The eggs, the size of rice grains, are laid down to 4 in. below the surface of the ground. They are held together by a frothy secretion which hardens to form an egg-pod $1\frac{1}{2}$–2 in. long, which usually contains 80–100 eggs. Above the pod the froth forms a plug which helps prevent the eggs from drying out and stops sand falling into the hole, so the hatchlings can escape. The egg stage lasts about 10–14 days in the main summer breeding areas but may be up to 70 days in the colder North African spring. The insects that hatch grow through a series of moults or skin-changes in the course of which they become gradually more like adult locusts and in the final 2 moults the wings form, becoming functional after the last moult, when the insect is adult. This takes 30–50 days, mainly depending on temperature. In a swarm the adults are pink at first, but after a few weeks or months, usually coinciding with the rainy seasons, they mature sexually and become yellow. The flightless immature locusts are traditionally known as 'hoppers'.

When they first hatch young solitary locusts disperse and unless some environmental factor forces them together they never do begin to associate in bands but settle down to the solitary life of grasshoppers. These are usually green or brown, blending well with their surroundings.

Jekyll and Hyde phase-change

Under certain conditions, depending on many variable factors, often associated with the weather, scattered solitary locusts may become concentrated into favourable laying sites. With every female locust laying two or three batches of 70–80 eggs each the numbers after hatching will have multiplied at least 100 times. With many more hoppers crowded into the same area, groups coalesce and they are then well on the way to the all important phase change from solitary to gregarious type which leads eventually to hopper bands and locust swarms.

When crowded together their colour

Left: Immature pink adult female. Millions of these exist in vast swarms, which follow the wind to arrive in new breeding grounds soon after rain.
Right: Hopper bands on the march, eating all the way. At first they move only a few yards a day, but in the later stages they hop for up to a mile.

changes to a bold pattern of black and orange or yellow stripes which probably helps them see one another and so keep together. The brightly patterned, crowded hoppers grow into pink adults which turn yellow at sexual maturity, solitary adults being sandy-coloured. Moreover, in the adults there are structural differences between the solitary and gregarious phases, notably in the wing, which is relatively longer in the gregarious phase. It is known that structural changes between one phase and another are associated with relative differences in the insects' hormonal balance.

Mutual stimulation leads to greater activity and they start to 'march'. Because an urge to keep close together is induced by development in the gregarious phase they march together in bands.

As adults they continue to migrate, and the urge to crowd together is maintained, but they are now airborne and move much faster. Weather conditions too can lead to the development of gregarious locusts and swarm formations. Scattered flying locusts fly downwind towards frontal systems of converging airflow and thus tend to accumulate in rainy areas. As the region inhabited by the desert locust is mainly arid, the result of persistently flying with the wind is to concentrate large numbers of locusts in areas when rain is likely to fall and provide them with food in the form of a flush of desert plants springing up after the rain. The gregarious phase develops in the offspring and migration then takes place in the usual way, following the prevailing wind and the favourable weather.

Locust plagues

When the swarm descends the locusts devour everything green. After mating takes place each female lays several hundred eggs. The young that hatch are still crowded and behave in just the same way, but the swarm that results can be many times larger. This swarm continues to migrate and again descends and multiplies its numbers. In this way a swarm may cover vast areas and build itself up into an aggregate of thousands of tons of locusts resulting in plague conditions. Plagues eventually come to an end due to adverse weather. The few survivors revert to the solitary phase, in which they are relatively harmless.

Perhaps the most important discovery made by the Anti-Locust Research Organisation has been that the African migratory locust and the red locust change from the solitary to the gregarious phase only in certain limited outbreak areas. These areas are effectively policed by regional locust control organisations and plague outbreaks have been prevented since 1944.

The desert locust is the locust of the Bible, and now by far the most damaging of all. It is hard to control because it has no geographically determined outbreak areas. It ranges over a vast area, from southern Spain and Asia Minor, the whole of northern Africa, through Iran to Bangla Desh and India, an area comprising about 60 countries. Between plagues lasting 6 or more years there are equally long recessions when only solitary locusts are to be found. The last plague ran from 1950 to 1962 and another showed all the signs of building up rapidly after the spring rains of 1967. In 1968 the situation looked very serious but by mid-1969 it was much quieter than expected 6 months previously. The last outbreak was in 1973–4 in New South Wales, Queensland and Victoria.

Natural enemies

If all the locusts in a swarm only 2 miles square were to breed successfully, in only four generations there would be a severe infestation of the whole 196 million square miles of the earth's surface. Fortunately there is enormous mortality from natural causes. Winds may fail to carry the locusts to a suitable breeding area. The soil may not be moist enough for the eggs to hatch. Or they hatch to find insufficient plant growth for their food or to protect them from the heat of the midday sun. There are also many predators, parasites and diseases of locusts. A little fly *Stomorhina* lays its eggs on top of the locust egg pods as soon as they are laid and the fly's grubs eat up the eggs. Larvae of the beetle *Trox* can destroy an egg field completely and ants have been seen waiting at the top of an egg froth plug and carrying away all the hatchlings. Flocks of birds often accompany both hopper bands and adult swarms and they can account for enormous numbers of hoppers. At this stage hoppers are particularly vulnerable and their predators take advantage of the feast.

Control by man

Concentrated insecticides and highly efficient spray gear using both aircraft and ground vehicles are used in enormous campaigns against desert locusts. One of the most effective, because it is simple and cheap, uses the exhaust gases from a Land Rover to produce a fine spray of poison. This will drift over the vegetation in the path of hoppers and is a very quick and economical way of killing hopper bands. Aircraft can match the mobility of a migrating swarm; searching greater areas, finding and following swarms and spraying them in the morning and evening when they fly low and are most vulnerable to spraying. A single light aircraft carrying 60 gallons of insecticide can destroy 180 million locusts.

Migrating swarms of locusts commonly travel between 1 000 and 3 000 miles between successive breeding areas and naturally cross many international frontiers. Regional locust control organisations within the desert locust invasion areas pool resources and facilitate the movement of supplies across frontiers. These organisations in turn are coordinated by the Food and Agriculture Organisation (FAO) of the United Nations with its headquarters in Rome. FAO cooperates with the Desert Locust Information Service run by the Anti-Locust Research Centre in London.

phylum	**Arthropoda**
class	**Insecta**
order	**Orthoptera**
family	**Acrididae**
genera & species	***Austroicestes cruciata*** Australian plague grasshopper
	Chortoicetes terminifera Australian plague locust
	Locusta migratoria manilensis Oriental migratory locust
	Locusta migratoria migratoria Asiatic migratory locust
	Locusta migratoria migratorioides African migratory locust
	Melanoplus spretus Rocky Mountain locust
	Nomadacris septemfasciata red locust
	Schistocerca gregaria desert locust

Left: Close-up of a yellow and black hopper. Right: Trio of swarming hoppers. These come together to form dense groups, which join others to become a massive band.

Like an unknown monster from outer space the mantis cradles a day-flying moth in its spined forelegs and delicately and neatly eats its live victim.

Mantis

The name Mantis is derived from a Greek word meaning 'prophet' or 'soothsayer' and refers (as also does the epithet 'praying') to the habitual attitude of the insect—standing motionless on its four hindlegs with the forelegs raised as if in prayer—it is waiting for unwary insects to stray within reach. The forelegs are spined and the joint called the tibia can be snapped back against the femur, rather as the blade of a penknife snaps into its handle, to form a pair of grasping organs which seize and then keep a hold on

any unfortunate victims.

Mantises, or praying mantises as they are often called, feed mainly on other insects, and are found mostly in tropical or subtropical countries. Most of the smallest are about an inch long. They have narrow, leathery forewings and large fan-shaped hindwings, which are folded beneath the forewings when not in use. Most mantises can fly, but they do not readily take to flight and seldom go far.

About 1 800 species are known, the most familiar species being the European mantis **Mantis religiosa**, *which lives in the Mediterranean region and has been introduced into eastern North America.*

Hidden terror
Most mantises spend their time sitting still among foliage, or on the bark of trees, waiting for insects to stray within reach of a lightning-quick snatch of their spined forelegs. Nearly all are shaped and coloured to blend with their surroundings. Many are green or brown, matching the living or dead leaves among which they sit, but some have more elaborate camouflage which serves two purposes. First, because they do not pursue their prey but wait for it to stray within reach, they need to stay hidden. Secondly, their grasping forelegs, although formidable to other insects, are usually useless against birds and lizards, and since mantises are slow-moving, they must be concealed to avoid being caught and eaten.

◁ As the female **Sphodromantis gastrica** lays her eggs she gives out a liquid which she stirs into a froth by movements of her body. The plastic-like substance then hardens enclosing the eggs. Each capsule, which is usually attached to a twig, contains about 80—100 eggs. One female may make as many as 20 such oothecae in her lifetime.
Overleaf: Close-up of mantis head.
▽◁ Section through an ootheca of **Sphodromantis** sp. showing the egg chambers. The spongy texture of the capsule is seen clearly here but it nevertheless gives good protection against hungry birds.
▽ Young mantids emerge from the ootheca. They may moult up to 12 times before becoming adult. Their wings, tiny at first, grow larger with each moult.

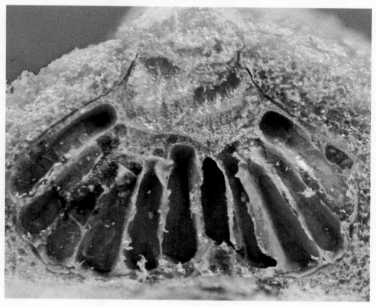

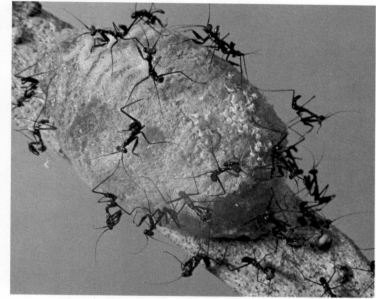

Mantises never take plant food. They seize their insect victims in their spined forelegs and eat them alive, neatly and delicately. Some of the largest species occasionally catch and eat small birds and lizards in the same way.

Unusual mating habits

To a female mantis a male is no more than just another piece of food. He must, therefore, be careful in his approach if he wishes to mate, rather than be the next meal. On seeing a ripe female, the male, justifiably enough, freezes, then starts to creep up on her with movements almost too slow for the eye to follow—sometimes taking an hour or more to move 1 ft. Once within range, he makes a short hop and clasps the female, to mate. If the pair is disturbed or the female sees her suitor, she will eat him, starting by biting off his head. As he loses his head, so he loses his inhibitions, because mantis copulation is controlled by a nerve centre in the head which inhibits mating until a female is clasped. If this nerve is removed (by an experimenter, or by a female mantis) all control is lost, and the body continues to copulate. The female, therefore, has much to gain from attacking and eating males; she ensures both fertilisation of her eggs and nourishment for her developing ovaries.

Eggs in a bag

The female lays 80—100 eggs at a time in tough, spongy capsules which she attaches to twigs, and she may produce 20 capsules in her lifetime. While laying her eggs she gives out a liquid which she stirs into a froth by movements of her body. The eggs become enclosed in this while it is still plastic, then it quickly hardens and dries.

The young mantises hatch together and at first hang from the egg capsule by silken threads which they give out from the hind end of the abdomen. After their first moult they can no longer make silk. They grow by gradual stages, moulting up to 12 times before becoming adult. The wings, tiny at first, grow with each succeeding moult.

The egg capsules are a protection against insectivorous animals and birds, but they are no protection against parasitic wasps of the ichneumon type, which are probably the most serious enemies of mantises.

Fatal flowers

Some mantises are even more deceptive, taking on the appearance of flowers and so luring insects such as bees and butterflies within reach. The orchid mantis of Malaysia and Indonesia, in its young or subadult stage, is coloured pink and the thigh joints of the four hindlegs are widely expanded so they look like petals, while the pink body

resembles the centre of the flower. When the mantis reaches the adult stage, however, its body becomes white and elongated as in a normal mantis. It still has the expanded, petal-like legs but its resemblance to a flower is largely lost. The African 'devil's flower' has expansions on the thorax and the forelegs which are white and red. It hangs down from a leaf or twig, and catches any flies or butterflies attracted to it.

When they are frightened, many mantises will suddenly adopt a menacing posture, rearing up and throwing their forelegs wide apart. One African species *Pseudocreobotra wahlbergi* improves on this display by spreading its wings, on which there are a pair of eye-like markings, so the enemy is suddenly confronted with a menacing 'face'.

class	**Insecta**
order	**Dictyoptera**
suborder	**Mantodea**
family	**Mantidae**
genera & species	*Hymenopus coronatus* orchid mantis **Mantis religiosa** European mantis **Idolum diabolicum** African devil's flower, others

*Incredible birth: this **Bactrododema aculiferum** has just hatched from its tiny egg shell, having first pushed off the top of the egg, the operculum.*

Stick-insect

*Stick-insects are today more commonly kept as pets than probably any other insect. They are sluggish and live among the foliage of trees and bushes or in low-growing herbage, relying for protection on their resemblance to their surroundings. They are always long and very slender, usually with smooth bodies, although some species are spiny. The larger kinds look like twigs and may be green or brown; the small species and the young of the larger ones are usually green and resemble the midribs of leaves or the stems and blades of grass. Some are very large and the Asian species **Palophus titan** is the longest living insect, sometimes exceeding a foot in length.*

Some stick-insects have wings but many are wingless, a condition that enhances their resemblance to twigs.

*Stick-insects, with the leaf-insects, comprise an order, the Phasmida, once included in the Orthoptera together with the grass-hoppers, mantids, cockroaches and others, but this group has now been divided into several separate orders. About 2 000 species of phasmids are known, the majority being found in the Oriental tropics. One species, **Bacillus rossii,** is native to Europe, ranging as far north as central France. Two kinds of stick-insects from New Zealand have become established in the extreme southwest of the British Isles: the prickly stick-insect **Acanthoxyla prasina** in Devonshire and on Tresco in the Scilly Isles, and the smooth stick-insect **Clitarchus**
hookeri** also on Tresco and on an island off County Kerry, Eire. The so-called laboratory stick-insect **Carausius morosus** is an Oriental species often kept in schools and laboratories and more generally as a pet. It is a very easy insect to keep and breed and can be fed on leaves of privet, ivy or lilac. It cannot, however, survive out of doors through the cold winter in northern Europe and it is important that it is kept inside during this period.*

Dazzle and hide

Most stick-insects feed and move about only at night. By day they remain motionless and often appear to be 'feigning death'. In fact they pass into a hypnotic or catalyptic state during the day. When they are in this condition the limbs can be moved into any position and will stay there, rather as if the joints were made of wax. Some of the winged species are active by day. In many of these the hindwings—which are the only ones developed for flying—are brightly coloured but are entirely concealed when the insect is at rest. If it is disturbed the wings are suddenly unfolded and the resultant flash of bright colour is confusing to a searching predator. Then, when the wings are closed again, the bright colour suddenly disappears, so the exact position at which the insect has alighted is effectively concealed. This is a well-known protective device and is called 'flash coloration'.

All stick-insects are plant eaters and occasionally they become numerous enough to defoliate areas of woodland. In Australia there are two species which occur in swampy areas but also feed on agricultural crops where they sometimes cause serious damage.

Eggs like raindrops

All the phasmids lay rather large, hard-shelled eggs which look very like seeds. In some cases they closely resemble the actual seeds of the plant on which the insect feeds. The eggs are dropped by the females at random. The tap of falling eggs is often heard from the cages of captive stick-insects and a North American species *Diapheromera femorata* is sometimes so numerous that the sound of thousands of its eggs falling on the forest floor is as loud as that of rain.

Several hundred eggs are usually laid, a few each day, and they take a long time to hatch. Those of the laboratory stick-insect hatch in 4—6 months at ordinary room temperatures, but this can be speeded up to 2 months by extra warmth or retarded to 8 months by cold conditions such as an unheated room in winter. The eggs of the Madagascar stick-insect *Sipyloidea sipylus* will hatch in as little as one month if kept at $24°C/75°F — 27°C/80°F$, but at lower temperatures may lie dormant for up to a year.

The young look very like the adults in all except size and, in the case of the winged species, in lacking wings, which develop gradually during growth.

Many stick-insects reproduce by parthenogenesis, that is the females lay fertile eggs without mating. In these species the males are usually rare; in cultures of the laboratory stick-insect, for example, they number about one in every 4 000 females. Of the two New Zealand species already mentioned, the male of the prickly stick-insect is unknown and possibly does not exist. In New Zealand, males of the smooth stick-insect are almost as common as females, but no males have been found in the small British colonies of the same species and the eggs develop without fertilisation.

Odd colours

The laboratory stick-insect occurs in various colour forms ranging from green to shades of brown. The colour is determined by green, brown, orange-red and yellow granules in the cells of the surface layer of the skin. Pure green individuals cannot change colour, but the others regularly change, becoming darker at night and paler by day. The change is brought about by movement of the pigment granules within the cells. Brown pigments may move to the surface and spread out, making the insect dark in tone, or they may contract into lumps and move to the inner part of the cell so the insect becomes pale. The orange-red granules can also move about in this way, but the green and yellow ones are unable to move about at all.

The alternation of colours becomes established by exposure to normal day and night, but once established it continues as a rhythm governed by the time cycle of 24 hours. A stick-insect conditioned to normal light change and then kept in permanent darkness will continue for several weeks to change colour every 24 hours, just as it did before. If it is kept in the dark by day and exposed to artificial light at night a reversed rhythm will develop in response to these conditions. This also persists for some time when the insect is kept continually in darkness with no light at all.

phylum	**Arthropoda**
class	**Insecta**
order	**Phasmida**
families	**Bacteriidae**
	Phasmidae

△ *Remarkable camouflage: head of* **Bactrododema aculiferum** *with its ear-like projections looking very like broken-off twigs.*
▷ *Rare shot: 7-inch* **Clemancatha regale**.
▽ *Precarious upside-down mating of* **Gratidia spp**. *The female holds onto the stem as the male clasps her — both beautifully camouflaged.*

Termite

Termites, often incorrectly called white ants, resemble true ants in their way of life, although less so in appearance, and the two are very distantly related. Ants are related to bees and wasps and termites are near relatives of cockroaches. Most of the 1 700 species live in the tropics, but a few are found in southern Europe and 55 in the United States. They are absent from northern Europe and are the only important order of insects not represented in northern Europe.

Fossil termites date back at least 250 million years. One very primitive genus **Mastotermes**, surviving in Australia, is very similar to a cockroach in the form of

its hindwings and also in the way the female lays her eggs, these being arranged in groups of 16 and 24 in two rows.

Termites and ants often resemble each other in being social insects living in colonies numbering hundreds or thousands of individuals. In both, the colonies consist of large numbers of 'workers' and 'soldiers' which are non-reproductive, and a few, or even just one, reproductives, the 'kings' and 'queens', which are the parents of all the others and may be very long-lived. In both, the non-reproductives are wingless, but the functional males and females have wings and fly in swarms from the nest. Before founding new colonies, or re-entering existing ones, they break off their wings. Both ants and termites have the habit of trophallaxis or mouth-to-

Harmonious community (above). A winged reproductive termite, two soldiers and two white workers: **Calotermes flavicollis** (×15).
Nest of activity (right), harvester termites **Trinervitermes trinervoides**. Note the long snout on the head of each soldier which can secrete a toxic liquid to repel enemies (×6).

mouth feeding. The 'royal' individuals are fed entirely in this way. Termites and ants are also alike in having some species that cultivate fungi underground for food.

The life histories of the two insects are, however, very different. In ants there are distinct larva and pupa stages and the larvae are helpless and have to be fed by the workers. In termites the young hatch as minute replicas of the adults and do not change their form as they grow. They

are first fed by trophallaxis, but soon learn to feed themselves and can take an active part in the work of the nest long before they are fully grown. Ant workers and soldiers are all non-reproductive females; in a termite nest all the castes are composed of both sexes. The queen ant mates only on her nuptial flight and is not joined by the male when she founds a colony. The king and queen termite, on the other hand, cooperate in founding the colony and live together in the nest, mating at intervals and being fed by the workers.

A termites' nest
One of the most intensively studied of all termites is the black-mound termite *Amitermes atlanticus*, investigated by Dr SH Skaife in the Cape Province of South Africa.

The nests consist of black, rounded mounds, 2 ft or less in diameter. The nest is made of a cement of the termites' faeces. It is watertight and very strong; a pickaxe or hammer is needed to break it. When broken open it has a sponge-like appearance, consisting of innumerable cells an inch or less in size connected by openings just big enough for the termites to creep through. The inhabitants of the mound live in a perpetual warm, moist fug, with 5—15% of carbon dioxide always present in the air. A man confined in such an atmosphere would soon lose consciousness. The temperature varies far less than that of the outside air. In extremes of heat and cold the termites huddle to the centre; when the sun rewarms a chilled nest or the summer dusk cools an overheated one, they crowd to the periphery. The king and queen black-mound termites are not confined to a 'royal

chamber' as in some termites, but move about from cell to cell through temporary enlarged openings made by the workers.

The outside crust of the nest consists of sand grains stuck together with faecal cement, and any break in it is quickly repaired with this same material. During the spring months of August and September the nest is enlarged about an inch all round.

Division of labour
The queen is $\frac{1}{2}-\frac{3}{4}$ in. long, depending on her age, which may reach 15 years. The king measures only $\frac{1}{4}$ in. Both had wings and flew at one time, but they broke their wings off when founding the colony. In addition to these 'primary reproductives' there are 'secondary reproductives', individuals of both sexes with rudimentary wings, which can produce fertile eggs if the primary pair meet with an accident or be-

come infertile with age. They are stimulated to do so by special feeding, but are never as prolific as a primary queen, and her place is taken not by one but by a number of female secondaries. In some nests a third, wholly wingless type of reproductive is found, but these are rare. The non-reproductives are either workers or soldiers. These go out at night for food, which in this species consists of decaying vegetation. The soldiers are simply a bodyguard against attack by ants, the arch-enemies of termites. They cannot even eat the natural food themselves but are fed, as the reproductives are, by the workers. A black-mound termite nest may last 40—50 years.

A two million termite tower
The more primitive kinds of termites, including *Mastotermes* and the family Kalotermitidae, live in wood, excavating galleries and chambers in it and feeding on it. Their natural role is to break up fallen timber and return it to the soil, but when they turn their attention to the timbers of buildings or to stored wooden crates and boxes they work havoc and are a serious problem in all tropical regions. Some of the more advanced types of termites make immense nests, towering as much as 20 ft above the

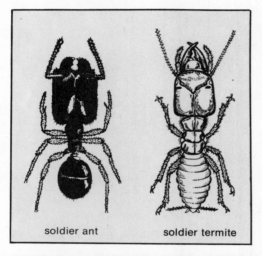

soldier ant   soldier termite

ground and containing perhaps a couple of million inhabitants. When ground is being levelled in tropical Africa for cultivation or building, the large termite nests sometimes defy even bulldozers and have to be destroyed with explosives. In northern Australia the remarkable compass termite *Amitermes meridionalis* makes termitaria 10—12 ft high. They are shaped like a flat wedge with its edge uppermost and stand in an exact north and south position, with the flat sides facing east and west. It is not certain how this arrangement benefits the termites, or how they manage to build with such exact orientation, although it has been suggested that the termites build to make full use of the sun's warmth.

Some termites make underground nests with little or no visible superstructure, others build carton nests of chewed wood pulp in trees, very like wasps' nests.

Need help to digest
Termites are primarily vegetarians. Those that live in wood and feed on it have microscopic protistans in their intestines which break down the cellulose of the wood, enabling the termites to digest it. The subterranean and mound-building termites subsist on various kinds of vegetable matter,

◁ *Comparison between a soldier ant* **Pheidole instabilis** *(left) and a soldier termite* **Archotermopsis**. *Both social insects, ants and termites live in colonies, each member or caste of the colony with a specific job. The soldiers, as their name implies, defend the colony. The most notable difference between these two soldiers is that the abdomen of the ant is waisted.*

▽ *Rulers of the colony, king and queen termites,* **Macrotermes natalensis,** *the longest lived members of the society. The king looks a mere weakling beside the queen who has her abdomen swollen disproportionately with eggs. Once fertilised she does nothing but lay eggs, the king staying with her, which is unusual among social insects, to help expand the new colony (approx ×2).*

living, dead and decaying. The fungi which are invariably present in decaying wood or leaves are probably important to many if not most termites, and some cultivate fungi in large chambers underground, just as the leafcutter ants do.

In a termites' nest of the black-mound type nothing is wasted. The bodies of the dead are devoured and excrement is eaten over and over again until every particle of nourishment is extracted from it. The paste that remains is used for building.

Free-for-all feast
When the winged males and females swarm out of the nests every insectivorous creature is their enemy. Birds, small mammals, lizards, toads and even some sensible opportunists among humans have a feast. Only a tiny fraction of the fragile fluttering princes and princesses live to become kings and queens. A few highly specialised mammals, such as anteaters, pangolins, the aardvark, and aardwolf, can break into the termitaria using strong claws and sweep up the termites with long sticky tongues. The termites' arch-enemies are, however, ants; a permanent state of war exists between the two insects. Termite soldiers are really specialised ant fighters. Some have powerful jaws which can snap an ant in two. Others have no jaws but instead the head is drawn into a spout-like snout from which an intensely sticky liquid can be squirted that effectively gums up any ant it touches. In spite of their seemingly effective armament, however, no termites are a match for ants in open battle, and they rely on the massive defences of their nests for their continued existence.

The long-lived queen
Most people know what a queen termite looks like—a great sausage-shaped egg-factory. Queen termites are unique among insects in growing after their last moult. The skin between the abdominal segments stretches, leaving the original segmental coverings as brown islands on the pale, bloated back. The queen black-mound termite can live 15 years; others, of larger and more highly developed species, may live longer. In Australia, in 1872, the top of a large termite nest had to be broken off to allow telegraph wires to pass over. In 1913 and again in 1935 the nest was examined and was found to have a flourishing population, although the broken top had not been renewed. No secondary reproductives have ever been found in nests of this species (*Eutermes triodiae*), so the original king and queen, founders of a nest already 14 ft high in 1872, were probably still alive in 1935. It is possible the original population had died and the nest had been recolonised, but it was more probably a case of an insect living as long as a man.

phylum	**Arthropoda**
class	**Insecta**
order	**Isoptera**

Top left: 'Watch it' — a threatened male raises his pincers. Top right: Birthday suit — a freshly-peeled female rests beside her old skin.

Above left: Female earwigs are model mothers. This one is pottering anxiously round her eggs, protecting and cleaning them.

Above right: Watching over a nursery of earwig toddlers, which stay with the mother until their second moult, eating their own skins.

Earwig

The fearsome-looking pincers of the common earwig are referred to in its scientific name — **Forficula auricularia** — since **forficula** is Latin for 'little scissors'. Curved in the male and straight in the female, they are carried at the hind end of the flattened brown body and when danger approaches they may be raised in the air and displayed as a threat. Although not as effective weapons as they look, they are nevertheless used in defence and the insect can use them to grip with some tenacity. Those of the males vary in length and fall into two more or less distinct size ranges.

At first sight, the earwig seems to have no wings, but in fact there is a serviceable pair neatly folded away beneath tiny wing cases overlapping the front part of the abdomen. These wing cases or 'elytra', like those of beetles, are the hardened front pair of wings, which in dragonflies, butterflies and other insects are still used in flight. The pincers of the earwig are said to assist in folding away the wings after use.

The tawny earwig is only half the size but otherwise much like the adult of the common earwig. There are a few other British species, including two that have been introduced, but these are much less common.

There are some 900 species of earwigs throughout the world, differing in size from $\frac{1}{4}$ in. to $1\frac{1}{2}$ in. but otherwise similar except that some are wingless.

Rarely seen on the wing

Earwigs spend the day hidden away in dry, usually upright crevices, and are often to be found under loose bark. The common earwig is also found tucked away among the petals of dahlias. Whether or not they are doing much damage is a disputed point though they are known to eat both petals and leaves. Gardeners often provide an alternative home in the form of an up-turned flower pot, preferably stuffed with newspaper or straw. Earwigs are active at night and it is partly for this reason that they have rarely been seen flying although some — and the tawny earwig is one — often take to the wing on hot days. When earwigs are seen on clothes hanging out on a line overnight, however, it is easier to believe they have flown there than climbed.

The common earwig is widespread in Europe and has also been introduced and firmly established in the United States, becoming a nuisance in some places.

Earwigs eat plant lice

The diet includes a great variety of both animal and plant matter. To a large extent, earwigs are scavengers, but they may sometimes eat large numbers of plant lice, and have been seen to capture larger insects like bluebottles with their pincers. They will also eat fruit, leaves, flowers and fungi.

The 'broody-hen' insect

The most remarkable feature of the earwig is its family life and the 'broody-hen' behaviour of the mother. The sexes come together in September. Then, throughout much of the autumn and winter, they may be found in pairs either in chambers dug about an inch down in the earth, or sometimes just in crevices among vegetation. Late in January or towards the end of March, the male leaves — or is perhaps driven out — and the female starts to lay her oval, pearly-white eggs. Within about 2 days some 20–80 are laid, the largest females tending to produce the greatest number. At first the eggs are scattered about the floor of the chamber, but the mother soon gathers them into a pile and thereafter gives them her continual attention. One by one she picks them up in her mouth and licks them all over. At this time she is more than usually aggressive, and her only food is the occasional egg that has gone bad. The rest hatch 3–4 weeks after being laid.

The behaviour of the mothers has been subjected to scientific scrutiny. It has been found, for instance, that they recognise their eggs, when collecting up after they are laid. A female earwig will quite readily collect little wax balls or rounded stones. Later on, however, the wax balls and stones are rejected as lacking the appropriate taste or smell.

It has also been found that the eggs must be licked by the mother if they are to hatch and that the female's urge to lick them is dependent on the presence of the eggs. The urge fades in a few days if the eggs are removed, and after that it cannot be revived even if the eggs are replaced, but it will persist as long as 3 months if the eggs are continually replaced by others as they hatch.

The young earwigs are not grubs or larvae but nymphs, essentially like the parents though smaller and more dumpy, with simple straight forceps. Like domestic chicks, they stay with their mother for a while, nestling under her body. Twice they cast and eat their skins while in her care, and after the second moult they disperse, to become fully grown by about July. This cosy family picture is spoiled, however, if the mother dies, for she is then eaten by her own offspring (along with the cast skins).

The family life of the earwig represents an early stage in the evolution of a social organisation, which is developed independently and far more fully in ants, bees, wasps and termites. A relative of the earwig (Hemimerus) protects its eggs in a very different way. It behaves more like a mammal than a bird. Its eggs are retained within the body, where they are nourished by a sort of placenta and the young are born alive.

Do earwigs enter ears?

To some people earwigs are endearing animals, for no very clear reason. To others, through a belief that they will enter the human ear, they are objects of apprehension. This belief is reflected in the name given to the animal not only in English but in other languages, *Ohrwurm* in German and *perce-oreille* in French, to name only two. It is sometimes suggested that the English name is derived from 'ear-wing' since the extended wings are somewhat ear-shaped, but 'wig' is from the Old English 'wiggle', to wriggle, and the wings are hardly likely to be seen often enough to compete with the pincers for commemoration in a common name.

Entomologists seem to discredit the notion of earwigs entering ears, but there are authentic accounts of its having happened in medical journals and in the case-books of medical practitioners. Moreover, there is a consistent note in the descriptions of the discomfort experienced by the patients, who complain of a 'noise of thunder' in the ear.

It must be agreed with the sceptics that the earwig has no special passion for ears, but it does have an instinct to insinuate itself into cracks and crevices, under loose bark or in folds of curtains—so why not on rare occasions in the ear of an unwary camper or, more often perhaps in the past, in the ears of our ancestors who lived closer to nature? For peace of mind, when sleeping under canvas, some cotton wool in the ears is a reasonable precaution. The first aid remedy is to float the insect out with oil.

It is interesting that earwigs themselves have been used in medicine, as a cure for deafness, on the principle that like cures like, or, as it is popularly known 'a hair of the dog that bit you'. The earwig was dried, powdered and mixed with the urine of a hare.

phylum	**Arthropoda**
class	**Insecta**
order	**Dermaptera**
family	**Forficulidae**
genera & species	***Forficula auricularia*** common earwig ***Labia minor*** tawny earwig others

Below left: Earwig couple. The male can be distinguished from the female by the scimitar curve of his pincers; the female's are straight. Below: Female earwig's wing pattern. Earwigs can fly quite well, but they are rarely seen doing so because they are most active at night.

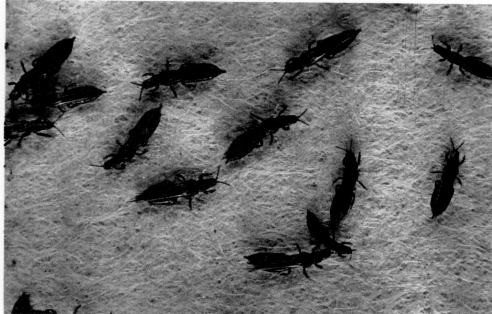

Left: Damaged corn ears: apart from direct damage, many species of thrips carry viruses and other diseases from plant to plant. Right: The culprit: **Limothrips cerealium.**

Thrips

Thrips are most unusual insects, in the structure of their wings, in their life history and, above all, because we normally neither see them nor hear them although they are frequently agricultural pests and can also annoy us in other ways. They form a small order of insects which numbers less than 2 000 species. Almost all of them are tiny, $\frac{1}{50} - \frac{1}{6}$ in. long, the giant among them being an Australian thrips which is $\frac{1}{2}$ in. long. Under the microscope they look like lice that have grown feathery wings. They have two pairs of wings, each consisting of a narrow strap fringed in front and behind with long hairs. The name of their order, the Thysanoptera, means 'fringe-wings'. On each side the wings are held together at the bases by a series of hooks, and they are folded over the back when at rest. A number of species lack wings.

There are two suborders, distinguished by the form of the ovipositor, or egg-laying organ. In the suborder Terebrantia the ovipositor is saw-like and used to insert the eggs into plant tissues. In the other suborder, the Tubulifera, the ovipositor is simple and hollow and used to lay eggs in crevices.

Force of numbers

Most of the thrips live on plants, especially on the blossoms and fruit, and feed by sucking the sap. For this they use their highly peculiar mouthparts, which form a piercing and sucking apparatus modified from the maxillae and mandibles. These are asymmetrical, the maxillae usually having a little asymmetry while only the left mandible is functional, the right-hand one being vestigial or lacking altogether.

Thrips occur in very large numbers and damage plants directly by disfiguring the flowers, spoiling the fruit and causing the tops of grasses to shrivel, a condition known as 'silvertop'. It is said that fruit, such as pears, may not even start to develop if thrips get onto the blossom in sufficient numbers. The greenhouse thrips excretes red drops that turn black and disfigure the foliage of ornamental plants. Some of the pest species have names which suggest, quite wrongly, that they live only on certain plants. The onion thrips, for example, attacks a wide variety of plants, and the honeysuckle thrips is a pest of the flowers and fruit of both blackberry and loganberry. The grain or corn thrips is, however, well named as it attacks cereals and grasses. Besides damaging the plants directly many species of thrips carry viruses and other diseases from plant to plant. Their powers of flight are feeble, but once air-borne they may travel long distances on the wind, thus spreading the disease over a wide area.

The species that are pests of crops belong mostly to the Terebrantia. Many of the Tubulifera feed on dead leaves and fungi and some form plant galls in which they live. A few are predatory, attacking aphides, and one species is regarded in Florida as beneficial because it preys on a destructive species of whitefly.

Mixed-up metamorphosis

The thrips are as freakish in their life history as they are in their appearance and structure. In the first two stages of their larval life the young thrips resemble the adults except in size and in lacking wings. They are, however, active and feed avidly. At the third moult they cease to be active and are often enclosed in a cell or cocoon. Before reaching the adult stage they undergo two more moults, three in the Tubulifera. The last stage before maturity is called the pupa and the one or two stages preceding this are called the prepupa. No other insects have a life history in any way resembling this unusual one.

Unseen misery

For most of their time thrips do little more than stay in one spot sucking sap with their tubes sunk in the tissues of plants. If disturbed, however, some crawl about in a leisurely manner, while others run quickly or even leap into the air. Although they do not often use it, some can fly. The smaller thrips, which are little larger than specks of dust, may get caught up in thermals. So, especially in hot weather, there may be droves of thrips circulating in the atmosphere and sometimes they land on humans. They are virtually invisible but cause an annoying tickling on the hands and face as they crawl over the skin. Some people are more susceptible to these irritations than others, and to those who do feel them they are worse than an actual pain.

phylum	**Arthropoda**
class	**Insecta**
order	**Thysanoptera**
genera & species	***Heliothrips haemorrhoidalis*** *greenhouse thrips* ***Idolothrips spectrum*** *Australian giant thrips* ***Limothrips cerealium*** *grain thrips* ***Thrips flavus*** *honeysuckle thrips* ***T. tabaci*** *onion thrips, others*

Mayfly

Mayflies make up one of the most distinct and peculiar of insect orders. They have features which are not found in any other group of insects, and all the species in the order are very much alike.

*The adult has large forewings and its hindwings are small, sometimes absent altogether. Each wing has a fine network of veins, and when the insect is at rest all four wings are held close together over the back in the manner of a butterfly. The legs are small and weak and the tail ends in three, sometimes two, long filaments or cerci. The eyes are large, especially in the males. In some genera, **Cloeon**, for example,*

the land. The compact mass of moving insects attracts the notice of females, which fly into the swarm. Each is at once seized by a male, the pair then leaving the swarm to mate. The males die almost immediately after mating and the females soon after laying their eggs, although they may have spent several years as aquatic nymphs.

The female mayfly always lays her eggs in water, but in some species she drops them from the air as she flies just above the surface. In many species the eggs are provided with fine threads which anchor them to water plants or pebbles. A few give birth to living young which have hatched from eggs retained in the mother's body. In the egg-laying species one female may lay several hundred, or several thousand, eggs.

The nymphs are always aquatic; breathing is supplemented by gills set along each side

the males have two pairs of compound eyes, one pair with small facets on the sides of the head and one pair with large facets on the top. The antennae are reduced to tiny bristles, suggesting that the insect is aware of its surroundings mainly through its sight. The jaws and other mouthparts are vestigial and functionless and adult mayflies never feed. They only gulp down air until the stomach becomes distended like a balloon. This reduces the insect's overall specific gravity and makes the mating flight easier.

About 1 000 species are known, but only those of Europe and North America have been thoroughly studied and there must be many species still undescribed.

Guiding light

The adult life of mayflies is concerned solely with reproduction. They nearly always hatch in great numbers together, and the males gather in dancing swarms over

of the abdomen. Unlike the adults, the nymphs show many differences from species to species. Some are adapted for swimming actively among water plants, others to living on the bottom, burrowing in the mud or clinging to rocks in rapidly flowing water. Nearly all are vegetable feeders, and they take from a year to as much as 4 years to reach full size. A recent discovery about free-swimming mayfly nymphs is that they orientate themselves in the water not by a sense of balance based on gravity, as had been supposed, but by the direction from which the light reaches their eyes. In an aquarium with a glass bottom, lit from below, they swim upside-down.

They mate and die on land

The event in the mayfly's life which sets the Ephemeroptera, as they are collectively called, wholly apart from all other insects is the change from a subimago to an imago. Before this happens, however, the fully grown nymph rises to the surface of the water and floats there, or crawls out onto

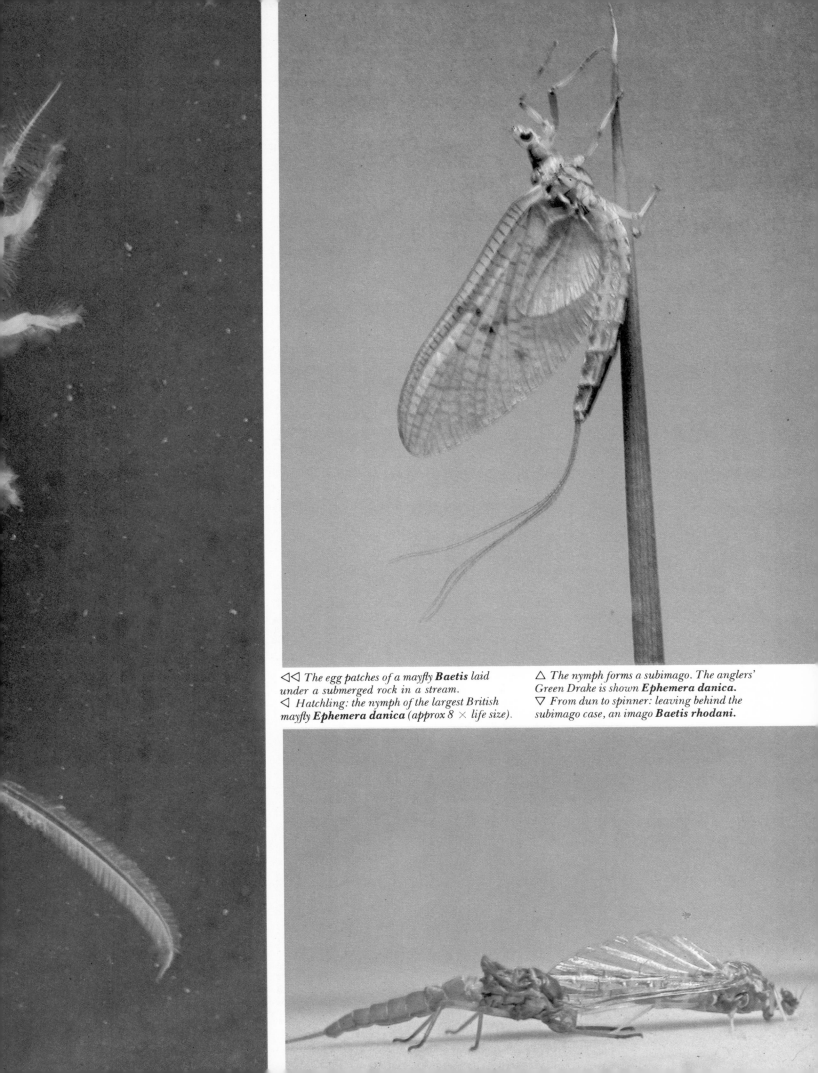

◁◁ *The egg patches of a mayfly* **Baetis** *laid under a submerged rock in a stream.*
◁ *Hatchling: the nymph of the largest British mayfly* **Ephemera danica** *(approx 8 × life size).*

△ *The nymph forms a subimago. The anglers' Green Drake is shown* **Ephemera danica.**
▽ *From dun to spinner: leaving behind the subimago case, an imago* **Baetis rhodani.**

a stone or reed. Its skin splits and a winged insect creeps out, resting for a time before making a short, rather laboured flight to a bush or fence or to a building near the water. Although it is winged, this insect that creeps laboriously out of the water is not the perfect insect or imago, as the final stage is called. After a few minutes or hours, varying with the species, the subimago moults again, shedding a delicate skin from the whole of its body, legs and even its wings. Then it flies away, much more buoyantly than before, but it will live at most for a few days and, in many species, only for a few hours. A subimago can be recognised by the wings which appear dark and dull due to the presence of microscopic hairs, which form a visible fringe along their hinder edges.

The fisherman's fly

Mayflies are of great interest to anglers, both on account of the part they play in supplying fish with food, and by their direct connection with the sport of fly-fishing. The hatching of a swarm of mayflies excites the fish, especially trout, and stimulates their appetites, so they take a lure more readily than at other times. The swarming is known as a 'hatch' and the fish are said to 'rise' to it. They feed both on the nymphs as they swim to the surface and on the flies, both subimagoes and adults, which touch or fall into the water.

A mayfly is far too delicate an object to be impaled on a hook like a maggot or a worm, and the flyfisherman's practice is to make replicas of the flies by binding carefully prepared scraps of feathers onto the shaft of a hook. These are then 'cast' and allowed to fall onto the surface of the water. A lure so used is called a 'dry fly', as opposed to a 'wet fly', which sinks under the surface.

The more exactly the artificial fly duplicates the species of mayfly which is hatching, the greater are the chances of success, so anglers study mayflies carefully and they have their own names for them. Any subimago is known as a 'dun' and the imagoes are called 'spinners'. Those of the species *Procloeon rufulum* are called the Pale Evening Dun and the Pale Evening Spinner respectively. *Rhithrogena semicolorata* are the Olive Upright Dun and the Olive Upright Spinner. The two stages of *Ephemera danica* have separate names, the Green Drake and the Spent Gnat.

If a well made artificial fly is swung, by means of a rod and line, into a swarm of the males whose species it represents, numbers of them will pursue it, losing interest only when actual contact reveals to them that they have been heartlessly deceived.

◁ *A short life but a gay one: having passed through all the hazards of a year or more of aquatic larval life this adult* **Ephemera vulgata** *will live only long enough to reproduce.*

class	**Insecta**
order	**Ephemeroptera**
families	**Ephemeridae**
	Caenidae (hindwings absent)
	others

Dragonfly

Colourful and powerful fliers, dragonflies are among the fastest of all insects. Most dragonflies are large insects which hold their wings stiffly extended on each side when at rest, whereas most other insects fold them over the back. The wings are capable of only simple up-and-down movement, have no coupling device joining the front and back wings, as in higher insects such as butterflies, and have a fine network of 'veins' supporting the membrane. All these characteristics show that dragonflies are primitive insects that have existed with little change for a very long time. The earliest known fossil dragonflies are from the late Carboniferous period, deposited about 300 million years ago. There were dragonflies similar to those living today in the Jurassic period, 150 million years ago, when the giant dinosaurs were roaming the earth.

The name is often used in England as an equivalent of the insect order Odonata, but the members of the suborder Zygoptera are very distinct in appearance. Living dragonflies consist of two very unequal suborders, the Anisoptera (all the familiar species) and the Anisozygoptera (only two species known, from Japan and the Himalayas respectively).

As in their relatives the damselflies, the wings of dragonflies are usually transparent and colourless, but may be tinted or patterned, and the body is often brightly coloured. They differ markedly from damselflies in having very swift, powerful flight. Estimates of their actual speed are difficult to obtain and vary from 35 up to 60 mph, but they are certainly among the fastest of all insects. The antennae are minute and the eyes enormous, occupying the greater part of the head. Each compound eye may contain as many as 30 000 facets.

Territorial instincts

Dragonflies fly a 'fighter patrol' over a fixed area. Although they are most often seen near water, which is where they breed, their powerful flight carries them far away from their breeding places, and they may be met wherever there are trees and bushes on which they can rest. One can often be seen flying back and forth over a definite 'beat', and when it lands it will do so on one or other of a small number of resting places. The beat may be an area selected as suitable for hunting prey or, especially if it is over water, it may be the territory chosen by a male dragonfly, which will then mate with any female of its own species which flies into this area. These males defend their territories strenuously against other males of the same species. After a while they begin to show signs of battle in the shape of torn wings and mutilated legs.

△ Male dragonfly **Orthetrum coerulescens.** The female of this British species is brown with black markings on the abdomen.

▽ African beauty of the family Libellelidae. The wings show the complex venation supporting the membrane which is found in all dragonflies.

Whether in hunting or fighting, the sense used most is sight; a dragonfly can detect movement 40 ft away.

Some species of dragonflies are migratory and may fly great distances over land and sea. One species *Libellula quadrimaculata* sometimes migrates in spectacular swarms. In 1862 a swarm was observed in Germany, estimated at nearly two-and-a-half thousand million strong, and in June 1900 the sky over Antwerp 'appeared black' with these dragonflies. In 1947 a huge migration of another species *Sympetrum striolatum* was seen flying overhead by observers on the south coast of Ireland.

Masked killers

Dragonflies are predatory in all their stages. The adults catch other insects on the wing, seizing them with their forwardly directed legs and chewing them with their powerful jaws. In the southeastern United States two large species *Anax junius* and *Coryphaeshna ingens* are serious predators of honeybees.

The larvae capture their prey by what is known as a mask, a mechanism that is shared with the damselflies but is otherwise unique among insects. The labium or lower lip is greatly enlarged and armed with a pair of hooks. At rest it is folded under the head,

△ *Skimming low over the surface, a female dragonfly dips her abdomen to lay eggs.*

but it is extensible and can be shot out in front of the head, the hooks being used to seize the prey like a pair of pincers. The victim is then drawn back within reach of the jaws. Other insects, tadpoles and small fish form the prey of dragonfly larvae, and those of the larger species can make serious inroads into the numbers of young fish in a rearing pond. On the other hand, the young dragonfly larvae perform a useful service by destroying great numbers of the aquatic larvae of mosquitoes.

The 'tandem'

Mating involves the same curious procedure as the damselflies, in which the male transfers his sperm from the primary sexual organ near the tip of his abdomen to an accessory organ farther forward, at the base of the abdomen. He then alights on the back of a female and curls his abdomen under his own body in order to seize her head (not her thorax as in damselflies) with a pair of claspers at the end of his abdomen. He then releases the hold with his legs but retains that with his claspers. The female then curls her abdomen round in such a way that the tip of it makes contact with the male accessory organ. Both before and after mating the two may fly together, with the female held by the male claspers, in what is known as the 'tandem position'. They may even maintain this position while the eggs are being laid.

Dragonflies almost always lay their eggs in water. One of two ways is used. Some insert their eggs into the stems of water plants, as damselflies do. These include the big hawker dragonflies, *Aeshna*. Others, like the golden-ringed dragonfly *Cordulegaster boltoni* force their eggs into the sand or gravel at the margins of shallow streams. The second method is to fly close over the surface of water and repeatedly dip the tip of the body, extruding eggs at the same time, so these are washed off and sink to the bottom.

Form of jet propulsion

Most dragonflies spend their early life under water. The larvae vary in shape. Those that live in mud are short, thick-set and covered with a dense coat of hairs to which the mud clings. When such a larva is at rest, only the eyes and the tip of the abdomen are exposed, the rest being buried. The golden-ringed dragonfly has a larva of this type. Those that live among water weeds are more slender and active, but no dragonfly larvae are as slender and delicate as those of damselflies. They have gills inside the intestine a short distance from their hind opening and the larvae breathe by drawing water into the rectum and then driving it out again. This mechanism is also used for another purpose. If suddenly disturbed, the larva drives the water out forcibly, so propelling itself rapidly forward, in a simple form of jet propulsion.

When fully grown, after 2 years or more in most European species, the larva crawls up a plant growing in the water, climbs above the surface and undergoes its final moult to become an adult dragonfly.

Destruction of their habitat by pollution, drainage, dredging and infilling of ponds is the most serious threat to dragonflies and this is increasing throughout the world. As larvae, their chief natural enemies are fishes, whose own babies the well-grown dragonfly larvae prey upon. In fact dragonfly larvae probably form an important source of food for freshwater fishes. When small they are also eaten by other predatory insects, including larger dragonfly larvae, often of their own species. The adults are so swift and active that they have few natural enemies, but one small bird of prey, the hobby, feeds extensively on them.

△ *Libellula quadrimaculata* — both male and female have very similar markings on the abdomen and wings.

▽ *Dragonfly of Transvaal Lowveld, South Africa, resting. Powerful fliers, dragonflies are among the fastest of all insects.*

Biggest insects ever

The present-day Odonata are among the largest living insects. In tropical America there are damselflies with bodies 5 in. long and wings spanning 7 in. These are slender, flimsy creatures and are greatly exceeded in bulk by a Borneo dragonfly *Tetracanthagyna plagiata* whose wings also span 7 in. and whose thick body measures about 5 in.

No modern dragonflies, however, compare in size with some which lived 300 million years ago, in the forests when our coal measures were being laid down. At Commentry, in France, fossil remains of these have been found, including impressions of wings, which show that the wingspan of the biggest of them *Meganeura monyi* was as much as 27 in., about equal to that of a crow. They are by far the largest insects known to have inhabited the earth, but it is interesting that no larval remains have yet been found.

class	**Insecta**
order	**Odonata**
suborders	**Anisoptera, Anisozygoptera**

Louse

A louse is a small wingless insect which lives as a parasite on the outside of a mammal or a bird. Lice fall naturally into two distinct groups which are regarded by entomologists as separate orders.

The sucking lice (suborder Anoplura) are parasitic on mammals only and feed by sucking their blood. The biting lice (suborder Mallophaga), which exist mostly as parasites of birds although a few live on mammals, feed mainly on the feathers or hair of the host. The members of both orders have a similar appearance. They are small, pale in colour and flattened, and they have tough, leathery skins. The last two features are adaptations to protect them against scratching and other attempts by their hosts to dislodge them. Their bodies have undergone many changes linked with the parasitic way of life. Their legs are short and so are the antennae. The eyes are very small, sometimes almost non-existent. The segments of the body, so noticeable in the abdomen of a normal insect, are often not very clearly marked. There is no metamorphosis. Both types pass the whole of their lives on the body of the host, and one species of louse is often confined to one species of mammal or bird or to a group of related species.

The so-called book-louse is neither a true louse nor a parasite, but belongs to the order Psocoptera. It lives among books and furniture in damp, badly ventilated rooms.

Sucking lice

The hollow, piercing mouthparts and the way in which the claws of the legs are adapted for gripping hair distinguish this order of only 230 known species. The human louse can be used as a typical example. Not only is it confined to man as a host, but there are two varieties: the body louse and the head louse. The former lives on clothing next to the skin and the latter among the hair of the head. The two varieties differ slightly in structure as well as in habits; they can be persuaded to interbreed under experimental conditions, but there is no evidence that they do so naturally. They have very similar life cycles. Their eggs, known as 'nits', are cemented on to the hair or fibres of the clothing. An adult louse lays about 10 eggs every day and in the course of its life lays about 300. At body temperature the eggs hatch in about a week, and the insects hatching from them are miniatures of the adults. They feed throughout their lives by inserting the hollow, piercing mouthparts into the skin and sucking up blood. They shed their skins three times before they are fully grown. Lice live for about 7 weeks.

The only other louse parasitic on man is the so-called crab louse which lives among the pubic hair. Its mode of feeding and life history are similar to those of the head louse.

Scratching can be fatal

In spite of its unpleasant associations, the crab louse does not convey disease, but this is very far from true of other species. By far the most serious disease carried by the human louse is epidemic typhus, which is caused by a virus-like micro-organism called *Rickettsia*. The body louse is the carrier and, rather curiously, the disease is not transmitted by its bite but by the entry of infected louse-excrement and the body fluids of crushed lice into abrasions in the skin. Scratching and seeking out lice and squashing them are therefore dangerous practices in conditions where typhus is likely to occur.

Such conditions are found in places where people are crowded together and have no opportunity to change and wash their clothes, or customarily fail to do so.

Flowers and fever

Up to quite recent times, gaols crowded with unfortunate people awaiting trial were subject to terrible epidemics of typhus. The hazard even extended to the courts of justice, because infected lice dropped out of the ragged clothing of the prisoners and transferred themselves to the court officials, witnesses and anyone else present. This risk was recognised, though no one associated it with lice, and judges were provided with a bouquet of flowers whose scent was believed to keep away the 'evil humours' of the disease. It is still traditional in some courts for the judge to receive a nosegay of flowers. The terribly crowded conditions of the crew on ships, especially naval vessels, also led to typhus epidemics, and both 'gaol fever' and 'ship fever' were among the names by which the disease was known.

In the First World War, when conditions in the trenches were very conducive to louse infestation, a curious disease called 'trench fever' occurred. It was conveyed by lice and seems to have been a sort of mild and seldom fatal variant of typhus. After the war it completely disappeared, and so has never been investigated by modern techniques.

Our own horror at the idea of being infected with lice is, of course, salutary, but it is quite a modern attitude. In mediaeval times the sanctity of holy men was enhanced in proportion to their lousiness. When the body of Thomas à Beckett was disrobed after his murder the lice in his hair-cloth garment, in the words of a contemporary chronicler, 'boiled over like water in a simmering cauldron'. The onlookers, far from being disgusted, were overcome with 'the joy of having found such a saint'.

Absence of lice from one's body used also to be regarded as a sign of lack of virility, and even today the religion of large numbers of people forbids them to kill a louse, though it is permitted to remove one from one's own person and deposit it unharmed on that of a neighbour. Evidently it will be some time before typhus goes the same way as trench fever.

Another quite distinct disease called relapsing fever is carried by human lice. It is easy to cure and not very prevalent.

class	**Insecta**	
order	**Phthiraptera**	
sub-order	**Anoplura**	
genera & species	***Pediculus humanus*** *human louse* ***Phthirius pubis*** *crab louse* *others*	

▽ *Photomicrograph of female human louse (× 20).*

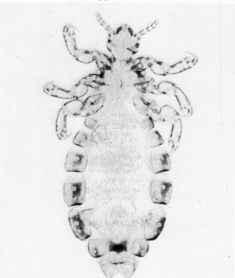

▽ *Eggs or 'nits' cemented onto human hair (× 25).*

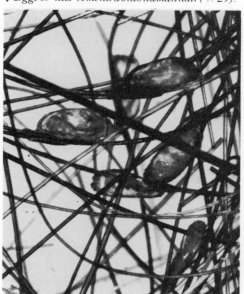

▽ *De-lousing in the fifteenth century.*

Flea

Fleas are small, wingless insects, parasites with the body flattened from side to side, making it easy for them to slip through the fur or feathers of the host. The legs are modified for rapid movement in this environment and also for powerful jumping, and the thick, hard skin is a good defence against the host's scratching.

The name 'flea' is used for any member of the insect order Siphonaptera, of which a little over a thousand species are known. The order is very distinct and isolated from other insects, but there are indications of winged ancestors and a relationship with, perhaps, the scorpion flies (Mecoptera). All fleas live, when adult, as blood-sucking parasites of mammals or birds. Their larvae live on the debris and dirt that accumulate in the lairs or nests of the animals which are the hosts of the mature insects.

The eggs are large for the size of the insect, about $\frac{1}{50}$ in. long, and white. The larvae are small whitish maggots, legless but having a pair of short antennae and biting jaws. The pupae grow in cocoons.

In a few species the female is sedentary, remaining attached and feeding in one spot. She may even burrow into the skin of the host, the tropical jigger flea **Tunga penetrans** being an example of this.

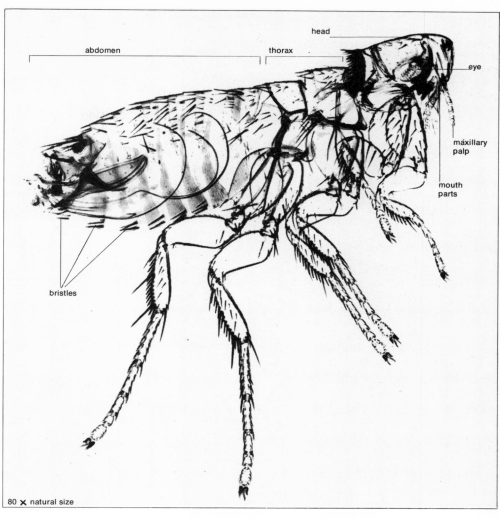

80 ✕ natural size

△ Flea showing the tough, bristle-covered shell – a good defence against scratching hosts.
▽ A prepared specimen displays its legs which are powerful for jumping.

Choice of targets

Fleas usually parasitise only mammals and birds which have a lair or nest in which they live and breed, or which congregate in large numbers in regular roosts. The majority of known species are parasites of rodents, most of which live in nests or burrows, and insectivores and bats are also much infested. Apart from man, primates are never more than casually infested. Monkeys do not as a rule carry fleas at all. Aquatic mammals such as otters and coypus are also not attacked by fleas and among the hoofed animals, the pig is one of the few animals regularly infested.

Among birds fleas are most numerous on the species which nest in holes such as woodpeckers, tits and the sand martin, the last being perhaps the most flea-infested of all birds. The rock dove and its descendant the domestic pigeon have a special flea of their own *Ceratophyllus columbae* and this is not found on wood pigeons. Possibly it is because rock doves and domestic pigeons nest in holes and on ledges while wood pigeons make an openwork nest in trees. This underlines the basic requirement for infestation by fleas, which is a suitable environment in the host's nest for the non-parasitic debris-eating larvae.

It is unusual for fleas to be confined to one host. Both the flea of the rock dove and the sand martin's flea *Ceratophyllus styx* are restricted to the one species. Most fleas will feed and breed on a variety of hosts; the

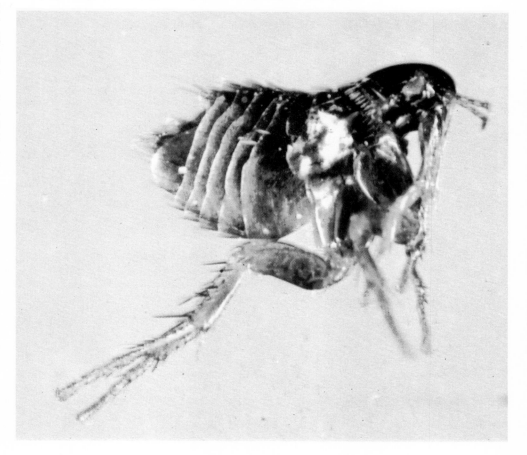

111

human flea *Pulex irritans* is found also on pigs, and the hen flea *Ceratophyllus gallinae* feeds on a great number of different birds and can live on mammalian, including human, blood as well.

Carriers of disease

Fleas will also casually infest hosts with which they have no breeding association. Cat fleas, finding themselves on a human, bite readily. The incidence of the dreaded bubonic plague is mainly due to a particular flea *Xenopsylla cheopis* that normally lives on rats, leaving these bodies when they die of plague and infesting people whose hygienic standards permit rats to live in numbers in their dwellings. The bacterium *Pasteurella pestis* that causes plague affects rats and men equally severely and is conveyed from one to the other in the saliva of the fleas. In mediaeval times practically no house was free of rats and the great epidemics of plague or 'black death' killed millions of people.

In the jigger flea, the female burrows into the skin of its human host. Both sexes start their adult life as very small fleas, hopping about in the dust around human habitations. After mating the females burrow into the skin of people's feet under the toenails and grow to the size of a pea, forming a cyst. This causes a great deal of pain and is difficult to remove without causing sores or abscesses due to secondary infection. The hen stick-tight flea *Echidnophaga gallinacea*

▽ *Flea sword-fight and chariot race.*

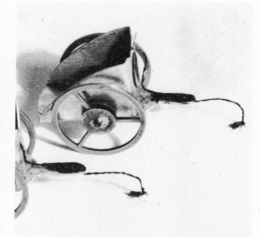

infests poultry and the females gather on the naked skin of the birds' heads and attach themselves permanently. This flea's choice of hosts is quite unusual; it infests poultry and various small mammals, clustering on their ears, and is particularly partial to hedgehogs.

Delayed hatching

The eggs of fleas are dropped into the nest of the host or may be laid among its fur or feathers, whence they are shaken out and many fall into the nest. Almost all fleas require a meal of blood before they can develop and lay their eggs. The tiny maggot-like larvae feed on dirt and debris, including dried blood, in the host's nest, or in dusty unswept corners in human habitations. When fully grown they make cocoons and pupate. The pupae often lie dormant for long periods and in some species, including the human flea, are sensitive to movement and vibration, which stimulates them to hatch. Campers, invading a deserted house that has been abandoned months before, may be greeted by hordes of fleas that hatch in response to the tramping and dumping of heavy luggage. This is an obvious adaptation to delay hatching of the pupae until a new host and source of blood appears on which newly-emerged adults can feed.

Special mouth parts

Like other blood-sucking insects fleas have special sucking mouth parts. The most important part is a narrow tube formed from three needle-like stylets, an anterior and two lateral ones. They are serrated towards the tip to increase their efficiency in piercing. An anticoagulant 'saliva' is injected before the blood sucking commences. It is this which causes the irritation associated with a flea bite, and which leads to disease organisms being passed into the blood of the host by infected fleas.

Fleas are very greedy feeders and only digest and assimilate a fraction of the blood they suck up, the rest being passed out of the intestine unchanged. It is thought that this apparently wasteful habit may have been evolved to provide a supply of dry coagulated blood for the flea larvae which are feeding in the nest of the host. If this were so it would be an example of a parent insect making provision for its larvae resembling, but far less elaborate than, that used by wasps and bees. The idea may not be as far-fetched as it appears. The larvae feed in the normal way, searching for edible particles among their surroundings and chewing them in their mandibles.

When parasite eats parasite

Fleas are regularly caught and eaten in small numbers by their hosts, usually in the course of licking, cleaning and preening. This benefits another form of parasite. The common tapeworm of dogs and cats *Dipylidium caninum* spends one phase of its life cycle in dog fleas and depends on the fleas being eaten to get from one host to another. Far more effective enemies of fleas are certain mites which live in nests and prey on the fleas in all their stages. Small beetles of the genus *Gnathoncus* are often found in birds' nests, and they also prey on fleas and their larvae.

Performing flea

At one time the flea circus was a familiar item of entertainment in country fairs. *Pulex irritans* was still an abundant and familiar insect 50 to 100 years ago when the forms of public entertainment were far less numerous and less sophisticated than they are now. At the present time the manager of a flea circus would be faced with two difficulties. He would probably have difficulty in finding an audience and he would certainly have difficulty in finding a sufficient supply of human fleas for his performers. He would therefore have to be content with dog or cat fleas, which are not easy to feed in captivity.

It was customary for the proprietor of one of these circuses to keep human fleas and feed them on his own arm. A large part of his skill lay in constructing tiny devices such as tricycles and 'chariots' which could be propelled by fleas attached to them in such a way that the crawling of the insect caused them to move. Another very delicate operation was the tethering or harnessing of the fleas with very fine gold or silver wire. There was never any question of the fleas being taught or trained in any way, though of course this was always claimed as part of his expertise by their owner. Advantage was simply taken of the natural movements of the insect when restrained in various ways. The real skill displayed by those who ran flea circuses lay in making the 'props'. One was a coach, of tiny proportions, perfect in every detail which was drawn by a team of fleas.

The relatively enormous size and rapidity of the flea's jump has puzzled naturalists since the time of Socrates. It has recently been shown that in addition to the powerful leg muscles and tendons, the flea's jumping apparatus incorporates a cap of resilin, a rubber-like protein which, when compressed and suddenly released, delivers power faster than most actively contracting muscle. Resilin is generally a component of the wing-hinge ligament of flying insects, such as dragonflies and locusts, and its presence in the thorax of fleas suggests that they have adapted and modified a flight mechanism to increase their mobility while living among fur and feathers. In other words fleas are insects which fly with their legs.

Adult fleas are remarkably long-lived. Supplied regularly with blood a human flea has survived 513 days, and a Russian bird flea is said to have lived for 1 487 days or a little over four years.

class	**Insecta**
order	**Siphonaptera**
genera	***Pulex, Tunga, Echidnophaga*** others

Shieldbug

Shieldbugs are also called stinkbugs — and for good reason. They represent a group of plant-bugs comprising four families of the suborder Heteroptera. All are flattened in shape and some have an outline like that of an heraldic shield. Most are $\frac{1}{4}-\frac{1}{2}$ in. long, but the colourful red, black, orange and blue **Oncomeris flavicornis** *of Australia, is 2 in. long. Shieldbugs are included in the great order of insects called the Hemiptera, which include the true bugs and cicadas, all of which are characterised by mouthparts formed for piercing and sucking. They also grow into adults by incomplete metamorphosis.*

Most shieldbugs have a superficial resemblance to beetles, but these develop by complete metamorphosis, involving distinct larval and pupal stages, and they have biting mouthparts. They also resemble beetles in using the hindwings for flying and the forewings as a protective covering for the hindwings. Not all shieldbugs can fly and most of those that can, do so only in hot weather. In the shieldbugs each forewing is divided into two parts, a thick leathery basal part and a thin membranous area towards the tip. This results in the backs of these insects being broken up into patterns of triangles, which is the most noticeable feature distinguishing them from beetles.

Shieldbugs are mainly insects of warm climates and are most numerous nearer the tropics. For example, less than 40 species occur in Britain, many more are found on the continent of Europe, especially towards the south, and, of course, the number increases greatly in tropical Africa.

Useful and harmful selection

Almost all shieldbugs are found crawling about on the foliage of trees or bushes or in low herbage, and many of them are found attached to particular species of plants on whose sap or fruit they feed. The birch, hawthorn and juniper shieldbugs take their names from their food plants and the last two types feed mainly on the berries. As might be expected some of them are pests of agriculture. One of the tortoise bugs *Eurygaster integriceps* is a serious pest of wheat in the USSR and Near East. The green vegetable bug *Nezare viridula* has a world-wide distribution in the warmer countries, including southern Europe, and does great damage to beans, tomatoes and other vegetables. It is sometimes encountered in imported vegetables in Britain and other northern European countries, but does not seem to be able to establish itself in these countries.

▷ *The bright colours of Australasian* **Catacanthus punctum** *warn predators; like most shieldbugs it can emit a foul-smelling liquid.*

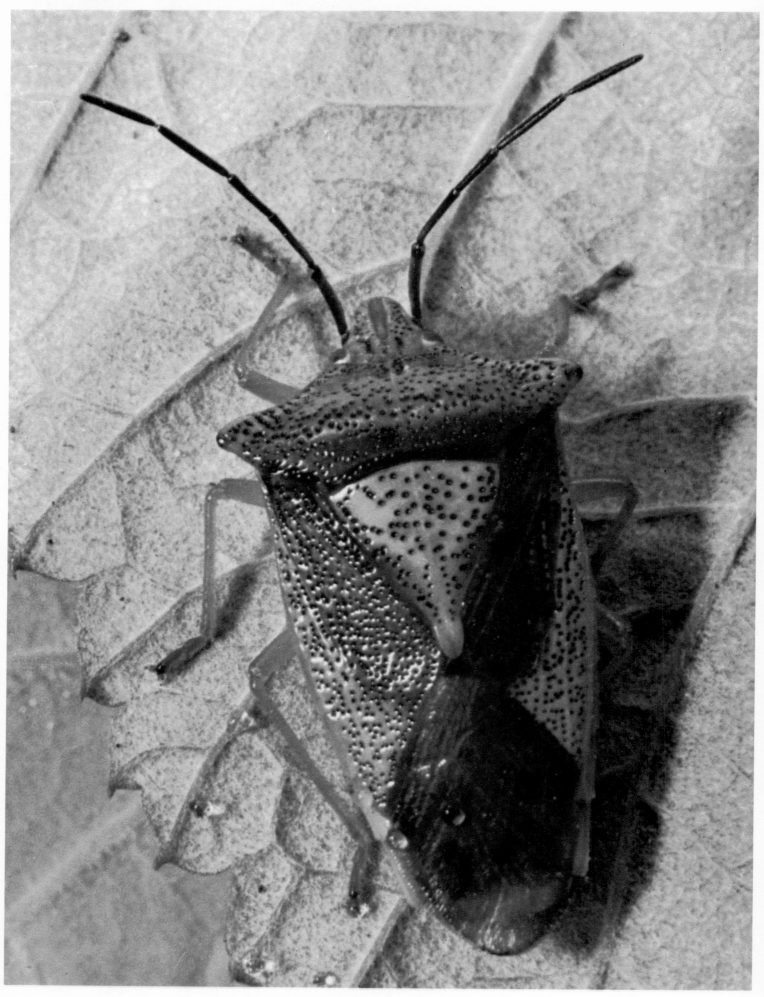

*◁ The hawthorn shieldbug **Acanthosoma haemorrhoidale** prefers the berries to the leaves; it will also feed on whitebeam and oak.*

Some of the shieldbugs are predatory and may be of service in destroying harmful insects. The North American genus *Podisus* is a useful enemy of the Colorado beetle.

Broody shieldbugs

Shieldbugs lay their eggs either on their food plant or on the ground. The eggs are laid in batches and look rather like those of butterflies and moths. They are usually developed in the insect's body 14 at a time and the batches often comprise multiples of this number. A few shieldbugs develop their eggs in dozens and lay them in two neat rows of six, lying side by side. In many species the eggs hatch by the opening of a definite lid on the top, so that under a microscope the egg cases look like little empty barrels.

The young grow by stages, changing their skins usually five times before reaching full size. Although the development is gradual there is often a startling change in colour and pattern when the adult stage is reached. *Sehirus dubius*, an interesting species quite common in continental Europe, is variable in colour. In one form of it the young are black on the forepart of the body, and red with black markings on the hinder part. After the last skin-change the adult is at first brilliant red, but it only retains this

coloration for a couple of hours; its colour then darkens until it assumes its final livery of steely black.

A number of the shieldbugs are known to brood their eggs, attending and protecting them up to the time they hatch. The parent bug *Elasmucha grisea*, which lives in birch woods, goes further than this. The female lays a batch of about 40 eggs on a birch leaf, the egg-mass being diamond-shaped and compact, the right shape for her to cover with her body, and she broods the eggs rather as a hen does, for 2—3 weeks until the young hatch. The mother and small larvae stay around the empty egg shells for a few days and then move away together, in search of the birch catkins which form the main part of their diet.

Why stinkbug?

Many of the shieldbugs have glands from which they can eject an evil-smelling and ill-tasting fluid if molested. Anyone picking a berry and not noticing the shieldbug on it may get an unpleasant taste in the mouth. A bug held in one's fingers will usually resort to this same mode of defence, and the smell is so strong and offensive that 'stinkbug' is used, especially in North America, as an apt alternative name for the shieldbugs. Some kinds feed on fruits and berries and render any they touch inedible. The forest bug *Pentatoma rufipes* sometimes infests cherry orchards and spoils a great deal of the fruit in this way. It can be prevented from

climbing up the trunks of the trees in spring by grease-banding the trunks.

Some species having this defence capacity are conspicuously coloured, usually black with white, yellow or red patterns. They are undoubtedly examples of warning coloration. By making themselves conspicuous to predatory enemies, especially birds, they derive protection from the fact that a bird, once it has tasted one of the bugs, will remember its distinctive appearance and avoid trying to eat others of the same species. The individual suffers but the species benefits.

Shieldbugs not protected in this way are preyed on by birds, especially tits, which seek out the hibernating bugs in winter. Far more serious enemies are the tachinid flies, whose larvae live as parasites inside the bodies of the developing bugs, killing them just before they reach maturity. These predators are in no way deterred by the bugs' repugnant fluids or lurid colours.

phylum	**Arthropoda**
class	**Insecta**
order	**Hemiptera**
suborder	**Heteroptera**
families	**Acanthosomidae** **Cydnidae** **Scutelleridae** **Pentatomidae**

*Patterns on a leaf, **Lyramorpha** and its young. The harlequin-like young grow by stages, changing their skins several times before the adult stage.*

Aphis

Aphides or 'plant lice' are a group of the Hemiptera (bugs) order of great importance to agriculture as they do considerable harm to crops, both directly, by sucking the cell-sap, and indirectly, by transmitting certain virus diseases, such as potato leaf-roll and sugar-beet yellows, from one plant to another. There are many species, some 500 in the British Isles alone, for example, but probably the best known are those referred to as greenfly and blackfly by the gardener who finds them, often in depressing numbers, on his roses and broad beans. Aphides have soft, oval bodies, small heads, compound eyes, long 6- or 7-jointed antennae, and a jointed beak or rostrum adapted for piercing plant tissues. Some have transparent wings, the first pair being much the longer. Aphides are usually about 2—3 mm long; rarely more than 5 mm.

Clouds of insects

Though most familiar as pests of cultivated plants, aphides begin their life on various wild trees and shrubs from which they migrate at intervals to other plants, both wild and in gardens. After mating in late summer or autumn, the black bean aphis *Aphis fabae* for example, lays eggs on the spindle tree or guelder rose. These hatch the following spring as winged females which fly to bean crops where they reproduce by parthenogenesis (that is, without mating). These are called 'stem mothers' as they are the beginning of a new population. Although they may reach the bean plants only singly in many cases, they breed at a tremendous rate forming large colonies, which explains the apparently quite sudden appearance of an infestation where none was visible a day or so previously.

How such a weak, delicate creature as the aphid manages to migrate so successfully from its host plant to another has been investigated thoroughly in recent years. The winged females usually leave the plants where they hatched in two main waves, one in the morning, one in the afternoon. But conditions must be favourable for the movement to take place. It never takes place at night or at temperatures below 17°C/62°F. Once airborne, the aphides are carried up on air currents, often to a great height. After several hours, descending air currents bring the aphides down and they seek out suitable plants. Sample catches taken in nets on balloons at heights up to 2,000 ft show that 30% of clouds of insects floating high up consists of aphides. They may be carried hundreds of miles over land and sea.

In preparing for flight, aphides appear to go through a kind of take-off procedure, which may be repeated several times before actual launching takes place. The centre pair of legs is raised and tucked into the hollow formed by the constriction between thorax and abdomen. Then, balancing on the remaining four legs, the aphid unfolds its wings and takes off. In spite of their apparent fragility, aphides are not easily

A winged black aphid being tended by an ant. Ants will farm large numbers of aphides, tending them carefully and milking them for the honeydew which is secreted by the aphides (approx × 12).

blown off plants.

The winged females settle on the alternative plants and produce mainly wingless offspring, but some winged individuals are produced at intervals, and these daily leave to seek out other uninfested plants.

Piercing and sucking feeders

As a family, aphides feed on many kinds of plants, but while some species may be catholic in their tastes, others can exist only on one species. The mouth-parts are modified for piercing plant tissues and sucking up the cell-sap, especially from the phloem, the main food stream of the plant. The mandibles and maxillae (mouth-parts) work together as extraordinarily fine needle-like stylets which are thrust deep

into the soft parts of the plant. The labium or tongue takes no part in the operation but has a groove in which the stylets are sheathed when not in use. Before feeding actually begins, a salivary secretion is injected into the wound made by the stylets. This prevents the sap coagulating as it flows up the stylets.

While many aphides feed externally on plants, others, far less familiar to us, form 'galls' or enclosed receptacles in which they are able to feed while hidden from the attacks of predators. Examples of aphid gall-makers may be found on trees such as poplars, elms, limes, spruce and cultivated currant bushes. Frequently, the galls form a refuge for passing the winter. In spring and summer a new generation may seek out quite different plants on which to feed without making a gall. In some species, there is simply a migration back and forth from one part of the tree, the leaves and shoots, to the roots. An example is the notorious woolly aphis or American blight of apple trees, which makes a characteristic fluffy 'wool' in which it feeds.

Oddly enough, it is their excretory habit which is undoubtedly the most striking and significant fact about aphides. In feeding, aphides take up large quantities of sap in order to get sufficient protein. The rest, the fluid rich in sugar, is given out through the anus as honeydew, often in great quantities. Being rich in sugars honeydew is much sought after by ants and some other insects.

Young without mating
For most of the year, aphid populations consist only of females which reproduce parthenogenetically at a great rate. Later in the year, winged females fly back to their primary host plants—usually trees—and lay eggs which hatch as males and females. These mate and lay eggs in crevices in the bark, which hatch in the following spring, producing only females.

A single parthenogenetic female may produce as many as 25 daughters in one day, and as these themselves are able to breed in about 8–10 days the numbers of aphides produced by just one female in a season can reach astronomical proportions. It has been estimated that if all the offspring of a single aphid were to survive, and each reproduced and multiplied, there would be in the

▽ *Greenfly bearing young actually giving birth. The offspring's body is just free of the mother (approx × 20).*

course of one year sufficient to 'equal the weight of 500,000,000 stout men'. Breeding is slowed down by adverse conditions, especially cold. If aphides are kept warm in a greenhouse, parthenogenetic females are produced continuously without a single male ever seeing the light of day.

Enemies everywhere
Many small insect-eating birds, such as tits and flycatchers, eat aphides. Ladybirds, lacewings, bugs, spiders and hover-fly larvae prey on them. In addition, certain parasitic wasps of the family Braconidae lay their eggs in aphides. The larvae consume the tissues of their hosts and eventually pupate inside the empty husk.

Some aphides have, however, evolved defensive mechanisms to guard against attack from these wasps. The aphides' blood cells secrete a capsule which envelops the parasite larva, arresting its development completely within 24 hours. Others form no capsule but appear to secrete some substance which stops the wasp larva's progress within a short period.

Aphides are also able to deter insect enemies by exuding a kind of wax from a pair of chimney-like stumps, called cornicles, on the rear end. This temporarily paralyses the attacker. Some aphides, too, are apparently so distasteful that a ladybird larva will vomit if it tries to eat one.

Ants, who rear aphides for the sake of their honeydew, also protect their charges from attack by predators. One way they do this is to eat the eggs of potential predators, such as those of ladybirds and hover-flies, which have been deliberately laid near an aphid population.

Ants' aphid farm
Long before history, man tamed and domesticated certain animals for his own uses: for pulling loads, for hunting, for companionship, but especially as food. Ants have been doing much the same thing with aphides for infinitely longer. They rear or at least closely associate with them, eating the honeydew and taking it back to the nest for the larva. Just as man is able to stimulate the production of milk in cows and goats, so too can ants encourage production of honeydew in aphides by improving conditions for their existence. This they may do by a variety of means, apart from repelling predators. They may 'herd' their charges, by forcibly confining them to the growing tips of plants which are the most nutritious, thus stimulating growth and breeding and, of course, the emission of honeydew. Where there are no ants present, the honeydew may eventually cover large areas of the plant, causing its death by wilting, by suffocation or by attracting fungi. By removing the aphides' honeydew, the ants ensure their charges' food sources.

Ants also take aphides into their nests, where they may lay eggs, or they may carry the eggs themselves from the plants on which they are laid. After emerging, the young aphides are carefully tended and 'milked' by the ants while they feed on the roots of various plants. Some aphides live only in ants' nests, and never see the light of day. For others, special shelters are built where the aphides can feed, protected from predators. Comparison with the human farmer's cattle-sheds is irresistible.

Presumably, the ants' habit of 'farming' aphides started haphazardly by attacking and killing them for food or simply by licking the drops of fluid which appeared periodically at the insects' vents. Honeydew is not produced continuously and the drop of liquid produced is in normal circumstances discarded by a flick of the aphides' hind leg. Under stimulation from an ant, however, the aphid does not discard the fluid but allows the ant to remove it, and goes on doing so, seeming to enjoy the caressings of the ant's antennae.

Under continued stimulation very large quantities of honeydew may be produced. One large aphid can produce nearly 2 cu mm in an hour, and a colony of the common ant *Lasius fuliginosus* can, it has been estimated, collect about 3–6 lb of honeydew in 100 days.

Control of aphides is something of paramount importance, but always difficult, and it is depressing for the gardener to know that the presence of ants in an aphid colony contributes directly to the increase of the problem. It has been calculated that in accelerating growth and reproduction in aphides and protecting them from predators, ants can indirectly double the loss in the yield of bean plants as compared with when aphides alone are present.

class	**Insecta**
order	**Hemiptera**
sub-order	**Homoptera**
family	**Aphididae**

117

Doodle bug

Doodle bug is the name given to insects of the family Myrmeleontidae, grouped in the order Neuroptera which includes the alderflies and which bear some resemblance to dragonflies, and more particularly to the lacewing flies, which they resemble in appearance and habits, in both larval and adult stages. The adults have long thin bodies and two pairs of slender wings of about equal size. Their heads are small with short, thread-like antennae, knobbed at the tips. The largest are little more than 3 in. The larva has a short, thick, fleshy body and dispro-portionately large calliper-like jaws which are armed with strong spines and bristles that help to grasp its prey, mainly ants. This habit of preying on ants has led to the English name ant-lion, a translation of the French name, which is 'fourmi-lion'. The name is also thought to be derived from the habits of the larva. There are several species of doodle bug in the United States, especially in the south and south-west. The student of etymology may be interested to know that this name was applied independently to the flying bomb in 1944. There are more than 600 species of doodle bugs. The typical European species is **Myrmeleon formicarius,** *the adult of which is about 1 in. long with a wing span of 2 in.*

Habits

Doodle bugs are found in woods, forests and plantations wherever there is a sandy soil. The larvae of many species burrow in the sand, the entrance of the burrow being at the bottom of a conical pit, 2 in. deep and 3 in. in diameter at the top, which is also dug by the larva. Groups of these pits can be readily seen in places in southern Europe where the soil is fine and quite dry, and sheltered from the weather, for a shower of rain would destroy the pits and smother the doodle bugs. Likely places are the entrances to dry caves, beneath over-hanging rocks and trees, below the eaves of houses, and in similar sheltered sites.

The adults are active from June to August, usually at dusk or during the night. Their flight is somewhat feeble and awk-ward. One reason why this type of insect is named after its larva is because the adults are very inconspicuous even in strong day-light, flying only when the light is failing or has gone, seldom being seen except when attracted to lights.

Pit-trapped victims

Adult doodle bugs have been relatively little studied. They are reported to feed on fruit and on small flies, and they may possibly feed on the honey-dew produced by aphids, as do the lacewings. The larva sets and springs one of the most spectacular traps

△ Doodle bug gripping an ant in its vice-like jaws.

◁ The delicate beauty of the harmless adult doodle bug is in vivid contrast with its vicious hunting larva.

▽ The gigantic calliper-like jaws or mandibles of the doodle bug larva which firmly seize its victim. Together with the secondary jaws or maxillae, two tubes are formed down which flows a paralysing fluid.

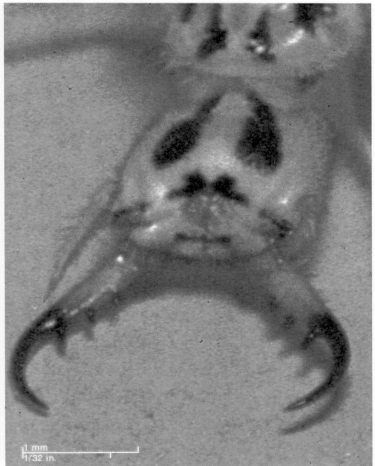

in the animal kingdom. Buried at the bottom of its pit, with only camouflaged head and strong jaws exposed, it waits for grains of sand disturbed by a passing ant or spider to fall and provide a trigger to spring its trap. Immediately sand is scooped on to the head by the jaws and the larva then jerks its head forwards and upwards, catapulting a stream of sand with great force and accuracy at its intended victim. This barrage, the steep sides of the pit, and the sand being undermined by the doodle bug's digging, together cause the victim to slide down to within reach of the doodle bug's jaws where it is immediately seized.

Sometimes the doodle bug gets only an unsatisfactory grip on its prey. In this event it may toss its victim rapidly against the sides of the pit until it gets a firm hold. It may even temporarily release its victim and again hurl sand at it if it shows signs of escaping. But once firmly held, the prey is drawn partially beneath the sand and then the second function of the calliper-like jaws comes into effect. These jaws are deeply grooved underneath. When the maxillae or secondary mouth parts are pressed against them, together they form two tubes down which a paralysing fluid flows, to be injected into the victim's body. When its struggles have ceased digestive juices are then injected in much the same way. These dissolve the tissues which the doodle bug then sucks up and swallows. Finally, the empty case of the insect's body is tossed up and over the edge of the pit by the doodle bug using the same technique as when catapulting sand grains.

Although the eyes of the larva are well-developed they seem to play no part in detecting the presence of food. If a few grains of sand at the edge of the pit are dislodged so they roll down the side and strike the doodle bug larva in wait at the bottom, it will immediately begin hurling sand upwards. Since it will react in this way when no prey is visible it is a fair assumption that the eyes play little part.

Occasionally doodle bug pits are grouped so close together that there is little chance of the occupants all getting sufficient food. This is offset by the larvae being able to fast without harm for up to 8 months.

Not all species of doodle bug dig pits. Some capture their prey by speed, others do so by stealth or ambush, perhaps lurking beneath stones and rubbish. It is interesting to note that while the highly specialised and somewhat sedentary pit-making species can only walk backwards, the more active species are able to do so in any direction.

Three-year life cycle
After mating, the female doodle bug lays her eggs singly in the sand. These are white and oval, and being sticky on the surface, immediately become encrusted with a layer of sand, which serves as a protective camouflage. Within a day of hatching, the young doodle bug has already dug a pit, of a size proportionate to itself. Thenceforth, the larva goes through three stages known as instars. At the end of each of these, the larva leaves its pit temporarily and hides beneath the sand for about a week to ten days. During this period it casts its old skin,

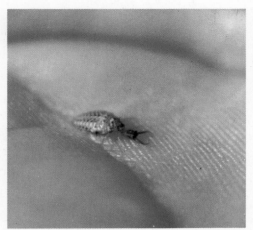

Doodle bug larvae although very vicious are quite small. Here a larva is held in the palm, clearly showing its size.

and then digs a new pit and begins to feed again. Probably the length of time spent as a larva depends to a large extent on the food available. But even with plenty of food it is estimated that the life-cycle from egg to adult takes from 1–3 years, and far longer under unfavourable circumstances. Once fully grown the larva pupates beneath the soil at the bottom of the pit, within a spherical silken cocoon. As in all insects of the order Neuroptera, the silk is produced by the Malpighian tubules; these structures are named after Malpighi, the 17th-century Italian microscopist who first described them. The silk is given out through the anus. This contrasts with caterpillars of butterflies and moths, for example, whose silk is produced by glands in the head. Almost as soon as the silk makes contact with the air, it hardens and, like the eggs, the cocoon is further protected by sand which sticks to its outer surface, although the innermost layers of silk never become sanded. Only when the cocoon is completed does the doodle bug larva shed its skin for the last time, revealing the cream-coloured pupa. The period of pupation to emergence of the perfect winged insect is usually about a month. Just prior to emergence, the doodle bug pupa cuts a hole in the cocoon with its pupal mandibles, and, using its 'free' pupal legs, crawls part way out of the cocoon before emerging as the perfect insect. At this stage, the pupal skin splits, and the adult works its way to the surface of the soil where it then climbs up a plant or tree from which it can hang while the body hardens and the wings expand and dry.

Innate abilities
Before man settled down to agriculture he lived by hunting and capturing wild animals. No doubt one of the first things he learnt to do was to build a pit in which to trap his quarry. Whether he merely stumbled on the idea or thought it out carefully in the first place is something we shall never know. Whichever way it was, however, he devised various methods of using the pit. He would camouflage it with branches of trees so that the animal passing that way did not suspect a trap. He would plant pointed stakes in the bottom of the pit or lurk nearby ready with a spear to make a kill. These and many variations have been used

for thousands of years and are still in use in various parts of the world even today. All the methods bear some resemblance to the tactics used by the doodle bug. Indeed, some of the things the doodle bug does seem to be an improvement on human techniques and therefore have the appearance of intelligence. We can be fairly sure that man started using pits because his better brain capacity enabled him to see the advantages and also to improve on method. Here is the essential difference between the things that insects do and the things we do. The insect merely follows an inherent behaviour pattern. We would find if we examined the pits and the behaviour of thousands of doodle bug of a given species that each individual trapped its prey in exactly the same way as every other individual of its species. Each doodle bug larva would start with the same method and would continue to use this method throughout its lifetime as a larva, without any improvement on it. Everything it does is therefore inborn or innate.

Nevertheless, those who study insects find themselves being forced to admit that there are times when even insects appear to depart slightly from the inborn pattern of behaviour, to adjust their actions to the varying needs of the moment or to the

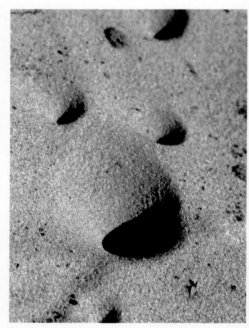

Doodle bug trapping pits. Should an ant or spider walk too near this steep-sided pit, it is doomed. The doodle bug disturbs the sand so the victim slides down to be gripped by its waiting jaws.

changing circumstances, in a way which suggests that some sort of thought or some sort of intelligence, no matter how rudimentary, is being brought to bear on it. As a result, scientists now tend to talk about insects having plastic, that is, flexible behaviour.

class	**Insecta**
order	**Neuroptera**
family	**Myrmeleontidae**
genera	*Myrmeleon, Palpares, Hesperoleon, and others*

Caddis-fly

Caddis-fly is the common name given to the insect order Trichoptera, of which between 4000 and 5000 species are known throughout the world. Their nearest relatives are the Lepidoptera (butterflies and moths). The antennae are long and many-jointed. The adult insects look rather like moths and fly mainly at night, often coming to artificial lights.

Most of the larvae are aquatic, living in freshwater and breathing by external gills on the sides of the abdominal segments. These are the well-known caddis-worms, which build tubular cases to protect their bodies, although not all caddis-fly larvae do this. All of them spin silk.

△ *Protective tubular cases, open at one end, are built by caddis-fly larvae from pieces of plant stems and leaves, and small stones and shells, bound together with silk (3 × natural size).*
▽ *The caddis-worm* **Lepidostoma hirtum** *partly emerges from its tubular case to feed (×16).*

Underwater builders

By far the most interesting feature of the caddis-flies is the life of the aquatic larvae, which varies in the different families and genera. They can be divided into two types, those which build portable cases, and are almost all vegetarians, and those which live free and are at least partly carnivorous. The case-builders use many materials in various ways to build their tubes. Members of the genus *Phryganea*, which includes the largest caddis-flies, cut pieces of leaves and stick them together with silk. The most familiar cases are probably those of *Limnephilus*, which are made of small stones, and pieces of plant stems or empty snail shells. If removed from their cases and given beads or similar objects, some of these caddis-flies will use the artificial material to make new ones. *Stenophylax* and *Heliopsyche* use fine sand grains to make their cases, the one a straight cylinder, the other a spiral tube that looks remarkably like a small snail shell. Cases made of stones or sand often have their weight reduced by a bubble of air trapped inside. *Heliopsyche* is American, all the others mentioned are found in Britain.

All the cases are tubular and open at the one end, where the larva pushes out its head and thorax to move about or feed. The rear end is closed with a silken mesh so that a current of water can flow through and aerate the gills. All caddis-larvae have a pair of hooked limbs at the back, used to hold onto the case — so tightly that attempts to pull the larva out invariably injure it. It can easily be made to leave its case, however, by pushing the head of a fairly large pin through the mesh of the rear opening.

Most of the larvae with non-portable cases live in silken tubes, in flowing water, some living under stones in swift upland streams. In the genus *Plectronemia* the larva is nearly 1 in. long and makes a silk tunnel with the open end facing upstream widely flared to form a trumpet-shaped net. Any small animal or piece of plant material carried into this trap by the current is seized and eaten by the larva, which thus gets its food in very much the same way as a web-spinning spider. A number of other stream-dwelling caddis-larvae make nets of various shapes to gather food. When they are damaged, or choked with inedible material, the larvae clean and repair them.

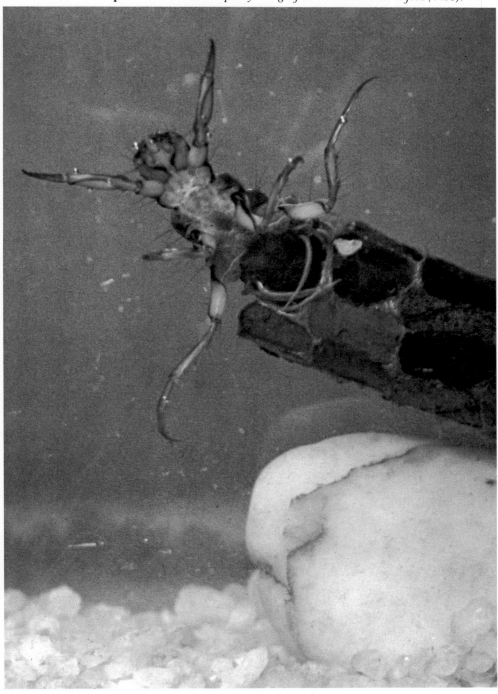

△ *Adult caddis-fly* **Stenophylax permistus** *has large wings and flies mainly at night. The adult is short-lived, for only a fraction of the annual life cycle (3 × natural size).*
▽ *Caddis-fly head magnified about 20 times. The compound eye's many facets can be clearly seen.*

Adult feeds on nectar

The mouth-parts of adult caddis-flies are vestigial, and if they feed at all as adults, they can probably take in only liquid food. In the wild they probably feed from flowers with exposed nectaries, but will take sugar and water in captivity. Fed in this way they can be kept alive for 2 or 3 months, but given only water they live for less than 2 weeks. The case-bearing larvae eat mainly the leaves and stems of live plants and may be a nuisance when one is trying to establish water lilies in a pond. A cabbage leaf tied to a string, thrown into a pond and left for a few hours, will often be covered with case-bearing caddis-larvae if it is taken out carefully. The large case-bearing larvae of *Phryganea* catch and eat water insects as well as plant food. Most of the tube-dwelling or free-living larvae have a mixed diet.

Life history

The eggs are laid by the females in spring and summer. Some kinds drop them on the surface as they are flying over, others crawl underwater and stick them to stones or plants in a jelly-like mass. Some of the larvae do not make cases or tubes until they have moulted their skins several times, others make tiny cases as soon as they hatch. When the larva is fully grown, nearly a year later, it pupates, inside the case if it belongs to a case-bearing species, otherwise in a silken cocoon. When the time comes for the adult insect to emerge, the pupa bites its way out of the case, being equipped for the purpose with strong mandibles, and swims to the surface of the water. There it splits open, releasing the adult caddis-fly, which can fly almost immediately on emergence. The life history usually takes a year to complete, of which the adult life is only a small fraction.

Anglers and caddis-flies

These insects are of interest to anglers for two reasons. The larvae, taken out of their cases, make excellent bait for the man who watches a float. The adults, when they hatch in quantity, cause a 'rise' of trout, that is to say the fish are stimulated to come to the surface and feed, and this is of prime interest to the fly fishermen.

Entomologists always speak of caddis-flies by their Latin names, but anglers use an English terminology that is hardly ever heard except in the context of fly fishing. They are known collectively as sedge flies, the large *Phryganea grandis* being the great red sedge or murragh. There is a group of species called silverhorns, and some have names of their own such as Grannom, Caperer and Halford's Welshman's Button.

Artificial flies are made in imitation of caddis-flies. To make a murragh a piece of dark grey-black or black-claret mohair or seal's fur is used for the body, a dark brown-speckled feather from a fowl's wing is used for the wings and two dark red cock hackles (the feathers from the neck) complete the job; only the soft fibres near the base of the feather being used.

class	**Insecta**
order	**Trichoptera**
genus	***Limnephilus, Phryganea***

Colorado beetle

*Familiar to many people from the pictures displayed in police stations and elsewhere, the Colorado beetle is a dreaded potato pest. It is $\frac{3}{10}$ in. long, a little bigger than a ladybird. The convex, shiny back is longitudinally striped black and yellow, and the thorax, the region just behind the head, is spotted black and yellow. The specific name **decemlineata** means ten-striped, as there are five black stripes on each wing-cover. The larva is equally conspicuous, orange-yellow with black markings on the head, black legs and three rows of black spots along each side. It has a characteristic hump-backed appearance.*

Potato pests

The Colorado beetle is a serious pest, feeding on potato leaves both as larva and adult, though it may occasionally resort to other plants of the potato family.

It passes the winter as a mature beetle, hibernating underground at a depth of 10 − 12 in. In late spring it comes out and, if it does not find itself surrounded by potato plants, flies in search of them, often for a distance of many miles. The female lays her eggs on the leaves, usually on the underside; they are yellow in colour and laid in batches. The larvae hatch in a few days, feed voraciously on the leaves and are fully grown in about 3 weeks. They then burrow into the soil to pupate, and a new generation of beetles emerges in 10 − 15 days. In Britain this second brood appears in late July or August, and if the weather stays warm a third generation may be produced. As soon as bad weather sets in, the beetles burrow into the soil and hibernate until the following spring.

The damage is done to the haulm, or above-ground part of the plant, which may be completely stripped of its leaves, so that the tubers cannot develop. The large number of eggs produced by each female and the rapid succession of generations are factors which make the Colorado beetle such a formidable pest. A single individual emerging in the spring may have thousands of descendants by the autumn.

33 insect enemies

The Colorado beetle seems to have no natural enemies that are effective in reducing its numbers. There are at least 33 different kinds of insects that prey on it, including bugs, beetles, wasps and flies, and one fly lays its eggs in the larvae of the Colorado beetle. Yet these account for only $\frac{1}{5}$ of the total. Spraying the potato foliage with a modern insecticide is the usual method of control. The important thing is obviously to spot any infestation as early as possible and exterminate local populations before they have a chance to spread. Anyone who finds a Colorado beetle, either in a potato field or casually, should immediately report the matter at the nearest police station. The specimen *must* be taken along for its identity to be checked. This surveillance has so far proved effective.

△ *In late spring a female Colorado beetle will lay a batch of yellow eggs on the potato leaf, which hatch in a few days.*

▽ *Fully-grown larva, about 3 weeks old. It is ready to burrow into the soil and pupate for about 15 days before emerging as an adult.*

An entomological curiosity

Like many insects which have become pests, the Colorado beetle is especially interesting. Almost all species of insects are conditioned to live in some particular type of climate. If the climate differs from that of their natural environment they will fail and die out at some stage in the life cycle. The Colorado beetle is a conspicuous exception to this rule. It can live the year round out of doors in Canada, where the winters are arctic in severity, in the hot deserts of Texas and Mexico and in the British cool wet climate. The beetle's habit of hibernating deep underground as an adult is probably the most important factor in promoting this quite unusual ability to adapt itself to any climate in which men can grow potatoes.

A potato bridge

Among the discoveries made in the Rocky Mountains by the American explorer Stephen Harriman Long, in the early 1820's, was a pretty black-and-yellow-striped beetle feeding on a sort of nightshade called buffalo burr *Solanum rostratum*. Neither it nor its food plant were particularly abundant, and it was simply an attractive insect living in a state of balance with its environment.

The buffalo burr is a member of the potato family. The potato is native to Peru and Ecuador, in South America. It was brought to Europe by the Spaniards and later found its way to the new colony of Virginia in North America. How this happened is not known. Neither Sir Walter Raleigh nor Sir Francis Drake, both of whom are credited with discovering it, took it there. In the course of the opening up and settlement of western America in the 1850's, potatoes were introduced and cultivated by the pioneers, and in Nebraska in 1859 it was found that the 'buffalo burr beetle' was turning its attention to the potato. Its numbers increased rapidly and it began to spread. No control measures were known at that time and the beetle spread from potato field to potato field, frequently destroying the whole crop. From Nebraska in 1859 it appeared in Illinois in 1864, in Ohio in 1869, and it reached the Atlantic coast in 1874. This indicates an average rate of travel of 85 miles a year. The potato fields of the United States had formed a bridge from west to east along which the beetle could travel. It also spread 400 miles northwards into Canada. The Atlantic formed a barrier, however, until 1922.

Then it was found in the Gironde region of France and from there it has extended its range all over continental Europe. It appeared in Tilbury in 1901, but the next outbreak in Britain was in Essex in 1933, where prompt control measures exterminated it. It has appeared from time to time in Britain since then, but has always been prevented from establishing itself. In 1946 there was a real danger it might become established. In 1947 infestations were discovered at 57 centres. In 1948 there were 11, and in 1949 not one was found. Prompt control measures had proved effective, much to the relief of the many British potato farmers.

class	Insecta
order	Coleoptera
family	Chrysomelidae
genus & species	*Leptinotarsa decemlineata*

Adults and larvae of the brightly-coloured Colorado beetle often live together on the same plant. Scourge of potato crops the world over, the Colorado beetle is an insect with an international price on its head, but if outbreaks are reported early, prompt control measures usually prove effective.

Glowworm

The glowworm is a beetle belonging to the family Lampyridae which also includes the fireflies. Many centuries ago anything that was long and crawling was called a worm. The female glowworm lacks wings and it was this and her general appearance that was responsible for the name.

Male and female of the common European glowworm **Lampyris noctiluca** are yellowish grey-brown. The male has large eyes and two very tiny light-producing organs at the tip of the abdomen. He also has wings covered by the usual wing cases of beetles, and his length is about $\frac{1}{2}$ in. The female, slightly longer than the male, differs little in shape from the larva and the last three segments of the body, on the underside, are yellowish and strongly luminescent.

A second species of glowworm **Phosphaenus hemipterus** is widespread over continental Europe.

△ *Fickle flasher: having attracted three males to her powerful light, a female glowworm mates with one, ignored by her disappointed suitors.*

▽ *Incandescent cousin: female African beetle of the closely related family Phengodidae waiting in the grass for response to her light.*

The lure of the lights

Adult glowworms are most active in June and July. Preferring slightly damp places, they may be found on hedgerow banks, hillsides and in rough meadows, especially where there is a plentiful supply of snails. By day they hide in cracks and crevices. After nightfall the female climbs onto a prominent piece of foliage and takes up a position head down so her luminous end is prominently displayed. The female glowworm's method of light-production is the same as in the firefly. Beneath the light-producing bands is a whitish, opaque layer which not only prevents absorption of the light into the body, but reflects it back, making full use of all the light. The winged male homes on the female's light for mating. The light may be visible to us over 100 yd or so under suitable conditions, but may be 'doused' as we approach and switched on again after an interval. By contrast, the larvae light up as a result of being disturbed, which suggests that in them the luminescence may serve as a defence, frightening away some enemies. The larvae's light also is slightly different from that of the adults, being more intensely green.

Short-lived adults

The pale yellow eggs are $\frac{1}{20}$ in. diameter. Usually they are laid in ones and twos over a period of a couple of days on grass stems or moss, or in or on the soil. They hatch in a fortnight, the larvae being almost exact miniatures of the adult females except for the simpler structure of the legs and a series of paler spots at the front corners of each body segment. Growing by a series of moults, the larvae reach the adult stage in three years. The pupa of the male differs from that of the female, reflecting the different appearance of the adults. Emerging from the pupae after about 8 or 9 days, usually in April or May, the adults live for only a short while after mating and egg-laying. During mating neither sex glows.

Making the most of youth: doomed to starvation as an adult, a glowworm larva gorges itself on a tiny garden snail (12 × life size).

Larvae feed, parents starve

Adult glowworms take no food, although it is often asserted that they do. The larvae feed on snails which they discover by following their slime trails. They drive their hollow, curved mandibles into the mollusc and inject a dark fluid, partly paralysing and partly digestive. This rapidly reduces the snail's tissues to a pre-digested soup-like liquid which the glowworm then sucks up. Newly-hatched glowworms are only $\frac{1}{5}$ in. long. They feed on the smaller snails. Sometimes the larvae feed communally, crowding round the lip of the shell and feeding side by side. After a meal the glowworm pushes out a white sponge-like device from its anus. With this it can clean away from its head and back any remains of slime resulting from its meal.

Lucky to survive

Glowworms fall victim to any insect-eating animal, despite the glowing lights on their bodies, but especially to toads and hedgehogs, both of which feed at night. Some are eaten by frogs and spiders, and there are mites which penetrate the soft joints between the body segments of the larvae and feed on their body fluids. The larvae are particularly vulnerable to mites when they have shed their skins at the periodic moults, making them fair game for these parasites.

On the decline

The twinkling lights of a modern city are an irresistible attraction to the eye of young and old alike. It is doubtful, however, whether any of the artificial illumination produced by man has the same aesthetic quality as that from a well-stocked colony of glowworms seen on a moonless night. It is not surprising that poets have made so much of this. Unfortunately, the chances of seeing it today are on the whole much smaller than in times past. Glowworms, useful and attractive insects, have died out from many areas where they were once common. The reasons for this are not easy to see, but it almost certainly springs from the pressure on land for housing, factories, intensive farming, combined with more efficient draining of the land. No doubt the use of insecticides is also partly to blame. What is quite certain is that it is not natural enemies that have brought about this fall in numbers, because toads and hedgehogs are all less numerous than they used to be.

Ironically, there may be another reason. Many insects are irresistibly attracted to artificial light, and in this the male glowworm is no exception, in spite of the fact that it has its own, highly individual 'bright light' to go to—that emitted by the female. Even the weak, flickering light of a candle-flame will attract a glowworm, as Gilbert White, one of the first naturalists, records. In many areas, it seems, modern artificial lighting systems have become a serious threat to glowworm survival, in that the male glowworms are finding them far more alluring than the more modest glow produced by the females, which as a result may languish in vain and even die 'old maids'! Once attracted to the lights of large buildings the male insects may damage themselves in hitting or being burnt by them, and then fall to the ground stunned or dazzled, to be subsequently eaten by a variety of small animals; or the attraction may simply disrupt the delicate balance of nocturnal flight activity. Fortunately there are still many areas where such hazards are less pronounced, as is indicated by the fact that the greatest numbers of glowworms are found in areas which are comparatively less developed industrially.

phylum	**Arthropoda**
class	**Insecta**
order	**Coleoptera**
family	**Lampyridae**
genus & species	*Lampyris noctiluca*

Ladybird

Small, brightly coloured beetles, oval or almost circular in outline, ladybirds were regarded with affection long before it was realised they are useful as well as pretty. The name ladybird (sometimes ladybug or lady beetle) dates from the Middle Ages when the beetles were associated with the Virgin Mary and called 'beetles of Our Lady'. Their coloration is generally red or yellow with black spots and the pattern tends to be variable, extremely so in some species. A few, like that known as **Coccidula rufa**, are brown without conspicuous markings, and are not usually recognised as ladybirds. The colourful species have a strong and unpleasant smell and they taste equally bad. Their bright colours doubtless serve as a warning to predators not to try to eat them. Both ladybird adults and their larvae prey on aphids, destroying them in great numbers.

The four commonest species in Europe are the two-spot, ten-spot, seven-spot and twenty-two-spot ladybirds. The first is red with a single black spot on each wingcase but black specimens with four red spots are common, and the beetle is sometimes yellow with black spots. The underside and legs are black. The second is reddish or yellow, usually with five black spots on each wingcase, but the ground colour may be black as in the last species. The underside is brown and the legs yellowish. The seven-spot is larger than the first two species and its colours hardly vary at all. It is orange-red with a black spot on the line dividing the wingcases and three others farther back on each side. The last is much smaller with 11 black spots on each side on a bright yellow ground. One of the largest and most handsome species is the eyed ladybird **Anatis ocellata**, which has black spots on a red ground, each spot being

▷ △△ The lunate ladybird of the South African high veld **Chilomenes lunata** laying a batch of eggs. There are 5–50 in a batch, but the beetle lays several batches, usually to a total of about 150 eggs, though 1 000 has been recorded. To provide for the young, the female lays them in an aphid-infested place. They hatch in about 3 weeks.

▷ △ Eggs of the lunate ladybird. The larvae will start their aphid massacre, made easy by the mother's consideration and the soft, defenceless prey, straight away. The massacre continues even after pupation. Some idea of the extent of aphid and scale insect control by ladybirds can be had from the record of a single larva's eating 90 adult and 3 000 larval scale insects. This appetite, and the high rate of reproduction, make it a very beneficial beetle.

▷ Scourge of the aphids: larvae of the S. African ladybird **Cryptolaemus** hunting. Protected by a waxy secretion, then by warning colours, and a vile taste as adults—an easy life at all stages.

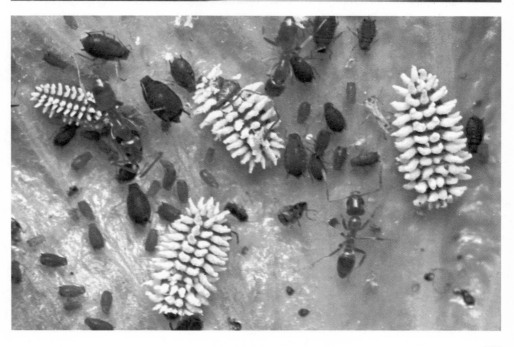

surrounded by a halo of yellow. It may be ⅖ in. long and lives among pine foliage.

The first four of these have been given the scientific names **Adalia bipunctata, A. decempunctata, Coccinella septempunctata** and **Thea vigintiduo-punctata** respectively. Even scientists sometimes jib at long names so these four ladybirds are usually referred to as **2-punctata, 10-punctata, 7-punctata** and **22-punctata.**

Winter hibernation

In summer ladybirds fly actively about among foliage. In winter they hibernate as adults, often in large groups. Sometimes 50 or 100 of them can be found crowded together under a piece of loose bark, on a post or in a porch. They often congregate in houses and usually go unnoticed until they come out in spring. In California crevices and caves on certain hilltops are well known as hibernation resorts where ladybirds gather in their thousands.

Hordes of ladybirds

Ladybirds usually lay their orange-coloured eggs on the undersides of leaves, in batches of 3—50. Several batches are laid by one female, totalling 100—200 eggs, sometimes more. Because the beetles themselves feed on aphids or greenfly they tend to choose places where these are abundant in which to lay, so the larvae find food handy from the start. The eggs hatch in from 5 to 8 days, turning grey shortly before they do so. The larvae are active, bristly and variously coloured in patterns of black, orange, blue and red. Like the adult beetles they feed on aphids, but since they are growing rapidly they are far more voracious. The larval stage lasts 3 weeks or so, during which time several hundreds of aphids are eaten.

When thousands of aphid-eating ladybirds are each laying hundreds of eggs and every larva is consuming hundreds of aphids, it can be imagined that very large numbers of greenfly are destroyed, and the benefit to plants, both wild and cultivated, is enormous. The pupa is usually attached to

◁ △△ *A pupa, the ladybird's only lull in feeding.*

◁ △ *Full circle: adult lunate ladybirds feeding on a liberal supply of aphids.*
Even man, for hundreds of years, has contributed to the ladybirds' mollycoddled existence by recognising the need to keep them alive. They have even taken their place in English folklore with the rhyme 'Ladybird, ladybird, fly away home, your house is on fire, your children alone', a reference to the custom of burning hop vines at the end of the season, no doubt with many larvae on them. The second stanza, 'Except little Nan, who sits in a pan, weaving gold laces as fast as she can' concerns the colourful larva weaving a pupal case. These lines, spoken when a ladybird landed nearby, must have saved many an extremely useful insect's life.

◁ *The black sheep: one of the few vegetarian ladybirds* **Epilachna dregei** *which spoil the group's fine reputation by feeding on potato leaves.*

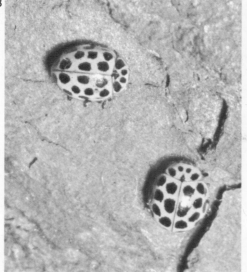

a leaf. The whole life cycle takes from 4 to 7 weeks, so several generations of ladybirds may be produced in a summer.

One small group of ladybirds are not predatory but feed as larvae on plant food. For example, there is a species, the twenty-four-spot ladybird *Subcoccinella viginti-quatuorpunctata* (certainly better written *24-punctata*), which eats clover.

Ladybird farms

The principle of using one species of insect to control the numbers of another is now well known, and is often advocated as being preferable to the use of poisonous insecticides. An early example of an operation of this kind concerns the use of a ladybird. Towards the end of the last century the Californian citrus orchards were devastated by the cottony-cushion scale insect, which was accidentally introduced from Australia. A brightly coloured ladybird *Rhodalia cardinalis* was found to be a natural enemy of the scale insect in Australia, and in 1889 some of these ladybirds were brought to California and released in the orchards. They effectively controlled the scale insect there and they have since been introduced to South Africa.

The Californian citrus growers were also troubled by aphids and other plant bugs, and use was made of a native ladybird, a species of *Hippodamia*, that hibernates, as mentioned earlier, in caves in the hills. These were collected and sold to the citrus farmers by the litre (8 000 to 10 000 beetles in each litre) and later by the gallon. This control was started in 1910, neglected, then revived during the Second World War.

Even this is not the end of the story of useful ladybirds in California. In the 1920s the orchards were attacked by another scale insect *Pseudococcus*. Again a ladybird was brought from Australia, by the name of *Cryptolaemus montrouzieri*. This failed to breed under natural conditions in Western America, so huge ladybird factories were maintained where they were bred, with careful control of temperature and other conditions, on potato shoots infested with *Pseudococcus*. In 1928 alone 48 million ladybirds of this species were set free in the Californian orange orchards.

*(1) Searching every nook and cranny of a rock face for prey **Propylea 14-punctata**.*
*(2) The writing on the wings: the unusual markings of **Coccinella hieroglyphica**.*
*(3) Beauty as well as usefulness: the black and yellow **Thea 22-punctata**.*
*(4) The lighter colour variation of **Calvia 14-guttata**.*
*(5) Mopping up the plant parasites on a leaf, a dark colour variety of **Calvia 14-guttata**.*
*(6) Not all ladybirds have spots: a striped ladybird **Paramysia oblongoguttata**.*
*(7) One of the best-known ladybirds, the two spot **Adalia bipunctata**.*

class	**Insecta**
order	**Coleoptera**
family	**Coccinellidae**

*The beautiful apollo butterfly, **Parnassius phoebus**, resting with wings outstretched.*

Apollo showing its bright spot markings.

Apollo butterfly

One of the family of butterflies known as the swallowtails, not unlike them in shape, but lacking the tail-like appendages on the hind wing which give the family its name. The apollo and its relatives are not brightly coloured, most of them being white, with spots and eye-like markings of black and red. They are nevertheless elegant and beautiful.

Range and habitat

The common apollo is found in mountainous regions of Europe, from Scandinavia to the Alps and Pyrenees. It flies at fairly low altitudes. There is, however, a related species, the alpine apollo, which occurs at higher altitudes. About 30 species of apollo butterflies are known, ranging through Europe and Asia to North America. Many are mountain butterflies and some species range up to 20,000 ft in the Himalayas. Owing to their inaccessible habitat some of the Central Asiatic species are extremely rare and highly prized by collectors.

Life history

The caterpillar of the common apollo feeds on orpine, a kind of stonecrop. The caterpillar is black with red spots and, when fully grown, spins a cocoon in which to pupate. Growth is slow and it takes 2 years to complete the life-history. So far as they are known the early stages of all the species are similar, and the larvae feed on stonecrops and saxifrages. The habit, very unusual among butterflies, of spinning a cocoon is no doubt correlated with the need for protection from frost at high altitudes.

Only the common apollo habitually flies at low altitudes, and there are indications that some of the bodily structures of apollos as a whole may serve as an alpine kit. The body is covered with hairs, like a fur coat. It is dark in colour, which may help to absorb heat from the sun. The wings, white with black spots, are proportionately larger than in other butterflies, so exposing a greater surface to the sun's rays, and also assisting the butterfly in its unusual soaring habit. Moreover, they are so thinly covered with scales as to be almost translucent, which probably assists the absorption of the sun's heat.

God-like butterflies

Apollo butterflies have been seen in the Alps soaring above hillsides on uprising wind currents with wings outstretched and motionless. Soaring flight, common in birds, is rare among insects. Apollo was a Greek god of the mountains and the vegetation and later the sun god. All this makes the choice of name for these butterflies singularly apt. The god-like character is, however, marred by a North American species, *Parnassius autocrator*. The caterpillar, brilliant orange in colour, gives off a most unpleasant odour from just behind its head whenever danger threatens. All apollo larvae (and swallowtail too) have an organ (the osmeterium) behind the head that gives off an odour, but this is usually faint and at any rate not unpleasant to the human nose.

class	**Insecta**
order	**Lepidoptera**
family	**Papilionidae**
genus	*Parnassius*

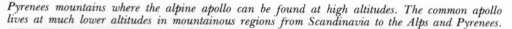

Pyrenees mountains where the alpine apollo can be found at high altitudes. The common apollo lives at much lower altitudes in mountainous regions from Scandinavia to the Alps and Pyrenees.

*Caterpillar of European apollo **Parnassius apoll**, which takes nearly 2 years to grow.*

△ *Male birdwing,* **Ornithoptera priamus,** *feeding. Only the male birdwings have the attractive iridescent markings on their wings. The unfortunate females have to make do with less spectacular markings.*

Birdwing

Imagine a butterfly with a wingspan that is sometimes more than 10 in. and you have some idea of the size of the birdwing butterfly. This amazing wingspan of some of the genera was what provoked naturalists to dub them 'Ornithoptera' (bird-winged). The males are somewhat smaller than the females. Their wings are large and velvety and usually of a black or purplish shade. These wings are made even more attractive by their beautiful iridescent markings in blue, green, pink, orange or gold. That is the male. The unfortunate female has to make do with less spectacular markings. Her wings are speckled with a uniform white instead of the fluctuating colour ranges that make the male so irresistible.

The birdwing's width and size comes from its long, graceful forewings. The hindwings, by comparison, are small. One characteristic of the swallowtail family, to which they belong, is the long tail on each of the hindwings. These tails can only be seen in the birdwings on the tailed birdwing **Ornithoptera paradisea** *and on one or two others. Butterfly collectors named several birdwings after*

their current heroes. One was named after Queen Victoria: Queen Victoria's birdwing **Ornithoptera victoriae;** *and one of the White Rajahs in Sarawak, Rajah Brooke, had the pleasure of seeing his name immortalised in butterfly-collecting circles by having perhaps the most beautiful of all the birdwings,* **Troides brookiana,** *called after him. Birdwings live in open woodland or forest, from southern India and Sri Lanka across to northern Australia, New Guinea and the Solomon Islands.*

Birdwings fool the entomologists

Very little is known about some of the species. It is only recently, for example, that the life cycle of Rajah Brooke's birdwing has been described. No one has ever succeeded in finding its caterpillars in the wild, but an entomologist in Sumatra has finally succeeded in breeding them in captivity.

For a long time, entomologists listed, as one of the unusual features of Rajah Brooke's birdwing, the fact that the female was rarely seen. They even put the ratio of males to females at as much as 1 000 : 1. They based their statistics on data they got from collections made at places where the birdwings congregate, such as river banks or seepages and other damp places.

Then it dawned upon somebody that the reason they were getting these extraordinary figures was because it was only the males of the species who congregated at these spots. This explained the unusual figure of 1 000 : 1, which was quite unlike the statistics they had obtained on other species, showing the males and the females to be almost 50 : 50. Enquiries in other sources revealed, as a matter of fact, that females of the common birdwing *Troides helena* are somewhat more numerous than the males.

Birdwings live in the trees, especially in the canopy of foliage at the tops of the taller trees. When the entomologists realised this they had the answer to the mystery of the 'elusive butterfly'. They were not rare at all.

It was just that the female of Rajah Brooke's birdwing and both sexes of other species did not come down to seepages and damp places and remained totally unattracted by the bait, such as carrion, which was put out for them. This made collecting them rather tricky. The collectors found that they had to resort to shooting the birdwings with 'dust shot' as if they were birds. However, when birdwings do fly low they are easy to catch because their flight is slow, direct and unsuspecting. It makes a welcome change for the collector who is constantly being frustrated by the bouncing, weaving flight of many other butterflies.

131

Above: Rajah Brooke's birdwing. It was thought that the males outnumbered the females by 1000 : 1, as only the males were usually seen. Females were then found in the treetops, making numbers equal (life size). Right: Wonderful action shot of birdwing, **Troides rhadamantus**, *alighting on a flowerhead. Its long thin feeding tube, the proboscis, is already extended so it can suck the flower's nectar.*

What they eat

Birdwing caterpillars feed on plants of the Aristolochiaceae family and on betel leaves. The adults feed on flowers. Some of the closely related swallowtail butterflies also feed on plants of the same family. These are known to be distasteful because of a chemical in the plant but it is not known whether the birdwings are also distasteful to their predators.

Life cycle of a birdwing

The eggs of the common birdwing are laid singly on the upper sides of leaves. From the eggs hatch caterpillars bearing six rows of fleshy tubercles which run the whole length of the body. The caterpillars also have a curious Y-shaped organ, called an osmeterium, on the head. This is connected with glands in the body. When a caterpillar is alarmed the osmeterium is worked in and out, exuding an unpleasant smell.

After the caterpillars have fed for a month, they turn into chrysalises on the vertical stem of the plant where they have been living. The chrysalis has the typical form of the swallowtail family. The lower end is anchored to the plant stem by a silken pad. The body and upper end is supported by a silk thread which passes around the stem of the plant, in very much the same way that a lumberjack is secured to a tree with a safety-belt. After

three weeks the adult butterfly emerges from the pupa.

The cost of rarity and beauty

Lots of people collect butterflies, from schoolboys with their little collections of the more common kind to professional entomologists with neat rows of specimens in glass-topped boxes marked 'Do Not Touch'. It is a hobby that can be taken to great lengths, like anything else. We are now all familiar with those tense scenes in auction rooms when paintings or postage stamps fall under the hammer for thousands, or even hundreds of thousands, of pounds. Many a non-collector has found it hard to understand why a painting suddenly becomes so amazingly valuable after being ignored by everyone for years and years.

How does one put a price on a painting or a stamp, which intrinsically is only worth the price of the materials it is made of? Two of the main criteria must obviously be its rarity or its beauty. Add to these the fanaticism of some buyers and the tension and competition in an auction room and you have some of the reasons why people pay such inflated prices.

Butterflies are just like paintings and stamps. Serious collectors have always been willing to pay for unusual specimens that they have been unable to catch themselves and the price is arrived at through a com-

bination of beauty and rarity. If a butterfly is spectacularly beautiful and rare it can be valuable. By contrast, a small, dull one, even if it is very rare, is usually not worth much. There has always been a trade in butterflies and they are even bred especially for the purpose. Not surprisingly birdwings have always been in demand. Many 'part-time collectors' supply them from New Guinea, the Solomons and Northern Australia. Good specimens of the common species are available at a pound or two, although rarer ones might cost £25 ($60) to £30 ($70).

In 1966 a large collection of butterflies was auctioned in Paris and a collector paid £750 ($1 785) for a specimen of the very rare birdwing *Troides allotei* from the Solomon Islands. It was an amazingly high price to pay for a specimen.

It should be very interesting to see, in years to come, whether this butterfly maintains its value or whether other collectors decide that even a very pretty butterfly is not worth that much and spend their money on a motor car instead.

class	**Insecta**
order	**Lepidoptera**
family	**Papilionidae**
genera	*Troides* *Trogonoptera* *Ornithoptera*

Burnet moth

The bright colours of the burnet moths make them very conspicuous. They are small with thick bodies, long forewings and short hindwings; the antennae are thickened near the tip and then pointed. Most are brightly coloured, the forewings dark metallic blue or green with scarlet markings and usually separate spots, the hindwings with a black border. This applies to all the British species, but in southern Europe white and yellow-spotted ones occur. In the beautiful **Zygaena carniolica**, of central and southern Europe and western Asia, the red spots are surrounded by white rings. Occasionally yellow-spotted forms occur as rare varieties of the normally red-spotted species.

Burnets from around the coasts of the Mediterranean occur in immense numbers and great variety. They extend in small numbers to temperate Asia and southern Africa and also into northern Europe. They belong to the family Zygaenidae which has many species with very metallic-looking colours and often bizarre-shaped wings. One subfamily of Zygaenidae has species where the hind wing, instead of the normal rather rounded shape, is thin and forms long trailing streamers behind the forewings.

Many of the brightly coloured species are day fliers, their colours warning predators that they are distasteful. In Europe some of the species are of very local distribution and many are confined to limestone districts where the soil is suitable for their food-plants to grow.

Moths in a meadow

Burnets usually live in colonies, often occupying only part of a hillside or a single meadow, and the colonies may persist for a few years and then die out. In a flourishing colony, the moths are often abundant, sometimes half-a-dozen or more being seen on a single flower-head.

The burnets are all day-flying moths and are most active when the sun is shining. The flight is slow and buzzing, and when at rest the moths are sluggish and can easily be captured without a butterfly net. They are on the wing at various times from June to August.

Tubular tongues for nectar

The adult moths feed on the nectar of flowers, sitting on the flower-heads and probing the nectaries with their long tubular tongues. The caterpillars feed on the leaves of low-growing plants. The food-plants of the three common British species are trefoils and clover. The mountain burnet feeds on crowberry, and one of the other northern species on thyme.

Annual life cycle

Normally the burnets have an annual life cycle, the caterpillars feeding during the late summer, hibernating through the winter and completing their growth during the

△ Burnet moth, **Zygaena trigonellae**, drying its wings (5 × life size).

▽ The beautiful **Zygaena carniolica** is found in central and southern Europe and western Asia.

spring and early summer of the following year. The mountain burnet is exceptional in taking more than one and possibly as much as four years to complete its life-cycle. Only a short time is spent as a pupa and the adult moths probably live only two or three weeks.

The caterpillars are thick and slug-shaped, green or yellow with a regular pattern of black spots. The pupa is enclosed in a characteristic spindle-like cocoon of parchment-like silk, shining yellow or white in colour. The cocoons are usually attached to a stem of grass or some other plant, those of the commoner species being conspicuous and easy to find. After the moth has hatched the black empty pupa shell always sticks out.

Safety in nastiness

Their habits would seem to make the burnets an easy prey for birds and other insect-eating animals, since they are slow-flying, conspicuous, and make no attempt to hide, and little to evade capture. They are all very ill-tasting, however, and to some degree poisonous, so that a bird which has pecked one of them is never likely to attack another. Their conspicuous appearance is associated with this, as it is to their advantage to be easily recognisable so that predators have no difficulty in learning to avoid them. Another day-flying moth, the cinnabar *Callimorpha jacobaeae*, of Europe and western Asia, quite unrelated to the burnets, has a

Burnet moth caterpillar, magnified 8 times, feeding on trefoil, one of its food-plants.

but this did not last for a very long time.

Within seconds it was almost literally running round in circles, stopping every so often to bite at cool grass blades or to rub its beak on the grass, the bare earth, or any stick or stone it came across, while saliva dripped from its beak. From time to time it spread its wings in the manner that has come to be associated with birds that have something acrid or pungent in the mouth.

Clearly the rook was agitated and going through an unpleasant experience, one it was unlikely to forget. The bill-cleaning and

agitated movement went on for some minutes. Moreover, during that time it repeatedly attacked its companion, with whom it had just been feeding harmoniously, chasing it with vicious stabs of the beak.

phylum	**Arthropoda**
class	**Insecta**
order	**Lepidoptera**
family	**Zygaenidae**
genus	**Zygaena**

Six-spot burnet, a common European species.

Five-spot burnet moths mating on an empty cocoon that has an empty pupa shell sticking out of it.

similar red and black pattern and is also protected by having a nasty taste.

The poison of the burnet moths is discharged in the form of a yellow fluid from the region of the neck, and it contains histamine and hydrogen cyanide.

Bad taste

A rook living in an aviary with a magpie as a companion was offered a burnet moth, experimentally, to see whether it would accept or reject it. It picked up the moth, dismembered it in rook fashion, by severing the wings and biting off the head. Then it took the body of the moth into its mouth—

Previous page: Turquoise Forester moth,
Procris statices.

Copper butterfly

The wings of these butterflies have the colour and lustre of polished copper and are marked with dark spots and bands, sometimes with blue or purple as well. They are a group of small butterflies in the family Lycaenidae, and are thus allied to the blues and hairstreaks. They are widely distributed in the temperate and cold regions of the northern hemisphere, both in the Old and the New World. There are, however, three species in temperate New Zealand. Presumably their ancestors arose from the same stock as those in the northern hemisphere and in time became separated.

The caterpillars are slug-shaped and, in the majority of species, feed on various kinds of dock or sorrel. Like those of many of the blues group, the larvae of some species are attended by ants for the sake of a sweet secretion which they produce. In the case of the coppers this exudes all over the body, unlike many others of the family, which have a single orifice connected with a special gland.

There are nearly a dozen species known in Europe and North Africa, but only two were known to reach Britain; one is a familiar butterfly of open country in general, the other is an insect which unhappily became extinct. They are known respectively as the small copper and the large copper.

Small copper

This is a pretty, lively and even rather aggressive little butterfly. The males establish territories and try to chase all other butterflies away, flying out and attacking individuals of their own species and other, larger ones as well. They have no weapons and are quite incapable of injuring each other.

The small copper has an enormous range extending from Europe right across Asia to Japan, over a large part of North America and northward to beyond the Arctic Circle. It is divided into distinct subspecies in different parts of its range but they are all very similar in appearance. Some of these subspecies range into Africa. Another ranges almost as far north as any butterfly, into Ellesmere Land, and is one of the five butterflies found in Greenland.

Three generations a year

The larva feeds on dock and sorrel and the life cycle is passed through so quickly that there may be three generations in a good summer. The caterpillar is green with a brown line along the back and clothed with short greyish hairs. It is not attended by ants. The pupa is pale brown or greenish and attached to a leaf or stem of the food plant. The species overwinters as a larva but not (as in most larval hibernators) at any particular stage of its growth. The butterfly is on the wing continuously from May to October.

▷ *Small copper at rest. These far-ranging butterflies often breed three times a year.*

137

not unlike those of the small copper.

The large copper was discovered in Britain a little before 1800, in the fens of East Anglia, a habitat that was rapidly shrinking due to artificial drainage. Butterfly collecting was already a popular pastime, and the coppers were persecuted without restraint. Not only did collectors visit their haunts, but dealers encouraged the local people to capture them in all their stages for sale at prices ranging from a few pence to a shilling, rich rewards for the poor of those days. The butterfly held out for half a century, the last specimens being taken in 1847 or 1848. The British large copper could probably have been saved if a reserve had been created where it could have been secure from the greed of collectors and from destruction of its habitat, but at that time the idea had not occurred to anyone that active measures might be taken to preserve rare animals from extinction.

The large copper is still found in many parts of Europe and Asia, but the British subspecies was larger and finer than any of the Continental forms. About a thousand preserved specimens of it exist, but as a living animal it has gone for ever. The great water dock is the food plant of the large copper. The caterpillar, which is attended by ants, is green and looks like a much flattened slug. It hibernates when young, feeds in the following spring, and the butterflies appear in July and August.

Two other species, the scarce copper and the purple-edged copper, were included as British by early entomologists. It is not impossible that they once lived in Britain and became extinct before collecting became methodical and widespread.

△ A small copper shows its wing pattern while taking a meal off a sprig of heather.

▽ One of the Dutch large coppers introduced to Wood Walton Fen on great water dock plant.

Small copper larvae feed on dock and sorrel.

The small copper is exceedingly variable, and its more extreme varieties or 'aberrations' are eagerly sought by collectors. Reduction or modification of the pattern of black bands and spots produces most of the varieties, but in one of the rarest and most highly prized the copper ground colour is replaced by silvery white.

Large copper

In this species the wing span is about $1\frac{7}{10}$ in. and the male and female are very different. In the male all four wings on the upper side are brilliant burnished copper with only narrow dark borders and small central dots. The female has dark markings

Butterfly naturalisation

In 1915 a subspecies of the large copper was discovered in the province of Friesland, Holland, and named *Lycaena dispar batavus*. It resembles the extinct English race more closely than any other and the idea occurred to some British naturalists to try introducing it to the fenland nature reserves in East Anglia. It is rare in its native haunts, and some difficulty was experienced in obtaining living specimens. This was overcome, however, and the first butterflies were released by the Society for the Promotion of Nature Reserves in Wood Walton Fen, Huntingdonshire, in 1927. The experiment was successful and later was repeated at Wicken Fen, owned by the National Trust, in Cambridgeshire. The Dutch large copper is still maintained at Wood Walton and is bred artificially and released every year to supplement wild stock and to ensure against any accident to the small wild population.

phylum	**Arthropoda**
class	**Insecta**
order	**Lepidoptera**
family	**Lycaenidae**
genus & species	***Lycaena dispar*** *large copper* **L. hippothoe** *purple-edged copper* **L. phlaeas** *small copper* **L. virgauteae** *scarce copper*

Purple emperor

*A large, showy and sometimes rare butterfly, the purple emperor is named after the purple iridescence on the wings of the male, which can only be seen when viewed from a particular angle. Otherwise they are dark-brown, almost black, with a line of white patches and an inconspicuous eyespot on each hind wing. The white patches are very occasionally missing and such purple emperors are known as the variety **iole**, much sought after by collectors. The underside of the wing has an intricate pattern of brown and grey with bands of white. The female is very much like the male but lacks the iridescence and is slightly larger. Her wingspan is 3 in. compared with $2\frac{1}{2} - 2\frac{3}{4}$ in. of the males.*

Purple emperors are found locally in many parts of Europe and Asia.

Two plants needed

Purple emperors' preference for oak woods is one factor which limits their distribution since these woods become scarcer year by year due to man's activities. Purple emperors do, however, survive in woodlands that have been stripped of all tall trees. They are on the wing in July and the first half of August but even in bright weather and in places where they are known to live they are not easy to see. They are not attracted to flowers like so many other butterflies and spend most of their time around the tops of oak trees. The dull coloured females are easier to find because they descend to lay their eggs in sallow bushes. The males spend their time perching on leaves and periodically flying high across a clearing or soaring up almost out of sight on their powerful wings. Sometimes several males may be seen chasing each other in circles.

Slug-like caterpillar

Purple emperors lay their eggs on the upper surfaces of sallow leaves. Each female ranges over a considerable area, laying one egg on each leaf, although she may revisit a bush later and so lay another egg on a leaf already bearing one. Other females may also use that leaf, so it is quite possible to find several eggs on one leaf. The egg is like a minute blancmange, $\frac{1}{25}$ in. high, almost hemispherical with about 14 radially arranged ridges. At first it is green, then the base becomes purple, and just before hatching it turns black. The caterpillar emerges about a fortnight after the egg is laid. It is yellow with a black head and measures just a little over $\frac{1}{10}$ in.

After 10 days of eating the sallow leaf on which the egg was laid the caterpillar sheds its skin. It is now green, the same colour as the sallow leaf, and it looks very much like a slug, with a pair of horns projecting from the head and a body tapering to a point at the rear end.

The caterpillar continues to feed through the summer and into autumn. It grows to $\frac{1}{2}$ in. and changes to brown, so matching the autumn leaves. When not feeding it lies along the midrib of the leaf so that it is very inconspicuous. In October the caterpillar retires to a twig or a fork between two twigs, and spins a mat of fine silk on which it rests for the winter. In the following April the caterpillar changes colour back to green, and starts feeding on the fresh leaves, growing to $1\frac{3}{4}$ in. before pupating in June. Pupation takes place on the underside of the sallow leaf where it lays a mat of silk and runs more silk up the leaf stem to the twig, presumably to act as an anchor. The chrysalis hangs from the silk mat by a number of small hooks. Just before pupating the caterpillar changes to a very pale green, matching the underside of the sallow leaf, and making the chrysalis very difficult to find. The adult butterfly emerges in about 3 weeks.

Lured to the ground

Although male purple emperors spend most of their short lives in the tops of the trees, they do sometimes come down, feeding on the sap that oozes from wounded trees and sometimes on the honeydew of aphides (page 116). They also descend to the ground to drink at puddles or to feed on animal carcases or horse droppings. At one time purple emperors were caught by placing the rotting corpse of a rabbit or other animal in a woodland ride, but this method is not successful now, probably because the

Brilliant beauty — a purple emperor sunning itself on a sprig of oak leaves. This attractive butterfly is, unfortunately, not very common and is seen even more rarely than one would expect as it spends most of its time at the tops of oak trees. Although it can survive in young oak plantations, mature oak woods are becoming fewer and fewer.

The butterfly's purple colouring, possessed by the male only, is normally seen only on one wing, as in this picture. In some lights both wings are iridescent, the purple scales changing colour with the incidence of the light. There are also dark scales caused by melanic pigment.

purple emperor has become so rare. They can also be attracted by bright objects and there are several stories of male purple emperors coming down to settle on car radiators, and even flying headlong into cars as they are being driven along.

phylum	**Arthropoda**
class	**Insecta**
order	**Lepidoptera**
family	**Nymphalidae**
genus & species	*Apatura iris*

Vanessids

*The Vanessids include some of the most colourful butterflies in the northern hemisphere, and some of these have a wide distribution. The scientific name, **Vanessa**, is now restricted to the Red Admiral, although this species, and all the others here included in the popular name Vanessids, are in the same family (Nymphalidae). Vanessids have the front pair of legs reduced in size, only the rear two pairs being used for walking. They are fairly large butterflies, with a powerful flight. Most of the species resident in northern Europe pass the winter hibernating as butterflies, others are continuously brooded in the subtropics and migrate northwards in summer. Their caterpillars bear an armature of branched spines and the pupae, or chrysalises, which are suspended by the tail, are ornamental with shining metallic spots. It was the ornamentation of these pupae which led the early butterfly collectors to call them 'aurelians', from the Latin **aureus**, golden. 'Chrysalis' has a similar derivation from the Greek chrysos also meaning golden.*

Species of Vanessid are found on all continents. Generally, they are large powerful fliers. Many of the tropical species feed on ripe fruit or even on the rotting carcass of a dead animal.

Peacock

This beautiful butterfly ranges from Britain eastwards to Japan. It is resident in Britain and spends the winter hibernating in dark sheltered places, often in attics and out-houses. It is quite easy to breed peacock butterflies, by keeping them in a cage in a cool, dark room for the winter. They can then be 'tamed' before releasing them in the spring, so they will remain in the garden and will come to be fed on sugar-water. They have only one generation a year, and the habit of hibernation results in the butterfly having an unusually long life in the winged state. A peacock butterfly in captivity lived for 11 months. Its food plant is nettles.

Red Admiral

The red admiral is the popular name for a butterfly which has several subspecies. One found in Europe, Asia and the Canaries, is the familiar European one. Formerly it was believed to occur in the United States but a distinct subspecies occurs there. This is found from Canada to Mexico and on some West Indian Islands and has been introduced to Hawaii. There is even one distinct species of Red Admiral which is known only from Hawaii. Other species of Red Admiral are found in India and the Far East.

Map butterfly

There are many species of Nymphalids known as Map butterflies from the appearance of the pattern on the wings. The European Map butterfly is widespread in France and elsewhere in Europe. Attempts to introduce it to Britain have failed. It is remarkable in being represented by two distinct seasonal forms. Unlike most vanessids it overwinters as a pupa, and the butterflies which hatch in May are chequered tawny and black and look rather like fritillaries. The larvae from the eggs of these spring butterflies feed and grow rapidly,

pupate and produce in July a generation of black-and-white butterflies totally unlike their parents. The length of day during the larval stage determines which form the mature butterfly shall assume. By exposing the caterpillars to long or short 'days', using artificial light, successive generations of either form can be bred. Its food plant is entirely nettles.

Camberwell Beauty

This butterfly is known as the mourning cloak in North America. It is, like the red admiral, distributed all over the northern hemisphere, and it also goes down the Andes, in South America. In spite of its wide distribution it is a great rarity in Britain. It appears to need the severe continental winter to induce proper hibernation. It feeds on willow, poplar and birch.

Small tortoiseshell

This gay little butterfly ranges right across the Eurasian continent to Japan. It is one of the commonest species in Britain and can be seen in gardens throughout most of the spring and summer as it goes through two generations in a year. The butterflies of the second generation hibernate and reappear in spring. Its food plant is nettles.

Large tortoiseshell

Up to the first two decades of this century this butterfly was not uncommon in southern England, but it has suffered a decline and is now by far the rarest of the resident vanessids in Britain. It is still occasionally seen in Essex and Suffolk and is common in central and southern Europe. Its food consists of elm foliage.

△ *Mourning cloak—a vanessid that hibernates as an adult, feeding on the sugar-rich sap from trees when it emerges in early spring.*
△ ▷ *Bird's eye view of a small tortoiseshell.*
▷ *The most widespread butterfly in the world— the painted lady. In the spring it migrates in vast numbers from North Africa to Europe.*
◁ *The rich-hued vanessid of European summer— each year the red admiral flies north from the Mediterranean to lay its eggs.*
▽ ◁ *Peacock butterflies on a spray of* **Buddleia**, *a favourite food plant of adult butterflies.*
▽ *The tattered look of the comma provides excellent camouflage when the wings are folded.*

They taste with their toes

As already mentioned, all the nymphalid butterflies (vanessas, fritillaries, emperors and others) are 'quadrupeds', the forelegs being stunted and not used for walking. Those of the males have only two terminal joints and are brush-like. In the females these legs are more slender with four terminal joints and are only sparsely haired. They are used as sense organs, the end joints serving as organs of taste. A red admiral can distinguish, by touching with its forefeet, between pure water and a sugar solution $\frac{1}{200}$ of the strength required to be detected by the human tongue.

Spare the nettles

Farmers and people obsessed with the idea of 'tidiness' wage a relentless war on nettles, spraying them ruthlessly wherever they grow. But nettles should be allowed to grow in places that are not needed for cultivation or pasture. Five of the vanessid butterflies described here depend on nettles for their larval food. If those who aim to exterminate this plant had their way we should see much fewer gaily coloured butterflies.

Comma butterfly

The recent history in Britain of this very attractive butterfly is in curious contrast to that of the large tortoiseshell. Up to about 1920 it was confined to a small area in South Wales, but about that time it began to spread over southern England and the Midlands and has maintained this wider distribution. Like the other resident British vanessids it hibernates as a butterfly, but remains in the open in woods and hedges, sheltering under leaves instead of seeking shelter in natural hollows or buildings. When its wings are closed the coloration and irregular outline make the butterfly look like a withered leaf. Without this the butterfly would never survive the hunting of winter-hungry birds. It goes through two generations in the summer and the larva feeds on nettles and elm.

Painted Lady

This is known as the thistle butterfly in North America. It has the distinction of being the only butterfly with a world-wide distribution, without the formation of any well defined races or subspecies. The reason for this is that the urge to migrate is so powerful and persistent in this butterfly that its populations are subject to constant mixing, which of course prevents the formation of local races. In Britain and northern Europe the painted lady is a summer migrant of the same type as the red admiral. The main breeding ground of the European painted ladies is North Africa, and travellers there have witnessed the hatching of thousands of pupae among the sand dunes and the start of the butterflies' massed flight towards the Mediterranean. Its food plant is thistles.

phylum	**Arthropoda**
class	**Insecta**
order	**Lepidoptera**
family	**Nymphalidae**
genera & species	***Aglais urticae*** *small tortoiseshell* ***Araschnia levana*** *map butterfly* ***Nymphalis antiopa*** *Camberwell beauty, or mourning cloak* ***N. io*** *peacock butterfly* ***N. polychloros*** *large tortoiseshell* ***Polygonia c-album*** *comma* ***Vanessa atalanta*** *red admiral* ***V. cardui*** *painted lady or thistle butterfly, others*

Mosquito

There are 2 000 species of mosquito living everywhere from the Tropics to Arctic latitudes, often in enormous numbers. While not all are troublesome to man, some species are notorious bloodsucking pests which transmit distressing diseases such as malaria, yellow fever, elephantiasis and filariasis.

Mosquitoes are slender-bodied insects, about $\frac{1}{4}$ in. long, with a single pair of narrow wings and long slender legs. In most of them the wing veins and the rear edge of each wing are decorated with small scales. The antennae are hairy in the female and copiously feathered in the male, except in members of the subfamily Dixinae. In most species the female has a sharp tubular proboscis adapted for piercing and sucking fluids, usually blood. Exceptions to this are again found in the Dixinae, which are also unusual in having transparent larvae, known quite appropriately as phantom larvae.

Basically 'mosquito' and 'gnat' have the same meaning, the first being Spanish, the second Old English. Today many people speak of small insects that 'bite' as mosquitoes, and similar but equally small, harmless insects, especially those seen in dancing swarms, as gnats. The confusion is the same among scientists—judging from popular books on the subject—who speak of **Culex pipiens,** the commonest mosquito in Europe, as the common gnat, but otherwise restrict the use of the word 'gnat' to the Dixinae.

There are two main groups of mosquitoes, the culicines and the anophelines, represented by the genera **Culex** and **Anopheles** respectively. The wings of culicines are transparent or slightly tinted, while the wings of anophelines are usually marked with dark and light spots or patches. Another difference is that the female culicine has a pair of very short palpi beside the long proboscis while the palpi of the anopheline female are as long as the proboscis. The best way of distinguishing the two is that when resting the culicine holds its body horizontal to the surface on which it is standing and the anopheline tilts its body upwards.

Eggs in any water

Mosquitoes lay their floating eggs in water, which may be fresh, brackish or salt, according to the species. With few exceptions each species chooses a particular kind of

▷△ *Blood transfusion. An adult mosquito* **Culex pipiens** *sucks up blood through its tubular proboscis. Most of them are specialised in their habitat also at this stage, each species usually preferring a particular type of host.* (14 × *life size*)
▷▽ *Bloated with blood. A female mosquito* **Culex pipiens** *has just taken her last blood meal before she lays her eggs.*

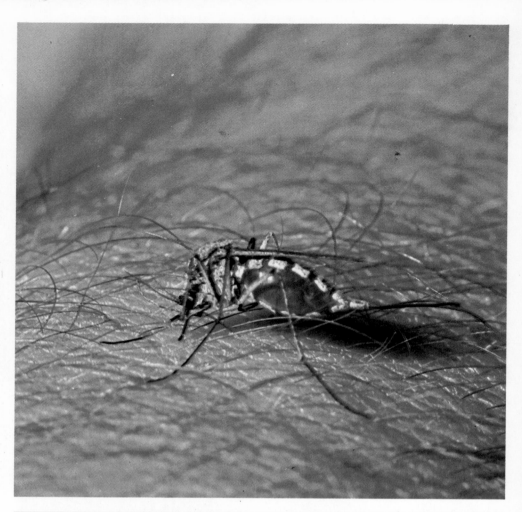

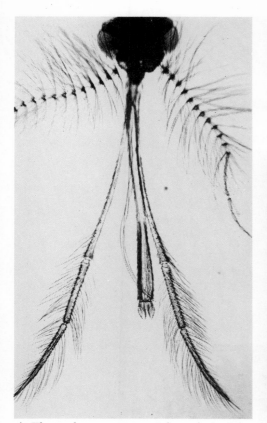

△ *The feathery antennae of the male (×60) are sensitive to sound vibrations, but only when the long hairs are erect. Some species keep them permanently erect so are always ready to mate while others erect them only at certain times of the day.* △ *Impending doom? A swarm of mosquitoes.*

watery situation, which may be the margins of ponds or lakes, in ditches, seepages, waterfilled cart ruts or hoofprints, polluted waters, water collected in holes in trees — usually at the top of a bole where branches fork — in aerial plants growing on trees or in pitcher plants. Water butts are often homes for mosquito larvae, but the eggs have even been seen in the water bowl put down for a pet dog. *Anopheles* lays single eggs, while *Culex* lays its eggs in compact masses or egg-rafts.

Each larva has a broad thorax in which all three segments are fused and an abdomen of 9 segments. The head bears the simple larval eyes and a pair of developing compound eyes. Brushes of bristles either side of it sweep fine particles of animal or plant food into the mouth, except in those larvae that extract dissolved food from the water, or prey on other insect larvae, usually other mosquito larvae. The thorax and abdomen are also decorated with long bristles. At the tip of the abdomen are four gills and a breathing siphon which can be pushed through the surface film of water to take in air. Some larvae feed on the bottom, others nearer the surface. They swim with twisting movements of the body, coiling and uncoiling spasmodically. Mosquitoes rest just beneath the surface hanging down more or less vertically. At the slightest disturbance of the water they quickly swim down but, after a while, they must return to hang from the surface film in order to breathe.

Lively pupae

Larval life lasts about a week in most species, depending on temperature, but in those feeding on other insects it is prolonged, with usually only one generation a year. The pupae are active but do not feed, and the pupal life is short, at the most a few days. Pupae are typically bulky, having a large rounded head and thorax combined, with a pair of breeding siphons on top, and the abdomen more or less curled around it. In the last stages of development the pupa rises to the surface of the water, its hard outer skin splits, and the adult mosquito pulls itself out of the pupal husk and takes to the air.

The love call

Soon after leaving their pupal skins, the adults mate, after which the males die. The females must take a meal for their eggs to develop, either of blood or, in some species, nectar or sap. A few can manage on food stored during the larval stage. Some species of mosquitoes take the blood of mammals, others the blood of birds or even of amphibians. Sometimes a female will take another drink of blood after laying.

In the interval between leaving the pupal skin and mating the mosquitoes must rest. If a male takes to the wing too soon, his wings do not beat fast enough to proclaim him a male and other males will try to mate with him. He may lose some of his legs in the process. If a female takes off too soon, her wingbeats will be so slow the males will not recognize her until she has been in the air for a while and the pace of her wingbeats has quickened.

Surviving hard times

In temperate latitudes the females of some species pass the winter in sheltered places, such as caves, hollow trees or houses, especially in cellars. A few species lay their eggs in dry places which will be flooded in late winter or spring. These eggs can withstand dry and cold conditions, and in some instances will not hatch successfully without them. When the female of *Anopheles gambiae*, a malaria-carrier, lives in desert areas, she gorges herself with blood and then shelters in huts, cracks in rocks or in rodent burrows, until the rains come. The dryness delays her egg-laying. Other species of desert mosquitoes lay thick-shelled eggs able to hatch even after 1 − 2 years, and in some cases up to 10 years later.

War on mosquitoes

Mosquitoes have many enemies. Airborne mosquitoes are eaten by birds such as swallows and flycatchers hunting on the wing. The larvae and pupae are eaten by small fish. The guppy, called the millions fish because of its large numbers in its native home, is used to control mosquito larvae and has been introduced into rivers in infested areas to keep down their numbers. Another control is to spray oil on waters of ponds and swamps. A small amount of oil will spread to cover a wide area with a thin film which prevents the larval mosquito from breathing at the surface of the water.

Homing on victims

When a female mosquito takes blood from a malarial patient, she will pass the malaria parasite by her saliva on to the next victim whose blood she sucks. It is the same with yellow fever, although a different species of mosquito is involved, and with elephantiasis, filariasis, and other mosquito-borne diseases. There are several defensive measures which can be taken to keep the mosquitoes away. This is usually achieved by netting or by deterrents, or by killing the larvae or the mosquitoes, or changing the habitat and

143

reducing the number of people carrying the disease who act as a reservoir for further infection. The use of deterrents depends on the behaviour of a mosquito in homing on its victim. An increase in the carbon dioxide in the air, as from human breathing, makes a female mosquito take off and fly upwind. As she draws near her victim the slight increase in temperature and humidity directs her more certainly towards her target until she can see where she needs to land. In these later stages the concentration of carbon dioxide is also greater, but certain chemicals (deterrents) will confuse her and make her swerve away.

Mysterious outbreaks

The ague was once prevalent in Europe but was stamped out largely by the draining of the marshes. When soldiers serving in the tropics during the First World War returned home after contracting malaria, it was feared they might act as a reservoir for malaria (or ague). With the air traffic of today there once again is the fear that infected mosquitoes may be introduced into countries at present free from their diseases, and steps must be taken against them. Thirty years ago an African mosquito *Anopheles gambiae* found its way to Brazil, and 60 000 people died before the malaria was brought under control. In the Second World War, in Colombia, yellow fever suddenly struck villages where it had been unknown. In due course it was traced to the monkeys living high in trees which formed a reservoir, the carrier being a mosquito whose larvae lived in water in aerial plants growing in the tree tops. Woodmen felling some of these trees were attacked by mosquitoes from pupae in the aerial plants. The disease was then spread by a species of mosquito living at ground level.

Odd behaviour

Not all mosquitoes are troublesome; some are highly interesting. The larvae of *Mansonia* do not need to swim to the surface of the water to breathe. They have a saw-like apparatus for piercing water plant roots and drawing off the air contained in them. The females of another species *Leicesteria* lay their eggs onto their hindlegs which they then push through small holes in bamboo stems where water has collected. The eggs fall into the water and later hatch. A New Zealand mosquito *Opifex* has unusual mating behaviour. The males fly over water waiting for pupae to come to the surface to release the females within. They then mate with the females before they can get out. A mosquito *Harpagomyia* of Africa and southern Asia settles on tree trunks waiting for ants to pass. It then flies over to an ant, holds the ant's body with its front pair of legs and does not let the ant go until it has brought up a drop of food from its crop. The oddest story of all is, however, of a tropical American carrier of yellow fever which seems to prefer laying its eggs in water in flower vases, even those in hospital wards. In dealing with an outbreak of yellow fever in New Orleans it was found that the mosquitoes were breeding in the water in flower vases placed on the graves of the unfortunate yellow fever victims.

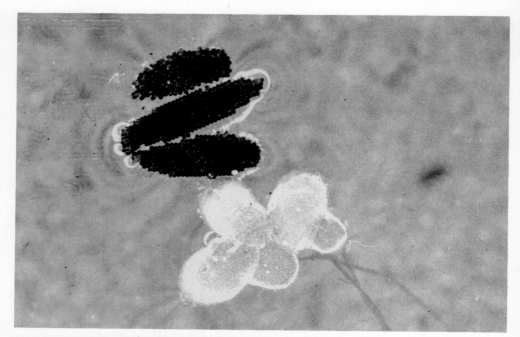

△△ *Life afloat. Compact rafts of the eggs of the common gnat* **Culex** *beside a duckweed plant. Between them mosquitoes lay their eggs in almost every type of water, although the majority live in fresh water. Each individual species is, however, very limited in its habitat.*
△ *Living down under? A mosquito larva hangs from the surface in still water. It breathes through the respiratory tubes which reach up to the surface. The head, thorax and abdomen are clearly visible as are the mouth brushes which hang like a drooping moustache and sweep particles into the mouth. (7 × life size)*
▷ *Bulky but active. Mosquitoes spend only a few days in this pupal stage, whether the life cycle lasts a year or 10 days. (13 × life size)*

phylum	**Arthropoda**
class	**Insecta**
order	**Diptera**
family	**Culicidae**

A housefly cleans itself by rubbing its first pair of legs together. This common fly spreads disease mainly as a result of its indiscriminate feeding habits. Bacteria may be carried on the legs or body, or in the proboscis and so be exuded onto food with the next flow of saliva.

Housefly

Many different kinds of flies come into houses. Some are accidental intruders that buzz on the window panes trying to get out into the open air again. Others enter houses in the autumn to hibernate in attics and roof-spaces. But there are two kinds that make our houses their home. One is the housefly, the other is the lesser housefly. The first is stoutly built and in both sexes the abdomen is yellowish or buff. Lesser houseflies are smaller and more slender, the females dull greyish, the males similar but with a pair of semi-transparent yellow patches at the base of the abdomen. The two are also distinguished by a difference in the veins of the wings which can easily be seen with a lens. This difference separates the two species regardless of sex.

Both have a wide distribution, the housefly being found throughout the tropics as well as in almost all inhabited temperate regions.

Kiss-in-the-ring flight

Houseflies pass their adult lives in houses, flying about the rooms and crawling over food that is left exposed. Both species breed in the sort of refuse that accumulates around the dwellings of people who live unhygienically, but their habits differ in detail. Lesser houseflies appear earlier in the season than houseflies, which build up their numbers rather slowly after the winter and are not usually abundant until July. The males of lesser houseflies fly in a very distinctive way. They choose a spot in a room, often beneath a hanging lamp or similar 'landmark', and fly as if they were following the sides of a triangle or quadrilateral, hovering momentarily at the corners and turning sharply at them; a single fly will continue to follow the same course for long periods. If, as often happens, more

than one fly is patrolling in the same area, one of them will intercept the other and the two whirl together for an instant and then part again. The expression 'playing kiss-in-the-ring' aptly describes this activity, but they are in fact all males, and always lesser houseflies.

Flies in summer—and winter

The breeding habits of the two species are similar but the larva of the lesser housefly prefers food rich in nitrogenous compounds, such as urine or bird droppings. These flies are nearly always abundant where chickens are kept. The larvae of the housefly are less particular. Manure and compost heaps, the night soil from old-fashioned privies and house refuse of any kind all provide them with breeding-grounds.

The eggs are laid on the larval food, and the adult flies also feed in places of this kind. The eggs are white, about $\frac{1}{25}$ in. long and a female housefly may lay as many as 900 in batches of about 150. They hatch in as little as 8 hours if it is very warm, otherwise in 1–3 days. The white legless maggots feed rapidly and may reach full size in under 2 days, but can live for 8 weeks in colder and less favourable conditions. At 15°C/60°F houseflies will breed continuously throughout the year, taking about 3 weeks from egg to adult, but in the tropics the cycle is completed in a week. The pupa is formed in an oval brown capsule called the puparium, which consists of the last larval skin; instead of being shed at pupation this is retained and plays the same part as the moth cocoon.

The lesser housefly has a similar life cycle, but its larva is very different in appearance, being flattened and beset with rows of short branched tentacle-like processes on the upper surface of the body.

Flies disappear in winter time, and the question where they go is often asked—and it once formed the theme of a popular song. There seems no simple answer to it. Houseflies may hibernate as adults or continue breeding slowly in warm places, especially

in buildings where cattle are kept. Probably the fly has different adaptations for wintering in different parts of its range. In warm regions it breeds all the year round.

Sucking up their food

Adults of both species feed by settling on moist organic matter of almost any kind and sucking up nutrient liquid from it. If the material is dry the fly regurgitates a drop of liquid on to it and sucks up the resultant solution. Crude sewage and a bowl of sugar are equally attractive and the insect may fly straight from one to the other. The feeding apparatus consists of a short sucking proboscis expanded at the end into a sponge-like organ with which the fly mops up its liquid food. Flies that have overfilled their stomachs will often regurgitate on any surface on which they happen to be resting, leaving little dirty spots.

People will sometimes assure you that they have been bitten by a housefly. The mistake is excusable because the stable fly *Stomoxys calcitrans* looks almost exactly like a housefly. Its mouthparts are, however, very different, consisting of a stiff piercing organ, and they feed, as horseflies do, by sucking blood. Their bite is quite painful and they can penetrate one's skin through a thick sock. The stable fly breeds in dung mixed with straw and is far less common now than when horses were kept in large numbers.

Bearers of disease

The most important disease-carrying insects are those which feed on our blood, taking micro-organisms from infected people and injecting them into the blood of healthy ones. Examples are the tsetse fly and some mosquitoes. Houseflies do not feed in this way, but by feeding on excrement and exposed foodstuffs they are potential carriers of gastro-intestinal diseases such as dysentery. Houseflies taken from a slum district have been found to carry on average over $3\frac{1}{2}$ million bacteria per fly, and over a million in clean districts. These are not all disease bacteria, but some of them are very likely to be. Infants and small children seem to suffer most from fly-borne disease. In a tropical village infant mortality dropped in one year from 22·7 to 11·5 per cent when flies were controlled by an insecticide.

It is not difficult to kill flies in vast numbers by spraying such substances as DDT and chlordane on the places where they feed and breed but they have a remarkable capacity for developing resistance to specific poisons. No individual fly develops resistance during its lifetime, but some will almost always survive a spraying and these will include individuals having, by an accident of nature, some degree of immunity to the pesticide being used. This immunity is inherited by their offspring, in varying degrees, and the most resistant of these will again survive and breed. Selection of this kind continues with every generation until the insecticide is useless in any concentration at which it is safe to use. The process is exactly the same as the natural selection through which evolution has taken its course. These examples of acquired resistance in insects are in fact examples of very rapid evolutionary change, and they form one of the most compelling arguments against relying too much upon pesticides in our efforts to control harmful insects.

Control of houseflies is best achieved by depriving them of breeding places. The modern civilised way of life has already gone a long way towards doing this with water-borne sanitation, the use of covered dustbins and the decline of the horse as a means of transport.

class	**Insecta**
order	**Diptera**
family	**Muscidae**
genera & species	***Musca domestica*** *housefly* ***Fannia canicularis*** *lesser housefly*

Top right : Photomicrograph of a leg. The last segment has a pair of claws and two suction pads which help the fly to walk on smooth surfaces (× 60).
Bottom right : Housefly just about to land.
▽ Wings of housefly (top) and lesser housefly (bottom). The differences in venation can be used to distinguish the two types of fly.

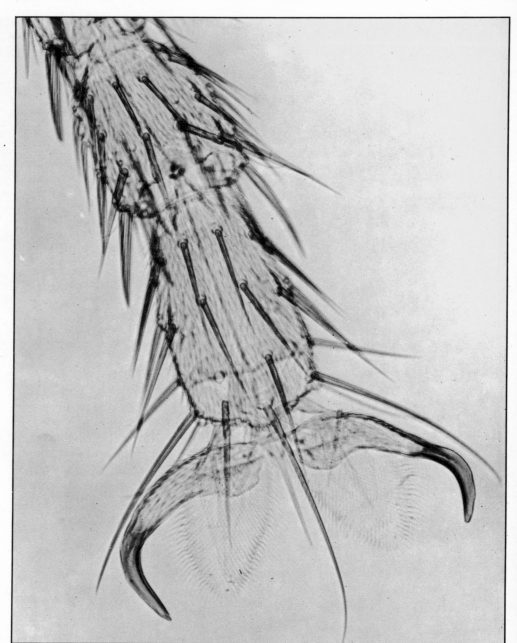

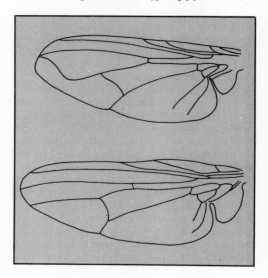

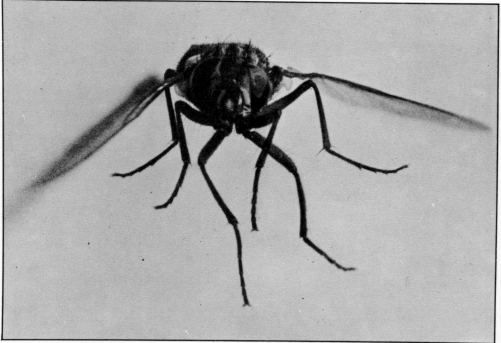

146

Bumble-bee

Bumble-bees are rather like honeybees (see page 149) except that they have a larger body which is covered with stiff yellow, orange or red hairs. The bumble-bee also has a sting which it can use to inject venom into the body of an enemy. The sting is a modified ovipositor—a tube-like organ used by other insects to deposit their eggs.

Bumble-bees are also known as 'humble-bees'. Both names come from the lazy humming sound made by the bee as it flies from one flower to another.

The bumble-bee is found all over the world. Most species live in the tropical or sub-tropical zones but they can also be found in places as far apart as Arctic Canada and Tierra del Fuego, and the equivalent of this range in the Old World. They are not native to Australasia, but were introduced there when settlers found that none of the local bees would pollinate the red clover plant which they had introduced. So the bumble-bee was brought in to do the job.

Buzzing around from flower to flower

Under a microscope the hindleg of a bumble-bee is an interesting sight. The outer face of the 'shin' is flat and polished but along each side there is a row of stiff bristles. These bristles make up what is called the pollen basket. If you watch a bumble-bee flying from one flower to another it is quite easy to see the large yellow balls of pollen attached to its hindlegs. When the bee forces its way into a flower the pollen is rubbed off onto its body hairs. The bee then brushes the pollen from its body, moistens it with a little nectar and sticks it onto the pollen basket. When it gets back to the nest it uses its forelegs to remove the balls of pollen from this basket and put them into the egg-cell.

The bumble-bee is attracted to the flower by the nectar, which it sucks up through a special extendible tube. The nectar is then stored away in the crop or honey stomach.

Flowers and bees depend upon each other for their existence. The bee benefits from the pollen and the flowers benefit by being 'cross-pollinated'. This cross-pollination occurs when some of the pollen from one flower is rubbed off onto another flower, thus fertilising it.

It is for this reason, to attract bees rather than people, that flowers have evolved their attractive colours and scents.

The life cycle of a queen bee

Usually it is a pure accident if an insect meets one of her offspring. This is because most insects lay their eggs and then leave them to hatch out by themselves.

Some insects, however, are different. They are called social insects. This kind of insect stays with her offspring and they, in turn, stay with her and help look after her next brood. Wasps, honeybees and ants are all well-known examples of social insects. In their case thousands of individuals live in one nest. Most of them are sexless or, rather, under-developed females. These workers care for the breeding female, the queen, and for her eggs and larvae. Bumble-bees are social insects too, but their communal life is not as well developed as the others. There are fewer workers in the colony and they all die before the winter.

The life of a bumble-bee colony begins in autumn. A young female bumble-bee leaves the nest, mates and finds a sheltered spot where she can spend the winter hibernating. When spring comes—the actual date depends upon the species—the young queen emerges and suns herself until she is fully active. Then off she flies in search of pollen and nectar from the spring flowers. The queen needs pollen because it contains large amounts of protein which is used to build up in her ovaries the eggs to be laid later.

Soon the queen starts looking for a suitable place to build her nest. She might take over the abandoned nest of a fieldmouse, a vole, or a hedgehog. Or she might pick somewhere else: a disused bird's nest, a thatched roof, a bale of hay or even a discarded mattress. Her favourite sites are along hedgerows and banks or in old, neglected corners of fields and gardens. Nowadays it is not easy for the queen bee to find this kind of place. Modern intensive and mechanised farming demands that these unproductive corners be ploughed up so that every square foot of ground pays its way. The result is that bumble-bees, which are in a sense vital to the pollination of crops, are themselves becoming scarcer.

The queen usually builds her nest at the end of a tunnel. The tunnel may be several feet long, if she has used an old mouse nest, but some species prefer tunnels only a few inches long, so they build their nests in thatch or similar places. Some kinds of bumble-bees, known as carder-bees, even manage to build their nests on the surface. They do this by combing grass and other material into a tight, closely-woven ball.

If the queen has taken over the nest from a former occupant there is always plenty of nest material readily available. She fashions this into a small inner chamber lined with only the finest grass and roots. She stays in here for a day or two drying it out with her body heat. Insects are cold-blooded, but the larger ones generate enough heat, especially with their flight muscles, to keep their bodies a few degrees above air temperature outside the nest.

Food in a 'honey pot'

By now the eggs are developing inside the queen bee. She begins to make an egg-cell out of wax. The wax is secreted from between the plates on the underside of her abdomen. She goes out to collect pollen which she stores in the egg-cell, in which 8—14 eggs are laid. The cell is then covered

*Male mating with queen bee **Bombus agrorum**. Young males are produced at the end of the season. After mating the queen finds a sheltered spot where she can spend the winter hibernating until the spring.*

*Bumble-bee queen, **B. hortorum**, incubating her first batch of brood which have reached the pupal stage. She stores surplus nectar in a wax 'honey pot' near the entrance of the nest to provide food in bad weather.*

with a cap of wax. The queen spends some of her time settled on top of the eggs to keep them warm. She also goes out feeding and brings home any surplus nectar which she stores in a 'honey pot' near the entrance to the nest. The 'honey pot' is made of wax and is about ¾ in. high and ½ in. across. It provides a source of food when the weather is too bad for the queen to go out foraging.

When the larvae begin to hatch out of the eggs. they are just helpless maggots with very little in the way of legs or sense organs. They do nothing except feed on the pollen which has been stored in the egg-cell and on the mixture of nectar and pollen which their mother regurgitates to them. But they grow amazingly quickly on this diet. They shed their skins several times and then spin a cocoon and pupate.

At this point the queen carefully removes the wax from around the cocoons and makes it into new egg-cells. She puts these on top of the cocoons and lays the next batch of eggs in them. Eventually the first brood emerge from their cocoons as fully developed workers. They spend a day or two drying out while their wings expand and harden. Then they are ready to go out collecting food and to tend the next batch of larvae.

Before long a whole colony of several hundred workers has been built up. The queen, however, never becomes a helpless egg-laying machine as happens with ants and termites. She can still make egg-cells and feed larvae although she hardly ever leaves the nest to forage.

Towards the end of the summer, some of the eggs produce males and fertile females. The males develop by parthenogenesis — that is to say, from unfertilised eggs. The females, the next generation of queens, appear at first to be exactly the same as the sterile female workers but they grow much larger and eventually leave the nest to mate with the males. The males differ from other bumble-bees by having larger antennae,
which they use to locate the females. They do not have a sting.

Once the old queen has produced the males and the new queens she stops laying worker eggs. Gradually the whole colony dies out. After mating the males also die. It is winter again and only the young queens are left to survive through to spring.

Bumble-bees fighting for their lives

Bumble-bees have many enemies, large and small. The worst ones are insect-eating birds like the bee-eater, but there are plenty of others. Badgers or skunks and other mammals will dig up bees' nests both for the honey and for the bees themselves.

Naturalists once observed a skunk scratching at a nest until the irate inhabitants flew out. The skunk caught each one in its forepaws and killed it by rubbing it against the ground.

Fieldmice and shrews also attack bumble-bee nests, and among the smaller animals that are enemies of the bees are robber flies. They grapple the bees with their legs and suck their blood. Then there are the 'mites' which live in the air-sacs or 'lungs' of the bees and also suck their juices. Another enemy is the wax moth. It lays its eggs in bumble-bee nests and its caterpillars ruin the egg-cells by burrowing through them.

The cuckoo-bee is a close relative of the bumble-bee and in its own way another enemy. Cuckoo-bees do not have pollen baskets with which to collect stores of pollen. So instead they invade the nests of bumble-bees and lay their eggs there. The eggs develop into males and females, but not workers, and they have to be tended by the bumble-bee workers.

In a fight the bumble-bee will defend itself by biting and stinging. It rolls onto its back, with its jaws open and sting protruding, and sometimes squirts venom into the air. Its sting is not barbed, like the sting of a honeybee, so it can be withdrawn from the corpse of an enemy and used again.

Economic importance

Charles Darwin began many controversies with his famous book *On the Origin of Species*. One of the things he mentioned in the book was that only bumble-bees visit the flowers of the red clover. This is because the red clover has a long, narrow flower and other bees do not have long enough tongues to reach the nectar which lies at the base of the flowers.

Darwin pointed out that if bumble-bees became rare or extinct the red clover would also die out. This would have serious economic effects, he said, because cattle are fed on red clover.

He went on to quote a Mr H Newman who said that more than two-thirds of bumble-bee nests in England are destroyed by mice. He claimed that bumble-bee nests were more common near villages and towns, where cats were plentiful. Therefore a large number of cats would mean a larger crop of clover because the cats would eat the mice who killed the bees.

Later a German scientist intervened to remark that a large number of cats would be good for England's economy because he considered England's wealth to be based on her cattle.

In a true Darwinian spirit, TH Huxley then stepped in to supply the final link. He suggested that, since old-maids were very fond of cats, the sensible way to strengthen the economy of the country would be to increase the number of old-maids. Less weddings and more spinsters was the short answer, according to Huxley.

class	**Insecta**
order	**Hymenoptera**
family	**Bombidae**
genus	*Bombus*

A batch of cocoons, two of which have been cut open to show the pupae inside. These will emerge as fully developed workers and will then spend a day or two drying out while their wings expand and harden (8 × lifesize).

*When the temperature of their nests becomes too high some of the workers fan currents of air with their wings to cool the nests (**B. ogrorum**).*

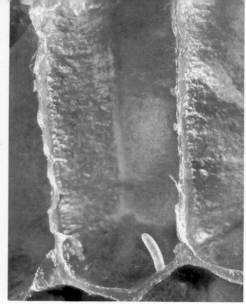

Left: A tree-suspended nest of wild bees. Centre: A queen struggles out of her cell. Right: Each egg is laid in a hexagonal cell.

Honeybee

*Any of the four species of social bees belonging to the genus **Apis** can be called honeybees but the name is most usually associated with the European domestic bee **Apis mellifera**, sometimes called the western honeybee. This differs from all other social bees and social wasps of temperate climates in forming colonies that survive the winter by living on reserve stores of food, so a particular dwelling site or nest may be occupied for an indefinite length of time. In social wasps and bumble bees all the members of the colony die at the end of the summer except the fertilised females or queens, which hibernate and found new colonies in the following spring.*

In the colonies of social bees, wasps and ants there are two kinds of females. The fertile females are called 'queens' and the sterile females are the 'workers', the latter doing all the work of maintaining the economy of the colony. In the wasps, most bees and some ants, the egg-laying organ or ovipositor of both types of female is transformed to a sting, connected with a poison gland. In the queens the eggs are extruded from an opening at the base of the sting.

Bees have been kept for their honey by man for many hundreds of years. Throughout most of history this has been mainly a matter of inducing them to make colonies in hollow receptacles of various kinds, such as earthenware pots, logs and straw baskets or 'skeps', and then robbing them of their honey. Until recently their breeding has been entirely uncontrolled and even now they are not domesticated in the same way as dogs, cattle, or even silkworms.

Household chores

The great majority of European honeybees are now living in hives although wild colonies may be found, almost always in hollow trees. In midsummer a strong colony normally contains one queen, 50 000 to 60 000 workers and a few hundred males or drones. The expectation of life of a worker bee at this time is only 4—6 weeks and her span is divided into two periods. For just under 3 weeks after emerging from the pupa the worker's duties lie within the hive, where she is fed at first by older bees, but later feeds herself from the stores of honey and pollen. Her first spell of work is as nursemaid to the developing larvae, to whom she passes on a great deal of the food she eats, partly by direct regurgitation and partly by giving them a jelly-like secretion from certain salivary glands in her head. By the time she is about 12 days old her wax glands have developed and she turns to building and repairing the comb of geometrically arranged cells in which the larvae are reared and food is stored. At this time she also goes out for short flights around the hive, learning the landmarks by which to guide herself home when she ventures farther afield.

From about 12 days to 3 weeks old she takes over the nectar and pollen brought in by returning foragers, converting the former to honey and storing it away. At the same time she helps to keep the hive tidy, carrying outside dead bees and other debris. At 3 weeks old she is ready to go out foraging herself for nectar, pollen, water and resin, which are the four substances needed for the hive's economy. The last is used to make a sort of varnish-like cement called 'propolis' with which crevices and any small openings in the hive are sealed up.

Searching for nectar

In searching for nectar-yielding flowers the worker bee is guided by her senses of smell and sight. Bees have good colour vision but it differs from our own. They cannot see red at all but can see ultraviolet 'colour', invisible to us but revealed by photography by ultraviolet light. Bees guide themselves to and from the hive by reference to the angle of the sun, or of polarised light from the sky, and have a time sense which enables them to compensate for the continuous change in the sun's position.

Foraging is very hard work and after 2—3 weeks of it the worker is worn out and dies. Workers hatched in the autumn have a much longer life before them, as they build up food reserves in their bodies and their activity is reduced through the winter. They keep warm by huddling together in a mass and feeding on the honey that they have stored.

The queen rules her great horde of daughters, not by example or wise counsel, but by secreting from her body a substance whose presence or absence controls their behaviour. Her chief role, however, is egg-laying, and at midsummer she may be laying 1 500 eggs a day, totalling more than the weight of her own body. This enormous fecundity is needed to compensate for the shortness of the workers' lives.

The idle drones

Mating with and fertilising the queens is the only useful part played in honeybee economy by the drones. During summer they usually live 4—5 weeks and are fed by the workers, not even seeking their own food among the flowers. In autumn the drones remaining in the colony are turned outside to die of starvation or chill.

New colonies are founded by what is known as swarming. As a preliminary to this extra queens are produced in the hive and then large numbers of workers, accompanied by some drones and usually one queen, leave the hive and fly together for some distance. Then they settle in a large cluster and search for a suitable place, where a new colony is made by some of the workers. At this stage they can easily be persuaded to settle down in artificial quarters of any kind merely by shaking the swarm, with its attendant queen, into a suitable receptacle, such as a beehive.

Natural and artificial breeding

Queens may be produced in a hive in response to ageing of the mother queen or to the urge to swarm. In either case they fly out to seek mates when they are about a week old. A drone that mates with a queen condemns himself to death. The reason for this is that his genital organs become so firmly fixed in the queen's body that they are torn out when the two bees part, and he dies almost immediately. The sperm is stored by the queen in an internal sac called the spermatheca, and sperms are released to fertilise the eggs as she lays them. Here there is a strange departure from the condition normally found in animals. All eggs that are fertilised produce females, either workers or queens; drones are only produced from eggs that develop without being fertilised.

The larva and pupa stages of honeybees (collectively known as the 'brood') are passed in the wax cells into which the eggs are laid, one in each cell. The larvae are entirely helpless and are fed by the workers. The development of a worker bee takes 21 days, 3 as an egg, 6 as a larva and 12 as a pupa.

The natural mating behaviour of queen and drone bees makes any control of pairing and breeding impossible, but in recent years a technique for artificially inseminating chosen queens with sperm from chosen drones has been developed. It is a difficult process requiring delicate manipulation under a microscope, but by this means selected strains of bees can now be bred.

'Common' and 'royal' food

The natural food of bees consists of nectar and pollen, the nectar supplying the energy-producing sugar and the pollen being a source of protein. The bees also make honey from nectar and store it for food. It is untrue to say that bees suck honey from flowers; nectar and honey are chemically distinct and the latter is much more concentrated. The larvae are fed partly on a mixture of nectar or honey and pollen and partly on a secretion from various glands of the young workers, the substance that is often called 'royal jelly'. When a fertilised egg is laid in a normal sized cell the larva is fed at first on jelly and later on pollen and honey, and it develops into a worker. When production of queens is needed the workers make larger cells into which the reigning queen lays ordinary fertilised eggs. The larvae from these, however, are fed until they are fully grown on royal jelly alone and they develop into queens. Drone larvae are fed similarly to those of workers but for 2 more days, 8 instead of 6.

Bees will readily drink a solution of sugar in water and are often fed on this during the winter by bee keepers who take most of their stored honey but are also concerned to keep their bees alive.

Enemies and disease

In spite of their stings bees are preyed upon by birds, dragonflies and some kinds of wasps. Certain moths called wax moths lay their eggs in the hives and the larvae live on wax, pollen and general comb debris, doing serious damage if they are at all numerous. The big death's-head hawk moth is said to invade colonies and steal the honey, piercing the wax comb with its short, stiff proboscis. It was called the 'Bee Tyger' by the early entomologists.

The greatest menace to honeybees, however, is disease and starvation.

Fierce relatives

Only four species of the genus *Apis* are known, and one of them, the eastern honeybee *Apis indica*, is so similar to *Apis mellifera* it is sometimes regarded as a subspecies. It is domesticated in tropical Asia.

Both the other species inhabit the eastern tropics. The giant honeybee *Apis dorsata* is a large bee which makes enormous hanging combs in the open. An overhanging surface is chosen at a considerable height from the ground. Large branches overhanging cliffs and buildings, especially water towers, are favourite sites for colonies. These bees may be dangerous if molested and there are records of people being attacked and stung to death. Nevertheless the Dyaks of Borneo climb by night with smoking torches, throw down the combs and gather the honey.

The little honeybee *Apis florea* is by contrast an inoffensive little insect, reluctant to use its sting. A colony consists of a single comb the size of the palm of a man's hand, which contains only 1 or 2 oz. of honey.

In tropical America stingless bees of the genus *Trigona* (not closely related to the Old World honeybees) make large colonies in hollow logs and similar places and they used to be domesticated for their honey by the Maya Indians of Mexico.

phylum	**Arthropoda**
class	**Insecta**
order	**Hymenoptera**
family	**Apidae**

A drone makes landfall beside the queen, who is surrounded by workers. From her body the queen secretes a substance whose presence or absence controls the behaviour of the great horde of her daughter-workers, who supply the hive or colony.

Method in their madness: this is a workers' conference, carried out in dance language. To tell each other where flower-nectar is to be found, worker bees have evolved two sorts of dance: a round dance for nearby nectar and a tail-wagging dance for distant nectar.

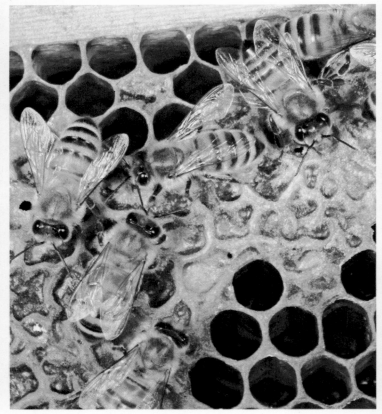

Wasp

To most people a wasp recalls the black-and-yellow insect often abundant enough in summer to be a nuisance, but in its broader sense the term 'wasp' includes any of the stinging Hymenoptera that is not a bee or an ant.

The common wasp **Vespula vulgaris** and the German wasp **V. germanica** are equally common in Europe, and so alike that the workers are difficult to distinguish, though the queens can be separated by the pattern of their yellow and black markings. Except to entomologists these two are just 'wasps', without any thought of there being more than one species. Almost all that is said here jointly concerns both.

The nearest European relative to the wasp is the hornet **Vespa crabro**, and they are more distantly related to the paper wasps **Polistes**. Their American equivalents, with similar habits, are known colloquially as 'yellowjackets'.

Four other species of **Vespula** are found in Europe, all very similar in appearance to the two common kinds. The red wasp **Vespula rufa** also nests underground, but the tree wasp **V. sylvestris** and the Norwegian wasp **V. norvegica** hang their nests in trees and bushes. Finally there is the cuckoo wasp **V. austriaca** whose queen enters the nest of a red wasp, kills some of the workers and supplants the queen. The parasitic invader's brood is reared by the red wasp workers, the offspring of the parasite consisting entirely of fertile males and females.

▽ *Lover of liquids – a wasp feeding.*
Adult wasps feed on nectar, fruit and tree sap.

Fear-inflicting German wasp. Wasps usually sting only when annoyed or if their nest is approached.

Elaborate paper building

The history of a wasps' nest really begins in the autumn of the year previous to its construction, when the big queen wasps leave the nests where they were hatched, mate and then hide themselves, to pass the winter in hollow trees, sheds and attics. The queen finds a rough beam or piece of sacking, clamps her jaws onto a fibre and hangs dormant for six or seven months. She emerges in late spring and seeks a crack in the ground or an old mouse's hole running under a tree root. Just below this she digs out a chamber, removing the earth in her jaws. Then she flies repeatedly to and from a fence post or dead tree, each time bringing home a little pellet of paste made by rasping away the wood and moistening the resultant material with saliva. This substance is plastered on to the underside of the root, where it hardens to form a kind of cardboard or paper. A little curved canopy is fixed onto this foundation and a paper stalk is made, pointing down from the centre of the canopy. A cluster of hexagonal cells, also of paper, is then made round the stalk, with their open ends downward. The queen lays an egg in each then encloses this first comb in a bag of paper about as big as a golf ball, with a hole at its lower end.

Building a city

All this time the queen has been feeding on nectar. When the eggs hatch into small white larvae she divides her time between feeding them on the juices of chewed-up insects—they are growing and so require a protein diet—and adding more cells to the comb, enlarging the enclosing bag as she does so. By the time the larvae from the earliest eggs have passed through the pupal stage to produce the first workers, she may have added a storey to her house, built below the first and hanging by little stalks of paper. To make room for the growing nest the queen may have to excavate more earth and carry it away.

When the worker wasps, which are non-reproductive females, appear in quantity, they take over from the queen the job of extending and enlarging their home. New storeys are added, one below the other, increasing to the maximum diameter of the nest and then decreasing again to give it a roughly spherical shape. Quantities of earth are removed by the workers and wood pulp is brought back for construction. The anchorage to the root is strengthened as the bulk and weight of the nest increases, and struts and stays are made between it and the surrounding earth. The queen stays at home, fed by her sexless daughters, who must also bring home animal food for all the growing larvae. As each cell is completed she places an egg in it until a population of as many as 5 000 wasps, or more in very big nests, is built up and maintained. The total number of the queen's offspring that hatch, live and die in the service of the nest throughout a summer may be five times this number.

Make do and mend

When complete the nest is a hollow sphere 8—9 in. wide, containing 6—10 horizontal combs which extend more or less right across it. The nest is comparable to a house built of bricks and mortar, yet there is a difference: although the nest has a basic external form, the inside is continually being nibbled away and repulped to be added, together with fresh pulp, to the outside and to the expanding combs, so the whole structure is constantly changing.

At the end of the summer a generation of males and functional females is produced. The latter are the queen wasps, similar to workers but larger; the males are about the same size as the workers but have much longer antennae. Eggs which produce workers and queens are always fertilised by spermatozoa from the store which the queen acquired at mating and keeps in her body. Males are produced from unfertilised eggs, from which the queen withholds sperm as she lays them. After mating the males soon die and the queens hibernate. At the end of the summer the workers become lazy and cease to maintain the economy of the nest, and they and the old queen die with the first frosts of autumn.

The workers feed on nectar and fruit juices and also accept drops of liquid exuded by the larvae. The larvae and queen are fed by the workers on the juices of captured insects; wasps destroy great numbers of bluebottle flies.

The larva is a white legless grub and it maintains its position in the upside-down cell by pressing its body against the sides. When fully grown it closes the cell by spinning a papery cover across the mouth. During its life its excrement accumulates at the end of the intestine and is voided all at once in the last larval skin when it changes into a soft white pupa. The wasp emerges 3—4 weeks after the eggs were laid.

Guests and parasites

A hoverfly *Volucella* enters wasps' nests and lays its eggs without any interference from the wasps. Its curious prickly larvae play a useful part in the nest as scavengers, living in the midden below the nest, where dirt and dead bodies accumulate, and also entering vacated cells and cleaning out the deposits of excrement. This helps in making the cells available for re-use. The larvae of the moth *Aphomia sociella* also live as scavengers in wasps' nests. Late in the season, when the nest is 'running down', these invade the combs and devour the grubs and pupae. The larva of a rare beetle *Metoecus paradoxus* lives parasitically on the grubs of wasps in underground nests. It is at first an internal parasite (like the larva of an ichneumon or a tachina fly), however, it later emerges and devours its host. It is a remarkable fact that *Metoecus* apparently invades the nests of only the common wasp, never those of the German wasp, although to our eyes the two species look exactly the same.

The wasp's sting

This formidable weapon is really an ovipositor or egg-laying organ that has become transformed into a tiny hypodermic needle connected with a poison gland. The eggs are extruded from an opening at the base of it. Wasps sting if they are squeezed or restrained, as when they accidentally crawl inside someone's clothing. They also attack and sting if the nest is interfered with or even simply approached. The inhabitants of large, well-populated nests are more aggressive than those of small ones. The two main constituents of the venom are histamine and apitoxin. Old-fashioned remedies such as washing soda and ammonia were based on the mistaken idea that the venom is an acid of some kind, and they are ineffective except in giving reassurance. Genuine relief is given by the application of antihistamine to the site of the sting and by taking antihistamine tablets.

phylum	**Arthropoda**
class	**Insecta**
order	**Hymenoptera**
family	**Vespidae**

Barnacle

TH Huxley once described barnacles as animals that 'stood on their heads and kicked food into their mouths'. No description could better fit the basic features of barnacles.

They are common sea creatures which encrust rocks and the piles of piers, or foul the bottoms of ships. They are often mistaken for molluscs, as they bear a resemblance to limpets or mussels, and until the early part of the 19th century this was the general opinion of zoologists. Then, in 1829, a surgeon by the name of Vaughan Thompson, discovered that barnacles had free-swimming larvae that had the characters of crustaceans, so they were, in fact, related to amphipods, shrimps and lobsters.

The barnacle's head is firmly cemented to rock or timber by secretions from the first pair of antennae, or antennules. The body is enclosed in five limy plates that give the barnacle its superficially mollusc-like character, and within the cavity formed by these plates and the body lie the six pairs of forked limbs that are fringed with stiff hairs, or setae. These limbs, or cirri, equivalent to the limbs used for walking or swimming by other crustaceans, beat in unison, flicking out through a gap between the plates then withdrawing again, in a grasping action. Food is collected on the setae or is drawn in by the current set up by the beating of the cirri. This also circulates water with dissolved oxygen around the gills for respiration.

One million on every yard of shore

Acorn barnacles are the most numerous animals on the shore, clustering in groups on rocks and seaweeds. Their numbers on a shore on the Isle of Man have been estimated as being one thousand million in a stretch of about 1 000 yd, and figures of 30 000/sq yd are often quoted.

There are two major types of barnacle. The acorn barnacle at first sight resembles a small limpet but the shell is made up of several plates. The common barnacle of British shores *Balanus balanoides* attains a diameter of nearly $\frac{1}{2}$ in. while the American *Balanus nubilis* reaches a diameter of nearly 1 ft. Acorn barnacles extend well up the shore, as well as living on ships, and may be exposed to the air for a considerable time each tide. A muscle running across the body contracts to pull the plates together preventing the barnacle from losing water when the tide is out, and this is why there is the impression of the barnacle having a solid shell. When the tide floods back, the plates are swung open and the feathery limbs commence their continuous clutching of food. While the barnacles are exposed, however, they are not completely shut. There is a small hole left through which air can percolate. Oxygen then dissolves into the water in the cavity between the plates and is absorbed into the body.

△ Acorn barnacles, **Balanus**, thrust their feathery feet through the mantle opening and withdraw them. in a grasping motion into their mouths. A shell of overlapping plates protects their bodies. (14 × life size).

△ Goose barnacles, **Lepas anatifera**, are arthropods which hang upside down on tough long stalks.

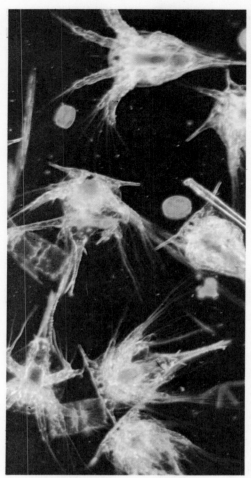

△ **Balanus** nauplii and diatoms in plankton. After several moults it passes into the cypris stage. (100 × life size).

▽ Cypris, enclosed in bivalve shell, will soon attach itself by antennal discs on top of head. (100 × life size).

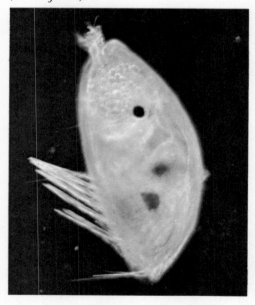

The other type, the goose barnacles, hang from a tough stalk that is formed from the front part of the head. They are occasionally found thrown up on the beach but normally live on floating timbers, buoys and ships' bottoms. They are also found on flotsam such as bottles, lumps of oil etc. Some species form a mucous bubble that hardens to act as a float from which several individuals may hang.

Both acorn and goose barnacles may live on other animals such as turtles and whales. One acorn barnacle, *Coronula,* is commonly found on whale skin. It reaches a diameter of 3 in., and may in turn have several goose barnacles attached to it.

The habit of settling on metal plates and timbers makes barnacles a considerable pest as a layer of barnacles on a ship's bottom severely reduces its speed. From early times it has been the practice to ground ships and careen them, scraping the encrustations from below the waterline. A foul-bottomed ship is at a tactical disadvantage in action, while shipment of cargo becomes more expensive as the time of the voyage is increased. Nowadays fouling by barnacles is reduced by special paints that deter the larvae from settling.

Filter feeders

Like other sedentary animals, barnacles can do little more than wait for food to come to them. They generally settle where there is likely to be a current of water passing over them which will carry fresh food for the cirri to sweep up as it passes. As the cirri sweep back into the shell they fold over rather like a clutching hand so any prey they have is firmly trapped in their meshes. The food is then swept down towards the mouth where it is wiped off the cirri by the appendages surrounding the mouth. These also sort out edible from inedible particles. Edible matter is pushed into the mouth and the rest is pushed away.

Small creatures up to 1 mm long can be caught in the net of the cirri. These include the larvae of other crustacea and of other marine organisms. Small organisms such as single-celled planktonic plants are also caught and eaten, as are bacteria which are only 1/500 mm long. The bacteria are too small to be caught by the beating cirri but are swept into the cavity by the current they set up. Here they are trapped in the net formed by two more pairs of stationary cirri which lie by the mouth. These cirri have an extremely fine net of setae with meshes only one micron across.

Remarkable fertilisation

Barnacles are hermaphrodite, each individual having both male and female organs. Fertilisation takes place within the cavity formed by the plates and the body. The eggs are fertilised by sperm cells of a neighbouring individual which unrolls a 1½in. long penis through the opening of its own shell and protrudes it into one of its neighbours. Normally barnacles are found in dense groups and there would be no difficulty in finding a mate. Occasionally individual barnacles are found by themselves and in some cases they produce young, presumably by self-fertilisation.

Development of the egg takes about four months, but the larvae are not released from the parent until conditions are favourable for their growth, when the adults secrete a so-called 'hatching substance'. This is secreted when the adults are well fed, so that larvae will be released when there is an adequate supply of food for them too. In British waters this is in early spring, at the time when the food source of minute planktonic plants is most abundant.

The newly-hatched larva is a minute creature called a nauplius. It has a round head tapering to a spiny tail and three pairs of limbs with which it rows itself around in a characteristically jerky fashion. The nauplius larva feeds and grows, moulting several times and eventually changing into a cypris larva, resembling a minute two-shelled shellfish like a mussel. The cypris larva has six pairs of limbs. It does not feed but drifts in with the incoming tide, feeling around with the first pair of limbs, or antennules, for a suitable place to settle. It searches around a rock or piece of timber, turning this way and that. As it reaches more suitable conditions it turns more frequently. This keeps it in the suitable place until it is almost turning in circles in the best place. Then it anchors itself by its antennules and rapidly changes into the adult form. The limy plates are secreted and the limbs change from walking legs to waving cirri.

Young barnacles feel for their future homes

Choosing a place to settle is very important, for once adult, a barnacle is unable to move for the rest of its life, which may be several years. It must find, therefore, a place with a rough surface in the shade and where there is a suitable current to bring it food. Some American species have been shown to need a current from ½−1 knot.

Experiments have shown that barnacles are stimulated to settle when they come into contact with other barnacles, or even with surfaces where other barnacles were once attached. Further research showed that the barnacles were secreting a protein called arthropodin. This is a substance secreted through the skins of crustaceans, such as crabs, and of insects. On reaching the surface of the skin the protein hardens. Some protein is left behind in a thin film on the attached surface when the barnacle dies, and it is for this film that the cypris searches with its antennules. Although the film may be too fine to see with a microscope, the cypris feels it rather than smells it. Somehow, it is able to detect the shape of the molecules of the protein.

This behaviour is important because if it can find some arthropodin, and barnacles can distinguish between arthropodin of their own and other species, the barnacle larva can settle in a place that is almost guaranteed to be a suitable environment because other barnacles have successfully settled there before. Moreover, it will mean that other barnacles will settle there, so ensuring cross-fertilisation.

phylum	**Arthropoda**
class	**Crustacea**
subclass	**Cirripedia**
order	**Thoracica**
genera & species	***Balanus balanoides*** common British barnacle
	B. nubilis American barnacle
	Lepas anatifera goose barnacle

Crayfish

The crayfish is a freshwater crustacean. It looks like a small lobster, 4 in. or more long, and coloured sandy yellow, green or dark brown. The head and thorax are covered with a single shell, or carapace, which ends in front in a sharp-pointed rostrum. Its eyes are compound and stalked. On its head is a pair of small antennules which are richly supplied with sense-organs, and a pair of long antennae, which are organs of touch. These have excretory organs at the base. The crayfish has a pair of strong jaws and two pairs of smaller accessory jaws, the maxillae. The second pair of maxillae drives water over 20 pairs of feathery gills on the bases of the thoracic limbs.

On the thorax there are three pairs of appendages, which are used to pass food to the jaws, a pair of stout pincers and four pairs of legs, which the crayfish uses to walk forward. The abdomen is divided into segments and has five pairs of limbs on its underside. The first pair are grooved in the males and are used to introduce sperm onto the female. The other four are swimmerets. The crayfish can swim speedily backwards with forward flicks of its abdomen, which ends in a fan-shaped tail. It does this to escape.

Preparing to carve: a freshwater crayfish about to feed off a male stickleback.

Crayfish in cooler waters

The two families of crayfish are confined almost entirely to temperate regions: the Astacidae in the northern hemisphere, the Parastacidae in the southern hemisphere. There are no crayfish in Africa, but they are present in Madagascar. There is none in the greater part of Asia, but they are found in Korea and the northern islands of Japan. The largest crayfish *Astacopsis franklinii* lives in Tasmania and may weigh up to 9 lb. Another large crayfish related to it is sold as Murray River Lobster in southeastern Australia. One of the Tasmanian crayfish, known as a land crab, habitually leaves the water and burrows in damp earth in forests. In the Mammoth Cave in Kentucky, in the United States, there are several crayfish living in the underground waters. They are colourless and blind; the eyes are gone, leaving only the stalks.

Naturalized aliens

Only one crayfish *Potamobius pallipes* is native to Britain. It is known as the white claw. A larger European crayfish *Astacus fluviatilis*, reared on farms especially in France, has been introduced into the Thames, and is known as the red claw. An American species, introduced into Germany, has become established there. The three species have similar habits. They live in rivers and lakes, especially those with hard water which contains the lime needed for their shell. They feed mainly at night, resting by day in burrows in the mud or under stones, but can sometimes be seen moving about by day.

They eat smaller aquatic animals such as insect larvae, snails, worms and tadpoles, and a small amount of plant food. In the Mississippi Valley they graze on rice during the night. This infuriates the local farmers who regard them as pests.

Unusual breeding habits

Crayfish mate in the autumn. The male turns the female over and sheds milt through the first pair of abdominal appendages onto her abdomen, where it sticks. The female then goes into a burrow to lay her hundred or so eggs. These become attached to bristles on her swimmerets where they are fertilised by contact with the milt. The eggs hatch the following spring. Unusual for a crustacean there is no larval stage. The newly-hatched crayfish are transparent, and tiny replicas of the adults. They remain attached for some time to the female's swimmerets, which they grasp with their claws.

Life and death in crayfish

In many parts of the world, crayfish are considered a delicacy. Sometimes they are eaten raw although this can prove to be hazardous, because crayfish carry a fluke larva. If this is swallowed with a crayfish it will migrate through the wall of the gut to the lungs, where it matures to the adult parasite. In time the adult lays eggs which are ejected with the sputum. From the eggs hatch first stage larvae which infest snails. The cycle of parasitic infection is completed if a snail is eaten by a crayfish.

One interesting aspect of the life of a crayfish is that it grows by periodic moults. This is common knowledge and is often stated in books on natural history. Most crustaceans and insects grow like this. But although it is always stated simply, the process itself is complex. In crayfish it takes place in four stages. First the calcium salts, the chalky matter in the old shell, are taken back into the blood, ready to be laid down again in the new shell being formed beneath the old one. Then the old shell, or such as remains of it, now merely a tough cuticle, is shed and the body takes up water and swells. Then the calcium salts are laid down in the new cuticle and this takes time to harden.

The moult of a crayfish takes 6 hours. During this time the crayfish fasts and stays in hiding. It is a very dangerous period for it; not only is it vulnerable especially to enemies, but it is also in danger from the many attendant difficulties of the process itself. It has only recently been realized, in fact, that many crayfish die during this complicated moulting process.

phylum	**Arthropoda**
class	**Crustacea**
order	**Decapoda**
families	**Astacidae** **Parastacidae**
genera & species	*Astacus fluviatilis* *Potamobius pallipes* *others*

Hermit crab

Hermit crabs live in abandoned sea snail shells, and in all of them the form of the body is modified accordingly. The banana-shaped abdomen, protected in its 'hermitage', is soft and curves to the right to fit the inside of the snail shell. The front end of the body has the hard covering typical of crabs and lobsters and the right claw, larger than the left, is used to close the entrance of the shell. The two pairs of legs behind the claw are used in walking, but the next two pairs are small and are used to grip the shell. The last pair of limbs on the abdomen, which in a lobster form part of the tail fan, are sickle-shaped and used for holding onto the central column of the shell. There are swimmerets on the left side of the abdomen only.

The robber or coconut crab **Birgus latro** of the South Sea Islands, is a land-living hermit crab several pounds in weight and 6 in. across. The adult has lost the shell-dwelling habit and although the abdomen is still twisted it has a hard covering and is kept tucked under the thorax. The stone crabs **Lithodes,** found off the coasts of Britain, although looking like true crabs, show their hermit crab ancestry in their small asymmetrical abdomen.

Strange houses

The common hermit crab of European seas is the soldier crab *Pagurus bernhardus*. Normally only the young are found on the shore, their red and yellow front ends projecting from winkle, topshell or dog whelk shells.

They are nimble despite their burdens and are well-protected from the pounding of waves and from drying up when the tide is out. The older ones reach a length of 5 in., live in deeper water and occupy the larger shells of common and hard whelks. On tropical coasts live semi-terrestrial hermit crabs of the genus *Coenobita*. These usually occupy ordinary snail shells, but East Indian coenobites have been seen wearing such odd substitutes as joints of bamboo, coconut shells and even a broken oil lamp chimney. *C. diogenes* of Bermuda lives in shells that are in fact fossil or subfossil, since they be-

*The face of a squatter: hermit crab **Pagurus megistos**. The massive right claw acts as a 'door' when the crab retreats into its shell. The legs are adapted to the crab's home-changing habits. Only the two pairs behind the claws are used for walking; the rest grip the shell.*

longed to a snail *Livona pica* now extinct in Bermuda. *Pylopagurus* is a hermit crab whose shell becomes encrusted with a bryozoan (moss animal). The shell is said to be dissolved leaving only the moss animal's chalky skeleton, which cloaks the crab and grows with it.

Another hermit crab *Pylocheles*, found in deep water in the Indian Ocean, lives in pieces of bamboo. Its abdomen is straight. *Xylopargus* of the West Indies lives at 600–1 200 ft in hollow cylinders of wood. The rear end of its body is shaped to make a kind of stopper. Some marine hermit crabs have less mobile homes. They live in holes in coral or sponge. This is a habit to some extent shared by lobsters and perhaps indicates the origin of the hermit crab's way of life. The coconut crab makes burrows at the bases of coconut trees and lines them with coconut husks.

Feeding on sago and coconut

Hermit crabs are mainly omnivorous scavengers, tearing up food with their smaller left claws and transferring it to their mouths. *P. bernhardus* also feeds on tiny animals and plants, tossed with sand and debris between its mouth parts with its left claw. Some other hermit crabs can filter particles from the water with bristles on the antennae. Every so often they wipe the antennae across the mouth to take the food collected. The land-living coenobites often climb bushes for plant food and may even attack young birds. The robber crab is said to hammer in the eye-holes of coconuts, but probably feeds mainly on coconuts already cracked open in falling from the tree. It also eats carrion, fruit and sago pith. It, too, is a climber, and can scale the trunks of sago palms and other trees. A local belief is that when the robber is up a tree it can be caught by tying a girdle of grass high up round the trunk. When the crab comes down and its body touches this it lets go, under the impression it has reached the ground, and falls and is stunned. In fact, it takes more than a fall of this kind to stun the crab.

Breeding and growth

P. bernhardus breeds through much of the year and females with 10 000–15 000 dark violet eggs attached to the swimmerets on their abdomen are to be found at most times. Such crabs, in berry as they are called when laden with eggs, come partially out of their shell from time to time and fan their swimmerets to aerate the eggs. As the larvae hatch, moulting at the same time to become zoea larvae, the mother crab sits partly out of her shell and gently wipes the swimmerets with a brush of bristles on her small fourth pair of legs. The tiny shrimp-like zoea larvae shed their skins four times, growing each time, but at the fourth moult the young hermit crab first seeks a snail shell for a home. This stage lasts 4–5 days. Sexual maturity is not reached for a year or more. The sexes differ externally only in the form of the swimmerets which have differing functions, but in many species the male is larger than the female.

Periodically, the growing hermit crab sheds its external skeleton. A split appears on the abdomen and the crab wriggles out of its old skin. As the hermit crab outgrows

△ *Free food and transport in exchange for what? Hermit crabs often pick and 'plant' anemones on their backs. It has recently been shown that this gives protection from octopuses, their main enemy.*

its 'home', this must be replaced with a larger one. The crab examines the new shell all over for several minutes with its claws, then, if it seems good enough and the coast seems clear, it hurriedly transfers its abdomen from the old shell to the new. Sometimes one hermit crab may try to drive another from its shell.

The 'terrestrial' hermit crabs *Coenobita* and the coconut crab *Birgus* must visit the sea to hatch their eggs, for their larvae are marine. Though the adult coconut crab does not carry a shell, the young stages coming ashore do so.

Strange partnerships

Like any hard object lying on the sea bed, the shell of a hermit crab tends to become encrusted with weed, sponges, barnacles and hydroids. Certain sea anemones, however, regularly associate with hermit crabs and form close partnerships with them. Large specimens of the common *P. bernhardus* often carry the anemone *Calliactis parasitica* on their shells, sometimes several of them. As the hermit feeds, the anemone sweeps the ground with its outstretched tentacles and gathers fragments left by the crab. The hermit crab may sometimes benefit from bits of food caught by the anemone. Another hermit crab, Prideaux's hermit crab *Pagurus prideauxi*, light reddish-brown in colour and 2 in. long, regularly carries the anemone *Adamsia palliata* which, unlike *Calliactis*, is to be found on hermit crab shells and nowhere else. The basal disc of the anemone wraps tightly around the shell,

completely enclosing it. As the crustacean grows, so does the anemone, adding to the effective capacity of the shell. Thus the shell does not have to be replaced. The mouth of the anemone, in this case, lies just behind that of the hermit crab. Anemones are armed with stinging cells and these help protect the hermit crab, discouraging, for instance, the attacks of octopus and squid. *P. prideauxi* is immune to the poisons of the stinging cells which can be fatal to other hermit crabs. *Paguropsis typica* goes a stage farther than *Pagurus prideauxi* in carrying *Anemonia mammilifera* without a snail shell. Another species of hermit crab *Parapagurus pilosi-manus* has large eyes in spite of the fact that it lives in water too deep for light to penetrate: it has been suggested that it finds its way about by light from the phosphorescent anemone which cloaks it.

phylum	**Arthropoda**
class	**Crustacea**
subclass	**Malacostraca**
order	**Decapoda**
family	**Paguridae**
genus & species	***Pagurus bernhardus*** ***P. prideauxi***
family	**Coenobitidae**
genera & species	***Coenobita*** ***Birgus latro***

Fishes: The First Vertebrates

It is an accepted convention to visualize the classification of the animal kingdom as starting with the Protozoa, the single-celled animals typified by the amoeba and ending with the mammals, which includes the human species. This resulted in a catch-phrase, less used today than formerly 'from amoeba to man'. When set down on paper in tabular form, such a classification gives the impression of a steady and continuous progression from the Protozoa, through the lower invertebrates and the higher invertebrates to the vertebrates. It must be nearer the truth to suppose that somewhere among the more organized echelons of the lower invertebrates there came a parting of the ways. One path led to the higher invertebrates, the other to the vertebrates. This bifurcation may have occurred at the level of the phylum Echinodermata (star-fishes, sea-urchins and others). There is, however, a distinct gap here in our knowledge that can be bridged only by speculation based on fragmentary information, and it is not our purpose here to discuss these questions.

It is sufficient to note that the first true vertebrates were jawless fishes and that there is living today a form of pre-vertebrate, the lancelet, which embodies all that could be expected in the ancestral vertebrate. How it was evolved from an invertebrate stock is, however, still shrouded in mystery. That a form like the lancelet must have preceded the fishes seems reasonable.

The earliest fossils of fishes have been taken from rocks of the Ordovician period, 450 million years old. They are recognizable as being fishes, though they lacked jaws. Relatively few species of these jawless fishes have been discovered and fewer still have survived. From this ancestral stock, however, sprang two main lines of descent: the cartilaginous fishes typified by the sharks, skates and rays, which were almost entirely marine, and the bony fishes, represented by the more familiar fishes in our present-day rivers and lakes as well as many others in the sea. The bony fishes outnumber the cartilaginous fishes by more than thirty to one. The latter have, however, the distinction of having produced one of the largest of all animals, the whale shark, reportedly having a maximum length of 60 ft and a weight of 20 tons or more. This leviathan is outmatched only by the larger whales, particularly the blue whale. On the other hand, the bony fishes include the smallest of all vertebrates, a goby from the freshwaters of the Philippines which, fully grown, is under $\frac{1}{2}$ inch long.

The first primitive jawless fishes of the Ordovician period found an environment inhabited by invertebrates, in which the only animals rivalling them in size and agility were the cephalopod molluscs, represented by the ammonites and belemnites, the ancestors of modern squids, octopuses and cuttlefishes. It was near to being an empty ecological niche and they took full advantage of it to diversify. By the middle of the Devonian period, a little over 50 million years later, they had evolved many species and spread widely through both salt and fresh waters of the world, so much so that the Devonian period has become known as the Age of Fishes. The jawless fishes, which appeared first, soon began to decline in numbers, and are represented today only by the lampreys and hagfishes. The cartilaginous fishes fared better but in numbers of species are poorer today than in those distant times. It was the bony fishes, the last of the three groups to appear, that finally became dominant, as they still are.

It is worth noting, within the context of what has been said previously about evolutionary trends, the courses followed by the three groups. The jawless fishes threw off relatively few species and there were no startling variations in form. So far as we know their colours were mainly unobtrusive, if not positively drab. Much the same can be said of the cartilaginous fishes. They did achieve a change in shape so that they are basically of two forms, the typical fusiform shark and the flattened rays and skates. Apart from this, in these two groups, the one free-swimming, the other bottom-living, there is no great diversity in behaviour, exploitation of environment or colour. The bony fishes, especially those of today, combine a remarkable range of size, a great diversity of colour and bodily adornment and an exploitation of almost every kind of aquatic habitat.

The major groups of fishes are as follows:

Class Agnatha
  (lampreys and hagfishes)   45 species
Class Chondrichthyes
  (cartilaginous fishes,
  sharks and rays)   600 species
Class Osteichthyes (or
  Pisces) (bony fishes)   20,000 species

Lancelet

A semi-transparent, elongated marine animal usually under 2½ in. long, the lancelet is shaped rather like a fish; it swims like a fish, too, by sideways undulations of its flattened body, which is pointed at each end. But it lacks the paired fins of a fish and—for other reasons—cannot qualify as a vertebrate. The various species are widely distributed in the seas throughout the world. On the coast of Amoy, China, 35 tons of lancelets are harvested for food each year.

Lancelets are found in tropical and temperate seas, generally close to the shore. Originally they were given the scientific name Amphioxus, which means 'sharp at both ends', but this has now been changed to Branchiostoma for reasons given at the end of this article, and amphioxus, the anglicised form of the scientific name, is now used as an alternative common name, especially in biological laboratories.

Taking evasive action

Most of the time, the lancelet lies with its hind end buried in sand or gravel, the head pointing more or less vertically upwards above the surface. The beating of cilia around its mouth creates a current drawing water in through the mouth and thence through a sort of sieve, known as the branchial basket, in the front half of the body. The water passes through the sieve and out through a pore near the middle of the body, on the underside. When disturbed, the lancelet leaves the sand, zig-zags rapidly around in the water above and then dives back into the sand a few seconds later.

Curtains of food

The branchial basket is an elongated oval in shape with vertical slits on either side. It serves as a set of gills for taking oxygen from the water flowing through it, and also for capturing food. Along the floor of the basket is a groove known as the endostyle. This constantly secretes mucus that is carried up the internal sides of the branchial basket by the beating of cilia lining the walls, in a kind of curtain. This curtain of mucus contains many minute gaps through which water can flow through the gill slits and so to the outside. Food particles, such as diatoms, are, however, trapped on the inside of the mucus curtain which continues to be driven upwards by the cilia until it reaches another longitudinal groove in the roof of the basket. There another set of cilia drive the mucus backward into the stomach where it is digested.

Lopsided larvae

The lancelet lives 1—4 years, varying with the species. The eggs and sperm of the lancelet are released into the sea to be fertilised. About 8 hours after the egg is fertilised a ciliated embryo has been formed which swims about and then changes into an elongated, lopsided larva. This eventually develops into the adult. The lopsided larvae is ⅓—⅔ in. long but sometimes it grows much larger than this and becomes sexually mature without changing into an adult. This process is called neoteny. These giant larvae of the lancelet were once regarded as a separate species and given the name *Amphioxides*.

Vertebrate/invertebrate?

In 1774 a strange little animal was picked up on the coast of Cornwall and sent, preserved in alcohol, to the celebrated Russian naturalist, Pallas. There seems to be no record of who picked it up or why it was sent right across Europe when there were many competent naturalists in Britain who might have examined it. At all events, Pallas described it in a footnote in a book he was publishing, giving a very brief description in Latin and naming the animal *Limax lanceolatus* under the impression that it was a slug. Half a century later, on December 21, 1831, Jonathan Couch, one of the leading English naturalists of that time, was walking along the shore near Polperro, in Cornwall, after a storm. It is the practice of some naturalists to go beach-combing after a storm to see what specimens may have been thrown ashore. Apparently Couch turned over a flat pebble lying on the sand about 50 feet from the ebbing tide and saw a tiny tail sticking out of the sand. He dug out the rest of the animal and was able to watch it in a sea-water aquarium and see how active it was. Couch sent the specimen to William Yarrell (the English zoologist) who in 1836 described it in a book *A History of British Fishes* as a fish of very low organisation to which he gave the name *Amphioxus*. He also recognised it as the same animal that Pallas had looked at. Previously, however, in 1834, the Italian naturalist Costa had published a description of the same animal collected from the shore at Naples and had given it the name *Branchiostoma lubricum*. This brief history accounts for the changing of the animal's name. It had become generally known as *Amphioxus* because Costa's description had been overlooked and was not brought to light until 45 years ago. The international rules of nomenclature state that the first name proposed for an animal must be the one used even if it has been overlooked for years. So the name given by Costa had to take precedence over Yarrell's *Amphioxus*.

The relationship of the lancelet with the rest of the animal kingdom remains one of the most interesting features of the animal. Amphioxus resembles the vertebrates in having a dorsal nerve cord lying above a stiffening rod, the notochord, and an arrangement of muscles along its tail much as in a fish. At the same time it lacks a backbone, jaws, or indeed any bone, and a brain as well as the eyes and other sense-organs associated with the brain. So it is not a vertebrate, yet comes very near to being one. The current view is that both amphioxus and the vertebrates evolved from the same ancestors as the sea-squirts or tunicates, which feed in much the same way as amphioxus but are anchored to a solid support when adult and look most unlike amphioxus. They do, however, have a free-swimming tadpole-like larva. If this were to become sexually mature without taking on the sessile adult form, like the 'amphioxides' larva, then we should have something like both the ancestral amphioxus and the ancestral vertebrate.

phylum	**Chordata**
subphylum	**Cephalochordata**
family	**Branchiostomidae**
genus & species	***Branchiostoma lanceolatum*** ***B. californiense*** *others*

Heads upwards, a pair of lancelets sift the water for food. The fish-like muscle blocks can be seen along the body. The squares showing through the skin of the belly are reproductive organs.

Lamprey

Lampreys look like eels and have sometimes been called lamprey eels or lamper eels. They are, however, jawless like the hagfish which is their nearest relative, and, like the hagfishes, lampreys are not true fishes but direct descendants of the jawless Ostracoderms. There are about 30 species, both marine and freshwater. Some are parasitic on fish, others are not. Lampreys live in temperate regions of northern and southern hemispheres. The sea lamprey, the best known, lives on both sides of the North Atlantic. Members of the genus **Lampetra** *are found in Europe and Asia as well as North America. In the southern hemisphere, species of* **Geotria** *and* **Mordacia** *are found off the coasts of Chile, Australia and New Zealand.* **Geotria** *has a large fleshy bag, of unknown function, almost hiding its mouth.*

Pump-like gills

The eel-like body of a lamprey has a slimy scaleless skin. Its fins are found along the centre-line of the body. There is a single nostril in the middle of the head, which leads behind into a blind sac. The eyes are well-developed. The head ends in front in a large funnel-like mouth with horny teeth lining the funnel, some of the teeth being on the muscular tongue protruding at the base of the funnel. Behind the head is a row of small circular gill openings running along each side of the body. Inside are seven pairs of gill pouches lined with blood-red gill-filaments which open into a tube that is blind at one end and opens into the back of the mouth in front. A lamprey can breathe by taking in water through its mouth to pass across the gills. More often, because the mouth is so much used as a sucker, a lamprey breathes by contracting muscles around the gill-pouches, driving the water out. As the muscles relax water is drawn in. This pumping action seems to be helped by movements of the sinuous latticework of cartilage, the branchial basket, surrounding the gill-pouches.

The lamprey feeds by pressing the circular edge of its mouth against the side of a fish which it finds by eyesight, not by smell as in the hagfish. It protrudes its tongue and punctures the fish's skin by rasping the teeth on it; the fish starts to bleed and the blood is sucked in by the lamprey. It sucks in a few fragments of flesh as well, but it feeds more on the blood than on the flesh. Not all adult lampreys feed in this way; some species do not feed as adults.

Lampreys barricade their nests

There are three species of lamprey in Europe. They are usually spoken of as the sea lamprey, river lamprey and brook lamprey. It is better to use the second's alternative name of lampern, because it also spends its adult life in the sea. The brook lamprey is also known as the pride. It lives all the time in freshwater. Those lampreys living in the sea enter rivers to spawn. The migration begins in winter and

△ *The hooded larva of a brook lamprey.*
▽ *Lamprey skeleton showing branchial basket, which supports the gill pouches, and the viciously toothed, circular mouth cartilage, which serves instead of jaws.*
▽▽ *Powerful sucker of a brook lamprey.*

by spring the lampreys are in the rivers and building nests. They swim strongly and can make their way over rocks or up vertical walls, hauling themselves up with the sucker mouth. The male lamprey makes a nest by holding pebbles in its sucker mouth and moving them downstream to form a barricade. In a depression made upstream of this, the eggs will later be laid.

The females arrive later than the males and then help build the nest, the two sometimes combining to move large pebbles. After spawning the adults drift downriver to die. The eggs are $\frac{1}{25}$ in. diameter and they hatch 2 weeks later. The larva, or ammocoete, was once thought to be a different species. It is small and worm-like, and lives by burrowing in the sand or mud and coming out at night to feed on particles of plant and animal bodies. These are strained through fleshy tentacles (cirri) on a hood-like mouth and passed into the gullet where they are caught by sticky secretions on a special groove, the endostyle. This endostyle becomes the thyroid gland—the chemical controller of growth—in the adult.

After 3–5 years of larval life the ammocoete, now 4–5 in. long, changes into an adult lamprey. The hooded mouth becomes funnel-shaped, the cirri are replaced by horny teeth, the nostril moves from the front of the snout to the top of the head, the eye grows larger. The sea lamprey becomes silvery and goes down to the sea, as does the lampern, but the latter does not parasitize fishes. Instead it feeds on molluscs, crustaceans and worms. The pride or brook lamprey, which remains in rivers, does not feed when adult.

Surfeit of lampreys

It is often said that King John died of a surfeit of lampreys. It was, in fact, Henry I. It was King John who fined the men of Gloucester 40 marks because 'they did not pay him sufficient respect in the matter of lampreys'. American history is more recent and has to do with a surfeit of lampreys in the Great Lakes. Gradually, over the years, the lampreys made their way up the New York State Barge Canal and the Welland Canal and became firmly established in the Great Lakes. There they ruined a commercial fishery that had been yielding a yearly catch of 11 million pounds of lake trout and other fishes. A big research programme was set going to find ways of killing off the lampreys. Weirs were built to stop further migrations into the lakes, the lampreys were poisoned and electrocuted. Some success was achieved but now that a poison that kills the larvae has been discovered lampreys are being wiped out and the fisheries are recovering.

class	**Agnatha**
order	**Petromyzoniformes**
family	**Petromyzonidae**
genera & species	*Petromyzon marinus* sea lamprey *Lampetra fluviatilis* lampern *L. planeri* pride others

Maneater shark

A single species of heavy-bodied shark bears the ominous name of maneater, or great white shark. It grows to 20 ft long or more and is bluish-grey to slate grey above, shading to white below, with fins growing darker towards their edges. It also has a conspicuous black spot just behind where the pectoral fin joins the body. Its snout is pointed and overhangs an awesome, crescent-shaped mouth which is armed with a frightful array of triangular saw-edged teeth. In large individuals the largest teeth may be 3 in. high. The pectoral fins are large. The pelvic fins, and the second dorsal and the anal fins, which lie opposite each other, are small. The tail fin is nearly symmetrical instead of having the upper lobe larger as in most sharks. There is a large keel along the side of the tail in front of the tail fin.

The maneater belongs to the family of mackerel sharks, which includes the porbeagles and mako shark. These are similar to the maneater but smaller, up to 12 ft long being about the limit. They feed on fishes such as mackerel, herring, cod, whiting, hake and dogfish. They also provide sport for sea anglers because of the fight they put up when hooked. Most mackerel sharks are dangerous to man.

The maneater is found in all warm seas and occasionally strays into temperate seas. It lives in the open sea, coming inshore only when the shallow seas are near deep water. One maneater was caught at a depth of 4 200 ft off Cuba and other evidence also suggests the shark is a deepwater fish.

Not as big as was believed

Maneaters may be much maligned monsters. They are neither as big as is generally said nor as voracious. Very little is known about the habits of the maneater except what can be deduced from its shape and the contents of the stomachs of individuals caught and dissected. Its shape suggests it can swim rapidly, but from those hooked and landed with angling tackle it is fairly certain the maneater is not as swift as the smaller mako. Since young have been found in a female's body the species is presumed to bear its young alive. The maneater is said to be of uncertain temper, yet skin divers report it to be wary and even easily scared. It is probably less dangerous than the mako which is known to attack small boats as well as swimmers. The maneater's bad reputation probably rests on its large size and fearsome teeth, coupled with occasional attacks that look deliberate. On the first of these two points it is hard to speak with certainty. The largest maneater of which we have reliable information measured 36½ ft long, and this one was caught a century ago, off Port Fairey, Australia. Most of the others are between 20 and 25 ft. One that was 21 ft long weighed 7 100 lb; another 17 ft long weighed 2 800 lb. Maneaters have been said by authoritative writers to grow to over 40 ft but there is no solid evidence.

Nothing refused

Several books have been published in the last 10 years which give details of shark attacks. Two are devoted solely to the subject. They are: *Shark Attack* by V M Coppleson, an Australian doctor who has collected the case histories of injuries from sharks, and *Danger Shark!* by Jean Campbell Butler, whose narrative is based on the New Orleans Shark Conference of 1958, at which shark researchers pooled their findings. Putting the information from these and other sources together, there is the general impression that sharks, the maneater in particular, will try to eat anything that looks like food. As a result they snap at living animals, including bathers or people who have accidentally fallen into the sea, as well as corpses and carrion, even inanimate objects such as tin cans. The attacks on boats, as in the attack on the 14ft cod boat off Nova Scotia in 1953, by a maneater, which left some of its teeth in the timbers, are probably due to mistake rather than malice. Several times whole human corpses have been taken from sharks' stomachs but they proved to be of people who had been drowned.

Maneater or corpse swallower?

There are several instances of maneaters found to contain the intact bodies of other animals. These include a 100lb sea-lion, a 50lb seal, and sharks 6–7 ft long. While human beings have been badly bitten, usually producing frightful wounds, some of which have proved fatal, there is little evidence of limbs being severed, and less of a person being swallowed whole. Two things have also emerged from the studies so far made. The first is that sharks digest food very slowly and animal remains swallowed take days, even weeks, to be digested. The other, which seems linked with this but is learned more from sharks in captivity, is that sharks seem to eat little.

Extenuating circumstances

When one speaks of malice in relation to shark attack one is only reflecting the attitude of mariners to these beasts. As a class they are hated. There are many stories of captured sharks being treated with savagery, being disembowelled and then thrown back live into the sea. Yet in the economy of the sea they are scavengers rather than evil predators. Moreover, in areas where shark attack is heavy there is reason to suppose man has not been blameless. For example, in the region around Sydney Harbour, Australia, and again at Florida, blood from abattoirs seeps into the sea, and sharks are drawn by the smell of blood. In the Bay of Bengal, where human corpses are floated down the Ganges from the burning ghats, shark attack is again high.

None of these things lessens one's sympathy for victims of shark attack, nor lessens one's own fear of the sharks themselves, but they put the subject in perspective zoologically. One of the first scientific conclusions we are led to is that while sharks may be ferocious they seem not to be voracious, as they are so often described. In fact, because they will engulf almost anything they come across, sharks have at times aided the course of human justice.

Silent witness

The classic example of this concerned the United States brig *Nancy* which was captured on July 3, 1799 by HM Cutter *Sparrow* and taken to Port Royal, Jamaica, Britain and the United States then being at war, to be condemned as a prize. The captain of the *Nancy* produced papers at the trial which were, in fact, false and he was about to be discharged when another British warship put in at the port with papers found in a shark caught on August 30. They proved to be the ship's papers thrown overboard by the captain of the *Nancy,* when capture seemed inevitable. They led to the condemnation of the brig and her cargo.

class	**Selachii**
order	**Pleurotremata**
family	**Isuridae**
genus & species	***Carcharodon carcharias***

Maligned monster: the maneater shark's bad reputation stems from its large size and supposed voraciousness. Most maneaters measure between 20 and 25 ft and not 40 ft as often quoted. They seem to eat anything that looks like food which results in bathers, corpses, carrion and rubbish being taken.

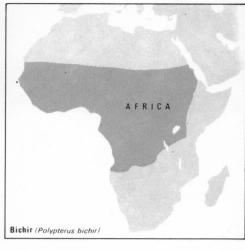

Bichir (Polypterus bichir)

◁ This strange fish not only breathes air but also uses its front fins like legs to stalk its prey. It will even die if it cannot gulp air from the surface. To do this, the bichir swims slowly to the surface, takes a quick gulp, then rapidly swims down to the bottom.

Bichir

A freshwater fish just over 2 ft long living in the Upper Nile, Lakes Rudolf and Chad, and their associated rivers. There are four other related species, all in tropical Africa. The bichir has a long body, small but broad head, and rounded tail, but its distinctive feature is a series of finlets along the back which may be raised or lowered. Each finlet is flag-like and consists of a single ray to which one or several fin-rays are attached. The pectoral fins, too, are peculiar. They are fan-like, almost as if stalked. The body is covered with an armour of hard rhombic scales, made of the hard protein, ganoin. Bichirs are fishes with many primitive features and in fact are surviving Palaeniscoids.

Air-breathing

The bichir lives hidden among the thickets of large water plants at the margins of rivers and lakes, from which it comes out at night, to feed. It has gills in addition to the lung-like swim-bladder, yet if denied air for even a short time it dies. To breathe air, a bichir swims slowly to the surface, takes a quick gulp, then quickly swims down to the bottom. In most fishes, even in those that gulp air, the swim-bladder is single. In the bichir it is paired, like the lungs of a land vertebrate, although the two parts are of unequal size.

A peculiar feature of its behaviour is its use of the pectoral fins almost as legs, as supports for the front part of the body. The fish may rest supporting itself on these fins, with the head raised, rather in the manner of a quadruped on land, such as a lizard. When hunting for food it behaves quite unlike other fishes. It prowls, moving forward slowly inch by inch, stopping, raising the head as if sniffing around, then moving forward again. Its unusual tubular nostrils, coupled with the small eyes, suggest that the sense of smell is used in finding food.

The almost cat-like prowl is seen, also, when a bichir is confronted with any new object. It moves forward much in the manner of a cat stalking a mouse, but its pectoral fins are fluttering and the finlets on its back are raised, all ready to swim backwards if need arise. When moving quickly, the finlets are laid back, the pectoral fins are pressed close to the body, and the bichir drives itself through the water with side-to-side eel-like movements of the body.

Predator of small animals

The food consists chiefly of small fishes, but small aquatic animals, mainly insect larvae and small worms, and small frogs are also taken.

Leaping courtship

Spawning takes place, usually in August and September, at the time of floods, when the rivers and lakes overflow to form marshes and swamps. The bichir moves out into these. Courtship begins with two bichir leaping out of the water, after which they chase each other, keeping close together. After a while the pursuit is broken off. There follows a brief rest which is ended by the male going over to the female and nudging her with his head or brushing her with his anal fin, which is said to be swollen and folded at the breeding season. Practically nothing is known of the spawning itself until the larval stage. The larvae are tiny miniatures of the adults but with external feathery gills, like those of newt larvae.

One of the missing links

The bichir has been described as one of the most interesting fishes for anatomical and evolutionary studies. To understand why, we need to go back nearly half a century. Then, anything that was fish-like and had fins was a fish, and this was true whether we were dealing with sharks, sturgeons or sticklebacks. Then came a change in outlook. Somebody put forward the idea that sharks were not fishes. That is, they were not true fishes, because they had a skeleton of cartilage instead of bone. Now the habit grew of speaking of two groups of animals, the sharks, or cartilaginous fish, and the true or bony fishes.

However, this is a point about which anyone who is not an ichthyologist or a student of fishes can rest easy. To anyone but an ichthyologist the old idea of what can be regarded as a fish is still workable. Moreover, even to the specialist, the division between the cartilaginous fishes and the bony fishes is anything but definite. In between are various links, of which the bichir is one. Its skeleton is bony but has more than the usual amount of cartilage in it. Its intestine has a spiral valve, one of the hallmarks of a shark. It has spiracles, openings behind each eye like an extra gill, which are a feature of many cartilaginous fishes. In its anatomy, therefore, it shows a mixture of shark and true fish. Also in its lungs, the limb-like pectoral fins and in features of its behaviour, it indicates the line along which, in all probability, the dramatic step was taken by which a land-living amphibian, some form of primitive salamander or newt, arose from an air-breathing fish able to use its paired fins as limbs. This, of course, fits in with the bichir's habit of breeding in marshes where the water contains little oxygen and a fish that can breathe air is at an advantage. There are others in this noble company, among them the bowfin, sturgeon, lungfishes and the celebrated coelacanth. One or other among the ancestors of this distinguished company took the evolutionary line which led to the first amphibian, later the first reptile, and through it to the mammals and birds.

class	**Pisces**
order	**Cladista**
family	**Polypteridae**
genus & species	***Polypterus bichir***, *others*

American paddlefish looks menacing but is really quite harmless, feeding on small planktonic organisms which it probably detects with its long snout.

Paddlefish

The paddlefish, a large freshwater bony fish, is related to the sturgeons. It has a long body, and looks like a shark. The skin of the paddlefish is naked except for a few scattered vestigial scales and patches of scales on the tail fin. It has a fairly large head drawn out at the front into a flattened snout shaped like the blade of a canoe paddle. The snout is between one-third and one-half the total length of the fish. At the base of the snout are the small eyes and beneath them a very wide mouth. The gill covers are large and triangular with the apex to the rear, and are drawn out into a point. The pectoral and pelvic fins are medium-sized, as are the single dorsal fin which is set well back on the body and the anal fin which is opposite it. The tail fin is only slightly forked.

There are only 2 species: one, also known as the spoonbill sturgeon, lives in the Mississippi Valley of North America, the other in the Yangtse river system in China. The first is up to 6 ft or more long and weighs 170 lb. The Chinese species, sometimes called the swordbill sturgeon, is reported to reach 23 ft long.

Paddling for food

Some people say the paddlefish uses its paddle to probe in the mud for food, while others say it uses the paddle to stir up the mud, but as others have suggested, this seems unlikely for such a sensitive and easily damaged organ. They maintain, and this seems more likely, that as the paddlefish swims slowly along, it swings its highly sensitive paddle from side to side to detect its food. When it opens its large mouth, the back of the head seems almost to fall away from the rest of the body as the gill covers sag, revealing the capacious gill chambers. This sudden opening of the mouth and gill cavities probably produces a suction which draws in small plankton. As the fish swims forward, the plankton is strained from the water by the long gill rakers on the inner sides of the gills. They sometimes eat other fish; shad, for example, have been found in their stomachs.

Vanishing mystery

Although paddlefish are living in a region where there are many people fishing and where there are many naturalists capable of keeping a watch on it, its breeding and spawning behaviour were unknown until a few years ago. Then CA Purkett, in 1960, noticed paddlefishes assembling over a gravel bar in the Osage River when the water level had risen several feet during a spate. He could see them swimming just over the gravel bottom and every now and then one would come to the surface, waggle its tail, and then go down to the bottom again. He assumed correctly that they were spawning and he was later able to work out the story, so ending a long-standing mystery.

The eggs are $\frac{1}{8}$ in. diameter. As they are laid they sink down to the pebbles and stick to them. The larvae hatch within 7 days at ordinary summer temperatures and they are then $\frac{1}{3}$ in. long, with a large head, no eyes, no paddle and no barbels, and each feeds on its large yolk sac. The larvae are encumbered with this yolk sac until it has been used up. They can be seen swimming erratically up to the surface and down again and when the flood waters begin to subside they are carried downstream or are washed among the rocks. Now we see why the spawning had escaped attention. It takes place on a flood, and when the flood waters recede, there is nothing left to show what has taken place.

The larvae begin to grow their eyes and their barbels within a few hours of being hatched but the paddle does not begin to grow for 2—3 weeks. At first it is only a small bump on the snout but once it appears it grows rapidly. One particular individual that Purkett had under observation grew to 2 in. long in 29 days and had a paddle $\frac{1}{3}$ in. long. Paddlefish kept in ponds grew 6—12 in. in a year, some growing as much as 2 ft in a year, but they are 7—8 years old before they begin to breed.

Missing links

In the early days of the settlement of North America, the paddlefish was not regarded as a fish worth eating. Even today it ranks as only second rate, although the greenish-black eggs are used as caviare. The chief interest in the fish is in its relationship with other fishes. It is classified in the class Pisces, which are also known as bony fishes, yet its skeleton, like that of sharks, is made of cartilage. It also has a short straight intestine with a spiral valve, like sharks. There are other small details of the anatomy which link the paddlefishes with the sharks although in most other respects they are more like bony fishes. They are, in fact, 'missing links', connecting these two main groups. They and the sturgeons are the only surviving members of an order dating back about 100 million years, which was an offshoot from the common ancestors of sharks and bony fishes. The fact that there are only 2 species, one in one part of the world and the other in a widely separated part, suggests that they are a dying race. If so, their end is being hastened, at least in North America, where the building of dams and river pollution have even further restricted their range.

class	**Pisces**	
order	**Acipenseriformes**	
family	**Polyodontidae**	
genera & species	***Polyodon spathula***	*American*
	Psephurus gladius	*Chinese*

A living fossil, the bowfin is the sole surviving member of a family which flourished 130 million years ago.

Bowfin

The bowfin, with many primitive features, is a living fossil whose ancestors abounded 130 million years ago. A single species now occupies a family and an order on its own. It is a freshwater fish found only in the lakes and streams of the eastern United States, although its ancestors were widely distributed over North America and Europe, where their fossils may be found. Normally about 2 ft in length, it may reach 3 ft. Long-bodied, pike-like, it has a long soft-rayed dorsal fin, a rounded tail and thin scales with an enamel-like covering of ganoine. The male has a dark spot circled with orange or yellow at the base of the tail fin. In the female it is either lacking or is merely a dark spot.

Air breathing fish

The bowfin, mudfish, or spotfin is quite a remarkable fish which can breathe air. It lives in still waters and sluggish streams, and can survive in water with little or no oxygen. As with several other primitive fishes the swimbladder of the bowfin has a spongy inner lining well supplied with blood-vessels and acts as a lung, the bowfin rising to the surface to gulp air. It can live out of water for as much as 24 hours. It is said to utter a bell-like note which is possibly due to exhaling before taking in more air. Another primitive feature, which is more pronounced in sharks, is the spiral valve in the intestine. There is only a vestige of this valve in the bowfin, but even that is unusual in the bony or true fishes, to which the bowfin belongs. Another feature characteristic of primitive bony fishes is the large bony gular plate on the underside of the head between the two lower jawbones. The bowfin swims by a motion of its dorsal fin.

Voracious feeders

The bowfin eats crustaceans, worms, frogs and fishes, as well as dead flesh. It is so voracious and takes such a wide variety of animal foods that where the fish is abundant it is considered destructive and steps are taken to eradicate it. In the southern United States it is used as food, smoked or dried and in fishballs and jambalaya. Fishing for bowfins is said to be exciting sport because they will snap at almost any bait, although frogs and minnows are most used. The bowfins' strong jaws, sharp teeth and predatory habits have earned them the names of freshwater dogfish and freshwater wolves.

Male nests and guards the young

Spawning takes place in May to June, when the male's dark spot with its ring of colour becomes more intense. The male selects a weedy area along the margin of a lake or stream. There he builds a circular nest among a clump of water plants. He is said to swim round and round pressing the vegetation down, much as a bird fashions a nest by pivoting in it. Several females lay their eggs in the nest and the male, after fertilising these by shedding his milt on them, guards the nest until the eggs hatch, which they do in 8—10 days. The eggs stick to the stems and leaves of the plants. The guardian male, by swimming round and round the nest, creates currents that aerate the eggs. He also guards the young until they are about 4 in. long, when his parental instinct wanes. Such parental care behaviour is obviously an advantage for a species living in sluggish and poorly oxygenated water. The young fishes have their own protective device in the form of cement organs at the end of the snout. With these they can cling to water plants when first hatched and until their rapid growth makes them large enough and strong enough to swim, when they leave the nest in a compact group with the male in attendance.

Link with the past

The bowfin is only one of many animals to have been called a 'living fossil'. This term was first used by Darwin for a tree, the ginkgo or maidenhair tree, which was worldwide in Mesozoic times 200 million years ago, when the giant reptiles roamed the earth, but was found by Europeans, in the 18th century, to be still surviving in China and Japan. It was about the same time, in the Mesozoic age, that large-mouthed predatory fishes first appeared. The family to which the bowfin belongs sprang from these and during the last 150 million years reached its zenith and then declined, the only species left being that now found in the eastern United States. Another species persisted in Europe until 50 million years ago and then died out. So this fish is a typical 'living fossil'; not a missing link but a link with the past. It has outlived its era and is the sole survivor from a past heyday.

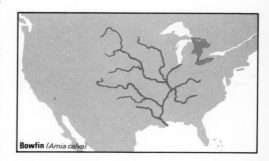

Bowfin *(Amia calva)*

class	**Pisces**
order	**Protospondyli**
family	**Amiidae**
genus & species	*Amia calva*

Despite a sleek and shark-like appearance, sturgeons are slow-moving fish. Here two Volga sterlets cruise gently above the sandy bottom, searching for food. They have poor eyesight and locate their food mainly by touch, using the sensitive barbels seen on the underside of their long snouts.

Sturgeon

The sturgeon is best known as the fish that gives caviare, the luxury food which could soon be a thing of the past. Of greater interest is the fact that the two dozen species are relics of a primitive race of fishes. They are more or less halfway between the sharks and the bony fishes, having a skeleton partly of bone and partly of cartilage. They are shark-like in shape and in the way the hind end of the body turns upwards into the upper lobe of the tailfin. The snout is tapered in the young fish, long and broad in adults, and in front of the mouth, on the underside of the head, are four barbels. The body is scaleless except for five rows of large plate-like scales with sharp points running from behind the gill-covers to the tailfin.

The largest is the Russian sturgeon or beluga (not to be confused with the mammal beluga, the white whale), of the Caspian and Black Seas and the Volga, Don, Dnieper and other rivers of that region. It is up to 28 ft long and

3 210 lb weight. One that was 13 ft long and weighed 2 200 lb was known to be 75 years old. It yielded 400 lb of caviare. The Atlantic sturgeon, on both sides of the North Atlantic reaches 11 ft and 600 lb. The white sturgeon of the Pacific coast of North America usually weighs less than 300 lb, but there are records of 1 285, 1 800 and 1 900 lb. The sterlet of the rivers of the USSR is up to 3 ft long. The rest of the two dozen species of sturgeon are all found in temperate waters throughout the northern hemisphere.

Numbers down everywhere

Sturgeons are slow-moving fish, spending their time grubbing on the bottom for food. Some, however, make long migrations. Individuals tagged in North American waters have been found to travel 900 miles. Most species live in the sea and go back up the rivers to spawn. The largest, the beluga, from which half the world's supply of caviare comes, is entirely freshwater. Today all sturgeons are fewer in number than they were a century or two ago, partly from overfishing and partly from the pollution of rivers and to some extent because

hydro-electric schemes have spoilt their spawning runs. In the 17th century a prosperous sturgeon fishery flourished in the New England States of America. In the mid-19th century they were still being caught, for their caviare and for a high quality lamp oil their flesh yielded. A century later the annual catch had fallen by 90%. Sturgeons were once abundant off the Atlantic coast of Europe. Now they are found mainly around the mouth of the Gironde river in western France, the Guadalquivir in Spain and in Lake Ladoga in the USSR. A few only are caught each year around the British Isles and adjacent seas. Around the Black Sea—Caspian area overfishing has brought the sturgeon yield to a low ebb and efforts have been made to establish hatcheries, to rear young sturgeon and so replenish the stock. It has been estimated that as many as 15 000 sturgeons have been caught in these seas and adjoining rivers in a day.

Rummages for food in the mud

The name of this fish in several European languages means the stirrer, from the way the sturgeon rummages among the mud for food. This it finds largely by touch, using its sensitive barbels. Sturgeon also have

165

A young sterlet barely drifts along, its sensitive barbels tracing food. As it grows the nose broadens and the fish may reach 3 ft in length.

taste-buds, which are normally on the tongue or inside the mouth in other fish, but in the sturgeon are on the outside of the mouth. These help in the selection of food. They protrude from the toothless mouth to suck in the food. Sturgeons are slow feeders and can survive several weeks without eating. In freshwater they eat insect larvae, worms, crayfish, snails and other small fishes. In the sea they take bivalve molluscs, shrimps and other small crustaceans, worms and more small fishes than are eaten in fresh water. The beluga feeds in winter mainly on flounder, mullet and gobies in the Black Sea, and on roach, herring and gobies in the Caspian.

When caviare hatches

Spawning takes place in depths of 18–20 ft. The eggs are blackish, $\frac{1}{10}$ in. diameter and sticky so they adhere to water plants and stones, or clump together in masses. A single female may lay 2–3 million in one season. These hatch in 3–7 days, the larvae being $\frac{1}{2}$ in. long but their first summer they may grow to 8 in.

Use for the swimbladder

Sturgeon have been fished for their flesh and their oil as well as for their caviare. They have also supplied isinglass. This is from the swimbladder and was first named by the Dutch in 1525. They called it *huisenblas* which became anglicized as isinglass. When prepared for use it looks like semi-transparent plastic sheets, and it is almost pure gelatin. It is still used today for special cements and water-proofing materials, but its main use is in clearing white wines, an ounce of isinglass being enough to clarify up to 300 gallons.

Royal fish

In the days of Ancient Rome the fish, garlanded with flowers, was piped into the banquet carried by slaves similarly crowned with flowers. It was, however, Edward II of England who made it a royal fish. His decree ran: 'The King shall have the wreck of the sea throughout the realm, whales and great sturgeons, except in certain places privileged by the King.' Sturgeon have ascended English rivers including the Thames

and at one time any caught above London Bridge belonged to the Lord Mayor of London. Henry I is said to have banned even that. Indeed, he forbade the eating of sturgeon at any table than his own. A royal fish indeed: and, in the 1950's, as Sir Alister Hardy recalls in his book *The Open Sea*: a sturgeon 'died in an excess of misplaced homage, and was covered with distinction, by burying itself in the condenser pipe of one of Her Majesty's aircraft-carriers: HMS *Glory*!' – a worthy burial.

class	**Pisces**
order	**Chondrostei**
family	**Acipensenidae**
genera & species	***Acipenser ruthenus*** sterlet ***A. sturio*** *Atlantic sturgeon* ***A. transmontanus*** *white sturgeon* ***Huso huso*** *beluga* *others*

The aptly named shovelnose sturgeon **Scaphirhynchus platorhynchus**; *the bizarre snout is used to dig snails, shrimps and other morsel from the gravel.*

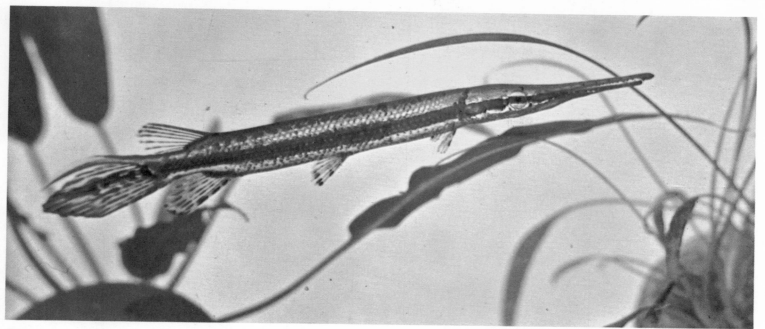

Gar

These slender pike-like fishes are living fossils of a family that reached its peak in the Mesozoic period 70—220 million years ago. There are seven species living in the rivers and lakes of North and Central America.

The commonest of these species is the longnose gar, which lives from the Great Lakes southwards. It is up to 5 ft long, its slim body covered with a tough armour of close-set diamond-shaped or rhombic enamelled (ganoid) scales which do not overlap in the usual manner of fish scales. The long snout is a beak; its jaws studded with small sharp teeth recall those of the gharial among crocodilians, the beak being twice as long as the rest of the head. The dorsal and anal fins are set far back on the body. The back is olive to silver, the underside white.

The shortnose gar, up to 2 ft long, lives mainly in the Great Lakes. The tropical gar of Mexico is said to reach 10 or even 12 ft, and the alligator gar which ranges from southern United States to Panama and Cuba is about the same size. Its snout is very like that of an alligator.

Indolent fishes

The gars live mainly in still waters, where they lie almost motionless among water plants, looking more like floating logs than fish. They move quietly and slowly to stalk passing prey, which is seized with a sudden sideways slash of the snout. Although apparently so lethargic, gars can move rapidly when necessary. Their food is mainly other fishes but little animal food is refused. Frogs, salamanders and worms are readily accepted and the young gar feeds largely on water insects. They soon take to catching fish, however, and a young 2 in. gar is on record as taking 16 young minnows in quick succession. It is easy to imagine from this the predatory nature of the gar and why

fishermen hate them, and gars also take bait from their hooks. A gar can, with one snap of its jaws, seize a whole group of small fishes. With larger fish the prey must be gradually worked round in the mouth into a position from which it can be swallowed head first. All food takes 24 hours to digest, which is slow compared with most other freshwater fishes.

Eggs and babies stick to rocks

The males mature in 3—4 years, the females taking 6 years. Spawning is from March to May in shallow waters, each female being accompanied by 3 or 4 males. The average number of eggs laid per female is about 28 000 but may vary from 4 000 to 60 000 according to her size. The eggs are sticky and cling to rocks and water plants. In a few days they hatch and the baby fishes fix themselves to water plants by cement organs, adhesive discs at the end of the snout, and hang there until the yolk sac has been absorbed. After this they swim freely, feeding at first on mosquito larvae.

Rapid growth

In spite of its reputation for voracity, justified if by nothing else by its almost shark-like teeth, a gar has a low food consumption, feeds irregularly and has a slow rate of digestion. Yet it is one of the fastest growing of freshwater fishes. In its first year a young male gar grows on average just over $\frac{1}{10}$ in. a day to reach $19\frac{1}{2}$ in. by the end of the first season, the female reaching 22 in. in the same period. After that growth slows down to 1 in. a year but continues for 13—14 years in the females, which outlive the males. Because it moves about so little—even its feeding is leisurely—and because it has a high metabolic efficiency (that is, its body makes the fullest use of all its food), the energy supplied by the food goes into growing in size instead of being dissipated by moving about quickly and continuously.

Scaly armour

In all probability it is because its scales are so closely set, forming such a rigid covering, that a gar must lead an inactive life. This

△ *The dart-shaped body of short-nosed gar helps it merge with surrounding water plants.*

tough scaly armour of the gar has, however, proved very useful and been used by different peoples in different ways. The original inhabitants of the Caribbean islands are said to have used the skin, with its diamond-shaped, closely fitting scales, for breastplates. Some of the North American Indians separated the scales and used them for arrowheads. The early pioneers in the United States found gar skin hard enough to cover the blades of their wooden ploughs.

class	**Pisces**
order	**Ginglymodi**
family	**Lepisosteidae**
genus & species	***Lepisosteus osseus*** longnose gar *L. platystomus* shortnose gar *L. spatula* alligator gar *L. tristoechus* tropical gar

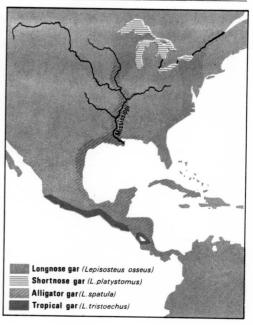

Longnose gar (Lepisosteus osseus)
Shortnose gar (L.platystomus)
Alligator gar (L.spatula)
Tropical gar (L.tristoechus)

△ *Suffering from exposure: waste eggs trapped in stream debris. Eggs are usually covered by sand.*

Pacific salmon

There are six species of salmon in the North Pacific, by contrast with the North Atlantic where there is only one species, called the Atlantic salmon. Except for the Japanese species, the masu, these range from about Kamchatka in Siberia to the American west coast as far south as California. Of these the chinook, also known as the tyee, quinnat, king, spring, Sacramento or Columbia River salmon, weighs 10—50 lb, with a maximum of 108 lb. The sockeye, red or blueback salmon weighs 5—7 lb, but may weigh up to 15½ lb; the silver salmon or coho weighs 6—12 lb, going up to 26½ lb; the chum, keta or dog salmon weighs 8—18 lb; but is sometimes as much as 30 lb, and the humpback or pink salmon which is 3—5 lb, may weigh up to 10 lb.

Drastic changes for spawning

Pacific salmon return to spawn in the same river in which they hatched, and when they do so they become brilliant red, and their heads turn pea green. The males grow long hooked snouts and their mouths become filled with sharp teeth. The females do not grow the hooked snout. Most of the returning salmon are 4—5 years old. The humpback matures the earliest at 2 years, the silver salmon at 3, but some of the sockeye and chinook may be as much as 8 years old.

The salmon return in early summer, even in late spring, or in autumn in the case of the chum. They stop feeding as their digestive organs deteriorate and head for the coast from their feeding grounds out in the Pacific. On reaching the mouth of a river they head upstream, except the chum which usually spawns near tidal waters. The

silver salmon moves only a short distance upstream. The chinook, on the other hand, has been known to travel as much as 2 250 miles up rivers. One exception to this is a subspecies of the sockeye which is non-migratory. In contrast with the Atlantic salmon, however, Pacific salmon never survive the spawning run.

Mating ends in death

By the time the salmon near the spawning grounds, they are mere bags of bones housing the eggs or the sperms. The males often look the worse for wear as they fight with each other. The females look for a place in the sandy or gravelly shallows where the water is clear with plenty of oxygen. Then they start digging troughs (redds) in the river beds with their tails; each one lying on her side and flapping with her tail. When her trough is deep enough, she lies in it to spawn, her mate swimming over to her to shed his milt to fertilise the eggs. Each female lays several batches of eggs, to a total of 3—5 thousand, in different troughs, by the end of which time she is completely exhausted. With her tail fins worn to stubs, her skin blackening and with blotches of grey fungus attacking it, she dies. The males share the same fate, and the carcases of both drift downstream or are stranded at the edge.

Down to the sea as infants

Each batch of eggs becomes buried under sand as fresh redds are dug and the loosened sand is wafted over them. Thus protected, the orange-pink eggs hatch 8 weeks later. The alevins or young salmon remain under the gravel feeding on their yolk sacs for some weeks before wriggling to the surface as fry. They feed heavily on water fleas and other small animals and in the following spring are carried downstream by the current. The humpback and chum go

to the sea as fry but the sockeye may go as fry or as 1—3 year fish, and the quinnat and coho go when 1—2 years old.

Finding their way home

There has always been a great interest in how salmon find their way back to the streams where they were hatched. The full story has not yet been pieced together but sufficient is now known to sketch in many of the details. There is evidence, for example, to show that the thyroid gland plays a part in the salmon's changing preference for water of varying salinity. When the coho was injected with a certain hormone it sought sea water. When the injections were stopped it sought fresh water. The opposite effect was found in the humpback. Probably other glands are involved, as well as the length of day and possibly the diet. The sense of smell may play a part, as it does in finding food. Temperatures also influence the fish, certainly once they have entered fresh water. When these are too low or too high the fish make no effort to surmount obstacles. There is some evidence also that celestial navigation, using the sun by day and the stars by night, as in migrating birds, keeps the salmon on their compass runs along the coast to the mouths of the rivers they came from.

Expert water-tasters

Of the different ways that salmon find their way back, one of the easier to test is the odour, or the taste of the water from which the fishes originated. Laboratory experiments have shown beyond doubt that fishes, including salmon, can recognize waters of only slightly different tastes; smell and taste are closely linked. This is not so very surprising since water-tasters dealing with the purification of drinking water are able to tell by tasting, in an almost uncanny way, where a particular glass of water came

△ *The remains. Reduced to blackened bags of bones after spawning, dead sockeye salmon are washed up at the river's edge.*

△ *On home ground. A pair of sockeye salmon, having swum from the Pacific Ocean up to the head waters of the river in which they hatched 4 or 5 years before, are now ready to spawn themselves — then die, starved and exhausted by their marathon journey on which they do not feed at all.*

from. These same tests show that the memory of a particular type of water persists for a long time in a fish, and that the younger the fish the longer the memory will probably be.

Controlled fishing

Many people living a long way from the Pacific are familiar with the Pacific salmon — in canned form. The salmon fishery is commercially highly valuable, with 2 – 10 million sockeye alone being caught and canned. The salmon are taken in gill nets, reef nets and purse seines on their way to the Fraser River in British Columbia. Unrestricted fishing could kill the industry,

so by an agreement between Canada and the United States, 20% of each race of fish are allowed through to continue their journey to the spawning grounds. This is taken care of by a joint International Pacific Salmon Fisheries Commission, which also arranges for the catch to be divided equally between the two countries. There is co-operation also in providing concrete and steel fishways to assist the salmon up the rivers. The Pacific salmon fishery is therefore as near as it has so far been possible to an actual husbandry of a wild resource. Moreover, research is being carried out to produce strains of salmon that can tolerate less favourable rivers than they

use at present, and to transplant fry which, when mature, will return to spawn in waters earmarked for cultivation.

class	**Pisces**		
order	**Salmoniformes**		
family	**Salmonidae**		
genus & species	***Oncorhynchus gorbuscha*** *humpback*		
	O. keta *chum*		
	O. kisutch *silver salmon*		
	O. masou *masu*		
	O. nerka *sockeye*		
	O. tshawytscha *chinook*		

Trout

The European trout, of very variable colour, is known by three names. The brown trout is small, dark and non-migratory. It can weigh up to 17 lb 12 oz and lives in the smaller rivers and pools. The lake trout is larger and paler. It lives in larger rivers and lakes and it may be migratory. The sea trout, large, silvery up to 4½ ft long and weighing up to 30 lb, is distinctly migratory. All three belong to the same species.

The European brown trout and lake trout are greenish brown, the flanks being lighter than the back, and the belly yellowish. They are covered with many red and black spots, the latter surrounded by pale rings. There are spots even on the gill covers. These two and the sea trout resemble the salmon in shape and appearance except that the angle of the jaw reaches to well behind the eye and the adipose fin is tinged with orange.

The North American species are similar. The cut-throat trout has two red marks across the throat. The Dolly Varden is named for its conspicuous red spots, coloured like the cherry ribbons worn by the Dickens character. In the brook trout the pattern is more mottled but it also has red spots on the flanks. The rainbow trout has a reddish band along the flanks. The lake or mackinau trout lives in deep water, down to 400 ft. The golden trout lives in water 8 000 ft or more above sea level.

▷ Like some figment of an angler's daydream, a big New Zealand rainbow trout jumps from its shoal for a flying titbit.
▽ Mixed bunch, with rainbow trout in front of brown. Because of aquarium glass, the red line on the rainbows' sides cannot be seen.

Temperature important

Trout grow best in clear, aerated waters and although they are sometimes found in turbid waters it is only when the surface layers are well supplied with oxygen. They are readily affected by silt; it may spoil their spawning sites, reduce their food supply or act directly on the fishes themselves. Laboratory experiments have shown that particles in suspension in the water, at a level as low as 270 parts per million, abrade the gills or cause them to thicken. The rate of growth of trout varies in other ways as well, often to a remarkable extent, with the conditions of their surroundings. Temperature, for instance, is highly important, and an example can be seen at the time when they resume feeding after the winter fast. Normally, trout stop feeding in autumn and resume in spring, in about March when the water reaches a temperature of 2°C/36°F or more. In a mild winter they may begin feeding in December and continue until the first cold snap of the following autumn.

The rate of growth also varies from one river to another, or from river to sea. Trout living in small streams grow more slowly than those in large rivers, and those in large bodies of fresh water grow more slowly than those living in the sea. A trout in a small river will grow 2½, 5 and 8 in. in its first, second and third years respectively. Corresponding figures for a sea trout will be 3−5, 4−5 and 10−11 in.

Diet changes

The diet of trout varies with their age. Fry eat mainly aquatic larvae of insects, rarely the adults. Later they eat large numbers of winged insects, as well as water fleas and freshwater shrimps. When adult they eat mainly small fishes as well as shrimps, insect larvae and adults, especially the winged insects. Sea trout feed on sprats, young herring and sand eels and also on a large percentage of small crustaceans, including shrimps and prawns.

Correct place to spawn

Male trout begin to breed at two years, females at three, returning to do so to the place where they themselves were hatched. This homing has been verified experimentally, by transporting marked trout to other parts of a river system, then finding them later, back on their 'home ground'. Breeding usually takes place from October to February, the time varying from one locality to another. Spawning is normally in running water, trout living in lakes going into the feeder streams.

For spawning the female makes a 'redd' in gravelly shallows, digging a depression with flicks of her tail. As she lays her eggs, the male, in attendance on her, fertilises them, stationing himself beside her but slightly to the rear. It has been found that a successful redd is one with a current flowing downwards through the gravel. The eggs hatch in about 40 days. The fry are ½−1 in. long at hatching, and the yolk sac is absorbed in 4−6 weeks.

Surrounded by enemies

WE Frost and ME Brown, in their book *The Trout*, state that 94% of fry are lost during the first 3−4 months of their lives. After this the mortality drops to 20%. Eels are often said to kill trout and especially to ravage the spawning grounds, but there is no evidence of this. The chief enemies of trout are water shrew, mink, the common rat, and to some extent otters and herons. Another enemy of trout is larger trout. Well grown ones have sometimes been found to have another trout, 5−6 in. long, in their stomachs. The record for the brown trout comes from New Zealand, where the fish were introduced. In 1967 a 20lb trout had a foot-long trout in its stomach. In their cannibalism, therefore, trout vie with pike, always regarded as a traditional enemy, which, with few exceptions, take only medium to large sized trout.

There are two other contributors to trout depletion—apart from man. Numbers of other animals compete with it for food, and of these, which include several water birds, the eel is probably one of the worst, more so in rivers than in lakes. The other natural 'enemy' is lack of oxygen, especially during the winter. When the pools and lakes are frozen over, trout must rely on oxygen trapped under ice. This is replenished by oxygen given out by water plants. When, however, the ice is blanketed by snow, light does not penetrate, plants cannot 'work', and trout are asphyxiated.

Many species

The wide variation in size and colour of the European trout is brought out by the history of its species. In 1758 Linnaeus named three species: the Swedish river trout, the sea trout and the lake trout. Dr Albert Gunther, leading authority on fishes, wrote in 1880: 'We know of no other group of fishes which offers so many difficulties . . . to the distinction of species'. He recognized 10 species in the British Isles alone—the sea trout, sewin, phinnock, Galway sea trout, Orkney sea trout, river trout, great lake trout, gillaroo, Welsh blackfinned trout and Loch Leven trout. Thirty years later, C Tate Regan, Günther's successor, put forward strong arguments for treating these and all species and races in continental Europe as one very variable species.

class	Pisces
order	Salmoniformes
family	Salmonidae
genera & species	*Salmo aguabonita* golden *S. clarki* cutthroat *S. gairdneri* rainbow *S. trutta* brown *Salvelinus fontinalis* brook *S. malma* Dolly Varden *S. namaycush* lake, others

Young brown trout, easily identified by the red spots on the side of its body, swims in clear river water; the clearer the water, the faster it grows.

Hatchet fish

Tiny, strangely-shaped fishes, looking like strips of shiny, crinkled tinfoil — such is the best description of the 15 species of deep-sea hatchet fishes, all of them distant relatives of the salmon. Most of them are 1—2 in. long, the largest being 3½ in. There are 450 of the smaller ones to the lb. Hatchet fishes have high bodies flattened from side to side, resembling the head of a hatchet, the lower surface corresponding with the sharp edge of the hatchet blade. They are covered with large scales which in a few species are missing from the breast and belly, leaving those parts transparent. In all of them the colour of the body is silvery and iridescent. Their eyes are large, their fins are of moderate size and transparent except for the rays supporting them, and along the lower edge of the body and on the underside of the tail are many closely-set light organs. The light from these is usually blue but in some a bright ruby red light has been seen.

The marine hatchet fishes should not be confused with the freshwater fishes given this name (see page 178).

Sensitive telescopic eyes

Marine hatchet fishes live in the twilight zone of the oceans, where only the green and blue rays of light penetrate. They can be found between 300 and 1 500 ft in all tropical and temperate seas. The human eye can detect light at these depths although sensitive photographic plates lowered into the sea register that a very small amount of light penetrates even farther, down to 3 000 ft. Since the human eye can detect a faint light down to 1 500 ft we can suppose the large eye of hatchet fishes, with its large lens, and retina composed of long rods only, is at least as sensitive as the human eye.

How much the light from the hatchet fish's own light organs (which are on the lower edge of the body) help the eyes is problematic. They probably help little, since the eyes are well up on top of the head or directed upwards in some species. In some of these last species the eyes are tubular and are usually described as telescopic. It is even suggested that they may truly be telescopic, magnifying objects seen by the fishes because their focal length, the distance between the lens and the retina, is greater than in the normal eye.

Submarine weightlessness

Hatchet fishes are very light, weighing on average about $\frac{1}{35}$ oz. They have a well-developed swimbladder. These two things together mean they have neutral buoyancy, that is, they neither float up nor sink, but maintain a balance. We are used to the idea of weightlessness in space travel; neutral buoyancy means much the same thing. So hatchet fishes can swim easily and make considerable vertical migrations daily, coming up almost to the surface at night and going down again by day. In these migrations they are following their food, which consists of planktonic animals such as copepods and the fry of other fishes. At the same time the hatchet fishes themselves become the prey of carnivorous fishes living near the surface and they are an important part of the food of tuna.

Submerged islands?

Since the end of the Second World War, with the refinement of the echo-sounder, observers on ships of the US Navy in the Pacific noted that their echo-sounder traces showed, in addition to a profile of the sea-bed, a second, sometimes a third or a fourth profile far above the seabed. During the day these 'deep scattering layers', as they came to be called, were at depths of 700 – 2 400 ft. At nightfall they moved up nearer the surface and became more diffuse. They proved to be made up of the larger animals in the plankton. They need to be about $2\frac{1}{2}$ in. long to reflect back the echoes of the echo-sounder, and the animals giving the traces that make up the deep scattering layers are jellyfishes, large numbers of crustaceans and the larger arrow-worms. In the trace of a deep scattering layer are blobs and marks like an inverted V. These marks were first called tent fish and blob fish, but were later found to be caused by hatchet fishes and lantern fishes. This is an indication of how numerous these two kinds of deep-sea fishes are. When echo-sounders were first being used they often indicated shoals where there should have been deep water. These submerged islands, as they were thought to be, are now known to be deep scattering layers, strata of plankton with the hatchet and lantern fishes feeding under them and forming a temporary and movable ceiling over the vast recesses of the abyssal depths of the oceans.

class	**Pisces**
order	**Salmoniformes**
family	**Sternoptychidae**
genera & species	***Argyropelecus gigas*** ***Sternoptyx diaphana*** *others*

△ *Dense masses of hatchet fishes help form the phantom sea floor of the deep scattering layer on echo-sounder screens.*

◁ *These are preserved museum specimens.*

▽ *Freshwater hatchet fishes, which do a butterfly-like dance in courtship. Like the marine version, they are named for their shape. These are pygmy hatchet fishes* **Carnegiella marthae.**

Arapaima

The arapaima, said to be one of the largest freshwater fishes, is rather like a pike. It has a long cylindrical body, with the unpaired fins set well back towards the tail, a small flattened head, and a jutting lower jaw. The fish is coloured green in front but the rear half of the body becomes increasingly reddish, the tail being crimson. In Brazil it is known as the pirarucu, pirá meaning fish and urucú being the name of a bush in Brazil bearing flaming red seeds from which is made the annato dye, used for colouring cheese and butter. In Peru it is known as paiche. It also occurs in Guyana, and probably in Venezuela and Colombia.

Freshwater fishes are generally smaller than marine fishes, and only a few of them attain giant size. The arapaima is one of the larger ones and is said to reach nearly 15 ft in length and 440 lb in weight, but usually it is 7–8 ft long. The family to which it belongs is characterised by stout, bony scales each containing canals that form a mosaic-like pattern. Rings on the scales indicate age. The arapaima matures at 4 to 5 years and can live 18 years or more.

The arapaima is placed in the family Osteoglossidae or bony tongues, fishes with a lineage that can be traced back over 100 million years. So the arapaima is a living fossil, and some of its more primitive features are the bony head, peculiar shape of the fins, lobe-like tail and the lung-like air-bladder.

△ A gigantic arapaima about to grab a tasty fish. The operculum which covers the gills has been raised so the gill arches are visible. The rings on the large scales indicate the fish's age. A lifespan of over 18 years is not unknown.

▷ The arapaima can grow to over 5 ft in length in 5 years from birth. Certain features, such as the head, the shape of the fins, the lobe-like tail and the lung-like swimbladder, indicate its primitiveness. Its family can be traced back over 100 million years.

Air breathing

The arapaima keeps to shallow water where it moves about lethargically, periodically rising to the surface to gulp air into the swim-bladder, which opens by a duct into the back of the throat, functioning as a lung. The swim-bladder is large and occupies the whole area above the gut. It is made of cellular, lung-like tissue, and it opens direct into the gullet. This system is probably aided by the arapaima's large human-like red blood corpuscles. (The blood also clots on exposure to air—another development in the direction of land-living.) This development of air breathing apparatus recalls that of lungfishes, and it is of interest that the Osteoglossidae have nearly the same distribution as the lung-fishes (see map), and both provide evidence suggesting that all continents were once joined and have drifted apart. The amphis-baena also provides similar evidence for the theory of continental drift.

Omnivorous feeder

Though essentially a fish-eater, the arapaima seems ready to eat anything. The fish it preys upon include the hassar, lukamani, and baira, but examination of 5,000 stomachs revealed the remains of many other items, including water snails, freshwater shrimps, worms, vegetable matter, freshwater turtles, snakes, frogs, crabs, grasshoppers, pebbles, sand, mud, and even coal. The young fry feed on microplankton, later take general plankton, and as they increase in size they take plankton and small fishes. When the young have reached this last stage they stand a risk of being eaten by their parents. There is an interesting adaptation of the fourth gill-arch, which was once thought to help in breathing. In one of the five species in the family this has now been shown to be a filter, which strains small particles from the water passing across the gills. These are trapped in mucus which is then carried to the gullet and stomach. When the water-level is low, in the dry season, this food is important.

Breeding season

The breeding season lasts from December to May. Spawning takes place in shallow water, at depths of 2½—5 ft. During April and May, when the rivers overflow and flood the low-lying land, the arapaima move into this shallow water, select sandy areas clear of vegetation and hollow out nests, digging with mouth, chin, and fins. These saucer-like nests are 20 in. across and up to 8 in. deep.

Normally there is little difference between male and female, but at the breeding season the female goes a chestnut shade, the male develops a black head and his tail turns a bright vermilion. Each female lays up to 180,000 eggs in several batches, each in its separate nest. The eggs, ⅛—¼ in. in diameter, hatch in 5 days. The larvae, ½ in. long and black, swarm in a group over the male's head near the surface. So as he rises to gulp air the larvae swarming round his black head are made invisible. They also swarm round his head when disturbed, protected no doubt by this camouflage. The female, meanwhile, swims around father and offspring, ready to drive off intruders.

Enemies

It is caught and eaten in large numbers, its flesh being salted or dried. The aboriginal American Indians kill it with bow and arrow or trap it in the shallows. Jaguars also are said to catch arapaima.

Size in question

While its lineage and anatomy are in little doubt, the arapaima's size has been the subject of much speculation. Nearly every book on fishes, every dictionary and encyclopedia, tells us that the arapaima reaches 15 ft in length and a weight of 400 or even 600 lb. This, it seems, is a myth. The fish is extensively eaten and therefore must be very well known. The numbers caught annually are high, as indicated by the investigator who, wishing to catalogue the things the arapaima eats, examined 5,000 stomachs in a short while. Yet nobody has so far recorded, from actual measurements, one longer than 7 ft or a greater weight than 246 lb.

When we look into this we find that the naturalist Schomburgk, writing in 1836 about his visit to Guiana, stated that 'the natives' told him 'the fish reached 15 ft long and 400 lb weight'. Every writer since has repeated these figures, most of them being unaware that the evidence was hearsay. Other writers have aided and abetted by using such phrases as 'too long and wide to fit into a 15-ft canoe' or 'I estimate 300 to 400 lb because one fish filled up to busting point 181 Indians. . . .'

Since Schomburgk's day hundreds of thousands of arapaima have been caught and eaten, many thousands have been examined by scientists. Yet the largest recorded is still only 7 ft.

class	**Pisces**
order	**Osteoglossiformes**
family	**Osteoglossidae**
genus & species	*Arapaima gigas*

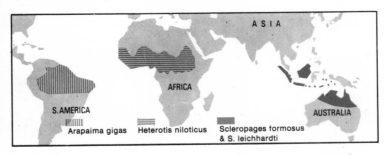

Distribution of the Osteoglossidae. Note the discontinuous distribution through South America, Africa, the Malay Archipelago and Australia.

Butterfly fish

It is virtually impossible to speak about butterfly fishes without confusion since the name is commonly used for different kinds of unrelated fishes. The same can be said of angelfishes. Attention is drawn to this on page 202, where butterfly fishes are described, together with their very close relatives, the marine angelfishes. Here we discuss this subject in order to deal with a freshwater fish that has been called a butterfly fish. At the same time this gives us the opportunity to contrast and compare it with the marine fishes, inhabitants of coral reefs especially, which are also called butterfly fishes. For our description of the habits of marine butterfly fishes we must refer to page 202. But here on the following pages we portray these fishes, belonging to the family Chaetodontidae, in a series of fascinating and beautiful photographs.

The one species of freshwater butterfly fish is sufficiently extraordinary to merit close attention on its own. Never more than 4 in. long, it lives in the rivers of tropical West Africa. Its head and body are boat-shaped, flattened above, bluntly rounded below. It is coloured grey-green to brownish-silver, marked with spots and streaks. The large mouth is directed upwards, and the nostrils are tubular. Another remarkable feature is its fins. The pectoral fins are large and wing-like.

Each pelvic fin has four very long filamentous rays not connected to each other, and the unpaired fins are large, transparent and supported by long rays.

For a long time the relationships of this fish, first discovered in 1876, have been in doubt, but it is now placed in a family on its own near that of the large South American fish, the arapaima. It has no relationship with the marine butterfly fishes of the family Chaetodontidae.

▽ The freshwater butterfly fish is not related to marine butterfly fishes of the tropical seas.

▽▽ Four-eyed butterfly fish, so-called because of the false 'eye' markings at its tail end.

▽ Vividly-striped marine butterfly fishes are deep-bodied and flattened from side to side

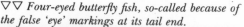

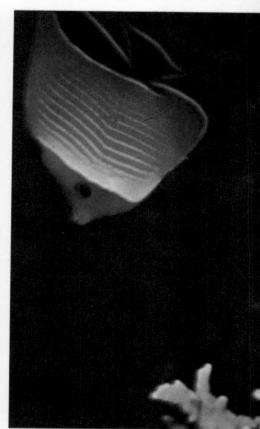

A fish that flies

This remarkable fish is reckoned to fly over the water, flapping its wings like a bat or a bird. The freshwater butterfly fish spends most of its time just below the surface of still or stagnant waters in the Congo and Niger basins, in the weedy backwaters and standing pools. But it is most renowned for its ability to leap out of water for distances up to 6 ft, its large pectoral fins being used, as are those of the true flying fishes, in gliding flight. It has also been credited with flapping these fins in true powered flight, as in bats and birds. By 1960, however, it had been generally agreed that this was not so.

Then came a remarkable sequel. PH Greenwood and KS Thomson investigated the anatomy of this fish. They found it had a most unusual shoulder girdle, the arrangement of bones to which the pectoral fins are attached. In fact, these two authors described it as unique among fishes. The bones were so thin that they had to be very careful not to damage them while dissecting them out. The whole of the shoulder girdle is broad and flattened to give support to a highly developed system of muscles, comparable with the large pectoral muscles that work the wings of birds. The two scientists also found that the fins could not be folded against the body, as is usual in fishes, but could be moved up and down. In brief, they concluded that, while it was still unproven whether or not the butterfly fish could make a powered flight, its shoulder girdle and muscles were such that it ought to be able to fly. The best that can be said is that the fish has been seen to beat its fins up and down when held in the hand. It has, however, been suggested that this is only used to give the butterfly fish a push-off from the water to become airborne.

Insect feeder

The food consists almost entirely of the small insects, such as flies, that fall on to the surface of the water.

Life history

Relatively little is known about the breeding, and such details as we have are from the few butterfly fishes that have bred in captivity. Numerous false matings have been seen, with the male riding on the back of the female, sometimes for hours at a time, holding her firmly with the long rays of the pelvic fins. Mating finally is effected by the two twisting their bodies together to bring the vents opposite each other. Fertilisation seems, however, not to be internal. As soon

▽▽ *Marine butterfly fishes* **Chaetodon** *live around coral reefs in shallow tropical seas.*

▽ *The butterfly fish* **Heniochus acuminatus** *lives in the warm seas around the Philippine Islands. It has a very deep body, most of the depth being due to a highly arched back.*

The freshwater butterfly fish Pantodon buchholzi found in the waters of western Africa is one of the strangest of the so-called flying fishes. It spends most of its time swimming just under the surface and is capable of leaping out of the water for a distance of 6 or more feet.

as they are laid the eggs float to the surface, and in 3 days these hatch. The fry remain at the surface feeding on the tiniest of the insects, such as springtails and aphides, which fall on them.

Flying or gliding
The ability to make either gliding or powered flights through the air is rare among fishes, although to be able to leap from the water is common enough. For years, scientists have argued among themselves whether or not the flying fishes of the oceans beat their wings when airborne. At present, evidence suggests that they do not. Similarly, it may be some years before we can be sure whether the West African butterfly fishes beat their wings or not. There is, however, one group of freshwater fishes that do beat their fins to achieve true

flight through the air. These are the hatchet fishes of northern South America, found from the River Plate to Panama.

As so often happens, another confusion of names arises. We already have it over butterfly fishes, as we have seen. There are also two kinds of hatchet fishes. One is marine (see page 172) and the other is freshwater. Both are named for their shape, the body being flattened from side to side, so that it looks like the blade of a hatchet:

The freshwater hatchet fishes beat their pectoral fins rapidly when making a take-off run over the surface before becoming airborne, and they continue to beat their fins when airborne.

To make the confusion even more confounded, it may be mentioned that freshwater hatchet fishes do a butterfly-like dance

during their courtship. Fortunately we can note the scientific names and there can be no doubt as to the animal referred to. Each animal has a binomial name of genus and species, rather like the surname and christian name used to identify humans.

class	**Pisces**
order	**Osteoglossiformes**
family	**Pantodontidae**
genus & species	*Pantodon buchholzi* *freshwater butterfly fish*

Piranha

Few accounts of travel in South and Central America fail to contain some references to the piranha or piraya, the small but allegedly very ferocious fish that inhabits the rivers of this region. In some places it abounds in such vast numbers as to be a serious pest, making the infested streams either very hazardous or quite impossible for fording or bathing.

The name piranha applies loosely to about 18 species, of which only 4 seem to be dangerous to humans. All are members of the genus **Serrasalmus,** having a general similarity of appearance and habits. Some scientists, however, classify them differently. Most of the

species average 8 in. in length but **Serrasalmus piraya,** of the River São Francisco in eastern Brazil, one of the most dangerous, may reach 2 ft. Most of them are olive-green or blue-black above and silvery or dark grey on flanks and belly. Some species have reddish or yellowish tinted fins. The colours seem to vary considerably from place to place and with age. For example, old specimens of the white piranha **Serrasalmus rhombeus,** found in the Amazon system and north-eastern South America, are often dark enough to be called black piranhas.

The body of the piranha is deep, short and rather compressed from side to side. A large bony crest on top of the skull supports a keel on the back, and a similar keel on the belly is strengthened by a firm

*Red piranha (**Serrasalmus nattereri**) ; close-up of fish lurking among weeds.*

row of enlarged scales bearing sharp, backwardly-directed points, so the deep and heavy forepart of the fish is provided with a cut-water above and below. There is a fleshy adipose fin on the back between the dorsal and tail fins. The tail is slender and muscular and together with the broad, tough, blade-like tail fin helps to drive the body through the water with great force. As in all really swift fish the scales are very small. The most striking feature is the mouth. The massive lower jaw has relatively huge muscles operating it. The teeth are large, flat and triangular with very sharp points. These points merely pierce the skin, the rest is done by the

179

usual erratic spawning behaviour of most of the other members of its family. The male guards the eggs as well as the fry, when they hatch. These became free-swimming about 5 days after hatching.

Ferocity exaggerated?

The ferocity of the piranha has become almost legendary. Stories are told of a cow or a pig, falling into a river, being stripped to a skeleton in a few minutes. One of the most famous stories is that of a man, fording a stream on horseback, who was brought down and killed by a swarm of piranha. Later the bones of horse and rider were found, picked perfectly clean, the man's clothes undamaged. It is probable that a lot of the stories have been exaggerated. Some travellers now say that they have waded in or swam in rivers infested with piranha shoals and have never been attacked. Yet others say they have come on villages where hardly a native had not suffered the loss of a toe or finger. It is difficult to know what to believe but there must be some truth in the danger from these fish.

It is possible that the ferocity of the piranha may vary with the species and from place to place, and it may be that they are much more aggressive at the beginning of the rainy season when the males are guarding the eggs. This could also explain why it is that they will attack bathers at certain places in a river, where perhaps they have laid eggs, leaving others unmolested not far away. Nevertheless, those aquarists who keep these fishes admit to treating them with respect and taking extra care in feeding them, or when netting them to transfer them from one aquarium to another.

edges, which are literally razor-sharp. The teeth of the upper jaw are similar but much smaller and fit exactly into the spaces between the points of the lower ones when the mouth is closed. The jaws are so strong and the teeth so sharp that they can chop out a piece of flesh as neatly as a razor. The fact that there is a reliable record of a 100lb capybara reduced to a skeleton in less than a minute shows the efficiency of the teeth.

A few of the smaller species are kept in aquaria, the most popular seen in tropical fish stores and public aquaria being *Serrasalmus nattereri*, the red or common piranha, up to 1 ft long and coloured red on the underside and fins.

Some piranhas are found only in certain river systems, such as the Rio São Francisco, Rio Paraguay or Rio Orinoco, while others range over a wide area.

Water alive with fish

Piranha hunt in shoals, sometimes of several thousands, so in places the water seems to be alive with them. Smaller fishes form their staple diet, but any animal entering or falling into the water accidentally may be attacked. They often attack each other. It is said that they will instantly be attracted by blood in the water but apparently anything out of the ordinary will attract them.

Waterplant hatcheries

It is thought that piranha breed when the rainy season sets in about January or February. The female deposits her eggs on water plants or roots. On hatching, the fry stay attached to the vegetation in clusters until they have absorbed most of the yolk sac, and then become free-swimming. *Serrasalmus spilopleura* is one of the few species which has been seen breeding in an aquarium. The female deposited her eggs carefully on aquatic plants, which is unlike the

class	**Pisces**
order	**Cypriniformes**
family	**Serrasalmidae**
genus & species	***Serrasalmus nattereri*** red or Natterer's piranha **S. piraya** piraya **S. rhombeus** white or spotted piranha **S. spilopleura** common piranha others

The electric eel, unrelated to the true eels, emits high-voltage discharges which stun or kill fishes or frogs, those dying near the eel being eaten.

Electric eel

The South American electric eel, which can kill a horse with an electric shock, is not even related to eels. It has less than 50 relatives, which include the gymnotid eels, and knife-fishes, all tropical American and probably generating electricity to a greater or lesser extent; but the most spectacular and notorious is the electric eel itself, which can discharge up to 550 volts when fully grown.

The electric eel has a cylindrical body, a uniform olive-brown, up to 6 ft long—the largest recorded 9½ ft—running to a pointed tail. It has no fins on the back, only very small paired fins behind the gills, and a long conspicuous anal fin running from the tip of the tail almost to the throat. Its eyes are very small. About ⅞ths of the body is tail, with the internal organs crowded into a small space behind the head. The tail contains the electric organs, made up of 5—6 thousand electroplates (elements) arranged like the cells in a dry battery. Moreover, there are three parts to the electric organ, two small batteries and the main battery. The electric eel is positive towards the head end, negative at the tail end, the reverse order to that of the electric catfish.

Poor gills, no lungs

The electric eel lives in waters poor in oxygen. It comes to the surface from time to time to gulp air. In its mouth are patches of superficial blood vessels which take up oxygen from the air gulped at the surface, so acting as auxiliary breathing organs.

It swims by undulating the long anal fin and is said to be able to swim forwards or backwards, up or down, with equal ease. So long as it is still its main electric organ at least is not working, but the small battery in the tail is working continuously. As soon as the eel starts to move it gives out electric impulses at the rate of 20—30 a second which later increases to 50 a second. These are used for direction-finding, it is now known, although they do not form an electric field, as in the Nile fish.

High-voltage jolts

It has been said that the second of the small batteries probably fires the larger battery, which gives out a series of 3—6 waves at intervals of 5/1000 of a second, each wave lasting 2/1000 of a second. These are the high-voltage discharges which stun or kill fishes or frogs, those dying near the eel being eaten. Larger animals coming into contact with a large electric eel are stunned. A stunned horse falls and is liable to be drowned. A man can stand the shock, but not repeatedly.

Unknown breeding places

Little is known of the breeding; there is no obvious difference between the sexes and the breeding places are unknown. The eels disappear from their usual haunts in the breeding season. When they return young eels 4—6 in. long come back with them, still guarded by the parents. Young eels are light brown with bands. Later they become marbled and finally olive-brown with the throat brilliant orange.

Millions of years ahead

Even more remarkable than the electric eel is the story of the first man to study its electrical discharge. From the beginning of the 16th century Spain had refused all non-Spaniards permission to visit her American colonies. In 1800, when rapid strides were being made in the study of electricity, the German naturalist, Baron Friedrich von Humboldt, applied for and was granted permission to visit South America. With a companion he arrived at the upper reaches of the Orinoco River and Calabozo, a town of exiles.

Von Humboldt took with him a large amount of scientific apparatus. Oxygen had only recently been recognized and von Humboldt took the latest apparatus in order to analyse the gases in the swim-bladders of fishes. He also took the latest electrical apparatus, only to find that Carlos del Pozo, resident in the town of exiles, had begun making similar apparatus thousands of miles from the centres of learning in Europe—a remarkable coincidence. And there also von Humboldt found large fishes that had developed their own electrical apparatus, but millions of years in advance of del Pozo and the European scientists.

This gifted German gave the world the first scientific accounts of the behaviour of the electric eel. He stood on one of these fishes and experienced a painful numbness. He also found that for the rest of the day he was afflicted with a violent pain in the knees and in the rest of his joints. Having studied the eel he made a remarkable prophecy: 'The discoveries that will be made on the electromotive apparatus of these fishes will extend to all the phenomena of muscular motion subject to volition. It will perhaps be found that in most animals every contraction of muscle fibre is preceded by a discharge from the nerve into the muscle.' He also predicted that electricity is the source of life and movement in all living things.

class	**Pisces**
order	**Cypriniformes**
family	**Gymnotidae**
genus & species	***Electrophorus electricus***

The South American electric eel lives in waters poor in oxygen. It comes to the surface from time to time to gulp air. In its mouth are patches of superficial blood vessels which take up oxygen from the air gulped at the surface, so helping with breathing.

Electric eel *(Electrophorus electricus)*

Trunkfish

The trunkfishes are the nearest we have to fishes masquerading as turtles. They are also known as boxfishes and cofferfishes because their bodies are enclosed within bony boxes made up of 6-sided bony plates fitting closely into one another, leaving only the tail unarmoured. Inside, the backbone is short with only 14 vertebrae between the skull and the beginning of the tail, all joined in a compact manner.

A typical trunkfish has a more or less conical head, the face sloping down at a steep angle to the small mouth, which is armed with strong crushing teeth. The eyes are large and there is only a small opening from the gill chamber. The length of a trunkfish seldom exceeds 1 ft. The single dorsal fin and the anal fin are fairly large, as are the pectoral fins, but there are no pelvic fins. The fleshy, naked tail ending in a large fanlike tail fin projects backwards from the bony box and, except for the other fins, is the only part capable of movement. The box enclosing the body is flat on the undersurface and it may be 3-, 4- or 5-sided in cross section, and one or more of its edges may be armed with strong spines.

Trunkfishes live at or near the bottom of warm waters, especially in tropical seas, all round the world.

Geometrical fishes: a comparison between the fishes above and overleaf will show the 3- and 4-faced arrangements of trunkfish armour. These arrangements vary according to species and serve as a rough means of classification.

△ Its transparent, fan-shaped fins beating rapidly, the cumbersome body of a smooth trunkfish moves slowly forwards. Unlike most fish, trunkfishes swim almost entirely by just a rapid beating of their fins.

◁ Passing beauty: **Ostracion meleagris** in the Hawaii reef. Like other trunkfishes, it can adopt a variety of colour schemes. The sexes and young of the same species are often quite differently patterned and coloured.

183

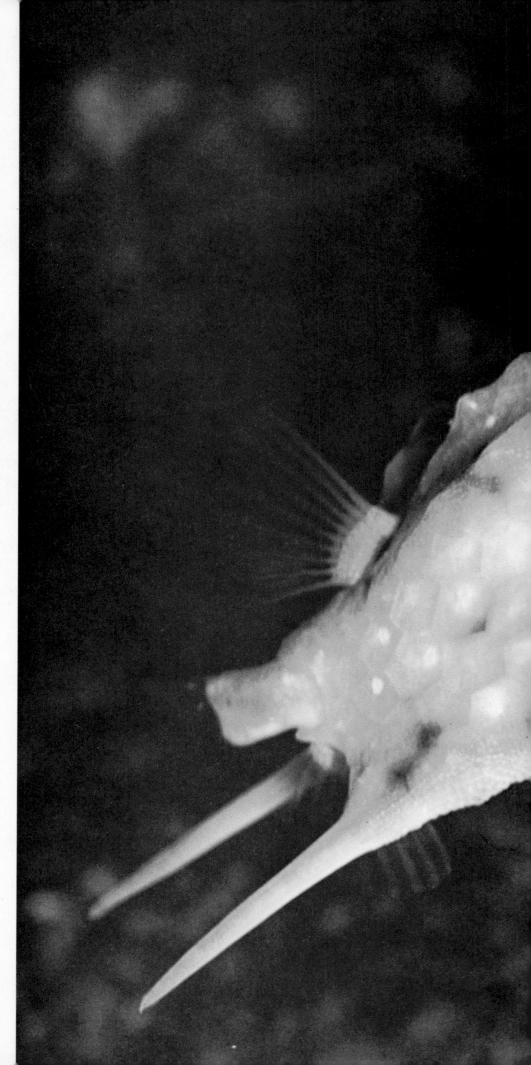

Slow moving

Like tortoises on land, trunkfishes are slow moving, and for much the same reasons. The normal fish swims by strong side to side movements of the whole body and, more especially, by the muscular tail. A trunkfish can move its tail only to a small extent. Its swimming is like a small boat being propelled by a single oar sculling from the stern. The only difference is that the hydrodynamic principles are more complex in the fish because the tail is flexible. The main swimming force is produced by side to side movements of the dorsal and anal fins, aided by the pectoral fins. A trunkfish is the very opposite of being streamlined—in fact the flat faces must create considerable resistance to progress—and when swimming it moves its fins very rapidly, giving the impression of a great expenditure of energy with only a little gain in forward movement.

Confusion of colours

Rapid movement is not necessary for so heavily armoured a fish, which can also rely on its colour and colour changes for security, and on its ability to poison other fishes. A common trunkfish found in the seas on both sides of the tropical Atlantic is the cowfish, so named because it has two sharp, forward-pointing spines on the forehead, rather like the horns of a cow. It is pale green in colour, marked with blue spots and lines, but it can change this to yellow with blue spots or brown with a network of light blue markings, or even to pure white. The colours also differ between the sexes. The 4-sided blue trunkfish of the Indo-Pacific is an example. The females and the young fish are purplish blue with numerous small white spots scattered thickly and evenly over the whole body. The male is very different, being purplish blue with a pale blue network except for the flat upper surface, which is a brownish purple with small white dots with a brick-red border. Even the eyes differ: in the females and young fish they are blue, in the males they have a red border.

Emit poison

It has been suggested that the gaudy colours act as warning colours, advertising to possible enemies that trunkfishes do not depend entirely on their armour but have other undesirable qualities. We do not know yet exactly how it is used, but we do know that trunkfishes can give out a poison. When one of them is placed in an aquarium it is not long before the other fishes begin to show signs of distress, coming to the surface to gulp air, and dying soon afterwards. The only fishes not affected are tough characters such as moray eels, the large groupers, and other trunkfishes. The poison persists even after the trunkfish have been removed.

Search for food in corals

Trunkfishes live among the corals, which they search for food, biting off pieces of coral to digest the polyps. At the same time, in biting pieces from the coral, they expose worms and other small invertebrates sheltering in it. Some trunkfishes use their spout-like snouts to blow jets of water at the sandy bottom to uncover and dislodge worms, molluscs and small crustaceans, which they immediately snap up.

Dingleberries

The breeding habits of the cowfish of tropical American waters are probably typical of the whole family. It lays buoyant eggs, $\frac{1}{32}$ in. diameter, which hatch in 2—3 days. The larvae begin to develop the hard cover in about a week and they become somewhat rounded in shape, and it is only as the young fishes mature that the box-like edges to the body become sharply defined. During the early stages of life young trunkfishes shelter under clumps of floating seaweed. Their rounded shape has earned them, in the United States, the name of dingleberries. At this stage they seem to have rather cherubic faces, with their large eyes, small mouths and what look like puffed cheeks.

Regarded as delicacy

The heaviest mortality among trunkfishes is in the early stages, when eggs, larvae and young fishes are often eaten. Once they reach maturity their protective boxes, and in some species the poison they give out, deter predators. Also, being so slow, they lack the large muscles that make the flesh of other fishes attractive. Yet trunkfishes are eaten, even by human beings, and in some places are regarded as a delicacy. They are cooked in their own boxes, and some people of the South Pacific are said to 'roast them like chestnuts'. There are, nevertheless, other opinions, one of which is that what little flesh there is cannot be praised for its flavour, although the liver is proportionately quite large and oily.

class	**Pisces**
order	**Tetraodontiformes**
family	**Ostraciontidae**
genera & species	***Lactophrys bicaudalis*** *large spotted trunkfish* ***L. quadricornis*** *cowfish* ***Ostracion lentiginosus*** *blue trunkfish* *others*

◁ *Always in shape, the complete covering of interlocking hexagonal plates of **O. cornutus** forms a rigid protective shield over the whole of the body except the flexible tail.*

185

Carp

Of the extensive carp family (Cyprinidae), this is the most widely distributed. Native of Japan, China and Central Asia, from Turkestan to the Black Sea and the Danube basin, it has been introduced into many European countries as well as the United States. It differs from other members of the family in its unusually long dorsal fin, with 17—22 branched rays, the strongly serrated third spine of the dorsal and anal fins, and in its four barbels, two at each corner of the slightly protrusible mouth. There are no teeth in the mouth, but there are throat-teeth. The colour of the wild form is olive to yellow-green on the back, greenish-yellow to bronze-yellow on the flanks, and underparts yellowish. The fins are grey-green to brown, sometimes slightly reddish.

Wild carp at home

Carp prefer shallow sunny waters with a muddy bottom and abundant water plants. They avoid clear, swift-flowing or cold waters. Wild carp are found in large rivers and, more commonly, in ponds. Their food is insect larvae, freshwater shrimps and other crustaceans, worms and snails, as well as some plant matter. The barbels, organs of touch, and the protrusible mouth are used for grubbing in the mud, much of which is swallowed and later ejected when the edible parts have been digested. In winter

feeding ceases and the fish enter a resting period, a form of hibernation. In May to June carp move into shallow water to spawn, the eggs laid on the leaves of water plants. Each lays over 60 000 eggs/lb of her body-weight. The larvae hatch out in 2—3 days, the adults return to deeper water, while the young fishes remain in shallow water, near the bank. They become sexually mature in 3—4 years. Small carp will be eaten by almost any fish significantly larger than themselves, including larger carp.

Domesticated varieties

As with many other domesticated animals, carp are found in a number of varieties, of two main types: leather carp and mirror carp. The first is scaleless, the second has large scales in two rows on each side of the body. Both can throw back to the original carp form. The shape of the body varies, from relatively slender to deep-bodied with a humpback. Some fish culturists claim these vary with the food, sparse feeding producing the slender forms, abundant feeding giving rise to humpbacks.

How old is a carp

Carp have probably been domesticated for many centuries, and have been carried all over the world for ornamental ponds, or for food. Surprisingly, therefore, in view of the familiarity that should have resulted from this, there is a conflict of opinion on important points—for instance, their longevity and maximum weights. Above all, there are serious discrepancies about when carp were introduced into Europe.

△ *Cyprinid fishes, for instance roach, tench and some carp, often show red forms which breed true to type. Aquarists take advantage, with results like these Japanese* **Hi-goi**, *golden carps.*

Gesner, the 16th-century Swiss naturalist, mentioned a carp 150 years old. Carp in the lakes of Fontainebleau, France, have been credited with ages of up to 400 years. Bingley, writing in 1805, records a carp in the pond in the garden of Emmanuel College, Cambridge, England, that had been an inhabitant more than 70 years. Tate Regan, authority on fishes in Britain in the first half of this century, was of the opinion that under artificial conditions a carp may attain 50 years but that 15 years would probably be the maximum in the wild state.

Perhaps one reason for the excessive claims is their hardiness when removed from water. This is also the reason why the fish could be spread over such a wide area by man. Wrapped in damp moss or water plants, it can survive transport over long distances. If Pennant is to be believed, this remark has the force of under-statement. In his *British Zoology* he tells of a carp wrapped in moss, with only its mouth exposed, placed in a net and hung in a cellar. It was fed with bread and milk and lived over a fortnight. It is only fair to add that it was 'often plunged in water'.

Carp usually grow to about 15 lb in the United States but in Europe a fish of over 60 lb and a length of 40 in. has been recorded. Claims have been made for 400 lb carp. Frederick II of Prussia is said to have caught one of 76 lb and a 140 lb carp is said to have

△ *Clarissa, the largest carp caught in Great Britain, was taken from Redmere Pool by R Walker in 1952. She was about 15 years old and weighed 44 lb. She lived in an aquarium until 1972.*

△ *The mirror carp is identified by rows of large scales along its back and sides.*

▽ *Some think carp found in Britain today came from carp cultivated in monastery stewponds.*

been caught at Frankfurt on Oder. There are several records of carp around 25 lb in Britain, but there is one for 44 lb taken by R Walker in 1952.

Historical uncertainty

The introduced form of the common carp was known to the Greeks and Romans, and has long been kept in ponds in parts of Europe. We know it is today found widely over England, the southern parts of Wales and in southern Scotland. The question remains: when was it first introduced into Britain?

Writers on the subject seem to have been fairly unanimous that all our carp must be regarded as descendants of fishes cultivated by the monks for centuries in their stewponds. Certainly, carp are still to be found in many of the surviving stewponds adjacent to ruins of monasteries and priories. That on its own is very little help in finding the date when they were first put there. Other than this, information comes from documentary evidence or guesswork, or a mixture of the two.

Eric Taverner, in his *Freshwater Fishes of the British Isles* (1957), suggested that carp were brought here from France and the Low Countries in the 14th century. Richard Fitter, writing in 1959, invokes an entry in *The Boke of St Albans* for dating their introduction prior to 1486. Emma Phipson, in *The Animal-Lore of Shakespeare's Time* (1883), speaks of Leonard Mascall, a Sussex gentleman, who has had the credit for importing the carp into England about the year 1514. She also points out that in the Privy Purse Expenses of Elizabeth of York, 1502, mention is made of a reward paid for the present of a carp. Izaak Walton, in *The Compleat Angler*, opined that the date was around 1530. Dr Albert Günther, celebrated authority on fishes in the last half of the 19th century, fixed the date at 1614.

The latest pronouncement is by Günther Sterba, in his *Freshwater Fishes of the World* (1962), that the carp reached England in 1512, Denmark in 1560, Prussia 1585, St Petersburg (Leningrad) 1729, and North America (California) 1872.

The dissolution of the monasteries began in 1535. A plan of a Benedictine monastery of the 12th century shows the site of a fishpond. Accepting the dates quoted here the fishponds of religious houses in England must have been stocked for at least two centuries with fish other than carp. Two of our seven authorities give dates about or after the dissolution of the monasteries, and three give dates only slightly before that event.

It is a romantic idea that English monks could supply themselves with carp to be eaten on fast days. But the evidence seems to be in favour of some other fish, probably the perch.

class	**Pisces**
order	**Cypriniformes**
family	**Cyprinidae**
genus & species	*Cyprinus carpio*

Swordtail

The swordtail is one of the more important as well as most popular of aquarium fishes, not only for its beauty but because it is a good subject for selective breeding. Swordtails are live-bearing tooth-carps, so they have the shape of that family. The dorsal fin is relatively large and so is the tailfin which is broad-based and rounded at the rear edge. The pelvic fins are at about the middle of the body. The females are up to 5 in., the males being up to 3¼ in. exclusive of the sword, which is formed from much elongated rays of the lower part of the tailfin. The outstanding feature of the swordtail is its colours.

Swordtails have been bred in so many colours and colour variations that a description of these in a small space would be impossible. What follows here can, however, be taken as a sort of standard colouring, the one most likely to be seen. The back is olive-green shading to greenish-yellow on the flanks and yellowish on the belly. The scales are edged with

them to take any food floating at the surface. They can also search on the bottom, the body held almost vertical with the head downward. They also snap at small swimming invertebrates. They are, in fact, omnivorous, taking anything small, both plant and animal, swimming or floating, and in the aquarium they spend much time grazing small algae growing on the glass or stones.

There seems to be a strong social hierarchy known as peck order in a community of swordtails which reveals itself in the aquarium by one of the males tending to bully the rest. Indeed, these fishes seem to be unduly spiteful, especially in small aquaria. Dominance in a community of any species is decided and maintained by fighting, or at least, by aggressive displays, and is closely linked with the strength of the sex hormones. Experiments with swordtails have shown, however, that a female maintains her position in the social hierarchy for 1–3 months after being spayed and a castrated male retains his for 1–6½ months. This is unusual because as a rule, when the gonads are removed, and with them the sex hormones, the individual usually drops more or less immediately to a subordinate rank in the social hierarchy.

brown so the whole body seems to be covered with a fine net. The fins are yellowish-green, the dorsal fin being ornamented with reddish blotches and streaks. From the tip of the snout to the base of the tailfin runs a rainbow band of colour made up of zigzag lines of carmine, green, cinnabar, purple or violet. The sword of the male is yellow at the base shading to orange, bordered with black above and below.

Swordtails live in the fresh waters of southern Mexico, British Honduras and Guatemala in Central America.

Bullying males

As is usual with popular aquarium fishes more is gleaned about their way of life from individuals kept in tanks than from those living in the wild. They live the usual uneventful lives of small fishes, most of their time being taken up with searching for food – or bullying each other. Their mouth is inclined slightly upward making it easy for

△ *A male swordtail with a black-edged yellow 'sword' swims alongside a female.*
◁ *Red and green swordtails: two males with females and young.*

Mystery of sex-reversal

Swordtails first became aquarium fishes about 1910, and not long after this the idea began to be current that these fishes undergo a remarkable sex-reversal. In 1926 Essenberg reported that females, after having had several broods, may become fully functional males. From the many reports that followed this the impression is gained that this is commonplace. There have, for example, been several authoritative books on freshwater or aquarium fishes written during the years since Essenberg's report was published, and all have given prominence to this idea. Gunther Sterba in his book first published in 1959 speaks of the quite remarkable and always astonishing sex-reversal in swordtails. He claims that in some strains as many as 30% of females later change into males. Yet in 1957 Myron Gordon, who had made a special study of the species, had already claimed that such

189

changes were extremely rare, quoting a substantial report on swordtails by Friess, in 1933, in support of his claim.

Subjects for heredity study

If the supposedly remarkable sex-reversal is still in doubt there are other aspects of the breeding for which we have more reliable information. Swordtails have been almost domesticated and by selective breeding a wide range of colour varieties exist, usually named according to their colours, such as the green, the red, the red-eyed red, the red-wag, the black, the golden, and the albino. According to Dr Myron Gordon, quoted by William T. Innes, there are wild specimens comparable to all the selected varieties produced up to 1935 except the golden. There have, however, been others since then, including the one seen below.

Swordtails have been much used for the study of genetics, by crossing the colour varieties. In addition many hybrids with the platy have been produced, which increases still further not only the range of colours but also the materials for further studies on heredity. These fishes are particularly suitable for laboratory work of this kind. The sexes can be readily recognized, which is always a help in such studies. The males not only differ from the females in having the 'sword', they also have a gonopodium for the insertion of milt, fertilisation being internal. They also breed rapidly. A brood may number up to 200, each ¼ in. long at birth. The newly-born must rise to the surface for air to fill the swim-bladder after which they can swim well and start to feed almost immediately. They also grow quickly. At first the sexes look alike but soon the males start to grow a sword. Swordtails live 2–3 years, so there is a rapid turn-over in populations. As a result swordtails, with their near relatives the platys, may be considered as a vertebrate equivalent of the fruit fly for genetical studies.

Hybridization

Probably the most remarkable feature of the sex life of the swordtail is the ease with which it hybridizes with platys in aquaria, yet although both species live virtually side by side in the fresh waters of Mexico and Guatemala no wild hybrids have been found. This is the more noteworthy since their breeding behaviour is so similar. There are, however, several small differences, hardly noticeable until close and critical study is made of them. To begin with, platys take about 5 minutes from the start of pre-mating behaviour to the actual mating, whereas swordtails take only one minute. The actual mating takes only half the time in platys that it does in swordtails and altogether the mating behaviour of platys is much the more vigorous. The differences are slight, and probably no one of them would be sufficient to form a barrier between the species, but taken as a whole they do. Under artificial conditions, as in an aquarium where the choice of mates is limited anyway, the barrier is readily overcome. In the wild, with a wide choice of mates, even small details count.

class	**Pisces**
order	Cypriniformes
family	Poeciliidae
genus & species	*Xiphophorus helleri*

▽ *Selective breeding results in a wide range of colour varieties: a recent breed is seen here.*

Zebra fish

There are several fishes with a common name that includes the word 'zebra'. The most noticeable of these is a small fresh-water fish of Bengal and eastern India. Less than 2 in. long, it is called the zebra fish or zebra danio and is a member of the large carp family. It is an extremely popular fish with aquarists.

It is a slim fish with the body only slightly compressed. The single dorsal fin and the anal fins are fairly large, and it has a relatively large tailfin and small pelvic and pectoral fins. There are two pairs of barbels. The back is brownish-olive, the belly yellowish-white and the flanks are Prussian blue with four golden stripes from the gill cover to the base of the tail. The dorsal fin is also blue with yellow at its base and a white tip. The anal fin is again blue-gold barred, and so is the tailfin. The effect of the stripes is to make the fish look even more streamlined than it is, and to give an impression of movement even when the fish is stationary.

Beauty in repetition

As so often happens with a fish of outstanding colour, subsequently popular with aquarists, there is little that is zoologically striking in zebra fishes. They swim among water plants or in schools—it is when they are all aligned, swimming in formation, evenly spaced, and all travelling in the same direction that they most catch the eye. Almost certainly their attraction owes much to the repetition of their stripes—termed the 'beauty in repetition' by Dr Dilwyn John in 1947. In 1935, William T Innes came very near to saying this in his comprehensive book *Exotic Aquarium Fishes* when he described it as a fish 'to show to advantage moving in schools, it scarcely has an equal, for its beautiful horizontal stripes, repeated in each fish, give a streamline effect that might well be the envy of our best automobile designers'.

Special precautions

Zebra fishes are carnivorous, feeding on any small animals they can swallow, which usually means small insect larvae, crustaceans and worms. After their colour, their strongly carnivorous tendencies provide one of their more interesting features. They are egg-eaters, and those who breed zebra fish in aquaria need to take special precautions to achieve success.

There is little difference between the sexes except that the female, especially just before spawning, is more plump than the male, and her stripes are more silver and yellow than the golden stripes of the male. In the pre-spawning behaviour the male leads the female in among the water plants and the two take up position side by side, she to shed her ova, he to shed his milt over them to fertilise them. As the eggs slowly sink there is a tendency for the two to snap up the eggs. The first precaution for the aquarist is therefore to provide a breeding aquarium with water so shallow that the fish have no chance to catch the eggs before they sink to safety in the spaces between the gravel on the bottom. The correct size of gravel pebbles must be used or the adults may become trapped between them. Marbles have been used, or else some sort of trap. An early trap used was a series of slender glass rods held together at the ends with soft wire and raised just off the bottom of the aquarium. This was later superseded by fine metal mesh or nylon.

Each female lays about 200 eggs which hatch in two days. The larvae are at first fairly helpless and inactive, but two days later they can swim and start to feed on microscopic plankton animals. They begin to breed at a year old. At two years they are old-aged, and a zebra fish of three or more years old is an extreme rarity.

Question of stripes

The name 'zebra' is from an Amharic or Ethiopian word and first gained currency in Europe in 1600. By the early years of the 19th century its use had been extended not only to cover all manner of striped animals but also materials showing stripes, and especially to striped shawls and scarves. In the world of fishes there is the zebra shark of the Indian Ocean, with black or brown bars on the body, more like the stripes of a tiger. So we have the anomaly of the common name being zebra shark and the scientific name *Stegostoma tigrinum*. In the extreme south of South America is the zebra salmon *Haplochiton zebra*. In pisciculture there is a hybrid of the trout *Salmo trutta* and the American brook trout *Salvelinus fontinalis*, which is called the zebra hybrid. A foot-long marine fish of the Indo-Pacific *Therapon jarbua* is sometimes called the zebra or tiger fish. It is, however, among the aquarium fishes that the name is most used —the striped or zebra barb *Barbus fasciatus* of Malaya and the East Indies is an example. The common killifish *Fundulus heteroclitus*, of North America, is also called the zebra killie, while the zebra cichlid *Cichlasoma nigrofasciatum* is also—and more appropriately—called the convict fish. Some of these fish have horizontal stripes and others vertical, and there has been some disagreement over which are more correctly termed 'zebra'. However, since a glance at a photograph of a zebra shows that the stripes run in different directions on the different areas of the body, there seems no reason why the name should not be applied to all.

class	**Pisces**
order	**Atheriniformes**
family	**Cyprinodontidae**
genus & species	***Brachydanio rerio***

▽ *On the right lines: the popular zebra fish proves that parallel stripes never meet.*

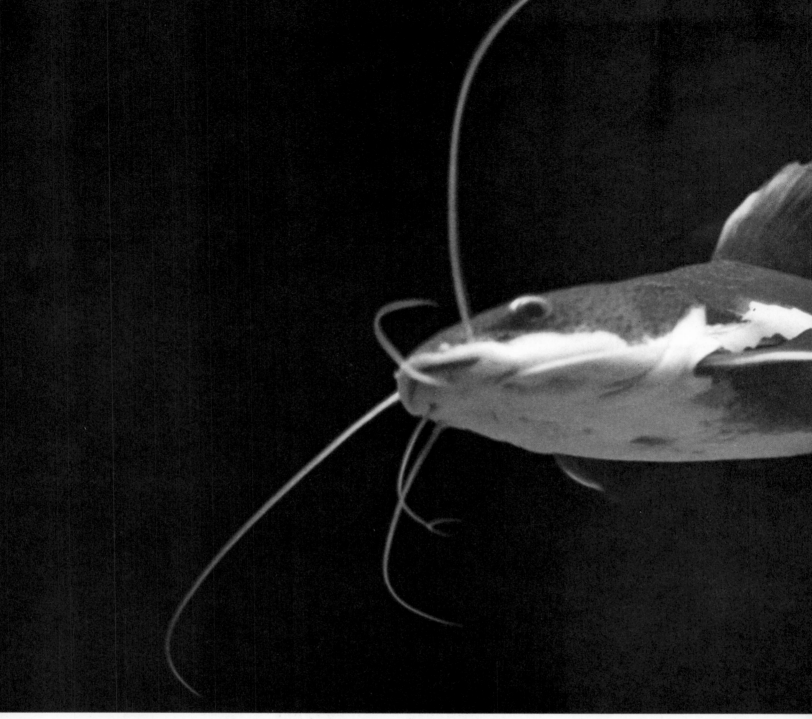

Catfish

The European catfish, or wels, grows to 9 ft or more in the rivers of central and eastern Europe and western Asia, and is the most famous of a large group called the naked catfishes. Its head is large and broad, the mouth has a wide gape and around it are three pairs of barbels or 'whiskers', the feature of all catfishes. In the wels the three pairs of barbels can be moved about and one pair is very long. The eyes are small. The body is stout, almost cylindrical in front, and flattened from side to side in the rear portion. The skin is slimy and has no scales. The fins, except for the long anal fin, are small. The colour is dark olive-green to bluish-black

on the back, the flanks being paler with a reddish sheen, the belly whitish, the whole body being marked with spots and blotches.

The wels has many common names: silurus, the name given it by the Romans, glanis, sheatfish, or sheathfish, said to be from a fanciful resemblance to a sword scabbard, and waller. It has been introduced to a number of lakes in different parts of England.

Night hunter

The European catfish lives in rivers or deep lakes with plenty of water plants. It spends the day under overhanging banks or on the mud in deep water, foraging in the mud with its barbels in search of small invertebrates. At night it hunts, feeding voraciously on fish, crustaceans, and frogs. The larger ones take small water birds and mammals.

In May to June, the breeding season, the catfish moves into shallow water, where the female lays her eggs in a depression in the mud formed by lashing movements of her tail. A large female may lay 100 000 eggs, which are said to be guarded by the male. The fry are black and tadpole-shaped.

Legendary criminal

It would be surprising if a large fish, with hearty appetite, that lurks in dark places did not gather an evil reputation. The wels has been accused of swallowing lambs, even children. Gesner, in the 16th century, reports that a human head and a hand bearing gold rings were taken from the stomach of one of these large catfish.

Many strange habits

Although related, the various naked catfishes show remarkable diversity in form and habits. The banjo catfishes of South America may live in rivers and brackish

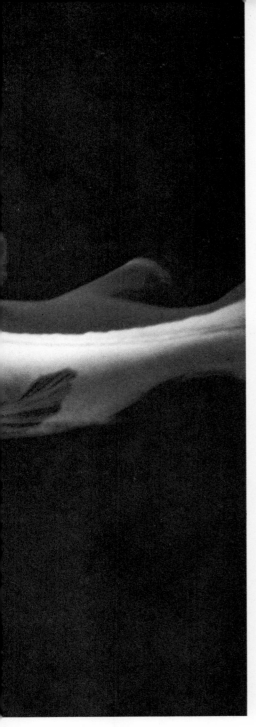

◁ *Most of the many different kinds of catfishes have three pairs of barbels round the mouth.*

△ *Glass catfish, like many catfishes, has no scales.*
▽ *The barbels are used to probe in mud for food.*

estuaries, some species in the sea. They are named for their flattened bodies with an unusually long tail. In one species *Aspredinichthys tibicen* the tail is three times the length of the body. In the breeding season, the females of this species grow a patch of spongy tentacles on the abdomen, and carry their eggs anchored to these.

Marine catfishes of the family Ariidae are mouth-breeders. That is, the male holds the eggs, which in some species are nearly 1 in. diameter, in his mouth, and when they hatch he continues to shelter the fry in the same way. For a month he must fast. Another name for these catfishes is crucifixion fish, because when the skull is cleaned, a fair representation of a crucifix is formed by the bones of the undersurface.

Another family of marine catfishes (Plotosidae) contains one of the most dangerous fishes of the coral reefs. The dorsal and the pectoral fins carry spines equipped with poison glands. Merely to brush the skin against these spines can produce painful wounds.

Equally dangerous are the parasitic catfishes. Some of this family (Trichomycteridae) are free-living but many attach themselves to other fishes using the spines on the gill-covers to hook themselves on, piercing the skin and gorging themselves on the blood. Others insinuate themselves into the gill-cavities, eating the gills. The candiru *Vandellia cirrhosa* is prone to make its way into the urethra of a naked person entering the water, especially, so it seems, if water is passed. A surgical operation may be necessary to remove the fish. Men and women in the unsophisticated areas of Brazil wear a special guard of palm fibres to protect themselves when wading into rivers.

North America has the flathead (family Ictaluridae), a useful catfish reaching 5½ ft long and 100 lb weight. The channel catfish is a most valuable foodfish. There are, however, the madtoms, 5 in. or less, but with pectoral spines and poison glands.

Mad in another sense are the upside-down catfishes of tropical African rivers. From swimming normally these catfishes may suddenly turn and swim upside-down, for no obvious reason. When courting, the male and female upside-down catfishes swim at each other and collide head-on, repeating this at half-minute intervals.

class	**Pisces**
order	**Siluriformes**
family	**Siluridae**
genus & species	***Silurus glanis*** *European catfish others*

Seahorse

The seahorse is a strange animal which looks like the knight of a chess set, but that is not the end of its oddities. It can wrap its tail round a seaweed or similar object, as a South American monkey wraps its tail round a branch. Each of its eyes is on a turret and can move independently. Although many other fishes can also move their eyes independently, this ability is more pronounced in seahorses. A final oddity is that the male carries the babies in a pouch.

A seahorse has a large head with a tubular snout, a moveable neck, a rotund body and a long tapering, slender tail, with a total length of not more than 8 in. The neck, body and tail are marked with circular and longitudinal ridges, on which there are bony bumps, so the fish looks almost like a wood carving. There is a pair of small pectoral fins and a single small dorsal fin. The colours vary widely but are mostly light to medium brown, scattered with small white spots, and often there are ornamental fleshy strands.

There are 20 species, half of which live in the Indo-Australian region. The others live off the Atlantic coasts of Europe, Africa and North America, with two species on the Pacific coast of America.

Swimming upright

Seahorses live in shallow inshore waters among seaweeds or in beds of eelgrass in estuaries. They swim in a vertical position, propelling themselves by rapid waves of the dorsal fin. When swimming at full speed this fin may oscillate at a rate of 35 times a second—which makes it look like a revolving propeller. The pectoral fins oscillate at the same rate, and the head is used for steering, the fish turning its head in the direction it wants to go. When a seahorse clings to a support with its tail it still keeps its body upright. If the fins are damaged they can be regenerated relatively quickly.

Tiny mouth

The seahorse eats any kind of swimming animal small enough to enter its tiny mouth. Prey is located by sight and quickly snapped up, or is sucked in from as much as $1\frac{1}{2}$ in. away. It is mainly tiny crustaceans such as copepods, but baby fishes are also eaten.

Male courts male

Breeding starts with males going through actions that look like a courtship, and a male seahorse of one species has even been seen to court a male of another species. This courtship probably brings him into condition to receive the eggs. He pairs up with a female, either swimming in front of her but without actually touching her or, in some species, the two may entwine tails. He seems to be bowing to her, but this is actually a pumping action to drive the water out of the pouch on his belly. The female inserts her long ovipositor into the opening of the pouch to lay her eggs, as many as 200 in

△ *Pregnant male seahorse* **Hippocampus erectus,** *his belly pouch extended with eggs.*
▽ *Proud parent with day-old young seahorses.*

▷ *The scene is set for the seahorse ballet; one wraps its prehensile tail round another.*
▽ *Young day-old seahorse (approx. × 7).*

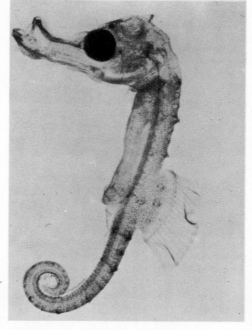

some species. During this time the mouth of the pouch is large but when laying is finished it closes to a minute pore, and stays like this until the baby seahorses are ready to be born, in 4—5 weeks. They are about $\frac{1}{2}$ in. long at birth, perfect miniatures of their parents and the first thing baby seahorses do is to swim to the surface to gulp air to fill their swimbladders. They feed ravenously on extremely small crustaceans, such as newly hatched brine shrimps, and grow rapidly. In the Steinhart Aquarium in the United States young seahorses *Hippocampus hudsonius* were found to grow from $\frac{3}{8}$ in. at birth to $2\frac{1}{2}$ in. in 2 months.

Placental fishes

The inside of the pouch changes just before and during courtship. The walls thicken and become spongy, and they are enriched with an abundant supply of blood vessels. As the female lays her eggs the male fertilises them and they become embedded in these spongy walls, which then act like a placenta. As the pouch is closed there must be some way by which oxygen reaches the eggs, and it is almost certain that the network of blood vessels in the wall of the pouch passes oxygen to the eggs and takes up carbon dioxide from them. Also food probably passes from the paternal blood into the eggs, just as it does from the mother's blood in the mammalian placenta.

Male labour

We are used to the idea that no matter what happens beforehand, in the actual bearing of offspring it is always the female that has the burden. In seahorses it is the reverse. As each batch of eggs is laid in his pouch the male seahorse goes through violent muscular spasms which work the eggs to the bottom of the pouch to make room for more. It seems also that there is a physiological reaction as the eggs sink into the spongy tissue, and he shows signs of exhaustion. When the young have hatched and are ready to leave the pouch, the mouth of the pouch opens wide. The male alternately bends and straightens his body in convulsive jerks and finally a baby seahorse is shot out through the mouth of the pouch. After each birth the male rests, and when all the babies are born he shows signs of extreme exhaustion. In aquaria the males often die after delivering their brood but this does not happen in a natural state, because the male soon looks around for another female to fill his pouch with eggs.

Seahorses have been described as having the head of a horse, the tail of a monkey, the pouch of a kangaroo, the hard outer skeleton of an insect and the independently moving eyes of a chameleon. It would, however, be difficult to find a suitable comparison for the labour pains of the father.

class	**Pisces**
order	**Gasterosteiformes**
family	**Syngnathidae**
genus	***Hippocampus brevirostris***
& species	***H. hippocampus,*** *others*

John Dory

This fish, of curious shape and habits, is included in an order known formerly as the Zeomorphi but now called Zeiformes. The non-classical scholar may be forgiven for translating these two names as god-like or god-shaped.

The John Dory has a very high and narrow body, flattened from side to side and rounded in outline, it is shaped like a plate. The large head has a mournful expression due to the drooping mouth and the jawbones are such that the mouth can be shot forward when seizing prey. The dorsal fin is in two parts, the front portion being high with the spines strong and, in older individuals, long and carried backwards to end in a line with the tail. The rear part of the dorsal fin and the anal fin that lies opposite it are soft and flexible. Along the bases of the dorsal and anal fins are spines, but the scales on the body are small and spineless, and the skin is smooth. There are also 8–9 spiny plates along the belly. The John Dory is grey to fawn or golden yellow with long blotches of reddish-purple, and on each flank just behind the gill covers is a large black spot with a yellow margin. The maximum length is $22\frac{1}{2}$ in. and it can weigh up to 18 lb.

It lives in the Mediterranean and eastern Atlantic as far north as the southern and southwestern waters of the British Isles and sometimes reaches Norway.

Cat-like stalking

The John Dory with its high plate-like body cannot chase its prey. Instead, it stalks its food, keeping its body rigid, swimming by waving its second dorsal and its anal fin, using the tail fin as a rudder. Its plate-like shape means it can slip easily through the water for short distances. Keeping its eyes on its prey, it gradually draws nearer and nearer to it, finally seizing it by shooting out its protrusible toothless mouth. While stalking it shows signs of excitement. It holds its dorsal fin erect and quivers its fins, its colours blushing and fading all the time. These signs of supposed excitement may have an added value. Seen from head-on the high and very narrow body looks like a thin vertical stripe. The colours coming and going and the quivering of the fins tend to blur even this, so the small fish being stalked is oblivious of impending danger and makes absolutely no attempt to swim away.

The John Dory lives at depths down to 300 ft and little is known about its way of life apart from what has been seen of occasional individuals kept in aquaria. It feeds almost exclusively on small fishes, especially young herring, pilchard and sand eels, although it has been seen to take shrimps in captivity. It takes only live food; a John Dory in an aquarium was seen to spit out a dead fish it had seized. Nevertheless, Dr Douglas Wilson at the Plymouth Aquarium was able, in due course, to persuade a captive John Dory to take strips of squid which looked like fish when dropped into water and slowly floated down.

Sexing the John Dory

There is no outward difference between the sexes. Only by dissection and by examining the roes is it possible to distinguish female from male. In the same way we learn that the eggs are $\frac{1}{10}$ in. diameter. The eggs are pelagic (that is to say that they float), and are laid at any time during the period from June to August.

Origin of the name

The John Dory is used as a food-fish but people are divided on the quality of its flesh. There is also a division of opinion so far as its name is concerned. It seems to have a romantic ring, almost reminding one of the tang of the sea, so one suspects the fish might have been named after some swash-buckling buccaneer or other adventurous seadog. Then there is the story that the black marks on its flank are where the finger and thumb of St Peter pressed when he took the coin from the fish's mouth, so getting the name *Peterfisch* in Germany. But there is the same legend about the haddock, and also about a species of *Tilapia*, but since the John Dory and the haddock are both marine, the *Tilapia*, being a freshwater fish, should take the credit.

Two other suggestions rob it of any glamour it might have. One is that its name is a corruption of the Italian word *janitore*, for a doorkeeper, the other that it is from the French *jaune dorée*, because of its golden yellow colour. The scientific name is *Zeus faber*, the first name being that of the overlord of the Greek gods; the second is Latin for a blacksmith.

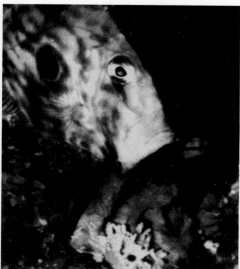

△ *Never seeing the bright side of life the John Dory swims around with a permanent gloomy expression on its face. Apart from the unfortunate pout this fish has strong dorsal fin spines and the large black flank spots. The legend goes that St Peter made these marks with his finger and thumb.*

◁ *Because of its high plate-like body the John Dory cannot chase its prey. Instead it stalks its food and seizes it by rapidly shooting out its toothless mouth.*

▽ *Head of John Dory with the mouth retracted (left) and protruded (right).*

class	**Pisces**
order	**Zeiformes**
family	**Zeidae**
genus & species	***Zeus faber***

Cardinal fish

This is the name of many small fishes, usually red or with red in the pattern of the body, that live mainly on coral reefs in tropical seas. A few live in freshwater streams on tropical Pacific islands. All but a few deep-sea forms are shallow-water fishes, usually not more than 4 in. long. The largest are up to 8 in. long and these live in the brackish water of mangrove swamps.

There are great numbers of cardinal fishes, suggesting that they are the mainstay of many predatory fishes. They easily form associations with sedentary animals.

△ *Cardinals are usually red in colour.*
▽ *Barred cardinal's striped body breaks its outline quite effectively.*

▷ *A group of cardinal fish sheltering amongst sea urchin spines. They are found in the limpid waters of Australia's Great Barrier Reef.*

Shelter in a shell

The best-known are two species of 2 in. conchfish of the Caribbean, Florida and Bermuda. These shelter in the large molluscs *(Strombus)* known as conches, resting in the mantle cavity and coming out at night to feed on small crustaceans. Not every conch contains a fish and not every cardinal fish shelters in a conch. Some shelter in sponges, empty conch shells or empty bivalve shells, in fact in any convenient hollow object or cavity.

American scientists studying a Hawaiian species of cardinal fish collected over a thousand specimens from a small area of dead coral. This gives a picture of the conchfish hidden away in all manner of cavities and shelters on the sea-bed by day, and swarming out at night to feed. As it is, the fish is mainly seen when a conch is taken from the sea for food. As the mollusc lies on the bottom of the boat it opens its mantle cavity and out flops the cardinal fish.

Sea-urchin host

One cardinal fish *Siphamia versicolor* of the Nicobar Islands in the Indian Ocean, lives in association with a dark-red sea-urchin. When nothing is happening to disturb the peace, the urchin parts its long spines so that they form pyramid-like clusters, and between these the fish moves, cleaning the sea-urchin's skin. At the slightest alarm, even a shadow falling on the urchin, the spines are spread defensively and the fish shelters among them, usually head-downwards.

At night the fish comes out to feed, but if driven from its sea-urchin host it will swim to another. If this urchin is a different colour the fish will change colour to match that of its new host.

Mouth-breeding

The breeding habits of the cardinal fishes are simple. As the female lays her eggs, the male takes them into his mouth and there they remain until they hatch. Sometimes, the males alone hold the eggs, sometimes the females, and in other species both parents may share the duty. There are a few species in which the eggs are picked up by the male only when danger threatens. Some idea of what this mouth-breeding involves can be had from a comparison of two species. The female of one in Australian waters lays eggs $\frac{1}{8}$ in. in diameter

and the male holds 150 in his mouth. In a Mediterranean species the eggs are $\frac{1}{50}$ in. in diameter and the male holds 22 000 in his mouth.

In this Mediterranean species the eggs are fertilised inside the female's body and there is a curious inversion in the copulation. The genital papilla of the female is long and she inserts it into the male's body to take the sperm for fertilising her eggs. This form of 'petticoat government' is completed by the male taking over the care of the eggs, as we have seen.

Death-like ruse

Little is known about the enemies of cardinal fishes. Consequently, it is possible to make only the generalization that they must be eaten by many small and medium-sized predatory fishes. This is supported by the behaviour of the brownspot cardinal fish. Animals at the mercy of others often use the tricks which used to be known as shamming dead or feigning injury, but which are now included under the comprehensive title of distraction displays. The 3 in. brownspot, so named from a dark spot above each of its breast fins, flops on one side and gives every appearance of being dead when one tries to catch it.

Elaborate light-organs

There are many animals and some plants which produce living light. In some there is an obvious advantage, as when the female

glowworm shines the light at the tip of her abdomen, so bringing the male to her side. In other instances it is hard to see what purpose is served, as with the fungus which grows inside hollow trees, glowing with a spectral light at certain times of the year.

Some bacteria are luminous, and they present much the same case as the fungus: it is hard to see what purpose is served by it. Coastal fishes that have light-organs are dependent on these bacteria for them, unlike deep-sea fishes which produce their own light. Several cardinal fishes have these light-organs. One of them *Apogon ellioti*, from southeast Asian seas, not only has a population of bacteria, but the gland in which this is located has a reflector. Moreover, the muscles below the gland are translucent and act as a lens. The result is that this small cardinal fish swims about at night with a lamp in its throat. The purpose of this elaborate light-organ is unknown.

More remarkable is the cardinal fish that has in its intestine three such lamps, each containing luminous bacteria and each with its reflector and lens. The absurd part of this story is that these lamps are directed towards the interior of the intestine.

class	**Pisces**
order	**Perciformes**
family	**Apogonidae**
genera	***Apogon**, others*

See-through skin: the translucent tissues reveal the bone structure as if by X-ray. △ **Chanda lala**. ▷ *Siamese glassfish* **Chanda wolfii**.

Glassfish

This is an obvious name for fishes that are transparent, with the skeleton and some internal organs clearly visible; yet although transparent they do not lack colour. A number of fishes are transparent or translucent but the name 'glassfish' is reserved for certain small fishes that are favourite aquarium fishes. Large game or commercial fishes, including the snooks and the Nile perch were once thought to be closely related. The glassfish and the Nile perch although so different to look at, have one thing in common: they have both, at different times, ended in the ground: the glassfish used as fertilizer, the Nile perch mummified by the Egyptians.

The body is deep and strongly compressed from side-to-side. The dorsal fin is in two parts, that in front being supported by hard rays, the rear portion having one hard ray and up to 18 soft rays. The tailfin is either rounded or deeply forked.

The 8 or more species are found from East Africa through southern Asia to eastern Australia, the majority being in southeast Asia.

The 8 species of snooks live in the seas of tropical west and east Atlantic and the eastern Pacific. They readily enter rivers and may be 4½ ft long with a weight of 51 lb. The Nile perch, up to 7 ft long and more than 250 lb weight, is only one of several related African game species. It looks much more substantial than the glassfish.

Living gems for fertilizers

The Indian glassfish looks like a piece of crystal floating and reflecting colours in water. It is up to 3 in. long, greenish to yellowish but shining gold or iridescent bluish-green in reflected light. The flanks are marked with bars made up of tiny black dots, with a delicate violet stripe running from the gill-cover to the root of the tail. The fins are yellowish to rusty-red, the dorsal and anal fins with black rays and bordered with pale blue. Rays of paired fins are red or bluish.

It is the best known of the small glassfishes, and lives in fresh and brackish waters of India, Burma and Thailand. Its uneventful life is spent among water plants feeding on small aquatic animals such as insect larvae, crustaceans and worms. Its breeding habits are almost equally uneventful. In aquaria, according to Günther Sterba, spawning is triggered by morning sunshine raising the temperature, and a brief separation of the sexes, by putting them in separate tanks for a short time then reuniting them. The pair take up position side-by-side, quivering all the time. As the female lays the pair turn over to an upside-down position. The female lays her eggs among water plants to which they stick. She lays 4—6 at a time, repeating this until 200 or more have been laid. After this the parents take no further interest. The eggs hatch in 8—24 hours, depending on temperature, the baby fishes hanging from the water plants for 3—4 days after which they swim freely. Their food is small crustaceans, such as water fleas. The young glassfishes do not go in search of food but snap up any hat drifts past them. It can be presumed that if food is scarce around the area at such times many young fishes will die of starvation. Nevertheless, large numbers survive for, as William T Innes remarks in his *Exotic Aquarium Fishes*, this little gem treasured by aquarists is caught in large numbers in India and Burma for use as a fertilizer.

Family likenesses

Two people when related even distantly often share what we call a family likeness. In height, girth, colour of hair and in almost every way the two may be wholly unlike yet there is something that marks them as belonging to a family. It may be something very small, for example, a peculiarity in the way they walk, the shape of the lower lip, and so on. It is the same in classifying animals, and the family we are considering here is a fine example. Included in it are glassfishes, small, transparent, delicate; as well as snooks that are large, sturdy and not transparent and the 7ft robust giant, the Nile perch. From a casual glance they look most unlike yet each has a similar outline, and each has at least one small feature we call a family likeness. In each the lateral line, the line of sense-organs running along the flanks of fishes, goes right to the end of the tailfin, which is most unusual.

class	**Pisces**
order	**Perciformes**
family	**Centropomidae**
genera & species	***Chanda ranga*** *Indian glassfish* ***Centropomus unidecimalis*** *snook others*

*Marine angelfish, **Holacanthus**, living among the coral reefs of tropical seas, outstanding for its varied patterns and colours.*

Angelfish

*The name 'angelfish' has been used commonly for two types of fishes. Both of these types are bony fishes, one of which is marine, the other freshwater. The latter has long been a favourite with aquarists who, perhaps to avoid confusion of names, developed the habit of using its scientific name, which is **Scalare**. Since not everyone followed their example, however, at least part of the confusion remains. There is another perplexing usage. Some scientists 'lump' the marine angelfishes into the butterfly fish family (see page 176), but the butterfly fish is only distantly related to them and belongs to an entirely separate family.*

There is little to choose between these angelfishes and butterfly fishes. Most are brilliantly coloured, mainly coral-reef dwelling fishes; the angelfishes, however, have a sharp spine on the lower edge of the gill-cover which is lacking in the butterfly fishes.

It hardly needs explaining that these vernacular names are prompted by the enlarged flap-like or wing-like fins.

Most angelfish are small, up to 8 in. long, but the marine ones reach 2 ft in length. The outline of the body, because of the well-developed fins, has much the shape of a flint arrowhead.

Colourful and curious

The marine angelfishes, and the similar butterfly fishes, which together number more than 150 species, live mainly in shallow seas and a few enter estuaries. They live in pairs or small groups at most, around reefs, rocks or corals.

They are inoffensive as adults, they are peaceable, they do not dash away as most fishes do when, for example, a skin diver intrudes into their living space. They move away but slowly, every now and then tilting the body to take a closer look at the newcomer.

The outstanding feature of these fishes is the wide range and the beauty of their colours and patterns. In many of them the young fishes have the same colours as the adults, but in others the differences are so great that it looks as if there are two different species involved. Their behaviour tends to be different also. Quite small —that is, up to a few inches long—they tend to be solitary, and individuals are usually found in the same places day after day, in each case near a shelter into which the fish darts when disturbed. The shelter may be under a rock bed or among seaweed. A tin can lying on the sea-bed will readily be used for shelter. In an aquarium the sub-adults will be aggressive towards each other, but one kept on its own readily becomes tame and learns to feed from the hand.

Probably the most beautiful of the angels is the rock beauty, coloured jet black in front and yellow in its rear half, its fins bright yellow with red spots. It has a strong sense of curiosity that makes it draw near to the underwater swimmer. The queen angelfish, when small, is largely dark brown to black with three bluish vertical bands on the sides of the body and a bluish band along the dorsal fin. Adult, it is mainly a startlingly bright yellow with irregular and diffuse patches of violet or red on various parts of the body. The French angel is black with strongly contrasting bright yellow vertical bands and a yellow face (see illustration page 204).

Feeding

Angelfishes have small mouths armed with many small teeth and they use these when they browse on the algae and coral polyps or catch the small invertebrates on which they feed. In some species the snout is somewhat elongate, and may be inserted in cracks and crevices in rocks or coral to capture small animals for food.

In certain species of butterfly fishes, such as *Chelmon rostratus*, the snout is very long and tube-like with the small mouth at the end. This enables the fishes to probe even deeper into the crevices of coral rock for their food.

Parental care

Little is known of the breeding habits of marine angelfish, but they probably conform to the pattern of their better known relations in that they show quite close care of the eggs and fry.

Both fish clean a patch of flat rock, and the female lays her eggs on it, the male swimming close over them shedding sperm for fertilisation. The eggs are tended for 4—8 days by the parents, when the fry hatch, and sink to the bottom.

The parents guard them until they are sufficiently free-swimming to hide in crevices and weed. The fry are unlike the adults in that their bodies are long and slim. They do not not assume full adult shape before three or four months have passed.

Conspicuous colouring

All angelfishes and butterfly fishes are conspicuous. To the underwater swimmer

△ *Angelfish are strongly territorial and use their colours both to advertise possession of their territory and to warn off an intruder of their own species. One of these freshwater* **Scalare** *is displaying at the other with a sideways flick of its bright pectoral fins like flashing signals.*
▽ *These freshwater angelfish,* **Scalare***, are favourites with aquarists, being easy to care for and attractive to look at.*

their colours stand out and 'hit the eye'. Especially striking are the patterns of the imperial angelfish or blue angelfish, with their inscribed patterns of white and black curves and half circles on a rich blue and violet background, dazzling to the eye when seen at close quarters.

We are used to the idea of colours and colour-patterns serving as camouflage to hide an animal from its enemies or enable it, if a predatory animal, to steal close to its prey undetected. We are used also to conspicuous colours, especially combinations of yellow, black and red, serving as warning colours, the wearer of these colours being poisonous or bad-tasting or having a sting. The colours of angelfishes certainly fail to hide their wearer. Although one writer has described angelfishes as nestling among coral heads like hummingbirds among brilliant blossoms, most underwater swimmers agree you can see these fishes clearly at a distance. There is no indication that angelfishes are poisonous or unpalatable, or have a sting. They are eaten by the local peoples wherever they occur, although their skins are said to be tough.

Perhaps the comparison with hummingbirds is not so far-fetched as it appears at first sight. Conspicuous colours in birds are associated with displays, especially aggressive displays, as they are in lizards such as the anole and the same may be true of angelfishes. Experimentally, a mirror was placed in an aquarium with a French angelfish. The fish drew near, nibbled at its reflection in the mirror, then threw itself sideways and flicked its bright blue pectoral fins like flashing signals. This suggests that angelfishes are strongly territorial and use their colours both to advertise possession of a territory as well as to warn off an intruder of their own species.

There was at least one angelfish that escaped attention for a long time despite its colouring, a bright orange head with a glowing dark blue contrasting body. This, the pygmy angelfish, was wholly unknown until 1908, when one was brought up in the trawl off Bermuda from a depth of 540 ft. It was dead when it reached the surface and its carcase was committed to a jar of alcohol to preserve it. It became something of a mystery fish and it was not until 1951 that it was given a scientific name, when one scientist examining it realized it was a new species of angelfish. The next year a second specimen was taken from the stomach of a larger fish, a snapper, caught in 240 ft of water off Mexico. In 1959, this fish, believed to be so rare, was caught in fair numbers by a skin-diver off the Bahamas, in 40 ft of water.

class	**Pisces**
order	**Perciformes**
family	**Chaetodontidae**

◁ *Marine French angelfish,* **Pomacanthus paru***, showing one of the bizarre shapes and patterns typical of these fish, which look quite different when they are seen from the side than they do from the front view.*

Pompadour fish

This fish from the rivers of the Amazon basin has been described as the noblest among aquarium fishes. Its name of pompadour is then quite appropriate although it is also known as the discus from its shape. The pompadour fish and its relative, which is divided into subspecies known as the green discus, brown discus and blue discus, are almost disc-shaped when fully grown and up to 8 in. long. The long dorsal and anal fins make the otherwise oval body look more nearly circular. The body is covered with small scales but the cheeks and gill covers are more markedly scaly. The mouth is small, with thick lips. There is a single row of small conical teeth in the middle of each jaw and instead of the usual two pairs, there is a single pair of nostrils.

The colours are not easy to describe because they change with age. A young pompadour fish is brown with several vertical dark bars down each side. At 6 months old, flecks of blue appear on the head and gill covers, and these spread until the sides are coloured with alternating bands of blue and reddish brown and there are nine vertical dark bands, the first running through the eye. The fins become blue at their bases, pale blue and orange on the outer edges, and there are streaks of blue and orange between. The pelvic fins are red with orange tips. The green discus is mainly green with 9 dark vertical bars, the brown discus mainly brown with 9 dark bars and the blue discus brown with 9 blue bars.

△ *Turning blue with age, pompadour fish* **Symphysodon aequifasciata.** *At 6 months the head and gill covers become flecked with blue and this gradually spreads across the sides.*

Hanging by a thread

Pompadour fishes usually spend the day sheltering in the shadows of water plants when they are not feeding and they avoid strong sunlight. They eat water insects, especially the larvae of midges and small dragonflies, small worms and similar invertebrates. There is a brief courtship, during which the pair clean the surface of a broad leaf of a water plant. When this is ready, the female lays rows of eggs on it. Sometimes the surface of a stone is used but only after being meticulously cleaned. Once the eggs are laid the male swims over and fertilises them. The parents take it in turn to fan them with their fins and they hatch in about 50 hours. As each baby breaks out of the egg it is removed in the parents' mouth and placed on a leaf, where each hangs by a short thread for the next 60 hours. The parents continue to fan with their fins and when, at the end of this time, the babies are about to swim, they swarm on the side of one of the parents and appear to hang there. After a time the parent gives a wriggle and the fry are shaken off towards the side of the other parent, who is swimming nearby. When 3—4 weeks old the fry become independent and feed on small animal plankton such as very small water fleas or their larvae. At first they are the normal fish shape, if a little plump in the body. The discoid shape comes with age.

Feeding the fry

There can be little doubt that baby pompadours get protection by swarming on the side of the parent, although sometimes they are eaten by the parents, at least in aquaria.

The question is whether they get something more. In 1959 Dr WH Hildeman reported observations that seemed to show that the babies fed on a slime secreted by the parents' skin. This seems to have been accepted by students of tropical fishes. In the 1969 edition of their book *All about tropical fish* Derek McInerny and Geoffry Gerard not only state that the parents secrete a whitish mucus over their bodies but that the fry will eat nothing else. They quote Mr R Skipper 'who has successfully raised several spawnings' and he claims they will not thrive on any alternative food. Indeed, he maintains the only hope of raising them is to leave them with their parents. Against this we have the words of Gunther Sterba, in his *Freshwater fishes of the world*, that not only do the young of some other cichlid fishes cling to the sides of their parents but that at least one aquarist has reared young pompadours away from

the care and protection of parents.

One reason why pompadours are not more often kept in aquaria is that young ones taken in the wild are infected with micro-organisms. The frequent changes of water necessary to keep them in captivity seem to favour the parasites, which get the upper hand and kill the pompadours.

class	**Pisces**
order	**Perciformes**
family	**Cichlidae**
genus & species	***Symphysodon aequifasciata*** brown, green and blue discus ***S. discus*** pompadour fish

▽ *Floating discs of colour,* **Symphysodon discus** *swim in the shadows.*

206

Tilapia

Tilapia is the name given to a hundred or so species of freshwater fishes which belong to the large family of cichlids. One species **Saratherodon galilaea** was probably responsible for the miraculous draught of fishes mentioned in the Bible. Other species are also used as food fishes and have been spread around the world. Tilapias are also kept as aquarium fishes and their study has brought to light several unusual features of fish behaviour.

They have large heads and deep bodies, strongly compressed from side to side. The long dorsal fin is spiny in front and soft-rayed in the hinder part, which usually rises to a point in the rear. The anal fin is larger and pointed behind. The tail fin is squarish along its rear edge. The pectoral fins are moderately large and the pelvic fins are more or less level with them. Most tilapias grow to a length of 8—12 in. and a few species may be 18—20 in. long. The colour varies from species to species and is often very variable within a species. The back may be yellowish to olive-brown, green, bronze, blue or violet, the flanks silvery and the belly even lighter. Usually there is a metallic sheen of bronze, golden or violet, and the body and fins are often marked with darker spots and bars.

Tilapias are widely distributed over Africa south of the Sahara, and from the Nile basin to Israel, Jordan and Syria.

Peripatetic tilapias

Tilapias live in lakes and the sluggish parts of rivers, estuaries and brackish lagoons, especially where there is shelter under banks, among water plants or among waterlogged branches. Large numbers of *Tilapia grahami* live in the soda lake Magadi, in Kenya, in water of 28—45°C/80—112°F. Tilapias readily acclimatise and several species have been transported all over central and eastern Africa; so many have become established in local rivers to which they are not native. There are five species now in Lake Victoria, for example, two native and three introduced. The precise mechanics of these introductions are not always known, so it is usual to speak of the fishes as having 'escaped'. For example, *T. mossambica*, of East Africa, turned up in Java in 1939. By various means, some of which can only be guessed at, it is now found in Sumatra, Bali, Lombok, Celebes, the Philippines, Taiwan and South Korea, as well as Malaya, Thailand and Sri Lanka. In the west it is established on Trinidad, St Lucia and Haiti and, recently, in Texas.

△△▷ *Mouth brooder: a female* **Paratilapia multicolor** *with young fry showing through the cheeks of her brood pouch—the young are released as soon as they can swim.*
△ ▷ *Aggression not affection: male* **T. variabilis** *fight each other by pushing with their mouths.*
▷ *Mouth-brooding* **Hoplochromis burtoni** *ignores her young to show aggression to male.*

How they get there

In 1961 a press report told of tilapia 'turning up' in large areas of Florida. Apparently a biologist had suggested that they should be introduced into a pond to provide new sport for anglers, but that does not explain their being found in 16 lakes, 4 creeks and 2 rivers in southern Florida. The press report gives a clue when it continues, that although it is illegal to put tilapia into waters that are free of them, many tropical fish fanciers tire of having them in their aquaria and dump them in the nearest water. Since tilapia has 'an elephant's appetite and a rabbit's reproductive ability' it is not long before it cleans out a pond of food needed by other fish. This is a danger that has to be watched, and in some places native fishes have been wiped out after tilapias have been introduced. On the other hand, several of the larger species, including *T. mossambica*, are an important source of protein, and are often bred in special ponds.

Artificial ponds

In 1951 *T. melanopleura* was established in special fish ponds in Madagascar. These were so successful that more ponds were made. By 1958 there were 40 000, by 1960, 80 000. An adult could catch 11 lb of these fish a day, and even a child could catch 4 lb a day. In South Africa, where tilapias are called kurper or freshwater bream, they are used to clear sewage ponds of mosquito larvae, and at the same time they multiply and the young can be transferred to other ponds and rivers to provide food fishes. One problem that occurs when the tilapia multiply rapidly is that they eat up the vegetation and insect larvae, starve out or eat up the other fishes, and in the end the pond is

▽ *Playing safe: young* **T. nilotica** *stay close to their mother; when danger threatens they all rush back into her mouth.*

overstocked with undersized tilapias. A suggested cure is to use hatcheries and to separate the sexes, putting the females in one pond and the males in another. In one experiment *T. mossambica* were crossed with other species of *Tilapia* and the hybrids were all males—which could be grown to maturity for food without the problems of a population explosion.

Mainly plant eaters

Tilapias are basically vegetarian, some species sieving the plant plankton, others eating the small algae on stones, and a few doing both. Some seem to turn readily to animal food, such as water insects and their larvae, or fish fry—even tilapia fry.

Mouth nurseries

Some tilapias lay their sticky eggs on the surface of a stone which the male and female have carefully cleaned beforehand. Once the eggs are laid the male swims over them and sheds his milt to fertilise them. The parents aerate the eggs by fanning them with their fins, and when the fry have hatched the female keeps them together in a tiny shoal, shepherding them by signals until they are old enough to swim away on their own. Most tilapias are, however, mouth brooders. To start with the pair dig a pit an inch or two deep and 5–12 in. across in the sandy bottom, scooping up mouthfuls of sand or small pebbles and spitting them a little way from the nest. Then the male swims head downwards and mouths the bottom of the pit. Soon he starts to swim slowly over the nest, rubbing it with his belly. The female joins in and they take turns in swimming across it. Finally the female lays her eggs and the male sheds his milt over them. This is repeated several times and when all the eggs are laid either the male or the female, or both—the pattern varies with the species—suck the eggs into

the mouth. The eggs hatch in the mouth and 8–20 days later the fry leave it and swim away. In some species the female first sucks up the eggs and then the milt as the male sheds it, so that the eggs are fertilised in her mouth.

Careful tests made with one species showed that if the eggs are removed from the mouth of a mouth brooder they fail to hatch and become diseased. It was finally discovered why: the movement of the eggs in the throat makes them rub against each other and against the sides of the pouch, and this cleans them of any bacteria that might damage them.

Counts have shown that tilapia begin to spawn at 2–3 months, may spawn 6–11 times a year, and that some species multiply 1 000 times in 2–3 months.

Miraculous draught

Tilapias are today an important item of food in tropical countries. Paintings on Egyptian antiquities show they were fished thousands of years ago. The miraculous draught of fishes recorded in the Bible was almost certainly tilapias. Canon Tristam, writing over a century ago, told of seeing *Saratherodon galilaea* 'in shoals of over an acre in extent, so closely packed that it seemed impossible for them to move, and with their dorsal fins above the water. They are taken both in boats and from the shore by nets run deftly round, and enclosing what one may call a solid mass at one swoop, and very often the nets break'. A man was stationed at a high point on shore to spot the shoals.

class	**Pisces**
order	**Perciformes**
family	**Cichlidae**
genus	***Tilapia, Saratherodon***

208

Moorish idol

This is one of the most striking of the small reef fishes. It has given inspiration to artists, designers and decorators and has been figured on wallpapers and fabrics. It is said to have been sold in the fish markets of Hawaii, and may still be sold there. It is mentioned and depicted in almost every book on fishes although practically nothing is known of its way of life or its life history.

There are three species of moorish idol, the largest being up to 8 in. long bu 4 in. is more usual. The body is strongly flattened from side to side, and when looked at from the side it is nearly circular. There is, however, a high dorsal fin in the mature fish and a triangular anal fin, making the outline almost diamond-shaped. In front the snout is drawn out and ends in a small mouth with small, very fine teeth in both upper and lower jaw. Two bony horns grow out over the eyes. The tail is short and it carries a tail fin that is almost triangular. The most striking feature is the colour pattern, the body being white and pale yellow with broad bands of brownish black running from top to bottom. The skin is shagreen-like, being covered with small sharp scales which have the effect of making it feel almost like fine sandpaper to the hand.

Moorish idols spread halfway round the world in tropical seas; they are found from East Africa around the coasts of the Indian Ocean, the East Indies, Melanesia, Micronesia and Polynesia to the coasts of Japan and the various islands off the Pacific coast of Mexico.

Hiding among coral

These fishes are often seen in shallow in-shore waters but their real home is on the coral heads in deeper waters, in coral lagoons, especially in the surge channels through coral reefs, and along the outer edges of the reefs. Although the outward appearance and colours, the shapes of their fins and other physical features have been repeatedly described in great detail in one scientific paper after another, nothing has been recorded of how they swim or what is their food. At best we can only deduce something of this. They probably swim by waving their tails, dorsal and anal fins, with the tail fin used as a rudder. This is how the butterfly fishes and marine angelfishes, to which they are distantly related, also swim. It is the way fishes swim that spend their time among irregular reefs or coral where quick movements and sharp turns are needed rather than swift forward movement.

Tweezer jaws

The narrow jaws of a moorish idol, with small teeth in front, act almost like tweezers. The snout is very like that of the butterfly fishes. From looking at moorish idols in aquaria, as well as guessing from the shape of the jaws and teeth, they probably feed on small crustaceans and other small invertebrates picked out with the 'tweezers' from small crevices.

Knife-like spine

The spawning times and mating behaviour are unknown. Young moorish idols are seldom seen, probably because of the difficulty of collecting them from among the coral heads. The few that have been caught show that the young fishes, up to $\frac{1}{2}$ in. long, have much the same shape as the adults but with long, low dorsal and anal fins and only one black band running from the top of the head, through the large eye

△ *At home among the colourful corals—the moorish idol has a very striking colour pattern and an exquisitely shaped dorsal fin.*

to the throat, where the pelvic fins are situated, the small pectoral fins being just behind the eye. In the front of the dorsal fin are three spines. Two of these are very short but the third is long and thin, about $1\frac{1}{2}$ times as long as the body, streaming out behind. As the fish grows this gets shorter and finally the whole dorsal fin assumes the well-known triangular shape. Another feature of the young fish is that it has a knife-like spine behind each corner of the mouth. These drop off when it has grown to about 3 in. long.

Why moorish idol?

Not the least puzzling aspect of these fishes is their common name. 'Moorish' is usually associated with the western Mediterranean region, where the Moors are best remembered for the way they spread across North Africa and into Spain centuries ago. But moorish idols do not live there. Moreover, the Moors would have nothing to do with idols. A possible key to the origin of the name may lie in the association of the word 'Moorish', meaning Mohammedan, with the language of southern India on the coasts of which the fish does live. This word is now obsolete but it was once used by Englishmen living in that part of India. Perhaps it would have been better to have adopted the name which the Hawaiians give to these fishes—*kihikihi.*

class	**Pisces**
order	**Perciformes**
family	**Acanthuridae**
genus & species	*Zanclus canescens* others

Follow the leader: a shoal of bluefin tuna migrate northward through the Florida-Bermuda channel.

Tuna

*Although the name 'tunny' was first used in England—from the Latin **thunnus**—at least as early as the 15th century, and the Spanish word tuna did not come into general use until the beginning of this century, tuna is rapidly becoming the accepted name for this large fish.*

The tunny or bluefin tuna of the Atlantic is said to reach 14 ft long and weigh 1 800 lb, but few exceed 8 ft in length. It has a sleek streamlined shape with a large head and mouth, and large eyes. The first dorsal fin is spiny and close behind it is a smaller soft-rayed second dorsal fin. The anal fin is of similar shape and size as the second dorsal, and behind these two, reaching to the crescentically forked tail, are finlets, nine on the upper and eight on the lower surface of the tail. The pectoral fins are medium sized, as are the pelvic fins, which are level with the pectorals. The back is dark blue, the flanks white with silvery spots and the belly white. The fins are dark blue to black except for the reddish brown second dorsal and the yellowish anal fin and finlets. There are three keels on each side at the base of the tailfin.

The bluefin is found on both sides of the North Atlantic as far north as Iceland.

Segregated by size

Tuna are oceanic fishes that sometimes come inshore but apparently never enter rivers. They move about in shoals in which individual fishes are all about the same size. The smaller tuna make up the largest shoals; the larger the tuna the smaller the shoal, and the really large individuals are more or less solitary. They swim near the surface in summer but are found between 100 and 600 ft in winter. Tuna are strongly migratory, their movements being linked with those of the fishes on which they feed and also on the temperature of the water. They are intolerant of temperatures below $10-12°C/50-54°F$, so although they move into northern waters in summer they migrate back to warmer seas in autumn. A cold summer will limit the northward migrations. There also seem to be movements across the Atlantic. Tuna tagged off Martha's Vineyard, Massachusetts in July 1954 were caught in the Bay of Biscay five years later and occasionally individuals from American waters turn up off the coasts of Norway. Two tagged off Florida in September and October 1951 were caught off Bergen, Norway 120 days later, having travelled 4 500 miles.

Tuna, like their relative the mackerel, swim with the mouth slightly open so that their forward movement forces water across the gills. Their oxygen requirements are high because of their great muscular activity which depends on a correspondingly abundant supply of relatively warm blood. Because of this high oxygen requirement they swim more or less continuously. Tuna are believed to reach speeds of up to 50 mph.

Feeding frenzy

Very young tuna feed largely on crustaceans especially euphausians but later they eat mainly shoaling fishes such as herring, mackerel, sprats, whiting, flying fishes and sand eels. They also eat some squid and cuttlefish. When a tunny shoal meets a shoal of food fishes it is seized with what has been called a feeding frenzy. It charges through, the tunny twisting and turning, often breaking the surface, and sometimes leaping clear of the water. The commotion usually attracts flocks of seabirds to feed on the smaller fishes that are driven to the surface.

Soon put on weight

Spawning takes place in the Mediterranean and to the southwest of Spain in June and July and off Florida and the Bahamas in May and June. The eggs are small and float near the surface. They hatch in about 2 days, the newly hatched larvae being less than ¼ in. long. The baby fishes grow quickly reaching a weight of 1 lb in 3 months. At a year old they weigh 10 lb, at 2 years 21 lb, 35 lb at 3 years and 56 lb at 4 years of age. At 13 years of age they reach a length of 8 ft and weigh 440 lb. The two tagged at Martha's Vineyard were 18 lb and nearly two years old, and they had reached 150 lb when captured later in the Bay of Biscay, at the age of 7 years.

Ancient fisheries

The many references to the tunny in classical literature show it to have been as important to the Mediterranean peoples as the herring was to the people of northwest Europe. The fisheries have continued through the centuries. Many methods have been used for catching the fish, such as harpoons, baited hooks and nets. The most spectacular are the net fisheries; very long nets are used to intercept migrating shoals and guide them into a final compartment or 'death chamber'. When this is filled with jostling fish the net floor is raised, the surrounding boats close in and the massed fish are clubbed, speared and dragged into the boats. Tuna fishing, or tunny fishing, according to whether it is carried out in American or British waters, has become a popular sport during the last half century. A large fish has been described as 'the tiger of the seas' and 'a living meteor' that strikes like a whirlwind and, played with a rod, will give a man the contest of his life, perhaps towing his boat for hours over a distance of several miles before becoming exhausted. The chief natural enemy is the killer whale.

Wide ranging tunas

There has long been some doubt whether the tuna of the American Atlantic is the same species as the tunny of the European side. They differ slightly in details of anatomy and in the time of the breeding season. Nevertheless, the tendency now is to treat them as separate populations of a single species. Other related species have similar wide distributions. A near relative, the Atlantic albacore, up to 4 ft long and 65 lb weight, with long scythe-like pectoral fins, has its counterpart in the Pacific albacore which ranges from the Pacific coast of North America to Japan and Hawaii. In the yellow-finned albacores or yellow-finned tunas, up to 9 ft long and 400 lb weight, the second dorsal and anal fins are also long and scythe-like. One species ranges across the tropical and subtropical Atlantic and another ranges across the Pacific and into the Indian Ocean. The actual identification of species is difficult because tuna, like many of the large fishes, seldom reach museums, where they can be effectively studied.

class	**Pisces**	
order	**Perciformes**	
family	**Scombridae**	
genus & species	***Thunnus alalunga*** albacore	
	T. albacares yellowfin	
	T. atlanticus blackfin	
	T. obesus bigeye	
	T. thynnus bluefin	
	T. tonggol longtail	

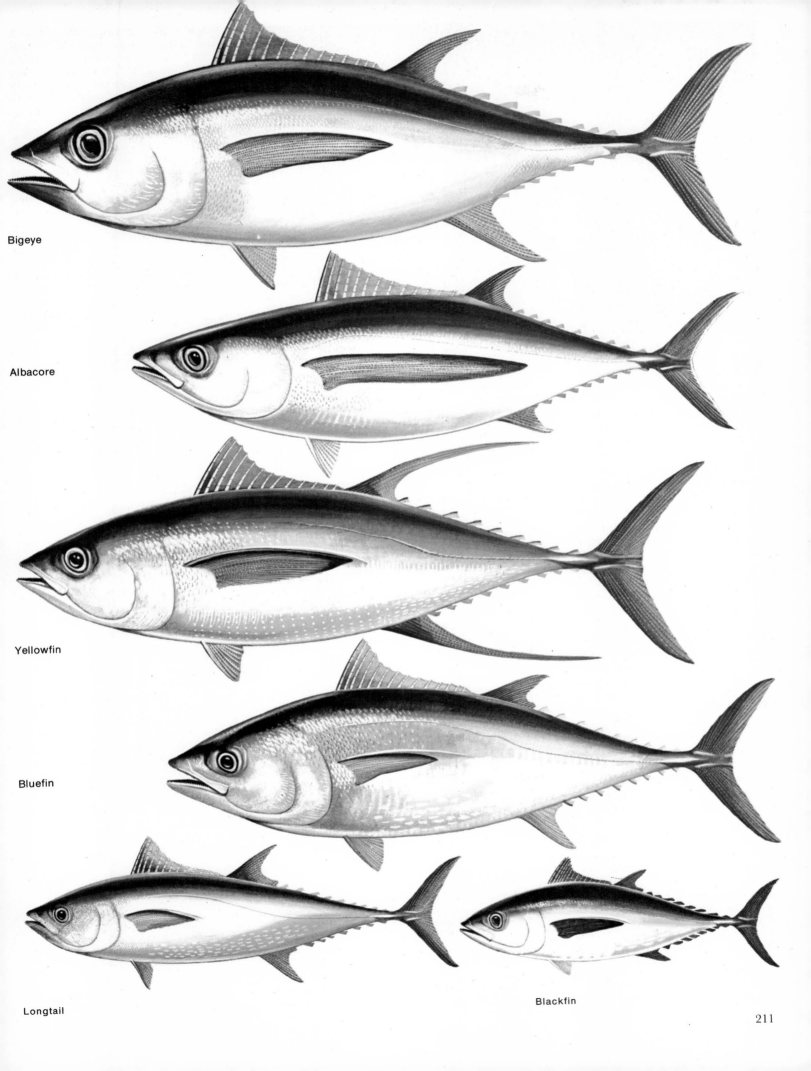

Bigeye

Albacore

Yellowfin

Bluefin

Longtail

Blackfin

211

△ *Helped by their streamlined shape and powerful tail, shoals of mackerel move very fast as they scour the upper waters for food.*

Mackerel

Diminutive relatives of the mighty tunas, mackerel share with them the streamlined shape, voracious feeding, and agile swimming which have made them favourites with fishermen and with anglers all over the world.

The common European mackerel has a plump but streamlined body, blue green on the back, silvery below. The back is patterned with darker ripple marks, but two varieties are occasionally seen. In one, the dotted mackerel, the ripple marks are replaced by spots. In the other, the scribbled mackerel, the ripple marks are finer and look like marbling. There are two dorsal fins, the one in front being spiny, and the pelvic fins are well forward, almost level with the pectoral fins. A line of finlets runs from the second dorsal to the tail fin, with a similar row of finlets on the underside of the body.

The range of the common mackerel in the eastern Atlantic is from Norway to the Canaries. The same species occurs in the western Atlantic from Chesapeake Bay to the Gulf of Maine. The Spanish or chub mackerel occurs in these same areas but does not extend so far north. The Pacific mackerel ranges from Alaska to the Gulf of California, and on the other side of the Pacific, with a similar distribution, is the Japanese mackerel.

The pygmy mackerels live in the Indo-Australian region. These are similar fishes, more deep bodied and up to 15 in. long. Rastrelliger kanagurta, of the Indian Ocean, known as kembong, is fished in large numbers all the way round the coasts of the Indian Ocean from East Africa to the Malay Archipelago.

The horse mackerel is not a mackerel but a member of the family Carangidae, although its habits are similar to those of true mackerel.

Spawning cycle

Mackerel live in shoals, but to a lesser extent than, for example, the herring. At the end of October they leave the surface waters, go to the bottom and lie densely packed in the troughs and trenches. Towards the end of December they spread outwards over the surrounding seabed. At the end of January they move up to the surface, coming together in shoals, and start moving towards the spawning grounds. One of the main spawning grounds is near the edge of the continental shelf, in a wide V to the south of Ireland. The period of spawning is from March to June, after which they move into inshore waters breaking up into small shoals, and they stay there until October, when they go down to the bottom again to repeat the cycle.

Seasonal change of diet

On the seabed, mackerel feed on shrimps and smaller crustaceans, marine bristle-worms and small fishes. When they return to the surface in January they change their diet, taking animal plankton, especially the copepod *Calanus*, selectively picking these from the water, snapping them up as a swallow snaps up flies. From June to October, while in inshore waters, the mackerel feed on small fishes, especially young herrings, sprats and sand eels. Mackerel hunt mainly by smell, as is shown by the Breton fishermen who lure them by pouring stale fish blood overboard and scooping up the mackerel attracted to it. They must use sight at close quarters, however. With their pelvic fins well forward they can turn in a tight circle to catch prey as fast as themselves but less manoeuvrable.

Sinking eggs

The female lays about half a million eggs, each $\frac{1}{20}$ in. diameter. Each egg has a small oil globule in it and floats at the surface for 2 days. Then it sinks slowly down to mid-water where it remains suspended for a short while. If the temperature is right, about 15°C/58°F, the eggs hatch and a larval mackerel $\frac{1}{10}$ in. long, still bearing a yolk sac, is born. The yolk lasts for about 9 days, after which the young mackerel begins to hunt minute plankton. Mackerel take 2 years to mature, at about a foot long.

Important food fish

Mackerel are preyed upon by fast swimming predatory fishes, especially in the young stages, their first two years of life, about which little is known. They are caught in nets or on long lines, or by spinning. Mackerel are only second in importance to herring among pelagic fishes. They are caught in seine nets from March to June and by hook and line from July to October.

Diver's discovery

Dr J Travis Jenkins tells us that it is a belief among fishermen that the first mackerel of the season are blind, that they have a cloudy film of skin over the eyes, which disappears in summer. One reason for this belief is that mackerel will not take bait until the summer. It used to be thought by marine zoologists that mackerel strained plankton from the sea, as a whalebone whale does. This seemed reasonable because mackerel have slender gill-rakers beset with fine spines making an efficient filtering apparatus. Both these beliefs were corrected in 1921 when an officer of the Royal Navy was hanging below a ship in a diver's suit during salvage operations. In the shadow of the ship the plankton animals showed up in dark silhouette against the sunlit waters beyond. The mackerel appreciated this advantage and the diver was able to watch them distinctly snapping up individual copepods—at a time when they should have had a film over their eyes.

class	**Pisces**
order	**Perciformes**
family	**Scombridae**
genus & species	*Scomber japonicus* Spanish or chub *S. scombrus* common others

Mudskipper

Mudskippers are fish which, instead of retreating with the falling tide, usually remain on the exposed mud. They can breathe air and move quickly over the mud, using their pectoral fins. Among some of the largest members of the goby family, they live on mud flats and mangrove swamps from West Africa to southeast Asia and the southwestern Pacific.

Mudskippers are 5—12 in. long, almost tadpole-like with a heavy head and long body compressed from side to side. They could well be described as pop-eyed, with their conspicuous eyes, placed well up on the head. These eyes can move

Three mud dwellers

Mudskippers show a zonation from the depths of the mangrove swamps, even up in the trees, through the mud of the forest floor down to the mid-tide level. There are three basic types of mudskippers. The eel-skippers *Scartelaos* so called because they have long slender bodies, live in the very soft mud at mid-tide level in the estuaries and are never far from water. Little is known of their habits. The second group, genus *Boleophthalmus*, live in large numbers on the mud at the seaward edge of mangrove forests. They may move into the margin of the forest, under the trees, but no more. They move their heads from side to side as they skitter over the mud skimming diatoms and algae from the surface. In a way not yet understood, they sort these

△ *Mudskipper profile: these are quite common in tropical parts of coastal Australia.*
◁ *Gill-chambers full of water, Malayan mudskippers **Periophthalmus chrysopilos** on mud.*

about in all directions. The front dorsal fin is high and spiny. The pectoral fins are fairly large and somewhat limb-like. The pelvic fins are joined to form a kind of sucker. The colour of the body varies from blue-grey to brownish, often with many small blue spots. The fins, especially the two dorsals, are decorated with coloured spots which vary according to the species.

In western Africa they live on the Saharan shores to the north and the Namibian shores to the south. In eastern Africa they range from East London to the Red Sea, and from there around the shores of the Indian Ocean and into the Indo-Australian region.

out from the water in the mouth, swallow the diatoms and algae and spit out the water. The third group includes the genera *Periophthalmus* and *Periophthalmodon*, the commonest mudskippers, found along the banks of creeks and throughout the mangrove forests. These feed on insects that have fallen into the mud, on crabs, worms and the smaller mudskippers.

The species of *Periophthalmus* fall into two groups: those represented by *P. kalolo* in which the pelvic fins are still separate, and those represented by *P. chrysospilos* with the pelvic fins joined and forming a sucker. Mudskippers of the first group can climb only onto the exposed roots of mangroves whereas those of the second group are able to climb the vertical shoots and trunks by means of their suckers.

▽▷ In these Malayan species the pelvic fins have moved anterior to the pectoral fins and joined to form a sucker which enables them to climb the vertical trunks of mangroves.

Living in air

All mudskippers spend much of their time out of water, but they constantly return to the pools left by the tide. The gill chambers are much enlarged to carry a supply of water but this has to be continually renewed in the pools although they can breathe air through the membranes lining the back of the mouth and the throat which are richly supplied with blood vessels. Mudskippers are said to dip their tails in water because they breathe through them. This is not so at all. They need to keep their skin moist, so they often splash water over themselves with one of the pectoral fins. They also have to keep their eyes moist. We have a supply of fluid on the surface of the eye supplied by the tear gland, and every time we blink we draw the lids over the eyes and

moisten them. Fishes have no tear glands and a mudskipper cleans and moistens its eyes by pulling them back into the head.

Double vision

The eyes themselves serve a dual purpose: the retina of the upper half is rich in rods, which means that it can detect small movements; the lower part has cones, which give colour vision. Presumably with the upper part of the eye they look down to detect insects and other small animals but watch other mudskippers for their colours, since these are used for signals. Eelskippers, when they meet, open their mouths at each other, showing the dark indigo blue inside. They also raise and lower the long spine of the dorsal fin. These movements are a challenge which may end in a pushing

match, after which the two separate.

Most, if not all, mudskippers have some form of signal which is often used while they are moving about over the mud. Usually it is a matter of raising and lowering the brightly coloured first dorsal fin every few seconds. One species throws itself in the air at frequent intervals, seeming to stand for a split second on the tip of its very thin tail before flopping back on the mud. This appears to be a matter of making those around keep off its territory, so all have their own feeding ground.

The mudskipper's pectoral fins are broad and mounted on a stubby limb, a sort of arm. In moving over the mud it uses these as crutches. It anchors its body with the anal fin and presses downwards and backwards with the pectoral fins, so it moves with a similar action to a sealion. In the water it swims in the usual way, that is by wriggling its tail, usually keeping its head above water.

Gymnastic courtship

Except in the breeding season, when the male has brighter colours, it is impossible to distinguish the male from the female except by dissection. At the breeding season in *Periophthalmus chrysopilos*, the only species whose breeding behaviour is at all well known, the colours of the male intensify and he has a brilliantly golden chin and throat. He displays this by doing 'press-ups' at passing females until he attracts one. She then follows him to his burrow. Mating seems to take place in the burrow, and the eggs are also laid there.

215

Mud sappers

Although it is generally believed that the first fishes to come on land, the ancestors of the salamanders, were probably of the coelacanth type (see page 228), the mudskippers show us some of the ways in which these ancestral land-water vertebrates must have lived. They are truly amphibious, some species spending most of their time on land, others most of their time in water, being able to stay submerged for up to 2 hours. They have overcome problems of breathing and movement on land, and have also solved the problem of shelters, by burrowing in the mud. The burrows are made up of a saucer-shaped depression leading into a vertical tunnel, with a rampart of mud round the saucer. The saucer may be anything from 6 in. to 2 ft across. One species makes a Y-shaped burrow with twin turrets of mud at the surface. The burrow is dug with the mouth, the fish bringing out mouthfuls of mud and spitting them on to the rampart to build it.

Leaping as well as bounding

The actions of any mudskipper out of water are quite remarkable, as we have seen. There is, however, one species which does more than probably any other to justify the common name of these relatives of the gobies. This is *Periophthalmus koelreuteri*, which is the most widespread species, round the shores of the Indian Ocean. It spends a great deal of its time, when the tide is out, perched on the margins of small pools in the mangrove swamps with the tip of its tail just in the water. The usual size of this mudskipper is about 5 in. in length. When disturbed it jumps to the next pool, which may be anything up to 2 feet away. Moreover it seldom misses its target. Such jumps are made by curving the body and then straightening it suddenly.

class	**Pisces**
order	**Perciformes**
family	**Gobiidae**

▷ *A giant mudskipper* **Periophthalmus** *displays by raising and lowering its dorsal and tail fin. This species lives on the banks of Malayan rivers where they dig 'castles' for themselves. This is a small pool with a muddy wall and perhaps a tunnel in the pool for the fish to retreat into. This species is about twice the size of* **Scartelaos** *being about 9 in. and also much fatter. It will sit on its 'castle' wall and defend its territory, evicting all rivals.*

▷▷ *Tail standing. This mudskipper* **Scartelaos viridis** *was filmed at the mouth of a small river near a Chinese hamlet in Malaya. It lives on the mud flat and is exposed only at very low tide. Every so often, as the series of frames show, it throws itself upwards until it is almost standing on its tail before flopping back onto the mud. This appears to be a matter of showing itself to warn those around to keep off its territory so all have a reasonable amount of feeding ground.*

In the ring: two wary males circle each other during a lull in combat, seeking an opening to attack.

Fighting fish

*Many fish fight, but the celebrated species is the fighting fish **Betta splendens** of Thailand. This is one of 7 related species in southeast Asia, ranging from Thailand to Borneo. It has been selectively bred for fighting qualities and used for sport, with bets placed, in Thailand.*

The wild ancestor is 2 in. long, yellowish-brown with indistinct dark stripes along the flanks. In the breeding season the male becomes darker and rows of metallic green scales on its flanks become brighter. Its dorsal fin is medium-sized, metallic green tipped with red. The anal fin is large and red edged with blue and the small pelvic fins are red tipped with white. The tail fin is rounded. The female is smaller, less colourful, mainly yellowish brown.

Short-lived

Fighting fish live in clear but weedy rivers and lakes, in irrigation ditches and ponds, and two species are also found in mountain streams. They mature rapidly and grow quickly, and they do not live much longer than two years. Because of their rapid growth they feed heavily on all kinds of small aquatic animals such as water fleas, mosquito larvae, worms or small pieces of dead flesh.

Endurance tests

Male fighting fish are pugnacious towards each other—one species has been named *Betta pugnax*—but to nothing like the extent of the selectively bred descendants. Wild fighting fish rarely keep up their fights for 15 minutes and usually it is much less. The cultivated varieties are considered to be poor samples if they fight for less than an hour and some will continue to attack for up to 6 hours.

A raft of bubbles

Mating is preceded by the male swimming around the female, with heightened colours and fins spread. There follows what can only be called dancing and embracing. Before this takes place, however, the male has built a nest, a raft of bubbles. He takes in bubbles of air at the surface and these become enclosed in a sticky mucus in his mouth, so the bubbles last a long time.

The courtship ends with the male turning the female on her side and wrapping himself round her. Then he tightens his grip, turns her upside down, and in a short while lets go and, as she remains suspended in the upside-down position, he stations himself beneath her. She begins to lay 3—7 eggs at a time, to a total of several hundred. As these slowly sink the male catches each in turn in his mouth, coats it with mucus, then swims up to his raft and sticks it on the underside. This is repeated until all the eggs are laid, the male looping himself round the

female each time to fertilise the eggs as she lays them. Finally, the male drives the female away. After that the male guards the nest. The young hatch 24—30 hours later, when the male's parental duties are at an end.

Head-on crash

The first *B. splendens* to be bred in Europe appeared in France in 1893 and in a very few years it was being kept by aquarists over a large part of the world. One of the earlier varieties was cream-coloured with flowing red fins. Then came the famous Cornflower Blue. After that there were various shades of blue, lavender, green and red ending in the best-known, the rich purplish-blue. All these varieties had flowing veil-like fins and, whatever their colour of body, all had red drooping pelvic fins.

There have been many stories, usually highly coloured, about the way the males fight. The facts are dramatic enough. When two males are put in an aquarium together their colours heighten and they take up position side by side, heads pointed in one direction, one fish slightly in advance of the other. Their fins are erected, their gill-covers expanded. Then, with lightning speed they attack. They try to bite each other's fins and in the end one may have some of its fins torn down to stumps. They may also bite patches of scales from each other's flanks. Sometimes they meet in a head-on clash with jaws interlocked.

Above: Male on the right surveys female. Below: Under the nest, a raft of bubbles, male mates with a female by wrapping himself round her.

The greatest damage is done when the cultivated fighting fish are unevenly matched. A small one matched against a large one is bound to suffer. So is a long-finned variety matched against a short-finned variety. Long flowing fins make it hard for their owner to turn quickly. More-over, the fishes attack the rear half of their opponents, where the flowing fins are.

Exploding with rage

One of the more exaggerated stories to be published was collected by the distinguished American fish specialist, Hugh M Smith. It is quoted in *Exotic Aquarium Fishes* by WT Innes. It tells how you go out and catch your fighting fish—assuming you live in Thailand—and bring it home in a bottle. Your neighbour does the same. You stand the two bottles together. The two fishes see each other, flash their colours at each other and blow themselves up. They hurl themselves in vain at each other, until finally one of them becomes so angry it literally bursts. If this is your fish you lose your bet!

class	**Pisces**
order	**Perciformes**
family	**Anabantidae**
genus & species	***Betta splendens*** ***B. pugnax*** others

Kissing gourami

This is a popular aquarium fish that has achieved fame for a single trick of behaviour that looks uncommonly like a familiar human action. Other than this the species would have remained in relative obscurity. 'Kissing' is by no means confined to this gourami, which is chosen here to show an interesting facet of animal behaviour.

There are several species of gouramis, all from southeast Asia, where they grow to a foot or more and are used for food. The kissing gourami may grow to a foot long, but when kept in an aquarium it is usually well short of this. Its body is flattened from side to side, oval in outline, with a pointed head ending in a pair of thickened lips. The greenish to grey-yellow dorsal and anal fins are long and prominent and both slope upwards from front to rear. The normal colour of the body is silvery green with dark stripes on the flanks but there is another colour phase, pinkish-white and somewhat iridescent.

Thick lips for breathing and eating

The kissing and other gouramis belong to the labyrinth fishes, which means they have an accessory breathing organ in the gills for taking in air at the surface, as well as breathing by gills. The kissing gourami not only rises to the surface from time to time to gulp air, and therefore can live in water that is slightly fouled, but it also feeds at the surface. The thickened lips probably have an advantage in these two respects. The food

consists of both animal and plant matter and in an aquarium kissing gouramis eat dried shrimps and powdered oatmeal, water fleas and dried spinach. To some extent they will feed on the small algae that grow on the sides of the aquarium.

Life history little known

There is still some doubt about their breeding habits. Many labyrinth fishes build bubble nests for their eggs but so far as we know kissing gouramis build no nest but lay 400–2 000 floating eggs. They seem to ignore these as well as the young which hatch in 24 hours. The baby fishes eat ciliated protistans for their first week, taking water fleas after this, graduating to the mixed diet as they grow older. They begin to breed when 3–5 in. long.

Mystery of the kiss

Nobody seems very clear whether this is an aggressive action or part of the courtship. Probably it enters into both. When several kissing gouramis are kept together in one aquarium the larger of them bother the smaller by 'sucking' at their flanks. They will do the same with fishes of other species. This is probably aggressive. When a pair are together, however, they can be seen to face each other, swaying backwards and forwards, as if hung on invisible threads, and then they come together, mouth to mouth, their thick lips firmly placed together in an exaggerated kissing action. Like other labyrinth fishes the male wraps himself around the body of the female when mating. This is preceded by the two swimming round and round each other in a circling movement, after which they again come together, lips to lips, in a seeming kiss.

A touching scene—like mirror images of each other two gouramis 'kiss'. It is not fully understood why this fish, a favourite among tropical fish fanciers, makes this familiar human action. It may be one of aggression but it also enters into the courtship ritual.

Mouth wrestling

The use of the mouth as a test of strength in fighting is common among the higher animals. It is frequently seen in aquarium fishes, especially among cichlids and labyrinth fishes. One fish butting another with its mouth is often used in courtship, especially by the smaller freshwater fishes, and it seems likely that the mouth-wrestling and the butting lead on to the kissing. At all events, A van der Nieuwenhuizen, in his book *Tropical Aquarium Fish*, takes the view that in the cichlid, known as the blue acara *Aequidens latifrons*, mouth-wrestling is used to defeat a rival as well as court a mate. He maintains that when a pair indulge in a bout of mouth-wrestling which ends in stalemate this means the two are physically and psychologically suited and the chances of their breeding are high. The mouth-tugging, as he calls it, may last for hours and be repeated day after day, to end in a genuine lovers' choice. The chances are that the kissing of the gourami has exactly the same importance, so it is a true lovers' kiss.

class	**Pisces**
order	**Perciformes**
family	**Anabantidae**
genus & species	*Helostoma temmincki*

The barracuda is one of the most feared and dangerous predatory fishes. Apparently they may be dangerous in one area and not in another.

Barracuda

Barracuda are pike-like fishes, not related to pike but having a similar long-bodied form, with a jutting lower jaw and a wicked-looking set of fangs. Fishermen, in handling even the dead fish, treat them with respect. There are more than 20 species, but most of them are harmless. The evil reputation of barracudas has perhaps been over-stated, and it is difficult to know what to believe. One eminent authority, speaking of the fear fishermen in the West Indies have for the barràcuda, has referred to merciless struggles waged between man and barracuda in the shade of the mangroves. This is at variance with all that one hears from skindivers, as well as with what is said of the speedy attack by this fish. Nevertheless, there are a number of authentic records of attack, especially from the great barracuda, also called picuda, or becuna, the giant of the family, which ranges through tropical and subtropical waters the world over, and may reach a length of 8 ft or more. The northern barracuda, or sennet, of the western North Atlantic, reaches only 18 in., but the European barracuda, barracouta or spet, of the Mediterranean and eastern Atlantic, may reach 3 ft. Other species are the Indian barracuda and Commerson's barracuda, both of the Indian Ocean, and the California barracuda.

Most voracious fish

More fearful to some people than even the shark, the larger barracudas are among the most voracious of predatory fishes. Long and torpedo-shaped, the barracudas swim swiftly and feed voraciously, especially on plankton-feeding fishes, charging through their shoals, attacking with snapping bites. It is said that when a pack of barracuda has eaten enough, it herds the rest of the shoal it is attacking into shallow water and keeps guard over it until ready for another meal.

Small or half-grown barracudas swim in shoals, the larger individuals are solitary. A solitary barracuda attacks swiftly, bites cleanly and does not repeat its attack (shoaling barracuda seldom attack people). It hunts by sight rather than smell, as sharks do, and advice given to bathers and divers reflects this. For example, murky water should be avoided because the fish, aware of every movement you make through its keen sight, may over-estimate your size, thereby over-estimating the danger you represent to it, and attack. A metallic object flashing in clear water looks to a barracuda like a fish and stimulates attack. An underwater spear fisherman towing a fish may be in trouble also, and it is not unknown for a barracuda to snatch a captured fish from a skindiver's belt.

Virtually all the interest in this fish has been concentrated on its behaviour towards man, apart from its use for food. On two occasions American scientists have collected all reports of alleged attacks on human beings. It seems these amount to fewer than 40, making the barracuda less dangerous in aggregate than sharks. To a large extent the reputation of this fish is the result of what appears to be an insatiable curiosity. It will hang around a skin-diver, watching his movements and following him, generating in him a very uncomfortable feeling. There is evidence that a barracuda is most dangerous—some say only dangerous—when provoked. Even so, there are records of a person standing in no more than 1 ft of water having the flesh bitten from the lower leg, or the bone almost severed.

One feature of barracuda behaviour, for which there is as yet no explanation, is that the fish may be dangerous in one area and not in another. Barracuda in the Antilles, for example, should be avoided, but around Hawaii they seem to be harmless.

Barracuda spawn over deep water offshore in the Caribbean, ocean currents distributing the larvae and young.

Reputation prejudiced

All barracudas are regarded as good food-fishes, but there is some prejudice against the barracuda because its flesh is, on occasions, highly poisonous. This may be a seasonal danger, the flesh being poisonous at some times of the year and not at others, it may be due to the flesh being allowed to go slightly bad before being cooked, but it is also due to what is known as ciguatera, which is due to toxins, originating in toxic algae and diatoms, building up from plant-eating fish to predators, and concentrating. The toxin is the cause of sickness, and even death, in humans who eat the predator (for example the barracuda). In the Caribbean, some species of fish are safe to eat from only one side of an island.

Prejudice is not confined to the fish. Sir Hans Sloane, writing in 1707, maintained that barracudas were more fond of the flesh of dogs, horses and black men than that of white men. Père Labat, in 1742, carried this prejudiced statement further. He declared that, faced with a choice of a Frenchman and an Englishman, a barracuda would always choose the latter. He attributed this to the gross meat-eating habits of the Englishman, which produced a stronger 'exhalation' in the water, as compared with the more delicate exudations of a Frenchman, who is a daintier feeder.

class	**Pisces**
order	**Perciformes**
family	**Sphyraenidae**
genus & species	***Sphyraena barracuda*** *great barracuda*
	S. borealis *northern barracuda*
	S. sphyraena *European barracuda others*

△ *The skull of the great barracuda showing its wicked-looking set of fangs and the jutting lower jaw.*

▽ *School of barracuda swimming past coral of the Great Barrier Reef, Australia. Shoaling barracuda seldom attack people.*

Plaice

The plaice is one of the best known of the flatfishes and commercially the most important. It has a flattened body, with the dorsal fin extending from the head almost to the tailfin, and the anal fin from behind the gill cover to the same point. The brownish, upper, or right side is marked with red spots, each of which is surrounded by a white ring in the adult. These may be pale when the fish has been resting on whitish pebbles. The underside is pearly white but can be partially or wholly coloured, a condition known as ambicoloration. It may take the form of scattered brown or black spots or patches on the white undersurface. Alternatively, only the hindend may be completely coloured as on the upper surface, including the red spots. When the pigmentation extends along the whole underside the undersurface of the head is usually white, but in exceptional cases even this may be coloured. The mouth is twisted, with the lower, or blind, side more developed and armed with a greater number of teeth. The small scales are embedded in the skin and there are bony knobs between the eyes. Plaice can grow to almost 3 ft long, but the usual size is much less.

They range from Iceland and the White Sea, along the coasts of Scandinavia, south through the North Sea to the coasts of France and the western Mediterranean. Plaice are not identical throughout their range but split into a number of races. They vary in area of distribution, time and site of spawning, and in their degree of pigmentation.

Living magic carpet
Plaice live on sandy, gravelly or muddy bottoms, slightly buried, swimming just off the bottom at intervals through the day and night. They are said to be demersal or bottom-living fishes. They swim with vertical undulations of the flattened body, like a living magic carpet, then, holding the body rigid, they glide down. On touching bottom they undulate the fins to disturb sand or mud, which then settles on the fins, disguising the outline of the body. In this position a plaice breathes with a suction-pump action of the gill-covers.

Young plaice seem to go into a state resembling hibernation in winter. They remain quiescent in shallow water, slightly buried in the sand. At the appropriate time they move from shallow to deeper water.

Chisel and grinder
The teeth in the jaws of a plaice are chisel-like, but the throat teeth are blunt crushers. The food is mainly small molluscs but other small bottom-living invertebrates, such as worms, are eaten. Plaice swim over the shore at high tide to feed on the cockle and mussel beds. They hunt by sight not raising the head much off the bottom, but shooting forward horizontally with great accuracy to take the prey. Very small molluscs are

△ Face to face with the adult plaice. With distorted mouth and transposed eye it now lives permanently at the bottom of the sea, lying on its left side.

In this plaice the upper surface is mottled light grey to suit its background of shell-gravel. The plaice in the bottom picture has a brown mottling because it is lying on differently coloured sandy gravel. A plaice can change its colour and patterns to blend in with its background. A hormone is secreted which alters the shape of the pigment cells thus changing the colour of the plaice's body.

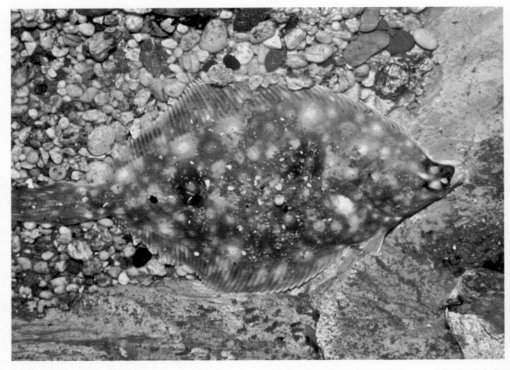

taken whole into the stomach. Larger ones are crushed by the throat teeth. They also bite off the siphons of molluscs or the heads of worms sticking out of tubes.

Prolific spawnings
There is little in their outward appearance to tell male from female, but if at any time they are held up to the light the female roe shows as a small dark triangle. The male roe is a curved rounded line. The males reach the spawning grounds first and are still there after the females have gone. Spawning time differs from one part of the sea to another. Off the east coast of Scotland it is

from early January to May, with a peak in March. In the Clyde estuary, on the west coast of Scotland, it is from February to June. In the southern North Sea it is from October to March.

To spawn, two plaice swim about $2\frac{1}{2}$ ft off the bottom, the female lying diagonally across the male, releasing a stream of eggs while he emits a stream of milt. Spawning lasts less than a minute, after which the two separate and return to the bottom. Each female lays 50–400 thousand eggs, the number depending, it seems, on the length of the fish. The transparent eggs, each in a tough capsule, are just under $\frac{1}{12}$ in. diameter.

They float at or near the surface, and many are eaten before they can hatch, which they do in 8—21 days, according to the temperature of the water. The larvae are about $\frac{1}{4}$ in. long, without mouth or gills, and with the remains of a yolk sac attached which supplies them with food. This is the most vulnerable part of the life of a plaice. Apart from those eaten by other animals only 1 in every 100 thousand survive the first few weeks of larval life, or 2—5 for every pair of parent plaice. Although this seems disastrous the figures are put in perspective by the knowledge that in one area alone, halfway between the mouth of the Thames and the coast of Holland, 60 million plaice come together each year to spawn. The adults are probably protected by their colour and their habit of lying buried, but seals find them, and predatory fishes, such as cod, eat the small ones.

Plaice are of great economic value but of the tens of millions of plaice eaten each year in Europe, few are eaten at the right moment. Plaice has the best flavour when it is cooked immediately after being caught. The sole however, develops its characteristic taste 2—3 days after death due to the decomposition of the flesh with the formation of different chemical substances.

Baby food
As the contents of the yolk sac are being used up, the larval plaice starts to feed on diatoms. At this stage it has the normal fish larva shape, giving no indication of the adult shape to come. As it grows it graduates from small diatoms to larger diatoms then to larvae of small crustaceans, such as copepods, and molluscs. At this stage an important item is the planktonic food *Oikopleura*. After 2 months the larva gradually metamorphoses into a young flatfish, this takes about 2½ weeks. The body becomes flattened from side to side, the young plaice starts swimming on its side, the skull becomes twisted by growing more quickly on one side than the other, causing the left eye to be swung over to the right side. At the same time the young plaice leaves the upper waters for the seabed, settling on its left side, so its right side and both eyes are uppermost. As these changes have been taking place the young plaice (still only ½ in. long) has been carried by currents to its inshore nursery ground.

The account given above of the feeding of the larvae is only a generalization. The food taken varies in different places, the plaice taking whatever is available. In Scottish coastal waters they eat mainly worm larvae, crustacean eggs and larval molluscs. Off Plymouth, copepods and other small crustaceans are eaten, in the Irish Sea the larvae feed on small copepods, and spores of algae, and in southern North Sea it is mainly *Oikopleura*. The survival of the larvae can be seriously affected if supplies of these foods are low in the area where they form the staple diet of the larvae.

How they grow
After the ½ in. young plaice has settled on the bottom it reaches 2¾ in. by the age of 1 year, 5 in. by 2 years, nearly 8 in. by 3 years, 10½ in. by 4 years and 13 in. by 5 years of age. These figures are for females, the males being smaller. On average, the males reach sexual maturity in 2—3 years, the females in 4—5 years. The figures must be read as approximations because average sizes of plaice have been found to vary: 17 in. in the North Sea, 15 in. in the English Channel, 13 in. in the Kattegat and 10 in. in the Baltic. These are, again, merely examples to show how size can vary, with environmental conditions. A 2ft plaice is 20 or more years old, and a 33in. plaice, which is one of the largest recorded, would be about 40 years old.

class	**Pisces**
order	**Pleuronectiformes**
family	**Pleuronectidae**
genus & species	***Pleuronectes platessa***

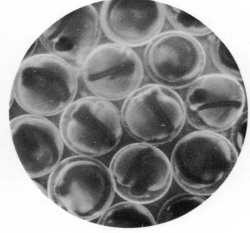
Plaice eggs with developing embryos.

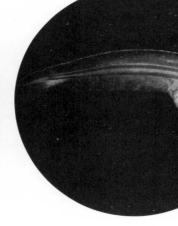
Larva lives in plankton, off its yolk sac.

As yolk sac is used up the mouth develops.

Like many marine fishes the plaice lays a large number of eggs to offset heavy predation. The dramatic part of the life cycle occurs after 2 months in preparation for life on the seabed. The body becomes flattened from side to side; the skull is twisted by growing more quickly on one side than the other, causing the left eye to migrate to the right side; then the young plaice settles with both eyes uppermost.

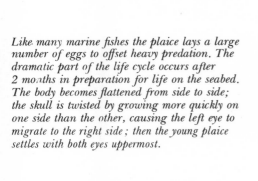

Left eye migrates as larva swims on its side.

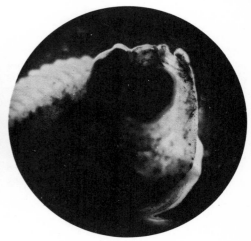
Eye migration complete, plaice settles on bottom.

Hippoglossus hippoglossus
The halibut is a rather mixed-up fish—being halfway between an ordinary fish and a proper flatfish.

Halibut

The halibut is little more than halfway between an ordinary fish and a thorough-going flatfish. It is longer in the body and more plump than most flatfishes, such as the plaice and the flounder. Its jaws have kept their original shape instead of being distorted, with one jaw weaker than the other, and they are armed with sharp teeth. The fringing fins (dorsal and anal) are somewhat triangular and the tail and tail fin are well-marked and powerful. The upper surface, which is in fact the right side, is uniformly olive brown, dark brown or black, the underside being pearly white.

There are two species, one in the North Atlantic, the other in the North Pacific. Exceptional heavyweights have reached a length of 12 ft and a weight of 700 lb. Small halibut live inshore but, as they mature, move into deeper waters, onto sandy banks for preference, at depths of 1 200 ft or more.

Matching its background

A halibut lies on the seabed where it can pass unnoticed by its prey because of its colour. It leaves the bottom to chase after smaller fishes. Most flatfishes swim by undulations of their fringing fins, but halibut do so by vigorous movements of the body and the powerful tail. While on the bottom the halibut's upper side is coloured like the seabed. Lying on mud a halibut will be black. If it moves onto a patch of sand it begins to grow pale. One with its head on a patch of sand and its body on mud will have a pale head and a black body. These changes are governed through the eyes. A flatfish blinded by injury remains the same colour whatever it is lying on. If we watch a flatfish in an aquarium we see the eyes standing well out on the head, each moving independently of the other, and commanding a view of the bottom all around its head.

Bludgeoning its prey?

Halibut eat crabs, molluscs, worms and other bottom-living invertebrates, but their main food is fishes, especially herring, also flounder, cod, skate, and many others. The fish evidently has a reputation as a killer with fishermen. Dr GB Goode, former Commissioner of Fisheries in the United States, has stated that fishermen declare a halibut kills other fishes with blows of its tail. Whether this is true or not, it tells us something of what fishermen think of the halibut.

Floating eggs

Spawning takes place in the Atlantic during May to July at depths of about 1 200 ft. The Pacific halibut spawns in winter at depths of 900 ft. The female roe is large. In a 250lb fish it may be 2 ft long and weigh 40 lb. A mature female may lay 2¾ million eggs, each ⅛ in. diameter and buoyant, so they float to the surface. The eggs hatch in a few days, the baby fish being the usual fish shape at first, with an eye on each side of the head. It remains at the surface and is carried by currents to inshore waters. After a while the left eye begins to migrate over the top of the head until it comes to lie close to the right eye. At the same time the young halibut turns more and more on to its left side while the dorsal and anal fins grow longer to become the fringing fins. As these changes are taking place the fish is sinking towards the bottom finally to rest on it, left side down. In about one in 5 000 it is the right eye that migrates and the fish then comes to rest on the right side. Until it comes to rest the young halibut is transparent, then it changes colour to become brown or black on the upper side. The halibut is fairly long-lived. One 4 ft long will be about 12 years old, and as much as 35 years of age has been recorded.

Evolution of flatfishes

In the Indian Ocean is one flatfish of the genus *Psettodes* that is more like sea perch to look at. The migrating eye stops short on top of the head, the dorsal fin begins farther back than in other flatfishes and both dorsal and anal fins have spiny instead of soft rays. They rest on their side on the bottom and, like the halibut, swim up to catch prey. Some sea perches also lie

on their sides on the bottom to rest, although their shape is normal, and they and *Psettodes* suggest how the flatfish condition probably arose during the course of evolution.

Enemies of halibut?

There are few details known about the enemies of halibut but we can be reasonably sure, by comparison with what is known about other fishes laying huge numbers of eggs, that there is a heavy loss of eggs, fry and young. Later, the growing halibut will suffer from fish-eaters among other species of fish, doubtless also from porpoises, dolphins and seals. There is a steady drain on their numbers from commercial fisheries, halibut being taken by trawl and long line.

Name is mediaeval

Halibut must have been fished for a very long time since the name dates from mediaeval times. It is believed to mean holy turbot, from the Scandinavian word *butta* used for turbot. Captain John Smith, founder of Virginia, wrote of 'the large sized Halibut, or Turbot', and followed this with the strange remark that some are so big 'that the fisher men onley eat the heads & fins, and throw away the bodies'. Later, the halibut became known as the workhouse fish. This may have been a term of contempt or a reference to the fact that one halibut could be large enough to feed many hungry mouths. The fish finally came into its own, not only for the table but for medicinal purposes, in the present century. As we know, the cod was finally recognized in the 1920s as a supplier of cod liver oil for medicinal purposes. A decade or so later halibut oil became popular and almost displaced cod liver oil.

class	**Pisces**
order	**Pleuronectiformes**
family	**Pleuronectidae**
genus & species	***Hippoglossus hippoglossus*** *Atlantic halibut* ***H. stenolepis*** *Pacific halibut*

Porcupine fish

When relaxed the porcupine fish has much the shape of an ordinary fish, but when it blows itself up its body becomes almost spherical with long spines bristling all over it. Its tail and mouth look very small compared with this greatly distended body. It has large eyes, and the dorsal, anal and pectoral fins are of moderate size. Porcupine fish are about 1 ft long but may be as much as 2½ ft. In the same family are the burrfishes which have short spines that are always erect.

Doubly armoured

When disturbed or alarmed, porcupine fish inflate their bodies by drawing in water. The body swells, and the spines, which have been lying flat, are erected, standing out almost at right angles to the surface. If a porcupine fish is taken out of water suddenly it blows itself up by drawing in air.

The spines, which may be 2 in. or more long, are sharp and anyone handling an inflated porcupine fish should wear gloves. Each of the long stout spines has a three-armed base, the paired arms of which overlap in the skin with those of their fellows, providing a more or less continuous 'coat of mail'. In some species the spines have only two arms at the base and can be raised and lowered without the fish inflating itself.

Porcupine fish which live in tropical seas, are slow swimmers; they swim by waving the dorsal and anal fins, helped to a small extent by the pectorals, the tailfin being used for steering.

Coral-eaters

The teeth of the porcupine fish form a continuous plate in the upper jaw with another plate in the lower jaw. Each plate has a sharp edge with a crushing surface behind it. The fishes feed by crushing molluscs and by biting off and crushing pieces of coral. The flesh of the coral is digested in the stomach. The stony matter in the coral,

△ *Submarine satellite. Free-swimming porcupine fish* **Diodon hystrix** *blown up with water.*

crushed by the dental plates, accumulates and one porcupine fish dissected had over 1 lb of crushed coral rock in its stomach.

Escape from shark's stomach

Nothing is known of the breeding habits or the enemies of porcupine fish. There are very few records of what happens when they are attacked but Dr William Beebe, distinguished American marine zoologist, watched some porcupine fishes threatened by a 4ft garfish bunch together for protection. They looked like one large round prickly fish. Then, for no obvious reason, from time to time one would leave the mass and swim away, to be promptly seized and eaten by the garfish. By contrast with this, Robert Hegner, in his *Parade of the Animal Kingdom*, takes the view that if a shark is foolish enough to swallow a porcupine fish it will pay dearly for it. According to him, when the prickly fish reaches the shark's

stomach it gives out what Darwin called a 'most beautiful carmine-red fibrous matter', which is supposed to protect the fish from the shark's digestive juices. Thus protected it starts to cut and crush the wall of the shark's stomach and body wall until it reaches the sea and freedom.

Sharks have been seen to swallow these fishes but we can only surmise what happens inside them. Craig Phillips, in *The Captive Sea,* says that the surest way to ruin a net is to catch a porcupine fish in it. The more tightly the fish feels itself imprisoned the more it blows itself up, and its body remains inflated with the spines sticking out. Phillips deals with this fish by inserting a plastic tube into its throat, which deflates it. Does a shark suffer the fate of the net, as Hegner suggests, or has it some trick of deflating its prickly victim?

Can be poisonous

South Sea Islanders used to make war helmets of the dried skins of porcupine fishes. In the Far East they have been used as lanterns, the dried skin hung up with a candle inside or, in more modern times, an electric bulb in it. In southern England it used to be common to see a dried dead porcupine fish hanging in a fishmonger's shop, acting as a sort of trade sign. These are about the only uses man makes of the porcupine fish except that in some parts of the world it is eaten. It has a bad reputation, however, and care and know-how are needed in preparing the fish for the table because a poison in its liver and skin can contaminate the flesh if the cook does not prepare it correctly.

△ *Porcupine globe fish swimming slowly along the sea bed, its spines lying flat. The spines are only erected when the fish inflates itself.*
▽ *Careful guidance for a porcupine globe fish. Its spines may be up to 2 in. long.*

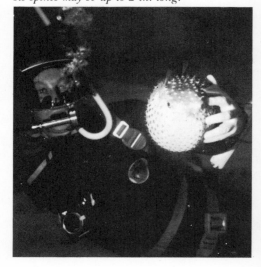

class	**Pisces**
order	**Tetraodontiformes**
family	**Diodontidae**
genus & species	*Diodon holacanthus* *D. hystrix* *porcupine globe fish, others*

Anglerfishes

There are more than 350 species of anglerfish, the Pediculati, but because of the distinct differences between them it is convenient to consider them as two groups: anglerfishes (225 + species) and deep-sea anglers (125 species). All have developed the characteristic habits of anglers: they keep still most of the time, using a rod and line to catch small fishes. The rod of the anglerfish is a modified spiny ray of the dorsal fin. Habitual immobility means little expenditure of energy, and less need for breathing. This is reflected in the small gills of anglerfishes with only a small gill-opening.

'Pediculati', the old name for anglerfishes, means 'small foot', referring to the elbowed pectoral fins used like feet to move over the seabed in short jumps. The pelvic fins are also somewhat foot-like but they are small, usually hidden on the undersurface in advance of the pectoral fins. Because of their squat shape, bottom-living habits and method of locomotion the anglerfishes have been given a variety of descriptive vernacular names: goosefishes or monkfishes, frogfishes or fishing frogs (because of the wide mouth) and batfishes. One of the best-known is **Lophius piscatorius**, up to 4ft. long with a large head, about 2½ ft across, and a wide mouth. Although the fish is so ugly the flesh is highly palatable and is widely used as fried fish.

Camouflaged and immobile

Anglerfishes of one kind or another are found at all depths throughout tropical and temperate seas. Bottom-living for the most part, their bodies are ornamented with a variety of warts and irregularities, as well as small flaps of skin. These, with their usually drab colours arranged in a broken pattern, serve to camouflage the fish as it lies immobile among rocks and seaweed. The sargassum angler specializes more than most anglerfishes in camouflage. It lives exclusively among the weed of the Sargasso Sea, and uses its pectoral fins to grasp the weed, so that it is not easily shaken from its position.

Angling for food

The general method of feeding is to attract small fishes near the mouth with some form of lure. In the goosefishes or monkfishes this is a 'fishing rod' bearing a fleshy flap at its tip, which is waved slowly back and forth near the mouth. In others the rod lies hidden, folded back in a groove, or lying in a tube, and is periodically raised or pushed out and waved two or three times before being withdrawn. The lure at the end of the rod often is red and worm-like in shape. A small fish seeing it swims near and then suddenly disappears!

Breeding

Several deep-sea species of anglerfish show a peculiar relationship between male and

Anglerfish's body is camouflaged by flaps of skin resembling surrounding seaweeds.

Small fishes attracted to the anglerfish's mouth by a lure are snapped up. (⅓ natural size.)

female; the dwarf male, about ½in. long, attaches itself to the female (whose length is up to 45 in.) so securely that the two grow together, even sharing a blood system. The female is then, in effect, a self-fertilising hermaphrodite, the male being reduced to a mere sperm-producing organ.

Another outstanding feature of the breeding cycle of some anglerfishes is the size of the egg-masses. The female goosefish or monkfish lays eggs in a jelly-like mass, up to 40 ft long and 2 ft in width. This floats at the surface. The relatively large pear-shaped eggs are attached by the narrow end to a sheet of spawn, which floats at the surface, and may contain nearly 1½ million of them.

The larva, even before it leaves the egg, begins to develop black pigment. Seen from above the spawn appears as a dark patch in the water, the enclosed larvae looking like currants in a cake. One of these masses, seen by rowers in a boat off Scapa Flow, was mistaken for a sea-monster and the rowers pulled away from it for dear life! The larva is in an advanced stage when hatched and already has the beginnings of its fishing rod. Later, other spines develop on the back and branched fins grow down from the throat, so the larva looks very unusual.

The compleat angler

It is an interesting pastime to list how many human inventions have been anticipated in the animal kingdom. Anglerfishes have used a rod and line (or a lure) long before man did. It is not surprising that both human and fish anglers should use similar methods because their aims are identical. But although attention is always drawn to this by writers on the subject, nobody seems to have commented on the other piece of apparatus the two have in common: the landing net. Both kinds of anglers play their fish but the anglerfish does not allow his quarry to take the bait. Instead, the lure is waved until a fish draws near, then it is lowered towards the mouth. As the victim closes in on it the rod and its lure is suddenly whipped away, the huge mouth is opened wide, water rushes into this capacious 'landing net' and the prey is sucked in, after which the mouth snaps shut. And it all takes place in a flash. Only when a fish is large, so that the tail protrudes

from the mouth after the first bite, can we see what has happened. The anglerfish's ability to snap up its prey like lightning is quite remarkable. One moment the small fish is there near its mouth, the next moment it is no longer there, and the speed with which the anglerfish moves its jaws is too fast for the human eye to follow.

The batfishes take their angling to even greater lengths. The whiskery batfish, of the Caribbean, for example, is covered with outgrowths of skin that look exactly like small seaweeds and polyps known as sea-fire, that coat rocks like so much moss. Small fishes are deceived to the point where they will swim near and try to nibble the flaps of skin. The final touch to this masterpiece of deception lies in the batfish habit of gently rocking its body, making the flaps of skin sway from side to side, just as polyps and seaweed gently sway as the slow currents in the sea move back and forth. This is so much an ingrained habit that a batfish, removed from its surroundings and placed in an aquarium, will periodically rock itself even although it is surrounded only by clear water and glass.

When the small fish, deceived in this way, swims near, out comes the rod with its lure, looking like a wriggling worm. With this the batfish 'plays' its quarry. It will dangle the lure in front of the fish then withdraw it to entice the little fish nearer. It will vary the wriggling of the lure, now waggling it in an agitated manner, now moving it slowly. Watching this one gets the impression of a fish 'playing cat-and-mouse' with a smaller fish until—'snap'—and only the larger fish can be seen, motionless, and with a dead-pan expression.

class	**Pisces**	
order	**Lophiiformes**	
families	**Lophiidae**	anglerfishes
	Antennariidae	frogfishes
	Ogcocephalidae	batfishes

Coelacanth

First made known to science in 1938, and belonging to an order previously thought to have become extinct 70 million years ago, the coelacanth is a 5ft long, 120lb primitive fish. Coelacanth means hollow spines, referring to those of the fins. The fish, first caught off the coast of Natal, and later off Madagascar, is of robust build, brown to dark blue, and outwardly shows several peculiarities. The first is that each of the pectoral fins, instead of coming straight off the body, is carried on scaly muscular lobes and seems to be halfway between a normal fin and the walking limb of primitive land animals. The rear dorsal and the anal fins are similarly lobed. The second peculiarity is in the tail. Instead of the junction between the body and the tail fin being marked by a constriction, the body merely narrows rapidly and evenly, and then continues backwards as a narrow strip, dividing the rays of the tail fin into two equal parts, one above and one below it. Another peculiarity is its scales. Each scale is a bony plate covered with dermal denticles (small tooth-like points in the skin) like those of sharks.

Scientists' clever forecast

In addition to its strange external appearance the coelacanth has a number of peculiar internal features which are just as significant as its ancient ancestry. Although it is a bony fish, the backbone is made up almost entirely of a large, tough cartilaginous rod, the notochord. In an evolutionary sense, the notochord came before the backbone, and in the developing embryo of vertebrates it appears first and is later enclosed by the vertebrae and lost, except in very primitive vertebrates (for example, lampreys). The heart of the coelacanth is very simple, even simpler than that of other fishes. Interestingly enough it is like the heart predicted by anatomists when trying to explain how the heart evolved.

The kidneys, instead of lying just under the backbone, are on the floor of the abdomen, and instead of being a pair they are joined. This is unique, and it is hard to see any explanation. It is not so much a primitive character as one quite unexpected. The stomach also is peculiar; it is just a large bag. The intestine has a spiral valve, a feature shared with sharks and other primitive fishes.

Armoured 'lungs'

Perhaps one of the more perplexing features of the coelacanth is the swimbladder (an elongated silvery bag, an outgrowth of the gullet). This probably arose in the first place as a breathing organ. The fossil coelacanths, which flourished 450–70 million years ago, had a swimbladder and lobed fins. It was largely among these fishes that scientists looked for a possible ancestor to the land vertebrates. That is, the coelacanths seemed to be distant ancestors of man, with the beginnings of lungs and of walking limbs. One drawback to such a theory was that the

*Highlight in natural history: Professor Smith poses with **Malania**, the second coelacanth to be discovered, together with South African Air Force personnel, Captain Hunt's schooner crew, and the French governor of the Comores (at right). The date is December 29, 1952.*

swimbladder of coelacanths was sheathed in bony scales, so it could not have served as a lung and it would have made a very poor hydrostatic organ.

Hopes frustrated

When it was realised that an actual living coelacanth had been found, the more sober scientists hoped it would shed light on the puzzle of the rigid swimbladder. The more excitable ones began to talk about the living coelacanth shedding light on man's ancestry. Some of them broadcast to this effect and the coelacanth became, in the minds of many listeners, a missing link of supreme importance. That proved, however, a nine days' wonder. The swimbladder was also a disappointment. The first modern coelacanth was almost decomposed before being examined by an expert. In addition it had been gutted in the hope of preserving it. When more living coelacanths were caught and dissected, the swimbladder was found to be slender and filled with fat. It, also, cannot function as a lung and even more certainly is not a hydrostatic organ.

There are a number of other features of the anatomy which are peculiar, and which are of interest mainly to the expert. To-

gether they suggest that the coelacanths were an aberrant offshoot of the early fishes, having gone off at a tangent from the main line of evolution. They show relationships with sharks, chimaera, lungfishes, and other primitive fishes. Above all, they indicate that the coelacanths, following an independent evolutionary line, were a dying race, with the living coelacanth as the last survivor, so far as we know.

One of the peculiarities, which has an interesting lesson to teach, is the skull. This is hinged midway, as in fossil coelacanths. The brain cavity in it is large. It has long been a puzzle how the brain managed to work if the skull containing it was hinged. The living coelacanth shows that the brain is small and confined to the rear portion of the skull, behind the hinge. It lies embedded in fat and cushioned on two large blood ducts. The brain itself is therefore very small by comparison with the cavity of the skull.

It is common, in studying fossil animals, to take a plaster cast of the cranial cavity in the skull to reconstruct the shape and proportions of the brain. The living coelacanth teaches us that this could well be misleading.

Trawler's lucky catch

considerate and curious seaman, a quick-thinking curator of a tiny museum, and a scientist who let nothing stand in his way: these three people brought to light one of the most exciting animals of the century. On December 22, 1938, a fishing boat shot her trawl off the mouth of the Chalumna River, west of East London, in South Africa. It was not the usual place for the trawlers to fish. On this occasion the ship stood 3 miles offshore, her trawl dragging the seabed at 120 ft. It came up with 3 tons of fish, which were emptied on the deck in the usual way. Half an hour later the trawlermen came to the last fish, 5 ft long, blue, and with unusual scales, a fish they had not seen before. It lived for 4 hours.

The skipper, Captain Goosen, realising he had something unusual, sent the fish to Miss Courtenay-Latimer, curator at the East London museum. She wrote to Professor JLB Smith at Grahamstown, 400 miles away. But it was now Christmas Eve, the mail was choked, and so Smith did not see the fish for some days after its capture. Nevertheless, although it was in poor shape he realised its importance, and it is to the credit of Smith, Miss Courtenay-Latimer and Captain Goosen that a priceless scientific treasure was brought to the notice of the world's scientists.

On December 20, 1952, a fisherman, Ahmed Hussein, landed a 5ft, 100lb fish with a hook and line, from 65 ft of water off the Comores Islands, west of Madagascar. Professor Smith was informed, and flew to the Comores in a South African Air Force Dakota placed at his disposal by the then Prime Minister, Dr Malan. Although Smith gave it the name *Malania anjouanae* after the Prime Minister, it was later realised this was the same as the first coelacanth, which had been named *Latimeria chalumnae*, after Miss Courtenay-Latimer. This second fish was the culmination of a 14-year campaign in which Smith flooded East Africa with leaflets in English, French and Portuguese, offering a reward of £100 for the first two specimens caught.

A lucky find

Madagascar, including the Comores, was then under French administration, and French scientists now took up the search. A third was found in September, 1953, and in 1954 two more were caught: on January 28 and January 31. Since then others have been caught, which suggests that the one caught off Natal in 1938 had wandered from its normal habitat.

This, one of the most interesting of living fishes, is known therefore almost entirely from a dozen dead individuals examined by scientists, or watched for the very short while a few survived in aquaria. Brought to the surface they have soon died due to the combination of decompression and exposure to warmer waters.

class	**Pisces**
order	**Crossopterygii**
family	**Coelacanthidae**
genus & species	*Latimeria chalumnae*

△ *The leaflet which offered East African fishermen £100 for the first two coelacanths caught. Skin divers have looked for the fish off the coasts of Madagascar and neighbouring islands, and some have caught a glimpse of large fishes believed to be coelacanths along the steep slopes where the rocky sea-bed suddenly dips in a vertical wall to very deep water.* ▽ *Skeleton of a coelacanth tail. The characteristic double tail has fins made up of hollow rays of cartilage. This is a link with the Rhipidistian fishes of 320 million years ago, the supposed ancestors of land animals.*

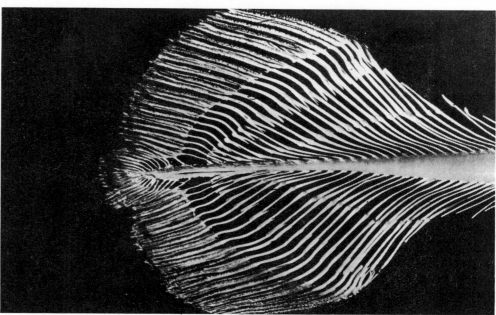

Amphibians and Reptiles

For reasons it would be difficult to define the custom has grown up of always speaking of amphibians and reptiles in one breath, as if the two must always be linked. Yet there is almost as much of a gulf between the living representatives of these two groups as between, say, birds and mammals. The features they have in common are that they are cold-blooded, air-breathing vertebrates typically living on land. The main differences between them are that amphibians, with rare exceptions, have a smooth scaleless skin whereas reptiles are scaly and that amphibians must go to water, or at least to a damp spot and this only exceptionally, to breed, whereas all reptiles have to come on land to lay their eggs.

The word 'amphibian' means more or less literally 'double life'. The typical amphibian spends the first part of its life in water and its adult life on land. There are plenty of exceptions to this, as there are to virtually every general statement made about living organisms. There are both salamanders and occasional toads that live their whole lives in water, examples being the salamander known as the olm and the Surinam toad. Conversely, there are frogs, the Stephens Island frog of New Zealand being one, that lay their eggs on land. The Stephens Island frog lives among boulders and its eggs are laid on damp earth. From them hatch fully formed froglets, the tadpole stage having been passed within the egg membrane.

The word 'reptile' is from the Latin *reptare* to creep and (very conveniently) *repere* to crawl. Therefore they should be, in fact, the 'creepy-crawlies' of modern vernacular, although this in practice embraces more commonly such creatures as centipedes, earthworms and slugs. Among reptiles the true creepers are the snakes and the few lizards, like the slow-worms, that are also legless. Tortoises and turtles may be said to crawl but most reptiles can employ a respectable walk, even a run, and it would tax the imagination to see in the Komodo dragon of today or the giant dinosaurs of past ages anything approaching a creepy-crawly.

Perhaps our habit of linking amphibians and reptiles dialectically is because of an intuitive feeling that both played an important part in the early colonization of the land masses by vertebrates. Among the diverse forms to emerge from among the multitudinous bony fishes were those that could breathe both by lungs and by gills. They were amphibious, and since they also had fins approximating to limbs, they could spend much time on land. There can be little doubt that it was from such pioneering fishes that the amphibians sprang.

The first fossil amphibians are found in the Lower Carboniferous rocks, 300 million years old. They are tailed amphibians of the type represented today by salamanders and newts. Tailless amphibians, the frogs and toads, did not appear for another 150 million years, in the Jurassic period. Meanwhile the first reptiles had put in an appearance in the Upper Carboniferous, and by the time frogs and toads had evolved reptiles were dominant on land and continued so into the Cretaceous period that followed, a period that was to become known as the Age of Reptiles.

The transition from an air-breathing fish to an undoubted amphibian is shown in one of the most complete series of fossils. A slightly less perfect series illustrates the development of reptiles from amphibian ancestors, but the indications that this was the true course of events are indisputable.

It is a common failing to think of the Age of Reptiles as including only the giant reptiles, the dinosaurs on land, the pterodactyls in the air and the plesiosaurs and ichthyosaurs in the water. In fact there were numerous other reptiles, small, medium and large, including the Rhynchocephalia, of which the tuatara is the only surviving representative, and the crocodiles and turtles, some of which also reached giant size. The lizards and snakes, by far the most numerous reptiles, came later, but meanwhile some groups of early reptiles had developed a temperature control and were partially warm-blooded (homoiothermic). One group gave rise to birds, the other to mammals, around 200 million years before the reptiles themselves achieved their domination in the Age of Reptiles.

The classification of Amphibians and Reptiles is as follows:

CLASS AMPHIBIA   3,000 species
Order Caudata or Urodela
   (salamanders, newts)
Order Anura or Salientia
   (frogs and toads)

CLASS REPTILIA   6,000 species
Order Rhynchocephalia (tuatara)
Order Crocodilia (crocodiles, alligators)
Order Testudines (tortoises, turtles)
Order Squamata
   suborder Sauria (lizards)
   suborder Serpentes (snakes)

Caecilian

The caecilian is a limbless amphibian with a long cylindrical body marked with rings, living wholly underground. The 158 species are worm-like or snake-like according to size, the smallest caecilian being only 4½ in. long, the largest, 4½ ft. Their colour is usually blackish but may be pale flesh-colour. The skin is smooth and slimy, but unlike that of other amphibians, it has small scales embedded in it, in most species. The eyes are small, sometimes covered with skin, and usually useless. There is a peculiar sensory organ; a tentacle on each side of the head lies in a groove running from eyes to tip of snout.

As in snakes, one lung is large and long, the other is reduced to a small lobe.

Caecilians live in warm regions, in America from Mexico to northern Argentina, in southern and south-east Asia and in the Seychelles and parts of Africa. They live from sea-level to about 6 000 ft.

Ancient burrower

Caecilians are the sole surviving relatives of the earliest land animals, large fossil amphibians which roamed the earth 400 million years ago. Burrows are made in soft earth, and caecilians seldom come above ground except when heavy rain floods the burrows. One species, at least, is aquatic, and a few species live in leaf litter which is found on the floor of rain forests.

Feeding

Little is known for certain but earthworms are probably the main diet for most species, and a few may eat termites. The sticky caecilian, of southeast Asia, the best-known species, also eats small burrowing snakes. They themselves are eaten by certain large burrowing snakes.

Life history

There is no difference between male and female externally. Fertilisation is internal and some species lays eggs, others bear live young.

More is known of the life history of the 15 in. sticky caecilian, the female of which lays some two dozen eggs, each about ¼ in. in diameter, connected in a jelly-like string. They are laid in a burrow near water, the female coiling her body around the egg-mass until they hatch. The larvae, which escape to water, have a breathing pore on either side of the head. This leads into internal gills, connected with the throat, as in fishes. External gills, present in the embryo, are lost before hatching. They have normal eyes, a flattened tail for swimming, and a head like a newt. At the end of its larval life the breathing pores close, lungs are developed and the young caecilian lives permanently on land, burrowing under-ground.

The aquatic species of caecilian has sometimes been observed swimming in an eel-like fashion.

Three-way links

The first mention of a caecilian was by Seba, in 1735, when he described it as a snake. Linnaeus, in 1754, also included it among the snakes. In 1811, Oppel put caecilians with frogs, toads and salamanders as amphibians, but these were generally regarded as reptiles as late as 1859. Then came a change, and the caecilians were thought to be degenerate salamanders. From 1908 on there followed studies of the anatomy, and it gradually became clear that caecilians provided an interesting link with the past.

Even now our knowledge of the caecilians is not extensive. They have always been regarded as rare animals, although it is now known that they are plentiful enough in suitable habitats. Yet, as with all animals living wholly underground, it is hard to find out anything about their way of life. What we can do, however, is study how they are made, and this is important, because it tells us that caecilians are a link with the large extinct amphibians that lived nearly 400 million years ago. Their large footprints are known from the Devonian rocks and their skeletons from the rocks of the next geological period, the Carboniferous (Coal Age). After that there is no trace of them, so they seem to have died out 300 million years ago. Some were crocodile-like, lived on land in the marshes where the coal measures were laid down, and they started life as aquatic larvae. They seemed to have been the first backboned animals to live permanently on land, and they almost certainly evolved from air-breathing fishes, the lobe-finned fishes which were the ancestors of the amphibians.

These ancient amphibians gave rise not only to the present-day amphibians but also to the reptiles. They link, therefore, the fishes, amphibians and reptiles, and the caecilians seem to be their direct surviving descendants. This relationship is seen not only in the degenerate scales found in the caecilian skin but also in the caecilian skull being so like that of these giant amphibians of 400 million years ago. It will be interesting to see if any fossil caecilians are found in the future and to compare them with the present day order. As yet no fossil caecilians have been found.

class	**Amphibia**
order	**Apoda or Gymnophiona**
family	**Caeciliidae**
genera	***Caecilia, Typhlonectes, Ichthyophis,*** *others*

Feeding habits of many caecilians are still unknown, but earthworms are probably important in their diet, as in this species **Siphonops annulatus.**

Axolotl

The axolotl is the Peter Pan of the amphibian world, being able to reproduce its own kind while still in its aquatic larval stage. This is unlike the usual development of amphibians such as the common frog, toads and newts, which as larvae, or tadpoles, are confined to fresh water. In the adult form they can live in water and on land, reproducing in water in the breeding season. Certain amphibians, the Mexican axolotl being the most famous, are able to complete their life cycle without ever leaving the water, as sexual maturity is reached in the larval stage.

The axolotl is a newt-like creature, 4—7 in. long, usually black, or dark brown with black spots, but albinos are quite common. The legs and feet are small and weak, while the tail is long, with a fin running from the back of the head to the tail and along the underside of the tail. It breathes through the three pairs of feathery gills on the sides of the head.

Habits and habitat

Axolotls are quite often kept in aquaria, especially in schools. This is rather surprising as they are rather dull animals, spending most of their time at the bottom of the tank, occasionally swimming about lazily for a few seconds before sinking again. A probable reason is that the axolotl can reproduce its own kind without ever leaving the water. Newts and most salamanders, kept in captivity, need water, land and very careful keeping if they are to survive and breed successfully.

Axolotls cannot be kept together with complete safety as they are liable to bite off each other's gills and feet, and bite pieces out of the tail. If this does happen, however, and they are then separated, the missing pieces will regenerate.

In the wild, axolotls are confined to certain lakes around Mexico City, where they are regarded as delicacies when roasted. The name axolotl is Mexican for 'water sport'.

Zoologists were unable to decide where to place axolotls in the classification of amphibians, until 1865 when, at the Jardin des Plantes in Paris, the problem was solved. Several specimens had bred successfully, when one day it was noticed that the young of one brood had lost their gills and tails, and had quite a different coloration. They had, in fact, turned into salamanders. This was the secret of the axolotl. It is one of several species of salamander, an amphibian which normally has an aquatic tadpole resembling the axolotl, that normally changes straight into the adult. The axolotl, however, usually becomes sexually mature while still a larva. This is because the axolotl fails to metamorphose.

Sperm capsule

In most frogs and toads, fertilisation of the eggs takes place externally. In other words, the female sheds the eggs into the water and the male simply releases his sperm near them, to make their own way to the eggs. The axolotls, related salamanders, and newts have a system of internal fertilisation but it is different from the normal method in which the male introduces the sperm into the female's body to meet the eggs waiting there. Instead, the male axolotl sheds his sperm in a packet called a spermatophore. It sinks to the bottom and the female settles over it and picks it up with her cloaca.

Albino axolotl **Ambystoma mexicanum**. *Externally it seems to be juvenile, but internally it is a sexually mature adult. For years zoologists were unable to decide where axolotls fitted into the classification, until they were observed changing into adult salamanders.*

The male attracts the female by a court-ship dance, secreting a chemical from glands in his abdomen and swishing his tail, pre-sumably to spread the chemical until a female detects it and swims towards him.

About a week later, 200—600 eggs are laid, in April or May. They are sticky, and the female attaches them to plants with her back legs. The young axolotls hatch out a fortnight to three weeks later, depending on the temperature of the water. At this stage they are only about ½ in. long and remain on the plant where the eggs are laid. After a week they start swimming in search of food and, if the water is warm and food plentiful, they will be 5—7 in. long by winter. They will then hibernate, taking no food, if the water temperature drops below 10°C/50°F.

Carnivorous feeders

The youngest axolotls feed on plankton, minute organisms that float in water. Later they eat water fleas such as daphnia, and when fully grown they hunt for worms, tad-poles, insect larvae, crustaceans and wound-ed fish. Their prey has to move, however, and axolotls will ignore still, dead food given to them but will snap up a piece of food that is waved about in the water.

Precocious amphibians

The axolotl's habit of breeding while in the larval stage is known as neoteny, or the retention of juvenile characteristics in the adult form. By 'adult' is meant a sexually mature animal. This habit is not restricted to the axolotl. Other amphibians, including some salamanders, sometimes exhibit neoteny, failing to emerge onto land, but continuing to grow in the larval form.

The basic cause of neoteny seems to be a lack of thyroxine, the hormone secreted by the thyroid gland, which controls metab-olism. If the secretion is upset in humans, several bodily disorders occur, including the formation of goitres, swellings in the neck caused by the thyroid gland enlarging. Administration of thyroid gland extracted from cattle, for instance, can often cure the goitre, and axolotls will change into adult salamanders if given thyroid gland.

It would seem, then, that there is some-thing lacking in the diet of both axolotls and humans with goitres. In Wyoming and the Rocky Mountain area the tiger sala-mander regularly exhibits neoteny and humans are liable to get goitres. This has been traced to a lack of iodine in the water, for iodine is an essential component of thyroxine. In these cases the adminis-tration of iodine, rather than thyroxine, is all that is needed either to effect the meta-morphosis of an amphibian or cure a goitre. However, iodine treatment is not the only way of making axolotls metamorphose. Sometimes a consignment sent to a dealer or a laboratory will change into adults shortly after being received. Apparently, the jolting during travel has been sufficient to start the change.

When faced with an odd occurrence like this, a zoologist asks whether it confers any advantage on the animal. The freshwater animal has an advantage over a land animal because it does not have to conserve its body water. This could well be the reason

△ *It is now known that several species of salamanders are able to breed while still in the gilled stage. The eastern mud salamander* **Pseudotriton montanus** *is one such amphibian.*

▽ *Adult of* **Ambystoma mexicanum**. *The axolotl in juvenile form can be made to change into an adult salamander by giving it extract of thyroid, or sometimes when given a physical jolt.*

for the axolotl's neoteny. The lakes where it lives do not dry up and there is an abund-ance of water, so it is an advantage to live and breed there, rather than risk life on the dry, barren land around. If the lakes dry up, then it can still change into a sala-mander, having the best of both worlds.

class:	**Amphibia**
order:	**Caudata**
family	**Ambystomatidae**
genus & species	**Ambystoma mexicanum**

Newt

Newts are amphibians of the salamander family. They have a life history very similar to that of frogs and toads in that the adults spend most of their life on land but return to water to breed. They are different in form, however, having long, slender bodies like those of lizards with a tail that is flattened laterally. The name comes from the Anglo-Saxon **evete** which became **ewt** and finally a newt from the transcription of the 'n' in an **ewt**. In Britain, newt refers solely to the genus **Triturus** but in North America it has been applied to related animals which are sometimes, confusingly, called salamanders.

Newts of the genus **Triturus** are found in Europe, Asia, North Africa and North America. There are three species native to Britain. The most common is the smooth newt which is found all over Europe and is the only newt found in Ireland. The maximum length of smooth newts is 4 in. The colour of the body varies, but is mainly olive-brown with darker spots on the upper side and streaks on the head. The vermilion or orange underside has round black spots and the throat is yellow or white. The female is generally paler on the underside than the male and sometimes is unspotted. In the breeding season the male develops a wavy crest running along the back and tail. The palmate newt is very similar to the smooth newt, but about 1 in. shorter and with a square-sided body. In the breeding season the males of the two species can be told apart because black webs link the toes of the hindfeet of the palmate newts, and its crest is not wavy. In addition, the tail ends abruptly and a short thread, about $\frac{1}{8}-\frac{1}{4}$ in. long protrudes from the tip. The largest European newt is the crested or warty newt. It grows up to 6 in. long. The dark grey skin of the upperparts is covered with warts, while the underparts are yellow or orange and spotted with black. The distinguishing feature apart from its size is the crest of the male. From the head to the hips runs a tall, 'toothed' frill — its crest, which becomes the tail fin.

▽ A male smooth newt with its spotted front, as seen from below.

234

Hibernating on land

When they come out of hibernation in spring, newts make their way to ponds and other stretches of still water where water plants grow. They swim by lashing with their tails, but they spend much of their time resting on the mud or among the stems of plants. They can breathe through their skins but every now and then they rise to the surface to gulp air. Adult newts do not leave the water immediately breeding has finished but remain aquatic until July or August. When they come on land the crest is reabsorbed and the skin becomes rougher. The crested newt keeps its skin moist from the numerous mucus glands scattered over the surface of its body. A few individuals stay in the water all the year round, retaining their smooth skins and crests.

Hibernation begins in the autumn, when the newts crawl into crevices in the ground or under logs and stones. They cannot burrow but are very adept at squeezing themselves into cracks. Occasionally several will gather together in one place and hibernate in a tight mass.

Two rows of teeth

The jaws of newts are lined with tiny teeth and there are two rows of teeth on the roof of the mouth. These are not used for cutting food or for chewing but merely to hold slippery, often wriggling, prey. They feed on a variety of small animals such as worms, snails and insects when on land, and crustaceans, tadpoles and insect larvae while living in water. Unlike frogs and toads, newts do not use their hands to push the food into their mouths, but gulp it down with convulsive swallows. Snails are swallowed whole, caddis flies are eaten in their cases and crested newts eat smooth newts.

Internal fertilisation

The mating habits of newts are quite different from those of common frogs and common toads. Fertilisation is internal and is effected in a most unusual way. The male stimulates the female into breeding condition by nudging her with his snout and lashing the water with his tail. He positions himself in front of or beside her, bends his tail double and vibrates it rapidly, setting up vibrations in the water. The female is also stimulated by secretions from glands in the male's skin. At the end of the courtship the male emits a spermatophore which sinks to the bottom. The female newt positions herself over it, then picks it up with her cloaca by pressing her body onto it.

After fertilisation the 200—300 eggs are usually laid singly on the leaves of water plants, although some American newts lay their eggs in spherical clusters. The female newt tests the leaves by smell and touch. When she has chosen a suitable one she holds it with her hindfeet, then folds the leaf over to form a tube and lays an egg in it. The jelly surrounding the egg glues the leaf firmly in place to protect it.

The eggs hatch in about 3 weeks and a more streamlined tadpole than that of a frog or toad emerges. It is not very different from the adult newt except that it has a frill of gills and no legs. Development takes longer than in frog tadpoles but the young newts are ready to emerge by the end of summer. A few spend the winter as tadpoles, remaining in the pond until spring, even surviving being frozen into the ice.

Unpleasant secretion

Newts have many enemies: the young are eaten by aquatic insects and the adults by fishes, water birds, weasels, rats, hedgehogs and many other animals. The crested newt has an unpleasant secretion that is produced in the glands on the back and tail and is exuded when they are squeezed. Grass snakes are known to be dissuaded from eating crested newts because of this.

Newt's nerve poison

The poison of the crested newt is not only unpleasant, but men who have tasted it have found it to be burning. A far more potent poison is that of the California newt. The poison is found mainly in the skin, muscles and blood of the newt, as well as in its eggs. Analysis showed that the poison is a substance called tetrodotoxin, which is also found in puffer fish. Tetrodotoxin extracted from newts' eggs is so powerful that $\frac{1}{8000}$ oz. can kill 7 000 mice. It acts on the nerves, preventing impulses from being transmitted to the muscles. Somehow, in a manner that is not understood, California newts are not affected by their own posion. Their nerves still function when treated with a solution of tetrodotoxin 25 000 times stronger than that which will completely deaden a frog's nerves.

△ *Left: Segmenting embryo of a crested newt. Right: The legless tadpole of the crested newt.*
▽ *Alpine newt* **Triturus alpestris.**

class	**Amphibia**	
order	**Caudata**	
family	**Salamandridae**	
genera & species	***Taricha torosa*** *California newt*	
	Triturus cristatus *crested newt*	
	T. helveticus *palmate newt*	
	T. vulgaris *smooth newt*	
	others	

Lungless salamander

The name 'lungless salamander' covers 200 species of salamanders living in Tropical and North America that have neither lungs nor gills but breathe through their skin and the lining of the mouth. A further peculiarity is that some of them cannot open their lower jaw to the normal gape. There is only one species outside America, **Hydromantes genei** represented by three subspecies.

Lungless salamanders range in size from $1\frac{1}{2}$ to $8\frac{1}{2}$ in. A few live permanently in water but most of them spend their lives on land. They are mainly sombrely coloured—black, grey or brown—but some have patches of red and the redbacked salamander occurs in 2 colour phases: red and grey with the belly of each spotted black and white. Varying proportions of red and grey individuals are found in any batch of larvae. Most lungless salamanders have the usual salamander shape, a long rounded body, tail about the same length, and short legs, the front legs with 4 toes, the back legs with 5. The four-toed lungless salamander has 4 toes on each foot. The longtailed salamander is so called because its 7 in. tail dwarfs a 4 in. body. The California slender salamander is snakelike, with vestigial legs, and lies under fallen logs, coiled up tightly like a watch-spring.

Some species are widespread. The dusky salamander ranges over the eastern United States from New Brunswick southwards to Georgia and Alabama and westwards to Oklahoma and Texas. Other species are very localised. The Ocoee salamander lives in damp crevices in rocks or on the water-fall-splashed faces of rocks in Ocoee Gorge, southeast Tennessee. One of the European subspecies lives in southeast France and north Italy, the second lives in Tuscany, the third in Sardinia.

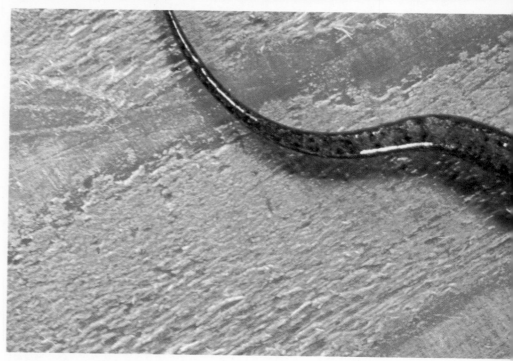

From deep wells to tall trees

Lungless salamanders mostly live in damp places, under stones or logs, among moss, under leaf litter, near streams or seepages or even in surface burrows in damp soil. The shovel-nosed salamander lives in mountain streams all its life, hiding under stones by day. Others live on land but go into water to escape enemies. The pygmy salamander, 2 in. long, living in the mountains of Virginia and North Carolina, can climb the rough bark of trees to a height of several feet. The arboreal salamander does even better, climbing trees to a height of 60 ft, sometimes making its home in old birds' nests. The Californian flatheaded salamander uses webbed feet to walk over slippery rocks and swings its tail from side to side as it walks, to help itself up a slope. On descent its curled tail acts as a brake.

Several species live in caves or artesian and natural wells as much as 200 ft deep. All are blind, one retains its larval gills throughout life and one cave species spends its larval life in mountain streams but migrates to underground waters before metamorphosis. It then loses its sight.

Creeping, crawling food

All lungless salamanders eat small invertebrates. Those living in water feed mainly on aquatic insect larvae. Those on land hunt slugs, worms, woodlice and insect larvae. One group of lungless salamanders *Plethodon* are known as woodland salamanders. They live in rocky crevices or in holes underground and eat worms, beetles and ants. The slimy salamander also eats worms, hard-shelled beetles, ants and centipedes as well as shieldbugs, despite their obnoxious odour and unpalatable flavour. The European species catches food with a sticky tongue which it can push out 1 inch.

Different breeding habits

There is as much diversity in their breeding as in the way they live. Some lay their eggs in water and the larvae are fully aquatic;

△ Mountain salamander, **Desmognathus ochrophaeus** lives near springs and streams where the ground is saturated.
▷ Red-backed salamander, occupant of old garden plots where there are tree stumps, rotting logs and moisture-conserving debris.

others lay them on land, and among this second group are species in which the females curl themselves round their batches of 2–3 dozen eggs as if incubating. In a few species the female stays near her eggs until they hatch, but without incubating them or giving them any special care. The woodland salamanders lay their eggs in patches of moss or under logs and the larvae metamorphose before leaving the eggs. A typical species is the dusky salamander. The male deposits his sperm in a capsule or spermatophore. He then rubs noses with the female. A gland on his chin gives out a scent that stimulates the female to pick up the spermatophore with her cloaca. Her eggs are laid in clusters of two dozen in spring or

◁ *The long-tailed salamander has a tail nearly twice as long as its body. It spends most of the day hidden under logs and stones.*

early summer under logs or stones. Each egg is $\frac{3}{16}$ in. diameter and the larva on hatching is $\frac{5}{8}$ in. long. It has external gills and goes into water, where it lives until the following spring, when it metamorphoses. The adults, $5\frac{1}{4}$ in. long, are dark brown or grey. When it first metamorphoses the young salamander is brick-red and light cream in patches. Later it takes on the colours of the fully grown adult but has a light band down the back and a light line from the eye to the angle of the jaw.

Not so defenceless

Lungless salamanders, like other salamanders and newts, seldom have defensive weapons, a possible exception being the arboreal salamander with its fang-like teeth in the lower jaw. It is known to bite a finger when handled. The slimy salamander gives

out a very sticky, glutinous secretion from its skin when handled and this possibly deters predators. The enemies are small snakes and frogs, which take their toll of the larvae and the young salamanders. It may be in an attempt to evade such enemies that the dusky salamander sometimes leaps about, several inches at a jump. The yellow blotched salamander, of California, has a curious behaviour that may be defensive. It raises itself on the tips of its toes, rocks its body backwards and forwards, arches its tail and swings it from side to side. It also gives out a milky astringent fluid from the tail. And it squeaks like a mouse.

Peculiar features

Peculiar features of these salamanders are that they lose their larval gills as they grow and they do not grow lungs. Instead, their skin has become the breathing organ with the skin lining the mouth acting the part of a lung by having a network of fine blood vessels in it, like the lining of a lung.

The arboreal salamander has a similar network of fine blood vessels in the skin of its toes, which may play the part of lungs (or should they be called terrestrial gills?). Another extraordinary feature is that others, like the yellow-blotched salamander, squeak, although they have neither lungs nor voice box. They do this by contracting the throat to force air through the lips or nose.

The loss of lungs in the lungless salamanders must be seen as a secondary condition. That is, the ancestral salamander had lungs and these had been lost in the later evolution. The most reasonable explanation for this would be that the losses correlated with the brook-dwelling habits. In the normal salamander the lungs function not only as respiratory organs, but also as hydrostatic organs, decreasing the total specific gravity of the animal, so bringing the salamander very near to having neutral buoyancy. The salamander needs then only a flick of its tail or slight movement of the limbs to propel itself through water and, more especially, to make it rise towards the surface. When it then becomes immobile again it does not immediately sink, as it would do if its specific gravity was greater, but slowly sinks. With the loss of lungs the lungless salamanders have increased their specific gravity and are therefore able the more readily to keep near the bottom in fast moving water.

The loss of lungs is compensated by the greater oxygen content of moving water and so has made their respiratory function also less important. The loss of lungs could be a disadvantage in another respect and a special adaptation has been needed to counteract this. Lungless salamanders have a nasolabial groove running from each nostril to the lips. It is believed that these act as gutters carrying from the nostrils water that has collected there when the head has been submerged.

class	**Amphibia**
order	**Caudata**
family	**Plethodontidae**
genera & species	***Aneides lugubris*** *arboreal salamander* ***Batrachoseps attenuatus*** *California slender salamander* ***Desmognathus fuscus*** *dusky salamander* ***D. ocoee*** *Ocoee salamander* ***D. wrighti*** *pygmy salamander* ***Ensatina croceator*** *yellow-blotched salamander* ***Eurycea longicauda*** *long-tailed salamander* ***Hemidactylium scutatum*** *four-toed salamander* ***Leurognathus marmoratus*** *shovel-nosed salamander* ***Plethodon cinereus*** *red-backed salamander* ***P. glutinosus*** *slimy salamander*

Mudpuppy

The mudpuppy is a kind of salamander living in the weedy streams, ponds and rivers of parts of North America. In the southern part of its range it is called water dog. Both names depend on a belief that it makes a barking sound.

It grows up to 20 in. long, although it is usually about 1 ft long, and is grey to rusty or dark brown with indistinct bluish-black spots and mottlings. There is a conspicuous dark mark on the side of the head running through the eye. Its short, weak legs are suitable only for crawling over mud and are held against the sides when swimming. Each foot has four fairly long toes. Just behind the head are three pairs of conspicuous, bushy and velvety red, plume-like gills. The head is flat and squarish with small eyes.

The mudpuppy ranges from southern Canada to the Gulf of Mexico, from the Mississippi and Missouri basins to New Jersey, and eight subspecies or forms are recognized. A dwarf mudpuppy lives in the Neuse River in North Carolina and the largest form lives in the rice field ditches of both North and South Carolina.

Asking to be caught

Mudpuppies, slow and sluggish salamanders, often take bait, getting themselves hooked, to the annoyance of fishermen. As well as losing his bait the fisherman finds the mudpuppy a slippery customer to handle, due to the slime-covered body. Inevitably this has led to the idea that the mudpuppy is poisonous, which is partly true. It has poison glands in its skin but the poison is not strong enough to affect human beings. Some people claim mudpuppies are good to eat, and one writer speaks of their fine quality and white flesh, rivalling frogs' legs in flavour,

The mudpuppy (above and below) is neotenous, it keeps its gills throughout its life.

Mudpuppies are mainly nocturnal, hiding during the day under stones or buried in the mud, but among dense weed they sometimes move about by day. They feed on worms, insect larvae, fish eggs, crayfishes, small fishes and frogs' eggs.

Never grow up

These salamanders are neotenous (see page 233); they never become fully adult but keep their gills throughout life. They do, however, become sexually mature. The size of the gills can vary. In cold, fresh water with plenty of oxygen the gills contract, but in warmer, more stagnant water low in oxygen they expand, becoming larger and more bushy so as to take up as much oxygen as possible. It is said that if the filaments of the plume-like gills become tangled the mudpuppy will rearrange them with its forefoot.

Delayed spawning

Before going into a dormant state in winter, the mudpuppies mate, and a male and female may share the same hole in the bank. In the following spring the female lays 18–880 yellowish eggs, according to her size, each in its jelly envelope and ¼ in.

across. She sticks them one by one in a crowded group on the underside of a log or large stone or boulder in about 5 ft of water. Sometimes they are laid in a sandy hollow on the riverbed. She stays beside them until they hatch in 38–63 days according to the temperature of the water. As in all such instances, the warmer the water, to some extent, the less time the eggs take to hatch. It is usual to say that the female guards the eggs. Whether this is so or not has never been investigated, but despite their defenceless appearance mudpuppies can give a sharp nip when handled. When first hatched, they still have the yolk sac hanging from their underside. This lasts them until they are 1½ in. long and about 2 months old, and able to find their own food. They mature in 5–7 years, at about 8 in. long and may live for 20 years.

Whining like a puppy

Newts do have a larynx and European newts can make faint squeaks like the sound made by drawing a wet finger over glass. As these newts have lungs the sound is probably made by air driven from the lungs across the vocal cords. The lungless salamanders of California (page 236) make a mouse-like squeak by contracting the throat and driving air either between the half-open jaws or through the nostrils. There is a legend that mudpuppies can bark like a dog. Perhaps this has arisen because when a mudpuppy is taken out of water it sometimes makes a sound like the whine of a puppy. If so, it would not be long before the story had grown to 'barking like a dog'.

class	**Amphibia**
order	**Caudata**
family	**Proteidae**
genus & species	***Necturus maculosus***

△ **Bombina variegata** *peers at the camera, showing its brightly-coloured throat and waistcoat. When faced with imminent attack, it throws itself on its back to show its yellow patches to better advantage, eyes closed and covered with its forepaws, and holds its breath until danger passes. If pressed, however, it exudes a corrosive white fluid.*

Firebelly

The firebelly is a toad with an unusual way of scaring its enemies. Less than 2 in. long, the males smaller than the females and sometimes only 1 in. long, the firebelly is dark grey over its back with black flecks. Its underside is blue-grey to blue-black with white spots and patches of orange or red. When disturbed or alarmed it throws its head up, arches its back and rises on stiff legs to expose its vivid fire-coloured belly. Faced with more immediate danger—for example, if someone goes to pick it up—the toad throws itself on its back displaying its vivid patches; at the same time glands in its skin give out a white poison fluid with caustic properties and a strong smell. So it remains motionless, its eyes closed and breathing suspended, until the danger is past. As in some other amphibians, including the common frog of Europe, the firebelly holds its paws over its eyes as if it cannot bear to look at its tormentor.

Close relatives are the yellow-bellied toad of Europe, sometimes called the variegated fire-toad, the firebelly of China and Korea, and another Asiatic species, the largest of all—but still not more than 3 in. long.

The firebelly is distributed from southern Sweden and Denmark, through Germany and the Balkans, east to the Ural mountains. The yellow-bellied toad, of similar size, habits and colour except that yellow replaces the red patches, extends from the Low Countries through France, Germany and Switzerland to northern Italy, but lives at higher altitudes, in ponds, on hills and mountains.

Toad with a musical voice

Both the firebelly and the yellow-bellied toad have melodious voices, the firebelly uttering a musical 'unk-unk'—it is known in Germany as the Unke—which often goes on all night. The yellow-belly sounds like soft bells which are ringing in the distance.

The firebelly feeds on insects, snails and worms. It belongs to the family Discoglossidae, or round-tongued toads, in which the rounded tongue is joined throughout to the floor of the mouth, so it must snap up its prey instead of shooting out its tongue. Feeding is mainly at night when the toad comes out on land. The firebelly is inactive for much of the day, floating among water plants in ponds and ditches. It is a good runner, as well as a good swimmer. It leaves the water to hibernate in soft ground.

Modest spawning output

In the breeding season black pads appear on the forearm and the first two fingers of the male. Then his 'unk-unk' call begins, made the louder by an internal vocal sac which acts as a resonator. Spawning is from May to June, during which time each female lays two or three times at well-spaced intervals. Each session lasts about 3 days. When the male embraces the female he holds her around the loins, to fertilise her eggs that are laid one at a time, or in small groups.

239

◁ *Tensed for take-off, a firebelly shows its full underside pattern through the glass of an aquarium wall.*
▽◁ *Top view. A submerging firebelly heads for the bottom with powerful strokes.*

She lays only a few dozen in all, certainly not more than 100, in contrast with the thousands of the common toad. The eggs stick to water plants or to vegetable rubbish on the bottom.

The eggs are $\frac{1}{8}$ in. diameter. They hatch in 7 days and the tadpoles grow to a length of 2 in. by autumn, then begin to shrink to toadlets $\frac{2}{3}$ in. long. The baby toads do not have warning colours at first; these appear gradually and are complete by the time the toad is mature, in its third year.

Safe from enemies

The firebelly probably has no serious enemies, and this seems borne out by the very large numbers living in some localities. These are not obvious to the casual eye partly because this toad will, if possible, escape, at the first disturbance, diving to the bottom and burying itself in the mud. Even if it only remains still its back looks so like a piece of mud that the toad is extremely difficult to see. Indeed, the firebelly, so long as it is the right way up, enjoys extraordinarily good camouflage protection. It is the more odd that it should have in addition, on its underside, the striking warning colours. Perhaps camouflage is its first line of defence, with warning coloration as a second.

No bluffing

These colours are no bluff. The white fluid given out by the firebelly at the same time as it shows its warning colours is caustic and corrosive. Naturalists collecting frogs and toads have found that to put a tree frog into a container with a firebelly half its size is to sentence it to death. Freshly caught firebellies soon become covered with a white froth when handled and merely the vapours from this quickly cause bouts of sneezing and running at the eyes.

class	**Amphibia**
order	**Salientia**
family	**Discoglossidae**
genus & species	*Bombina bombina* *B. variegata* *B. orientalis* *B. maxima*

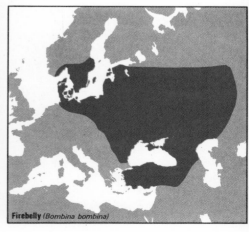

Firebelly *(Bombina bombina)*

240

Midwife toad

The midwife toad is named after its most peculiar mating habits, in which the male apparently helps the female in laying her eggs. Its total length is $1\frac{1}{2}-2\frac{1}{2}$ in., the female being a little larger than the male. The head is relatively small, the snout pointed and the back is covered with small round warts. The feet are partly webbed, the webs extending only about $\frac{1}{3}$ of the way along the toes. The upperparts are greyish or light brown with a darker patch between the eyes. The underside is dirty white with spots of dark grey on the throat and breast. Females have rows of reddish warts down the sides of the body.

Midwife toads are found in western Europe from Belgium and Germany as far north as Hameln, near Hanover, and southwards to Spain and Portugal, and as far east as Switzerland. They live at heights of 5–6 000 ft in the Pyrenees where snow lies for most of the year.

Seldom seen

Towards evening these shy, nocturnal toads give away their presence by a whistling call that sounds like a chime of bells when several toads call together. This sound gives them the alternative name of bell toad. Although very abundant in some places, they are seldom seen as they spend the day in holes which they dig with their forelegs and snout, or in crevices between stones and the deserted burrows of small mammals. Midwife toads are quite common in towns, where they hide in cellars or under woodpiles.

When they come out at night midwife toads crawl slowly, rather than hop, in search of insects, slugs and snails. Even when disturbed they can hop only clumsily. They are protected from enemies by the poison in their skin which is secreted from the warts. There is sufficient poison in one midwife toad to kill an adder in a few hours, so any predator that takes a fancy to a midwife toad is unlikely to last long enough to kill another.

Father carries the eggs

The breeding habits of midwife toads are notable for two unusual features; the male stimulates egg-laying by manipulating the female's cloaca, and after the eggs are laid, he carries them wrapped around his hindlegs until they hatch. These habits were not described until 1876 when a Frenchman spent 3 years studying midwife toads.

Breeding starts in April and continues throughout spring and summer. The females are attracted to the males' burrows by their calls. Mating is difficult to watch because it takes place under cover at night, and does not last long. Other frogs and toads stay in amplexus for as much as one day, but in midwife toads amplexus lasts for less than one hour.

The male midwife toad seizes the female around the waist and strokes her cloaca with his hindfeet, even pushing his toes into the cloaca. After a period of up to 20 minutes these movements suddenly stop, the female stretches her hindlegs and the eggs are extruded onto them. The male moves forward, transferring his grip to the female's neck, and fertilises the eggs. At the same time he urinates, soaking the jelly surrounding the eggs, making it swell up.

After fertilisation, the male wraps the string of 20–100 yellowish eggs around his hindlegs and walks off with them. For the next 3 weeks he carries the eggs, resting in his burrow by day and feeding by night. The eggs are kept moist by the dew, but on dry nights he goes to water and immerses them. He may mate again with another female, so carrying two or more strings of eggs. The females also mate again and may produce three or four lots of eggs in one season. When the eggs are ready to hatch, the male enters water and the tadpoles force their way out of the jelly and swim away. How he is aware the eggs are ready to hatch is not known.

The tadpoles are quite advanced when they hatch, being just over $\frac{1}{2}$ in. long and having one gill on each side. Most of them change into frogs before the autumn but some spend the winter as tadpoles and emerge the following spring.

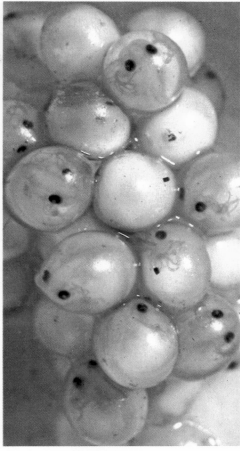

◁ △ *Male midwife carrying the developing eggs. This behaviour is one of the most peculiar types of breeding yet to be seen in amphibians. The male, after fertilising eggs as the female lays them, walks through them so they are wrapped round his hind legs. After about 3 weeks they are ready to hatch and the male enters water so the tadpoles can swim away.* △ *Eggs with visible tadpoles about to hatch.*

Melting their way out

In early descriptions of the life history of frogs and toads it was assumed that tadpoles bit their way out of the egg capsule. Closer examination revealed that during hatching tadpoles of the midwife toad kept their mouths shut. A hole appears in the egg apparently by the capsule being dissolved away. The whole process of hatching takes about $\frac{1}{2}$ hour. First the tadpole moves so its snout pushes against the capsule which then becomes pointed. After 15–20 minutes the capsule softens, then liquefies completely where the tadpole's snout is pressing against it. Then the tadpole forces its way out.

Between the nostrils of the tadpole is a gland which secretes an enzyme that dissolves the egg capsule. A similar gland had been found in the tadpoles of other frogs and toads whose eggs hatch in water. Those that hatch on land, such as the greenhouse frog, bite their way out of the egg.

class	**Amphibia**
order	**Salientia**
family	**Discoglossidae**
genus & species	***Alytes obstetricans***

Common toad

Despite a superficial resemblance to the common frog, few people have difficulty in recognising a common toad, even if they recoil in horror on seeing it. It has a flatter back and relatively shorter legs. Instead of the moist, bright skin of the frog, the toad has a dull, wrinkled, pimply skin. Its movements are slow and grovelling, and, although it can jump a short distance on all fours, it usually walks laboriously over the ground.

The rough skin blends well with the earth, so a toad can easily be over-looked as a clod of earth. This impression is heightened by the dark

Common toads mating.

brown or grey colouring which can change, although only a little and slowly, to match the surroundings, becoming almost red in a sand pit, for instance. Its jewel-like eyes are golden or coppery-red, and behind them lie the bulges of the parotid glands that contain an acrid, poisonous fluid.

Male toads measure about $2\frac{1}{2}$ in. and the females 1 in. longer.

The common toad ranges over Europe, north and temperate Asia and North Africa.

Hibernating toads

The common toad, like the common frog, hibernates from October to February, but in drier places. Dry banks and disused burrows of small mammals are chosen, and hibernating toads are sometimes found in cellars and outhouses. In the spring they migrate to breeding pools, preferring deeper water than frogs. Where the two are found in the same ponds, the frogs will be in the shallows and the toads in the middle.

The migrations of these toads are more spectacular. Toads give the impression of being slower movers and the migration route becomes littered with the remains of toads that have fallen foul of enemies. The route is especially well marked where it crosses a road and passing cars have run over the toads.

Although the migration may be long and arduous, perhaps covering 2 or 3 miles at

a rate of ¾ mile in 24 hours, the toads are very persistent, and laboriously climb stone walls and banks.

Outside the breeding season toads live in hollows scooped out by the hindlegs. In soft earth they bury themselves completely, otherwise the hole is made under a log or stone. These homes are usually permanent, the toad returning to the same place day after day. One toad was recorded as living under a front-door step for 36 years until it was attacked by a raven. Occasionally the retreats may be in places that must cost the toad some effort to reach. One is known to have made its home in a privet hedge, 4 ft above the ground, and others have been found in birds' nests.

Every now and then there are stories of toads being found in even odder places. Quarrymen and miners tell of splitting open a rock or lump of coal revealing a cavity in which lies a toad that leaps out hale and

with glass plates. The toads in the compact sandstone soon died but the ones in the porous limestone lived for a year or more. These rather macabre experiments suggest that the toads found in rocks and tree trunks could not have been there for long. It is most likely that either they had crawled into a crack or cavity which had later been filled in, or perhaps the miner or quarryman had hit a rock that happened to have a cavity in, thereby causing a toad hidden nearby to leap out suddenly, so creating the impression that it had come out of the hole.

Prey must be moving
At night and during wet weather, toads come out to feed on many kinds of small animals, but they must be moving because toads' eyes are adapted to react to moving objects. Any insect or other small invertebrate is taken, ants being especially favoured, and the stomach of one toad was found to

Spawn in strings
There is little to distinguish the breeding habits of common frogs and common toads. Both breed at roughly the same time of year and may be seen in the same pools. Male toads start arriving before the females but later the males may arrive already in amplexus on the females' backs. There is no external vocal sac and, unlike many of its relatives, a male common toad has a very weak croak.

The spawn is laid in strings rather than in a mass. The eggs are embedded three or four deep in threads of jelly that may be up to 15 ft long. Each female lays 3–4 thousand eggs, which are smaller than those of a frog, being less than $\frac{1}{16}$ in. in diameter. The jelly swells up but the spawn does not float, because it is wrapped round the stems of water plants.

The eggs hatch in 10–12 days and the tadpoles develop in the same manner as

The coppery-golden eye of the toad, its most attractive feature, shown with pupil expanded (left) and contracted (right).

hearty. Another story is told of two sawyers working in a saw pit, some 90 years ago. They were sawing the trunk of an oak into planks when they noticed blood dripping out of the wood. Examination revealed the now grisly remains of a toad in a cavity in the trunk. In every story there is speculation as to how the toads came to be imprisoned. It is hardly likely that they were trapped when the coal or rock was first formed millions of years ago, as was once believed. They could not have lived that long, as was shown by the following experiments performed over a century ago. Holes were drilled in blocks of sandstone and limestone, toads put in and the holes sealed

contain 363 ants. Some distasteful animals such as burnet moth caterpillars or caterpillars covered with stiff hairs are left well alone, but toads are known to sit outside beehives in the evening and catch the workers as they come back home. Snails are crunched up and earthworms are pushed into the mouth by the forefeet which also scrape excess earth off them. Young newts, frogs, toads and even slow-worms and grass snakes are eaten. One toad had five newly-hatched grass snakes in its stomach, while another had the head of an adder in its mouth. Toads will often return to a favourite retreat after hunting and will use the same home for years.

frog tadpoles, becoming shiny, black, ½ in. toadlets in about 3 months. Sexual maturity is reached in 4 years, before the toads are fully grown.

Poisonous toads
Toads suffer from all the enemies to which frogs fall prey, despite the poisonous secretions of the parotid glands. The poison is certainly effective against dogs, that salivate copiously after mouthing a toad, and show all the signs of distress.

Toads react more strongly to danger signals than frogs do, possibly because, not being leapers, they are more vulnerable and need added protection from enemies. One

Strings of spawn rope through the water during mating, to be wrapped around the stems of water plants and convenient pebbles.

reaction is to inflate the lungs more than usual, so increasing the volume of the body by as much as 50%. Snakes, their chief enemies, know fairly accurately when an object is more than they can swallow, but how far the inflated body of the toad deceives them has never been tested.

Unless the snake is only small, the swelling of the toad will make little difference to the outcome if attacked by a constricting or a poisonous snake.

The defence mechanism of the toad of inflating itself against enemies is instinctive. This is seen by the following experiment. Any long cylindrical object, such as a length of thin rubber tubing, moved across its field of vision, will cause it to blow itself up. This reaction becomes progressively weaker when the experiment is repeated, and in a short time no reaction is produced.

In old age, toads fall victim to flesh-eating greenbottle flies, which lay their eggs on them. The larvae then crawl into the nostrils, hampering breathing, and eat their way into the toad's body, eventually killing it.

Many superstitions

Toads are often regarded with horror, and in folklore they generally play an unpleasant role. Their mere presence was said to pollute the soil, but one method of preventing this from happening was to plant rue, which toads could not abide. Without it, tragedies could occur of the kind that befell a mediaeval couple strolling in the garden. The young man plucked some leaves of sage, rubbed his teeth with them and promptly fell dead. His young woman was charged with murder and, to prove her innocence, took the judge and court to the garden to demonstrate what had happened, and fell dead too. The judge suspected the cause and had the sage dug up. There was a toad living in the ground beside it.

By contrast, 'the foule Toad has a faire stone in his heade', as the 16th-century writer John Lyly declared. To obtain this jewel the toad was placed on a scarlet cloth which pleased the toad so much that it cast the stone out. The toadstone was then set in a ring, for it had the valuable property of changing colour in the presence of any poison that an enemy might put in food and drink. It was also effective as a cure for snakebite and wasp-stings.

class	**Amphibia**
order	**Salientia**
family	**Bufonidae**
genus & species	*Bufo bufo*

Arrow-poison frog

Arrow-poison frogs are found only in Central and South America where the Indians have long extracted poison from their bodies for use on arrow-heads. Many amphibians have at least a trace of poison in their bodies or secrete poison from glands in the skin, and quite a few can cause a good deal of pain to any human that handles them. Only the arrow-poison frogs and one or two others secrete such a strong poison as to cause rapid death.

Most arrow-poison frogs can be distinguished by the nail-like plate on each toe. Many species are brilliantly coloured. The two-toned arrow-poison frog is brick red with patches of blue-black on its legs. More brilliant is the three-striped arrow-poison frog, which is yellow with stripes of black running lengthways down the head and body and around the limbs. Some species have 'flash colours' which are suddenly exposed as the frog jumps. It is thought that the bright colours, especially the 'flash colours' are warnings to other animals that they are not fit to eat.

A Cuban member of the family, **Sminthillus limbatus** *is the smallest frog in the world, measuring less than $\frac{1}{2}$ in.*

Each female lays only one egg. The egg is large in comparison with the size of the mother's body and is laid in a moist spot on land, the larva completing its development and undergoing metamorphosis before hatching. This particular frog is by no means uncommon and its slow rate of breeding is in striking contrast to most frogs that ensure the perpetuation of the species by laying large numbers of eggs.

Habits

The various species of arrow-poison frogs are found in forests of different parts of Central and South America, some living in trees, others living on the forest floor.

Feeding

Arrow-poison frogs conform to the usual amphibian diet. As adults all amphibians are carnivorous. They take insects or other small invertebrates which are full of protein to restore worn-out tissue, and salts, fats, vitamins, and water needed for their metabolism. They also need carbohydrates which can be rebuilt from surplus protein.

Male carries the tadpoles

There are several peculiar features about the breeding habits of arrow-poison frogs. Courtship or courtship rituals are rare amongst frogs and toads, but probably the golden arrow-poison frogs, and probably other species, 'play' together for as much as two or three hours. They repeatedly jump at each other, sometimes landing on one another's backs, as if fighting. Following the 'play', the eggs are laid, but there is no 'amplexus', the process in which the male, as in the common frog, perches on the female's back and fertilises the eggs as they are laid. The female arrow-poison frog lays her eggs on the ground and the male, who has been waiting nearby, comes over and fertilises them.

The absence of amplexus may be linked with the occurrence of the courtship play, because in frogs using amplexus it is often the pressure of the male hugging the female that causes the eggs to be extruded. When there is no amplexus, it may be necessary for another stimulus, in this case leaping about with the male, to initiate egg-laying. Both methods ensure that there is a male present to fertilise the eggs which is the primary purpose of animal courtship.

When the eggs have been fertilised, the male carries them on his back where they become attached to his skin although how this is done remains to be discovered. After they hatch, the tadpoles remain on their father's back, getting no moisture except from rain. Up to twenty tadpoles can be found on one arrow-poison frog, and, as they grow, their father has to seek larger and larger holes in which to rest. Eventually he takes them down to the water and they swim away to lead an independent life.

Predator deterrent

Snakes, predatory birds and some carnivorous mammals will often prey on the majority of frogs. The arrow-poison frogs, however, possess the ultimate deterrent of the animal world—their flash colours give a warning to the predator, not to attempt to eat them because of their poisonous nature, giving the frogs a much safer life in their hazardous jungle existence.

It is very usual for an animal that carries a venom, or is in some other way unpleasant or unpalatable, to be brilliantly coloured in red, yellow or black or in some combination of these colours. Among arrow-poison frogs which are so highly poisonous these colours tend to predominate and are accentuated by the use of flash colours, as we have seen. This makes it even more puzzling that one species, *Dendrobates pumilio* should be dark blue and very difficult to see in the dark forests which are its home. The warning colours, red, yellow and black are very conspicuous, and it is their purpose to be conspicuous, because they are advertising a warning to predators. Yet *Dendrobates pumilio* seems to be doing its best to efface itself although it has eight times more poison in its skin than those arrow-poison frogs that are bright red and very conspicuous.

Self-effacing relative

Although it is usual to speak of the Dendrobatidae as the family of arrow-poison frogs, not all its members are poisonous. It is of interest to compare the case of a Brazilian species *Dendrophryniscus brevipollicatus* with other members of the family being discussed here. Apparently this particular species has no venom or very little of it. It is coloured brown, tan and buff, it lives among the leaf litter of the forest floor, and when molested its flattish body becomes stiff and the front part of the body bends upwards and backwards so that it looks like a dried leaf.

Poison arrows

The Indians of South America are renowned for their use of poisoned-tipped arrows,

△ *Golden arrow-poison frog (* **Dendrobates auratus** *).*
Overleaf: Arrow-poison frog **Dendrobates leucomelas.** *The poison secreted by these amphibians is so strong it kills very rapidly. Their bright colours give other animals warning of their poisonous nature so they are not eaten.*

which are reputed to cause death if they do no more than scratch the skin of their target. The best known of the poisons is curare, which is extracted from certain plants, but even this is a mild poison compared with that of the arrow-poison frogs.

The Indians collect the poison by piercing the frog with a sharp stick, and holding it over a fire. The heat of the fire forces the poison through the skin where it collects in droplets. These are scraped off into a jar. The amount collected from each frog, and its potency, varies with the species. The kokoi frog of Colombia secretes the most powerful poison known. This is a substance called batrachotoxin which has recently been shown to be ten times more powerful than tetrodotoxin, the poison of the Japanese puffer fish which had previously held the record as the most powerful known animal venom. 1/100,000 oz. of batrachotoxin is sufficient to kill a man.

One kokoi frog, only 1 in. long, can supply enough venom to make 50 lethal arrows. But the arrow-poison frogs are now being sought for more peaceful purposes. In the same way as curare has become an important drug because of its muscle-relaxing properties, so the venom of arrow-poison frogs is now being used in the laboratory for studies on the nervous system. It has been found that it acts in the same way as the hormones secreted by the adrenal gland, blocking the transmission of messages between nerves and muscles. Large amounts rapidly cause death, but in tiny doses it could well have medicinal value.

class	**Amphibia**
order	**Salientia**
family	**Dendrobatidae**
genera	*Sminthillus*
	Dendrobates, Phyllobates

△ *African bullfrog,* **Pyxicephalus adspersus,** *can puff out its vocal sacs to bellow like a calf.*

△ *With its powerful back legs, the bullfrog can leap over 3 ft. This ability helps in catching its prey; it lies in wait and leaps out on passing prey, catching it while it is in the air.*

Bullfrog

The bullfrog is a large species of North American frog. The adult grows to be about 8 in. long. Its skin is usually smooth like that of a common frog but sometimes it is covered with small tubercles. The colour varies; on the upper parts it is usually greenish to black, sometimes with dark spots, the underparts are whitish with tinges of yellow. The females are browner and more spotted than the males. The best way of telling them apart is by comparing the size of the eye and the eardrum. In females they are equal, but in males the eardrum is larger than the eye.

The natural home of the bullfrog is in the United States, east of the Rockies, and on the northern borders of Mexico. They have also been introduced to the western states of America, as well as to Cuba, Hawaii, British Columbia, Canada.

The bullfrog's damp world

Bullfrogs are rarely found out of the water, except during very wet weather. They like to live near ponds and marshes or slow-flowing streams, lying idly along the water's edge under the shade of shrubs and reeds. In winter they hibernate, near the water, under logs and stones or in holes on the banks. How long they hibernate depends upon the climate. Usually they are the first amphibians in an area to retire and, in the spring, they are the last to emerge. In the northern parts of their range they usually emerge about the middle of May, but in Texas, for example, they may come out in February if the weather is mild enough. In the southern areas of their range they may not bother to hibernate at all.

A voracious appetite

The bullfrog gets most of its food from insects, earthworms, spiders, crayfish and snails. Many kinds of insects are caught including grasshoppers, beetles, flies, wasps and bees. The slow-moving larvae and immobile pupae, as well as the active adults, are taken. The unfortunate dragonfly is usually caught when it is in the middle of laying its eggs.

The bullfrog captures small, active prey like this by lying in wait and then leaping forward as the prey passes. Its tongue flies out by muscular contraction and wraps around the prey like a whiplash wrapping itself around a post. The frog then submerges to swallow its victim.

Its diet of insects, however, is usually supplemented by bigger prey. This can include other frogs and tadpoles and small terrapins and alligators. The bullfrog even eats snakes, including small garter and coral snakes. The fact that it eats these snakes is a measure of its voracity. Garter snakes themselves feed largely on amphibians and coral snakes are venomous. There is one case on record of a 17 in. coral snake being taken by a bullfrog. It can even capture small animals like mice and birds and especially ducklings. Even swallows, flying low over the water, are not safe from its voracious appetite and leaping ability.

Unusual mating call

When the water temperature reaches about 21°C/70°F mating takes place. This can be about February in the south of its range, to June or July in the northern parts. At night the males move out from the banks to call, while the females stay inshore. They join the male only when their eggs are ripe.

Find an empty barrel somewhere and shout into it, as deeply as possible, the word 'rum' and, according to Clifford Pope, the American herpetologist, the hollow, booming sound which will emerge is very like the mating call of the bullfrog. The call has also been described as sounding some-thing like 'jug o' rum' or 'more rum' and the alcoholic allusion is carried a bit further in some parts by referring to the bullfrog as 'the jug o' rum'.

The bullfrog makes this extraordinary sound 3 or 4 times in a few seconds. Then, after an interval of about 5 minutes, it repeats it. The sound is made by air being passed back and forth along the bullfrog's windpipe, from lungs to mouth, with the nostrils closed. Some of the air enters the airsacs in the floor of the mouth and they swell out like balloons and act as resonators, amplifying the sound so that the noise can be heard half a mile away.

After the mating the female bullfrog lays 10−25 thousand eggs which float in a sheet on the surface of the water, in among the water plants. With its envelope of jelly, each egg is just over ½ in. It is black above and white below. The eggs usually hatch within a week of being laid. If the temperature is low, however, they may take 2 years, sometimes more, to change into an adult frog, by which time they are 2−3 in. long. They feed on algae and decaying vegetation with occasional meals of small pond animals. After about another 2 years the young bullfrogs are almost fully grown and are ready to breed.

Many enemies

Both the tadpole bullfrog and the adult have a lot of enemies. Fish, snakes, birds and mammals, such as skunks and raccoons, all take their toll. A particular enemy of the tadpoles is the backswimmer, which grapples with a tadpole, inserts its 'beak' and sucks out the body fluids. All the bullfrog can do to protect itself from any enemy, apart from hiding at the bottom of the pool or stream, is to use its tremendous jumping powers to leap several feet clear.

Man is another enemy of the bullfrog. Men hunt them for their legs which are considered as much of a delicacy as those of the edible frog. In California, where they multiplied rapidly after their introduction half a century ago, limits had to be set on the numbers that could be collected in an attempt to prevent them being wiped out altogether. The usual method of killing them is to search for them after dark, dazzle them with a flashlight and then shoot before they can leap clear.

The jumping-frog

There are many ancient legends about 'jumping-frogs' and how their owners have been double-crossed. Mark Twain tells one of the best versions in a short story about one Jim Smiley of Angel's Camp, Calveras County, California. In the story Jim Smiley catches a frog. He calls it Dan'l Webster. The frog is a terrific jumper and Jim makes a lot of money betting on it in contests with other frogs. Then a stranger arrives in the camp and says that he does not think that Dan'l, the frog, is that good a jumper. He's quite prepared to back his word with 40 dollars. The trouble is that, being a stranger, he does not have a frog. Unwilling to let 40 dollars slip by so easily Jim Smiley goes off to find a frog. He leaves his frog with the stranger.

Eventually the new frog is lined up alongside Dan'l Webster. The starting signal is given and both frogs are prodded. The new frog leaps away. Dan'l Webster doesn't move an inch. The stranger collects his 40 dollars and smugly takes his leave. Jim Smiley is baffled and furious.

He can't imagine what's happened to his champion frog. Maybe it's ill. So he picks it up to have a look.

'Why, bless my oats,' he exclaims, 'if he don't weigh a double handful of shot!' So he turns Dan'l Webster, the champion frog, upside down and out pours a couple of pounds of lead shot.

Mark Twain's story was a roaring success. In 1928 when a celebration was held in Angel's Camp, to mark the paving of the streets, the ceremonies included, naturally, a frog-jumping contest. The winner was an entrant called 'Jumping Frog of the San Joaquin' with a leap of 3 ft 4 in.

The contest became very popular and it is now held every year. Allowances are even made for the unpredictable natures of the frogs. Because the first jump might be short and the second record-breaking the contest is judged on the distance travelled by the frog in three consecutive leaps. The record now stands at over 16 ft. So many entries are attracted every year that a stringent set of rules is enforced. One can surely presume that all entries are weighed before jumping so that competitors are spared the embarrassing experience of Jim Smiley—whose tortured ghost is said still to haunt the arena.

class	**Amphibia**
order	**Salientia**
family	**Ranidae**
genus & species	*Rana catesbeiana* *bullfrog*

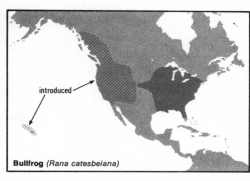

Bullfrog (Rana catesbeiana)

◁◁ Bullfrog, **Rana catesbeiana**. It will take quite large prey including other frogs, small terrapins and alligators, and even coral and garter snakes.

◁ Australian bullfrogs, **Limnodynastes dorsalis**. The female lays eggs in a mass of jelly which she beats up as the eggs are extruded so the eggs are coated and given protection.

▽ The bullfrog rarely leaves the water except during very wet weather. It lives in ponds, marshes or slow-flowing streams, and is often seen lying idly along the water's edge under the shade of reeds and shrubs.

Edible frog

Edible frogs are rather larger than common frogs, 2½—4 in. when full grown and with darker and bolder markings, especially the marbling of bright yellow and black on the hinder parts. The head is more slender than that of the common frog and lacks the dark patch running back from the eye. The marbling on the upper surface of the thigh and pale stripe down the back also distinguish the edible frog. The general colour varies from one to another; an edible frog is usually green when exposed to the sun and brown at the end of hibernation.

The most distinctive feature is found in males only. Just below the ear, there are external vocal sacs that swell to the size of large peas when the frog is croaking. They act as resonators, the volume of sound depending on the amount of air in the sacs.

The ranges of the edible and marsh frog, which is nearly related to the edible frog, overlap in central Europe, where the marsh frog breeds some two weeks earlier. If, however, bad weather causes it to breed late, interbreeding with the edible frog may take place, but it is not known whether the offspring are fertile. Despite this interbreeding, opinion is now strongly in favour of regarding the two as separate species.

Newcomers to England

The native home of the edible frog is in continental Europe and northern Asia, but it has been introduced into England on several occasions. The first recorded introduction was in 1837, when 200 were set free in Norfolk. During the next 5 years some 1 700 were brought over by a Mr Berney. His motive is not known, but he seems to have gone to some trouble, making special hampers, each having a series of movable shelves with water lily leaves stitched to them 'so that the frogs might be comfortable and feel at home'. Initially these colonists flourished, but land drainage has destroyed many of their homes and only a few scattered colonies are left. Since then more colonies have become established from frogs brought over from the Continent, in Surrey, Hampshire, Oxfordshire and Bedfordshire, but the colonies usually die out after a time. It would seem that conditions in England are, for some reason, not very favourable for edible frogs.

Edible frogs spend more time in the water than common frogs. If their ponds dry up, the frogs will migrate to other stretches of water, and they will sometimes come on land to feed at night; but young edible frogs do not wander like young common frogs.

Adult edible frogs hibernate in the mud at the bottom of ponds or by the water's edge, but young will come ashore and crawl into crevices or under logs and stones. They emerge from hibernation in April, the exact date depending on the weather.

Leaping on its prey

The prey, especially of young frogs, is mainly insects, including ants, wasps, flies, beetles, butterflies and moths. The frog lies in wait, hidden by water weed, and jumps at its prey, sometimes bringing down flying insects. The extensible tongue is used to capture small insects, but large ones such as dragonflies, or even larger prey such as newts, small fish, small mammals and birds, are caught in the jaws and crammed into the mouth by the forelegs.

▽ *Edible frogs mating. The male is showing a distinctive feature of edible frogs which is found only in the male: the vocal sacs just below the ears, which swell to the size of peas when the frog croaks, amplifying his call.*

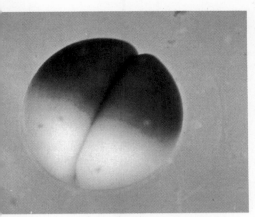

△ *Start of a life: a frog's egg divides for the first time after fertilisation.*
▽ *Edible frog tadpoles often grow fast, turning into froglets in as little as 3—4 months.*

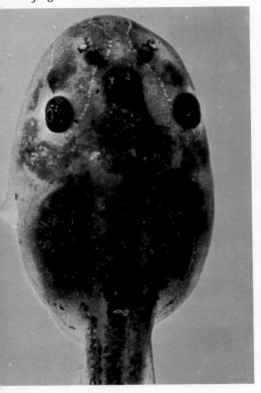

Giant tadpoles

The life history of the edible frog resembles that of the common frog. Mating takes place a month or more after emerging from hibernation. Croaking is heard most at this time although it continues all through the summer. A chorus of several hundred male frogs can be heard over a mile, sounding like the quacking of many ducks.

At the spawning pond males outnumber the females by 8 or 10 to 1. There is, however, no fighting or jostling between the males as one might expect from the breeding behaviour of most other animals. A mated pair can continue spawning in the middle of a crowd of unattached males without interference. Yet, should a pair in process of spawning become separated the female will immediately be seized by another male. Since the male's grasp during amplexus is not tenacious as in most other frogs such separation is not uncommon and the separate parts of the spawn from a single female may have been fertilized by two or more males.

Spawning takes place in shallow water at the edges of pools. Each female can produce up to 10 000 eggs, but in the British Isles they have never been found to lay more than 2 000. The spawn is laid in groups of 250, rather than in large masses as in the common frog. It does not float to the surface because it is laid among water weeds. The tadpoles leave the eggs in 10 days and develop in a similar fashion to the tadpoles of the common frog, but the rate of development varies considerably. Some tadpoles develop rapidly and turn into froglets, about 1 in. long, 3—4 months after hatching, but others will fail to complete their development before winter. Most will die, but some survive and grow to perhaps 2½ in. before changing into froglets. Sometimes they fail to metamorphose and continue to live as tadpoles. This is an instance of neoteny (see axolotl, page 232) and one edible frog tadpole caught in Surrey lived for 11 months in captivity, dying when 4¾ in. long.

Edible frogs reach sexual maturity at 2 years but are not fully grown until their fourth or fifth year.

Fishing for frogs

Edible frogs have all the enemies that afflict common frogs, but they have the added disadvantage of being prized as food by man. Edible frogs are by no means the only frogs that are eaten; common frogs are caught before the edible frogs have emerged from hibernation, and in other parts of the world various species are eaten—the bullfrog in the United States, for instance. The edible frog, however, provides the traditional dish of frogs' legs, which may be fried crisp like whitebait, or served with sauce or in a risotto.

The usual way of catching frogs is by rod and line. No hook is used, instead a brightly coloured lure is dangled in front of the frogs. This must be kept on the move for the frogs to strike at it. They are then flipped out of the water before they can let go of the lure.

The lure is traditionally a piece of red flannel or a skein of thread formed by winding a few yards of thread around the finger. The colour is immaterial and the important factor is that the lure must be on the move. A frog's vision is such that it reacts only to moving prey. Since the normal feeding habits of the edible frog include leaping upwards from the water to capture insects flying just above the surface, almost any small dancing lure will bring this reaction. The frog leaps, grips the lure with its jaw and must be immediately pulled up to be caught.

Frog fishing is best done on warm summer days because, like all cold-blooded animals, the edible frog is most active and will the more readily bite in proportion as the temperature rises. The experienced frog fisher will then be able to capture one frog after another as rapidly as he can raise and lower his line slipping each expertly into his hand.

It has been estimated that 15 to 20 frogs are needed to make a meal for one person and a single fisherman may take hundreds a day in favourable weather.

Frogs and electricity

The story goes that in 1786 Galvani, an

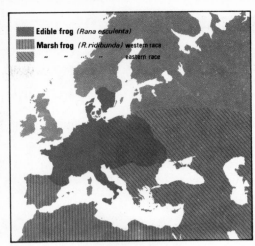

In the east and west of the edible frog's range, it overlaps the territory of the marsh frog. The marsh frog, however is isolated in that it breeds two weeks earlier than the edible frog. If bad weather brings the breeding seasons together, interbreeding may take place.

Italian physiologist, noticed that the skinned legs of an edible frog twitched when they were touched with a scalpel that had been charged with electricity. Sometimes this story is elaborated, and one can read that it was Signora Galvani who first noticed this when she was using a scalpel, accidently charged by one of her husband's electrical gadgets, to prepare frogs' leg soup. The truth is that Galvani had known of this effect for some years; ever since he had suspended some edible frogs, on copper hooks from an iron railing, and they had started to dance. According to Galvani, the muscle contractions were due to 'animal electricity' which was conducted from nerve to muscle by the two metals. Convinced of this, Galvani continued to investigate this strange source of power for the rest of his life, although other experimenters showed that the linking of these two different metals was the basis of an electric charge that stimulated the muscles to contract. The only contribution made by the frog's legs was that they provided a ready conductor for the electricity. The edible frog, however, had had its moment of glory in the advancement of science, even if its actions had been misunderstood.

class	**Amphibia**
order	**Salientia**
family	**Ranidae**
genus & species	*Rana esculenta*

Mouth-breeding frog

Also known as the vaquero, in Argentina, and as Darwin's frog and Darwin's toad, the mouth-breeding frog is probably the most remarkable of all the amphibians. First discovered by Darwin, it is only 1 in. long and its tadpoles mature to tiny froglets inside the father's vocal sacs.

This midget frog is an inconspicuous greenish brown with darker stripes and patches and a dark line running from behind each eye to the hind end of the body. There are many warts arranged in irregular rows on the body and legs. In front of the large eyes the snout rapidly narrows to a pointed, false nose, the nostrils lying halfway between the eyes and the tip of this 'proboscis'. The front legs are fairly short with long, slender toes, the hindlegs being long as in a normal frog.

*The mouth-breeding frog was found by Darwin in the Argentine during his famous **Beagle** voyage, and has since been found to range through southern Chile as well as southern Argentina.*

Weak voice

The home of this frog is in the beech woods where it hops around in a lively manner, rising well up on its hindlegs before making a short hop forward. The male has a small bell-like voice—weak for the size of the vocal sacs which, as we shall see, have a more important function. These form a large pouch under the throat which extends backwards under the belly to the groin and upwards on each side, almost to the backbone. Inside the mouth is a pair of slits, one on each side, that lead into the vocal sacs, which lie between the skin and the muscles of the body.

Strange nursery

In the breeding season the females lay 20—30 eggs over which the males stand guard for 10—20 days. As the eggs are about to hatch the males pick them up with their tongues, several at a time, and they slide through the slits into the vocal sacs which have now become much swollen. Each male may have anything up to 17 large eggs in his vocal sacs, and quite naturally he now becomes silent. The males do not have to fast while the tadpoles develop. The tadpoles can take no food, however, except for the yolk contained in the eggs which becomes enclosed in their intestines. When about ½ in. long, and with just a stump of a tail left, they leave the vocal sacs. Everything now goes back to normal in the male parent's body. The vocal sacs shrink and his shoulder girdle and internal organs, which had become distorted to make room for the growing tadpoles, go back to their former shape.

The males do not necessarily tend their own offspring; the females lay their eggs in masses and the males take whichever eggs are nearest at the time.

The earliest voice

The first voice in the history of the earth was probably that of a frog, and it may have sounded some 200 million years ago. Plenty of other animals made sounds, the crickets and grasshoppers, for example, as well as many fishes, but a voice-box in the throat came first in the tailless amphibians. Even the tailed amphibians, the salamanders and newts, who can hear, although they were once thought to be deaf, use only a very weak voice, though they have a larynx. By recording the calls of frogs and toads and playing these back to the animals during the breeding season and at other times the value of the voice was discovered. First and foremost, it seems, the voice is used as a mating call. The frogs and toads react most to calls when they are ready to breed. Males move towards any source of calls as a potential breeding site. Once the females have spawned, the voices of the males have no charms for them. So the mouth-breeding males suffer little from having to fall silent, as the females have already spawned. When the voice is used outside the breeding season it is to keep individuals spaced out.

class	**Amphibia**
order	**Salientia**
family	**Rhinodermatidae**
genus & species	***Rhinoderma darwinii***

The mouth-breeding frog was first found by Darwin and so is named after him. It is just over 1 in. long and has a peculiar false nose.

The colouring and patterning of the skin of this tiny frog varies tremendously from one frog to another as pictures 1, 2 and 3 show.

The tadpoles, picture 4, develop in the swollen vocal sac of the male. This sac is opened, picture 5, showing the tadpoles inside.

1

3

2

4

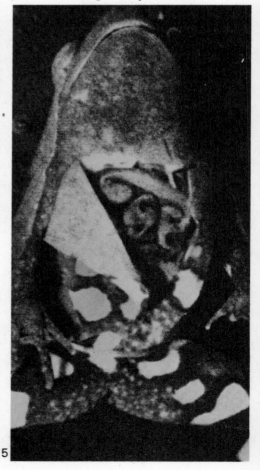

5

Reed frog

There are over 200 species of reed or sedge frogs, all living in Africa. Many are beautifully patterned and coloured, and can change colour in response to temperature or background. They are small, about 1 in. long. The five-lined reed frog, from Angola to Tanzania, is pale, almost golden brown with five mauve-brown stripes running down its back. These stripes are more distinct in the male than in the female. The painted or marbled reed frog has intricate patterns on its back. The patterns and their colours vary from frog to frog and with the background. Painted reed frogs may be black and white, black and green, black and yellow, brown and

△ A tiny painted reed frog clings onto a twig by the sucker-like discs on its fingers and toes. The beautiful pinky-red belly and markings on the head and arms are typical of this frog, which often proves difficult to identify because its colour and patterning varies so widely in different parts of its range.

yellow as well as several other variations. The painted reed frog ranges from the Cape to Rhodesia and Angola. At the

253

◁ *Nocturnal serenade—a male reed frog sings to attract a female. Actually, both sexes sing but only the male has the well-developed vocal pouch. The noise is produced by the vibration of the elastic edges of a pair of skin folds in the vocal cords. Air is passed backwards and forwards between the lungs and the large pouch which inflates and deflates like a balloon.*

▽ *The long reed frog,* **Hyperolius nasutus,** *is widespread in the coastal belt of eastern southern Africa. Often seen sunbathing on reeds at the edges of swamps, it is said to feed mainly on mosquitoes.*

their new background. The arum frog basks with its legs drawn under it but it may suddenly stretch its legs and leap away. If only slightly disturbed, however, it swings around and disappears behind the lily.

class	**Amphibia**
order	**Salientia**
family	**Rhacophoridae**
genera & species	**Afrixalus** *small golden spiny reed frog* **A. fornasinii** *brown and white spiny reed frog* **Hyperolius horstocki** *arum frog* **H. marmoratus** *painted reed frog* **H. tuberilinguis** *green reed frog* **H. quinquevittatus** *five-lined reed frog*

southern end of its range it is green or brown with light green spots, each spot ringed with a narrow black line. By contrast, the rare green reed frog is a plain brilliant green with no markings but is white on the belly and pink on the hindlegs.

The two spiny reed frogs live up to their name, for with the aid of a magnifying lens minute spines can be seen on their heads and backs. They differ from the other reed frogs in that the pupil of the eye is vertical instead of horizontal.

Sun-loving frogs

Apart from the spiny reed frogs, which hide during the day, reed frogs like to sunbathe, and can be found clinging to reeds or other plants even in hot sun. They are, however, always ready to leap to safety. Usually this means that they leap back into the pond but the painted reed frog that often lives miles from water escapes by long bounding leaps. During the dry season reed frogs disappear into cracks and crevices in the ground or bury themselves in the earth. Reed frogs feed on flying insects such as mosquitoes.

Varied breeding habits

The life histories of reed frogs have been largely made known through the studies of Vincent Wager, the South African expert on frogs. While the majority probably have life histories similar to other frogs such as the common, edible or bullfrogs, some reed frogs have unusual habits. The life history of the arum frog appears straightforward. Clusters of about 30 eggs

are laid among water plants and the surrounding jelly is sticky so the eggs become camouflaged with mud. The tadpoles feed on minute floating organisms rather than scraping at the slime of algae on stones.

The giant reed frog lays its eggs above water. About 300—400 are laid in a sticky mass on floating plants or on the leaves of plants overhanging water. At first the jelly is stiff, then it softens and hangs down. The tadpoles develop within this mass and wriggle about until the jelly liquefies, when they break out and fall into the water. The painted reed frog lays its eggs in clusters on stones or plants underwater, but the southern spotted form, called the pondo reed frog, sometimes loses its eggs through an unusual habit. The mated pair jump onto an erect stalk and bend it over with their weight until its tip hangs into the water. Some eggs are laid on the submerged part which sometimes springs up again after the frogs have let go. The eggs dry out in the sun and die. The egg-laying habits of the spiny reed frogs recall those of newts (page 234). The eggs are stuck to a leaf which is folded over to make a protective tube. The golden spiny reed frog lays its eggs under water, the brown and white spiny reed frog on plants up to 3 ft above the water.

Flower frog

The arum frog lives in flowers of the arum lily, where its ivory colour makes it inconspicuous as it basks in the sun. It is also overlooked by insects that are attracted by the scent of the arum lily and so fall prey to the frog. When arum lilies are not in flower the frogs move to other plants and change their colour to dark brown to fit

Tuatara

The tuatara is the sole survivor of the beak-heads, a group of very ancient reptiles that flourished during the Age of Reptiles, which lasted from 250 to 70 million years ago. It is the only species of reptile in an order and family of its own. Outwardly it looks like a fairly large lizard but internally it has many fundamental differences from modern lizards. With a length of 2 ft or more, it has a large head with teeth set along the edges of the jaws and a pair of enlarged front upper teeth. The nostrils are double and there is no external opening to the ear. The body and limbs are strongly built and there are powerful sharp claws on the partially webbed, five-toed feet. There is a crest of enlarged spines along the neck, back and tail and the back and sides are covered with small granular scales interspersed with tubercles. The scales of the underparts are larger and more regularly arranged. Like many of the modern lizards the tuatara is able to regenerate its long compressed tail, but not so efficiently. The tuatara's ground colour varies from blackish-brown to olive green or grey with a small yellow spot on each scale, which is brightest after the skin is shed and fades as the animal gets older. The scales of the crest are green.

It is only when the tuatara's anatomy is examined that the distinctions are found that cause it to be placed in a separate order and which make it so interesting to zoologists. In particular the skull is much stronger and firmer than that of other lizards, being more like the skull of a crocodile, with its parts joined together by bony arches. The backbone is primitive in structure, the vertebrae being concave at both ends. The ribs have hook-like processes about halfway along their length for attachment to the muscles. These are found also in birds and some fossil reptiles. The so-called abdominal ribs are well developed, forming a shield made up of several segments. Another unusual feature of the tuatara is the absence of an organ of copulation in the male.

Up to the middle of the 19th century the tuatara was common on the New Zealand mainland but today it is confined to a few rocky islands off the northeast coast of North Island and in Cook Strait between

▷ Of the many 'beak-heads' – reptiles that flourished 100 million years ago – only the tuatara survives, on a few islands around New Zealand.

△ *A tuatara on guard outside its burrow, which it shares with various species of shearwaters.*
△ ▷ *Looking seaward – a tuatara and its young.*

North and South Island. On some of these islands it is now plentiful owing to the New Zealand Government's policy of strict protection.

Three-eyed lizards

Perhaps the tuatara's most interesting feature to zoologists is the presence of the third or parietal eye, which is a feature of so many fossil vertebrates. This parietal eye is not, however, peculiar to the beak-heads; it is shared with many other species of lizards but it is better developed in the adult tuatara than in any other animal. Its presence in many embryos confused early ideas on evolution's relation to embryology. It is situated on the top of the brain, with a hole in the skull just above it, and has the vestiges of a lens and retina' but no iris. It connects with a glandular body in the brain, but in adults the skin thickens over the opening in the skull and it is unlikely that any light from outside is conducted to the brain. The parietal eye was probably an important sense organ in some of the earlier reptiles but it is not known for sure what function it serves in the tuatara.

One breath an hour

The tuatara may dig its own burrow or share one with a petrel. As far as is known the tuatara lives only on islands where the top soil has been so manured and worked over by these birds' numerous burrows that there is a layer of loose upper soil 18—24 in. deep. The tuatara can often be seen basking in the sun in the morning or evening but spends most of the day in its burrow, coming out to hunt for food only at night. It is active at quite low temperatures, sometimes as low as 7°C/45°F, the lowest temperature recorded for any reptile activity. Its rate of metabolism is very low; the normal rate of breathing even when it is moving about is only one breath per seven seconds, but it can go for at least an hour without a breath.

Although good-tempered when handled gently, a tuatara will scratch and bite in self-defence. Its voice is a harsh croak, and it

resembles the well-known croak of a frog.

The tuatara's diet consists largely of spiders, crickets, beetles and other insects, although snails and earthworms are also taken. Contrary to the popular image of bird and reptile living amicably together, the tuatara sometimes eats petrel eggs and chicks, even an occasional adult bird.

Unusually long gestation

Nothing is known of the courtship habits of the tuatara. Pairing occurs during January but the sperm are stored in the female's body until the following October or December when 5–15 white, oval, soft-shelled eggs are laid in a shallow depression in the ground which has been scooped out by the female, and covered over with earth. The

eggs receive no attention from either parent and do not hatch out until 12–15 months later, the longest incubation period known for any reptile. The young tuataras, which are brownish pink in colour, break the shells of their eggs and dig their way to the surface. They are about $4\frac{1}{2}$ in. long at this stage but their growth rate is very slow and they do not breed until they are over 20 years old, and they continue to grow until they are 50.

The tuatara has been kept in captivity on a number of occasions, one specimen in New Zealand having been kept for over 50 years. In the wild it lives to well over 50 years, and some claim that it may live to be 100 to 300.

Island sanctuaries

The tuatara probably became extinct on the

mainland of New Zealand because it was preyed upon by the many rodents, feral cats and pigs introduced by the English immigrants to New Zealand and which now inhabit the bush. These predators are not present on the islands to which the tuatara is now confined and it can consequently live and breed freely with little disturbance.

Dinosaur contemporary

The beak-heads flourished during the Age of Reptiles, along with the earliest turtles and long before the great dinosaurs trod the earth. They evolved into a remarkable variety of forms which are known from fossils found in many parts of the world. Some of these were larger than the tuatara as we know it today but none reached a

257

length of more than 5–6 ft. After the Jurassic period most of the beak-heads became extinct, the tuatara being the only member of the group to survive until today. It was first named by Dr John Edward Gray, an English zoologist who was on the staff of the British Museum, from a specimen received there in 1831, who thought it was merely a new species of lizard. It was not until 1867 that his successor at the Museum, Dr Albert Günter, realised that the animal was no ordinary lizard but was related to the ancient beak-heads, and was truly a living fossil.

class	**Reptilia**
order	**Rhynchocephalia**
family	**Sphenodontidae**
genus & species	*Sphenodon punctatus*

▽ *The islands on which the tuatara lives have a remarkable soil and vegetation. Beneath a canopy of low trees of the genus **Coprosoma** is a deep layer of soft humus. This is largely maintained by the burrowing activities of the shearwaters which mix leaves, twigs and excreta into an even composition. The islands' vegetation has suffered due to the introduction of goats, but fortunately their numbers have now been checked.*

Terrapin

The name terrapin is derived from an American Indian word for 'little turtle' and is one of those common words about which there is confusion as to the precise meaning, in the same way as there is confusion about 'turtle' and 'tortoise' (see tortoise, page 261). In Britain 'terrapin' is often used as the name for any small freshwater member of the order Testudines, particularly those kept as pets in aquaria. West of the Atlantic, however, the word has a more restricted meaning and some writers insist that terrapin should refer only to the diamondback terrapin **Malaclemys terrapin**. This is a very sensible idea and will certainly save the confusion that occurs when American natural history books are published in British editions with no explanation of the terms 'turtle', 'tortoise' and 'terrapin', and vice versa. The diamondback terrapin is well known gastronomically as the basic ingredient of 'Terrapin à la Maryland', and because of its economic importance as food, its biology has been studied in detail. It is so named because of the bold, rhomboidal or whorled markings etched in each plate of the carapace. The small plates that border the carapace like the scalloping on a pie crust, are hollowed and lighter in colour. The plastron is yellow and is speckled and lined with small black dots, as is the skin of the head and limbs. Female diamondback terrapins grow up to 8 in., the males to 6 in. and they weigh up to 2 lb. They range from Cape Cod, Massachusetts to Florida, Texas and Mexico.

Other freshwater turtles or tortoises sometimes known as terrapins, are the red-eared terrapin or pond terrapin **Pseudemys scripta**, the Spanish terrapin **Clemmys leprosa** of Spain, Portugal and North Africa and the geographic or map terrapin **Graptemys geographica** of the St Lawrence, the Great Lakes and the Missouri. Confusingly, the box turtles of North America are in the genus **Terrapene**.

Salt essential for health

The diamondback terrapin is never found far from the coast and is restricted to brackish waters, such as tidal estuaries and salt marshes, or the sea, where it may be found in bays. It is found up rivers only as far as the tide penetrates. It seems strange that diamondbacks should be restricted to brackish water but if captive terrapins are kept in fresh water they develop a fungus on the skin, which is cured by adding some salt to the water.

Terrapins come onto rocks to bask in the sun but they spend most of their time swimming with their webbed feet. They have the habit of floating with their shells hanging vertically with only the snout showing above water and with the hindfeet slowly moving to keep them steady. During the winter months terrapins hibernate under the mud of their habitat.

The diamondback terrapin, so called from the bold sculpturing of the plates of the carapace, is famous as a delicacy in the southern USA.

Crushed food

Apart from a few water plants, terrapins feed mainly on small animals such as fiddler crabs, periwinkles, insects and worms, which are crushed in the powerful jaws.

Males not always needed

Most of our knowledge of the breeding habits of diamondbacks comes from observations at terrapin farms where they are bred commercially for their flesh. In the wild, however, they lay their eggs in nests not far above the high water mark. The females, and probably the males as well, mature when about 7 years old. They may lay 1–5 clutches a year, younger terrapins laying fewer, and each clutch consists of 7–24 elliptical white eggs, 1½ by ¾ in. The laying season depends on the climate, being from early May to late July in North Carolina. The young hatch in about 90 days.

Observations at terrapin farms showed that female terrapins can lay fertile eggs although they have been separated from males for several years. In one test 10 females laid 124 eggs one year after being separated from males. Only one failed to hatch. After 3 years they laid 130 eggs and 91 failed to hatch but in the fourth year only 4 out of 108 hatched. It seems that the live sperms are stored in the ovaries and it is now known that this also occurs in other turtles and in snakes.

Gourmet's turtle

The diamondback terrapin has had a varied career as human food. During the 18th century it formed a cheap source of food for slaves, then over the course of the 19th century its fortunes changed as some whim of fashion decided its taste was superior to any other turtle. 'Terrapin à la Maryland' is a rich dish of terrapin meat cooked with vegetables, wine and eggs, with sherry added before serving. By 1920 diamondbacks were fetching $90 a dozen. As a result their numbers decreased so protection laws were passed and they were reared artificially. In recent years, however, there has been a decrease both in demand and price for terrapins.

class	**Reptilia**
order	**Testudines**
family	**Emydidae**
genus & species	*Malaclemys terrapin* diamondback terrapin

▽ *Horny lips, goggle eyes and spotted wrinkled chin and throat – close-up of the diamondback terrapin.*

Tortoise

Tortoises are well known for their slowness of movement and for their long life span. They live longer than any other animal today; and they are about the most heavily armoured. There is a difference between American and British usage. In the United States the name 'tortoise' is used only for land-living chelonians belonging to the family Testudinidae. In British usage some water-living chelonians, such as the European pond tortoise, are also given the common name of tortoise.

There are about 40 land tortoises, the best known of which are the so-called garden tortoises and the giant tortoises. Since the way of life of all of them is much the same, most attention will be given here to the Iberian or Algerian tortoise and the Greek or Hermann's tortoise, both garden tortoises. They have high domed shells, up to 1 ft long. The legs are covered with hard scales which often have bony cores and the five toes on the forefoot and the four on the hindfoot all have stout claws. When disturbed a tortoise pulls its head and limbs into the shelter of the bony box covered with horn which is usually spoken of as its shell. The head is completely withdrawn. The front legs are pulled back to make the elbows meet in the middle, protecting the entrance with their scaly skin. The hindlegs and tail are similarly withdrawn, the soles of the hindfeet sealing the entrance.

Tortoises live in tropical and subtropical regions. The Iberian or Algerian tortoise is found in northwest Africa and Spain, the Balkans, Iraq and Iran. The Greek tortoise ranges from southern France through parts of Italy to the Balkans. The star tortoise of southern Asia has pale star-shaped markings on its shell. The gopher tortoises of the southern United States get their name from the French **gaufre**, a honeycomb, an allusion to their burrowing. There are other land tortoises in southern Asia, Africa, Madagascar and other islands of the Indian Ocean, South America and the Galapagos Islands.

△ A leopard tortoise **Testudo pardalis** about to enjoy a refreshing mouthful of cactus.

The warmer, the faster

Tortoises live in sandy places or among rocks or in woodlands. They are active by day and generally slow in their movements, yet they can at times reach a speed of 2 mph over short distances. This may be slow compared with the speed of most quadrupeds but it is nearly the walking speed of a man and is faster than we normally consider tortoises' speed. The behaviour of a tortoise is geared to the temperature of the surrounding air. Its movements are faster in warmer temperatures but like other reptiles it is intolerant of the higher air temperatures. Tortoises spend some time every day basking. In temperate latitudes garden tortoises hibernate from October to March, fasting for a while prior to digging themselves into soft earth or under dead vegetation.

Seedlings a favourite meal

It was once widely believed that the smaller tortoises fed on insects and slugs and for this reason people, in England at least, bought tortoises to keep in their gardens. The idea is not yet wholly dead. It may be that a garden tortoise will sometimes eat the smaller garden vermin, but anyone who has seen a tortoise travel along a row of seedlings just showing through the ground will need little convincing that tortoises are wholly or almost exclusively vegetarian, eating low growing vegetation such as seedlings, succulent leaves, flowers and fallen fruits, and only occasionally insects.

Battering ram courtship

Males and females look alike but in most species there is some small difference in shape. In Hermann's tortoise, for example, the plastron, or underside of the shell, is flat in the female, concave in the male. In the Iberian tortoise the tail shield is flat in the female, curved in the male. Another sign is that a male in breeding condition butts the female in the flank, at the same time hissing slightly. Male garden tortoises, when there is no female around, will butt the shoes of people sitting in the garden or the legs of garden chairs. The female lays 4—12 whitish spherical eggs, each 1½ in. diameter, in a hole which she digs in soft ground. The eggs hatch 3—4 months later.

Man the enemy today . . .

The solid box of bone with its horny covering and the tortoise's habit of withdrawing into this fortress at the slightest disturbance, seem the best possible protection against enemies. The Bearded Vulture is a traditional enemy, flying to some height with a tortoise and then letting it drop to the ground to crack its shell. Rats attack and eat tortoises. Apart from these the natural enemies must be limited. On the other hand, tortoises are probably very vulnerable to the elements, especially to such catastrophes as grass and woodland fires. After a grass fire the number of dead tortoises of all sizes, and especially the small ones, gives an indication of how numerous these animals can be in places where normally little is seen of them. The greatest danger today is the trade in tortoises for pets. Once a tortoise has been bought and installed in a garden it will be treated with the greatest care. The method of packing them for transport has meant, however, that in recent years there has been a hideously high mortality between their being collected, mainly in North Africa, and their reaching the dealers.

. . . and in the past

The four species of gopher tortoises, which may be up to 13 in. long, have also suffered from the pet trade. Two, the Texas tortoise and the desert tortoise, are now protected by law but the Mexican is very rare and may be extinct. The giant tortoises which live on the islands of the Galapagos and on islands in the Indian Ocean have also suffered in numbers, but in a different way. The largest of them have reached nearly 5 ft long, stood $2\frac{1}{2}$ ft high and weighed 200 – 300 lb. Those of the Galapagos especially were taken by the crews of whalers, sealers and buccaneers for fresh meat. Between 1811 and 1844, a mere 105 whalers took 15 000. The giant tortoises of the Indian Ocean suffered even more, and in recent years a population on Aldabra Island was threatened through a proposal by the British Ministry of Defence to make the island an air staging post.

A ripe old age

Keeping tortoises as pets has been the only reliable way of estimating how long they can live.

The longest authentic record we have is for one of the giant tortoises, Marion's tortoise. It was taken to Mauritius, when full grown, by Marion de Fresne in 1766. In 1810 the British captured the island and the tortoise continued to live in the artillery barracks until 1918. It was, therefore, at least 152 years old, and probably 180 years or even more. Another famous giant was the Tonga tortoise, presented by Captain James Cook in 1774, when it was already 'a considerable age'. There is some doubt about this tortoise, largely because in Tonga the records are oral, not written, but there seems no reason why the present tortoise should not be the same as the one Captain Cook handed over.

class	**Reptilia**
order	**Testudines**
family	**Testudinidae**
genera & species	**Gopherus agassizi** *desert gopher tortoise*
	G. berlandieri *Texas*
	G. flavomarginatus *Mexican*
	Geochelone elephantopus *Galapagos giant*
	G. gigantea *Indian Ocean giant*
	Testudo graeca *Iberian or Algerian*
	T. hermanni *Greek, others*

▷ *Galapagos giant tortoises: some of the few remaining members of a species once numerous enough to give its name to the islands but numbers are now greatly diminished. In the 19th century they were easy prey for the crews of passing ships, and their hardiness enabled them to be kept on board as a live source of meat.*

Early morning and the leathery turtle completes her task of egg-laying by filling in the nest hole. This rare sea turtle spends more time in deep water than any other turtle. The females come onto land only to lay eggs. Each comes ashore, usually late at night, about four times a season.

Leathery turtle

The leathery or leatherback turtle or luth is the largest sea turtle, and also differs from the others in the structure of its shell. The upper shell or carapace is made up of hundreds of irregular bony plates covered with a leathery skin instead of the characteristic plates of other turtles. There are seven ridges, which may be notched, running down the back, and five on the lower shell, or plastron.
Leathery turtles are dark brown or black with spots of yellow or white on the throat and flippers of young specimens. They grow to a maximum of 9 ft, the shell being up to 6 ft, and may weigh up to 1 800 lb. The foreflippers are very large; leathery turtles 7 ft long may have flippers spanning 9 ft.

Rare wanderer

The leathery turtle is the rarest sea turtle and lives in tropical waters, probably spending more time in deeper water than other turtles. Little is known about its habits and even its breeding haunts are not well known. Leathery turtles are known to breed in the West Indies, Florida, the northeastern coasts of South America, Senegal, Natal, Madagascar, Sri Lanka and Malaya. The breeding populations are quite small and predation of eggs by men and dogs endangers the populations of some beaches. Although generally restricted to warm waters, leathery turtles are occasionally found swimming in cooler waters or washed up on beaches, especially when carried by adverse winds or currents. They have been seen off Newfoundland and Norway in the north, occasionally straggling as far south as New Zealand.

Unlike some other turtles leathery turtles do not carry encrustations of barnacles and seaweeds. This may be due to the very oily skin. The oil has been found to have antibiotic properties but it is not known whether this prevents other organisms settling on the skin. Also, like the other turtles without barnacles, they are fast swimmers. Leathery turtles are regularly escorted by pilot fish, which are more commonly associated with other fishes, such as sharks.

Although the leathery turtle is described here as the rarest of the turtles, it is of interest to note that it has been increasingly reported in recent years, especially in the North Atlantic. One reason for this, possibly the main reason, is that fishermen have switched to faster, motorized vessels.

A soft diet

The stomach contents of leathery turtles show that they feed on jellyfish, salps, pteropods (planktonic sea snails) and other soft bodied, slow-moving animals, including the amphipods and other animals that live in the bodies of jellyfish and salps. Leathery turtles have been seen congregating in shoals of jellyfish and the 2–3in. horny spines in the mouth and throat are probably a great help in holding slippery food.

Breeding in bands

Female leathery turtles come ashore in small bands to lay their eggs, usually late at night. They come straight up the shore to dry sand, stop, then start to dig the nest. They do not select the nest site, by digging exploratory pits and testing the sand, as in green turtles. A hollow is excavated with all four flippers working rhythmically until the turtle is hidden. She then digs the egg pit, scooping out sand with her hindflippers until she has dug as deep as she can reach. About 60–100 eggs, 2–2¼ in. diameter, are laid, then she fills the nest with sand and packs it down. Finally she masks the position of the nest by ploughing about and scattering sand, then makes her way back to the sea. Each female comes ashore to lay about four times in one season. The eggs hatch in 7 weeks and the babies emerge together and rush down the shore to the water.

The Soay beast

In September 1959 a large animal was seen in the sea off Soay, a small island off the Isle of Skye, western Scotland. There was much speculation at the time about what it could be. The two men who saw it gave a description and each made a rough sketch of it. The interest was increased by the fact that on at least one occasion many years previously a similar animal had been reported from these same waters. So the Soay Beast, as it came to be called, passed into history as an unsolved mystery, possibly a sea monster, probably one of the several different kinds of sea-serpent reported at various times. All these things seemed possible when one looked at an artist's impression published at the time. In due course Professor LD Brongersma had little difficulty in showing that, beyond reasonable doubt, the animal was nothing more than a large leathery turtle. In this he confirmed the opinion of Dr JH Fraser of Aberdeen, expressed in May 1960, a few months after the sighting was reported.

If the artist's impression was misleading we cannot blame him. He had only the verbal statements to go upon, together with two crude sketches. The real moral is that one should pay more attention to Occam's Razor. William of Occam (now Ockham) was a 14th century English scholar and philosopher who expounded the principle that if there are two or more theories to account for something, choose the simplest.

△ *Why do leathery turtles cry? The answer might be to remove sand from its eyes on the rare occasions when the turtle comes ashore to nest and lay eggs. The accepted theory is that the tears a turtle sheds get rid of the excess salt that has been swallowed with gulps of sea water.*
▽ *The leathery turtle belongs to tropical waters, but sometimes ranges into temperate seas in summer.*

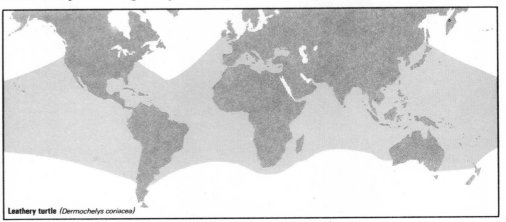

Leathery turtle (Dermochelys coriacea)

class	**Reptilia**
order	**Testudines**
family	**Dermochelidae**
genus & species	***Dermochelys coriacea***

With a shell length of little more than 4 in. this tiny turtle, the common mud turtle, is one of the smallest freshwater turtles of North America.

The common musk turtle has a much reduced plastron without hinges. The shields of the plastron are separated along the mid-line by soft skin.

Mud turtle

The mud turtles and musk turtles of the family Trionychidae are some of the smallest North American turtles: the adult eastern mud turtle has a brown or olive shell which is little more than 4 in. long. The young of this species has three ridges on the carapace, the upper part of the shell, but these disappear as it grows up. The plastron, or underpart of the shell, is light brown or yellow and the turtles have yellowish green spots on the head. The central part of the plastron is joined to the carapace while its front and rear portions are hinged to this central portion by strong connective tissues forming movable lobes. When the turtle withdraws its head, limbs and tail it draws these lobes over the openings, completely sealing itself in. Musk turtles are similar to mud turtles except that the plastron is very much smaller in proportion to the carapace and is without hinges, but the two kinds of turtles are alike in having musk glands along the sides of the body. The musk is much stronger in the musk turtles which are often called stinkpots as a result. Male mud turtles differ from females in having larger heads and longer tails and, when adult, their plastrons are concave. They also have patches of horny scales on the hindlegs, which are used to hold the female in mating.

There are about 17 species of mud turtle, 4 or 5 in the United States, and the rest in Central and South America. One large South American mud turtle has enlarged lobes on the plastron that make a perfect fit with the edges of the carapace, so the turtle inside is fully protected. The musk turtles live in the United States.

Quiet life

Mud and musk turtles live in pools and sluggish streams where there are plenty of water plants. They crawl over the bottom and occasionally wander out over the land or bask on banks and tree stumps. The

Stinkpot—a three day old common musk turtle.

common musk turtle is rarely seen out of water but the keel-backed musk turtle of the southeastern United States often comes out to bask in the sun. The mud turtles are more likely to be found on land and they often live in very small pools and roadside ditches.

An unpleasant catch

Mud turtles and musk turtles feed on tadpoles, snails, worms, water insects and fish. They also eat a large amount of carrion and are unpopular with anglers because they often take their bait. After giving an angler the impression that he has hooked a large fish the turtle adds insult to injury by discharging its foul-smelling musk when lifted from the water.

Leisurely courtship

The courtship of mud turtles usually takes place in the water but the female comes on land to lay her eggs. To mate the male approaches the female from behind and noses her tail to confirm her sex. He then swims beside her, nudging her just behind her eye. She swims with him for some distance then stops suddenly. This is a signal for the male to climb onto her back, grasp the edges of her carapace with his toes and hold her tail to one side with the scaly patches on one of his hindlegs. Several fertile clutches may result from one mating and females isolated for 3–4 years have laid fertile eggs.

The eggs are laid under rotten logs and stumps or in nests dug in the earth. The musk turtles sometimes lay their eggs in muskrat nests. Up to 7 eggs with hard, brittle shells are laid in each clutch. They hatch in 60—90 days, depending on the heat provided by the sun and the decaying vegetation around them. The newly-hatched turtles have shells about 1 in. long. Males mature in 4—7 years and the females in 5—8 years. In captivity mud turtles have lived for 40 years but in the wild they fall prey to several predators; crows attack the adults, while king snakes, raccoons and skunks eat the eggs.

The turtle frame

It is natural to assume that the plastron is no more than a breast plate to protect the underside of a turtle or tortoise, but in some species it is so small that it can offer very little protection. Even so, it still has an important part to play. In all turtles and tortoises the ribs are incorporated into the carapace and the plastron takes over to some extent the work of the ribs in bracing the body and in providing an anchoring surface for the muscles of the shoulders and hips. In the snapping turtle, for instance, in which the plastron is very much reduced, scientists have calculated that this small plastron is just sufficient to give the necessary strength and support to the body. It is much the same in the mud and musk turtles when they are young; they have a soft carapace and a rigid plastron which braces the carapace. As the turtles grow older and the carapace hardens the plastron is freed from this duty. Then, in mud turtles, it develops the hinges which, acting like lids, close over the turtle when it withdraws into its shell so giving it maximum protection from its enemies.

class	**Reptilia**
order	**Testudines**
family	**Trionychidae**
genera & species	***Kinosternon subrubrum*** common mud turtle ***Sternotherus carinatus*** keel-backed musk turtle ***S. odoratus*** common musk turtle others

Crocodile

The crocodiles and their close relatives alligators, caimans and gharials are the sole survivors of the great group of reptiles, the Archosauria, that included the well-known and awe-inspiring dinosaurs. The crocodile family itself includes the dwarf crocodiles and the false gharial as well as the dozen or so species of true crocodiles.

Crocodiles are often distinguished by the shape of the snout. This is long and broad in the Nile crocodile, the best-known species, short in the Indian marsh crocodile or mugger, and long and narrow in the false gharial. The differences between crocodiles and alligators are set out under alligator, page 272.

As with many large, fearsome animals, the size of crocodiles has been exaggerated. There is reliable evidence for the Nile crocodile reaching 20 ft and American and Orinoco crocodiles have measured 23 ft. At the other extreme the Congo dwarf crocodile has never been found to exceed 3 ft 9 in. Now that crocodiles have been hunted too intensively, large ones have become extremely rare.

Cold-blooded lover of warmth

Crocodiles are found in the warmer parts of the world, in Africa, Asia, Australia and America. Unlike alligators, they are often found in brackish water and sometimes they even swim out to sea. Estuarine crocodiles swim between the islands of the Malay Archipelago and stray ones have been found in the Fijis and other remote islands.

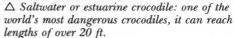

▽ *Smaller relative, different jaw structure: the broad-fronted crocodile of West Africa only grows to 5 — 6 ft and does not attack man.*

△ *Saltwater or estuarine crocodile: one of the world's most dangerous crocodiles, it can reach lengths of over 20 ft.*

Reptiles are said to be cold-blooded because they cannot maintain their body temperatures within fine limits, as can mammals and birds. A reptile's body temperature is usually within a few degrees of that of its surroundings. It cannot shiver to keep warm or sweat to keep cool. Many reptiles, however, can keep their body temperatures from varying too much by following a daily routine to avoid extremes of temperature. Crocodiles do this. They come out of the water at sunrise and lie on the banks basking in the sun. When their bodies have warmed up, they either move into the shade or back into the water, escaping the full strength of the midday sun. Then in the late afternoon they bask again, and return to the water by nightfall. By staying underwater at night they conserve heat, because water holds its heat better than air.

Stones in their stomachs

When crocodiles come out of the water they generally stay near the bank, although occasionally they wander some distance in search of water, and can cause great consternation by appearing in towns. They are generally sluggish, but, considering their bulky bodies and relatively short legs, they are capable of unexpected bursts of speed. They have three distinct gaits. There is a normal walk, with the body

lifted well off the ground with the legs under the body – a gait most unlike the popular conception of a crocodile walking. More familiar is the tobogganing used when dashing into the water. The crocodile slides on its belly, using its legs as paddles. The third method is used by a young crocodile which will occasionally gallop along with the front and back legs working together, like a bounding squirrel.

In the water, crocodiles float very low, with little more than eyes and nostrils showing. They habitually carry several pounds of stones in their stomachs, which help to stabilise their bodies. The stones lie in the stomach, below the centre of gravity and work as a counterpoise to the buoyant lungs. This is particularly useful when the crocodiles are fairly young. At that age they are top heavy and cannot float easily at the surface.

Maneaters: myth and fact

For the first year of their lives, young crocodiles feed on small animals, frogs, dragonflies, crabs and even mosquito larvae. Young crocodiles have been seen cornering the larvae by curving their bodies and tails around them. Larger animals are stalked. The baby crocodile swims stealthily towards its prey then pounces, snapping at it with a sideways movement of the jaws, necessary because the crocodile's eyes are at the side of its head.

As a crocodile grows the amount of insects in its diet falls, and it turns to eating snails and fish. The adult crocodiles continue to catch fish but turn increasingly to trapping mammals and birds. They capture their prey by lying in wait near game trails or waterholes. When a victim approaches the crocodile will seize it and drag it underwater or knock it over with a blow from its tail or head. Once the victim is pulled into the water the crocodile has a definite advantage. Drowning soon stills the victim's struggles, and, grasping a limb in its jaws, the crocodile may roll over and over so that the victim is dismembered.

Crocodiles are well-known as maneaters – but how true is this reputation? The maneating habit varies and it may be that only certain individuals will attack man. In parts of Africa, crocodiles are not regarded as a menace at all, while elsewhere palisades have to be erected at the water's edge to allow the women to fetch water in safety. It seems that crocodiles are likely to be more aggressive when their streams and pools dry up so they cannot escape, or when they are guarding their young.

In the crocodile's nest

The Nile crocodile breeds when 5–10 years old. By this time it is 7–10 ft long. The full-grown males stake out their territories along the banks and share them with younger males and females. They defend the territories by fighting, which may sometimes end in one contestant being killed.

A male crocodile approaches a female

Like an extra for a film on the first amphibious reptiles, a small saltwater crocodile comes ashore in Queensland, Australia. Unlike alligators, crocodiles can be found in brackish waters, estuaries, and swimming out at sea.

crocodile and displays to her by thrashing the water with his snout and tail. They swim in circles with the male on the outside trying to get near her so he can put a forelimb over her body and mate.

Up to 90 eggs are laid during the dry season. They hatch 4 months later, during the rainy season when there are plenty of insects about for the babies to feed on.

The Nile crocodile and the marsh crocodile dig pits 2 ft deep for their nests, but the estuarine crocodile of northern Australia and southeast Asia makes a mound of leaves. The nests are built near water and shade, where the female can guard her brood and keep herself cool. During the incubation period she stays by the nest defending it against enemies, including other crocodiles, although in colonies they sometimes nest only a few yards apart.

The baby crocodiles begin to grunt before hatching. This is the signal for the mother to uncover the nest. The babies climb out and stay near her, yapping if they get lost. They follow her about like ducklings and forage for insects, even climbing trees, and grunting and snapping at one another. They disperse after a few days.

The young Nile crocodiles are about 1 ft long at hatching and for their first 7 years they grow at a rate of about 10 in. a year.

Cannibals

The mother crocodile has to be on her guard all the time as many animals will wait for their chance to eat the eggs or the baby crocodiles. Their main enemy is the monitor lizard. They are bold enough to dig underneath the crocodile as she lies over her nest, and once a male monitor was seen to decoy a crocodile away from the nest while the female stole the eggs. Other crocodiles, herons, mongooses, turtles, eagles and predatory fish all eat baby crocodiles. Adult crocodiles have been killed by lions, elephants, and leopards, and hippopotamuses will attack crocodiles in defence of their young.

Crocodiles are cannibals, so basking groups are always sorted out into parties of equal size and the smaller crocodiles keep well away from the bigger ones.

Crocodile tears

If we say that someone is shedding crocodile tears it means that they are showing grief or sympathy that they do not really mean. The idea that crocodiles are hypocrites is an ancient one, and is described in TH White's translation of a 12th century bestiary: 'Crocodiles lie by night in the water, by day on land, because hypocrites, however luxuriously they live by night, delight to be said to live holily and justly by day.' The hypocrisy seems to be manifested in the form of tears, and malicious or misunderstanding comparisons are made with women's tears. Thus when Desdemona weeps, Othello complains:

'O devil, devil!
If that the earth could teem with woman's tears,
Each drop she falls would prove a crocodile.'

John Hawkins explains crocodile's tears as meaning 'that as the Crocodile when he

△ Hatching out: while still in the egg, baby Nile crocodiles grunt a signal to the mother to uncover the nest.

▽ Prelude to feeding: prey trapped in its vice-like jaws, a crocodile returns to the water where it will take its meal at leisure.

crieth, goeth then about most to deceive, so doth a woman commonly when she weepeth'. The deception practised by the 'cruell craftie crocodile' is that it lures unwary travellers into drawing near to find out what is the matter.

The story, like many myths and legends, may have a basis of truth. It could have sprung from the plaintive howling that crocodiles make. Crocodiles, however, do have tear glands to keep their eyes moist and tears, or water trapped in their lids, may run from the corners of their eyes. This, with the permanent grin of their jaws, could have led to their legendary reputation as hypocrites.

class	**Reptilia**
order	**Crocodilia**
family	**Crocodylidae**
genera & species	***Crocodylus niloticus*** *Nile crocodile*
	C. porosus *estuarine crocodile*
	C. palustris *marsh crocodile*
	Osteolaemus *dwarf crocodiles*
	Tomistoma schlegeli *false gharial*

▷ *'African crocodiles at home': a romanticized print shows waterfowl scattering in panic from the threat of an evil-looking flock of crocodiles.*

▽ *Although in parts of Africa crocodiles are not regarded as maneaters, the Nile crocodile has a very bad reputation. One crocodile (15ft 3ins long) shot in the Kihange River, Central Africa, was reported to have killed 400 people over the years.*

When annoyed, alligators open their vast jaws and roar. Male alligators also roar during their quarrels in the breeding season and to attract females.

Alligator

Two species of reptiles which, with the caimans, belong to a family closely related to the crocodiles. Alligators and crocodiles look extremely alike: the main distinguishing feature is the teeth.
In a crocodile the teeth in the upper and lower jaws are in line, but in the alligator, when its mouth is shut, the upper teeth lie outside the lower. In both animals the fourth lower tooth on each side is perceptibly larger than the rest: in the crocodile this tooth fits into a notch in the upper jaw and is visible when the mouth is closed, whereas in the alligator, with the lower teeth inside the upper, it fits into a pit in the upper jaw and is lost to sight when the mouth is shut. In addition, the alligator's head is broader and shorter and the snout consequently blunter. Otherwise, especially in their adaptations to an aquatic life, alligators are very similar to crocodiles.

One of the two species is found in North America, the other in China. The Chinese alligator averages a little over 4 ft in length and has no webs between the toes. The American alligator is much larger, with a maximum recorded length of 19 ft 2 in.
This length, however, is seldom attained nowadays because the American alligator has been killed off for the sake of its skin; whenever there is intense persecution of an animal the larger ones are quickly

eliminated and the average size of the remainder drops slowly as persecution proceeds.

*It is sheer accident that two such similar reptiles as the alligator and the crocodile should so early have been given different common names. The reason is that when the Spanish seamen, who had presumably no knowledge of crocodiles, first saw large reptiles in the Central American rivers, they spoke of them as lizards – **el largato** in Spanish. The English sailors who followed later adopted the Spanish name but ran the two into one to make 'allagarter' – which was later further corrupted to 'alligator'.*

Long lazy life
Alligators are more sluggish than crocodiles; this may possibly have an effect on their longevity. There is a record of an American alligator living for 56 years. They spend most of their time basking on river banks.

The American alligator is restricted to the south-eastern United States and does not penetrate further north than latitude 35. The Chinese alligator is found only in the Yangtse River basin.

Meat eaters
Alligators' food changes with age. The young feed on insects and on those crustaceans generally known as freshwater shrimps. As they grow older they eat frogs, snakes and fish; mature adults live mainly on fish but will catch muskrats and small mammals that go down to the water's edge to drink. They also take a certain amount of waterfowl. Very large alligators may

occasionally pull large mammals such as deer or cows down into the water and drown them.

Alligator builds a nest
It seems that the female alligator plays the more active role in courtship and territorial defence. The males apparently spend much of the breeding season quarrelling among themselves, roaring and fighting and injuring each other. The roaring attracts the females to the males, as does a musky secretion from glands in the male's throat and cloaca. Courtship takes place usually at night, the pair swimming round faster and faster and finally mating in the water with jaws interlocked and the male's body arched over the female's.

A large nest-mound is made for the reception of the eggs. The female scoops up mud in her jaws and mixes it with decaying vegetation; the mixture is then deposited on the nest site until a mound 3 ft high is made. The eggs are hard-shelled and number 15–80; they are laid in a depression in the top of the mound and covered with more vegetation. The female remains by the eggs until they hatch 2–3 months later, incubated by the heat of the nest's rotting vegetation.

The hatchling alligators peep loudly and the female removes the layer of vegetation over the nest to help them escape. Baby alligators are 8 in. long when first hatched and grow 1 ft a year, reaching maturity at 6 years.

The biter bitten
Young alligators fall an easy prey to carnivorous fish, birds and mammals, and at all stages of growth they are attacked and eaten

by larger alligators. This natural predation was, in the past, just sufficient to keep the numbers of alligator populations steady. Then came the fashion for making women's shoes, handbags and other ornamental goods of alligator skin. So long as these articles remain in fashion and command a high price, men will be prepared to risk both the imprisonment consequent on the laws passed to protect alligators and the attacks of the alligators themselves.

There is also another commercial interest, detrimental both to the alligator and to the fashion industry. For, while the fashion for skins from larger individuals shows no sign of abating, a fashion for alligator pets also persists—though it may have dropped in intensity since its inception. Baby alligators are still being netted in large numbers for the pet shops, but—as so commonly happens with pets taken from the wild—not all those caught are eventually sold. Of a consignment of 1,000 hatchlings that reached New York City in 1967, 200 were already dead and putrefying, and many others were in a sorry condition and unlikely to survive.

In addition to persecution, land drainage has seriously affected the numbers of the American alligator. The Chinese alligator is an even worse case. Its flesh is eaten and the various parts of its body are used as charms, aphrodisiacs and for their supposed medicinal properties. The New York Zoological Park has recently announced plans to try and breed the Chinese alligator and so protect it from complete extermination.

Unwanted pets

The fashion for alligator pets has its disadvantages for owners as well as the alligator populations. Even setting aside the largest recorded lengths for the American species of 19 ft upwards, it still achieves too large a size to be convenient in the modern flat, and people who invest in an alligator often find it necessary to dispose of it. Zoos have proved unable to deal with the quantity offered them—Brookfield Zoo near Chicago has built up an enormous herd from unwanted pets—and it is widely said that unfortunate alligators are disposed of in such a way that they end up in the sewers. One result of this is that every now and then, despite official denials, reports have appeared in the press to the effect that the sewers of New York are teeming with alligators that prey on the rats and terrorise the sewermen.

△ A female alligator builds a nest of rotting vegetation for her clutch of 15—80 eggs. She stays for 2—3 months by the nest until they hatch.

▽ Alligators spend much of their time basking on the banks of jungle rivers. Here they have made a lagoon by their thrashing about.

class	**Reptilia**
order	**Crocodilia**
family	**Alligatoridae**
genus & species	***Alligator mississipiensis*** American alligator
	A. sinensis Chinese alligator

273

Gecko

Geckos form a family of lizards noted for the large number of species, the structure of their feet, their voices, the differences in the shape of their tails, and for the ease with which some of them will live in houses. The smallest is $1\frac{1}{3}$ in. long; the largest—the tokay—may be 14 in. long.

Geckos are found in all warm countries: 41 species in Africa, 50 in Madagascar, about 50 in Australia, the same in the West Indies, with others in southern and southeast Asia, Indonesia, the Pacific islands and New Zealand, and South America. There are geckos in the desert regions of Mexico and southern California. Several have been introduced into Florida from the Caribbean islands. Spain and Dalmatia, in southern Europe, have the same wall gecko as North Africa.

A liking for houses

The majority of geckos live in trees, some live among rocks, others live on the sandy ground of deserts. Tree geckos find in human habitations conditions similar to, or better than, those of their natural habitat: natural crevices in which to rest or take refuge and plenty of insects, especially at night when insects are attracted to lights. Because geckos can cling to walls or hang upside-down from ceilings they can take full advantage of these common insect resting places, and so many of them are now known as house geckos.

Hooked to the ceiling

Most geckos can cling to smooth surfaces. Their toes may be broad or expanded at the tips with flaps of skin (lamellae) arranged transversely or fanwise. The undersides of the toes bear pads furnished with numerous microscopic hook-like bristles that catch in slight irregularities, even in the surface of glass, or have bristles ending in minute suckers. So a gecko can cling to all but the most highly polished surfaces. The hooks are directed backwards and downwards and to disengage them the toe must be lifted upwards from the tip. As a result, a gecko running up a tree or a wall or along a ceiling must curl and uncurl its toes at each step with a speed faster than the eye can follow. Some of the hooks are so small the high power of a microscope is needed to see them, yet a single toe armed with numbers of these incredibly small hooks can support several times the weight of a gecko's body. In addition to the bristles, most species have the usual claw at the tip of the toe which also can be used in clinging. In one species there are microscopic hooks on the tip of the tail which enable the animal to cling.

△ *Close pursuit. As firm as the flies it is hunting, a diurnal gecko* **Phelsuma vinsoni** *pauses on a vertical tree-trunk, unaware of the apparent impossibility of its position.*
▷ *Living crampons. Geckos get a grip from tiny hooks in the flaps of skin on their feet.*
▷▷ *After partial loss, regrowth and healing, the result is a three-tailed gecko.*

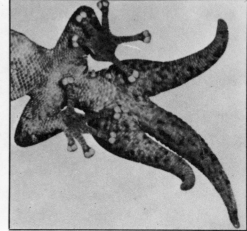

Leaf-like tail

The tail is long and tapering, rounded or slightly flattened and fringed with scales, according to the species, or it may be flattened and leaf-like. A South American gecko has a swollen turnip-shaped tail. It has been named *Thecadactylus rapicaudus* (*rapi* for turnip, *caudus* for tail). The flying gecko of southeast Asia has a leaf-like tail, a wide flap of skin along each flank, a narrow flap along each side of the head and flaps along the hind margins of the limbs. Should the gecko fall it spreads its limbs, the flaps spread and the reptile parachutes safely down.

Geckos can throw off their tails, like the more familiar lizards, and grow new ones. In some species 40% have re-grown tails.

Sometimes the tail is incompletely thrown and hangs by a strip of skin. As a new tail grows the old one heals and a 2-tailed gecko results. Even 3-tailed geckos have been seen. Temperature is important in growing a new tail. It has been found that when the wall gecko of southern Europe and North Africa grows a new tail with the air temperature at 28°C/82°F it is short and covered with large overlapping scales. With the temperature around 35°C/95°F the new tail is long and is covered with small scales.

Cat-like eyes

One difference between snakes and lizards is that the former have no eyelids. In most geckos the eyelids are permanently joined and there is a transparent window in the

lower lid. The few geckos that are active by day have rounded pupils to the eyes. The rest are active by night and have vertical slit-pupils like cats. In some species the sides of the pupils are lobed or notched in four places, and when the pupils contract they leave four apertures, the size of pinholes each one of which will focus the image onto the retina.

Surprisingly small clutches

All geckos except for a few species in New Zealand, which bear live young, lay eggs with a tough white shell. Usually there

are two in a clutch, sometimes only one. The eggs are laid under bark or under stones and take several months to hatch.

Harmless creatures

Geckos eat only insects. They are harmless and wholly beneficial to man, yet among the people of Africa, South America, Malaysia and the aboriginals of Australia there are widespread beliefs that their bite makes them dangerous to handle. Possibly such beliefs spring from some of the more remarkable species, like the gecko that stalks insects as a cat does a mouse, even lashing its tail from side to side just before the final pounce. Then there are the web-footed geckos living on the sand dunes of Southwest Africa. They not only use the webbed feet

to run over loose sand but also to burrow. They scrape the sand away with the forefoot of one side and shovel it back with the hindfoot of the same side while balancing on the feet of the other side. Then they change over. They walk with the body raised high and the tail held up and arched.

One web-footed gecko has a delicate beauty. It is pinkish-brown with a lemon yellow stripe along its flank. Its eye has brilliant yellow lids, the iris is black, patterned with gold and coppery tints, while the edges of the vertical pupil are chalky white. Its skin is so transparent the spine and some internal organs can be seen clearly. In *African Wild Life*, GK Brain claims its two ear openings are almost in direct connection; by looking into one earhole light coming in

△ *A regrown tail shows that, despite excellent camouflage, only desperate measures saved this gecko's life.*

through the other can be seen.

class	**Reptilia**
order	**Squamata**
suborder	**Sauria**
family	**Gekkonidae**
genus & species	*Gekko gecko others*

△ *Defiance: a cornered lizard unfurls its frill.*

Frilled lizard

One of the so-called dragons of Australia, the frilled lizard grows to about 3 ft long, with a slender body and long tail. It is pale brown, either uniformly coloured or with patches of yellow and darker brown. Its most conspicuous feature is the frill around the throat, like the ruff fashionable in Europe in the Middle Ages.

Apart from its size the only remarkable thing about this lizard is its frill. Normally this lies folded over the shoulders like a cape. It is a large area of skin supported by cartilaginous rods from the tongue bone which act like the ribs of an umbrella. In moments of excitement, muscles pulling on these raise the frill to 8 in. or more across, about as wide as the length of the head and body together.

It lives mainly in sandy semi-dry areas of northern and northeastern Australia.

Hindleg sprinter

The frilled lizard lives in rough-barked trees, coming to the ground after rainstorms, to feed. When disturbed on the ground it runs on its hindlegs with the frill laid back over the shoulders, tail raised, and the forelegs held close into the body. It may sprint for a considerable distance, or it may seek safety by climbing a tree. When brought to bay it turns, opens its mouth wide and extends its frill. The best description of what happens next is given by Harry Frauca in *The Book of Australian Wild Life*. It does not raise its tail, as it has often been reported to do, and as some other similar lizards are known to do, but keeps it flat on the ground. It sways from side to side and with its open mouth, coloured dark blue inside edged by pinkish yellow, surrounded by the greenish-yellow frill splashed with red, brown, white and black, it looks like a large flower among broad leaves. The colours of the lizard vary from one region to another. In Queensland the general colour is a sombre grey, in the Northern Territory it is pinkish, often with a black chest and throat. The colours of the mouth and frill also vary.

The open mouth and spread frill are a warning display. If the warning is ignored it passes to an aggressive display. The lizard steps boldly towards the intruder, keeping its mouth open and frill fully extended, and from the mouth comes a low hiss. The remarkable thing is that people who know very well the lizard can do nothing to harm them, tend nevertheless to be intimidated by all this show. Even a dog used to attacking larger lizards will retreat before it.

Meals of ants and eggs

The frilled lizard eats insects, including large quantities of ants, as well as spiders and small mammals. It is also said to be an egg thief. One of the many difficulties found in keeping this animal in captivity is that of getting enough of the right kind of food. In 1893, when the time it took to travel from Australia to Great Britain was much longer than it is today, the naturalist W Saville Kent brought a frilled lizard to London, the first to reach Europe alive. When it was exhibited before an audience of learned gentlemen one eminent zoologist is said to have followed it, in his excitement, on hands and knees, to watch it careering round on its hind legs and displaying its frill. Unfortunately, there is no record of how Saville Kent managed to feed his pet, but, like many reptiles, the frilled lizard can probably go without food for months.

Umbrella trick

Neither does history record whether any of the learned gentlemen noticed a comparison between the lizard and a lady. At that time ladies carried parasols and it was not uncommon for a lady, confronted by a cow as she crossed a field, to frighten the cow away by suddenly opening her parasol in its face. Konrad Lorenz, in *King Solomon's Ring*, tells how his wife kept geese from devastating her newly-planted flower beds. She carried a large scarlet umbrella and this she would suddenly unfold at the geese, with a jerk, causing the geese to take to the air with a thundering of wings. It is almost instinctive for a woman carrying an umbrella to use it in this way against a powerful and persistent opponent. It is a matter of no small interest to find that this same effective defence should have been evolved by a lizard.

class	**Reptilia**
order	**Squamata**
suborder	**Sauria**
family	**Agamidae**
genus & species	***Chlamydosaurus kingii***

Frilled lizard *(Chlamydosaurus kingii)*

Moloch

Moloch was a Canaanite god to whom children were sacrificed and was also one of Milton's devils. It is therefore not surprising that the name should have been given to this uncouth Australian relative of the colourful agama lizards. The moloch is, however, much maligned by its name as it is a most inoffensive lizard, yet the Australian aborigines treat it with care as they believe it is harmful. The alternative names of the moloch are mountain devil or thorny devil. The latter is the most descriptive. The moloch is covered with thorn-like spikes over its head, body, tail and legs. They are triangular in section and as pointed as any rose thorn. The lizard's total length is 6 in. and the body is round, so a moloch looks like a walking horse chestnut burr.

Molochs are found in many parts of South and Western Australia and in Northern Territory.

Lizard with a hump

Molochs are prickly lizards that move slowly even when in a hurry. When frightened they tuck their heads between their front legs, presenting a thorny hump that stands on the back of the neck. It is, how-

△ *An advancing moloch looms up over a fallen tree trunk.*
▽ *A walking thorn bush. The moloch, harmless in itself, is a mass of spikes to any aggressor.*

ever, difficult to see how this can enhance the general prickly reception a predator gets. Another suggested function for the hump was that it is a food store, but as it does not shrink when a moloch goes hungry this seems unlikely.

Molochs live in deserts and semi-desert regions and, as with so many other desert animals, although they are active by day their behaviour is adapted to avoid the worst of the sun's heat. They can also change colour but this ability is often exaggerated. When transferred from one background to another they change colour slowly, taking several minutes. Against a sandy background a moloch may be a dull light grey but against other backgrounds it is sometimes prettily coloured with orange, chestnut and black markings.

Painstaking ant eaters

A favoured method of feeding is for a moloch to sit by a trail of ants, flicking them up with its tongue as they run past. It has been estimated that they pick up 30—45 ants a minute, and that a moloch eats 1—5 thousand ants at one sitting, each one being picked up separately, so one meal takes a long time. Molochs eat little else but ants, taking only those without stings. Their jaws are weak but their teeth have complex serrated crowns which are well suited for crushing the hard outer skeletons of ants so their soft interiors can be digested.

Outsize eggs

The breeding habits of molochs are known from those that have laid eggs while being kept in captivity. Mating takes place in October and November, and eggs are laid in January. The maximum recorded clutch was 10 eggs, each about 1 in. long and $\frac{1}{2}$ in. wide—enormous eggs to be produced by a fairly small lizard like the moloch.

Before laying eggs the female moloch spends 2−3 days digging a nest in soft sandy soil. She does this according to a set pattern. Having started a hole and thrown out a small pile she removes the surplus by scraping earth backwards from the top, and gradually digs her way forwards into the hole. When she has reached the 'pit face' and dug out more soil she turns and goes back to the pile outside and starts again. In this way she continually throws the soil backwards, so the entrance and the tunnel are kept clear. The finished tunnel is 2 ft long, running downwards and ending 10 in. below the surface. It takes a long time to dig be-

cause the moloch often stops to rest. Having completed her task she lays her eggs at the bottom of the tunnel and fills it up again, leaving an air cavity around the eggs so the developing molochs can breathe. When the tunnel has been completely filled, the surface is levelled and swept so the entrance is concealed. The moloch then leaves the eggs to develop and the young to emerge on their own. Hatching takes place 10−12 weeks later and the young molochs, $2\frac{1}{4}$ in. long, dig their way out and disperse.

Dew-trap skin

It has been said that molochs can absorb water through their skin, because a drop of water placed on the back of one of them rapidly disappears. If this were so, the skin would be most unusual, because at the same time it must prevent water from leaking out, otherwise molochs would not be able to live in deserts. It is now known that the drop disappears because it spreads rapidly by flowing along minute grooves in the skin.

△ *Tiny grooves spread any moisture all over its body extremely quickly.*
△△ *A moloch spends a long time over its meal, picking each ant up singly. This meal may last it for several weeks.*

If the tip of the tail is dipped into water the whole of the skin becomes wet in a few seconds. When the water reaches its lips the moloch starts to sip it. No one has studied the use of this mechanism but it may be a way of collecting dew, forming on the moloch's body during the cold desert night.

class	**Reptilia**
order	**Squamata**
suborder	**Sauria**
family	**Agamidae**
genus & species	*Moloch horridus*

Chameleon

The chameleons are a family of lizards renowned for several unusual features. The body is high in proportion to the length and is flattened from side to side. The tail in most species is prehensile, is often held in a tight coil, and can be wrapped round a twig for extra grip. The toes of each foot are joined, three on the inside of the front feet and on the outside of the hindfeet, resulting in feet like pairs of tongs that can give a tenacious grip on a perch. Above all, a chameleon is remembered for three things: its ability to change colour, its eyes set in turrets that can move independently of each other, and its highly extensible tongue which can be shot out at speed to a length greater than the chameleon's head and body. To add to their bizarre form, some species have rows of tubercles down the back or a 'helmet' or casque like the flap-necked chameleon or horns like Jackson's chameleon.

A few species grow to 2 ft long, while dwarf species measure less than 2 in.

There are about 80 species of chameleon most of which live in Africa south of the Sahara and including Madagascar. One species, the common chameleon, ranges from the Middle East along the coast of North Africa to southern Spain. Two others live in the southern end of the Arabian peninsula and a third in India and Sri Lanka.

Chameleons live in slow motion

Chameleons live mainly in forests, and seem to spend most of their time virtually rooted to the spot, the only movement being of the eyes, each independently sweeping from side to side searching for food or danger. When they move they creep slowly along a twig. Sloth-like, a fore foot is released on one side and the hind foot on the other, and both are slowly moved forward to renew their grip on the twig while, equally stealthily, the other two advance. Although most chameleons keep to the trees as much as possible, the stump-tailed chameleons can often be found on the ground.

Periodically chameleons shed their skins. Before it comes off the old skin comes away from the new skin under it, leaving an air-filled gap that gives the chameleon a pale, translucent appearance as if it were neatly wrapped in polythene. Then the old skin splits, first just behind the head, and chunks of it flake off exposing the brilliant new skin.

Extensible tongue

Chameleons eat the usual food of small reptiles, that is, insects and other small invertebrates, but the larger species will also catch small birds, lizards and mammals. The similarity with other reptiles ends here, for the method of capture is unique except in frogs and toads. Chameleons capture their prey by shooting out their long tongue, trapping the victim on the tip and carrying it back to the mouth. The whole

△ Portrait of **Chamaeleo bitaeniatus** taken on Mt Elgon, Kenya. It lives above 9 000 ft.

◁ A chameleon in the later stages of shedding its skin. A new skin has first grown under the old. Notice that it even sheds the skin on its eyelids.

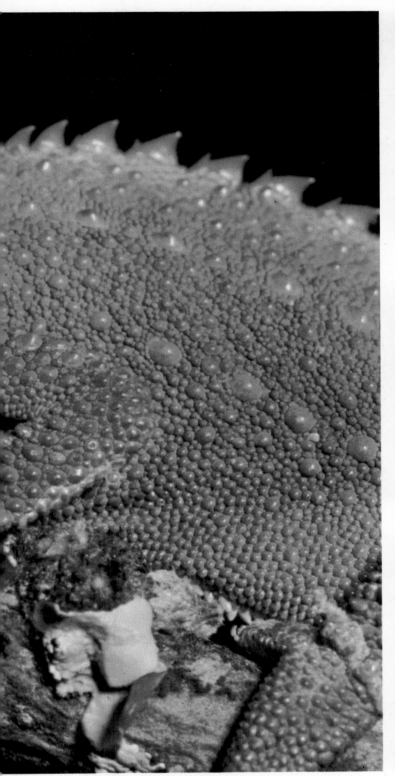

△ *Stage one: lining up on the target with tongue protruding. Note the spider in the top right corner.*
▽ *Stage two: muscles shoot the tongue to its full extent.*

▽ *Stage three: muscles contract, withdrawing the tongue. Despite its speed, the spider was quicker!*

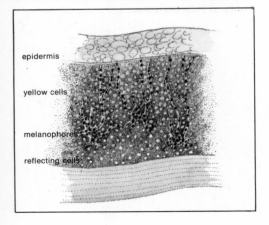

epidermis

yellow cells

melanophores

reflecting cells

◁ *Simplified diagram of section through skin: colour change is mainly due to melanophores moving dark pigment into or out of upper layers.*
▷ *Catapult mechanism of the chameleon's tongue: special bone with its own muscles pushes tongue forward and circular muscles squeeze it out. Longitudinal muscles withdraw the tongue.*

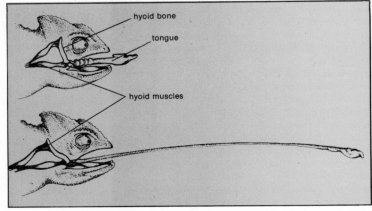

hyoid bone

tongue

hyoid muscles

action is so rapid that high-speed photography is needed to show the mechanism at work. By using a ciné camera it has been found that a 5½ in. tongue can be extended in $\frac{1}{16}$ second and retracted in $\frac{1}{4}$ second. Without such aids all one sees is the chameleon watching its prey from its perch, or slowly edging towards it, for chameleons only take sitting prey. When in range it directs both eyes at its victim and rocks from side to side, improving its stereoscopic vision and range-finding capacity by looking at the target from different angles. While doing this the tip of the tongue protrudes from the mouth like a wad of chewing gum, then suddenly the insect disappears from its perch and is seen to be crushed in the chameleon's jaws. Young ones begin eating insects when a day old, and with a little practice become expert.

How the chameleon shoots out its tongue has been deduced by a careful study of its anatomy. Two mechanisms throw the tongue forward, both of them activated by powerful muscles. At the back of the jaw lies a V-shaped bone with the point of the V pointing backwards. Attached to this bone by a flexible joint is the tongue bone, over which the tongue fits like a glove on a finger. When the chameleon is about to shoot the V-bone is moved forward slightly to push the tip of the tongue out of the mouth. Then, the circular muscles in the thick tip of the tongue contract violently so that the tongue is forced out in the same way as an orange pip squeezed between the fingers, and simultaneously the V-bone is thrust further forward, giving added impetus.

The end of the tongue is sticky with saliva but an insect can settle on a chameleon's head and walk across its protruding tongue with no difficulty. On the other hand some people who have kept chameleons as pets report that the end of the tongue does feel adhesive, but this may be due to the minute hooks or hairs or other rougheninings of its surface. Finally, there are photographs that show the tongue apparently grasping an insect. It may be that a combination of all three may be operating as in toads.

Breeding poses problems

Male chameleons hold territories which they guard against other males, keeping them out by bluff. The lungs of chameleons have branches spreading through the body and by inflating its lungs a chameleon can blow itself to a most impressive size. Females, of course, are allowed to enter the territories and the males chase after them and mate with them, unless dissuaded by a female already pregnant.

Some chameleons lay eggs, others bear their young alive. The former course has some disadvantages for chameleons lay up to 50 eggs in a clutch, each has a diameter of perhaps ½ in. Places to hide such a large clutch must be rare in a tree and the chameleon, who is bulky and ungainly when carrying her eggs, has to climb down the tree and dig a hole in the ground. A common South African chameleon has been described as digging the hole with her head and front feet, pushing the loose soil away with her hind feet. It takes a long time but eventually she has a hole nearly the length of the body. She then backs into it and lays

Independently-swivelling eyes and palsied gait.

her eggs, pressing each one into place with her hind legs. When she has finished she fills in the hole, tamps it down, camouflages it with sticks and pieces of grass and leaves it. In due course the young hatch out and fight their way to the surface.

Other chameleons bear their young alive. Before the birth the female's body becomes greatly distended. The young are born in a translucent membrane. As each one is due the mother presses her cloaca against the twig on which she is perching and the membrane sticks to it. After a short interval the baby chameleon struggles out and walks off down the twig. The mother takes no more interest in her offspring, except that, if she is very hungry, she may eat them. The young start to feed when a day old, and with a little practice become expert at catching insects.

Quick colour change

Although other reptiles, as well as many fish and squid, can change colour, it is the chameleon that is renowned as a quick change artist. This is epitomised by the story of the chameleon put on a red cloth that changed to red, then when put on a green cloth turned to green, but had an apoplectic stroke when placed on a Scottish tartan. This greatly exaggerates the chameleon's power of colour change. The truth is that most species of chameleon have a basic colour and pattern that suits their particular habitat and do not really change colour to resemble the background but in response to

light intensity, temperature, or emotional state. Thus, colour change serves two purposes: to camouflage the chameleon and to act as a signal telling other chameleons its mood. An angry chameleon, for instance, goes black with rage. How the colour change is controlled is still not properly known. There is evidence for control by nerves and also by the secretion from the brain of chemicals which act on the colour cells; probably both act in different circumstances.

What is better known is the mechanics of colour change. The specialised colour cells lie under the transparent skin in four layers. The outermost is made up of xanthophores or yellow-bearers, together with erythrophores, the red-bearers. Under this layer are two reflecting layers, one reflecting blue light, the other white light. Beneath is the most important, and most complicated, layer of melanophores. These contain a dark brown pigment called melanin, the same substance that colours human skin brown or black. The main body of each melanophore lies under the reflecting layers but it sends tentacle-like arms up through the other layers.

To alter the colour of the skin, the colour cells alter in size, so that by variation of the amounts of yellow, red and dark brown, different colours are produced by mixing. The reflecting layers modify these effects. When the blue layer is under yellow cells, green is produced and where the blue layer is missing, light reflected from the white layer enhances the yellow or red coloration. The melanophores control the shading of the colours. When the colours are bright all the melanin is concentrated in the bodies of the melanophores. If the melanin spreads along the 'tentacles' to obscure the white layer, greens and reds become darker and if the melanin is dispersed completely, the chameleon becomes dark brown.

class	**Reptilia**
order	**Squamata**
suborder	**Sauria**
family	**Chamaeleontidae**
genera & species	***Chamaeleo chamaeleon*** common chameleon ***C. dilepis*** flap necked chameleon ***C. oweni*** three horned chameleon ***C. jacksoni*** Jackson's chameleon ***Brookesia spp.*** stump tailed chameleons others

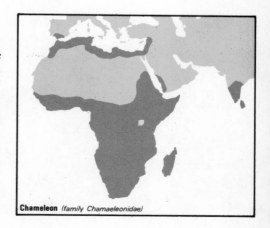
Chameleon (family Chamaeleonidae)

Iguana

The iguana family contains lizards such as the anole, the basilisk, the horned toad and many others, some of which are called iguanas in everyday English. The marine iguana is discussed under a separate heading; here we are dealing with the green iguana, the ground iguana, the land iguanas and the desert iguana or crested lizard.

The ground iguana is one of the most primitive members of the family. It has a crest like the teeth in a comb running down its back starting behind the head and petering out in the middle of the heavy tail.

One kind, the rhinoceros iguana, has two or three hornlike scales on its head and a large swelling on either side of the chin. Ground iguanas reach a length of 4 ft, 2 ft shorter than the green iguana which has been introduced to the Virgin Isles and the Lesser Antilles where it has driven out the ground iguana. The native home of the green iguana is Central and northern South America. It is pale green in colour, has a crest similar to that of the ground iguana and an erectable sac under the throat. The males are larger than the females, their crests are longer and their bodies are more orange or yellow compared with the females' light green. The males

△ Flowers on the menu: although it eats mainly insects when young, this green iguana seems to be interested in the more adult diet of tender young buds. They often clamber in trees.

also have a row of pores on the underside of each thigh, whose function is unknown.

The desert iguana lives in the deserts of North America. It measures 1 ft and is cream coloured with brown or black lines and spots. The land iguana of the Galapagos islands grows up to 5 ft. It is yellow with brown spots on the sides and legs.

High diver

The green iguana is an agile climber and adults are rarely found far from the trees of the tropical forests in which they live. It can scramble from one tree to another providing the twigs are interlaced to give reasonable support for iguanas cannot leap far. Green iguanas will, however, throw themselves from a branch 40—50 ft up and land on the ground unhurt, sprinting away to the undergrowth with barely a pause for breath. For an animal that appears so clumsy, with a heavy tail and legs splayed sideways, an iguana is remarkably fast and is extremely difficult to catch. Its reflexes are very rapid and unless one has nets the only way to catch an iguana is to throw oneself at it and even then a fullgrown iguana will be very hard to hold, as it can inflict nasty bites and scratches. Iguanas often take refuge in water and their favourite haunts are in trees overhanging pools and rivers. If disturbed they leap from the branch where they were lying and dive into the water. They swim underwater, propelling themselves with their tails, and surface under cover of vegetation along the bank.

The green iguana comes down to the ground in cold weather and hides under logs or in holes, but the other iguanas are usually ground-living and only occasionally climb trees. The desert iguana is a very fast runner and races about on its hindlegs.

Vegetarian lizards

As adults green iguanas eat a variety of plant foods, including young shoots, fruits, flowers and leaves, but the young ones also eat insects. Other iguanas are also vegetarian. The desert iguana prefers the yellow-flowered creosote bush but also eats other flowers, and after the flowering season is over it eats insects and carrion. Land iguanas feed on cactus and the larger species eat small rodents.

Eggs need constant temperature

Male land iguanas of the Galapagos form territories which they defend against other males. Each keeps watch from a rock and if another male intrudes he climbs down from his vantage point, walks slowly over to his rival and displays at him, pointing his snout at the sky and jerking his head up and down. If this does not scare the intruder into running away a fight breaks out, each trying to grab the loose skin on the other's flanks.

The female land iguanas live in the same burrows as their mates or in separate burrows alongside. Iguanas generally lay their eggs in nests well separated from each other but on a small island in Panama green iguanas were found nesting in great numbers close together on a sandy beach. Each female spent up to 2 weeks on the shore. For the first few days she probed the sand and dug small holes seeking a suitable site. Then she dug a large burrow 1—2 yd long and 2—3 ft deep. Because the beach was so crowded some were seen digging up other nests and scattering the eggs. Eggs were laid at the bottom of the burrow which was

▷ *The Barrington Island iguana of the Galapagos* **Conolophus pallidus**. *Local people prize its flesh, goats destroy its home.*

filled in afterwards. The females spent some time filling the hole and at the same time filling in adjacent holes. Sometimes this meant filling in the burrows of other females who might be trapped and buried.

The green iguana lays 20—70 eggs in a clutch. The eggs are spherical, white and about 1½ in. diameter. They hatch in 3 months and it has been found that an almost constant temperature is needed for their development. A few degrees too high or too low and they fail to hatch. Although the female abandons her eggs after they are laid she ensures their survival by burying them in a suitable part of the beach. She chooses a spot where the temperature fluctuates only 1°—2° either side of 30°C/ 86°F. The young iguanas measure about 10 in. when they hatch and grow to 3 ft in one year.

Fooling the iguanas

Man and his domestic animals are the iguanas' worst enemies. Their flesh is relished in many parts of the world. Hawks are also serious enemies, for they catch iguanas as they lie basking in trees. In parts of South America iguanas are hunted by men imitating the screams of hawks. The iguanas' reaction to the cries is to 'freeze' and they are then easily caught. Snakes also hunt iguanas; a 6 ft boa constrictor has been found with an adult green iguana in its stomach.

Vanishing iguanas

When Charles Darwin visited the Galapagos islands in 1835 land iguanas were extremely abundant. Darwin wrote 'I cannot give a more forcible proof of their numbers than by stating that when we were left at James Island, we could not for some time find a spot free from their burrows to pitch our single tent.' Since then man has settled on the island, bringing with him dogs, cats, pigs, rats, goats and other animals and the iguana population is now a fraction of its former size. On some islands, however, where there are no goats, there are still large numbers of iguanas. The link between goats and iguanas is that goats strip the vegetation, depriving iguanas of cover. Some islands seem to be populated by adult iguanas only. They can survive in the open but young iguanas need cover to protect them from the Galapagos hawk. Without this cover they are killed off, and when the old lizards die there will be none left.

class	**Reptilia**	
order	**Squamata**	
suborder	**Sauria**	
family	**Iguanidae**	
genera & species	***Conolophus subcristatus*** land iguana	
	Cyclura cornuta rhinoceros iguana	
	Dipsosaurus dorsalis desert iguana	
	Iguana iguana green iguana	

Marine iguana

The marine iguana is unique in its way of life, being the only truly marine lizard. It is found only in the Galapagos Islands, some 600 miles west of Ecuador. Because of its exceptional home, it is of great interest, but physically it is not so exciting. The accounts of early visitors to the Galapagos testify to the marine iguana's ugly appearance. One account describes them as having the most hideous appearance imaginable, and the same author, a captain of the Royal Navy, says that 'so disgusting is their appearance that no one on board could be prevailed on, to take them as food'. Marine iguanas grow up to 4 ft long. They have blunt snouts, heavy bodies, clumsy-looking legs with long toes and a crest that runs from the neck to the tail. The tail is flattened sideways and is used for swimming. Most marine iguanas are black or very dark grey, but on Hood Island at the south of the Galapagos Archipelago their bodies are mottled with black, orange and red and their front legs and crests are green.

Lizard heaps

Outside the breeding season, when they are not feeding at sea, marine iguanas gather in tight bunches, sometimes even piling on top of each other. They lie on the lava fields that are prominent but unpleasant features of the Galapagos. In the heat of the day they seek shelter under boulders, in crevices or in the shade of mangroves. At the beginning of the breeding season, the males establish small territories, so small that one iguana may be on top of a boulder while another lies at the foot. Fights occasionally break out but disputes are generally settled by displays. A male marine iguana threatens an intruder by raising itself on stiff legs and bobbing its head with mouth agape, showing a red lining. If this does not deter an intruder, the owner of the territory advances and a butting match takes place. The two push with their bony heads until one gives way and retreats.

While marine iguanas are basking, large red crabs will walk over them, pausing every now and then to pull at the iguanas' skin. The lizards do not resent this pulling and pinching and with good reason, because the crabs are removing ticks from their skin. Darwin's finches (named after Charles Darwin) perform the same service.

▽ 'It's a hideous looking creature of a dirty black colour, stupid and sluggish in its movements. The usual length of a fullgrown one is about a yard, some even 4 ft long.'
Voyage of HMS Beagle, Charles Darwin 1890.

Diving for a living

As the tide goes down the marine iguanas take to the water and eat the algae exposed on the reefs and shores. They cling to the rocks with their sharp claws, so as not to be dislodged by the surf, and slowly work their way over the rocks tearing strands of algae by gripping them in the sides of their mouths and twisting to wrench them off. At intervals they pause to swallow and rest. Some marine iguanas swim out beyond the surf and dive to feed on the seabed. They have been recorded as feeding at depths of 35 ft but usually they stay at about 15 ft. The length of each dive is about 15–20 minutes but they can stay under for much longer. When Darwin visited the Galapagos in HMS *Beagle* he noted that a sailor tried to drown one by sinking it with a heavy weight. An hour later it was drawn back to the surface and found to be quite active.

Marine iguanas normally eat nothing but marine algae. Unusual exceptions are the marine iguanas that haunt the home of Carl Angermeyer. He has trained them to come at his whistle to be fed on raw goat meat, rice and oatmeal.

Easy courtship

When the males have formed their territories, the females join them. They are free to move from one territory to another but the males soon gather harems of females around them and mating takes place without interference from other males. Courtship is simple: a male walks up behind a female, bobbing his head, then grabs her by the neck and clasps her with his legs.

When the males leave their territories, the females gather at the nesting beaches. There is competition for nest sites and fighting breaks out. Each female digs a 2ft tunnel in the sand, scraping with all four feet. Sometimes they are trapped and killed when the roof falls in or when a neighbour scrapes sand into the hole.

Only 2 or 3 white eggs, 3¼ by 1¾ in., are

△ Like a lichen encrusted monument — the marine iguana presents his best side to the camera and shows off his metallic colours. In profile his snout is seen to be blunt and the clumsiness of his legs and heavy body is apparent. But against the blue sky the red and green mottling of this otherwise rather grotesque reptile is given full due.
▽ The marine iguana is the only modern lizard that uses the sea as a source of food. It is herbivorous, and feeds exclusively on seaweeds.

laid. Then the female iguana fills up and camouflages the tunnel. When the eggs hatch in about 110 days, 9in. iguanas emerge.

Apart from man the main enemies of full grown marine iguanas are sharks, but the iguanas usually stay inshore where sharks are not likely to venture. Young iguanas are caught by herons, gulls and Galapagos hawks, as well as introduced cats.

Warmer on land

While he was on the Galapagos, Darwin found that it was impossible to drive marine iguanas into the sea. They would rather let themselves be caught than pushed in and if thrown into the sea they would hurriedly make for the edge and clamber out. This is a surprising habit for an aquatic animal as most animals that habitually swim, such as turtles and seals, make for the safety of the sea when frightened. Darwin assumed that the marine iguana behaved in this strange way because it had no natural enemies on land but that the sharks were waiting for it in the sea. If this were so, it would mean that marine iguanas would have to be pretty hungry before setting out to feed. Recently another explanation has been put forward. While basking, marine iguanas regulate their body temperatures to within a range of 35–37°C/95–99°F. The sea temperature around the Galapagos is 10°C/50°F less, so the marine iguanas are reluctant to escape into the sea, as this makes them too cool.

class	**Reptilia**
order	**Squamata**
suborder	**Sauria**
family	**Iguanidae**
genus & species	*Amblyrhynchus cristatus*

Skink

Skinks have none of the frills or decorations found in other lizard families; they all have an ordinary 'lizard shape' with a rather heavy tail and very often limbs that are reduced or missing. These are adaptations to the burrowing way of life which is characteristic of skinks and many spend most of their lives underground. Skinks are usually only a few inches long, the largest being the giant skink of the Solomon Islands, which is 2 ft long. The skink family contains over 600 species, and they are found all over the warmer parts of the world. In some areas, such as the forests of Africa, they are the most abundant lizards.

*Within the skink family there are all gradations from a running to a burrowing way of life. The little brown skink of the southeastern United States has well-developed legs and toes and is a surface dweller; the burrowing Florida sand skink is almost limbless. In the **Scelotes** genus of Africa there is a whole range of limb reduction. Bojer's skink of Mauritius has well-developed legs; the black-sided skink of Madagascar has very short legs; others have lost their forelegs altogether and have a reduced number of toes on the hindlegs; and the plain skink of South Africa has completely lost all its legs.*

Other adaptations for burrowing include the streamlining of the scales, the provision of a transparent 'spectacle' over the eye and the sinking of the eardrum into a narrow tube.

Diverse habits

Skinks are found in a variety of habitats, both on the ground and beneath the surface, from the damp soil of forests to the sands of deserts. A few live in trees, but only one has any adaptation for aboreal life. This is the giant skink which has a prehensile tail. Some skinks, such as the keel-bearing skinks, named after the projections on their scales, live on the banks of streams and dive into the water if alarmed. Some of the snake-eyed skinks live among rocks on the shore and feed on sea creatures such as small crabs and marine worms.

▷ *A young **Eumeces skiltonianus**. Like many other lizards skinks can shed their tails when they are attacked by a predator. The young of some skinks, including the type shown, have bright blue tails as an added safety device. When attacked the tail is broken off and it bounds continually; as it is the most conspicuous thing in sight, the predator is confused and the skink can scuttle safely away while the predator pursues the bounding tail. The tail is bright blue only when the skink is young, when the hazards of life are greatest. The blue-tailed Polynesian skink is exceptional in retaining its blue tail throughout its life.*

◁ *Foot-long mother* **Tiliqua rugosa** *and enormous newly-born.*

◁ ▽ *The largest of the skinks – the prehensile-tailed giant skink of the Solomon Islands.*

Teeth to fit the diet

The main food of skinks is insects and other small animals, including young mice and birds' eggs. The insect-eating skinks have pointed teeth with which they crush their hard-bodied prey and some types of skink which feed on earthworms have backwardly curving teeth which prevent the worms from escaping as they are being swallowed. The larger skinks are vegetarians and have broad, flat-topped teeth used for chewing.

Some lay eggs

Skinks lack the wattles and fans which other lizards use to display their superiority to rivals, but some male skinks develop bright colours during the breeding season. When they meet the males fight vigorously and may wound each other. Courtship is simple: the male follows a female, who allows him to catch her if she is ready to breed.

About half the skinks lay eggs; the others bear their young alive, the eggs being hatched just before they leave the mother's body. The eggs are usually laid under a log or rock and some skinks such as the five-lined skink of North America guard their eggs. The female curls around the eggs and stays with them until they hatch 4–6 weeks later, only leaving them to feed. As with other reptiles which stay with their eggs, it is difficult to decide what function they are performing. There is no evidence that skinks incubate the eggs and they desert them if disturbed, but it is known that skinks regularly turn their eggs which may be to prevent them from rotting.

Swimming in the sand

Some of the desert skinks are called sand-fish from the way they appear to swim through the sand. Their legs are well-developed but they are held close into the body when moving. Propulsion comes from the flattened tail which is reminiscent of the tails of amphibians or aquatic reptiles such as the marine iguana (page 286). Another adaptation is a sharp chisel-like snout that can cleave a way through the sand. Like other lizards, skinks have flexible skulls but their heads are strengthened for sand-swimming and burrowing by the fusing of the scales on the head.

class	**Reptilia**
order	**Squamata**
suborder	**Sauria**
family	**Scincidae**
genera & species	*Corucia zebrata* giant skink *Eumeces fasciatus* five-lined skink *Lygosoma laterale* little brown skink *Neoseps reynoldsi* Florida sand skink *Scelotes bojeri* Bojer's skink *S. inornatus* plain skink *S. melanopleura* black-sided skink others

Teiid lizard

Because only a minority of this family have common names it is customary to speak of them with an anglicized form of their scientific name. The Teiidae is a family of American lizards. The 200 or so species in the family are very varied, particularly in the form of their scales, but there are no really bizarre types. Their ways of life are also very varied and teiids are found in a great number of habitats, from the high Andes to the seashore.

The largest teiid is the 4ft caiman lizard, which has a flattened tail and is amphibious. One foot smaller is the tegu of Brazil. Apart from a few giants such as these, teiids are usually 1 ft or less in length, the smallest being 3 – 4 in. long. Most of the teiids have a typical lizard form but some have almost lost their legs and live by burrowing.

The family is most numerous in the American tropics but one lives as far south as central Chile and the racerunners and

whiptails are distributed over most of the United States except the far north. One of these, the six-lined racerunner, is the best known of the teiids. It is the smallest species in the United States, growing up to 10 in. long, of which half is tail. The skin is dark brown and there are six narrow lines running down the body. Other racerunners and whiptails have yellowish lines or spots but they often lose them when they are fully grown. The male of the six-lined racerunner has a bluish belly while that of the female is whitish. As the name suggests, racerunners can move fast and they are reported as being able to run at 18 mph over short distances.

Must live in the open

As might be expected of a member of a predominantly tropical family, the six-lined racerunner is active only in warm weather and may stay in its burrow on cloudy days. Similarly it spends a greater part of the year hibernating than other lizards living in the same area, being inactive for $\frac{1}{2} - \frac{2}{3}$ of the year. Racerunners live

△ *Whip-tailed and splay-footed* **Cnemido-phorus maximus,** *one of the many variations within the 200 species of the family Teiidae.*

in colonies on open, sandy soil, from which they disappear if the cover is increased, by agriculture, for instance. On warm days the lizards can be seen foraging, basking, chasing rivals or courting.

Each racerunner has a home range of $\frac{1}{5} - \frac{1}{4}$ acre, over which it forages. The range is not the same as a territory as it is not defended and the ranges of several individuals overlap. The frequent chasing and biting that can be seen in a colony are the result of a social hierarchy. One or two members of the colony are more aggressive than the others and the smallest lizards are harassed most. Within its range each racerunner has a burrow which it does defend. It may dig its own burrow or use the abandoned burrow of a mouse or vole. The burrow is used as a shelter from enemies and extremes of temperature.

The habitat of the six-lined racerunner is an average habitat for the teiid family as some live in deserts and others, such as the caiman lizard, are amphibious. The worm teiids and the snake teiid burrow in leaf mould. The Guiana earless teiid has minute legs on which it can walk slowly, but it wriggles like a snake when disturbed or even throws itself forward with a flick of its tail.

Teeth tell teiid's diet

Teiid lizards have a variety of diets as well as habits. This is reflected in their teeth. The front teeth are always conical but those in the side of the mouth may be conical, cusped or flattened. The caiman lizard has flattened teeth with which it crushes snail shells. The racerunners and the ameivas of Central America have cusped teeth and feed mainly on insects. The six-lined racerunner can catch active insects like grasshoppers but also digs in the soil for insects which it locates by scent. The tegu feeds on insects, frogs and lizards and occasionally raids poultry runs for eggs and chicks. It also eats fruit and some teiids eat almost nothing but plant food.

Blue-tailed babies

The few teiid species whose reproduction has been studied are egg-layers and this is likely to be the case throughout the family. Detailed studies have been made on the six-lined racerunner and one of the ameivas. The males in a colony fight each other and mate with any females that are responsive. When courting the male rubs his pelvis against the ground then, having found a receptive partner, rubs her with his pelvis and hindlegs. Racerunners lay one or two clutches a year, with 1—6 eggs in each clutch. The eggs are laid in sandy soil or under rocks and hatch in 8—10 weeks. The hatchlings are $1\frac{1}{2}$ in. long and have blue tails at birth.

Unusual teiids

The tegu sometimes lays its eggs in termite nests built in trees. The walls of the nests are extremely hard and it must be very difficult for the female tegu to force her way in, let alone for the baby tegus to get out, for the termites repair the damage caused by the female's entry and so quickly seal the eggs in.

The tegu eggs are undoubtedly safe inside the termite nest, whereas most reptile eggs are very vulnerable to predators. The adult teiids are also eaten by a number of predators such as snakes, armadillos and coyotes, but the rough teiids of the tropical American rain forests are protected because their slender, rough bodies make them look like dead sticks on the forest floor. Furthermore if touched they become as rigid as a stick. Another teiid *Proctoporus shrevei* indulges in advertisement rather than concealment. It lives in caves on Trinidad and the males have a row of spots on each flank which glow in the dark.

class	**Reptilia**
order	**Squamata**
suborder	**Sauria**
family	**Teiidae**
genera & species	*Ameiva spp.* ameivas
	Bachia cophias earless teiid
	Cnemidophorus sexlineatus
	six-lined racerunner
	Dracaena guianensis
	caiman lizard
	Tupinambis nigropunctatus tegu

▽ *More snake-like than lizard:* **Euspondylus**. *Some teiid lizards resemble snakes even to the extent of losing their legs.*

Green lizard

This is the second largest lizard in Europe; the male is 15 in. long, of which 10 in. is tail. Europe's largest lizard is the eyed lizard, 24 in. long of which 16 in. is tail, and there are records of 36 in. total length. The eyed lizard is often dark green spotted with yellow and black. There are blue spots forming rosettes on the flanks.

The head of the green lizard is large, its legs stout and the toes, especially on the hindfeet, long. The length of the toes is most marked in the males although the females are usually slightly larger than the males in total body size. The colour varies and while usually bright green in the male it may be yellowish-green or brown and yellow on the flanks of the female. Males are noticeably thick at the root of the tail.

Green lizards range across southern Europe from northern Spain and the south of France to southwest Russia and northwards to parts of Germany. They are also found in the Channel Islands, but attempts to acclimatize them a few degrees farther north, in southwest England, have failed.

Lovers of dampness

Green lizards live among rocks and on rough ground especially along the margins of woods, where the ground is not too dry. They are particularly found on river banks, but they may also occur in meadows, especially where there are damp ditches. They climb well and are reputed to be good swimmers and to take readily to water when disturbed and seek refuge on the bottom. They are active by day, hunting or basking, but seek the shade when the sun is hot. Hibernation is from October to March, in holes in the ground, under buttress roots of trees or under vegetation litter, the period of hibernation being shorter in the southern than in the northern parts of the range.

Shell-cracker jaws

Green lizards feed on insects, spiders, woodlice, earthworms and other small invertebrates but also eat smaller lizards and small rodents. They sometimes take birds' eggs, cracking the shells with their powerful jaws which can give a strong but non-venomous bite on the hand. They occasionally eat fruit.

Submissive females

The breeding season starts in late April and continues into May. The male's throat goes cobalt blue, and is used as a threat in the many contests that take place between males. He also uses the same intimidating displays towards females and it is the fact that she responds submissively, that is, she does not return his menacing attitude, which tells him she is a female. A short time after mating the female lays 5—21 dull white oval eggs, about ¾ in. long, in soft earth. She stays near her eggs and will come back to them even after being driven off. They hatch 2—3 months later, the newly-hatched young being 2—3½ in. long, brown with one or two rows of yellowish-white spots. They gradually turn

△ Green lizards fighting.
▽ The second largest lizard in Europe.

293

green as they reach maturity. Green lizards may live for 10 years in captivity although their life in the wild is doubtless generally less than this.

Victims of pet-keepers
This lizard is attacked by the usual enemies of lizards, particularly the larger birds of prey, and it has the usual lizard defence of casting its tail and growing a new one. The chief danger to the green lizard, as with several other southern European reptiles, notably the Greek tortoise and the wall lizard, is their export for pet-keeping. Thousands each year find their way northwards to central and northern Europe to be kept in vivaria, to be used in laboratories, or to re-stock the many zoos.

Unsuccessful habitat
Some idea of the traffic in these attractive reptiles can be gained from the attempts to naturalize them in England. In 1899 an unspecified number of green lizards were liberated in the Isle of Wight and for a while they bred there. The last were seen in 1936. In 1931 some were introduced into Caernarvonshire, in North Wales. These did not breed and survived for only 4 years or so. In 1937, 100 green lizards were set free at Paignton, in south Devon. A few were still alive in 1952.

The wall lizard, a medium-sized European lizard, 8 in. long, was also introduced at Paignton in 1937, 200 being set free. They lasted only a few years, yet the wall lizard is a more northerly species than the green lizard, ranging from Jersey, in the Channel Isles, across Holland, Germany and Poland to the southern European mountain ranges.

South Devon is only a few degrees farther north than the Channel Islands, but it seems this is enough to make the difference between survival and extinction for the green lizard. Subtropical plants grow well in south Devon so, while temperature may be important, there must be other factors working against the lizards. An animal set down in a foreign environment must find suitable hiding places, suitable food and other necessities for successful living. Everything around is strange and, far more than for a plant, it is a gamble whether an animal will settle down. Nevertheless, we have the instances in which one group of green lizards survived in the Isle of Wight for at least 37 years and another group in South Devon continued for at least 15 years. The climate of the British Isles is said to be slowly getting warmer. It may well be that future attempts at acclimatization might prove more successful, provided there is then more sunshine than is usual now. Experience with captive green lizards shows that without sufficient sunlight they are prone to skin complaints that shorten their lives.

△ *A meal of a brimstone butterfly.*
▽ *A male in the mating season.*

class	**Reptilia**
order	**Squamata**
suborder	**Sauria**
family	**Lacertidae**
genus & species	*Lacerta viridis* green lizard *L. lepida* eyed lizard

294

Slow-worm

The snake-like slow-worm, alternatively known as the blind-worm or dead adder, is in fact a legless lizard. Internally there are vestigial shoulder- and hip-girdles, evidence that its ancestors once moved on four legs. A slow-worm has eyelids like other lizards, the two halves of its lower jaw are joined in front, another lizard characteristic, and its tongue is notched, not forked like that of a snake. An average large slow-worm is about 1 ft long, the record is a $20\frac{3}{5}$ in. female.

The head of a slow-worm is small and short, not so broad as the body immediately behind it and larger in the male than the female. Fully-grown males are more or less uniform in colour above and on the flanks. They may be light or dark brown, grey, chestnut, bronze or brick red and one variety is even copper-coloured. The belly usually has a dark mottling of blackish or dark grey. The female often has a thin dark line down the centre of the back and another on the upper part

underground ensures fairly constant temperature conditions.

The slow-worm is not inappropriately named. More often than not when we come upon it, it will lie motionless, making no attempt to escape. At most it may move away in a leisurely manner and generally its actions are slow and deliberate. Occasionally, however, by contrast, it will move with astonishing speed.

In October the slow-worm hibernates in an underground burrow, in a hollow beneath a large stone, or even beneath a pile of dead leaves. As many as 20 may be found in one hibernaculum, the largest being underneath, the smallest on top.

Slow-worms cast their skins or, more correctly, their cuticle, about four times a year. The frequency of sloughing depends upon whether or not it is a good slug year, the chief food of the slow-worm, the shedding being in response to the need for more space for the growing body. The skin is shed whole as in snakes. Although a slow-worm readily sheds its tail the new tail is shorter and never as perfect as the old one. There is usually a ragged end to the old part, the narrower new part appearing as if thrust inside the fringe of old scales.

moment of birth or shortly afterwards. Litters of 6–12 – although as few as 4 or as many as 19 young have been recorded – are born in late August or September, but if the weather is cold this may be delayed until October or later. The young are up to $3\frac{1}{2}$ in. long, silver or golden in colour with black underparts and a thin black line running down the middle of the back. Very active, they are able to fend for themselves from the moment of birth, catching insects, but showing a marked preference for any slugs small enough to eat.

Slow-worms have been known to live in captivity for up to 30 years or more, the record being held by one that lived in the Copenhagen Museum for 54 years.

Numerous enemies

Probably thousands of slow-worms are killed each year by man under the impression they are young adders. The slow-worm has many enemies, especially when young. Its main enemies are hedgehogs and adders. Frogs, toads, lizards and small snakes also eat it, as well as foxes, badgers and rats, and many birds, particularly birds-of-prey; and even the mistlethrush has been seen to take one.

▽ *Spritely youngsters: black-striped and golden or silver coloured, young slow-worms are able to fend for themselves from birth.*

of each flank, and her belly is usually black.

The slow-worm is found throughout Europe including the British Isles and eastwards into the Caucasus, Asia Minor and northern Iran. In Scandinavia and Finland it extends as far as latitude 65°N. It is also found in North Africa.

A variety of the slow-worm, known as the blue-spotted slow-worm, is widely distributed over Europe including the southern counties of England. The colour which may vary from a light blue to deep ultramarine may be present in spots or stripes, sometimes so closely set that the animal appears blue all over. All blue-spotted slow-worms are males.

Name not inappropriate

The slow-worm lives in open woodlands, commons and heathland. It is seldom seen during daylight apart from the spring and late summer or autumn. It spends the daytime under flat stones or logs or in burrows sometimes as deep as a foot below the surface, often lying in the earth completely buried except for its head. Life

The gardener's friend

The slow-worm eats spiders, small earthworms and tiny insects. There is a marked preference for the small white slug *Agriolimax agrestis* so often a pest on tender green vegetables. This is consumed in quantity, but where this slug is missing the slow-worm takes others. The prey is seized in the middle and chewed from end to end. The slow-worm also eats snails. The principal feeding time is soon after sunset, or after rain, when the slugs themselves come out to feed.

Ovoviviparous female

Mating is from late April to June, when there is a great deal of fighting between the males, each trying to seize the other by the head or neck. Once a hold has been obtained there is much writhing and rolling together. In mating the male seizes the female by the neck and twines his body around hers. The female is ovoviviparous, the eggs hatching within the body. On rare occasions the eggs are deposited before hatching. The young are enclosed within a membranous envelope which is punctured by a feebly developed egg-tooth, either at the

Deceptive appearance

Since the slow-worm's snake-like appearance can so easily deceive us, it is possible that other animals it is likely to encounter in the wild can make a similar mistake. Alfred Leutscher, writing in the *Illustrated London News* for June 3, 1950, tells the story of how he once placed a slow-worm in a vivarium containing three tame common frogs. They made repeated attempts to swallow the 'worm'. 'Suddenly these frogs began to behave as if frantic with fear, making every attempt to escape and dashing madly against the glass sides of their enclosure.' He came to the conclusion that the frogs had at first taken the slow-worm for a likely meal and had then mistaken it for a snake.

class	**Reptilia**
order	**Squamata**
suborder	**Sauria**
family	**Anguidae**
genus & species	***Anguis fragilis***

△ *Massive-headed, belly-dragging, obese and ugly, the Gila monster is among the more repulsive of reptiles and one of the only two poisonous lizards. Surprisingly, many people have kept it as a pet; enough, in fact, to have made it rare. It is now protected by law to save it from extinction.*

Gila monster

Only two out of about 3 000 kinds of lizards are poisonous: the Gila monster (pronounced 'heela') and the beaded lizard. They look alike and live in deserts of the southwestern United States and adjacent parts of Mexico respectively. The first is named for the Gila basin in Arizona where it is plentiful, the second after the beaded nature of its scales.

The Gila monster is up to 23 in. long and weighs up to 3¼ lb. It is mainly pink and yellow with black shading. The beaded lizard, up to 32 in. long, is mainly black with pink and yellow patches. The Gila monster has 4—5 dark bands on the tail. The beaded lizard has 6—7 yellow bands. Both have a stout body, large blunt head, powerful lower jaw, small eyes, an unusually thick tail, short legs with 5 toes on each and remarkably strong claws.

Alternate gluttony and fasting

These lizards move about very slowly, although when captured they can move swiftly and struggle actively, hissing all the while. They spend long periods of time in their burrows in the sand, coming out at the rainy season and even then mainly at night. Being slow movers they must eat things that cannot run away. These are mainly eggs of birds and other reptiles, baby birds and baby mice and rats. They track them down partly by smell but more especially by taste, using the tongue to pick up scent particles on the sand from birds' nests or rodents' burrows. These are conveyed by the tongue to Jacobson's organ, a sort of taste-smell organ in the roof of the mouth. They eat insects and earthworms in captivity and from the behaviour of these captive animals it seems unlikely that venom is used to kill prey. Eggs are either seized, the head raised and the shell crushed so the contents flow into the mouth, or bitten in two and the tongue used to lap up the contents as the shell lies on the ground. The Gila monster drinks liquid food by lapping it up and holding its head back to let the liquid run down its tongue.

While active these lizards eat all they can find and store the surplus as fat in the body and especially in the tail. When well-fed their skeleton represents a small part of the total weight of the body and the lizards can then survive long periods of fasting. The fat tail will shrink to a fifth of its former girth, the rest of the body being little more than skin and bone. The lizard will quickly recover once it can find food. One that had survived three years drought, during which it took no food, was taken into captivity and in 6 months its tail had doubled in size and the body was as plump as usual.

Inefficient venom apparatus

The venom glands are in the lower jaw although teeth in both jaws are grooved. Each gland has several ducts that open into a groove between the lower lip and the gum, and the poison finds its way from this to the grooves in the teeth. Neither of the lizards can strike as a snake does but must hold with the teeth and hang on with a vice-like grip sometimes chewing to help conduct the venom. If bitten by a monster, the main problem is to free the tight-gripping jaws.

Nests in the sand

Mating takes place in July and eggs are laid a few weeks later. These are laid in a hole dug by the female with her front feet and covered with sand. There may be 3—15 in a clutch, each egg about 1½ by 2½ in. and oval, with a tough leathery shell. They hatch in about a month, the young lizards being 3½—4¾ in. long, and more vivid in colour than the parents.

Legally protected monster

Little is known of the natural enemies of the two poisonous lizards but by 1952 the Gila monster was becoming so rare it had to be protected by law to save it from extinction. It was being caught and sold in large numbers as a pet. Those who caught them were paid 25—50 cents an inch, and the lizards were then sold at 1—2 dollars an inch.

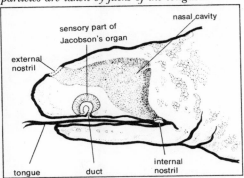

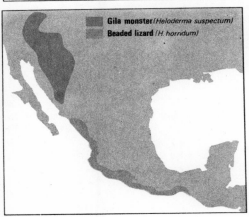

▽ *Section through Gila monster's head, showing Jacobson's organ in the roof of the mouth. This is specialised for taste and smell; scents are carried to it through the external nostrils (visible in both the pictures above), and particles are taken by flicks of the tongue.*

nasal cavity

sensory part of Jacobson's organ

external nostril

tongue   duct   internal nostril

Gila monster *(Heloderma suspectum)*
Beaded lizard *(H. horridum)*

Lizard with a bad name

In striking contrast with the popularity of the Gila monster as a pet are many erroneous beliefs that have gathered around it in the past. One is that it cannot eliminate body wastes, which is why it is so poisonous. For the same reason its breath is evil-smelling. Another is that it can spit venom, whereas at most, when hissing, it may spray a little venom. The lizard has been credited also with leaping on its victims, largely the result perhaps of the way it will lash out from side to side when held in the hand. Its tongue has been said to be poisonous, the lizard itself impossible to kill and possessed of magical powers. Lastly, it has been said to be a cross between a lizard and a crocodile.

More than 400 years ago, a Spaniard, Francisco Hernández, wrote that the bite of the lizard though harmful was not fatal, that it threatened no harm except when provoked and that its appearance was more to be dreaded than its bite. Although his writings had been overlooked the first scientists to study it seem to have taken much the same view when they named it *Heloderma suspectum*, because they were not sure whether it was poisonous, only suspected of being so. They were more certain about the beaded lizard which they named *H. horridum*. Now we know that the poison is a neurotoxin which causes swelling, loss of consciousness, vomiting, palpitations, laboured breathing, dizziness, a swollen tongue and swollen glands. Not all these symptoms appear in one person, however. The swelling and the

△ *Using tongue and 'nose' a Gila monster tests its surroundings.*

initial pain are due to the way the poison is injected. The lizard must hold on and chew with a sideways action of the teeth.

In 1956 Charles M Bogert and Rafael Martin del Campo published in America the results of their thoroughgoing investigation into the injuries suffered by human beings from the bite of the Gila monster. They found only 34 known cases of which 8 were said to have been fatal. Most of those who had died were either in poor health at the time or drunk. In several instances there were signs of repeated biting, as in the case of the man who carried the lizard inside his shirt, next to his skin. This may explain the drunks who fell victim. They teased the lizards in zoos and probably did not realise they were being repeatedly bitten.

class	**Reptilia**
order	**Squamata**
suborder	**Sauria**
family	**Helodermatidae**
genus & species	***Heloderma horridum*** *beaded lizard* ***H. suspectum*** *Gila monster*

297

Earless monitor

Earless monitors are flesh-eating lizards, and up to 1961 less than 10 had been found, all in Sarawak. These had been enough to show that the lizard is sufficiently unusual to be of great interest to zoologists, although to the non-specialist it is undistinguished in appearance. It was not considered a true monitor and was placed in a family of its own. It even seemed to have some affinities with snakes.

Because of this interest and because so few had been found, the Sarawak Museum offered a reward of $50—2 weeks' wages for an unskilled labourer—but no earless monitors turned up until January 1961, when someone found one while hoeing his garden. It was 13 in. long, probably about average size, the largest ever found being about 17 in. Its legs were small and the body was brown and covered with pimples or nodules. Other features of the earless monitor, which are shared by various other lizards, are the forked tongue that can be flicked in and out like that of a snake and the transparent lower eyelid. The earless monitor is so called because the ears cannot be seen from the outside; in other words, the eardrums are covered.

Rare because it hides

Since a Sarawak gardener found a specimen while hoeing, at least 25 more earless monitors have been collected, all from the flat coastal plains of Sarawak, and some have been kept in captivity so their behaviour has been studied. The first to be collected lived for 3 months in captivity, but several times during that period it worried its captors by giving every appearance of being dead. It would spend several hours at a time, flopped down and breathing very slowly, but if touched it would react by flattening its body against the ground or twisting and moving away.

Further observations showed that earless monitors are active only at night, usually after midnight. Like other short-legged lizards, such as skinks, the earless monitors move like snakes, with a side-to-side swimming movement. The animal sometimes moves by pushing with its hindlimbs, while the forelimbs are dragged passively or are used for scrambling over obstacles. Earless monitors also swim well, apparently preferring shallow water where they lie on the bottom. The longest recorded time underwater is 36 minutes.

Together with what could be seen when catching them, these observations give us some idea of the earless monitors' life in the wild. They have been caught either in fish traps or by being dug up. The original 1961 specimen was found 6 in. underground, and in captivity they have been seen burrowing, forcing their heads into crevices. So it seems that earless monitors are nocturnal, living underground but coming to the surface where they apparently make for water. They seem to be able to go for a long time without food, perhaps because of their ability to relax so completely, so they probably spend long periods underground. As they surface at night it is not surprising that so few have ever been found and that they are unknown to the local peoples. If this were not enough, their rough, brown skin makes them very easy to overlook.

As they live in flat, readily flooded areas, it may be that they deliberately wait for floods before coming out, or at least get washed out during floods. In January 1963, for instance, during serious floods, a dozen specimens were collected from one small river.

Before earless monitors became so relatively well known it was thought that they may have been venomous. This was largely because at one time they were thought to be related to the venomous Gila monsters. Captive specimens, however, have shown no inclination to bite when handled, and close examination shows no sign of poison apparatus.

Egg-suckers

In captivity the only food earless monitors have taken has been turtle or chicken eggs. They nibble and suck the yolk with the mouth hardly opened, so presumably do not eat large or hard food items in the wild.

A missing link?

The reason for the great interest in earless monitors is that they appear to be a missing link. Before 1961 an eminent authority on reptiles suggested that to see an earless monitor alive would be the fulfilment of a dream. In the event they seem to be remarkably uninspiring, but to the anatomist, they are of great importance.

After the first specimen had been described in 1878 the earless monitor was classed sometimes with the monitors and sometimes with the Gila monsters. Now it seems that it is also related closely to some extinct lizards and may be a link between the snakes and the lizards.

It has always been presumed that the snakes arose from lizards that gradually lost their legs. This is a trait that has developed in several types of lizard such as amphisbaenids and slowworms, although these lizards are not related to snakes. The lizards previously reckoned to be fairly closely related to snakes were the monitors, although they are not directly linked. The earless monitor now seems to be a more likely candidate, for it shares several features with snakes, and has fewer of the special features that separate other lizards from them. Among these characters are similarities of teeth and skull, the absence of the external ear and the long, forked tongue in which the forked end retracts into the root. The transparent lower eyelid may be the forerunner of the 'clear spectacle' covering a snake's eye.

class	**Reptilia**
order	**Squamata**
suborder	**Sauria**
family	**Lanthanotidae**
genus & species	***Lanthanotus borneensis***

Sluggish and dull-coloured, the earless monitor is not an exciting-looking animal—but it may well be a missing link, for no other lizard has so many of the features shared by snakes.

Anaconda

The largest snakes are to be found in the boa family, and the largest of these is **Eunectes murinus**, *the anaconda or water boa. Probably no animal has been the subject of such exaggeration in respect of size. The name itself is said to come from the Tamil words* **anai** *for elephant and* **kolra** *for killer. Properly this name must have originally referred to the anaconda's relative, the Indian python. Claims for 140-ft anacondas have been made and 40 ft often occurs in travel literature. The famous explorer, Colonel Fawcett, claimed to have killed a 62-ft anaconda and was pronounced 'an utter liar' by London opinion. In fact, a 20-ft anaconda is a large specimen, although it must be presumed that larger individuals do occur. It is difficult to find an authentic record for the largest anacondas. The measurement of 37½ ft for one specimen has been widely accepted by scientists but not by all. Long ago, the New York Zoological Society offered a prize of 5,000 dollars for a 30-ft anaconda. This has never been won.*

The anaconda is olive green with large, round black spots along the length of its body and two light longitudinal stripes on the head. It lives throughout tropical South America, east of the Andes, mainly in the Amazon and Orinoco basins, and in the Guianas. It extends north to Trinidad. The species is variable in colour and size giving rise to numerous sub-specific names. However, these can be regarded as merely geographical variations. The closely related **Eunectes notaeus** *of Paraguay is known as the Paraguayan or southern anaconda.*

Life by jungle streams and swamps

Water boa is a good alternative name for the anaconda, the most aquatic of the boas. It is apparently never found far from water; sluggish or still waters being preferred to rapid streams. It is this preference that limits the species to the basins east of the Andes. Swamps are a favourite haunt.

Anacondas have, as a rule, fixed hunting grounds and generally live alone, but they are occasionally seen in groups.

Largely nocturnal in habit, anacondas lie up during the day in the shallows or sunbathe on low branches, usually over water. On land they are relatively sluggish, but they are able to swim rapidly and often float motionless, allowing the current to carry them downstream.

Killing by constriction

Anacondas usually lie in wait for their prey to come down to the water's edge to drink, whereupon they strike quickly with the head, grabbing the luckless prey and dragging it underwater so that it drowns. At other times anacondas may actively hunt prey on land.

The usual prey caught by lying in wait are birds and small mammals—deer, peccaries

Anaconda is the largest of snakes, reaching up to 37 ft, although exaggerated claims give lengths of 140 ft. They kill their prey by constricting. Each time the victim breathes out, the anaconda tightens its coils until the animal dies of suffocation.

and large rodents such as agoutis. Fish also form a large part of the diet, a fact not surprising in so aquatic an animal. More surprisingly, turtles and caimans are sometimes attacked. There is a record of a 25-ft anaconda killing a 6-ft caiman. The special jaw attachment that snakes have allows an anaconda to swallow such a large victim. After a meal of this size, which will suffice an anaconda for several weeks, the snake rests for a week or more until digestion has taken place. Normally the diet will consist of more frequent smaller meals.

Most snakes are adapted for swallowing prey wider than themselves: the upper and lower jaws are only loosely attached, and the brain protected from pressure by massive bones. Also a valve on the breathing tube allows the snake to breathe while swallowing.

The method of killing the prey is the same as in other constricting snakes such as the pythons. The prey is not crushed, but merely contained; each time the victim exhales, the coils of the anaconda tighten around its chest so that the ribs cannot expand, thus preventing inhalation until it suffocates. Stories in travelogues refer to anacondas' prey having every bone in the body broken and being squashed to pulp. In reality, bones are rarely broken during the process just described, which is one of strangulation. The fallacy is due to confusion between freshly-killed and regurgitated prey. This is covered with mucus, which gave rise to the story that anacondas smear their prey with saliva to facilitate swallowing.

Breeding

Few observations have been made on the breeding cycle of the anaconda. Males of southern anacondas studied in captivity were apparently aroused by the scent of the females. The male moves up alongside the female, flicking his tongue over her, until his head is resting over her neck. When in this position, he erects his spurs, two claw-like projections which are the last visible remnants of the hind limbs. The spurs are moved backwards and forwards against the female's skin and when the cloacal regions are in opposition, a hemipenis is inserted and copulation takes place.

Anacondas, like other boas, are viviparous. From 20—40, sometimes up to 100 young are born in the early part of the year. Each baby is 2—3 ft long.

Anacondas in folklore

It is not surprising that such a large, and malevolent-looking creature should be the subject of folklore and fallacy. The South American Indians have numerous stories about the anaconda, from the belief that it turns itself into a boat with white sails at night, to the mythology of the Taruma Indians who claimed to be descended from an anaconda. Several factors have led to tales of giant snakes. For one thing size is notoriously difficult to estimate unless a comparison can be made with something of known dimensions. Exaggeration is more likely if the animal is moving and writhing around, or if the observer has had a shock, as he might well have on suddenly seeing an anaconda. Secondly, snake skins stretch very easily when being prepared so that the length of a skin gives no concrete evidence. It is not therefore difficult to see how stories of giant snakes could have arisen, and, once started, how this has led to unwitting or deliberate embroidery. Along with stories of venomous qualities and body size, there is exaggeration about the danger involved in meeting an anaconda. This is not unique; all large carnivorous animals become surrounded by stories of their man-eating habits. Many accounts are pure fiction. Only a few years ago a book was published describing a 140-ft anaconda, and how the author narrowly escaped from a 45-ft specimen by shooting its head off.

Other stories are reported truthfully but are not evidence of man-eating habits, but of self-defence, for when man blunders into an animal it is not surprising that it tries to defend itself. There are, however, remarkably few authentic stories of people killed and eaten. Rolf Blomberg, who has made many searches for record-sized specimens, has been able to find only two fairly definite instances of anacondas killing human beings. In only one case was it claimed that the victim, a 13-year-old boy, was eaten. Even this was somewhat doubtful because the story goes that he disappeared while bathing with friends. On discovering his absence, one of them dived down to search and saw an anaconda. The victim's father then hunted down the snake and shot it. Blomberg states that the boy's body had been vomited up but does not say whether,

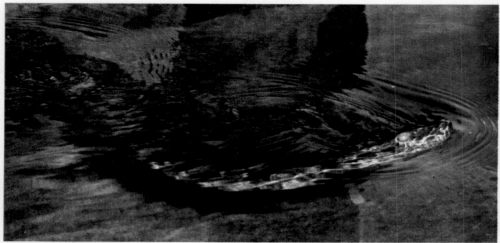

△ *An alternative name for the anaconda is water boa as it is never found far from the sluggish forest streams or swamps. Anacondas move relatively slowly on land but can swim rapidly and often float motionless, allowing the current to carry them downstream.*

▽ *Anacondas often lie up during the day in branches over the water's edge and wait for their prey to come down at night to drink, when they strike quickly with the head, grab the prey in their coils, often dragging it down into the water, to drown.*

in fact, it was recovered or whether this was only surmise. In the other incident a grown man was captured by an anaconda while swimming and was drowned. His body, when later found, had distinct marks of having been subjected to a powerful squeeze, but there was no indication of his having been swallowed.

Here then are two reports of the death of human beings, caused by anacondas. As we have seen, there is some doubt about one of them and in the second the man may have been killed but there is nothing to show he was eaten. In fact, few anacondas would be large enough to swallow a man. Nevertheless, such stories, perhaps in a garbled form, would travel through the country, so giving the impression that anacondas are man-eaters. After this, anyone who disappeared

and was last seen at the water's edge would be presumed to have been eaten by the anaconda, especially if one of these large snakes was seen in the vicinity. Such stories are so sensational that nobody asks for details or unequivocal evidence and the travellers would then take home a supposedly authentic story to relate to eager and uncritical audiences.

class	**Reptilia**
order	**Squamata**
suborder	**Serpentes**
family	**Boidae**
genus & species	*Eunectes murinus* *E. notaeus*

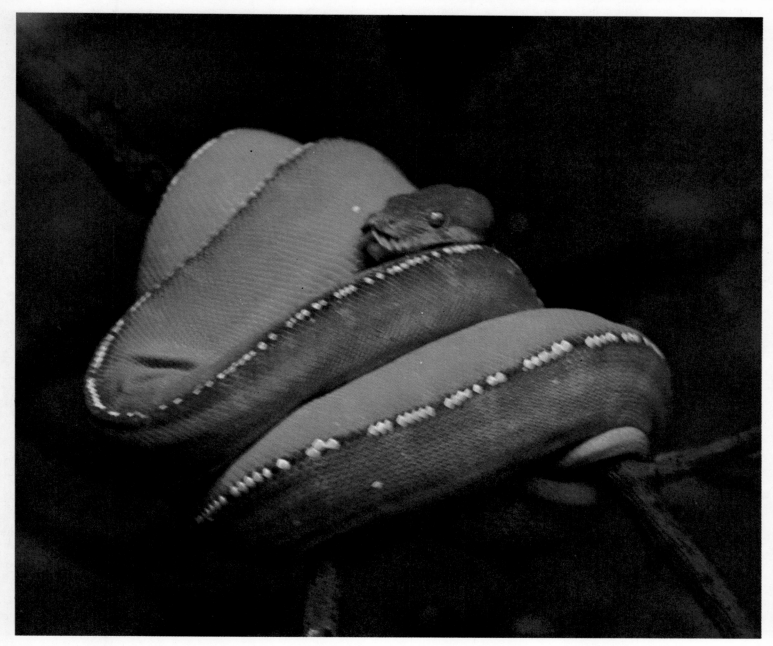

Python

Pythons are the Old World equivalent of the New World boas. Like the boas they have small spurs that represent the vestiges of hind limbs. The largest and best-known pythons belong to the genus **Python**. Not only are these large pythons at home in jungles, climbing trees, but they are often found near water. The African rock python which reaches about 32 ft long is not quite as long as the accepted record figure for the anaconda ($37\frac{1}{2}$ ft.), the largest of the boas. It lives in most parts of Africa in open country except the deserts. The other African pythons are the ball python and Angolan python of West Africa. There are no pythons in southwest Asia but several species are found from India to China and the East Indies. The Indian python reaches about 20 ft and ranges through southeast Asia from India to China and on some of the islands of the East Indies. The reticulated python,

reaching a length of 33 ft, has a more easterly distribution, from Burma to the Philippine Islands and Timor. The short-tailed python lives in the Malayan Peninsula, Borneo and Sumatra and the Timor python lives on the islands of Timor and Flores in Indonesia.

As well as the true pythons there are several other genera of pythons, including the carpet snake, that are found in the East Indies and Australia. Of the rock pythons the largest is the 20ft amethystine rock python or scrub python. A smaller group is the Australian womas which eat other snakes. The green tree python of New Guinea hunts in trees. The burrowing python, which lives in West Africa, in Liberia and throughout the rain forest of Zaire, spends its time underground chasing rodents and shrews.

Good travellers

The large pythons are often found near water and the Indian python is almost semi-aquatic. They also live in jungles and

△ *A green tree python wraps its coils around itself as it waits for some unsuspecting prey which it grasps with its enlarged front teeth. Its leaf-green colour with white spots along its back and its extremely prehensile tail, make it admirably adapted for life in the trees.*

climb trees, except for the African python which prefers open country. The reticulated python shows a preference for living near human settlements. At one time it was a regular inhabitant of Bangkok, hiding up by day and coming out at night to feed on rats, cats, dogs and poultry. One individual was caught in the King's palace. This habit of associating with buildings must account for its turning up in ships' cargoes. One reached London in good condition; but it is a good traveller under its own steam. It swims out to sea and was one of the first reptiles to reach the island of Krakatoa in the Malay archipelago, after it erupted in 1888, destroying all life.

Any live prey accepted

Pythons kill their prey by constriction, wrapping themselves around the body of the

prey so that it cannot breathe. The coils then hold the body steady while the python works it into its mouth. Prey is caught by ambush; the python lies in wait then springs out knocking the animal with its head and seizing it with its jaws until it can wrap its body round it. The list of animals eaten by pythons is too long to enumerate. Mammals are preferred, followed by birds, but young rock pythons have been caught in fish traps. African pythons eat many small antelopes such as duikers, gazelle, impala and bushbuck. A large python can swallow prey weighing up to 120 lb but this is exceptional and usually smaller animals are taken such as dassies, hares, rats, pigeons and ducks. Jackals and monkeys are sometimes eaten and one 18 ft African python is known to have eaten a leopard, with very little damage being sustained in the process of catching it. Pythons sometimes suffer from their meals. They have been found with porcupine quills and antelope horns sticking through their stomach wall. Usually such dangerous projections are digested before causing any serious damage.

A large animal will last a python for a long time but they sometimes kill several small animals in quick succession. An African python has been credited with capturing and eating three jackals and a small python was seen to kill two sparrows in quick succession, then pin down a third with its tail.

There are a few authentic accounts of men being attacked by pythons, and there is good reason to believe the case of the 14 year old Malay boy attacked and eaten on the island of Salebabu.

Devoted mother pythons

The courtship of pythons is less lively than that of smaller snakes. The male crawls after the female, trying to climb over her and sometimes they rear up and sway to and fro. The spurs or vestigial limbs that lie either side of the cloaca are used by the male to scratch the female and stimulate her to raise her body so that he can wrap his body around hers and bring the two cloacas together. The eggs, 100 in a single clutch, are laid 3—4 months after mating. The female gathers the eggs into a pile and wraps herself around them, brooding them throughout the 2—3 month incubation period, only leaving them for occasional visits to water and more rarely to eat. Most pythons merely guard their eggs but the Indian python incubates them by keeping her body a few degrees above that of the surrounding air. Reticulated pythons are 2—2½ ft long when they hatch and for the first few years they grow rapidly at a rate of about 2 ft or more a year. An Indian python nearly trebled its length in its first year of life. Pythons may live for over 20 years.

Courageous otters

Even the great snakes are not free from enemies. Young pythons have many enemies but as they grow larger fewer animals can overcome them. Crocodiles, hyaenas and tigers have been found with the remains of pythons in their stomachs and Jim Corbett writes of finding a 17ft Indian python killed by a pair of otters which had apparently attacked from either side, avoiding harm by their agility. When the ball python of Africa is molested it rolls itself into a tight, almost uniformly round ball, its head tucked well inside.

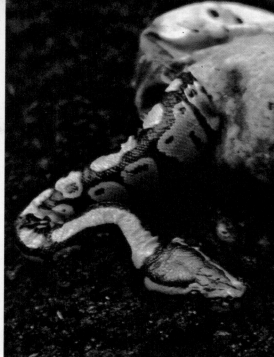

Beating elephants

Both African and Indian pythons were well known to the Greeks and Romans and have taken their place in folklore and religion. They are, for instance, responsible for one of the many dragon legends. Dragon is derived from the Greek word for snake, and the ancient writers were obviously talking about big snakes. It was mediaeval naturalists who turned them into fabulous creatures. Edward Topsell has left us a delightful description of how dragons capture elephants. In his *Historie of Serpentes* 1608 he writes how they 'hide themselves in trees covering their head and letting the other part hang down like a rope. In those trees they watch until the Elephant comes to eat and croppe off the branches, then suddainly, before he be aware, they leape into his face and digge out his eyes, and with their tayles or hinder partes, beate and vexe the Elephant, untill they have made him breathlesse, for they strangle him with theyr foreparts, as they beat him with the hinder.' Apart from the impracticability of an elephant being attacked, this is a reasonable account of a python killing its prey.

◁ *Strangled! A flying fox, caught in the jaws of a scrub python, is being strangled to death by the python's tightening coils.*

△ *A carpet python* **Morelia spilotes** *curls over and around her eggs, rarely leaving them. The temperature within her coils is up to 12F° warmer than the surrounding atmosphere.*

▷△ *A ball python emerges from its egg, after an incubation period of up to 80 days. It may be one of a hundred snakes in the clutch.*

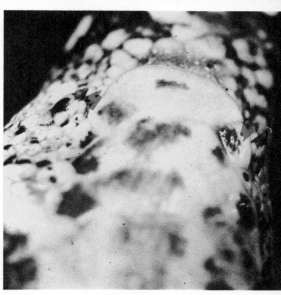

▷ *Superfluous legs. The two claws (arrowed) on either side of the anal vent of this African python are vestigial hind limbs, reminding us that snakes evolved from legged reptiles.*

▽ *The African python's skull shows the typical arrangement of teeth of a non-poisonous snake. The even sized teeth all point backwards, which ensures a firm and fatal grip on their prey.*

class	**Reptilia**
order	**Squamata**
suborder	**Serpentes**
family	**Pythonidae**
genera & species	***Calabaria reinhardti*** *burrowing python* ***Chondropython viridis*** *green tree python* ***Liasis amethystinus*** *amethystine rock python* ***Morelia argus*** *carpet snake* ***Python anchietae*** *Angolan python* ***P. curtus*** *short-tailed python* ***P. molurus*** *Indian python* ***P. regius*** *ball python* ***P. reticulatus*** *reticulated python* ***P. sebae*** *African python* ***P. timorensis*** *Timor python*

Egg-eating snake

Although many snakes eat eggs, only the Indian and African egg-eating snakes live almost exclusively on eggs and have a remarkable device for dealing with them.

There are five species of egg-eating snake in Africa, and one, related to them, in India. They are slender with blunt, rounded snouts and narrow heads not distinct from the neck, as are the arrowhead-shaped heads of many other snakes.

The common egg-eating snake, found in many places from Egypt to South Africa, is usually around 2½ ft long, a 3ft one being a large specimen. Its colour varies from slate-grey to olive-brown, with large, square black patches on the back that sometimes form a zig-zag line. The East African egg-eating snake, about the same size, ranges from the southern borders of Kenya to Mozambique. It is pinkish to reddish-brown with darker Vs and transverse bars running down the back. The largest species is the southern egg-eating snake. This averages 3 ft, and there are records of individuals of 3¾ ft.

Egg-eating snakes are mainly active at night and spend much of their time gliding through the foliage of trees, searching for birds' nests. They are harmless to man; they have no venom and only a few weak teeth at the back of the mouth. These are incapable of breaking the skin—not that the snakes will even attempt to bite.

Egg-crushing throats

An egg-eating snake, with a head and neck the diameter of a man's finger, can swallow whole a chicken's egg with a diameter of 1¾ in. It is a characteristic of snakes that they are able to swallow objects wider than themselves. Their jaws are specially hinged to engulf their prey (anaconda, page 299) and their throats can expand to accommodate the food. When swallowing an egg, the scales on the head and neck get pulled apart as the skin underneath becomes stretched to tissue-paper thickness.

The snakes seek out eggs by smell. On finding an egg, a snake investigates it carefully with its tongue, rejecting it if it is addled, and, if the egg is large, measuring its size by running the head and neck over it. Satisfied with its find, the snake then coils itself around the egg to hold it steady, yawns a few times as if limbering up and proceeds to engulf the egg from one end, drawing it in with slow, deliberate gulps.

Having swallowed the egg (which may take ¼ hour) the snake breaks it open with a most remarkable device that grips and saws through the shell. Along the roof of the throat there are about 30 teeth which are projections from the backbone that stick through the skin of the throat. The first 17 or 18 of these teeth are long and knife-shaped, the next few are broad and flat and the remaining 6 or 7 are stout pegs

projecting forwards. The egg is held against the teeth by throat muscles contracting around either end. The snake then raises its head off the ground and bends it backwards and forwards so the long teeth saw through the shell, releasing the contents. Next, the snake arches its neck upwards, so the shell is forced against the flat middle teeth which fold the shell into a rolled-up, boat-shaped sausage. The contents of the egg are swallowed and a valve in front of the stomach closes to keep them in while the snake wriggles and contorts to eject the empty shell.

In the tropical forests, egg-eating snakes will have a plentiful supply of food as birds nest all the year round, but in South Africa or northern India their food supply is seasonal. It is very likely that egg-eating snakes in these regions have to fast for the greater part of the year, living on fat stored up during the birds' nesting season.

△ *The big swallow: after a few experimental yawns to limber up, the snake lets out its elongated jaw hinges and begins to work the egg down its throat towards the 'teeth'. These saw through the shell which then rapidly collapses under the onslaught of repeated throat spasms. When the egg's contents have been swallowed, the flattened shell is regurgitated, with the sharp fragments (still attached to the membrane beneath the shell) wadded together into a neat pellet.*
▷ *Blue-grey version of the egg-eating snake, draped tastefully in the branches. Colour variations run from slate-grey to olive-brown.*

▽ *How the snake goes to work on an egg: these 'teeth' are in fact projections from the spine which grow down through the skin of the throat.*

Egg-laying

Because so much of the egg-eating snake's behaviour is unique, attention has been directed to that and their breeding habits have been largely overlooked. They lay 12–15 eggs which hatch in 3 to 4 months.

The newly-hatched young measure 9—10 in. It would be interesting to know whether they are able to swallow eggs when still small. Presumably they would have to select the smallest of birds' eggs.

Putting on a fierce front

Although egg-eating snakes are not venomous, their behaviour when disturbed is sufficient to deter any enemy that did not know better. At the first sign of danger an egg-eating snake inflates the front part of its body and hisses violently. Then it coils itself up and strikes at its adversary, for all the world like a cobra or other venomous snake, but cannot inflict any damage.

The body does not coil properly. Instead it is thrown into parallel folds which curve round in a C-shape, and are continually moving so that the scales hiss as they rasp against each other.

Many disguises

The common egg-eating snake is further protected by its resemblance to venomous snakes. This is more than coincidence, because throughout its range from Egypt to the Cape this snake varies in colour to match different venomous snakes in each area. In Egypt it resembles the brown saw-scaled viper whose venom is the most powerful of all vipers. It also hisses by rubbing its scales together in the same way as the egg-eating snake. Farther south, in Tanzania, the egg-eating snake mimics the young of the lowland viper, and in the southern half of Africa three snakes are mimicked. In Southwest Africa the horned adder is the model, and in South Africa the egg-eating snakes can be mistaken for a Cape mountain adder. In many parts they resemble night adders, which have the same dark squarish marks running down the back. In one part of Rhodesia night adders lose their dark markings, and here the egg-eating snake also has a uniform colour.

Mimicking poisonous snakes may well help to deter such enemies as baboons or warthogs, but may not work against predatory snakes such as the boomslang. Against man, the mimicry is positively disadvantageous. The usual reaction is to kill any snake in case it should prove dangerous, and to resemble known dangerous snakes is to provoke this reaction.

class	**Reptilia**
order	**Squamata**
suborder	**Serpentes**
family	**Colubridae**
genera & species	***Dasypeltis scabra*** *common African egg-eating snake* ***D. medici*** *East African egg-eating snake* ***D. inornata*** *southern egg-eating snake* ***Elachistodon westermanni*** *Indian egg-eating snake*

King snake

These are North American snakes, harmless to man—as are most members of their large family, the Colubridae. A special feature of king snakes—and the reason why they are so named—is that they eat other snakes, including venomous species like rattlesnakes. Another feature is that they show many colour varieties.

The common king snake, also known as the chain snake or thunder snake, is up to 6 ft long. The typical form, along the east coast area of the United States, is shiny black, criss-crossed by bands of yellow or white forming a chain-like pattern on its sides. Its underside is black with white or yellow blotches. The head is narrow and there is a slightly marked neck. In the Mississippi Valley the king snake is greenish with white or yellow speckling. In Georgia, Alabama and Florida it is black or dark brown marked with yellow. The Californian subspecies is in two colour phases: one with yellow rings, the other with yellow stripes, the background colour of both being black or brown. These and other species and subspecies range over most of the United States northwards into southern Canada and southwards into Mexico. The milk snakes, up to $3\frac{1}{2}$ ft long, are closely related to the king snakes. Their name is sometimes applied to king snakes in different localities.

Some king snakes are ringed red, yellow and black and look very like the venomous coral snakes. So they are sometimes called false coral snakes, a name also given to other colubrid snakes such as the rear-fanged **Erythrolamprus** of South America, red with black rings.

Terrorising the rattlers

King snakes, active especially in afternoon and evening, do not pursue other snakes. They eat small mammals, usually rodents, as well as lizards and frogs, caught in meadows and wooded areas. Should one of them meet another snake, however, it will eat it. It strikes it with its teeth and grasps the neck of its victim, at the same time throwing its body round the other snake, killing it by suffocation, just as pythons and boas kill their prey. King snakes are immune to snake venom, even that of rattlesnakes and copperheads, and the danger they represent to other snakes is shown by the behaviour of a rattlesnake in the presence of a king snake. Instead of coiling its body, raising its head to strike with its teeth, and raising its tail to shake its rattle, it keeps its head and neck on the ground and raises part of its body in a high loop, trying to beat off its attacker by blows from this loop.

The smaller milk snakes of North America take similar prey but the snakes they eat are younger and smaller. They are named for an alleged habit of taking milk from cows. This same story is current in parts of the world for other species of snakes. Not only

△ **Lampropeltis getulus splendida**, Sonora king snake, has distinctive black marks along its back.

▽ **Lampropeltis doliata amaura**, Louisiana milk snake or 'false coral snake' as it is sometimes called.

is there no evidence to support it but the way a snake's teeth work make it virtually impossible to believe that any snake could take a cow's teat into its mouth without lacerating it badly.

Brightly coloured babies

Mating takes place in spring, the female laying 10—30 white parchment-shelled eggs in summer. Sometimes these are laid on the ground, more usually they are under leaves and plant litter. In some species, she may coil her body around the eggs for the first day or so, but afterwards leaves them. They hatch in 4—6 weeks, the baby snakes being 7—8 in. long, coloured like the parents but with the colours brighter.

Snake eats snake

There are many stories, and photographs have appeared in the Press, of one snake swallowing another. This happens in zoos when two snakes seize the same food. Sooner or later their noses touch as they both try to swallow the same thing, and the one with the larger gape swallows the other. There was a case of a 38 in. king snake eating a 40 in. corn snake, a 15 in. grass snake and an 8 in. Dekay's snake all in one day. Doubtless this happens in the wild also, but rarely. There are, however, snakes like the European smooth snake *Coronella austriaca* which, besides eating frogs, lizards and mice, also eats snakes. One of the lizards it eats is the legless and snake-like slowworm,

King snake (Lampropeltis getulus)
Milk snake (L. doliata)

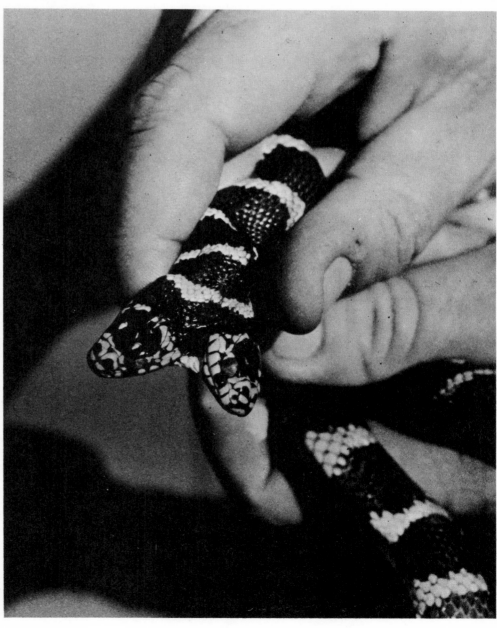

but smooth snakes, themselves only 18 in. long, will also eat young adders. Other snakes are snake-eaters to the extent of being famous for this habit, like the file snakes *Mehelya* of Africa. They behave like king snakes, in constricting their prey, and seem also to be immune to poison. The mussurana *Clelia clelia* of tropical America is another snake-eater. One mussurana which reached 6½ ft in length and looked unduly swollen was found to have swallowed a 6 ft fer-de-lance, the dreaded poisonous snake. The most famous snake-eater is perhaps the king cobra or hamadryad *Naja hannah*, of southeast Asia. It does not constrict its victims and it is not immune to poison, which is why it usually eats non-venomous snakes. It will, however, eat the other kind – including smaller king cobras.

Were it possible to know the truth we should doubtless find that many snake-eating snakes are cannibalistic, if only by accident. A snake is a snake to a snake-eating snake, whatever its species. Even more bizarre things than this have been seen. FW Fitzsimons, the distinguished South African specialist in snakes, tells of a Cape file snake that intervened when two deadly night adders had each seized a leg of a frog. The file snake settled the argument by swallowing all three. Then there was Dudly-Duplex, the two-headed king snake of San Diego Zoo. One night one head tried to swallow the other. This was rescued the following morning. Later, the aggrieved head tried to take revenge—with fatal results for the two heads and the body to which they belonged.

class	**Reptilia**
order	**Squamata**
suborder	**Serpentes**
family	**Colubridae**
genus & species	***Lampropeltis getulus*** common king snake ***L. doliata*** milk snake, others

Cobra

*Immortalised in Kipling's story of the hardy mongoose Rikki-Tikki-Tavi, the true cobras of the genus **Naja**, from the Sanskrit word 'naga' for snake, are medium-sized snakes. Several species average 6 or 7 ft. The Indian cobra has a dark body encircled by a series of light rings, and like all cobras, it has the characteristic hood behind the neck. The neck is flattened horizontally by long, moveable ribs being swung out to stretch the loose skin of the neck, rather like the ribs of an umbrella stretching out the fabric. The cobra rears up and expands the hood when frightened or excited, and, in the Indian cobra, this displays the distinctive spectacled pattern*

the hood has the typical 'spectacle' markings, but towards the eastern side of India a single ring-like marking becomes more common, while in the Kashmir and Caspian region the hood is marked with black transverse bars.

There are four species in Africa, the black-and-white cobra, the Cape cobra, the spitting cobra and the Egyptian cobra, which is also found in Asia.

Some cobras, such as the Egyptian cobra, are diurnal, others nocturnal like the Indian cobra, retiring by day to a favoured shelter in a burrow or under rocks. Some are found only near water.

Inoculating nerve-poisons

The cobra's venom is secreted from glands which lie just behind the eyes. It runs down

The Indian cobra is regarded by many experts as being one of the most dangerous snakes and death has been recorded as little as 15 minutes after the bite. Figures of 10 000 deaths a year have been given for India, which represents 1 in 30 000 of the population. Snakebite is so common in Asia and Africa because so many of the country people go about barefooted. Some cobras, notably the spitting cobra, of Africa, defend themselves by spitting venom over a distance of up to 12 ft. They aim for the face and the venom causes great pain and temporary blindness if it gets in the eyes.

Cobra venom has a different effect on the body than that of vipers which acts principally on the blood system, destroying tissues. Some tissue damage is done by cobra venom causing swelling and haemorr-

One of the four African species, the Cape cobra eats snakes as well as rodents, and is not averse to cannibalism.

Indian cobra, with its distinctive pattern. A cobra's hood works like an umbrella, with long, flexible ribs spreading the thin skin.

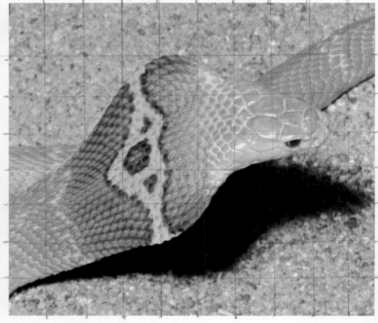

as the scales slide apart. The pattern is on the back of the neck but it can be seen from the front as the stretched skin is translucent.

Another well-known species is the Egyptian cobra, depicted on Ancient Egyptian headdresses rearing up with its hood inflated. Average length of adults is 5½–6 ft and there are reports of their reaching 10 ft, although the longest reliable measurement is over 8 ft. The body is yellowish to almost black, the lighter forms often having darker spots.

Cobras are found in Africa and Asia, although fossils have been found in Europe, presumably dating from a time when the climate was warmer. There are two or four species in Asia, the number depending on different authorities' methods of classification. One of these is the Indian cobra that is found from the Caspian across Asia, south of the Himalayas to southern China and the Philippines, and south to Bali in Indonesia. Throughout its range, the markings vary. In the west

ducts to the fangs that grow from the front of the upper jaw. Each fang has a canal along the front edge, and in some species the sides of the canal fold over to form a hollow tube like a hypodermic needle, so resembling the hollow fangs of vipers. The cobra strikes upwards, with the snout curled back so that the fangs protrude. As soon as they pierce the victim's flesh, venom is squirted down the fangs by muscles that squeeze the venom gland. When a very aggressive cobra tightens these muscles too early venom dribbles from its mouth.

Cobras' fangs are fairly short, but after it has struck the snake hangs on, chewing at the wound and injecting large quantities of venom. The seriousness of the bite depends very much on how long the cobra is allowed to chew. If it is struck off immediately, the bite will probably not be too serious. It is always difficult to assess the dangers of snake bite. Even where good medical records are kept, some of the less severe cases will probably not be reported, and the severity depends so much on the condition of the victim. Young and old people and those who are sick, especially with weak hearts, are most likely to succumb.

hage, but the principal ingredients are neurotoxins acting on the nervous system causing paralysis, nausea, difficulty in breathing and, perhaps, eventually death through heart and breathing failure.

Rat-catching snakes

Cobras eat mainly rodents, coming into homes after rats, which is a cause of many accidents. Frogs, toads and birds are also eaten, the cobras climbing trees to plunder nests. The Egyptian cobra often raids poultry runs. The Cape cobra often eats snakes, including its fellows, and the black-and-white cobra is reported to hunt fish. When food is short they will eat grasshoppers and other large insects.

Cobras' mating dance

Before mating, the pair 'dance', raising their heads a foot or more off the ground and weaving to and fro. This may continue for an hour before mating takes place, when the male presses his cloaca to the female's and ripples run through his body.

The Cape cobra mates between September and October and the eggs are laid a month later. These dates vary through the cobras' range as they mate and lay eggs at the season most likely to provide abundant food for the young. Eggs number 8—20, and are laid in a hole in the ground or in a tree. The female may stand guard and during the breeding period is irritable and aggressive. She is liable to attack without provocation with dire results for passers-by if her nest is near a footpath. Newly-hatched cobras measure about 10 in.

Enemies

The traditional enemies of cobras are the mongooses, but genets also attack them. The mongoose's tactics are to leap backwards and forwards, around the cobra, keeping it continually on the alert until it tires and cannot hold its body raised in striking position. The mongoose is protected by the speed of its movements and by being very resistant to the cobra's venom. Mongooses do not always win, however. It has been suggested that the inflated hood serves as a protection, making it difficult for any enemy to bite the cobra's neck. Cobras also sham dead, going limp until danger passes.

Snake-charmer's bluff

Cobras, especially the Indian and Egyptian species, are the favourite performers in the snake-charmer's act. It is perhaps fairly common knowledge now that the snakes are not reacting to the music but to the rhythmic movements of the charmer. The pipe is merely a stage prop, and is not used by all performers, because snakes are deaf, or, in other words, they cannot perceive airborne vibrations. They have no eardrum that in most other terrestrial animals vibrates in time to the airborne waves, and

The legendary 'asp' or Egyptian cobra may grow to a length of 8 ft; and length for length it is much heavier than the Indian cobra.

they do not have the systems of bones and ducts that convey the vibrations from the eardrum to the sense cells of the inner ear. They can, however, detect vibrations through the earth.

The explanation of the cobras' dance is that the basket is suddenly opened, exposing the snakes to the glare of daylight. Half-blinded and somewhat shocked, they rear up in the defensive position with hoods inflated. Their attention is caught by the first moving object they see, which is the swaying snake-charmer, whose actions they follow.

Part of the act consists of the cobras being handled and even kissed on the head. This is not such a dare-devil act of bravado as it may seem for it is said that cobras cannot strike accurately in the full light of day, and, anyway, their fangs will have been

drawn or their lips sewn up. If this has not been done, the chances are that the charmer is immune to their venom.

class	**Reptilia**
order	**Squamata**
suborder	**Serpentes**
family	**Elapidae**
genus & species	***Naja naja*** *Indian cobra* ***N. haje*** *Egyptian cobra* ***N. nivea*** *Cape cobra* ***N. nigricollis*** *spitting cobra* ***N. melanoleuca*** *black-and-white cobra* *others*

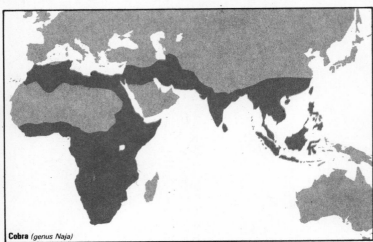

Cobra *(genus Naja)*

△ *When cobras 'dance' for snake-charmers it is because, shocked and half-blinded by sudden exposure to daylight, they rear into their typical defensive position with their attention fixed on the first moving object they see—the hand or pipe of the snake-charmer.*

Adder

A snake, member of the viper family, the adder has a relatively stout body and a short tail. The average male is 21 in. long, the female 2 ft – the record length is 2 ft 8 in. The head is flat, broadening behind the eyes to form an arrow-head shape.

The colour and body-markings vary considerably; adders are among the few snakes in which male and female are coloured differently. Generally the ground colour is a shade of brown, olive, grey or cream; but black varieties in which all patterning is obliterated are fairly common. The most characteristic marking is the dark zig-zag line down the back with a series of spots on either side; the head carries a pair of dark bands, often forming an X or a V.

It is often possible to distinguish the sex of an adder by its colour. Those which are cream, dirty yellow, silvery or pale grey, or light olive, with black markings, are usually males; females are red, reddish brown or gold, with darker red or brown markings. The throat of the male is black, or whitish with the scales spotted or edged with black; females have a yellowish-white chin sometimes tinged with red.

Distribution and habits

The adder ranges throughout Europe and across Asia to Sakhalin Island, north of Japan. In the British Isles it is absent from Ireland and the northern isles. It is usually to be seen in dry places such as sandy heaths, moors and the sunny slopes of hills where it often basks in the sun on hedge-banks, logs and piles of stones. It is, however, also found in damp situations.

Its tolerance of cold allows the adder to live as far north as Finland, beyond the Arctic Circle. It escapes cold weather by hibernation, which starts when the shade temperature falls below 9°C/49°F. It emerges again when the air temperature rises above 8°C/46°F – even coming out onto snow –

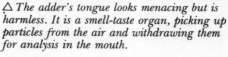

▽ *The hedgehog is one of the adder's arch-enemies. It is protected by its spines while it alternately bites and rolls up, until the adder is dead.*

△ *The adder's tongue looks menacing but is harmless. It is a smell-taste organ, picking up particles from the air and withdrawing them for analysis in the mouth.*

but a cold spell will send it in again. The duration of hibernation depends, therefore, on climate: in northern Europe it may last up to 275 days, whereas in the south it may be as little as 105 days. In Britain, adders usually hibernate for about 135 days in October-March, depending on the weather.

Unlike many other snakes adders do not burrow but seek out crevices and holes where they lie up for the winter. The depth at which they hibernate depends, like duration, on the climate: in Britain the average depth is 10–12 in., but in Denmark, where winters are more severe, adders are found at depths of 4 ft.

Very often many adders will be found in one den, or hibernaculum. As many as 40 have been found coiled up together, along with a number of toads and lizards. This

massing together is a method of preventing heat loss, but it is not known how the adders come to congregate in the hibernacula, which are used year after year. It may be that they can detect the scent left from previous years.

It is uncertain whether adders are nocturnal or diurnal. Their eyes are typical of nocturnal animals in that they are rich in the very sensitive rod cells: such eyes will see well at night, but during the day they need protection, and the adder's slit pupils cut down the intensity of light. On the other hand, despite these adaptations, adders are often active during the day. Courtship and some feeding are definitely diurnal; feeding depends on how hungry the adder is.

Rodent killer

The adder's main prey is lizards, mice, voles and shrews. Young adders subsist at first

A black adder. Adders range in colour from cream, through dirty yellow to silvery grey or olive (male); and from red to gold (female).

on insects and worms. Larger victims are killed by a poisonous bite, the effects of which vary with the size of the prey. A lizard will be dead within a few minutes, or even within 30 seconds; but an adder's bite is rarely fatal to humans. There were only seven authenticated records of fatalities through snakebite in England and Wales in the first half of this century, and four of these were children.

The adder's method of hunting is to follow its prey by scent, then poison it with a quick strike of the head. While the venom acts, the victim may have time to escape to cover, in which case the snake will wait for a while then follow to eat its dead prey.

Dance of the adders

The mating period is from the end of March to early May, though it has been known to last until autumn. In the north of Europe the summer is too short for the eggs to mature in one year, so breeding takes place in alternate years.

At the beginning of the breeding season, there is a good deal of territorial rivalry between males, culminating in the 'dance of the adders'. Two males face each other with head erect and the forepart of the body held off the ground. They sway from side to side, then with bodies entwined each attempts to force the other to the ground by pushing and thrusting. They do not attempt to bite each other.

Finally one gives up and departs. The female, who is frequently waiting close at hand, will accept any victorious male, if she is ready, and a male will mate with any female. He crawls up behind her and loops his coils over her body, rubbing his chin (which has especially sensitive skin) on her back until he reaches the back of her neck, and mating takes place.

Adders are ovoviviparous: that is, the eggs remain inside the mother's body until they are fully developed, and the young are born coiled up in a membrane which is ruptured by their convulsive movements. They have an egg tooth, which in other animals is used to rupture the egg membranes, but in adders it is degenerate as they have no need of it, and the tooth is so situated that it is of no use for this purpose. It is shed a few days after birth.

The young are born in August or September and the number ranges from five to 20: 10-14 are most common, each measuring 6-8 inches in length. They are immediately capable of independent existence, but often they appear to stay with the mother. Young adders disappear so quickly when disturbed that there is an ancient legend, an account of which appears in Holinshed's Chronicle of 1577, that in times of danger the mother adder swallows her offspring. This legend could be due to early observers cutting up an ovoviviparous mother and finding unborn adders inside. Not knowing that adders hatch from the egg inside the parent they would think she had swallowed them.

△ *Male (left) and female adders are always differently coloured.*

▽ *Adder with day-old young.*

The adder has no external ear or ear drum, but picks up vibrations from the ground through its lower jaw. The vertical slit pupil gives quick perception of horizontal movement.

Enemies although poisonous

Like most animals—even those well capable of defending themselves—adders are most likely to flee if confronted with danger, and they usually bite only if suddenly frightened. But, despite not having the excuse of self-defence, man is their chief enemy. However, the killing of adders on sight has not led to their decline, although nowadays increased urbanisation is destroying their habitat.

Undoubtedly many carnivores will take adders. Foxes and badgers kill them, and they have been found in the stomachs of pike and eels. Surprisingly, perhaps, the hedgehog is a great adversary of adders: one reason is that it can tolerate large doses of venom without harm. Its method of killing is to bite the adder, then curl up leaving nothing but a palisade of spines for the snake to strike at. It repeats the process of biting and curling until the snake is dead, after which the hedgehog eats it.

A confusion of names

The Anglo-Saxon name for the adder was *naedre*, which became 'a nadder' or 'a nedder' in Middle English. Later the *n* was transposed, so that we now have 'an adder'. The alternative name viper comes from the Anglo-Saxon *vipere* or *vipre*, itself derived from the Latin *vipera*. This was a contraction of *vivipara*, from *vivus* (alive) and *parere* (to bring forth)—alluding to the animal's method of reproduction. In general 'viper' was used to mean any venomous snake. There being only one such snake in England, viper and adder became synonymous for the one species (viper also being used to describe a venomous or spiteful person).

The two words have spread with the English language all over the world, being used not only for snakes of the genus *Vipera*. There are the near relatives such as the gaboon viper, more distant, like the pit vipers and mole vipers, and the death adder, which is not even in the viper family.

class	**Reptilia**
order	**Squamata**
suborder	**Serpentes**
family	**Viperidae**
genus & species	***Vipera berus***

311

Puff adder

There are 8 species of puff adder in Africa and they range in size from the Peringuey's desert adder, 1 ft long, to the Gaboon viper, 6 ft or more long. They are stout bodied snakes with short tails. The head is very broad compared with the neck, and is covered with small overlapping scales. There is a deep pit of unknown function above the nostrils, and in many species one or more erectile scales on the snout form 'horns', as in the rhinoceros viper. Not all puff adders are given this name, although they all belong to the same genus, and they fall into two groups. These are the highly coloured Gaboon viper and rhinoceros viper, of the tropical African forests, and the sombrely coloured brown and grey puff adders of the savannah and deserts. One of this second group, the common puff adder, is yellow to brown with darker bars or chevrons on the back. It ranges from Morocco southwards across the Sahara to the Cape and is also found in Arabia. The others have less extensive ranges, the Cape puff adder, for example, being found only in the mountains of Cape Province, South Africa.

Melting into the background

Savannah and desert puff adders, with their duller colourings, tend to harmonize with the differently coloured soils on which they are living. So also do the Gaboon and rhinoceros vipers in spite of their bright colours, for their colour patterns are disruptive. The Gaboon viper has a gaudy pattern of yellow, purple and brown arranged in geometric forms. The rhinoceros viper, even more brilliantly coloured with more purple, and blue as well, has green triangles margined with black and blue on its sides. But both snakes are virtually invisible on the carpet of dead and green leaves on the forest floor. The smaller species of puff adder live on sandy soils. Several of these smaller adders are able to climb into bushes, but generally puff adders keep to the ground, hunting mainly during the night.

Inoffensive yet deadly

The broad head of the puff adder houses the large venom glands and although the effect of this snake's bite is less rapid than that of a mamba or a cobra it is just as deadly. Fortunately, these snakes strike only to disable prey or in self-defence, and need a fair amount of provocation to make them hit back. Africans are said to be more afraid of harmless geckos than of the Gaboon viper, and Herbert Lang tells of a small boy dragging a 5 ft live specimen into his camp to sell it to him. If their venom is slow-acting it is nonetheless potent. R Marlin Perkins, curator of reptiles in the St Louis Zoological Gardens, nearly died from the bite of a Gaboon viper. Some years

◁ *The attractive 'horned' head of the rhinoceros viper is deceptive; it houses the venom glands.*

later, in 1964, the Director of the Salt Lake City Zoo died from a puff adder bite received while handling the snake. Puff adders can give out as much as 15 drops of venom at a time—4 drops are enough to kill a man. But usually snakes give a first warning by hissing. The hissing sound is produced by forcing air from the lungs and windpipe through the glottis. Puff adders have an especially loud hiss. Their puff makes a sound more like the noise of a horse when it forces air through its lips.

Beckoning their food

The food of puff adders varies widely between the species. Small prey, such as a frog, is grabbed and swallowed without being poisoned. Larger prey is struck with the fangs and allowed to run away to die. The snake later follows its trail to eat it. The carcase is dragged into the snake's mouth by the teeth in the lower jaw. Once part of the victim has reached the throat, muscular swallowing movements carry it down, the snake holding its head up to assist this. Some scientists claim that the long fangs, which may be 2 in. long in a 5ft Gaboon viper, are used to drag the victim into the snake's mouth. South African herpetologists do not support this, but suggest the long fangs make it possible to inject the venom deeply.

The common puff adder and the Gaboon viper eat rats and mice, ground-living birds, frogs, toads and lizards. The Cape Mountain adder feeds on the same but is known to eat other snakes. The many-horned adder and the horned puff adder bury themselves in the sand, except for the eyes and snout, to catch lizards. The horned puff adder leaves the tip of its tail sticking out of the sand and waggles it to attract its victims within striking distance.

An enemy to many small animals, the puff adder has few adversaries itself, mainly birds of prey, mongooses and warthogs, and man. Puff adders can store large quantities of fat and this is sold by African herbalists as a cure for rheumatism.

Large families

Puff adders are ovoviviparous. That is, the eggs are hatched inside the mother so the young are born alive or else they wriggle out of the egg capsule soon after it is laid. Mating is usually from October to December, the young being born in March and April. The young from a mother 3 ft long, are about 8 in. at birth. There are 8—15 in the litter of the smallest species, 70—80 or more in the large puff adders.

Fasting to grow

The paradoxical frog is named because of the paradox that the tadpole is much greater than the froglet into which it changes. The puzzle is, where does all the spare flesh go? The situation is reversed in the baby puff adder. As soon as it is born it can kill and eat small mice although it moults first before looking for food. It can, however, happily go without food for as much as 3 months. The ability to fast is not unusual. What is extraordinary is that the baby puff adder still grows 25% in length and increases its girth by a quarter while doing so.

△ Sedate mating, two love-locked common puff adders, the male is on the right. Mating usually takes place from October to December. Fertilisation is internal and sperm may survive inside the female for long periods. Most reptiles lay their eggs but puff adders are ovoviviparous, the female retains the eggs until the young are ready or nearly ready to hatch 5—6 months later.

◁ Submerged for the day, a small Peringuey's puff adder spends the day well hidden. Alerted by the photographer the snake raises its head so giving its position away. But its sandy colouring blends well with the soil making the snake very inconspicuous.

class	**Reptilia**
order	**Squamata**
suborder	**Serpentes**
family	**Viperidae**
genus & species	***Bitis arietans*** common puff adder ***B. atropos*** Cape Mountain adder ***B. caudalis*** horned puff adder ***B. cornuta*** manyhorned adder ***B. gabonica*** Gaboon viper ***B. inornata*** Cape puff adder ***B. nasicornis*** rhinoceros viper ***B. peringueyi*** Peringuey's puff adder

314

Pit viper

Some of the most-feared snakes are to be found among the 60 species of pit vipers (family Crotalidae) including well known forms like the fer de lance, (named so because of its lance-shaped head and body), and the sidewinder and the rattlesnakes, which we shall come to later. Here we shall consider others, such as the American water moccasin, copperhead and bushmaster, as well as the Asiatic pit vipers. Pit vipers are a diverse group with several interesting specializations, which is why we have given them three entries. Here, while dealing with the family in general terms, we pay special attention to what has been called their sixth sense, the two pits on the head that give them their name.

Pit vipers are solenoglyph. That is, they have fangs which fold back and are erected when about to be used. Most pit vipers are land-living, some are tree-dwellers, a few have taken to water and others lead a partially burrowing life. Water moccasins are heavy-bodied, up to 5 ft long, and while living on land they readily take to water when disturbed and they hunt in water. They are slate black to olive or tan with indistinct brown bands. The copperhead, a brown snake with hourglass markings along the back, is up to 3 ft long. It lives in rocky outcrops and quarries and among piles of rotting logs. The bushmaster is the longest of the American pit vipers, up to 12 ft, mainly grey and brown with large diamond blotches along the back. It has large venom glands and unusually long fangs. Its generic name **Lachesis** is from one of the Fates that influenced the length of life of people – a grim pun by the scientist who named it, for the bushmaster is one of the most dangerous of snakes. The Asiatic pit vipers are of two kinds, tree-dwelling and ground-living, the first having prehensile tails that assist their climbing. The Himalayan pit viper lives at altitudes of 7 000–16 000 ft, sometimes being found even at the foot of glaciers.

The Asiatic pit vipers are found mainly in eastern and southeast Asia with one species extending as far west as the mouth of the River Volga. Wagler's pit viper is kept in large numbers in the Snake Temple in Penang. The water moccasin and the copperhead are widespread over the eastern and middle United States, the bushmaster ranges from Costa Rica and Panama to northern South America.

Warm-blooded food

The warning posture of the water moccasin, mouth open showing its white lining, gives it the alternative name of cottonmouth. It also vibrates its tail at the same time, like its relatives the rattlesnakes, although it has no rattle to make a warning sound. Pit vipers, apart from their pits, are very

△ Trimeresurus gramineus.

ordinary snakes. Some take a wide range of foods, like the water moccasin which eats rabbits, muskrats, ducks, fish, frogs, other snakes, birds' eggs, and nestlings. The copperhead eats small rodents, especially the woodmouse, other snakes, frogs, toads, and insects, including caterpillars and cicadas. The bushmaster, by contrast, takes mainly mammals, and pit vipers generally tend to hunt warm-blooded animals more than cold-blooded, as one would expect from snakes with heat-detector pits. They have one on each side of the head between the eye and the nostril. Using these a pit viper can pick up the trail of a warm-blooded animal.

'Seeing' heat

Each pit is $\frac{1}{8}$ in. across and $\frac{1}{4}$ in. deep. A thin membrane is stretched near the bottom and temperature receptors, 500–1 500 per sq mm, are packed within this membrane. These receptors are so sensitive they can respond to changes as small as 0·002 of a C°, and they allow a snake to locate objects 0·1 of a C° warmer or cooler than the surroundings. In more understandable terms a pit viper could detect the warmth of the human hand held a foot from its head. The membrane with its receptors can be compared to an eye with its retina. The overhanging lip of the pit casts 'heat shadows' onto it, so the snake is aware of direction, and since the 'fields of view' of the two pits overlap there is the equivalent of stereoscopic vision, giving a rangefinder. A pit viper hunting by day has the advantage of being able to follow an animal's heat trail through low vegetation after the animal has passed out of sight. It could, of course, do this equally well by scent. The facial pits come into their own in night hunting, when prey can be tracked by scent with the facial pits guiding the final strike. At first it was thought they had something to do with an accessory aid to smell or as an organ of hearing—snakes have no ears. Another suggestion was that they might be organs for picking up low-frequency air vibrations. Then, as late as 1892, it was noticed that a rattlesnake, one

of the pit vipers, was attracted to a lighted match. Then came the discovery that pythons have pits on their lips that are sensitive to heat. The first experiments on pit vipers were made in 1937, and left no doubt that the pits are heat detectors and further studies since have shown just how delicate they are.

Snakes in cold climates

Pit vipers usually bear living young. There are a few exceptions, the bushmaster being one, and that lives in the tropics. Pit vipers extend from the Volga across Asia and across America. There may be a direct connection between these two facts. One of the advantages of bearing living young, as against laying eggs, is that the offspring are protected not only against enemies but also against low temperatures until they are at an advanced stage of development. At some time pit vipers must have crossed the land bridge that used to exist where the Bering Straits are now. This is well north, and it would have been far easier for snakes able to bear live young to survive in these latitudes and so make the crossing. It probably explains also why the Himalayan pit viper can live so near glaciers, and why the most southerly of all snakes is a pit viper named Bothrops ammodytoides, living in the Santa Cruz province of Argentina.

class	**Reptilia**
order	**Squamata**
suborder	**Serpentes**
family	**Crotalidae**
genera & species	*Ancistrodon contortrix* copperhead *A. himalayanus* Himalayan pit viper *A. piscivorus* water moccasin **Trimeresurus wagleri** Wagler's pit viper

Rattlesnake

These are heavy-bodied and usually highly venomous snakes, best known for the rattle, sometimes called a bell, cloche, buzzer or whirrer, on the tail. When disturbed the rattlesnake vibrates its tail, or rattle, as if giving warning that it is about to strike. Rattlesnakes are found almost entirely in North America, from southern Canada to Mexico, where there are 30 species and over 60 subspecies, with one species in South America.

There are two groups of rattlesnakes, each represented by one genus: the pygmy rattlesnakes **Sistrurus** *have short slender tails and very tiny rattles, and they never exceed 2 ft in length; and the rattlesnakes proper* **Crotalus**, *which are usually around $3\frac{1}{2}$–5 ft but exceptionally grow to 8 ft or more. The timber or banded rattlesnake of the eastern States is marked with dark chevrons on the back. In the prairie rattlesnake the markings are irregularly oblong. Most others have diamond markings. Rattlesnakes share with other pit vipers (page 315) a tolerance of low temperatures. The Mexican dusky rattlesnake lives at altitudes of up to 14 500 ft.*

Sound varies with size

The rattle is made up of a number of loosely interlocked shells each of which was the scale originally covering the tip of the tail. Usually in snakes this scale is a simple hollow cone which is shed with the rest of the skin at each moult. In rattlesnakes it is larger than usual, much thicker and has one or two constrictions. Except at the first moult, the scale is not shed but remains loosely attached to the new scale, and at each moult a new one is added. The rattle does not grow in length indefinitely. The end scales tend to wear out, so there can be a different number of segments to the rattle in different individuals of the same age, depending on how much the end of the rattle is abraded. It seldom exceeds 14 segments in wild rattlesnakes no matter how old they may be, but snakes in zoos, leading a more untroubled life, and not rubbing the rattle on hard objects, may have as many as 29 pieces in a rattle. The longer the rattle the more the sound is deadened, 8 being the most effective number to give the loudest noise. The volume of sound not only varies with the size of the snake and the length of the rattle, but it also varies from species to species. At best it can be heard only a few feet away.

◁ Threatening tiger rattlesnake. Between its coils is a large rattle, a unique organ composed of horny segments of unshed skin. The fact that rattlesnakes shed their skin three or four times a year during the first years of their lives disposes of the popular idea that the number of rattles corresponds to the years of the snake's age. The best reason to be found for the evolution of the rattle in an animal that is deaf is that it acts as a warning device to large animals that may molest or tread on the snake.

Rattlers not all black

It is hard to generalize on the size and effectiveness of the rattle as it is on any other feature of rattlesnakes. For example, these snakes have a reputation for attacking people, and of being bad tempered. It applies only to some of them. Unless provoked or roughly treated the red diamond rattlesnake may make no attempt to strike when handled. It may not even sound its rattle. The eastern and western diamond backs, by contrast, not only rattle a warning but they will also pursue an intruder, lunging at it again and again. How poisonous a snake is also depends on several things, such as its age—the younger it is the less the amount of poison it can inject—and whether it has recently struck at another victim, when the amount of venom it can use will be reduced. Cases are known in which a snake has taken nearly two months to replenish its venom to full capacity. Rattlesnakes of the same species from one part of the range may be more venomous than those from another part. Prairie rattlesnakes of the plains are about three times as venomous as those of California, and half as poisonous again as those of the Grand Canyon.

Waterproof skin

Rattlesnakes feed on much the same prey as other pit vipers (page 315), mainly small warm-blooded animals and especially rodents, cottontail rabbits and young jack rabbits. Young rattlesnakes, including the pygmy rattlesnakes, take a larger proportion of coldblooded animals, such as frogs, salamanders and lizards. Studies have also been made on how much rattlesnakes drink, and the remarks that follow probably apply to all snakes. Their needs are not as great as those of active and warm-blooded animals because the water loss from the body is not high. They need about one-tenth as much water as a mammal of similar size. In one test it was found that twice as much water is lost from a rattlesnake's head, and this mainly in its breath, as from the whole of the rest of its body, which suggests that its skin is almost waterproof. When it does drink it sucks up water from a pond or stream. There is no evidence that it laps it with the tongue, as is sometimes stated, or that it drinks dew.

Two years to be born

All rattlesnakes give birth to live young. Whether they have one litter a year or less depends on the climate. The prairie rattlesnake has one litter a year in the southern part of its range, but in the northern part it may be two years before the young are ready to be born. Mating is in spring and the number in a litter may vary from 1 to 60 according to the size of the mother, the usual number being between 10 and 20.

Slaughter of infants

Their venom does not spare rattlesnakes from being killed and eaten. Hawks of all kinds kill them, so do skunks and snake-eating snakes. Pigs, deer and other hoofed animals trample them, especially the young ones, and many die of cold or excessive heat, or from starvation. Indeed few from a litter survive their first year.

Sensitive eyes

Snakes are known to be deaf yet they often seem to be reacting to sounds. In fact, they seem at first glance to be able to hear but there is more to it than this, as Laurence Klauber found in his celebrated tests on rattlesnakes. First, having placed a rattlesnake under a table, he clapped two sticks together making sure his hands and the sticks could not be seen by the snake. It reacted, apparently to the sound. Puzzled at first, Klauber finally found the reason. He was sitting on a stool, his feet dangling, and every time he clapped the sticks together his feet moved and the snake reacted to sight of them. So he put a screen between the snake and his feet, and still the snake reacted when he clapped the sticks—it was seeing a reflection of Klauber's feet in a nearby window.

He found his red diamond rattler highly sensitive to footsteps on a concrete floor 15 ft away, and it still reacted to footsteps that distance away after he had placed it on a blanket. He decided to test this further. He put the snake in a fibreboard box, suspended this by a rubber band from a stick held each end on a pillow, to insulate it from vibrations through the ground. It still reacted to clapped sticks and to the radio. It was, in fact, as Klauber finally found, picking up the heat from the valves of the radio as these warmed up, and it was reacting to vibrations in the floor and sides of the fibreboard box, against which its body rested. So the box was changed for a Chinese woven bamboo basket hung from the same stick. Still the snake appeared to react to sound, but further tests showed it was reacting to Klauber's hand movements seen through the very tiny cracks between the bamboo withies. Apart from anything else, these experiments show how hard it can sometimes be to test a particular animal sense. They also show, among other things, how sensitive a snake's eyes are to small movements.

class	Reptilia
order	Squamata
suborder	Serpentes
family	Crotalidae
genus & species	*Crotalus adamanteus* eastern diamond back
	C. atrox western diamond back
	C. horridus timber or banded rattlesnake
	C. pusillus Mexican dusky rattlesnake
	C. ruber red diamond back
	C. tigris tiger rattlesnake
	C. viridis prairie rattlesnake

◁ *Sparring partners—two western diamond back rattlesnakes engage in combat. Although it is difficult to observe both snakes simultaneously during the fight it seems that the twining of the necks is a manoeuvre for an advantageous position from which one snake may forcefully throw his opponent.*

Sidewinder

Also known as the horned rattlesnake, the sidewinder is named after its peculiar form of locomotion which allows it to move over soft sand. Sidewinders are small rattlesnakes, the adults being only 1½ – 2 ft long. The females are usually larger than the males, whereas in other rattlesnakes it is the reverse. The body is stout, tapering to a narrow neck with a broad head like an arrowhead. Above each eye there is a scale that projects as a small horn. There is a dark stripe running backwards from each eye. The body is pale grey or light brown with a row of large dark brown spots running down the back and smaller ones on each side. The tail is marked with alternate light and dark bands and the underparts of the body and tail are white.

The single species of sidewinder lives in the deserts of the southwest United States, including Nevada, Utah, California, Arizona and in the northern part of the state of Baja California in Mexico.

Sand snake

Sidewinders are most common in areas of loose, windblown sand and although they can be found among rocks or on compacted sand there is usually loose sand nearby. Although other rattlesnakes live in deserts and can be found on loose sand, the sidewinder is the most characteristic of this type of habitat. It is likely that in this habitat the sidewinder has an advantage over the other snakes. By adapting to life in moving sand the sidewinder does not compete with other snakes. These can move over sand by the usual eel-like wriggling. The sidewinder's unusual looping movement enables it to get a good grip on loose sand and so move faster.

Sidewinders are most active in the early part of the night when air temperatures are not dangerously high and when their prey is also active. They spend the day in mouse-holes or buried in sand, usually under the shelter of a creosote bush or a yucca. They bury themselves by shovelling sand over themselves with looping movements of the body until they are coiled like springs, flush with the surface of the sand. Their mottled brown colour makes them very difficult to see as they lie there half buried.

Desert prey

The shallow saucers in the sand where sidewinders have been resting are often found near mouse and rat burrows as the sidewinders are probably attracted to these areas where they will find prey plentiful. Their main food is small rodents, such as deer mice, kangaroo rats and spiny pocket mice, and lizards such as the tree-climbing utas and other sand-dwelling iguanids. Sidewinders also eat a few snakes, such as the glossy snake and even other sidewinders, and a few small birds.

The breeding habits of sidewinders are the same as those of other rattlesnakes (page 317). Mating takes place when they emerge from hibernation in spring and the young are born alive.

The sidewinder is a small squat rattlesnake that is perfectly adapted for living in deserts.

How snakes move

Sidewinding is like a coiled wire rolled along the sand making a series of oblique parallel tracks. Only the white areas touch the ground.

In serpentine movement the body literally skates along in a series of shallow curves which get a grip on any projecting object.

Concertina movement: with the tail anchored the head and neck dart forward, the neck grips the ground and the rest of the body is then pulled up.

Sidewinding

Many snakes will perform 'sidewinding' movements if placed on a sheet of glass, throwing their bodies into loops to get a grip on the smooth surface. The sidewinder, and the horned viper and puff adder of African deserts, make a habit of sidewinding, leaving characteristic tracks in the sand. These are a series of parallel, wavering lines each with a hook at one end made by the sidewinder's tail.

It is very difficult to see how the track is made without seeing a sidewinder in action. In normal, or rectilinear, movement, a series of waves passes down a snake's body, pushing against the ground and driving the snake in the opposite direction to the waves. Sidewinding is very different; it is more like a coil spring being rolled or the movement of the tracks of a caterpillar tractor. The snake throws its body into curves and, when moving, only two points of the body touch the ground. These two points remain stationary while the raised parts move at an angle to the direction of the waves that pass along its body. As the snake progresses the part of the body immediately behind is raised, so that the body is laid down and taken up like a caterpillar track. When the point of contact reaches the tip of the tail, a new point is started at the head end and the snake moves along a series of parallel tracks.

class	**Reptilia**
order	**Sauria**
suborder	**Serpentes**
family	**Crotalidae**
genus & species	*Crotalus cerastes*

Birds

There is no doubt that among non-scientists birds are the most favoured of all animals, largely because they are the most obvious, because of their colours and their songs. They have also received more than their fair share of attention from scientists and one result of this is that it is unlikely that new species will be discovered in the future.

Another consequence of this attention is that the classification of birds has reached a stable form. In this classification 27 orders of living birds are enumerated, with two more for the recently extinct moas of New Zealand and elephant-birds of Madagascar. This is a higher proportion of orders to a single class of animals than in any other area of the animal kingdom.

Side by side with this, it has to be recognized that there are few, if any, other major groups of animals so poorly represented by fossils, as are birds. Fortunately, there are the remarkably complete fossils of the earliest known bird, the Archaeopteryx, the so-called lizard-bird, that indicate very clearly the evolution of birds from reptilian ancestors. This paucity of fossils is probably to be correlated with the flying habits, so that, as has often been said by palae-ontologists, "birds do not make good fossils". The situation is similar for bats – but not for the pterodactyls or flying reptiles. This absence of all but a few scattered fossils is the more remarkable when it is recalled that birds have certainly been in existence for about 180 million years.

The class Aves used to be divided into two main divisions: the Ratitae and the Carinatae, the first including the large, flightless, running birds, such as ostrich, emu, cassowary, rhea and kiwi, the second including all the rest. Today, both names are used, if at all, merely as convenient group names, the surviving ratites being assigned to four separate orders, the Struthioniformes (ostriches), Rheiformes (rheas), Casuariiformes (emus, cassowaries) and Apterygiformes (kiwis), on the assumption that these birds are not necessarily related but look alike as a result of convergent evolution.

Of the remaining 23 orders, one is by far the largest and contains the most familiar of all birds. It is named the Passeriformes, after *Passer domesticus*, the house sparrow, the most familiar of all birds in the western world, where the main work on the early classification of birds was carried out. This order, sometimes referred to merely as Passeres, contains more than half the known species of living birds and includes 56 of the 149 families of the 'Carinatae'.

In its turn, the Passeriformes, also known as the perching birds, is divided into four suborders, the Eurylaimi (broadbills), Tyranni (woodcreepers, antbirds, antpipits, ovenbirds, tapaculos and others), Menurae (lyrebirds, scrub-birds) and Oscines (songbirds). The first three of these account for only 15 of the 56 families and about 1040 species out of the 5000 or more species of Passeriformes.

The Passeriformes therefore bear comparison with bony fishes in having been evolved, geologically speaking, in a very short space of time. They have proliferated into numerous species, are worldwide, have successfully adapted to environments most of which are man-made, nesting or roosting on buildings and making use very often of 'unnatural' foods. Like the bony fishes, they have exploited a wide variety of habitats. Since they use agricultural land and buildings so much they are brought into close contact with people, whether in rural or urban districts, so that the Passeriformes can reasonably be said to have played a major role in the social phenomenon of the 20th century known as bird-watching.

It has been said, doubtless with a fair degree of truth, that we hold as favourites those animals having characteristics similar to our own. The passerines have these in generous degree. Most birds are deficient in the sense of smell, and this is especially true of passerines. With rare exceptions, birds are 'eyesight animals', like humans, meaning that sight is the most important sense. Above all, the Passeriformes are especially vocal, if not vociferous, a feature of human behaviour almost without parallel in the animal kingdom.

Ostrich

The ostrich is the largest living bird and one of the most familiar because of its bizarre appearance. A large male may stand 8 ft high of which nearly half is neck. The plumage of the male is black except for the white plumes on the wings and tail. It is these plumes that first led to the numbers of ostriches being greatly reduced in many places and later to ostriches being raised on farms. The plumage of the females is brown with pale edging to the feathers. The head, most of the neck and the legs are almost naked, but the eyelids have long, black eyelashes. There are two strong toes on each foot, the longest being armed with a large claw.

A few million years ago, in the Pliocene era, there were nine species of ostriches, but only one survives today. About 200 years ago five subspecies of this species ranged over much of Africa, Syria and Arabia, in desert and bush regions. They are now extinct or very rare over most of this area. The Asian subspecies was last recorded in 1941. Ostriches are still plentiful in East Africa, and they live wild in a few places in south Australia where they were introduced.

Strange social life

Ostriches are extremely wary, their long necks enabling them to detect disturbances from quite a distance. As a result it is very difficult to study ostriches in the wild and until recently our knowledge has been based mainly on observations on domesticated ostriches. Incomplete observations in the wild have led to many mistaken ideas about the habits of these birds which have now become legendary. A husband and wife team of zoologists, the Sauers, studied ostriches in South West Africa by the ingenious method of disguising their hide as a termite mound. Ostriches and several other animals treated this hide with complete indifference with the result that the Sauers were afforded a grandstand view of ostrich social life, and they found that in some respects this is almost as strange as the legends.

Ostriches often live in very dry areas and they move about in search of food, often in quite large groups. During wet spells the herds break up into family groups, consisting of a pair with chicks and immatures. The herd is led by a cock or hen that chooses grazing grounds and makes decisions as to when to move. If the herd leaves familiar territory or comes to a water hole where no other animals are drinking, the dominant ostriches push the immature birds forward to spring any ambushes.

Eats nearly anything

Ostriches feed mainly on plants including fruits, seeds and leaves. In deserts they get their water from succulent plants. They also eat small animals and are even said to eat lizards and tortoises. Their reputation for eating almost anything including lumps of metal and tins of paint is widespread and perhaps exaggerated but ostriches swallow considerable amounts of sand to aid digestion and it is said that it is possible to trace the movements of an ostrich by examining the kinds of sand and gravel in its stomach.

Unstable society

Until recently there was considerable doubt as to whether ostriches were polygamous or monogamous. Proponents of monogamy pointed out that there was never more than one male or one female seen at a nest or leading a group of chicks. It is now known that ostriches may be monogamous but more usually they are polygamous. The Sauers found that the social organisation of ostriches is very flexible and that a male accompanying a female with chicks need not be the father of the chicks.

Breeding takes place at any time of the year, depending on the time of the rainy season. At first the males develop a red pigment on their heads and feet and they display to each other, chasing around in groups with wings held out to show off the white plumes. Later they establish territories away from the communal feeding grounds, and here they are joined by the females. A male ostrich usually has three hens in his harem but it is not unknown for him to have up to five.

The courtship ceremony is elaborate. The male separates one female from the group and the pair feed together, synchronising the movements of head and neck. The male then sits down and opens his wings to show the white plumes. At the same time he rocks from side to side and twists his neck in a corkscrew. The female walks around him and eventually drops into the mating position.

Each female lays 6—8 eggs which are about 6 in. long and weigh up to 2½ lb. The members of a harem all lay in one nest, which consists of a depression in the ground that may be about 3 yd across. It may take nearly 3 weeks for all the eggs to be laid, after which the dominant hen drives the others away and the nest is guarded by the single hen and the cock. Incubation consists of keeping the eggs cool by shading them rather than keeping them warm. Towards the end of the 6-week incubation period some eggs are rolled into pits on the edge of the nest. These eggs are those that are most advanced and this is probably a mechanism to synchronise the hatching of the eggs as much as possible.

The chicks can run almost as soon as they hatch and after a month can attain a speed of 35 mph. When they leave their parents they form large bands, breeding when 4—5 years old.

Running to safety

Adult ostriches have little to fear from predators. They are very wary and can run at 40 mph, but the eggs and young ostriches may fall prey to jackals and other predators. The adults lead their chicks away from enemies and perform distraction displays while the chicks scatter and crouch.

▷ *A bizarre creature with a long naked neck: the ostrich is the largest living bird.*

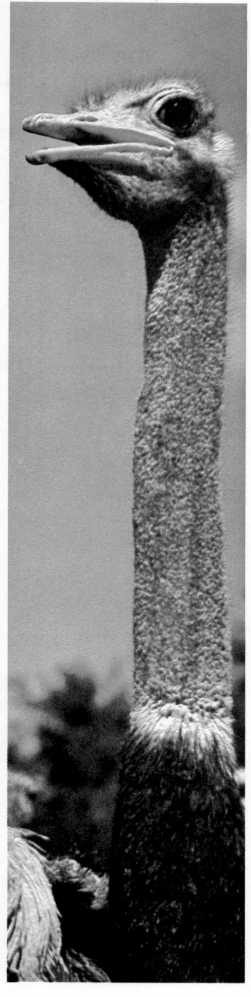

Beating their wings and calling loudly the ostriches run to and fro presenting a broadside to the enemy and occasionally dropping to the ground and setting up a cloud of dust with the wings. Sometimes the male continues the display while the female leads the chicks away.

Burying their heads
One of the popular notions about ostriches is that they bury their heads in the sand when danger threatens. The action is used to describe the behaviour of a person who thinks that a problem can be solved by ignoring it, and has been the subject of many jokes and cartoons. This idea is very old, for the Roman writer Pliny says '. . . the veriest fools they be of all others, for as high as the rest of their body is, yet if they thrust their head and neck once into any shrub or bush, and get it hidden, they think then

◁ *Too many eggs? At the end of the incubation period the most advanced eggs are rolled into a pit beside the nest to synchronize hatching.*
▽ *Arrival date. Ostrich chicks hatching.*

they are safe enough, and that no man seeth them.'

Like so many legends there is a basis of truth in the ostrich burying its head and the story is probably due to the difficulty in observing ostriches. When an ostrich is sitting on the nest, its reaction to disturbance is to lower its head until the neck is held horizontally a few inches above the ground. The ostrich is then very inconspicuous and the small head may well be hidden behind a small plant or hummock.

class	**Aves**
order	**Struthioniformes**
family	**Struthionidae**
genus & species	*Struthio camelus*

▷ *A handsome male ostrich gives chase to two females busy displaying.*
▽ *Ostriches on the march. Flocks of them move about in the dry season, looking for food.*

Rhea

The flightless rhea is the largest American bird. It stands about 5 ft high and weighs about 50 lb. Its head and neck are covered with short feathers, body plumage soft and wings longer than those of the ostrich, which it resembles. The long, powerful legs have three toes each, compared with the two toes of the ostrich. The sexes are similar but the males are a little taller.

There are two species of rhea of which the common rhea is the more abundant. It is brownish grey above, whitish below and bluish-grey on the flanks. There are patches of black on the head and neck. There is also a white variety. The common rhea ranges from northeast Brazil to central Argentina. Darwin's rhea is smaller; its plumage is brownish with white spots. It ranges from southern Peru to Patagonia in southern Argentina.

Tripping rheas

Rheas live in flocks of 20—30, sometimes more, but old males are always solitary. They live in open country of the pampas and highland plateaus where they escape from danger by running, or crouching if there is enough cover. When running fast rheas hold their necks out horizontally. They are extremely agile and can change direction with ease, holding one wing out like a sail when cornering.

The flocks sometimes mix with herds of bush deer or guanacos and even with cattle in areas where they are not molested. The common rhea is, however, less abundant than it once was. The spread of agriculture has destroyed parts of its habitat and it is often hunted. The traditional hunting method of the South American Indians was to encircle a flock of rheas. When horses were introduced by the Europeans, rheas were hunted from the saddle and brought down with bolas—three stones joined by thongs which were thrown at the quarry to entangle its legs and so cripple it.

Rheas are omnivorous, eating both plants and animals. They pluck leaves and seeds or grub roots, and catch insects, molluscs, worms and lizards. They also have a habit of snapping up bright objects.

Broody fathers

At the beginning of the breeding season there is intense rivalry between the males. They threaten each other with neck lowered into a U-shape. If both hold their ground they fight, twisting their necks together and biting and kicking. When one is vanquished and breaks away it is chased by the victor who spreads his wings and holds his neck in an S-curve.

The victorious males court the females which live in small groups. The first indication that a male is about to start courting is

◁ *A young rhea has a long way to grow! An adult rhea stands about 5 ft tall on long legs, adapted for running on the ground.*
▷ *Preliminary advances: a male common rhea ruffles its neck feathers at two females.*

when he ruffles his neck plumage. The ruffling later extends over his body, then he runs to and fro with his neck stretched and wings spread. At the same time he calls, uttering a two-note roar more like that of a mammal than a bird. He then approaches a female with neck lowered and wings spread and drooping to the ground. If the female responds to this display mating takes place.

Male rheas mate with several females and each female mates with a number of males, so rheas are both polyandrous and polygynous, but as no lasting pair bond is formed between the birds it might be better to describe them as promiscuous. Nesting and care of the eggs and young is left entirely to the males. The nest is merely a shallow hollow in the ground lined with grass. It is about 3 ft across and 1 ft deep. Each female lays 11—18 eggs, depositing them in several nests, or even on bare ground if she is ready to lay before the males have built their nests. At first a male leads one female after another to his nest to lay their eggs. The male starts to incubate these and then any

females coming near him are greeted with hissing and snapping. They have to persevere before the male will get up and allow them to lay further eggs.

One male may incubate up to 80 eggs but the clutches are usually 10—30. The chicks hatch in 35—40 days and soon leave the nest in the care of the male. They keep in contact with each other by plaintive whistles, but if one gets lost it will join another brood. As a result a 'family' may consist of young at different ages and parentage is even more muddled.

Who are their relations?

The large flightless birds such as rheas, ostriches, kiwis, cassowaries, emus and the extinct moas and elephant birds are often grouped together as 'ratites'. At one time these birds were placed in a single family Ratitae, on the basis of similar characters such as powerful legs for running, small wings and the lack of a keel on the breastbone, which in flying birds is the anchor for the powerful flight muscles. The evolution

of this group has long been debated, but study has been made difficult because of lack of fossils. It is, however, generally agreed that these birds are descended from ancestors that could fly and that far from belonging to a single family, they form 5 separate orders. Their similarity is due to convergent evolution as they have all adopted running on the ground as a way of life. The term 'ratites' is, however, still used as a loose term for these rather similar birds, as opposed to 'carinates' a term used for birds with keels on their breastbones.

class	**Aves**
order	**Rheiformes**
family	**Rheidae**
genera & species	***Pterocnemia pennata*** *Darwin's rhea* ***Rhea americana*** *common rhea*

Emu

One of Australia's flightless birds, the emu is the second biggest bird in existence. It stands 5–6 ft high, 2–3 ft less than the ostrich and dwarfed by the giant moas of New Zealand that became extinct a few centuries ago. Emus are related to cassowaries and share with them the coarse, drooping plumage and small wings hidden by the feathers. The feathers are double, as in cassowaries, with the aftershaft—the small tuft at the base of the vane in many birds—the same length as the main vane. The feathers are also downy, like the feathers of chicks, for the barbs do not have hooks linking them to make the stiff vane. The downy feathers, together with other anatomical features, suggest that emus and the other flightless birds known as ratites, such as ostriches, rheas and kiwis, are neotenous—that is, that juvenile characters have been retained in the adult (see axolotl, page 232).

Before Europeans settled in Australia there were several species of emu, but all except one have been wiped out. At one time Tasmania, Kangaroo, Flinders and other islands, had their own emus, but they were killed off so rapidly that hardly any specimens reached museums.

Apart from the female being slightly the larger, it is difficult to tell male and female emus apart. Their voices, however, are very different. The male makes guttural cries, whereas the female has a resonant booming call made by a large air sac connected to the windpipe.

Pests in the dry season

Emus live in most parts of Australia, except where building and agriculture have driven them out. They are found in the deserts, on plains and in forests—but not in the dense rain forests of northeast Australia, where their place is taken by the cassowary. Outside the breeding season emus live in small parties, sometimes banding together into large herds. They are nomadic, moving about the country in search of food and water. In the dry season they become a pest. They move from the arid areas into agricultural land, raiding crops and using water holes that in bad years are barely enough to support domestic stock and farmers shoot on sight of them.

Like their flightless relatives, emus are strong runners. When pressed they reach 40 mph in short bursts, covering over 9 ft in one stride. Normally they run at a slower and steadier cruising speed that enables them to cover long distances. They are extremely inquisitive, investigating any new object. This may explain the habit, shared with ostriches, of swallowing all sorts of strange objects: keys, nails, bottle tops, coins and so on. One emu is reported to have drunk the contents of a tin of paint, then eaten the tin. Another chased a man for 4 miles, having been attracted to his shiny bicycle; but they will follow men apparently just to look at them.

△The second largest of living birds—the emu. The external ear opening is visible as only downy feathers cover the head and neck.

▽ In the nonbreeding season these huge Australian birds congregate in small flocks, moving through the outback in search of food and water.

Keeping down harmful insects

Fruit of many plants, leaves, grass and insects are the food of emus. During the winter months insects, especially caterpillars probably make up the bulk of the diet. Wheat crops are attacked when they ripen and for this reason emus are often persecuted. Nevertheless, eating insects must repay the debt to a large extent. One emu killed in an official campaign had nearly 3 000 harmful caterpillars in its stomach.

Father guards the eggs

Emus breed when 2 years old, laying their eggs in February or March, the Australian autumn. The male builds the nest, about 3 ft across, making a shallow bowl of grass and weeds, usually under a tree or bush. After the female has laid her clutch of 8–10 dark green eggs, she leaves the nest and the male incubates them for 8 weeks. During this time he rarely leaves the nest, and when he does, he may cover it with leaves to make the already inconspicuous eggs almost impossible to find.

At the end of the 8 weeks the eggs, which were rough, have become smoother and darker. They are often collected and turned into curios or souvenirs by etching the thick shell, revealing the paler layers under the surface in a cameo-like effect.

The chicks leave the nest shortly after hatching. They are miniature versions of the adults but very pale grey with conspicuous black stripes running along the body. The father guards the chicks for up to 18 months, until they are nearly mature. The young chicks feed themselves, mainly on insects, but there is a legend that emus lay a sterile egg either for the chicks to eat or to support a colony of fly maggots for the chicks to eat after hatching.

Oil and outsize omelettes

The natural enemies are wedge-tailed eagles that take young emus; and nest robbers such as various lizards, mammals and birds raid unguarded nests. Black-breasted buzzards, however, drive male emus off their nests then drop stones on the eggs to break them.

The early destruction of emus living on islands was brought about by seal hunters and early settlers killing the emus not only for their flesh but for the oil that can be extracted from their bodies. About 4 gallons of oil can be got from one emu, and it was used for lighting and as an embrocation. Eggs were also taken, if they could be found. To make an omelette, the egg was broken into a basin and left overnight so that the oil could be skimmed off before cooking it in the morning. One emu egg, weighing 1½lb, made an omelette sufficient for the hungriest of families to go to work on and feel well-filled.

The great emu war

It is ironical that both the emu and the kangaroo, which appear on the Australian coat-of-arms, should be considered vermin. Both have had bounties on their heads, and in Queensland 121 768 emus and 109 345 eggs were destroyed in one two-year period alone. This slaughter had its lighter side, however. In 1932 some farmers persuaded the government to declare war on the emus on a large scale. On November 2 a battery of the Royal Australian Artillery engaged the emus with machine-gun fire, but the emus resorted to guerilla tactics and split into small parties, so spoiling the hopes of pouring a hail of fire into the serried ranks of birds. Next, ambushes were tried, with the emus being driven towards the guns. When the emus were at point-blank range the gunners opened fire. A dozen birds fell and the gun jammed. From then on the war got bogged down and after a month the offensive was discontinued.

The government, feeling perhaps that public money had been wasted, asked the farmers for £24 each to offset the cost of ammunition. In reply they received the following claim from one of them:

To victualling H.M.'s troops...............£ 9
To transporting of troops...................£10
To damage of transport vehicles.........£ 5

£24

A 4 days old emu chick surveys a 1½lb emu egg. The father guards the 8—10 chicks for 18 months. The chicks feed mainly on insects, but there is a legend that emus lay a sterile egg either for the chicks to eat or to support a colony of fly maggots for the chicks to eat after hatching.

class	**Aves**
order	**Casuariiformes**
family	**Dromaiidae**
genus & species	***Dromaius novaehollandiae***

Kiwi

The kiwi is the smallest flightless running bird in the southern hemisphere, the other runners being the emu, cassowary, ostrich and rhea. There are three species in New Zealand, each about the size of a domestic fowl, with a rounded body, no tail, stout but short legs, strong claws on their three toes and a long slender bill with slit-like nostrils at its tip. They range in size from a bantam to an Orpington and in weight from 3—9 lb, the females being larger than the males. The wings are very small, 2 in. long, and completely hidden by the hair-like body feathers that make up the plumage. The eyes are small but there are many long bristles at the base of the bill which are probably used as organs of touch. The ears are large and are the chief sensory organs used in detecting danger.

Kiwis are so different anatomically from the other running birds that they are probably only distantly related to them. They are more closely related to the extinct moas of New Zealand.

Waddling nightbird

The home of the kiwi is in the kauri pine forests with their tree ferns and swampy ground. Here they spend the day in burrows or under buttress roots of large trees. They are shy, retiring and hard to see in the forest because of the gloom and the birds' dark brown colouring. They come out at night and waddle along, their legs being set well apart. Their run is a long-striding waddle, with the bill held well out in front.

Food for all seasons

When feeding a kiwi moves quietly, probably feeling its way to a large extent with the bill bristles. At the slightest alarm it dashes rapidly to cover. Its main food, when the ground is moist, is earthworms and insects and their larvae. The tip of the long bill overlaps the lower half, so the bill can be thrust deep in the ground, driven by the short, thick neck. The bird tracks its prey mainly by smell. When the ground is dry in summer, the kiwi picks up fallen forest fruits and eats a large number of leaves.

Testing its sense of smell

It has always been assumed that the kiwi finds its food by smell, although most birds have a weak sense of smell. In December 1968, Bernice M Wenzel, of the University of California, published an account in *Nature* (Vol 220, p 1133) of a series of experiments carried out in New Zealand. Sets of tapering aluminium tubes were sunk into the ground in two kiwi aviaries. The tests, repeated over a period of 3 months, consisted of placing food in one tube, earth in another and a strong odorant in a third. By ringing the changes, such as using different odorants and different ways of masking the contents of the various tubes, it was proved beyond doubt that a kiwi can smell food several inches down in a way that no other bird is able to do.

Unusually large eggs

Although kiwis' nests have often been found, not much is known about the breeding or nesting habits. The nest is made in a hollow log or among the roots of a large tree. Sometimes it is in a hole or burrow in a soft bank, enlarged by the bird itself. Kiwis lay 1 or 2 very large chalky-white eggs, each about 5 in. long, weighing about a pound. This is $\frac{1}{8}$ of the hen kiwi's body weight, not $\frac{1}{4}$ as is sometimes stated. The male, as is usual with running birds, does the incubating, which lasts for 75—80 days. The chicks are small balls of soft hair-like feathers with a spindly beak. They remain in the nest for 6 days after hatching, receiving no food during this time. Then they follow their parents on their nightly forays, finding their own food, after the male has helped by clearing the ground for them. The normal call of the male is thin and reedy; that of the female is more hoarse. It is a two-note call, made only at night, and sounds like 'k-wee', with the accent on the second part.

At Hawke's Bay a colony of kiwis is kept under protection. Nesting boxes are provided and there it was noticed that during the incubation period the hen tapped at intervals on the box and the male inside tapped back. This may be a means of communication between the two partners.

Increased popularity

The kiwi population has decreased over the past century. They were prized by the Maoris as a delicacy, and their feathers were woven into cloaks for the chieftains. Then the early settlers hunted them for food. The birds also suffered from dogs, cats, stoats, weasels and other introduced animals. Their habitat has been reduced through the country being opened up for agriculture. In contrast with their falling numbers, their popularity has increased. Their image is seen on postage stamps and coins and on the trademarks of many products from shoe polish to textiles. The name became most familiar to people in Britain and in other parts of the world during the First World War because the New Zealand troops were called Kiwis. The Royal Air Force also perpetuated the name to some extent when its non-flying members were nicknamed Kiwis.

class	**Aves**
order	**Apterygiformes**
family	**Apterygidae**
genus & species	***Apteryx australis*** common or brown kiwi ***A. haasti*** great spotted or large grey kiwi ***A. oweni*** little spotted or little grey kiwi

The flightless kiwi of New Zealand, with beak outstretched, walks through undergrowth in long-striding waddles, in search of earthworms.

Tinamou

The tinamous are partridge-like birds that present a fine puzzle; in spite of looking like small game birds they are probably more nearly related to the large South American running birds, the rheas (page 324). They range in size from a quail, 7 in. long, to a grouse, 14 in. long. They have rounded, bulky bodies in which the well-developed feathers on the rump often hide the very short tail feathers. The wings are short and rounded, the legs short, with the hind toe, or hallux, minute or missing. The head is small and the neck slender. The plumage is dull, brown or grey with spots and bands, so tinamous are extremely inconspicuous. They have some powderdown plumage, like herons and parrots.

The martineta or crested tinamou is large, about 14½ in. long. It is a dull mottled brown with a long crest that is spread when the bird is excited. The ornate tinamou also has a crest which can be erected when excited. One of the smallest tinamous is the 9in. little tinamou. Its upperparts are rich brown with the sides of the head grey and the chin and throat white, gradually turning grey on the underparts of the tinamou.

The 50 or so species of tinamous live in the New World from southern Mexico to southern Chile and Argentina, including the island of Trinidad.

△ *Grey outlook of a martineta tinamou.*

Accident prone birds

Tinamous live in a variety of habitats from wet rain forests to open scrubland and the ornate tinamou can be found at over 13 000 ft in the Andes. They spend most of their time on the ground, keeping in touch with each other by attractive, fluting calls. They take flight only when startled, suddenly exploding into the air with a rush of wings, but they never fly far. Although their flight muscles are well-developed, sustained flight seems to be impossible because the heart and lungs are small. The tinamous' powers of co-ordination also seem to be limited as, when flushed, they sometimes hurtle headlong into branches and may kill themselves. Similarly, although fast runners, they soon tire and if pressed they may stumble. As tinamous are widely hunted for their extremely palatable flesh, it is surprising that these clumsy birds have survived; but they escape detection by remaining motionless or slipping quietly away through the undergrowth, camouflaged by their drab plumage.

A wide diet

Tinamous feed mainly on plants, particularly seeds and fruit, but they also eat insects and other small invertebrates. The ornate tinamou eats more animal food than most tinamous, including beetles, caterpillars and grasshoppers. Occasionally tinamous have been seen eating larger animals, such as mice. The plant food includes small leaves, flowers, fruits, seeds and, very occasionally, roots.

Father plays mother

Outside the breeding season tinamous are solitary. During the breeding season they are seen in twos and threes, and towards the end small coveys, consisting of parents with half-grown young, are formed. The breeding habits of tinamous are unusual in that the birds are usually polygamous and the females, which are slightly larger, with brighter colours than the males, play the dominant role in courtship. Some species live in pairs, as in the ornate tinamou where the sex ratio is 1:1, but in the variegated tinamou there are four times as many males as females. Each female may lay eggs in more than one nest, and several females may lay in a single nest. This is possible because the males build the nest and also incubate the eggs.

In the ornate tinamou courtship is fairly simple. The female is the most aggressive in defending the 6-acre territory and she courts the male by following him, both feeding as they go. The male displays by raising his rump and spreading the feathers to show a conspicuous dark patch. The variegated tinamou has a more elaborate courtship. The female runs to and fro, calling to attract the male and on approaching him, she lowers her wings and raises the tail and rump feathers to display a beautiful and elaborate pattern.

The male tinamou builds a nest in the undergrowth, which is little more than a poorly lined depression in the ground. The number of eggs that he incubates varies from 1 to 12 and they hatch in a little less than 3 weeks. The male may sit so tight during incubation that he can be lifted off the nest. After the chicks have left the nest he stays with them and defends them.

Doubtful honours

Tinamous are probably preyed upon, as partridge and grouse are, by both birds of prey and ground predators, such as foxes and the small and medium-sized members of the cat family. Sportsmen rate them as one of the finest gamebirds—always an unhappy situation for a bird. Frozen tinamou have also been exported to the United States as 'South American quail'.

Resembles the rhea

The tinamous are classed in their own order the Tinamiformes, low down in the scale of bird classification. They are not closely related to any other birds. Their resemblance to guineafowl, partridges and their relatives is only external, a consequence of their similar, ground-living habits. From a study of their anatomy it seems that tinamous are most closely related to the rheas, although the latter are flightless ratites, a group which includes ostriches and emus, that lack a keel on the breastbone. Yet the tinamous are 'carinates'. That is, they have a well-developed carina or keel on the breastbone, like the great majority of living birds. The breeding habits of tinamous are like those of rheas, with aggressive females and motherly males. There are physical similarities in the structure of the palate and in the shape of the rhamphotheca—the horny covering of the bill, and also there are chemical similarities in the composition of the eggs.

class	**Aves**
order	**Tinamiformes**
family	**Tinamidae**
genera & species	***Crypturellus soui*** *little tinamou* ***C. variegatus*** *variegated tinamou* ***Eudromia elegans*** *martineta tinamou* ***Nothoprocta ornata*** *ornate tinamou, others*

King penguin

King penguins look very much like emperor penguins, to which they are very closely related. They have the same stately walk as the emperors, with their long knife-shaped bills held up. King penguins are the smaller of the two, 3 ft long instead of 4 ft, but are otherwise similar in appearance. They both have blue-black backs and white fronts with yellow and orange patches around the neck, but in the king penguin the patches are separated into two comma-shapes on the side of the neck with a 'bib' of yellow on the breast.

King penguins live farther north than emperor penguins, in the ice-free sub-Antarctic seas between the Falkland Islands southwards to the South Sandwich Islands and Heard Island. There are very small colonies on Staten Island, near Cape Horn, and on the Falkland Islands. The largest colonies are found on islands such as South Georgia, Kerguelen, Macquarie and Marion.

Feeding at sea

Like other penguins, king penguins live at sea when they are not breeding and sometimes swim long distances, turning up on the fringes of the Antarctic pack ice. The latitudes in which the king penguins live are those of the roaring westerly gales, but these are unlikely to affect the penguins much except to drive them off course. Penguins are perfectly adapted to life at sea. Their bodies are streamlined and a layer of blubber under the skin insulates them from the cold water. The large king and emperor penguins can dive to considerable depths to hunt squid and fish which they catch in their sharp bills. The eyes of aquatic animals are designed to see underwater. Light is not bent so much as it passes from water into the eye as when it passes from air. To compensate, the lens is very strong. As a result aquatic animals are short-sighted out of water.

Prolonged childhood

The king penguin has the same problem of child care as the emperor penguin. Both are very large birds and their chicks take a long time to grow, yet the Antarctic summer is very short. The emperor penguin has solved the problem in an unexpected way by starting the 7-month nursery period in midwinter so the chicks become independent before the following winter. The king penguin has a different method. It lives farther north where the sea does not freeze and the adults are able to feed near the colony. So instead of laying their eggs in midwinter, the king penguins lay in spring or summer and when the chick hatches after 7½ weeks it is fed throughout the following winter, becoming independent the next summer.

Just before they start breeding king penguins come ashore to moult. They spend a fortnight ashore shedding their old feathers to reveal the brilliant new coat, then retire to sea to feed and build up reserves of food before breeding. Returning to land, they make their way to the colony among the tussack grass and mud where each male takes up position and advertises for a mate. He stretches his neck, ruffs out his feathers and tilts his head back and calls, braying like a donkey. If an unmated female hears him, she wanders over and the two penguins introduce themselves by flagging their bills up and down. They then set off on an 'advertisement walk', strutting along on their toes, waving their heads from side to side, showing off their brilliant patches of colour. The colours are important—if they are covered with black paint a penguin stands no chance of getting a mate.

At first these partnerships do not last very long. The male displays at any female and keeps company with a succession of prospective mates. Gradually, however, he pays attention to one particular female and the bond between them strengthens and they perform another display; standing side by side they raise their beaks and stand on their toes as if stretching themselves.

The king penguin, like the emperor penguin, makes no nest but balances the single large egg on his feet, protected by a fold of skin. He does, however, defend a small territory rather than wander about with his egg. The first eggs are laid in November,

*Yetis of the Antarctic! The little sheath bill **Chionis** is dwarfed by the big brown penguin chicks.*

and more are laid until April. After laying the female goes off to feed and make up the food reserves she lost forming the egg. The male is left guarding the egg until the female's return 2 weeks later. Thereafter, there is a shuttle service, each parent taking a turn in guarding the egg or chick.

As the chicks get older they spend more time on their own and eventually form crèches where they huddle together while parents go fishing. On its return a parent king penguin finds its chick by sound. It walks up to the crèche and calls, and one chick out of hundreds replies. They both walk towards each other, calling, and may even walk past, until another call brings them back to each other. Several pounds of food are transferred at each feed and the chicks put on weight rapidly, but as winter sets in feeding becomes very infrequent and the chicks huddle in their crèches, protected by their thick, woolly down but gradually losing weight. Then, in spring, when food becomes abundant again, the chicks put on weight, lose their down and the adult plumage emerges.

The chicks take to the sea 2 months later and learn to fish for themselves. This is well-timed because food is abundant at this season. The young king penguins stay at sea for most of their early life, spending more time ashore as they get older and begin to practise their courtship displays. At 6 years old, they come ashore and start courting in earnest.

Boiled for blubber

The enemies of king penguins are leopard seals. They lie in wait off the colonies, but the seals will find them difficult to catch as the penguins have an alarm system. When a king penguin sees a leopard seal, it panics and rushes towards the shore. Its flippers beat on the surface of the water and the clattering sound they make alerts other king

penguins, and they all rush clattering to the shore. Not only are all the penguins alerted but the leopard seals are probably confused and will be able to catch only weak or unwary penguins.

At one time, man was a far greater enemy. As elephant and fur seals became scarce sealers killed king penguins for their blubber, which was used for tanning leather. Their eggs were taken and their skins sometimes used for fancy clothing.

Slow breeding

It took only a few years for the sealers to reduce the numbers in a king penguin colony to such an extent that it was not worth their while to exploit them further. The reason for this is the extremely slow rate of breeding. After the egg has been laid, a pair of king penguins spends a year incubating, guarding or collecting food. By the time they are free of their offspring it is too late in the year to begin again and they leave the colony to feed during the winter and start breeding the following spring.

Therefore, king penguins, like the larger albatrosses (page 334) which also spend their first winter on the nest, cannot raise more than one young every two years. Furthermore, not all their offspring survive the first winter. If the egg is laid too late in the summer the chick will not have had time to accumulate enough fat with which to survive the winter. Without the attentions of the sealers, king penguins flourish; they are long-lived and generally survive to rear enough offspring to keep numbers constant.

class	**Aves**
order	**Sphenisciformes**
family	**Spheniscidae**
genus & species	***Aptenodytes patagonica***

Grebe

Grebes are waterbirds with long necks and short tails that give them a distinct, blunt-ended appearance. Many species have plumes on the head. The feet are set well back on the body, as in the divers. They are not webbed but each toe has a horny fringe that acts as a paddle. The feet are used for steering both in the air and in the water, the vestigial tail being useless for this purpose.

The largest grebe is the 19in. long great crested grebe, whose behaviour has been studied in great detail. It is found in most of Europe except northern Scandinavia, in many parts of Asia, Africa and in Australia and New Zealand. Its upperparts are light brown and the underparts white. The black ear tufts and, in the breeding season, chestnut and black frills on the sides of the head are particularly distinctive. The Slavonian grebe is darker on the upperparts than the great crested grebe. In the breeding season it has a glossy black head with a golden stripe running through the eye, and chestnut neck and flanks. Its range is circumpolar, from Iceland, Faeroes and Scotland through parts of Scandinavia and a broad belt across Asia to North America. Another widespread species is the little grebe or dabchick, the smallest of grebes, which has dark plumage. It breeds in Europe as far north as southern Sweden, in Asia as far as the East Indies and Japan and in most of Africa.

Of the 18 species of grebe, 10 are confined to the New World. In comparison with the wide-ranging species described above, others are extremely restricted. One is restricted to Madagascar, another to New Zealand and a third to the Falkland Islands. In the highlands of South America there are three species tied to single lakes. The flightless Titicaca grebe lives on Lake Titicaca, 2 miles high in the Andes, another lives on Lake Junin in Peru, while the giant pied-billed grebe, also flightless, lives on Lake Atitlan in Guatemala.

Shy stay-at-homes

Grebes live on lakes, reservoirs and flooded gravel pits, only rarely on slow-moving rivers. Some stay in one place all the year round but others, such as the great crested grebe, migrate to the coast in winter. Generally, however, grebes do not fly much and have to run across the water to take off. When disturbed they scutter to safety or dive and, like cormorants and darters, can swim half submerged by flattening their plumage, so squeezing the air out. Grebes are not gregarious, only occasionally are they seen in small parties. More often they live in pairs not straying from their territories, which in great crested grebes are about 2 acres. The great crested grebe can often be seen swimming slowly about in open water and can be watched diving re-

Penguin dance: a rare and complicated ceremony in which both male and female come high up out of the water and shake their heads with nesting materials in their bills.

Rearing display: the male, or the female, climbs onto the nest, rears up, and with bent neck moves the head from side to side as an invitation to coupling.

Invitation to coupling: as courtship proceeds the female takes more turns at mounting the nest (often only a copulation platform) and makes this final display.

Mating begins as the male jumps onto the female. This remarkable series of photographs by George Rüppell illustrates the now famous observations of JS Huxley in 1914 and KEL Simmons in 1955

peatedly for food, but the little grebe lives a very secluded life among reeds and other vegetation surrounding its lake or pond. It can be seen only by accident or by patiently waiting for its occasional trip from one reed bed to another.

Eating fish and feathers

Grebes eat fish, aquatic insects and crustaceans together with a few newts, tadpoles and some plant matter which they find by swimming underwater. A grebe usually stays underwater for $\frac{1}{2}$ minute or less, depending no doubt on the depth of the water, abundance of food and so on. They have been known to stay submerged for as long as 3 minutes. In calm, clear water a grebe can easily spot its prey while swimming with its neck raised, but in ruffled water or if searching for small animals it may swim with its head just underwater, waiting to submerge suddenly and plunge after its prey. Insects are sometimes picked off the surface or snatched out of the air.

Fish are swallowed alive, head-first. They may have to be juggled before being in the right position for swallowing. Grebes usually eat 4–6 in. fish, but larger ones are sometimes caught and the grebe can only gulp them down slowly. It is not unusual for dabchicks, and other waterbirds, to be choked by the spines of bullheads they are attempting to swallow.

A strange habit of grebes is feather eating. They regularly eat their body feathers, or soak them, and give them to their young. In the stomach the feathers break down to a felt-like mush which is thought to make sharp fish bones easier to regurgitate.

Floating nests

Grebes are famed for their spectacular courtship dances. Both sexes have plumes and ear tufts and both take the initiative in courtship. The great crested grebe has several displays with various functions. They vary from simple head-shaking to the penguin dance. Both birds dive, surfacing with weed in their bills, then rise up breast to breast and sway from side to side before relaxing. In the 'cat display' the grebe lowers its head with ear tufts spread and holds its wings out with the forward edges turned downwards. The western grebe of North America performs incredible dashes over the water. The two grebes rear up out of the water and dash across the surface side by side with their necks arched forwards. The dash is ended by both birds diving.

Some of the courtship is carried out on the nest, which is a large pile of waterweed built by both birds among the weeds, or occasionally floating freely. The adults take turns in incubating 3–10 faint white or blue-green eggs. If they are frightened off the nest they will often cover the eggs with nest material before creeping away.

The eggs of large grebes hatch in a month and those of small grebes in 3 weeks. The nest is abandoned as soon as the chicks dry out and the young chicks are carried on the parents' backs for a week or more. They occasionally get carried under when the parent dives or carried aloft when it flies. As they grow older they spend less time on the parent. This behaviour protects them from enemies, the worst of which, in Europe, is the pike. In a survey carried out in Britain, pike were the main cause of chick mortality, followed by foxes, otters, herons, trout and eels.

The young begin to dive when 6 weeks old and are independent by 10 weeks. Some species raise two broods in a season, the male guarding the first clutch while the female incubates the second.

Save the grebes

In 1860 the British population of great crested grebes fell to below 50 pairs because grebe feathers were once in great demand as decorations for women's hats. Since then, however, their numbers have increased, and now the bird is by no means rare. It is now the turn of another species, the giant pied-billed grebe, to be endangered. It is one of the rarest birds in America, only 100 surviving in 1965 on the 10 by 12 mile Lake Atitlan. The reason for their decrease seems to have been the introduction of largemouth bass as a gamefish. This on the face of it was an admirable scheme designed to enrich the area, but as all too often happens the project backfired. Largemouth bass, which weigh 10–12 lb, are predatory and live on the same small fish and crustaceans that the grebes hunt, and it seems that they also take young grebes. More seriously the bass have upset the delicate balance of the lake animals and the 50 000 people living round the lake are feeling the effects of this on their important fishing industry.

Steps have been taken to save the grebes. A small bay has been isolated from the lake by wire mesh, the bass killed off and grebes introduced. Rigorous patrolling against poaching has allowed the grebe population to increase. This is very encouraging, but expensive and one wonders whether it will be possible to eliminate the bass to allow both grebes and men to continue their fishing in peace.

class	**Aves**
order	**Podicipediformes**
family	**Podicipedidae**
genera & species	***Podiceps auratus*** *Slavonian grebe* ***P. cristatus*** *great crested grebe* ***P. ruficollis*** *little grebe* ***Podilymbus gigas*** *giant pied-billed grebe* *others*

Changeover: great crested grebe male takes on the job of incubating the last egg of the clutch while his mate prepares to leave with the chick.

333

Albatross

A family of birds in the petrel order. They are the largest members of the order and among the largest of flying birds. They have goose-sized bodies with very long, slender wings: of the 13 species, the largest is the wandering albatross, which has a wingspan sometimes exceeding 12 ft. The plumage is black and white or, in a few species, brown. In only some of the species is it possible to tell the sexes apart.

Ocean wanderers

Nine species of albatross are confined to the Southern Hemisphere, breeding mainly on the sub-Antarctic and oceanic islands. The other four are found in the North Pacific. None breed in the North Atlantic, although fossil remains have been found in England and a few have been recorded as vagrants in modern times. These vagrants include wandering, black-browed, yellow-nosed, grey-headed, and light-mantled sooty albatrosses. One black-browed albatross appeared in a Faroese gannet colony in 1860 and for 30 years—until it was shot—it accompanied the gannets on their annual migrations. Another visited the Bass Rock gannet colony off the Scottish coast in 1967 and returned in 1968.

The doldrums, the windless belt around the Equator, are possibly one of the reasons why so few albatrosses have been recorded in the North Atlantic, as albatrosses need a sustained wind for flight. They are heavy birds with comparatively small wing muscles, but they can remain airborne for long periods and cover vast distances because of the difference in the speed of the wind at the water's surface and some 50 ft above, due to friction slowing down the air at the surface. The albatross glides swiftly downwind and surfacewards, gathering speed. When just above the water it swings sharply round into the wind and soars up. As it rises it loses momentum and its ground speed (*i.e.* in relation to the water surface) decreases. Its air speed, however, does not decrease so fast, as the bird is rising and so continually meeting faster wind currents. By the time the air speed has dropped completely the albatross will have gained sufficient height to start the downward glide again. Thus it progresses in a series of zig-zags.

*1. Yellow-nosed albatross (**Diomedea chlororhyncha**) landing, showing its large wingspan. This enables it to soar for hours in the oceanic air currents.*
2. The albatross nests on cliff tops where it can easily take off. The chick is guarded by its parents for several weeks.
3. Later both parents can be away feeding for ten days at a time.
*4. Black-browed albatross (**Diomedea melanophrys**) ranges over the oceans between 30° and 60° latitude south, breeding on such islands as Tristan da Cunha, South Georgia, and the Kerguelen and Auckland Islands. It has been recorded as a vagrant to the British Isles and even to the Arctic.*

The main haunt of albatrosses is the sub-Antarctic zone where the Roaring Forties and Howling Fifties sweep around the world and there is nearly always enough wind to keep the albatrosses aloft—although they can glide in quite gentle breezes. To increase speed the albatross 'close-hauls', partly closing its wings to reduce air resistance without seriously affecting lift.

With their great wingspan and weak wing muscles albatrosses have difficulty in taking off. When there is enough wind—especially if there are thermal currents or eddies around the cliffs on which they nest—takeoff is not so difficult; but on still days they have to taxi, running along and flapping their wings until they have gained sufficient air speed to take off.

Some species are fairly confined in their range, like Buller's albatross in New Zealand; others, like the wandering, black-browed and sooty albatrosses circle the world from Tropics to Antarctic.

Marine feeders

All species of albatross feed on marine organisms living at the surface of the sea, such as fish, squid and crustaceans. They also take small sea birds on occasions, and they like refuse from ships, flopping down into the water as soon as a bucketful is tipped overboard. Sailors who have fallen overboard have reputedly been viciously attacked by albatrosses.

Cliff top breeding sites

Breeding grounds, where albatrosses gather in tens of thousands, are usually on the top of cliffs where the birds can take off easily. They are extremely faithful to their nest sites, and populations have survived such calamities as volcanic eruptions or pillage by man because the immature birds that were absent at the time later returned to breed.

Albatrosses are very long-lived birds: one recaptured 19 years after being ringed as an adult must have been at least 26 years old. They do not start breeding until at least seven years old, but young birds return to the breeding ground before then and court halfheartedly. Courtship displays, which are to be seen throughout the breeding season, are most spectacular. The two birds of a pair dance grotesquely and awkwardly with outstretched wings to the accompaniment of nasal groans and bill snapping. At the beginning of the breeding season several males may dance around one female.

A single egg is laid in a cup-shaped nest of mud and is incubated by both parents for periods ranging from 65 days in the smaller species to 81 days in the larger ones. The chick is also brooded for a short time and is guarded by the adults for several weeks. It is then left by itself and both parents can be away feeding at once. They return every 10 days to give the chick a huge meal of regurgitated squid and fish. The young of the smaller albatrosses fledge in two to three months, but larger ones may spend eight or nine months in the colony, sitting out the severe southern winter until the following summer. The parents feed them the whole time, so breeding is only possible in alternate years.

The young albatrosses leave the breeding grounds to glide away around the world, driven by the winds of the Westerly Drift. Before they return to start courting several years later they may circle the globe many times.

No natural enemies

Albatrosses have no natural enemies, living as they do on remote islands. Any introduced carnivores would, however, wreak havoc among the densely packed nests, for the sitting albatross's reaction to disturbance is just to sit tight on the nest and clack its bill. It also spits oil from digested crustaceans and fish—as does the chick—but this is hardly likely to discourage a determined predator.

The sailors' curse

Albatrosses have been known to sailors since the days of Magellan. Their inexpressive, fixed facial expression as they glide alongside a ship for miles on end without a flicker of the eye has brought them various nicknames: Mollymawk (from the Dutch Mallemok, 'stupid gull'), Gooney (English/American for a stupid person), Bakadori (Japanese for 'fowl-birds').

But they not only had a reputation for idiocy; they were considered to be harbingers of wind and storms—not, perhaps, surprising in view of their difficulty in remaining aloft in calm weather. They were also regarded as the reincarnations of seamen washed overboard, and it was thought extremely unlucky to kill them.

But, despite the chance of having an albatross hung round one's neck and suffering the far worse experience that later befell the Ancient Mariner, sailors have not always treated albatrosses kindly. Their capture on baited hooks trailed from the stern of a ship often relieved the monotony of life and diet.

More seriously, albatrosses were once favourite material for the 19th-century millinery trade, the wings sometimes being cut off the still-living birds. The North Pacific colonies bore the brunt of this fashion for plumage which, luckily, ceased before all the birds were dead.

Since the Second World War there has been another crisis for the albatross. Long-range aircraft flights have made oceanic islands necessary as staging posts, and one such is Midway Island, the home of the Laysan albatross. Not only are albatrosses using the United States Navy's runways for taking off, they also soar in the thermals above them, providing a serious danger to aircraft. Of the many methods that have been tried to reduce this danger, the most effective has been the bulldozing of dunes by the runways which cause the updraughts that the albatrosses need for flying.

class	**Aves**
order	**Procellariiformes**
family	**Diomedeidae**
genus & species	***Diomedea spp.*** ***Phoebetria spp.***

Pelicans often found their colonies in tall trees. The nests, unlined structures of dry twigs, are large and ungainly.

Pelican

The pelican is known to many people only from seeing it in zoos or on ornamental lakes where its ungainly appearance often makes it the subject of ridicule. In the wild, however, it is a superb flier and swimmer.

There are eight species, two of which occur in the New World and six in the Old, distributed over the tropical and warm temperate parts of the globe. The species differ only in the smaller details of size, colour and geographical range. Both sexes are alike and all have massive bodies, supported on short legs with strong webbed feet. They have long necks, small heads and a thick, harsh plumage. They are among the largest living birds, from 50—72 in. long. The most conspicuous feature is the enormous beak; the upper part is flattened and the lower part carries a pouch that can be distended to grotesque proportions. It can hold about 17 pints of water and is used, not for storing food, but as a dip net for catching fish.

Apart from the brown pelican, in the majority of the species the adult plumage is mainly white, tinged with pink in the breeding season in some species such as the pink-backed pelican of Africa. The primaries are black or dark. Some species have crests and in some there is yellow, orange or red on the bill, pouch and bare part of the face. The brown pelican, the smallest member of the family, with a wing-span of up to 6½ ft and weighing about 8 lb, has a white head with a yellow tinge. In the breeding season the neck turns a rich brown with a white stripe running down each side. The wings and underparts are dark brown. The larger white species may have a wing-span of 10 ft and weigh 24 lb.

The brown pelican, which is a sea bird that does not venture far from the shore and breeds on small islands, is found along the south Atlantic and Gulf coasts of North America through the West Indies to Venezuela. Along the Pacific it ranges from central California to Chile with one population on the Galapagos Islands. The other New World species is the American white pelican that breeds on inland lakes from western Canada to southern Texas. In the Old World there are pelicans in Africa, southern Asia, including the Philippines, and Australia and in southeast Europe there are isolated colonies of the large silvery white Dalmatian pelican which ranges eastward from there into central Asia, visiting Egypt and northern India in winter. It nested at least as far north as Hungary until the middle of the last century and according to Pliny it nested in the estuaries of the Elbe, Rhine and Scheldt.

Fishing cooperation

Pelicans feed mainly on fish but crustaceans are also taken. The white pelicans fish while floating on the surface or wading about in the shallows. They thrust their heads under the water, using their pouches as dip nets to catch the fish. Occasionally a large flock of birds will cooperate by forming a line across the water and swimming abreast, beating the surface violently with their wings to drive schools of small fish into shallow water where they can easily scoop them up.

Community breeding

Pelicans are very sociable and all the species nest in large colonies sometimes of tens of thousands. Most of the white species breed on isolated islands in large inland lakes usually making their nests on the ground but occasionally they nest in low trees. On the ground the nest is sometimes just a depression scooped out of the earth. The brown pelican which breeds on small islands on the coast, makes a loose nest of sticks in mangrove trees and low shrubs or sometimes on the ground.

In all species the breeding season varies from place to place and from year to year. In some tropical areas they may even breed throughout the year. Chalky white eggs numbering 1—4 are laid which both parents help to incubate for 29—30 days. The babies are born naked and blind but quickly grow a soft white down. Both parents feed the young, at first dribbling regurgitated food out of the ends of their beaks into the chicks' open mouths, but after a few days the chicks are strong enough to stick their heads into their parents' pouches to get the food. Before the chicks are 2 weeks old they leave the nest and form noisy juvenile groups but the parents continue to feed them for some time. The young mature slowly, only acquiring adult plumage after several years. They seldom breed until they are 4 years old. Pelicans are long lived birds. Although the accepted record is 52 years, there are less well authenticated accounts of birds living to a much greater age. The Emperor Maximilian is said to have had a pelican which lived for more than 80 years.

Many hazards for the young

Mature pelicans have few natural enemies. Sometimes they may be killed by sea lions in the Pacific or occasionally eaten by sharks but among the young mortality is very high. When the young birds congregate after leaving the nest many fall from trees or get caught in the branches or even trampled on by clumsy adults. When a baby pelican is hurt a larger fledgling is likely to eat it. The adult birds do little to protect their young and sometimes entire nesting colonies are wiped out by predatory animals. It is doubtful if even half the young birds survive. Fishermen have been known to destroy colonies of pelicans to prevent them taking so much fish. At Pelican Island, Florida, in 1911 a plague of mosquitoes caused an entire colony of breeding birds to abandon the rookery, leaving 600 nests containing nestlings. In Peru the guano diggers often damage the nests, knocking young birds out of the way and frightening away the parents, so leaving the chicks an easy prey for predators. Nowadays the pelican colonies are often in danger when marshes are drained or lakes dry up due to large water schemes.

Superb in flight

The pelican has often been described as a clumsy bird, a statement no more justified than it would be to speak of a duck or a swan as clumsy merely because they walk on

land with a waddle and because the body is heavily built. When a pelican has managed after much effort and flapping to become airborne it is a strong and graceful flier, and it is no less graceful in the water. With legs up, head well back on the shoulders and its large bill resting on the front of the neck it can sail through the air with little effort.

Pelicans seem to possess quite unnecessary powers of flight considering that all their food is taken from the water and everything about them suggests adaptation to an aquatic mode of living. They fly at about 26 mph and there is an authentic record of their having maintained this speed for 8 miles, so it seems they also have the quality of endurance in flight. There is one record of the common pelican having achieved 51 mph. They regularly fly in formation either in line astern or in V-formation, all members of the flight beating their wings in perfect unison. The sight of a flock gliding down like a squadron of flying-boats is spectacular. They also have the vulture's trick of using thermal currents, soaring in spirals to

a great height, even as much as 8 000 ft, where by alternately flapping and gliding they may circle for hours.

Symbol of piety

The principal myth concerning the pelican is that the parent bird, if unable to find food for her brood, pierced her breast with the tip of her bill and fed the youngsters on her own blood, and that is how the bird is figured in the earliest pictures of it. It was because of this belief that the pelican was chosen as an emblem of charity and piety and became a favourite heraldic emblazonment. There is a different version of the story according to Bartholomew. Writing in 1535 he says that the young pelicans smite the parents in the face, whereupon the mother retaliates, hitting them back and killing them. Then, on the third day, the mother smites herself in the side until the blood runs out onto the bodies of her youngsters, bringing them to life again.

These two stories may have arisen because in feeding its young the parent presses its

△ *Fish scoop. A yawning common white pelican shows its enormous pouch for catching fish.*

bill against its neck and breast in order to make the contents of the pouch more readily available to the young, who thrust their bills into the pouch to take the food. The red tip on the common pelican's mandible may also have made the story more plausible.

class	**Aves**
order	**Pelecaniformes**
family	**Pelecanidae**
genus & species	***Pelecanus crispus*** Dalmatian pelican ***P. erythrorhynchos*** American white pelican ***P. occidentalis*** brown pelican ***P. onocrotalus*** common white pelican ***P. rufescens*** pink-backed pelican others

Flamingo

Beautiful but bizarre, flamingos, like giraffes, have an appearance of unreality bordering on disbelief. Their necks and legs are proportionately longer than in any other bird; they feed with their heads upside down in foul, alkaline or saline water yet keep their delicately pink plumage immaculate.

There are four species of flamingo in both Old and New Worlds. Their plumage is tinged with pink, except for the black flight feathers. The greater flamingo, standing about 4 ft high, is found in America from the Bahamas to Tierra del Fuego, including the Galapagos Islands, and in the Old World from southern Europe to South Africa across to India. The lesser flamingo lives in eastern Africa and India. The two remaining species live in the Andes, 14 000 ft above sea level, in Bolivia, Chile, and Argentina. The Andean flamingo is common locally, but the James' flamingo is very rare and at one time was feared to be extinct.

Vast flocks of beautiful waders

Flamingos are gregarious, living in vast flocks of many thousands. One colony of the lesser flamingo in East Africa, the commonest species, numbers at least 1 million pairs. Flamingos breed, feed and travel in flocks and a flock of flamingos wading or swimming in a lake or flying in skeins, like geese, with necks and legs outstretched and wings slowly beating must be amongst the most beautiful sights in the world.

Flamingos are always found on lakes or lagoons of brackish water, where they breed and feed in shallow water. Many of them are migratory, and in recent years greater flamingos from the Camargue have been found to be flying south across the Mediterranean to spend the winter in Africa on the same lakes as the lesser flamingos.

Upside-down filter feeding

Shallow lakes and lagoons are the invariable homes of flamingos because it is here that minute plants and animals exist in the vast concentrations needed to feed the flamingo flocks. Flamingos extract their food from the water by a filtering mechanism which is very similar to that used by the blue whale. They wade through the water with necks lowered and heads upside down, sweeping from side to side. They adopt this unlikely position to sieve their food from the water. The upper and lower mandibles of the bill are fringed with bristles which trap particles as the flamingo sucks in water. The outer layer of coarse bristles keep out large particles while minute algae such as diatoms are collected on an array of bristles inside the bill. The collected algae are then worked off onto the tongue and swallowed after the water has been expelled.

The greater flamingo has a more varied diet than other species. The other flamingos sweep their heads through the surface water but the greater flamingo feeds nearer the bottom. Its bill has fewer filtering bristles

and has a flatter upper mandible. With it the greater flamingo sweeps up small snails and shrimps, as well as quantities of mud from which it extracts the organic matter, rejecting the inedible silt. The greater and lesser flamingos feed together in mixed flocks in the lakes of eastern Africa as the slight difference in feeding ground and feeding habits is sufficient to prevent them from competing for food.

They nest on hummocks

Flamingos breed in colonies. In East Africa where they are most abundant the colonies may be enormous. Several with over 900 000 pairs are known and at one time it was estimated that one had over 1 million pairs. Sometimes a particular colony may be deserted for several years in succession. Then the flamingos may perhaps rear two broods in very quick succession.

The erratic nature of the breeding is most likely due to changes in the water level of the breeding lake. The nests are towers of mud some 6—14 in. high with a depression in the top for the eggs. The water level has only to rise a foot or so for the colony to be

▷ *Rarity in captivity: the James' flamingo, which lives in the Andes, 14 000 ft above sea level. Very scarce, it was once believed extinct.*

▽ *A stilt-legged trio of greater flamingos, showing off their balance on dry land.*

A scintillating moment of breathtaking beauty as greater flamingos take to the air.

A single egg is laid in the saucer-shaped depression in the nest and is incubated for a month by both parents in turn. After the chicks hatch they stay on the nest for 2—3 days then they join the other chicks in bands which can run readily, and swim when 10 days old. The chicks look very much like goslings. They are covered in grey down and their bills are straight, not sickle-shaped like their parents'. Because of the resemblance of young flamingos to goslings and the goose-like flight of the adults, flamingos have been thought to be related to geese, but most ornithologists now think that the flamingos are related to storks and ibises.

Until its bill has developed the characteristic shape, a young flamingo is unable to feed itself and has to rely on its parents. To feed a chick a parent stands behind it and lowers its neck so the chick may take the tip of its bill in its own. The adult regurgitates liquefied food which runs down into the chick's mouth. The parents seem to be able to recognise their own chicks even when they are among a dense crowd of other chicks which may be running or swimming together. The crowds of chicks are always accompanied by adults that lead them away from danger.

Many enemies

The main enemies of flamingos are the fish eagles that can pick the young flamingos out of the rafts and carry them off. Hyaenas, cheetahs and jackals also kill any stragglers they find. In Roman times flamingo tongues were a delicacy and flamingos are still eaten by local hunters. At one time they were prized for their plumage but now the main human menace to them is disturbance of the breeding colonies, especially by low flying aircraft.

How do they sit down?

While idly looking at the more grotesque animals at the zoo, one is often led to wonder how they carry out simple everyday functions. How, for instance, does a heron or a flamingo sit down on its nest? Strangely, this was long in dispute, perhaps because the ornithologists writing about flamingos had never seen them at their nests and could only theorise. In 1697 William Dampier thought that the flamingo leaned back on its nest as if sitting on a shooting-stick. Even a century ago there were still some strange ideas on this point. One was that it sat astride its nest, another that it sat with the legs sticking straight out behind. The correct answer is that it sits like any other bird. The legs are doubled up beneath it, the 'knees' (actually the ankles) hinge backwards, so the folded legs stick out behind the sitting bird.

Aftermath of disaster: smashed and deserted eggs in the potash-ridden waters of Lake Magadi, Kenya.

inundated. On the other hand, if the water level of an alkaline lake drops, thick deposits may form and become caked on the legs of flamingo chicks when they leave their nests. In 1962 Lake Natron in Kenya was flooded and the flamingos moved to Lake Magadi to breed. Thousands of chicks perished, caked with soda that formed heavy anklets round their legs. A rescue operation was launched and many chicks were saved. A flamingo is long lived, however, and produces many chicks in its lifetime, so it is very unlikely that such a catastrophe would have a serious long term effect on the population.

At the beginning of the breeding season the flamingos indulge in spectacular courtship displays. Banding together in tightly-bunched flocks the male flamingos run to and fro with the necks held straight up and bills pointed skyward. At the same time there is a continual guttural uproar while the flock appears to be shimmering because the flamingos are jerking their heads sideways, fitfully and never in unison. At other times they bend their necks, sweeping their bills across their backs. Within the colony of thousands of flamingos these tightly-knit flocks of males flow and eddy.

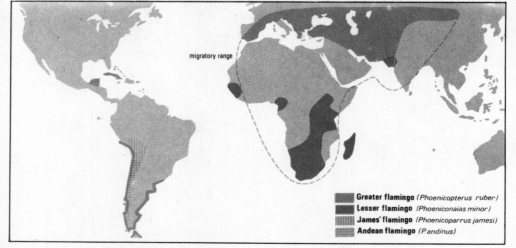

migratory range

- Greater flamingo (*Phoenicopterus ruber*)
- Lesser flamingo (*Phoeniconaias minor*)
- James' flamingo (*Phoenicoparrus jamesi*)
- Andean flamingo (*P. andinus*)

class	**Aves**
order	**Ciconiiformes**
family	**Phoenicopteridae**
genera & species	***Phoenicopterus ruber** greater flamingo* ***Phoeniconaias minor** lesser flamingo* ***Phoenicoparrus jamesi** James' flamingo* ***P. andinus** Andean flamingo*

Mallard

Although there are many species of wild duck the mallard is the one that most people think of as the 'wild duck'. It is the ancestor of most of the domesticated ducks. It is about 2 ft long and weighs 2½ lb. The male, or drake, is brightly coloured from September to June. His belly and most of his back are grey. His head and neck are a dark glossy green and a white ring at the base of the neck separates the green from the brown of the breast. He has small curled feathers on the tail and his voice is a low hoarse call. The female, or duck, is a mottled brown, her voice is a loud quack and she has no curly tail feathers. From July to August the drake is in eclipse plumage, and is unable to fly. That is, he moults his colourful feathers at the end of June, is clothed in a mottling similar to that of the duck, and resumes his coloured plumage at the end of August. Both sexes have wing patches (specula), which are dark or purplish-blue with white edges.

Mallard breed in Europe and Asia from the Arctic Circle southwards to the Mediterranean, Iran, Tibet and Central China, and in northern and central North America. Throughout the range there is a movement south in autumn to Africa, southern Asia and, in America, to Mexico and Florida.

Make your own duck pond

Wild duck are attracted to any water: from a small pond in woodland to large lakes, to rivers, streams and marshes, although they often live on dry land well away from water. This habit is taken advantage of by wildfowlers and bird-lovers alike as they can be encouraged to breed quite easily by digging a pond with small islands or floating basket nests. Mallard spend much time on land even when water is available, but whether on water or on land, and apart from feeding, they do little more than stand or sit about, preening from time to time. Indeed, ducks spend a large part of their time simply doing nothing. On land they waddle apparently awkwardly; on water they swim easily and dive only when alarmed. In the air they fly with rapid wingbeats and with neck outstretched, taking off in a steep ascent.

Wide choice of food

Mallard feed by day or by night, mainly on leaves and seeds, grain, berries, acorns, as well as much small animal life such as insects and their larvae, worms, tadpoles, frogs' spawn, small frogs and small fishes. They dabble in mud on land and at the edge of water and upend in deeper water to feed from the mud at the bottom.

Ritual courtship

Mallard form pairs in autumn and begin breeding in spring. Pairing is preceded by a ritualized courtship. This is initiated by a duck swimming rapidly among a group of drakes with an action that has been called nod-swimming or coquette-swimming. She swims with the neck outstretched and just above water and head nodding. This makes the drakes come together in a tighter group and they begin their communal displays. These are made up of stereotyped actions known as mock drinking, false preening, shaking, grunt-whistling, head-up-tail-up and up-and-down movements. These same movements are seen more easily when the drake and duck are courting.

The duck chooses a drake, who follows her away from the group. She symbolically looks back by turning her head, inciting him to drive away other drakes that may be following. The 'inciting' has become ritualized and is carried out even if no other drakes are there. Mock drinking is a formalized gesture of peace and two drakes meeting head on will 'pretend' to drink. It is a sign they have no intention of attacking each other. In false preening a drake lifts one wing slightly, reaches behind it with his bill as if to preen. Instead, he rubs the bill over the heel of the wing making a rattling sound. In shaking the drake draws his head back between his shoulders so the white ring disappears. The feathers on the underside of the body are fluffed out, so the drake appears to ride high on the water. The head feathers are raised so the green sheen disappears and the head rises high so he is almost sitting on his tail on the water, and then he shakes his head up and down.

When a drake grunt-whistles he thrusts his bill almost vertically into the water then throws his head back, scattering a shower of water drops, and as he does this he grunts. Head-up-tail-up is fully descriptive of the

▽ *Tired of just dabbling in things, a pair of mallard take to deeper water. The male will lose his lovely plumage once the breeding season is over.*

next movement, and in the up-and-down movement the bill is quickly thrust into the water and jerked up again with the breast held low in the water. Another movement is known as gasping; one drake utters a low whistle and the rest give a kind of grunt.

These actions may be made in sequence by a group of drakes facing into the centre or by one or two drakes, or between drake and duck. Also, one or other may be seen as isolated actions. Together they form a ritual pattern of courtship carried out in the autumn but actual mating does not take place until spring. More remarkable, in spite of the complicated courtship, there is a high degree of promiscuity in mallard; a drake will mate with a duck while the drake with whom she is paired looks on.

High-diving ducklings

The nest, built by the duck, is a shallow saucer of grass, dry leaves and feathers lined with down. It may be on the ground, usually under cover of bushes or in a pollarded willow, in the disused nest of a large bird such as a crow, or in a hollow in a tree up to 40 ft from the ground. Up to 16, usually 10—12, greyish, green or greenish-buff eggs are laid, from March to October, incubated by the duck alone, for 22—28 days. When the ducklings have dried, soon after hatching, the duck calls them off the nest and leads them to water, or if far from water to a feeding ground. Sometimes the drake is in attendance but takes no part in the care of the ducklings. Even when the nest is 40 ft up in a hollow tree the ducklings leave the nest when the duck calls, each in turn tumbling to the ground without injury. The ducklings are covered with yellowish down broken with large patches of brown. They take nearly 2 months to fledge.

Mother is one enemy

The natural enemies of mallard are birds of prey and ground predators such as foxes. These probably have little effect on mallard populations. The main losses are at the duckling stage. A duck may hatch a brood of 12 and in a fortnight be left with only one duckling. Crows, rooks, magpies, rats and other ducks attack the ducklings. The duck herself may tread on one or more or sit on them in the water, drowning one or two. By contrast, the same duck may then lay a second clutch of 12 and rear all the ducklings to fledging.

Tongue acts as a piston

When a duck dabbles its bill in mud it is doing much the same as when a large whalebone whale opens its huge mouth and swims through a mass of krill. Both are using a highly efficient filter in which transverse plates on the inner edges of the duck's bill play the part of the baleen plates of the whale. As the duck dabbles its tongue acts as a piston sucking water or mud into the mouth and driving it out again. Only the edible particles are left behind on the transverse plates, but how the sorting out is done nobody knows. It used to be thought birds had no taste buds, the groups of cells on the tongue that give a sense of taste. Mallard have, however, 200 arranged in rows along the sides of the tongue. It may be these that tell the duck how to sort out edible from inedible particles.

class	**Aves**
order	**Anseriformes**
family	**Anatidae**
genus & species	***Anas platyrhynchos***

▽ *These obedient children always follow when their mother calls them to water very soon after they have dried out from hatching.*

Swan

The six species of swan are very closely related to the geese. Together they make up a tribe of the order Anseriformes separate from the various tribes of ducks. One possible exception is the Coscoroba swan of South America, which is the smallest swan and has a comparatively short neck; it is thought to be in some way related to the whistling or tree ducks.

The most familiar swan is the mute swan that originally bred in parts of Europe and Asia, but has been domesticated and introduced to many parts of the world such as North America and Australia where it has gone wild. It is thought that it was introduced to Britain by the Romans. The mute swan is 5 ft long and weighs about 35 lb. The plumage is all white and the bill is orange with a prominent black knob at the base. The Bewick's swan and the whooper swan are two other species that breed in Eurasia. Bewick's swan breeds in the tundra of northern Russia and Siberia and visits Europe in the winter. The whooper swan breeds farther south, including northern Scandinavia and Iceland, with a few pairs nesting sporadically in Scotland. Both have black bills with a yellow base, the pattern differing slightly between the two, and Bewick's swan is rather smaller than the whooper with a shorter neck. There are two swans in North America; the whistling swan has a black bill, sometimes with a yellow spot at the base, and is smaller than the trumpeter with a completely black bill. The whistling swan breeds mainly north of the Arctic Circle and migrates to the southern coast of the United States. The trumpeter used to breed over much of North America but is now confined to the northwest United States and southwest Canada where there are now about 1 500 individuals under protection. The only swans in the southern hemisphere, apart from the Coscoroba swan, are the black swan of Australia, and the black-necked swan of South America, from Brazil to Tierra del Fuego and the Falkland Islands. The black swan is all black but with white primary wing feathers, and a red bill. It has been introduced to New Zealand. The black-necked swan has a black head and neck, a white eyestripe and a red bill.

▽ Mute swan takeoff. Their heavy bodies clear the water of the pond with difficulty.

Not so mute

Compared with other swans the mute swan is quiet, but its name is a misnomer for it has a variety of calls. A flock of mute swans can be heard quietly grunting to each other as they swim along a river. When disturbed or in defence of the nest mute swans hiss violently. The sighing noise during flight is caused by the wings. The whooper swan has a bugle-like call when flying and a variety of quiet calls when grounded. Bewick's swan has a pleasant variety of honks and other sounds and the trumpeter is named after the trombone-like calls produced in the long, coiled windpipe. It is said that the swan-song, the legendary song of a dying swan, is based on a final slow expiration producing a wailing noise as it passes through the long windpipe.

A danger to cables

Despite their great weight swans are strong fliers. They have four times the wing loading (the body weight divided by the surface area of the wings) of a herring gull or crow and they have to beat their wings rapidly

1 Profile: head of a whooper swan.
2 Swan song? A black swan stretches up its neck and wails through its long windpipe.
3 Reflecting swan: the Coscoroba swan has features of both ducks and swans.
4 Black-necked swans guard their young.
5 A pair of Bewick's swans sit upright on the water while their young paddle around.

to remain airborne. A high wing loading makes take-off and landing difficult and swans require a long stretch of water over which they can run to gain flying speed or surge to a halt when landing. Swans are also unable to manoeuvre in flight and the chief cause of mortality in built-up parts of the world is collision with overhead cables.

Shallow water feeders

Swans feed mainly on plants but they also feed on water animals such as small fish, tadpoles, insects and molluscs. They often feed on land, grazing on grass like geese, but more often they feed on water plants, which they may collect from the bottom by lowering their long necks underwater, sometimes upending like ducks. This limits the swans' distribution to shallow water because they very rarely dive and are only occasionally seen on deep water.

Centuries-old colonies

Swans nest near water. Male mute swans set up territories, each defending a stretch of river from which they drive other males and young swans. Intruders are threatened

△ *A pair of nesting mute swans, seen through the reeds, renovate their nest.*

by an aggressive display in which the neck is drawn back, the wings arched over the back and the swan propels itself in jerks with the webbed feet thrusting powerfully in unison, instead of alternately as in normal walking. There are a variety of displays between the male, the cob, and the female, the pen, involving tossing and swinging the head and dipping it into the water.

Mute swans mate for life and nest in the same territory each year, some violent fights taking place if a new pair tries to usurp the territory. The nest is a mass of water plants and twigs, roughly circular and cone-shaped with a depression in the centre. Wild mute swans nest among reeds on small islands in pools but semi-domesticated ones may nest in the banks of ponds in parks or in other inhabited places. Occasionally, mute swans nest in colonies rather than spaced out territories.

There are usually 5−7 eggs, sometimes twice as many, and they are incubated mainly by the female, the male taking over only when she leaves to feed. In the smaller swans incubation lasts 4 weeks, but it is 5 weeks in the larger species and 5½ weeks in the black swan. While the last eggs are being brooded by the female the male takes the cygnets to the water. The family stays together until the cygnets fledge at 4−5 months. When young they swim together in a tight bunch with the female leading and rooting up plants for them to eat.

class	**Aves**
order	**Anseriformes**
family	**Anatidae**
genera & species	**Coscoroba coscoroba** *Coscoroba swan* **Cygnus atratus** *black swan* **C. columbianus bewickii** *Bewick's swan* **C. c. columbianus** *whistling swan* **C. cygnus buccinator** *trumpeter swan* **C. c. cygnus** *whooper swan* **C. melanocoryphus** *black-necked swan* **C. olor** *mute swan*

Swan (Breeding grounds)

Mute *(Cygnus olor)*
Bewick's *(C.columbianus bewickii)*
Whistling *(C.c.columbianus)*
Trumpeter *(C.cygnus buccinator)*
Whooper *(C.c.cygnus)*

Martial eagle

The martial eagle is the largest of the African eagles. Like many other eagles it bears a crest. It has long wings and a relatively short tail and in flight can be confused with only one other eagle, the serpent eagle. The upperparts are dark grey with light grey bars on wings and tail. The underparts, including the feather 'leggings', are white, barred and spotted with black. The bill is black and the legs and toes, which are armed with long curved talons, are blue-grey. The total wingspan may be as much as 8 ft. The females have larger spans than the males and are more powerfully built. They are easily distinguished, being more spotted on the underparts than the males.

The martial eagle lives in Africa from the southern borders of the Sahara to the Cape, but not in the thickly forested regions such as Zaire.

Shy eagle

A pair of martial eagles inhabits a range of as much as 50 sq miles, soaring over the countryside for hours at a time, often at great heights where they are almost invisible to the naked eye. Martial eagles are shy birds as compared with other eagles, and shun human settlements, which is to their advantage as they are often persecuted for taking farm stock. Because of persecution and their dislike of inhabited areas, martial eagles are much rarer than they once were. They are found in savannah, semi-desert and other

▷ *A martial eagle discourages intruders on its reptile repast – monitor lizard.*
▽ *A golden glower from Africa's largest eagle.*
▽▷ *Grounded: sub-adult martial eagle showing its white chest and abdomen.*

open country, and breed only in forested regions when there is open country nearby.

Swoops down on prey

Martial eagles spot their prey from a great height, swooping down on it in a well-controlled glide. The speed of the descent is regulated by the angle at which the wings are held over the back. When they are held almost horizontal the glide is shallow and the descent slow, but if the wings are raised in a 'V' they get less lift and the eagle drops at a steep angle.

They usually prey on small mammals and birds that live in the open, but the species vary from place to place. Their favourite foods seem to be game birds such as francolin, bustard and guinea fowl and mammals, like hyraxes. They will even eat impala calves. Jackals, snakes and lizards are sometimes taken but martial eagles rarely eat carrion. Domestic poultry, lambs and young goats are often eaten, but Leslie Brown, the authority on African eagles, has suggested that on the whole martial eagles are beneficial to man and that their destruction of livestock has been exaggerated.

Choice of nests

Martial eagles build large nests of sticks in tall trees, often on hillsides so there is a clear run-in to the nest. The female builds the nest, which may be 4 ft across and 4 ft deep, while the male collects sticks, or even small branches. The nests are used year after year and usually the female has to do no more than repair the nest and add a lining of fresh green leaves. Some pairs of martial eagles have two nests, each being used in alternate years.

Nest repair may take several weeks and when complete a single white or pale greenish-blue egg with brown markings is laid. The laying date varies between November in Sudan to July in South Africa. The female alone incubates and broods the chick

when it hatches out after about 45 days. For about 2 months the male brings food to the female who then gives it to the chick. Later, the female also hunts for food for the chick. The chick makes its first flight when it is about 100 days old. For some days it returns to the nest to roost and thereafter it stays fairly near the nest. Young martial eagles have been seen near their parents' nest when 3 years old. Unlike the crowned eagle that breeds in alternate years, the martial eagle may breed several years in succession, then fail to do so for several years.

Separate interests

In the course of his remarkable studies on African eagles, Leslie Brown found a hill on which five, and in one year six, species of eagles nested. The hill was appropriately named 'Eagle Hill'. There seemed to be no reason for this gathering except a natural gregariousness; there was no special abundance of food and there were plenty of other suitable nesting places nearby.

While on 'Eagle Hill' the different species did not interfere or compete with each other. The martial eagles fed on game birds caught in open country whereas African hawk-eagles hunted those in bush country. Brown snake-eagles caught snakes. Verreaux's eagles ate hyraxes that they hunted among rocks; the crowned eagles preyed on duikers and monkeys in the forests and Ayres' hawk-eagles took small birds from the trees. So, although crowded, the eagles did not have to compete for food.

class	**Aves**
order	**Falconiformes**
family	**Accipitridae**
genus & species	***Polemaetus bellicosus***

Vulture

The name 'vulture' was originally applied to only the large, scavenging birds of prey of the Old World, but after the discovery of America the term was extended to the condors, turkey vultures and other members of the New World family of birds of prey. They resemble the Old World vultures in appearance, presumably through convergent evolution, both groups having similar habits.

Vultures have naked or nearly naked heads, and sometimes naked necks, which is an asset to birds that regularly thrust their heads into carcases. Unlike other birds of prey, which kill their food, they have relatively weak feet which are adapted for running rather than holding prey. Both groups of vultures have heavy bodies but they soar effortlessly for hours on their long, broad wings.

There are 15 species of Old World vultures, with dark brown or black plumage, except in a few cases. The bare skin of the head and neck may, however, be orange, pink or white. The European black vulture is the largest bird in the Old World. It has a wingspan of over 8 ft and weighs over 15 lb. The plumage is almost wholly dark brown or black, with pale skin on the head and neck. It ranges from Spain to Korea and Japan. At the other end of the scale there is the lammergeier, or bearded vulture, and the Egyptian vulture. The latter has a wingspan of over 5 ft and is almost pure white except for black on the wings. The Egyptian vulture ranges through Africa, southern Europe, the Middle East and India. Only a little larger is the hooded vulture which is dark brown with a pinkish head and neck. It is very common in Africa south of the Sahara. The seven species of griffon and white-backed vultures are, perhaps, the 'typical' vultures. They are found throughout southern Europe, Africa and Asia, often in large groups, and they nest in colonies. They are medium-sized and have a ruff of long feathers around the naked neck. The remaining vultures are the palm-nut vulture, which has a feathered neck and black and white plumage, the white-headed vulture with blue at the base of the bill and the lappet-faced vulture. All of these live in Africa and have wattle-like folds of skin on the head and neck. There is also the Asian black vulture, which has a bright red head and neck.

◁ Gregarious griffons. Cape vultures gorge on a common zebra carcase. Most vultures are not strong enough to rip the hide so have to wait for it to decompose.

349

△ *White-backed vultures:* **Gyps africanus**.

Ripe food only

Vultures hunt by sight, detecting carrion from vast distances by watching the behaviour of other vultures and other carrion-eating animals. Large carcases may attract large flocks of vultures but despite their heavy bills most vultures have difficulty in breaking through the skins of large animals. Therefore they have to wait for the carcase to decompose or for another animal to attack it. The large vultures, such as the lappet-faced vulture, are powerful enough to rip through hide and, although solitary in habits, they take precedence over the gregarious griffon and white-backed vultures at a carcase. These, in turn, keep away the small vultures which have to be content with scraps.

The rasp-like tongues of vultures enable them to pull flesh into the mouth and their long necks allow them to probe deep into a large carcase, while the lack of feathers means that they have no problems about preening blood-stained feathers. Vultures do not feed on carrion exclusively, however. The largest vultures sometimes prey on the chicks of flamingos or on small rodents and the palm-nut vulture feeds on oil-palm nuts as well as shellfish from the seashore and sometimes hunts in shallow water for small fish.

Huge nests

Unlike the condors and many other birds of prey, the Old World vultures build their own nests instead of laying their eggs on the ground or in the abandoned nests of other birds. The lammergeier and the Egyptian vulture nest in caves or rock crevices, as do the griffon vultures which nest in colonies of over 100 on cliffs. The Indian griffon and the white-backed vultures often nest in trees, with up to a dozen nests in one large tree. The large vultures, the hooded vulture and the palm-nut vulture, nest singly in trees. The nests are huge cups of sticks and twigs lined with leaves, pieces of hide and refuse.

There is usually a single egg, two in smaller species, which is incubated by the female. Incubation ranges from 46 to 53 days, depending on the size of the vulture, and the chicks stay in the nest for up to 4½ months. The male feeds the female while she is incubating, then both parents feed the chicks by regurgitation.

Decreasing scavengers

Vulture numbers are decreasing wherever modern agricultural methods and methods of hygiene are being introduced; there are fewer carcases left lying about, and those that remain have often been poisoned. Although the vultures are not so useful nowadays as scavengers around human settlements they still help to clear up the carcases of stock, which are a potential source of infection. Unfortunately they are not always seen in this light and are persecuted for allegedly killing livestock, although only the largest vultures could possibly attempt to do so.

Riding the thermals

Vultures are most common in dry, open country where they can soar effortlessly in ascending air currents. They are also found in mountain country, up to 20 000 feet. Apart from supplying the air currents necessary for flight, these areas are also those where there is likely to be an abundance of carcases of large animals easily visible from the air. Vultures are rarely found in forests, except for the hooded vulture. This is the most widespread, although not the commonest vulture in Africa. It regularly scavenges around towns and villages, providing a valuable garbage disposal service, and even follows people as they till the soil, to feed on insects that are turned up. Because of its exploitation of man it is able to penetrate forests where there are human settlements.

To be able to soar at great heights, the heavy-bodied vultures make use of thermals, the 'bubbles' of hot air that rise from the ground as it heats up. A thermal is like a smoke-ring with a stream of air rising through the centre of the ring, which is spinning rapidly. The vultures glide around inside the ring, using the rising air to hold them aloft. This is the same principle as is used by glider pilots. The dependence of vultures on thermals is shown by their daily habits. They do not take off in the morning until the ground has warmed up and thermals begin to form. The lighter species of vulture take off before the heavier vultures, which need more lift.

Tool-users

There are very few animals that use tools – the Galapagos woodpecker finch, the chimpanzee and the sea otter are probably the best known examples – but in 1966 another was added to the list. This is the Egyptian vulture, which throws stones at eggs. The habit is so well developed in a population in Tanzania studied by Jane Goodall that it is surprising that there are no previous records. These vultures smash the tough shells of ostrich eggs either by throwing them against a rock or another egg, or by throwing a stone at them. If there is no stone nearby a vulture may search for one up to 50 yards away, fly back with it in its bill then sling it with a violent downward movement of the head. The action is repeated until the shell cracks. One vulture managed to throw a 2lb rock, and continued to do so for some time, no mean feat for a raven-sized bird.

class	**Aves**
order	**Falconiformes**
family	**Accipitridae**
genera & species	***Aegypius monachus*** European black vulture ***Gypohierax angolensis*** palm-nut vulture ***Gyps africanus*** white-backed vulture ***G. coprotheres*** Cape vulture ***G. indicus*** Indian griffon ***Necrosyrtes monachus*** hooded vulture ***Neophron percnopterus*** Egyptian vulture ***Sarcogyps calvus*** Indian black vulture ***Torgos tracheliotus*** lappet-faced vulture ***Trigonoceps occipitalis*** white-headed vulture, others

Chicken

When we say somebody 'keeps chickens' in his backyard, we mean that the person owns domesticated fowls of the kind known scientifically as **Gallus gallus.** This is also the name of the red jungle fowl of southern and south west Asia, from the foothills of the Himalayas to Java. It is from this the domestic fowl is believed to have been bred, although some scientists believe that other wild fowl of the same region may have been involved, and they prefer to call the domestic fowl **Gallus domesticus.** The red jungle fowl lives in forests from sea level to 5 000 ft.

The cock of the wild fowl is mainly red and black, the black feathers having a greenish iridescence. The hen is russet and brown. The cock has a high arched tail, twin wattles on the throat and a saw-edge comb. The beak is short and strong, the legs powerful, the toes on each foot are armed with strong claws used in scratching the earth. Of the four toes one is directed backwards, set at a higher level than the rest and, in the cock, armed with a long spur. The wings are small and rounded, capable of strong but not sustained flight, consisting of bursts of wing beats alternating with glides. Their food is leaves, roots, bulbs, seeds and berries, earthworms and insects. The nest is on the ground. The chicks, able to run about soon after hatching, feed mainly on insects.

The cock's voice is a loud crowing, used to advertise his possession of a territory. He is polygamous and defends his territory if necessary by fighting with beak and spurs.

Early domestication

The date of domestication of the jungle fowl is uncertain. It may have been as early as 3 200 BC but had certainly taken place by 2 000 BC in India. There were domestic chickens in China by 1 400 BC as well as in Egypt and Crete, and they reached south-eastern Europe by 700 BC.

The evidence from archaeological relics, such as pottery, figurines, coins and mosaics, suggests that the birds were kept primarily for religious and sacrificial purposes, as well as for the sport of cockfighting. They were later valued for their egg-laying. According to Aristophanes (about 400 BC) every Athenian, even the poorest, kept his hen for laying eggs. The Greeks also invented the capon, or castrated cock, for fattening, but the eating of chicken flesh was the least of the economic uses until the 19th century. Another use for the bird was as an 'alarm clock' for the farmer.

From Ancient Greece to Ancient Rome was but a short step, and with the Roman conquest of much of Europe the domestic chicken was taken farther afield, although it seems also to have been taken along the trade routes in advance of the Roman legions. The Celts of northern Europe, for example, had it before Caesar invaded Britain.

▽ *Barnyard family. Cockerels are polygamous and defend their territories, if necessary, by fighting with beak and spurs. There are more than 100 breeds or varieties of chickens, but the number kept for egg or meat production is limited. Modern farming is so specialised that hens are now rarely found scratching around for a living. They tend to be kept in large flocks under standard conditions by poultry farmers only, either in deep litter houses or in batteries of cages. Separate units are maintained with some breeds kept as table birds and others as layers.*

Ornamental and commercial breeds

The modern breeds are divided into Mediterranean and Asiatic types. Of the former there are now 37 breeds used commercially, as well as 24 ornamental breeds. In addition to show birds and fighting cockerels, the breeds tend to be grouped into prolific layers and table birds. The names of some are almost household words: the white leghorn, the best egg-layer, closely followed by the Rhode Island red and the Plymouth. Among the ornamental breeds the most spectacular is the long-tailed Yokohama, bred for the long tail, which in the cock may reach 20 ft.

The peck order

In the scientific field chickens have been responsible for one of the biggest advances in our knowledge of animal behaviour. In 1922 the idea of a peck order was first published. It was discovered by observation of the common or farmyard domestic hen. Briefly, it amounts to this: if a dozen hens new to each other are put into an enclosure, they will separate into couples and start to fight. One of each couple will triumph over the other, either because she is stronger than her opponent or because her opponent refuses to fight. She will be dominant, the other will be subordinate.

Then the dominants will face each other in couples, from which half will emerge once more as dominants, the other half as subordinates. In the end a hierarchy will have been established which can be expressed as follows. If we identify the hens by the letters A to L there will be the boss hen (A) which can peck all the others and they will not peck back. The next in succession (B) will be able to peck all except A, C can peck D–L, but not A and B, and so it will go down the line, until the lowest in the hierarchy (L) will be subordinate to all the rest, the one which gets pecked by all the others.

Any hen can change her position in the hierarchy by winning a fight with a superior hen, but without such a challenge the positions in the hierarchy are accepted by all.

This is a simplified version but the principle is there, and subsequent research in a large number of animal species has confirmed it. In most animal communities (including our own) there is a social order of dominance and subordinance, among males as well as females. It is generally referred to as a peck order, because the first discovery was with domestic hens. And the discovery has revolutionized our study of the social behaviour of animals as well as human beings.

Chicken fortune tellers

The behaviour of chickens in their peck order has become almost a symbol in the philosophy of the modern scientist. Chickens have served as symbols in other ways in earlier civilizations. Hens were symbols of fertility, because of their egg-laying, and this was later transferred to the cock, largely from the elaborate display he uses in wooing the hen. He became an erotic symbol as well as a symbol of health.

The Romans went further and used chickens for prophecy, the *oraculum ex tripudio*. Hens were put in a cage with food. If they

△△ *Wild relative — the jungle fowl, which lives in forests from sea level to 5 000 feet. It is characterised by the iridescence of its feathers.*

△ *One of the more exotic breeds: the long-tailed Yokohama. Many varieties have been specially bred for their attractive plumage patterns.*

ate greedily, the omens were good. Should they show little taste for food, the omens were unfavourable. The method was open to abuse. One had only to starve the hens beforehand to obtain a good omen.

In the first Punic War a consul, angry with his hens because they refused to eat when he needed a good omen, cast them into the sea saying: 'Let them drink if they won't eat.' He was subsequently defeated in a battle at sea, a fate which the people of Rome attributed to his lack of respect for the hens.

class	**Aves**
order	**Galliformes**
family	**Phasianidae**
genus & species	*Gallus gallus*

Sunbittern

The sunbittern is a large and little-known inhabitant of tropical American forests. It is related to the coots, cranes and bustards rather than the true bitterns of the heron family. It is, however, heron-like in appearance, about 18 in. long, with a long slender neck, small head and long bill. The bright orange legs are also long and slender and the toes are unwebbed. The wings and tail are broad. The plumage is soft like that of an owl and is mainly brown and grey with black bars and spots. The crown of the head is black and two white streaks run across the face. There are two broad black bands across the tail. The bill is black on the upper mandible, yellow on the lower. When a sunbittern opens its wings a pattern of chestnut and orange becomes visible on the back with white and black patches on the wings.

Sunbitterns are found from southern Mexico to Bolivia and central Brazil.

Sunset display

Sunbitterns, like herons, live singly or in pairs along the banks of rivers or in swampy woodland and wade slowly through the shallows in search of food. Captive sunbitterns have been described as standing with their bodies swaying from side to side in the same manner as bitterns, reputedly to make them less conspicuous among the waving reeds. They also spend a considerable time motionless with the neck withdrawn as herons do. Sunbitterns are reluctant to fly preferring to walk and to swim across streams. When disturbed, however, they fly into trees. Their flight is very quiet, presumably because of the soft plumage, and their broad wings give them the appearance of gigantic fluttering moths. Sunbitterns are usually silent but sometimes they utter quiet whistles or rattles.

The display of the sunbittern is most spectacular. The forepart of the body is lowered while the head is raised and the wings are spread with the rear edges raised and the tail fanned and brought up, so that the whole of the beautifully patterned plumage is displayed in a semi-circle. The bright chestnut and orange of the back and wings have been described by Alexander Skutch as looking like 'a sun darkly glowing in a sunset-tinted sky'. During the display a harsh rattle is given. This display is used during courtship and also as a threat.

Sunbitterns feed on insects, crustaceans, small fish and other small animals found in shallow water along the banks. Their feeding behaviour is very much like that of herons; they stalk slowly or stand motionless then suddenly shoot out their necks and grab their prey in the dagger-like bill.

Nests rarely seen

Very few sunbittern nests have been found in the wild. Alexander Skutch describes one which consisted of a 12in. mass of decaying leaves, twigs, moss and mud, lined with green

△ *Out on a limb: an unusual photograph of a brooding sunbittern on its nest of moss and mud.*

leaves and perched on a 2in. branch. A tree is the usual place for a sunbittern to build its nest but they may build on the ground.

The first record of the nesting behaviour of the sunbittern was the description given of a pair that nested in London Zoo in 1865, and a century later it is still the most detailed account, although sunbitterns have since nested in other zoos. The pair built their nest of straw, grass, mud and clay on a specially provided platform, 10 ft up. The first egg was found broken under the nest but a second was laid shortly afterwards and was incubated by both parents for 27 days. The chick was like that of a snipe and was fed by both parents on food carried in their bills until its wing feathers had grown enough for it to fly to the ground, at the age of 21 days. The parents continued to feed it and 2 months after it had hatched another egg was laid and incubated mainly by the male while the female continued to feed the original chick. In the wild the normal clutch seems to be 2 eggs.

Mixed crowd

The order Gruiformes, to which the sunbittern belongs, contains some unusual birds. There is the large family of rails, some of which are flightless, the buttonquails in which the female plays the leading role in courtship, the mesites of Madagascar which are probably flightless, the cranes, finfoots and the bustards. Some of the Gruiformes resemble birds outside the order, such as the stork-like kagu, the ibis-like limpkin and the heron-like sunbittern. Despite a variety of external form and habit the gruiform birds have many similarities in the form of their skeletons and muscles. One habit which is, however, very common in the group is that of nesting on the ground and producing chicks that can walk soon after hatching. The sunbittern is an exception because it nests in trees and although its chicks are hatched with a coat of down and appear well-developed, they are fed in the nest for some time.

class	Aves
order	Gruiformes
family	Eurypygidae
genus & species	*Eurypyga helias*

Oystercatcher

*The oystercatchers are large waders that are found in many parts of the world. Some species have black and white plumage, hence the old name of 'sea-pie' but others are all black. The most widespread oystercatcher **Haematopus ostralagus** is found in Europe, the Canaries, South Africa, Asia, Australia, New Zealand and North and South America. It is largely black above with white underparts and has a long red bill and pink legs. Another pied oystercatcher is the American oystercatcher **H. palliatus** that ranges from New Jersey and California to Argentina and Chile, while a third **H. leucopodus** lives in southern South America. The sooty oystercatcher **H. fuliginosus** lives on the coast of Australia and other black oystercatchers **H. bachmani** and **H. ater** live in western North America, southern South America and Australia. In some places the common oystercatcher is all black, as in the Canaries, Africa and America.*

Moving inland

Oystercatchers are usually seen on rocky shores or sandy beaches, on mudflats, or in sand dune areas just behind the shore but they sometimes breed inland. They have nested inland in Scotland for centuries and they are now breeding inland in northern England. In New Zealand, oystercatchers are found by the snow rivers of South Island. Outside the breeding season oystercatchers gather in large flocks, and those that breed in high latitudes migrate to warmer regions in the winter. The Burry Inlet in South Wales, for instance, is the winter home of oystercatchers from Scotland, Iceland, the Faeroes and Norway.

The pied plumage and red bill of the oystercatcher are unmistakable, yet, surprisingly, they are sometimes difficult to see if they are motionless. They often give away their presence by their loud shrill calls of 'kleep-kleep' or a shorter, rapid 'kic-kic'. Oystercatchers are wary and run rapidly or take flight when approached.

Musselcatchers

It is difficult to see how the oystercatcher got its name. The authoritative *Handbook of British Birds* does not include oysters in the diet of the oystercatcher, and it would be surprising if it did because oysters live below the lowtide mark and oystercatchers feed between the tides or on land. A better name would be the old local name of musselpecker. Mussels, together with limpets, cockles, winkles, crabs and worms, make up a large part of the oystercatchers' diet. Cockles and worms are found by probing the sand with their bills. They also eat insects, especially their larvae, some plant food and occasionally eggs of other birds. The composition of the diet depends on the animal life living in the oystercatchers' habitat; whether sandy or rocky shores, farmland and so on.

The methods by which oystercatchers eat molluscs that are protected by strong shells, have been studied in detail. Limpets are dealt a sharp blow with the tip of the bill. Small ones are dislodged and large ones are shifted so they can be levered off or holed. The oystercatcher can then insert its bill and tear the strong muscles that hold the limpet down. Two different ways are used for opening bivalve molluscs such as mussels and cockles. If the shellfish is covered with water and its valves, or shells, are agape, the oystercatcher stabs downward then levers and twists to sever the adductor muscle that closes the valves. These fall open and the flesh is rapidly pecked out. If the shellfish are exposed to the air and firmly closed the oystercatcher has to smash its way in. Examination of mussel shells that were the remains of oystercatcher meals, shows that they are regularly smashed on the bottom edge and tests have shown that this side of the shell is much weaker than the top edge even in large mussels. The oystercatcher carries a mussel or cockle to a patch of firm sand, places it with its ventral margin upwards, and starts to hammer it. If the shell falls over it is righted or if it sinks it is carried to a firmer patch. On average, five blows of the bill are needed to penetrate a mussel shell and the bill is then inserted to cut the adductor muscle and prise the two halves apart. Cockle shells are not attacked in any particular position as their shells are weaker than those of mussels. Small crabs are flipped onto their backs and killed with a stab through the brain. The shell is then prised off and the flesh cut out with the same scissoring movements that are used for eating other shellfish.

In some places, such as the Burry Inlet

Posed on a cliff top beside a clump of thrift before flying down to feed at the mussel beds between the tide lines below. The strong red bill for prising open mussels and the thick red legs add flashes of colour to the oystercatcher's stark black and white plumage.

*S. African black oystercatcher **Haematopus moquini.***

in Britain, oystercatchers are considered a pest because of the damage they do to the cockle beds. Each oystercatcher eats about one cockle every minute and consumes on average 336 cockles per tide. As flocks number several thousands, they eat many millions of cockles each winter; but oystercatchers are only one of several enemies of cockles and it is debatable whether they seriously affect the cockle industry. In the Faeroes, they are considered beneficial as most of their food is insects and other invertebrates in grassland.

Piping display

Oystercatchers arrive at their breeding grounds in flocks but then split up into pairs. Each pair forms a territory which it defends against the other oystercatchers. Among their several displays there is the quite spectacular piping display in which a group of birds, or sometimes just a pair, run rapidly to and fro with necks outstretched and open bills pointing at the ground. At the same time they utter a piping call that varies from a clear 'kleep-kleep' to a quavering trill.

The nest is a shallow depression in shingle, sand or turf, sometimes with no lining but at other times lined with stones, shells, or dead plants. There are usually three eggs, yellowish or light brown with spots or streaks of dark brown. Both parents incubate the eggs which hatch in 24–27 days. The chicks leave the nest after a day or two and are fed by both parents. They fly in about 5 weeks and are fed by their parents for another 5 weeks.

Family traits

The careful study of the way oystercatchers open mussels was made by M Norton-Griffiths of Oxford University. He found that some oystercatchers regularly stabbed open mussels while others hammered the shells. Furthermore, young oystercatchers developed the same feeding habits as their parents. This is, perhaps, not so surprising as the chicks were learning to feed on only those animals which their parents brought

to them. First the chicks practise pecking empty shells and picking up pieces of flesh left in them, learning the scissoring movements of the adults. Later they take opened shellfish from their parents and remove the flesh by themselves. Eventually they open the shells themselves, starting on small ones and graduating to large ones as they become more proficient. Norton-Griffiths never saw a 'crab-eating' chick attack a mussel and when a 'mussel-eating' chick found a crab it was frightened of it. The differences in feeding habits are so marked that a population of oystercatchers is distinctly divided by them and 'mussel-eaters' mate only with 'mussel-eaters' and 'cockle-eaters' with 'cockle-eaters'.

class	**Aves**
order	**Charadriiformes**
family	**Haematopodidae**
genus & species	*Haematopus ostralagus* oystercatcher, others

Puffin

The puffin, a small auk about 12 in. long, with a massive, brilliantly coloured and decidedly bizarre bill, is perhaps the most popular and well known of sea birds. The comical effect of the bill is enhanced by coloured horny patches above and below the eyes. The plumage is basically the same as that of other auks; black above and white underneath, with the black extending around the neck as a collar. The legs are bright orange and the sides of the face ashy grey. The triangular bill has red, yellow and blue stripes with a thick yellow skin in the corners of the mouth. Outside the breeding season the basal part of the horny covering of the bill, including the blue parts and the yellow skin, are shed, leaving the base of the bill narrower and horn-coloured. At the same time the red tip becomes yellow. The bill of young puffins is more conventional, narrower and plainly coloured, the inner half greyish brown, the outer half reddish brown.

The puffin breeds along the coasts of the North Atlantic from Greenland to the Gulf of the St Lawrence in the west and from Spitzbergen and Novaya Zemlya to the British Isles and northern France in the east. Some spread as far south as the Canaries and into the Mediterranean as far as the Adriatic. British puffins have been found wintering in American waters but not all puffins migrate away from their breeding places. Puffins regularly spend the winter in Baffin Bay and in mild winters they stay near Amsterdam Island, north of Spitzbergen, despite the low temperatures and continual darkness of the Arctic winter. The horned puffin, which lives in the North Pacific and is a close relative of the Atlantic puffin, has fleshy growths over the eyes and differs in the colouring of the bill. It breeds on either side of the Bering Sea. Another Pacific puffin is the tufted puffin, all black but for a white face and long tufted feathers sprouting from above the eyes. The bill is red and green.

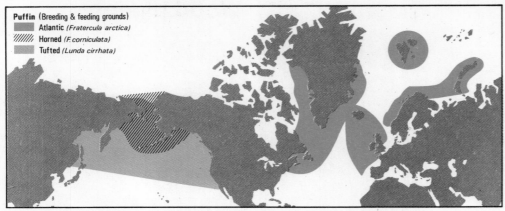

▽ *These two puffins are engaged in a ritualised courtship ceremony known as billing.*

Cliff nester

From spring until the end of the breeding season puffins contribute to the masses of auks that fly continually to and from the nesting cliffs. Instead of shuffling on their haunches like other auks such as the guillemots, puffins walk quite easily with a waddling gait. When they take off from the cliffs their wings appear to be too small to support them and they plunge steeply until their rapidly whirring wings become effective. When cornering in flight or coming in to land the orange feet are spread out to help in steering or braking.

Mysterious fish stackers

Puffins feed on small fish, such as sand eels and cod fry, together with crustaceans, floating molluscs and other planktonic animals. Outside the breeding season they go far out to sea, usually out of sight of land. Food is caught by diving, the puffins swimming underwater with their wings. If puffins have chicks to feed they carry their catch back in the bill. Puffins are quite tame on their breeding cliffs and can be watched from close quarters landing with fish draped crossways in the bill. They can carry up to 30 fish in this way, but this is exceptional. How they arrange the fish in the bill is still

a mystery. Presumably each fish is killed by a nip with the bill but how it is then placed alongside ones caught previously without dropping them is difficult to visualize. The tongue and the serrated floor of the upper mandible may be used to manoeuvre and hold them. Pictures of puffins with fish arranged in the bill head-to-head or alternating head-to-tail are based on either imagination or coincidence. Working the fish into a pattern would be very difficult and would serve no useful purpose.

Slow development

When puffins arrive at the breeding ground they start digging burrows or clearing out old ones. They dig with their heavy bills and scrape the loosened soil out with their feet. In large colonies burrowing can be so extensive as to cause a landslide. Sometimes they take over shearwater or rabbit burrows.

Puffins arrive at the breeding grounds already paired but there is a considerable amount of displaying around the burrows. The large colourful bill is used as a signal, being thrust forward in threat or shaken in appeasement. Mating takes place on the water after the male has chased the female.

A single egg, white with faint markings, is incubated for 40–43 days. The parents

share the task, but at intervals they leave the egg and parade together outside the burrow. The chick is fed on fish by both parents, but when 6 weeks old it is deserted by the parents who go out to sea to moult, during which time they become flightless. The chick stays in the burrow for another week then flutters down from the cliffs and paddles out to sea. The young puffins leave the burrows at night when there is less danger from gulls and skuas. Until they can fly they avoid danger by diving. Seven weeks is a very long fledging period for an auk, but puffins are reared in the safety of a burrow, whereas guillemots, razorbills and other auks breed on cliff ledges where their chicks are vulnerable to predation by gulls. These auks also leave the nest before they can fly, but unlike puffins are not independent and remain in the care of the adults.

Rat and oil problems

A certain number of puffins fall prey to gulls and skuas; on the island of Foula in the Shetlands, for instance, the cliffs are sometimes littered with the remains of puffins eaten by skuas, but their numbers are more severely reduced when rats are introduced to their breeding grounds. At one time the puffin population of Ailsa Craig was described as phenomenal, but in 1889, rats got ashore from a wreck and the population has since declined almost to extinction. A similar decrease has also occurred on Lundy, the name of this island being Norse for Puffin Island.

Recently there has been another threat to puffins, and other auks. Oil pollution is particularly serious to auks, because of their gregariousness and their habit of diving out of trouble and resurfacing in the oil patch. They are also particularly vulnerable when flightless during the moult.

Cliff crop

Man is another predator of puffins. The islanders of Faeroe, Shetland, St Kilda and other places have for a long time relied on sea birds for food, although the practice has declined in recent years. On St Kilda where sea birds formed the mainstay of the islanders, more puffins were killed than any other bird, including gannets and fulmars. They were the main food during the summer, eaten roasted, and their feathers were collected and sold. Catching puffins was usually the women's work, assisted by dogs who helped locate nests. They were hauled out of their burrows, snared or caught in nets as they flew in. On Foula, the sheer cliffs where many of the puffins nested were divided so that each man had a section where he could hazardously collect his crop.

class	**Aves**
order	**Charadriiformes**
family	**Alcidae**
genera & species	***Fratercula arctica***
	Atlantic puffin
	F. corniculata
	horned puffin
	Lunda cirrhata
	tufted puffin

Wood pigeon

From being a harmless rarity up to the end of the 18th century, the wood pigeon, or ring dove, has become one of the most common and most destructive pests of agricultural land, especially in certain parts of Europe. It is a handsome, rather heavily built bird, about 16 in. long with a wing span of about 18 in. The upper parts are bluish-grey with darker grey on the upper wings and black on the upper tail and wing quills. The breast is vinous shading to pale grey or lavender on the belly, flanks and under the tail. The rump and head are a bluer grey than the rest and the sides of the neck are a metallic purple and green. The base of the bill is pink, the rest yellow shading to pale brown on the tip. The base of the bill expands into a soft fleshy lump over the nostrils. The legs and feet are pink with a mauve tinge. The straw colour of the eye and its unusual pear-shaped iris give the bird a very alert expression. The wood pigeon can always be distinguished from other doves by the white patch on the sides of the neck, which is absent in young birds, and the broad white band across the wing. The male and female are alike except that the males tend to be slightly larger and their plumage brighter.

The typical race of the wood pigeon is found throughout Europe, except in the extreme north. It ranges eastwards to Russia and in the south extends to the north coast of the Mediterranean and to the various Mediterranean islands from the Balearics to Cyprus, and around the Black Sea. It is replaced by allied races in northwest Africa, the Azores, Madeira, Turkestan and Transcaspia to Iran, Baluchistan, Kashmir and Sikkim.

Wary in the country

The wood pigeon is primarily a bird of the woods but since the spread of agriculture it has taken to feeding on cultivated land. It is also a familiar bird in town parks and suburban gardens and is often found on downs and on coasts, some way from woods.

From autumn to spring and sometimes also in summer it congregates in large flocks to feed, although single birds and small groups may also be seen. In the towns and parks it may become quite tame but in the open country it is wary of humans and will

△ *Just beginning to lose their sparse yellow down, a pair of large young wood pigeons wait for the arrival of one or other of their parents with some food. After their first three days, when they are fed with pigeon's milk, their main diet is ripe cereal grain.*
◁ *One of the greatest enemies of farmers in Europe, the gentle-looking wood pigeon is easily distinguishable from other doves by the white patch on the sides of its neck. In order to reduce their numbers, the most effective method has proved to be nest destruction.*

359

Wood pigeon (*Columba palumbus*) Breeding grounds

△ *Two greedy young wood pigeons eagerly reach out of the nest trying to get more food from their ever-patient parent.*

take off with a loud clatter of wings at the slightest disturbance. Its normal flight is fast and strong with quick regular wing-beats and occasional glides. On the ground it struts about, restlessly moving its head to and fro. It roosts in trees, sometimes in large numbers.

The wood pigeon's voice, which is heard at all times of the year but more frequently in March and April, is often said to be a series of coos but the phrase 'two coos, Taffy take' repeated several times gives a better idea. The alarm note is a short, sharp 'roo' sound.

Agricultural menace

Originally the wood pigeon fed on acorns and beech mast as well as seeds, nuts, berries and the young leaves of many trees. Since the spread of agriculture and the disappearance of many woods it has turned, to a large extent, in many areas to cultivated crops and found them just as palatable and in greater abundance. Cereal grains are the most important food for both adults and young in late summer and autumn and in some areas peas and beans are taken in large quantities. In winter the birds depend mainly on clover, turnip tops and young greens. The pronounced hook at the end of the bill makes it easy for the pigeon to tear off the leaves of these plants. Some animal food is taken including caterpillars, earthworms, slugs, snails and insects.

The wood pigeon needs quite a large quantity of water and drinks greedily, not in sips like most other birds.

Billing and cooing

The courtship of a pair of wood pigeons begins while they are still in flocks. A pair separate from the main body and on the ground or a perch in a tree they bow to each other, their breasts touching the ground or perch, with their tails raised and spread, all the time cooing to each other. This bowing and cooing is often interrupted by a nuptial display flight in which the bird rises steeply with strong wingbeats then glides down and rises again with stiff set wings in an undulating course. At the top of its rising flight it usually makes several

claps with its wings, caused by a strong downbeat of the wings and not, as so often supposed, by the wings clapping together. Also at this time pairs of birds start to establish territories in the trees, the males driving away any intruders with aggressive posturing or actual attacks.

Young fed on milk

The breeding season is long, usually from April to September, but there are records of nests in every month of the year for the southern parts of the wood pigeon's range. The peak of breeding activity seems to be July, August and September in the British Isles when there is plenty of ripe corn for feeding the young. There are usually three broods a year. The nest is built in almost any kind of tree or in tall hedgerows, sometimes on top of the old nest of crows or sparrowhawks or on a squirrel's drey. Very occasionally it is built close to the ground or on ledges of rocks. In towns, buildings are used. The nest is a flimsy structure of intertwined sticks, often used for several years in succession. The male brings the material but only the female builds. Usually two, occasionally one or three, white, fairly glossy eggs are laid and are incubated for about 18 days, by both parents.

When the young birds hatch they are covered in sparse yellow down and for the first three days are fed at frequent intervals on a fluid from the parents' crops known as 'pigeon's milk'. After this, ripe cereal grain is the main food with some green food and weed seeds supplemented with animal foods. They stay in the nest for about 22 days, and afterwards are still fed by one or both parents for at least another week.

The average age attained by a wood pigeon in the wild in the British Isles is only 38 months but the oldest one recorded was in its 14th year.

Large numbers shot

Apart from man the adult wood pigeon has few enemies, but many of their eggs are taken by jays and magpies. The losses among young birds are due mainly to starvation, especially when they leave the nests and compete for food with the adult birds. In really severe winters the mortality among wood pigeons is very high but their numbers soon seem to increase again.

Owing to the widespread destruction of crops by wood pigeons a great deal of research has been done into methods of keeping down their numbers. Shooting the birds is still the most widely used method although some sportsmen contend that wood pigeons are difficult to shoot as the shot glances off their feathers. There is no evidence to show that widescale shooting makes any impression on their numbers.

Migrant or not?

The subject of migration of wood pigeons to and from the British Isles has provided a constant source of argument amongst countrymen, sportsmen and bird-watchers for many years. Apparently the wood pigeons in the British Isles are mainly sedentary but with a tendency to move south in the winter. Only a small proportion of the population undertakes long flights and these are usually young birds. There is probably a latent urge, inherited from migratory ancestors, which shows itself in only a few individuals. The only birds recovered abroad reached no farther than France. In continental Europe the migratory behaviour is rather different. Wood pigeons in Scandinavia and the Baltic are forced to migrate south in winter to escape the snow and some of these do arrive on the east coast of Britain, but the numbers vary considerably from year to year. Observers have told of hordes of wood pigeons arriving from the Continent and although large numbers may arrive in some years, confusion very often arises because of the flocks of wood pigeons that seem to fly out to sea from the British Isles and then fly back again!

class	**Aves**
order	**Columbiformes**
family	**Columbidae**
genus & species	*Columba palumbus*

360

Macaw

The 18 species of macaw include the largest and most colourful members of the parrot family. They live in tropical America, from southern Mexico through Central America to Paraguay. They have large beaks, the upper mandible being long and strongly hooked. The skin on the cheeks and around the eyes is naked except for a scattering of very small feathers.

The largest is the scarlet or red and blue macaw, of Mexico to Bolivia, 3 ft long, of which 2 ft is tail. It is mainly scarlet except for the yellow wing coverts and the blue of the flight feathers, the lower back feathers and outer tail feathers. The blue and yellow macaw, ranging from Panama to Paraguay, is only slightly smaller. It is a rich blue on the crown, nape, back, wings and upperside of tail, golden yellow on the underside, including the underside of the tail. There is a large black patch on the throat, the bill is black and the white sides of the face are marked with black wavy lines. The military or great green macaw, 30 in. long and ranging from Mexico to Brazil, is green, shading to blue on flight feathers, rump and tail coverts, with a crimson band on the forehead and red on the upperside of the tail. Less gaudy but probably more beautiful, certainly more prized by fanciers, is the hyacinthine macaw, 34 in. long, a cobalt blue throughout its plumage. Its range is limited to the interior jungles of the Amazon basin. The smaller species are usually green.

Commuting parrots

Macaws move about in screeching flocks except when breeding. Their day starts with a screeching chorus as individual birds leave their roosts to gather in a tree. There they bask in the early morning sun before setting off to feed. As the midday heat builds up they seek the shade, but when the sun's rays begin to weaken they come out again to feed. At dusk they return to their assembly point, usually a bare tree, before dispersing to roost.

Steamhammer beaks

Most macaws feed on seeds, nuts and fruits, the larger of them cracking even hard-shelled nuts such as Brazil nuts with their beaks and extracting the kernels with the

▽ Rendezvous at Felipe Benavides Fountain — red and blue and blue and yellow macaws.

beak helped by the fleshy tongue. Precise details of their feeding in the wild are hard to come by, but in captivity, although these form their basic foods, they seem to show a liking for such things as bread and butter and cake, and tame macaws have been known to take meat readily. It may be, therefore, that they take some insect food in the wild. This possibly explains, at least in part, their readiness to pull wooden structures to pieces, such as the edges of nesting boxes or woodwork frames in the aviary. In the wild the same activities would expose insect grubs.

Bashful male

Except for the hyacinthine macaw, which is said to nest in holes in earth banks, macaws nest in hollows in trees, sometimes high up from the ground. Once the eggs are laid macaws are aggressive towards anyone approaching their nest. Even tame macaws will defy their owners trying to see what is happening. A fairly clear account can, however, be given of the breeding behaviour of the blue and yellow macaw, based mainly on observations published by Mr Donald Risdon, in the *Avicultural Magazine* for 1965. He found little distinction between male and female except that the male blushes when excited, the bare skin of his face going a deep pink. The female seldom blushes and when she does the colour hardly shows. At the same time as he blushes the male nods his head up and down and contracts the pupils of his eyes. When Risdon's pair showed signs of breeding he gave them rotten wood, which they chewed up in typical macaw fashion. The eggs are slightly larger than pigeon's eggs. The nestling is still naked and blind at a week old. The wing quills begin to erupt at 4 weeks, the bill darkens and the eyes open. The back then begins to grow feathers followed by the tail and later the rest of the body and head, the young macaw becoming fully feathered by 10 weeks of age. It does not leave the nest for another 3 weeks, except to sit at the entrance. The parents feed it during this time by regurgitation. At 6 months the young macaw is as large as its parents and looks like them.

Vulnerability

With so formidable a beak a macaw could be a match for most small predators. Its main enemy is the harpy eagle. Their habit of feeding in flocks combined with their garish colours have made macaws vulnerable to the South American Indians with their blowpipes and arrows.

class	**Aves**
order	**Psittaciformes**
family	**Psittacidae**
genera & species	*Anodorhynchus hyacinthinus* hyacinthine macaw *Ara ararauna* blue and yellow macaw *A. macao* scarlet macaw *A. militaris* military macaw, others

Cuckoo

*The cuckoo is regarded in sharply contrasting ways; it is to some the harbinger of spring, to others, a base parasite. Of the many species, only the common cuckoo of Europe and Asia gives the loud insistent call that has given rise to the name. It is called **coucou** in French, **Kuckuck** in German, **Kukushka** in Russian and **Kak-ko** in Japanese.*

The common cuckoo has distinctive black and white barring on the underparts and a grey head and neck. The tail is long and the wings narrow, so in flight the cuckoo looks very much like a hawk. It can be distinguished, however, by its longer neck, the shape of the head and a pale streak under the wing.

Other cuckoos are gaudy by comparison with the common cuckoo. The red-winged Indian cuckoo has a magpie-like tail and a black head, back and tail. Related to it is the great spotted cuckoo, similar in shape but with white spots on the wings and back. The emerald cuckoo of South Africa is a brilliant golden green, except for a yellow belly.

Cuckoos belong to two subfamilies, with their relatives the anis, roadrunners, couas and coucals in other subfamilies. One subfamily, to which the common cuckoo belongs, ranges across the Old World from western Europe to Polynesia, while the other belongs to both Old and New Worlds. The former are all parasitic; the female lays her eggs in other birds' nests. It is for this habit that the cuckoos are best known, but it is by no means widespread in the family as a whole.

The lodger awaits acceptance in hedge sparrow's nest. When the foster parent is away the cuckoo flies down, lifts an egg out, swallows it or drops it and lays one of her own in its place.

Long migrations

Many cuckoos migrate over thousands of miles, from the tropics to the temperate regions. The common cuckoos begin to arrive in the British Isles in the last few days of March and leave during July to early September, each bird flying on its own bound for tropical Africa although exactly where is not known. The shining cuckoo of New Zealand makes an even more impressive migration, across 2 000 miles of ocean to the Solomon Islands. How they find their way over vast distances is especially puzzling as the young birds migrate from the breeding grounds several weeks after the adults have gone. This is sure proof that the urge to migrate, the ability to navigate, and the knowledge of the route are inherited, for there is absolutely no chance of the young cuckoos learning from their elders.

Feeds on many pests

Cuckoos eat insects, especially the larvae, but they will also eat worms, spiders, and centipedes. The beetles, flies, dragonflies, butterflies and moths eaten often include those harmful to agriculture; for instance, cockchafers, cabbage white butterflies and wireworms. In particular they eat hairy or toxic caterpillars including those of the cinnabar moth which are usually left alone by other birds. The yellow-billed and black-billed cuckoos of North America are useful because they eat the tent caterpillars that weave large communal shelters, from which they sally forth to strip trees of their leaves. Fruit is sometimes eaten, especially by the koel, a cuckoo of Asia and Australia.

Boarding out the children

It has been well-known since ancient times that the common cuckoo does not build a nest of its own, but lays its eggs in those of other birds. Other members of the cuckoo family do the same, as do other kinds of birds; for example, the cowbird and the honeyguide. It is far from easy to watch the cuckoo lay an egg in the host nest as so much depends on being in the right place at the right time. Nevertheless, the amazing ways in which she ensures that her offspring have a good chance of surviving until independent are now well-known.

The female cuckoo keeps a watch for small birds building their nests. When the nest is complete and the unwitting foster parent has laid an egg, the cuckoo flies down. Choosing a time when the foster parent is away, she lifts an egg out of the nest, swallows or drops it, and very quickly lays one of her own in its place and departs before the foster parent returns.

Cuckoo eggs are sometimes found in domed nests of willow warblers and it was once thought that the cuckoo laid her egg on the ground then carried it to the nest in her bill, but it is now known that she presses her body against the nest and ejects the egg through the entrance. In Australia and New Zealand the shining cuckoo lays in domed nests of wrens by forcing its head in through the entrance then out through the far wall. The egg is laid while it straddles the nest, then it scrambles out through the hole it has made. The foster parent, when it returns, merely repairs the gap in the nest.

Observations have shown that clutches with a cuckoo egg are more likely to be deserted than normal clutches, but usually the cuckoo egg is accepted. It hatches in 12½ days and often the chick emerges before its nestmates. This advantage is used by the baby cuckoo to evict the other eggs and any newly hatched young. It is perhaps this part of the parasitic habit, more than any other, that has earned the cuckoo its bad name. The baby cuckoo manoeuvres itself in the bottom of the nest so that an egg or chick becomes balanced on its back, between the wings. It then hoists the unfortunate creature out of the nest, to be followed by the others. Occasionally two cuckoo eggs may be laid in one nest, when two female cuckoos are keeping watch in one area. After a few days jostling, the urge to empty the nest of competitors dies away and both young cuckoos grow together.

If the cuckoo did not evict its nestmates they would surely die in any case, for the young cuckoo grows rapidly, and its foster parents are hard put to feed it. After 3 weeks it leaves the nest which it has outgrown, and the foster parents keep feeding it, often having to perch on its back to drop insects in the gaping beak.

The African emerald cuckoo is a brilliant golden green.

Almost ready to moult at the end of the season, hedge sparrow feeds its giant foster child.

The common cuckoo arrives in Britain in late March leaving between July and September.

Common cuckoo *(Cuculus canorus)*

Winter range

The baby cuckoo usually hatches first and begins to evict the other eggs.

The second egg does not survive long, being ejected from the nest in the same manner.

A newly-hatched tree pipit receives the same treatment being unable to defend itself.

Matching egg colours

Surveys of clutches containing cuckoo eggs show that the cuckoo egg is often very similar to the foster parents' eggs, and it has also been found that in any area cuckoos use certain host nests more than others. In Hungary, the chief dupe of the common cuckoo is the great reed warbler, and the cuckoo lays greenish eggs blotched with brown and black, like those of the warbler. In Finland, cuckoos' eggs are blue like those of its hosts the whinchat and redstart. Nearly all over its range, there are these preferences for certain hosts with a mimicking of their eggs. It seems that this reduces the chance of the foster parent abandoning the nest.

In the British Isles, however, cuckoo eggs differ surprisingly from their hosts'—yet they all tend to be of one pattern. The explanation for this seems to be that a cuckoo may lay in nests of another host if it cannot find the right one, and in Britain, where the countryside is divided into many small habitats with a large variety of possible host species, the cuckoo has not been able to form any set preferences for any particular host.

The final deception

Before the mysteries of bird migration were revealed it was thought the cuckoos turned into sparrowhawks in the winter and, even now, it is not unusual for a cuckoo to be mistaken for a sparrowhawk because of the similarity of shape and plumage. Bird watchers are not the only ones to be deceived as, when the cuckoo returns in spring, small birds will gather to mob it as if it were a hawk. There is some evidence that the cuckoos make use of this mistake. Cuckoos have been seen flying in an even more hawk-like fashion than usual, flapping and gliding in a soaring flight very much like a bird of prey. When they settle they are sometimes mobbed by meadow pipits and other small birds. On a few occasions this behaviour has been followed by the cuckoo alighting near a meadow pipit's nest, and one was seen flying away with a pipit's egg which it swallowed. It seems then that the cuckoo indulges in this hawk-like flight just before egg-laying, to lure the owners of the nest away by false pretences so that it can sneak in and lay its own egg.

Evidence for this is not conclusive but similar behaviour has been seen in other cuckoos. An Indian hawk-cuckoo that imitates sparrowhawks has been seen to lure birds from their nests in a more positive fashion, and the koel mimics a crow which is its main host in India. The male koel is black and it flies up to the host nest, calling, and is promptly chased away by the crows. Apparently they do this not so much to ward off a parasitic bird but for the same reason of ownership for which they would drive away another crow. Meanwhile the brown female koel slips in to lay her egg. The baby koel, moreover, does not eject its nestmates but it looks so like a young crow that it is hardly distinguishable from its fellow nestlings.

Of all the parasitic birds, however, the cuckoos, by reducing egg size and incubation time, and by mimicry of host birds' eggs, have applied the greatest resource to their underhand art.

class	**Aves**
order	**Cuculiformes**
family	**Cuculidae**
genera & species	***Cuculus canorus*** *common cuckoo* ***C. varius*** *hawk-cuckoo* ***Clamator coromandus*** *red-winged Indian cuckoo* ***C. glandarius*** *greater spotted cuckoo* ***Chrysococcyx cupreus*** *emerald cuckoo* ***Chalcites lucidus*** *shining cuckoo* ***Coccyzus erythrophthalmus*** *black-billed cuckoo* ***C. americanus*** *yellow-billed cuckoo* ***Eudynamys scolopacea*** *koel others*

Barn owl

The barn owl's body is not as white as it appears when it is seen flying about at dusk. The upper parts are orange-buff, often speckled with grey and white. The underparts and face are pure white.

Although widespread, barn owls are not common throughout the British Isles, and are absent from the North of Scotland. In North America they do not breed north of Massachusetts, southern Ontario and Michigan, Iowa, Nebraska and northern California but they are regularly recorded as visitors farther north.

There are ten species of barn owl in various parts of the world. They differ from other owls in small details of the skeleton and proportionately smaller eyes set in a heart-shaped facial disc.

The typical barn owl is widespread, found in most parts of Europe, America, Africa, India, South-east Asia and Australia. There are about 32 races.

Ghost-like habits

The barn owl has probably given rise to many ghost stories. It often lives in churches or empty houses and is likely to give anyone not expecting it a bad shock, when it flies silently past them, a ghostly white in the gloom of night, or when they hear its eerie, long drawn out shrieks.

In Britain barn owls were formerly subject to unnecessary persecution, especially by gamekeepers. In the early 20th century, however, they made some recovery, but in the late 1940's a general decrease became apparent and by 1955 they had disappeared from many areas, especially in eastern Britain. The decrease is largely the the result of the owls' dependence on man. Old buildings and hollow trees provided roosts and nest sites and the barn owls' main prey were the rats, voles and mice that fed on man's crops. Since the Second World War, agriculture in Britain has been changing. Derelict stables and rotten trees are no longer tolerated and intensive agriculture has changed those parts of the countryside that barn owls used to frequent. The most rapid decrease in numbers over the last decade or so has, without much doubt, been due to the increased use of pesticides sprayed onto crops. These poisons accumulate in the bodies of the small animals that eat the crops and are then accumulated even further when they are eaten by owls, with the result that the barn owls often become sterile and their eggs fail to hatch.

Sometimes barn owls may be seen in broad daylight, but more usually they come out at twilight. With their white plumage, they are easy to see, flying about 15—20 ft above the ground, with fairly rapid but long wing-beats. They have regular routes which they patrol night after night, circling about and occasionally dropping to the ground to catch their prey.

Prey is taken to the nest or to a regular roost, which is identifiable by the pellets of indigestible bones, insect bodies and fur

△ *Barn owl having just swallowed its prey, indicated by the blood on the ground.*

▽ *Parent barn owls with 3-month-old chicks. At 4 months the young fly off to find their own territories.*

that are regurgitated and dropped, littering the ground about the roost. The barn owl's pellets are blackish with a varnished appearance, easily distinguishable from the greyish, soft pellets of tawny owls.

Owl pellets identify prey

It is from their pellets that the food of barn owls, and other predatory birds, can be identified. As the owls regurgitate their pellets in set places and the pellets accumulate, it is possible to get a very good idea of the diet by collecting them at intervals and pulling them apart to find the bones and other remains of the owls' prey.

A few years ago a large number of pellets were analysed in Poland. The remains of nearly 16 000 vertebrates (back-boned animals) were found and identified. Of these, 95.5% were of small mammals, 4.2% birds and the small remainder, amphibians. In Britain, similar proportions have been found. Mammal remains appear in the following order of frequency: common shrew, long-tailed field mouse, field vole and bank vole. Others, such as brown rats, house mice, even moles, bats and rabbits are taken, while several species of bird, night-flying beetles and moths, and occasional frogs and fish are found in the pellets. It is this kind of analysis which exposes the folly of persecution. Barn owls, as we now see, rarely take birds and are not a significant menace to poultry or pheasants.

Rodent control

The large number of small mammals included in the barn owls' diet shows the

useful role they play, for these mammals feed on man's crops. The numbers that a barn owl can catch are shown by the observation made on an American barn owl. In only 20 minutes it had caught 16 mice, three gophers, one rat and one squirrel. It must be added that this impressive number of animals was captured for the owl's babies.

A nest of pellets

In April or May, and again in July, piles of prey can be found at a barn owl's nest site. This is a sign that they are about to breed, for the male collects extra food to feed to the female. There is no nest made, the eggs are merely laid on an accumulation of pellets. Usually four to seven white eggs are laid, but there may be as few as three or as many as eleven. They are incubated for nearly 5 weeks by the female alone, who remains on the nest, being fed by the male.

The young hatch out at different times because the female begins incubating the first egg as soon as it is laid, so each egg begins its development before the next is laid. It has been suggested that the staggered hatching of barn owls' eggs helps to reduce the strain of providing enough food for them, because they will not all be requiring large quantities of food at once. The chicks leave the nest after 9–12 weeks to find territories of their own, where they stay for the rest of their lives.

At one time it was thought that barn owls hunted by sight. But experiments have shown that they can catch their prey in total darkness, where it is absolutely impossible to see anything. A tame barn owl was put in a pitch black room and a mouse was allowed to scuffle through leaf litter on the floor. After a short pause the owl would swoop at the ground and when the lights were put on it was back on its perch with the mouse. The experiment was repeated 17 times, and the only four misses were near misses.

A detailed examination of a barn owl's ears shows them to be very well developed, and there are flaps of skin forming 'outer ears', hidden under the feathers. These flaps are not placed symmetrically about the head, so sound coming to one ear follows a slightly different path from that going to the other ear. Thus a sound is picked up by one ear slightly before or after the other. It is this slight difference that enables an owl to judge the prey's position.

To make life even more hazardous for a small animal, the long, flight feathers of an owl's wings are tipped with down on the leading, trailing and upper surfaces. This deadens the noise of the owl's wingbeats so the intended prey has no warning of attack, unless they, too, have specially sensitive ears.

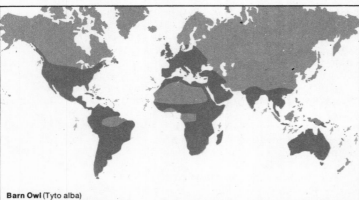

The barn owl has the distinction of being the most widely spread land bird in the world; varieties are found in every continent except Antarctica.
△ *Barn owl returning to its nest after a successful foray.*
▷ *Barn owl with captured prey.*

Barn Owl (Tyto alba)

class	**Aves**
order	**Strigiformes**
family	**Tytonidae**
genus & species	*Tyto alba*

366

Nightjar

The nightjar, unlike the ideal child of Victorian days, is more often heard than seen. It starts to fly soon after sundown and is active throughout the night. By day its remarkable camouflage keeps it hidden. Yet despite this nightjars have probably been given more common names than any other bird. Fern-owl, churn-owl, eve-jarr, dorhawk, nighthawk are only a few of them. In South Africa a nightjar is called a brain-fever bird because its insistent churring through the night can drive nearby campers almost crazy. The most frequent name, and one appearing in many languages, is goatsucker.

The original nightjar or goatsucker, called **caprimulgus** (goatsucker) by the Romans, is the one that winters in Africa as far south as the Cape and spends its summers in North Africa, Europe and Asia. It is 10½ in. long, its plumage is grey, barred and streaked with buff, chestnut and black, and its beak is small although the gape is very wide with strong bristles around the mouth. The adult male has white patches on the tail and wings.

There are 70 species all much alike in plumage and habits, including the American poor-will, whip-poor-will, chuck-will and night-hawks. In southern Europe and western North Africa is the red-necked nightjar which has a distinctive reddish collar. The Egyptian nightjar, of southwest Asia and northern Africa, lives in deserts and is sandy-coloured. In eastern and southeast Asia are the jungle nightjar and the large-tailed nightjar. The long-tailed nightjar in Africa has very long central feathers in the tail. The pennant-winged nightjar, 11 in. long, has the innermost pair of primaries 2 ft. long, while the male standard-winged nightjar in the breeding season, has one bare-shafted feather in each wing 2 ft long and a 6in. flag-like vane at the tip. In Australia the large-tailed, white-throated and spotted nightjars are similar to the European nightjar but larger.

△ Sitting pretty — a European nightjar. During the day nightjars sit motionless among dead leaves and bracken camouflaged by their speckled, barred, brown and buff plumage.

▷ An evil stare from the large eye typical of a nocturnal animal — **Caprimulgus pectoralis**. Whether the bristles around the mouth act as organs of touch is not really known.

Although it is normal for the white-throated nightjar to produce two broods each summer it was not until these photographs were taken that there was any evidence of an overlapping brood occurring in this species. During the day the parents incubated the second egg while concealing the hatched chick of the first brood. The second egg was laid exactly in the same spot as the first one.

1 The egg is laid on the ground unconcealed.
2 Both sexes take part in incubating the egg.
3 Chick hatches with a complete down cover.
4 18-day-old chick sits beside the second egg.
5 First chick threatens the photographer.

1

2

3

4

5

Cloak of invisibility

The European nightjar is almost invisible during the day as it rests on the ground on heaths, bracken-covered slopes and open woodland. To say that its plumage harmonizes with its background is less correct than to say that its colours are so broken up that the bird defeats the eye and appears to dissolve into nothing. Whether the nightjar is among bracken, on lichens, on rocks or on sand it is almost impossible to see and one may almost tread on it before it moves. The invisibility is increased by the nightjar closing its eyes and watching an intruder through slits, so its large eyes do not give away its presence. By contrast, the rays of a torch shone into bushes at night may be reflected in a pair of red-glowing eyes suggestive of a large animal.

Insect catcher number one

Nightjars become active at about sundown. They fly with a silent, almost moth-like flight, with strong, deliberate wingbeats alternating with graceful glides and easy wheeling movements. The characteristic churring or jarring call is heard most when the sky is clear. When the skies are overcast, the birds are silent. Nightjars call, almost invariably, perched lengthwise along a branch.

It used to be said that a nightjar flies with mouth agape, the bristles around the mouth acting as a sweepnet to catch insects or at least to direct them into the mouth. This is now disputed. Its food is almost wholly insects, from moths and large beetles to mosquitoes, but there are records of small birds being caught, perhaps accidentally. One nightjar examined had 500 mosquitoes in its stomach. Whether the bristles also act as organs of touch, as has been suggested, is problematical. On the third toe of a nightjar, on the undersurface, is a series of saw-like notches. This is used to comb the bristles around the mouth, and, so it is said, to remove the scales of moths that have been caught.

Gun-shot wedding

The white patches on the wings and tail of the male stand out in courtship. This probably helps the recognition of the sexes. The male flies around the female in wide circles, either beating his wings or holding them stiffly and obliquely over his back, with his tail depressed and fanned. Every now and then he claps his wings with a sound like a pistol shot. Other nightjar males use their long feathers for display. The standard-winged nightjar, for example, holds his two flagged primaries vertically over his back, whereas in normal flight they are trailing. At the end of May the female lays two elliptical eggs, creamy white mottled with brown and purple. No nest is made. The eggs lie on the ground, incubated for 18 days by both male and female, the male taking his turn at dusk and dawn. The young birds are fed by the parents for a further 18 days.

Drawing the enemy away

When disturbed at the nest the parent nightjar performs its distraction display, flopping over the ground as if with a broken wing. When this display is performed in the still of night the beating of the wings on the ground sounds uncannily loud. After the eggs are hatched the distraction display is still used to draw the attention of an intruder away from the young birds, which stay very still. Should the intruder go near the babies, however, they spread their wings, open wide their mouths and lunge at it — a disconcerting bluff.

Egg-carrying parents

Audubon, the celebrated American ornithologist, described seeing a chuck-will, an American nightjar, remove its eggs with its mouth when danger threatened. He saw one of the pair wait beside two eggs that had been disturbed, then he saw the two parents each take an egg in their mouth and fly away with it. Audubon's story was long doubted but this same behaviour has been seen since in other species of nightjars. Moreover, nightjars are reported to carry their chicks held between their thighs, as do woodcocks.

Ghost-like flight

Few birds show themselves in as many varying ways as nightjars. One may fly past your face in semi-darkness in smooth silent, almost ghost-like flight. A pair may circle over your head in courtship flight, when the crack of the male's wings has a startling, rather frightening quality, in the gathering gloom. In semi-desert parts of the world it is not unusual for a nightjar to be seen lying on the ground in the headlights of a car. Usually, even on the brightest moonlit night, it is impossible to see the bird or to track it as it moves churring from one perch to another.

class	**Aves**
order	**Caprimulgiformes**
family	**Caprimulgidae**
genera & species	***Caprimulgus aegyptius*** *Egyptian nightjar* **C. europaeus** *European nightjar* **C. indicus** *jungle nightjar* **C. macrurus** *large-tailed nightjar* **C. ruficollis** *red-necked nightjar* **Eurostopodus mystacalis** *white-throated nightjar* **E. guttatus** *spotted nightjar* **Macrodipteryx longipennis** *standard-winged nightjar* **Scotornis climacurus** *long-tailed nightjar* **Semeiophorus vexillarius** *pennant-winged nightjar, others*

Hummingbird

There are over 300 species of these minute, beautiful birds living in the New World. The largest is the giant hummingbird, an 8½ in. monster compared with the bee hummingbird of Cuba which is little more than 2 in. long; half this length is bill and tail, the body being the same size as a bumblebee. Hummingbirds are very diverse in form, although all of them are small and have the characteristic rapid wingbeats producing the hum that gives them their name. They have brilliant, often iridescent, plumage which has led to their being given names like 'ruby' and 'topaz'—and also to their being killed in thousands and their skins exported to Europe for use in ornaments. A feature of many hummingbirds is the long narrow bill, often straight but sometimes curved, as in the sicklebill. The sword-billed hummingbird has a straight bill as long as the head, body and tail put together.

Hummingbirds are most common in the forests of South America, but they range from southern Alaska to Tierra del Fuego. Some species are so rare that they are known only from collections of hummingbirds' skin exported to Europe. Loddige's racket-tail was known from a single skin found in 1840 and was not found alive for another 40 years, when it was discovered in a small valley high in the Andes.

Hummingbird stamina . . .

Considering the diversity of habitats and food in the South American forests it is not surprising that there should be so many kinds of hummingbirds living there. It is rather surprising, however, to learn that hummingbirds breed as far north as southeast Alaska, or in the heights of the Andes. The rufous hummingbird breeds in Alaska, migrating to South America for the winter, an incredible journey for so small a bird. The ruby-throated hummingbird also migrates to and from North America, crossing the Gulf of Mexico on each trip. Unlike non-migratory hummingbirds, it stores a layer of fat equal to half its body weight before setting off. At a normal rate of use, however, this would not last through a non-stop crossing of the Gulf. Yet the hummingbirds complete this marathon, so we must presume that they have some method of economising on food reserves.

. . . and speed

Even ignoring the mystery of their migration, the flight of hummingbirds is truly remarkable. Their wings beat so fast they appear as a blur. Small species have wingbeats of 50—80 per second and in courtship displays even higher rates have been recorded. The fast wingbeats enable the hummingbirds to dart to and fro, jerking to a halt to hover steadily. They are also extremely fast in straight flight—speeds of 71 mph have been recorded. Specialised filming has shown that hummingbirds do not take off by leaping into the air like other

birds but lift off with rapid wingbeats. The photographs showed that a hummingbird on a thin twig actually pulls the twig up as it rises before letting go.

Flying with such rapid wingbeats requires a large amount of energy, so hummingbirds must either feed constantly or have plentiful reserves. Even at rest their metabolism—the rate at which they produce energy—is 25 times faster than a chicken's. At night when they cannot feed they conserve their food reserves by becoming torpid—going into a form of nightly hibernation. In the Andes a hummingbird's temperature drops from 38°C/100°F to 14°C/57°F, about the temperature of the surrounding air—and their metabolism is reduced six times.

Nectar seekers

Hummingbirds feed on nectar and small soft-bodied animals. To sip nectar they hover in front of flowers and insert their pointed bills down the corolla or, if that is too long, pierce it near the base. The nectar is sucked through a tubular tongue that is very similar to those of flowerpeckers. Pollen is often brushed onto the hummingbirds' heads and transferred to other flowers, so pollinating them. To the flowers of the South American jungle, hummingbirds are as important as pollinators as bees are in a clover field. Hummingbirds can readily be attracted to tubes containing sugar-water and they become so tame they will feed at a tube held in the hand.

Small insects are caught on the wing and spiders are taken from their webs. Most hummingbirds are unable to manipulate insects in their bills and have to rush at them so they are forced into the mouth. Some pick insects and spiders from flowers.

Tiny babies

Courtship antics of hummingbirds are difficult to watch as they flit about among dense vegetation too fast for accurate observation. The males fly about in arcs, singing songs that are almost too high-pitched for humans to hear. They are usually promiscuous, mating in the air with several females, but in a few species such as the violet-eared hummingbirds (which have similar plumage for males and females) the male helps rear the family. The nest is a delicate cup of moss, lichen and spiders' webs placed on a twig or amongst foliage. The two eggs are incubated for 2—3 weeks and minute naked chicks hatch out. They are fed by the parent hovering alongside, putting its bill into theirs and pumping out nectar. The chicks grow very rapidly and leave the nest when 3 weeks old.

Hovering skill

When feeding, hummingbirds can be seen hovering steadily and even flying backwards. They can do this because their wings can swivel in all directions from the shoulder. When hovering the body hangs at an angle of about 45 degrees so the wings are beating backwards and forwards instead of up and down. In each complete beat the wing describes a figure of eight. As it moves forwards (the downstroke) the wings are tilted so they force air downwards and the bird upwards. At the end of the stroke they

flip over so that the back of the wing is facing downwards and on the upstroke air is again forced downwards. To fly backwards the wings are tilted slightly so air is forced forwards as well, and the hummingbird is driven back.

The flight of a hummingbird can be compared with that of a helicopter with its blades moving in a circle to achieve the same effect of driving air downwards as the hummingbird's wings do by moving back and forth. In the flight of most birds the power is in the downstroke, the upstroke being merely a recovery phase, but in hummingbirds both strokes are powerful. The breast muscles of a hummingbird weigh a third of its total weight and the muscles drawing the wings upward are half as powerful as those driving the wings down. Non-hovering species have comparatively much smaller muscles for the upstroke.

class	**Aves**
order	**Apodiformes**
family	**Trochilidae**
genera & species	***Archilochus colubris*** ruby-throated hummingbird **Ensifera ensifera** sword-billed hummingbird **Eutoxeres aquila** sickle-billed hummingbird **Loddigesia mirabilis** Loddige's racket-tail **Mellisuga helenae** bee hummingbird **Patagona gigas** giant hummingbird **Selasphorus rufus** rufous hummingbird, others

Hummingbirds
(family Trochilidae)

The form of individual species of hummingbird is very varied. This male black-throated train-bearer **Lesbia victoriae,** from Ecuador, has long ornamental feathers that do not appear to hinder its aerial acrobatics. Its body is only 2 in. long but the tail is 6 in. with widely forked feathers which help make a marvellous picture when it turns sharply doing its fast manoeuvres in the air. The iridescent throat is absent in the female.

Top: Banana and jerker. A male velvet-purple coronet **Boissonneaua jardini** greedily sips nectar from **Heliconia jaquinii,** a relative of the bananas. Centre: The white-lipped sicklebill is perfectly adapted for sucking nectar from flowers. Bottom: The tiny ruby-topaz hummingbird **Chrysolampis mosquitus,** a beautiful Brazilian species, vibrates its wings at about 100 beats per second, fast even for the hummingbirds.

Mousebird

Mousebirds or colies are the size of a house sparrow, but they also have long tails, up to 10 in. The tail is made up of 10 feathers of graduated lengths, the outside being the shortest and the two innermost the longest. The wings are short and rounded. The powerful bill is short and curved, and all species have crests. The feet are strong, and the four toes, with their sharp claws, are occasionally turned forwards.

The plumage of mousebirds is generally dull. The red-cheeked mousebird is grey with a greenish tinge, and is darker on the wings and tail than on the belly. The legs are light pink and the cheeks crimson. The blue-naped mousebird is buffish-brown with a blue tint and there is a patch of blue on the nape. The bill is red and black. The vanes of the tail feathers are very narrow and virtually fade away on the two long, central tail feathers. Other species are also distinguished by their colours, such as the white-headed, bar-breasted and white-backed mousebirds.

Mousebirds inhabit savannah and steppe country in Africa south of the Sahara.

Miniature pheasants

Mousebirds get their name from their habit of running along branches with their body and tail horizontal, in the same manner as a rodent. They are unusual in that they run on the backs of their legs like a fulmar or diver rather than on their toes. Their sharp claws, strong feet and long tail make them very agile and they swing about like titmice, sometimes hanging upside down. They often use their bills as an extra support in climbing, like parrots. In flight they look like miniature pheasants with their rounded wings and long tails. Their direct flight with an alternate flapping and gliding is similar to that of pheasants.

Mousebirds live in flocks of 5–30 birds which fly, chattering, from tree to tree, where they often preen each other. If flushed they usually stream out of a bush one after the other rather than rush out in a group. The flocks roost together, perching in a line along a branch, sometimes upside down, or on a vertical trunk with their long tails hanging downwards.

Menace to fruit

The fruit-eating habits of mousebirds make them very unpopular with farmers and often strict control measures have to be taken. The flocks strip berries and fruit from the trees, tackling the large fruit by making a hole in the skin and eating out the pulp, so only the empty skin is left. Flower buds and young tender leaves are also eaten. The mousebirds work systematically through the trees, starting from the base of the foliage and working upwards. When they get to the top of one tree, they fly to the bottom of the next.

They also eat insects and young birds. Nest-robbing is such a common habit that other small birds mob mousebirds.

△ *Bane of the farmers – a speckled mousebird satisfies its hunger by a tasty meal of figs.*

Replaceable lining

At the start of the breeding season mousebird flocks break up into pairs. Courtship displays consist of two mousebirds facing each other on a branch and bobbing up and down. They also rub bills and preen each other. The nest is built in dense foliage 6–25 ft above the ground. A platform of twigs is woven onto a branch and a cup of grass and roots is built on it. The lining is of green leaves which are replaced as they wither. Nests are often built within a few yards of each other and it is suspected that two pairs sometimes share a nest. Usually 2–4 eggs are laid. They are white with a few dark red or brown spots or streaks and are incubated by both parents for 2 weeks. At first the chicks are naked but within a few days they can leave the nest and crawl along neighbouring branches using their bills and wings to help climbing. They return to the nest at night to be brooded, leaving it at 3 weeks old, with the tail only partly grown. The parents accompany them everywhere for the first few days and feed them for another month.

Where do they belong?

The mousebirds are placed in an order of their own, the Coliiformes, as they have many peculiarities, both in structure and behaviour, and very few points of similarity with other kinds of birds. It has been suggested that they are distant relatives of the parrots, from the way they climb about in the trees, and from their general appearance. Internally, the heart, pelvis, palate and other organs are parrot-like, but other structures are decidedly unparrot-like.

class	**Aves**
order	**Coliiformes**
family	**Coliidae**
genus & species	***Colius indicus*** *red-faced mousebird* ***C. leucocephalus*** *white-headed mousebird* ***C. macrourus*** *blue-naped mousebird others*

Quetzal

Also known as the resplendent trogon, the quetzal ranks as one of the most beautiful birds. It measures 14 in. from bill to tip of tail, but, like the peacock, the tail coverts are extremely long, trailing behind the quetzal as shimmering plumes up to 2 ft in length. The head, which bears a tufted crest, the neck, chest and wing coverts are iridescent golden green. The wing covert feathers are plume-like, overhanging the crimson lower breast and belly. The back shimmers with blue and green and the long tail coverts are iridescent green. The female is duller, lacks a crest and the tail coverts are much shorter.

Quetzals are found in the forests of Central America, from southern Mexico to Panama, but are now becoming increasingly rare.

△ *Not just a pretty bird. The quetzal is the Guatemalan unit of currency.* ▷ *Deceptive beauty. The true tail feathers are hidden under the long iridescent green tail coverts which may be up to 2 ft in length. The wing coverts form shimmering golden green plumes which overhang the crimson lower breast and belly.*

Careful with tail

The forests of the Central American highlands are extremely humid, bathed continuously in rain and mist. This high humidity favours the growth of epiphytic plants which grow in great profusion on the trunks of the tall trees that form a canopy over 100 ft high. The quetzals live among this rich profusion of plants, feeding on the fruits and berries, which they pluck while in flight in an action reminiscent of flycatchers. Flying from its perch, a quetzal takes a berry in its bill, tears it off and returns to its perch. The male quetzal has an unusual habit of launching itself backwards from its perch. If it flew straight from its perch in the normal manner the long feathers in its train would be torn to shreds in no time. The female does not appear to take this precaution.

Quetzals usually stay in the dense forests but sometimes come out to feed in clearings. In the forest the quetzals give away their position by their habit of rapidly fanning their tails to show flashes of white. They also call loudly in flight, and during the breeding season the males have a variety of deep, powerful calls and songs that match their beautiful plumage. The males also have a display flight, circling above the forest canopy and calling loudly.

Inaccessible nests

Quetzals nest in holes in tree trunks, either enlarging existing woodpecker holes or excavating their own. Their bills are short and blunt, suited for eating soft fruit rather than chiselling wood and so quetzals can make their holes in only the most decayed trees. Both male and female take part in nest building, biting and tearing strips of soft wood until they have made a hole with an entrance about 4 in. across and up to about 1 ft deep.

The clutch of two light blue eggs is laid on the unlined floor of the hole and incubated by both parents in turn. According to Guatemalan folklore the quetzal's nest has two entrances, so that the male may sit on the eggs without ruining his train. He is supposed to enter through one side, incubate with his train hanging out, then depart through the other side. In Costa Rica the quetzal is supposed to have found a different remedy. He is said to sit on the eggs with his head facing inwards and his train trailing out through the single entrance. Few people have seen quetzal nests because of the inaccessibility of the forests and the difficulty of locating nest holes in trees covered with a rich growth of epiphytic plants. Presumably the problem of how the quetzal protected his train occurred to some people and these were the solutions they proposed. In fact, the train is sufficiently hardy to dispense with such elaborate behaviour. We now know that the male quetzal incubates facing the nest hole with the tail pressed vertically against the back wall. The train curves over his back and projects some inches through the entrance.

The eggs hatch after 17 – 18 days' incubation. The chicks are naked and blind at first and for the first few days are brooded by their parents, who also keep the nest clean by removing the eggshells and droppings. The chicks are fed on insects and other small animals until they are nearly 2 weeks old. Then fruits, especially those of the laurel family, are brought by the parents and later snails, small frogs and lizards. The nestlings fly when about a month old.

The feathered serpent

Considering the beauty of the quetzal it is not surprising to find that it is the national bird of Guatemala. It is not only figured on postage stamps but also on the national flag, and the Guatemalan unit of currency is the *quetzal*. A pretty story has it that a captive quetzal soon dies of a broken heart. Such reverence for the quetzal has not saved it from the feather trade. After its discovery by Europeans it soon became so rare that some people declared it was a mythical bird, but in the 19th century it was rediscovered, and only the inaccessibility of its home in the forests has saved it from the fate of many other creatures, that of extinction.

Before the Spanish Conquest the Aztecs of Mexico had also held the quetzal in high esteem and their mythology contained a 'feathered serpent' – *quetzalcoatl*. Quetzal feathers could only be worn by nobles and the long plumes were plucked from live quetzals who were then freed to grow new feathers—and sire more quetzals.

class	**Aves**
order	**Trogoniformes**
family	**Trogonidae**
genus & species	***Pharomachrus mocino***

Kingfisher

There are over 80 species of kingfisher living mainly in the tropics. They are stockily built with long bills, quite short tails and often brilliant plumage, of which the common kingfisher of Europe and Asia is a good example. The common kingfisher is found throughout much of Europe and Asia, south into North Africa and east to the Solomon Islands and Japan. It is one of the most beautiful of birds, 6½ in. long with a 1½ in. dagger-like bill, its upperparts a shining iridescent blue or green.

▷ *Psychedelic forest kingfisher of Malaya.*
▽ *A giant kingfisher* **Megaceryle maxima** *glares from a vantage point over a stream.*

▷ *King of the world: perched aloft, a greyheaded kingfisher* **Halcyon leucocephala** *watches carefully for passing insects. It also feeds on beetles, grasshoppers and small reptiles.*

The underparts are chestnut, the legs red and there are patches of white on the neck. The pied kingfisher of Africa south of the Sahara and southwest Asia is dull-coloured for a kingfisher but is nevertheless striking with its black and white plumage. Like many kingfishers it has a crest. The Amazon kingfisher, also crested, has brilliant green upperparts and white underparts, with a chestnut breast in the male. The Texas kingfisher, ranging into the southern USA, is very similar.
In some species where the sexes differ in plumage, the female is the more brilliant. On the other side of the Pacific the yellow sacred kingfisher is found in many parts of Australia and is the only kingfisher in New Zealand.

A blur of colour

Kingfishers are usually seen as little more than a blur of colour as they fly low over the water on whirring wings to disappear into waterside undergrowth. If lucky one sees it perched on a branch, rock or post on the bank and its true colours can then be appreciated. Kingfishers are very much alike in habit as well as form; their feeding and breeding behaviour follow a pattern although some kingfishers rarely, if ever, go near water. Even the common kingfisher, associated so much with streams and rivers, sometimes nests some distance from water.

When thousands of exotic birds were being slaughtered and their carcases and feathers sent to Europe and North America as decorations and ornaments, it is not surprising that the dazzling kingfisher did not escape persecution. It was used for decorating hats and stuffed kingfishers in glass cases were a common household ornament. Later kingfishers were shot because they were alleged to eat enough trout fry to damage breeding stocks. The pollution of rivers and streams now threatens their wellbeing. Hard winters have a very severe effect on kingfisher populations.

Fishing over land and water

The method of catching prey is similar in nearly all species. The kingfisher waits on a perch, then darts out, catches its prey and carries it back to its perch. The common kingfisher flies out, hovers momentarily just over the water then dives in. Having caught a small fish or water insect it uses its wings to 'fly' through the water then up into the air without pausing. Larger prey are beaten against the perch to subdue them and may be tossed and caught again to get them into a suitable position for swallowing. Common kingfishers take mainly fish such as minnows, sticklebacks and gudgeon, also small perch and small trout. These last two are the reason for the persecution of kingfishers, but they also feed on water beetles, dragonfly larvae and waterboatmen which also kill small fish. Small frogs, tadpoles and pond snails are also taken.

The majority of kingfishers, however, take mainly land animals, although they hunt from a perch like the common kingfisher. They dart down from their perches like shrikes or they hawk passing insects like flycatchers. The racquet-tailed kingfisher, living in the area from the Moluccas to northeast Australia, hunts for lizards, centipedes and insects in the leaf litter of humid forests, swooping on them and sometimes driving its bill into the soft earth. The stork-billed kingfisher of India, 14 in. long with a large scarlet bill, catches fish as well as frogs, lizards, crabs and insects. It also robs other birds' nests, taking nestlings even from nests in holes in trees, but, true to its kind, it returns to its perch to swallow its prey. An exception to this is the shoe-billed kingfisher of the forests of New Guinea. It digs for earthworms with its flattened bill.

◁ *Malachite kingfisher* **Corythornis cristata**, *a very common African species. It feeds on fish, water invertebrates and flies.*

Common kingfisher with a prospective meal.

Hole nesting

Kingfishers nest in holes, those that hunt fish usually nesting in holes in banks near water while the more land-living kingfishers nest in holes in trees or abandoned termite nests. The striped kingfisher of Africa uses ready-made holes and may even dispossess swallows from their nests under eaves.

The nest hole is dug by the kingfishers repeatedly flying at one spot on the bank, loosening a bit of soil with their bills each time. When they have formed a ledge they can perch and dig more rapidly until the tunnel is 1½–3 ft long. The 6 or 7 spherical white eggs are laid on the floor of the tunnel and incubated for 3 weeks. During this time a revolting pile of fish bones and droppings piles up around the eggs, a squalid contrast with the magnificent plumage of the adult birds. Until Ron and Rose Eastman made their prizewinning film 'The Private Life of a Kingfisher' in 1966 it was thought that pieces of fish were fed to the young. Their remarkable patience and technique, however, showed the young inside the nest burrow swallowing whole fish almost as big as themselves, the bones being later regurgitated. The chicks, which live in the tunnel for 3–4 weeks, are hatched naked but soon acquire a covering of bristle-like wax sheaths which are shed to reveal a plumage like that of the parents just before they leave the nest.

class	**Aves**
order	**Coraciiformes**
family	**Alcedinidae**
genera & species	***Alcedo atthis*** *common kingfisher* ***Ceryle rudis*** *pied kingfisher* ***Chloroceryle amazona*** *Amazon kingfisher* ***C. americana*** *Texas kingfisher* ***Clytoceyx rex*** *shoe-billed kingfisher* ***Halcyon chelicuti*** *striped kingfisher* ***H. sancta*** *sacred kingfisher* ***Pelargopsis capensis*** *stork-billed* *kingfisher* ***Tanysiptera galatea*** *racquet-tailed* *kingfisher*

Bee-eater

These are most spectacular birds of the Old World. There are several species of bee-eater, varying from 6—14 in. long, with characteristically brilliant plumage. The Australian bee-eater is aptly named the rainbow bird.

Most bee-eaters have bright plumage in which green often predominates with yellow, blue and shades of red, adding to the pattern. Even the relatively dull species have some patches of colour. The European bee-eater that is sometimes seen in the eastern and southern counties of England during the summer, has chestnut and golden upper parts with greenish breast and belly, a bright yellow throat and a greenish-brown tail. It can be easily told from any other British bird by the long, curved bill and the long feathers extending from the middle of the tail. The flight is also characteristic. A flock of bee-eaters continually circles around, flapping rapidly then gliding buoyantly on outstretched, pointed wings, all the time calling with a liquid, and rather monotonous, twittering.

Tropical habitat

In many parts of the tropics, flocks of hundreds, or even thousands, of bee-eaters wheeling and gliding gracefully over their nesting colonies or feeding grounds are a most impressive sight.

They live mainly in tropical regions, with a few species living in the milder temperate areas. Several species are migratory, moving towards the tropics outside the breeding season. The Australian bee-eater migrates to New Guinea and the Celebes, and the Madagascar species crosses to the mainland of Africa for the winter.

In 1946 and 1947 the European bee-eater began to extend its range northwards from the Camargue in southern France, northern Italy, Yugoslavia, Hungary and Rumania to Czechoslovakia where they bred in 1948, and Denmark, Belgium and northern France where a few pairs bred in the 1950's. Three pairs bred in England in 1955, but they have not bred there since.

Burrowing nesters

The nest is a burrow dug with bill and feet in sandy banks by the sides of rivers or roads. In Africa nest-chambers are sometimes made in the burrows of aardvarks. The tunnel is 2—3 in. in diameter and 2—5 ft long, sometimes up to 8 ft, depending on the softness of the soil. Burrowing starts with the bird flying repeatedly at the wall with bill partly open. When a sufficient hole has been made, the bee-eater can land in it and dig more rapidly. Excavation takes 10 days to a fortnight and the tunnel ends with a chamber usually set off to one side. No nest is made, but a pile of insect remains builds up as the birds eject pellets of the indigestible parts of their meals, and the eggs are laid on this. The burrows are used from year to year, being refurbished by having some of the insect remains removed.

In the Camargue, the bee-eaters arrive from Africa in April or early May, breeding taking place in late May and June. The burrows usually face south, so avoiding the severity of the seasonal Mediterranean wind, the mistral. Before the eggs are laid, the pair vigorously defend a favoured perch in a tree against other bee-eaters. Why there should be this territorial behaviour unconnected with either feeding or the nest is not known. It may allow courtship and mating to proceed undisturbed, for once the eggs are laid the fighting and threatening ends.

Four to ten white eggs are laid. The eggs of birds that nest in burrows are usually white, presumably because there is no pressure to evolve a camouflage to keep them hidden from predators. It has been suggested that the white eggs of bee-eaters act as reflectors so that the parents can see better in the burrow, but this is useless when the burrow is crooked and so pitch-black. They are incubated for 22 days, each bird taking spells of 10 minutes to ½ hour. The female generally spends the night on the eggs while the male roosts in a tree. During incubation the male feeds the female, and when the chicks have hatched, both parents feed them. Fledging is complete in about 3 weeks, each feather being retained in a membrane until it is nearly full grown, then bursting out, which is unusual. The chicks may wander some miles from the nest but usually return there to roost at night. The bee-eaters leave Europe in September.

Insectivorous feeders

Bee-eaters feed on insects, catching them while flying, either by circling around or waiting on a branch or telegraph wire. Their chief food is dragonflies, beetles, butterflies, wasps and bees. In Africa they are beneficial to man in taking a large toll of locusts. The indigestible parts are regurgitated in the form of pellets.

The carmine bee-eaters of the Sudan will ride on the backs of bustards, flying off to catch the insects that these large birds disturb as they walk about.

Bee-eaters in different parts of the world have often been reported as plunging into rivers and flying up with food in their beaks, but what exactly they are catching is not known. Presumably they are catching fresh-water insects or crustaceans.

Reptiles are main predators

In southern France the black kite, the Montpellier snake and the ocellated lizard are important predators of bee-eaters. Probably snakes and lizards are important predators all over the bee-eaters' range, where they can crawl down the burrows to take eggs, young, and adults.

Flocks of bee-eaters will take communal action, swooping down on men, kites and snakes to drive them away from the colonies.

Carmine bee-eaters hold insects in their beaks which have been caught in the air, either in the course of continuous hawking or during short flights from the perch.

Why does a bee-eater not get stung?

Bee-eaters are aptly named and in some parts of the world their habit of catching bees has led to their being persecuted as pests by bee-keepers. Nowadays they are generally regarded as taking more harmful insects than honey bees. Nevertheless stinging insects such as wasps and bees are an important item in their diet and the question arises as to how the bee-eaters avoid being stung. It could be that they are stung but are immune to bee or wasp venom. However, some observations on a captive bee-eater show that the sting is avoided.

The captive was an Australian rainbow bird. When it was given bees it would pick them up in the tip of its bill, holding them by the narrow 'waist'. Then it rapped the head of the bee against the perch once or twice, shifted its grip to the tip of the bee's abdomen, just behind the sting and rubbed it vigorously against the perch. This usually resulted in the sting being torn out, or if not, the venom was probably squeezed out. After this the bee was again held by the 'waist' and banged against the perch, then tossed to the back of the bill and swallowed.

This sequence of events was invariable whenever a bee was given to the rainbow bird, yet it never did this with other insects which were swallowed immediately. Thus the bee-eater could recognise stinging insects but its fixed pattern of actions suggests that it was instinctive. What would be interesting to know is whether a bee-eater has to learn by painful experience if an insect is poisonous or whether this, too, is instinctive knowledge.

Flocks of hundreds, or even thousands of bee-eaters, are a most impressive sight, whether circling in flight or at rest – and this is but part of a nesting colony.

class	**Aves**
order	**Coraciiformes**
family	**Meropidae**
genus & species	***Merops apiaster*** *European bee-eater* ***M. nubicus*** *carmine bee-eater* ***M. ornatus*** *rainbow bird*

Woodpecker

No birds are better adapted for a life on the branches and trunks of trees than the woodpecker.

There are about 200 species of woodpecker which are spread over the wooded parts of the world, except Madagascar, Australia and oceanic islands. They are up to nearly 2 ft long and are usually brightly-coloured with patterns of black, white, green or red. A few woodpeckers have crests. The bill is straight and pointed, the legs short with two toes facing backwards and the tail is made up of pointed feathers with stiff shafts.

The 15 species of green woodpeckers inhabit the woods and forests of Europe and Asia from the British Isles to Borneo and Java. The familiar green woodpecker of Europe is 12 in. long, and has a green plumage, which is brighter below, a bright yellowish rump and a red crown. The male has a red and black stripe under the eye, while the female has a plain black stripe. The pied or spotted woodpeckers form a widespread group, the 30-odd species being distributed across North America, Europe and Asia. They are black or grey with white patches, bars or mottling. The males often have red crowns. The three-toed woodpeckers are unusual in having one toe missing from each foot. They too have a circumpolar distribution. The ivorybills of America are the largest woodpeckers and inhabit forests of large trees. As a result of these forests being cut down these species are in danger of extinction. The ivory-billed woodpecker of North America and Cuba was thought to be extinct but in 1966 a few pairs were found in Texas.

Expert tree climbers

Woodpeckers are usually seen as just a flash of colour disappearing through the trees. They live solitarily in woods and can be identified by their characteristic undulating flight: 3—4 rapid wingbeats carrying them up, followed by a downward glide. They are more likely to be given away by their harsh or ringing calls, such as the loud laugh of the green woodpecker, or by their drumming, a rapid tattoo which they make with their bills on dead branches, or even on metal roofs.

Woodpeckers spend most of their time hopping up tree trunks in spirals, searching for insects. When a woodpecker has searched one tree it flies to the base of the next and repeats the operation. In climbing vertical trunks, woodpeckers are assisted by having two backward-facing toes, sharp claws, and stiff tail feathers, which are used as a prop while climbing, rather like a shooting stick.

Above: Female African **Campethera abingoni**. *Below: Great spotted woodpecker* **Dendrocopos major**.

Boring for insects

The woodpecker's food is largely insects and their larvae. The green woodpeckers often hunt on the ground for ants and sometimes attack bee hives. The red-headed woodpecker of North America catches insects on the wing. Otherwise woodpeckers feed on insects which are prised out of crevices in the bark or drilled out of the wood. The pointed bill is an excellent chisel and the skull is toughened to withstand the shock of hammering. When drilling, a woodpecker aims its blows alternately from one side then the other, like a woodman felling a tree. Insects are removed from the hole by using the woodpecker's second useful tool – an extremely long tongue; it can protrude up to 6 in. from the tip of the bill in the green woodpecker. The tongue is protruded by muscles running round the back and top of the skulls. It is often tipped with barbs or bristles or coated with mucus for brushing up the insects.

Some woodpeckers eat fruit and seeds or drink sap. Red-headed woodpeckers and acorn woodpeckers store acorns, drilling separate holes in trees for each acorn or else using a natural cavity. There is a story of an acorn woodpecker that spent an autumn feeding acorns into a knothole in the wall of a cabin. As the hole never filled, the woodpecker 'posted' several hundred acorns in it.

Nesting in holes

With the exception of the African ground woodpecker, which burrows in the ground, woodpeckers nest in holes that they excavate in trees. They drill into a trunk then tunnel downwards to make a cavity up to 1 ft deep. There is no nest lining and the 2–8 white eggs rest on the bottom of the cavity. The eggs hatch in 11–17 days and the chicks fledge in 2–3 weeks, depending on the size of the woodpecker. Both sexes bore the nest hole, and takes turns at incubating and feeding the chicks.

Evacuating the home

Boring a nest hole several inches across does considerable damage to a tree and may weaken it sufficiently for it to fall. This happened at a nest of a pileated woodpecker observed by FK Truslow in the Everglades National Park. The tree split off at the level of the entrance to the nest, revealing that the trunk had been hollowed to leave a shell only $\frac{1}{4}-\frac{1}{2}$ in. thick. Truslow stayed in his hide hoping to watch the reactions of the woodpeckers—the female was incubating at the time. About 10 minutes later the female woodpecker did a most remarkable thing. She returned to the tree, disappeared into the nest cavity and reappeared with an egg in her bill. She then flew off with it and did not drop it for the 75 yd she was in sight. All three eggs were removed in this manner. Unfortunately this extraordinary story has no satisfactory ending as he never found out what became of the eggs. It is, however, one of the few positive records we have of birds rescuing their eggs by carrying them away.

▷ *The lesser spotted woodpecker is widespread in the woods of Europe; but, although numerous, it is seldom seen.*

class	**Aves**
order	**Piciformes**
family	**Picidae**
genera & species	***Campephilus principalis*** *ivory-billed woodpecker* ***Dendrocopos major*** *great spotted woodpecker* ***D. minor*** *lesser spotted woodpecker* ***Dryocopus pileatus***

pileated woodpecker
Geocolaptes olivaceus
ground woodpecker
Melanerpes erythrocephalus
red-headed woodpecker
M. formicivorus
acorn woodpecker
Picoides tridactylus
three-toed woodpecker
Picus viridis
green woodpecker

Lyrebird

In 1798 the early explorers of the mountain forests of eastern Australia found what they called a mountain pheasant. It was also called Native Pheasant and New South Wales bird-of-paradise. It was not until the 1820's that the name lyrebird came into use.

The male lyrebird has a body the size of a bantam cockerel, with strong legs and feet. His plumage is ash-brown tinged with red on the wings. His 2ft tail is made up of 16 feathers. The two outer feathers are broad and shaped like the frame of a lyre. The remaining feathers lying between them are delicate lacelike plumes. The female has a similar plumage but with an ordinary tail. Males do not grow the distinctive tail until they are 3 years old.

Unique display

In mountain forests where the rocky slopes, running down to fast flowing streams, are covered with large tree ferns, the almost legendary lyrebirds act out their unique and inspiring display. In the autumn each male lays claim to a territory of 3—6 acres. With his strong legs and feet he scrapes together large mounds of earth and leaves on which to display. He may make a dozen of these in his territory. Having sung from the top of a log or from a low branch of a tree as a preliminary he flies to the top of one of the mounds and begins to sing in a loud penetrating voice. After a few minutes he unfolds his tail feathers which he has so far carried like a peacock's train. He raises these and swings them forward over his back, like a canopy, the two outer broad feathers that form the frame being swung out until they are at right angles to the body. Half-hidden under this shimmering canopy he begins to dance, pouring out a torrent of bubbling notes. The song rises higher and higher then suddenly stops. The tail is swung back into the normal position and the male lyrebird walks away, his display finished. Sometimes he will shake his tail feathers violently while they are spread over his back, making clicks and drumming noises at the same time.

People have written about this display being performed for the benefit of the hen, but there is little to suggest that it is more than a matter of advertising his possession of a territory.

One-chick family

Mating is during April and May, when the hen alone takes 3—4 weeks to build a large nest of sticks, lining it with moss. The male is polygamous and gives no help. The nest is roofed and may be built on the ground, on a rocky ledge, an old tree stump or in a high tree fork. In this she lays one greyish-purple egg about the size of a domestic hen's egg, having deserted the nest for several days. She deserts the egg for several days also, but when she begins to incubate it she does so for 6 weeks. The downy chick hatching from it loses its down in 10 days and begins to grow feathers but does not leave the nest for 6 weeks from hatching.

Superb lyrebird sings in Sherbrooke forest, 26 miles from Melbourne, Victoria.

During that time the hen brings insects and snails to feed it. Adult lyrebirds feed by scratching the ground with their strong toes and claws, like domestic chickens, for seeds, insects and other small invertebrates.

Traffic in tails

The adult lyrebird has no large natural enemies although it is likely the thylacine or Tasmanian wolf may have preyed on it before being exterminated. One enemy is the introduced red fox. The chief danger is from snakes, large lizards, and birds like the kookaburra raiding the nest. The only other enemy is man, whose raids are now curbed as the bird is protected by law. As soon as the lyrebird had been discovered a demand arose for its beautiful tail-feathers, and even in the early years of this century the tails were still being hawked around the streets of Sydney by the basketful. AH Chisholm, the Australian ornithologist, tells us that one Sydney dealer sold 498 tails in 1911 and another had exported 800 in the same year. Another ornithologist declared that 2 000 tails had been exported in 3 years at about the same time, although their export was prohibited. Fortunately the bird has long been protected by law so its future is ensured.

Unnatural position of feathers appears on stamp.

An artist's error

The lyrebird figures on Australian seals and stamps with its lyre-shaped tail held upright. This it never does except for a brief moment when swinging the tail from the train position to the canopy position over its back. Whether the person who designed the stamp had only the tail of the bird, which he stood against the wall of his studio to draw, or whether this was the only way to get the whole bird on to a vertical stamp, is unknown. Tradition dies hard, however, and even now artists are still drawing the lyrebird with his tail held in this unnatural position.

Alarm-raising mimic

The fame of the lyrebird rests not only on its remarkable tail but also on its voice. Its natural song is one of beauty and power and those who have heard it in the fern-covered glades of eastern Australia are loud in its praise. The bird is also an accomplished mimic. It has even been called Australia's mockingbird and at least one Australian zoologist was prepared to argue that nowhere in the world is there a bird mimic to touch it. Lyrebirds have been heard to imitate the crack of the whipbird, the chant of the pilotbird, the melody of the grey thrush and the screams of cockatoos. They will mimic a chorus of cockatoos, even to the whirring of their wings, or the solitary voice of a tiny sparrow. There seems the possibility that these mimickings are learned by young lyrebirds from their parents, and the suggestion has been made that some of the lyrebirds' notes are songs of extinct birds passed on from generation to generation. Certainly lyrebirds are unusual in using mimicked songs to answer each other.

Lyrebirds also mimic mechanical sounds, such as the rattling of chains and the sounds of a saw, as well as human speech. Chisholm tells of a timber mill in Victoria where three blasts of a whistle were used to signal an accident and six blasts meant a fatality. One day six blasts were heard and men came running from all directions. It was a lyrebird that had heard the three blasts, which were not infrequent, had copied them, and one day repeated them in succession.

△ *Threat display by female at intruder.* ▽ *Shimmering feather canopy as a male displays.*

class	**Aves**
order	**Passeriformes**
family	**Menuridae**
genus & species	*Menura novaehollandiae*

Goldfinch

The goldfinch is a very handsome bird, 5¼ in. long, named for the golden-yellow bar on each wing. Its back is a tawny brown, its underparts paler. The head is boldly marked with red, white and black. The wings are black with a gold bar and white tips to the flight feathers. The forked tail is black with white tips. The beak is short and conical: a seed-eater's beak.

The young goldfinch lacks the red, white and black of the adult's head. Instead it has lines of spots or streaks on head, back and breast and, except for the golden bar on the wing, looks very like several other closely related finches. One of these is the siskin **Carduelis spinus**, which is about the same size and belongs to the same genus but has more yellow in its plumage. It spends the summer in pinewoods and the winter among the alders along the riverside. Another is the twite **Carduelis flavirostris**, a finch of Scandinavia and northern Britain. The serin **Serinus dermus** is very like the siskin in appearance and habits. It is a European bird that occasionally visits Britain, which also has the lines of dark streaks. In an evolutionary sense all three are less 'grown up' than the goldfinch and show their immaturity in the streaked plumage of the adult.

The goldfinch ranges across Europe into western and southwestern Asia, also North Africa.

A charm of goldfinches

The goldfinch is a showy bird that appears to come from nowhere at certain seasons, especially late summer, when it feeds on the seed heads of herbaceous plants. Except in the breeding season, it goes about in small flocks and attracts attention by its musical twittering and its bold and conspicuous colours seen at close range. When not feeding it perches high up in trees, on the outer twigs, and seen then in silhouette so that its coloured head is obscured, it passes for any one of a half-a-dozen small finches. At night the flocks roost in trees and in winter use oak and beech, especially those in hedges, that are late in shedding their dead leaves. As with other small finches the flight is bounding or undulating.

A flock is usually spoken of as a charm of goldfinches. Originally this was spelled 'chirm', and meant a chorus of sounds and was applied to the chatter of any birds. In recent years it has become restricted to goldfinches. It was this musical twittering that made goldfinches, as well as the related linnets, popular as cage birds.

Diet of seeds

Goldfinches seldom feed on the ground although they may take insects, especially in summer. Their feeding is traditionally associated with the seeding thistle heads but they will visit the seeding heads of other

An agility at performing tricks with string made the goldfinch a popular cage bird in the past.

members of the daisy family Compositae. They also take seeds of pine and birch and may visit alders to feed from their catkins, in company with siskins, serins and redpolls. One goldfinch was seen to climb a dandelion stem until it bent over, then nip it, the stem folding at the weakened point. Then she held the top of the stem, as well as the part she was standing on, in her feet and ate the seeds. She did this repeatedly.

Away from the comparative safety of the nest, a young goldfinch faces the world.

Resourceful goldfinch hen

The breeding season begins early in May. The male flashes his golden wing bars at the female, as part of his courtship display, while swaying from side to side. The nest of interwoven roots, bents, wool, moss and lichens, lined with thistledown and wool, is built by the hen, usually well out on a branch but sometimes in a hedge. There have been a number of instances of goldfinches untying the strings of labels used on fruit bushes and weaving the strings into the nests. The 5—6 eggs are bluish white with red spots and streaks, each nearly ¾ in. by ½ in. The hen alone incubates for 12—13 days, fed by the cock, but both parents feed the chicks by regurgitation for another 12—13 days. There are sometimes 3 broods a year.

Hauling in the lines

The note included above under breeding behaviour, about goldfinches untying the strings of labels, may appear remarkable, but this is not beyond their known abilities. We are used to stories of tits pulling up strings of nuts to a perch in order to eat but for centuries, according to Dr WH Thorpe, the eminent authority on animal behaviour, goldfinches have been kept in special cages so people could watch what they do. In the 16th century the goldfinch was called the draw-water or its equivalent in several European languages. These captive goldfinches were in cages so designed that to survive they had to do precisely this. On one side was a little cart containing seed and this was held by a string. The goldfinch had to pull the string with its beak, hold the loop with one foot, then pull in another loop with the beak, hold that, and so on until it could take the seeds. Another string held a thimble of water. To drink, the bird had to draw this up in the same way.

Canaries and other captive birds have been seen to do similar things, and the performances are not confined to cage birds. In 1957, it was reported from Norway and Sweden that hooded crows were stealing fish and bait from fishermen's lines set through holes in the ice. A crow would take the line in its beak and walk backwards away from the hole. Then it would walk forward again, carefully treading on the line to stop it slipping back. It would repeat this until the fish or the bait was drawn to the edge of the ice, when it would seize it.

class	**Aves**
order	**Passeriformes**
family	**Fringillidae**
genus & species	**Carduelis carduelis**

Waxbill

The waxbills are a group of small, colourful, seed-eating birds, that are popular cage birds. Waxbills are related to the sparrows and weavers and the waxbill subfamily includes the mannikins, munias, cordon-bleus, silvereyes and many others well known to bird fanciers. Unfortunately, several have different common names which makes the term waxbill open to confusion. The cordon-bleus, for instance, are also called blue waxbills. The waxbills proper belong to the genus **Estrilda** which also includes the striking avadavat.

Waxbills are small, usually about 4 in. long and many have finely barred upperparts. The species, known as the Waxbill, the common waxbill or sometimes the St Helena waxbill, is brown with fine barring. There is a scarlet patch around the eye, the cheeks and throat are white and in the male there is a pink tinge to the underparts. It is found in many parts of Africa and has been introduced to St Helena and Brazil. Other waxbills have a similar confusion of names. The grey or red-eared waxbill is also called the common waxbill. The upperparts are grey-brown with a pink tinge and the underparts light grey with a pink tinge turning to crimson on the belly. There is a crimson stripe through the eye and the rump is black. The grey waxbill has recently become established in Portugal from aviary escapes. One of the smallest is the 3½in. locust finch that flies in dense swarms. Its plumage is almost black with red on the face and throat. The smallest waxbill of all is the zebra or orange-breasted waxbill with a crimson streak through the eye and a crimson rump. The throat is yellow becoming scarlet underneath and the sides are barred with yellow. Waxbills live in Africa south of the Sahara apart from the avadavat in Asia and the Sydney waxbill that lives in eastern Australia.

Grain eaters

Outside the breeding season waxbills are gregarious, living in parties, sometimes of only a few birds, but others, such as the locust bird, in large flocks. The members of a party continually call to each other with shrill or soft monosyllables designed to inform each waxbill of its fellow's position and to keep the party together. Waxbills are mainly found near rivers or in swampy country where they feed on seeds, particularly those of grasses, and are particularly abundant in grassland and in crops of cereals, in association with other seedeaters such as mannikins and whydahs. In Sierra Leone the flocks are followed by rats which feed on the seeds they spill. In general, waxbills occur in too few numbers to be pests. They also eat some insects and catch flying termites.

△ The distinctive southern grey waxbill of western Africa.

Husband's annexe or decoy?

The typical waxbills differ from their near relatives by building nests with tubular entrances projecting from a ball of grass that are very much like the nests of sparrows and weavers. The nest is built of grass stems or flowering heads woven into an untidy mass and fastened to vertical stems or placed on the ground among grass or herbage. Some waxbills decorate the nest with paper, damp earth, feathers and other materials and a peculiar feature of the nests of true waxbills is that there is a so-called 'cock nest' incorporated into the top or side of the nest or built a short distance away. It has been said that the cock nest is used as a roost by the member of the pair that is not incubating the eggs. There is, however, no proof of this and Derek Goodwin has suggested that the cock nests may mislead predatory birds into overlooking the real nest.

The nest is built by the female waxbill but the male helps with the decoration and with lining the nest with feathers. Both sexes incubate the 4—6 white eggs, which hatch in 2 weeks. They feed the chicks by regurgitating seeds when chicks solicit by gripping their parents' bills with their own. The young waxbills are able to fly in 16—17 days.

Getting their own back?

Many waxbills are parasitised by some of the related whydahs, also known as widow birds. The whydahs lay their eggs in the waxbills' nests and their young are brought up with the young waxbills. Not all the whydahs are, however, parasites and one waxbill, the zebra waxbill, has to a certain extent reversed the situation: it lays its eggs in the nests of whydahs and bishops, but only when they have been abandoned. Bishops and whydahs finish nesting in March and the waxbills then start their nesting season taking over the nests of the bishops and whydahs and relining them.

class	**Aves**
order	**Passeriformes**
family	**Ploceidae**
genus & species	*Estrilda astrild* common waxbill *E. locustella* locust finch *E. melpoda* orange cheeked waxbill *E. perreini* southern grey waxbill *E. subflava* zebra waxbill *E. temporalis* Sydney waxbill *E. troglodytes* northern grey waxbill others

Mammals

Although mammals, like birds, are descended from reptiles, the two groups are sharply contrasted in form and behaviour. They share a warm-blooded (homoiothermic) physiology and are air-breathing. But whereas all birds lay eggs, the characteristic feature of mammals is that the females bear their young alive. The bodies of birds, moreover, are clothed in feathers, those of mammals bear hair. Birds use sight as the main sense, mammals use smell except for the Primates (lemurs, monkeys, apes and man) which are mainly 'eyesight animals'. Except for man, mammals are relatively silent animals although all have voices, which mainly come into use at the breeding season.

One of the features of birds which lends credibility to the notion that they are descended from reptiles is the presence on their bodies of scales. It is true these are restricted to the legs and feet, but there they so strongly recall the corresponding structures on reptiles as to still any remaining doubts of the close relationship of birds to reptiles. When scales do occur in mammals these are of a different character and structure. Thus, the scales of the scaly-anteater or pangolin are made up of what can conveniently be called compressed hair.

When Captain James Cook visited Australia and opened the way to the settlement of that continent by Europeans, he could not have foreseen that one result would be to rescue the zoologists of those times from a dilemma. It would have been hard to convince anyone that mammals are descendants of reptilian stock without knowledge of the duckbill or platypus, of Australia, and the echidna or spiny anteater, of Australia (and also New Guinea) which

the early settlers found when they first arrived there.

Both these are undoubted mammals. They both have hair on the body and the females nourish their young in the early stages of life with milk. But both lay eggs, a feature unique among mammals. Moreover, in the shape of some of their bones, in certain other features of their skeleton, as well as in the anatomy of their reproductive, excretory and digestive systems, they bear the hallmarks of true reptiles.

Also in Australia, though not exclusively so because they occur as well in adjacent islands and in America, are the marsupials or pouch-bearers, epitomized for most people by the kangaroo. These are also undoubted mammals but they are only a degree or so removed from the egg-laying mammals in possessing some undoubted reptilian characters.

We have travelled far in this book from the point where reference was made to the phrase 'from amoeba to man'. Although in principle it is still valid and useful as a convenient catchphrase, it has been rendered outmoded, and the history of this sheds an important light on the classification of mammals.

Man has always placed his own species at the apex of the pyramid formed by the animal kingdom. Consequently, when constructing a classification of mammals, he began with the most primitive, the egg-laying mammals, and ended with the Primates, those with the most highly-organized brains, of which man is a member. This classification was accepted and used for decades.

In 1945, the eminent zoologist, Dr George Gaylord Simpson published a monograph

in which he suggested a new classification of mammals. The revolutionary idea it embodied was to give first consideration to the physical or bodily specializations, ignoring the matter of brain-development. The result can be seen in the table of classification appended here.

The classification of mammals is as follows:

Class Mammalia   3,700 species
SUBCLASS PROTOTHERIA
Order Monotremata
    (egg-laying mammals)
INFRACLASS METATHERIA
Order Marsupialia
    (marsupials or pouch-bearers)
SUBCLASS THERIA
Order Insectivora
    (shrews, moles, tenrecs)
Order Dermoptera (flying lemur)
Order Tupaioidea (tree shrews)
Order Chiroptera (bats)
Order Primates
    (lemurs, monkeys, apes, man)
Order Edentata
    (anteaters, sloths, armadillos)
Order Pholidota (pangolins)
Order Lagomorpha (pikas, rabbits, hares)
Order Rodentia (rodents)
Order Carnivora (dogs, bears, cats, etc.)
Order Pinnipedia (seals, sealions, walrus)
Order Tubulidentata (aardvark)
Order Sirenia (dugong, manatee)
Order Perissodactyla
    (horse, ass, rhinoceros, tapir)
Order Artiodactyla
    (pig, hippopotamus and other
    cloven-hoofed animals)
Order Cetacea
    (whales, dolphins, porpoises)

Platypus

Today the platypus is accepted as an unusual animal of quaint appearance, but it is not difficult to imagine its impact on the scientific world when it was first discovered. So strange did the creature appear that one scientist named it **paradoxus,** and a paradox it was with duck-like bill, furry mammalian coat and webbed feet.

Known as the duckbill, watermole or duckmole, the platypus is one of Australia's two egg-laying mammals, the other being the spiny anteater. The platypus is about 2 ft long including a 6in. beaver-like tail and weighs about $4\frac{1}{2}$ lb, the males being slightly larger than the females. The 'bill' is a sensitive elongated snout and is soft, like doeskin, not horny as is popularly supposed.

Although bizarre in appearance, the platypus is well adapted to its semi-aquatic life. The legs are short with strong claws on the toes and the feet are webbed. The webbing on the forefeet extends well beyond the toes, but can be turned back when on land, leaving the claws free for walking and digging. The eye and the opening to the inner ear lie on each side of the head in a furrow which can be closed when the platypus submerges. There are no external ears, thus the platypus is blind and deaf when under water. Young have teeth, but these are replaced in the adult by horny ridges.

Thick loose skin makes the barrel-shaped body of the platypus appear larger than it is. The pelt consists of a dense woolly undercoat and long shiny guard hairs. The colour varies from sepia brown to almost black above and is silver, tinged with pink or yellow underneath; females can be identified by the more pronounced reddish tint of their fur. Adult males have hollow spurs, connected to venom glands, on the ankle of each hind limb. The poison from them can be quite harmful to a man, although not fatal.

The platypus was not discovered until 1796, nearly 200 years after the first wallaby, for instance, had been seen by a European. This is not as strange as might appear at first sight, for aquatic animals tend to be elusive particularly if, like the platypus, they are nocturnal.

Its range can be seen on the map. The western limits are the Leichhardt River in North Queensland, and the Murray, Onkaparinga and Glenelg rivers, just within the border of South Australia. It is found in all fresh water, from clear icy streams at 5 000 ft to lakes and warm coastal rivers.

▷ Out of its front door and into the river. When underwater the platypus is blind and deaf so it relies mainly on its sense of touch, highly developed in the soft rubbery bill.

Hearty appetite

Like many small energetic animals the platypus has a voracious appetite, and probably needs more food, relative to its weight, than any other mammal. It feeds mainly in the early morning and late evening, on crayfish, worms and other small water animals. It probes for these with its bill and at the same time takes in mud and sand, which are apparently necessary for breaking up the food. During the day the platypus rests in burrows dug out of the banks, coming out at night to forage for food in the mud of the river-bottom.

Egg-laying mammal

The breeding season is from August to November and mating takes place in the water, after an elaborate and unusual courtship. Among other manoeuvres, the male will grasp the female's tail and the two will then swim slowly in circles. The female digs a winding, intricate burrow in a bank 25−35 ft, sometimes as much as 60 ft, long, 12−15 in. below the surface of the ground. At the end, a nesting chamber is excavated and lined with wet grass and leaves. The female carries these by wrapping her tail around a bundle. Usually two soft-shelled white eggs are laid, each ½ in. diameter. They often stick together, which prevents them rolling, and the wet leaves and grass keep them from drying out. Before retiring to lay her eggs, 2 weeks after mating, the female blocks the tunnel at intervals with earth, up to 8 in. thick, which she tamps into position with her tail. During the incubation period of 7−10 days she rarely leaves the nest but each time she does so these earth blocks are rebuilt. Presumably this is a defensive measure, but in fact today the platypus has virtually no natural enemies, although a carpet-snake or goanna may occasionally catch one. The inference is that in past ages natural enemies did exist in some numbers and the earth-block defences were very necessary. This is an example of what is known as 'fossil behaviour' and the platypus itself is a living fossil.

Blind for 11 weeks

The young platypus is naked and blind, and its eyes do not open for 11 weeks. It is weaned when nearly 4 months old, at which age it takes to the water. The mother has no teats; milk merely oozes through slits on her abdomen where it is licked up by the babies. A platypus matures at about 2½ years and has a life span of 10 years or more.

Competing with rabbits

Formerly hunted ruthlessly for its beaver-like pelt, the platypus is now rigidly protected. Too often, however, it falls foul of wire cages set under water for fish. Should the platypus enter one it cannot escape and will drown, as it is not able to stay under water for much more than 5 minutes. The introduced rabbit of Australia threatens the platypus in a different way. Where rabbits have driven too many tunnels the platypus cannot breed: it needs undisturbed soil for its breeding burrows. Fortunately, although reduced in numbers, it is now well protected by the Australian authorities and it is in no danger of extinction.

Creature of contrast

Fortunately for the sanity of naturalists, the paradoxical facts that the platypus, a mammal, laid eggs and suckled its young were not known when it was first discovered. In 1884, WH Caldwell, who had gone to Australia specially to study the platypus, dissected a female which had already laid one egg and was ready to lay another. Thrilled by this discovery he electrified members of the British Association for the Advancement of Science, then meeting in Montreal, with his laconic telegram — 'Monotremes oviparus, ovum meroblastic' (monotremes egg-laying, egg only partially divides). Delegates stood and cheered, for controversy over this point had raged in the scientific world for some years.

Long before this, in 1799, the first dried skin reached London and came into the hands of Dr Shaw, then assistant-keeper in the Natural History section of the British Museum. When Dr Shaw saw the skin he literally could not believe what he saw. At that time visitors to the Far East were bringing back fakes such as the 'eastern-mermaid', made from the skin of a monkey skilfully sewn to the tail of a fish. It is not surprising, therefore, that Dr Shaw should suspect someone had grafted the bill of a duck on to the body of a quadruped. He tried to prise off the bill, and today the marks of his scissors can still be seen on the original skin which is preserved in the British Museum (Natural History).

class	**Mammalia**
order	**Monotremata**
family	**Ornithorhynchidae**
genus & species	*Ornithorhynchus anatinus platypus*

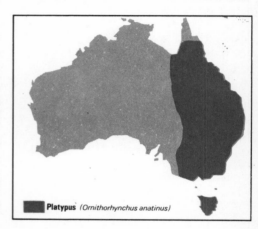

Platypus (*Ornithorhynchus anatinus*)

▽ *In the water the platypus uses its strong webbed forefeet for swimming and its hind legs as rudders. On land its forefeet are used for digging and to press the water out of its fur before it enters its burrow.*

Kangaroo

The best-known of the five kangaroos are the great grey and the red. The great grey or forester is up to 6 ft high, exceptionally 7 ft, with a weight of up to 200 lb. Its head is small with large ears, its forelimbs are very small by comparison with the powerful hindlimbs and the strong tail is 4 ft long. The colour is variable but is mainly grey with whitish underparts and white on the legs and underside of the tail. The muzzle is hairy between the nostrils. The male is known as a boomer, the female as a flyer and the young as a Joey. The great grey lives in open forest browsing the vegetation. The red kangaroo is similar to the great grey in size and build but the male has a reddish coat, the adult female is smoky blue, and the muzzle is less hairy. Unlike the great grey kangaroo it lives on open plains, is more a grazer than a browser, and lives more in herds or mobs, usually of a dozen animals.

The 55 species of kangaroo, wallaby and wallaroo make up the family Macropodidae (**macropus** = big foot). Only two are called kangaroos but there are 10 rat kangaroos and two tree kangaroos. A third species is known as the rock kangaroo or wallaroo. There is no brief way of describing the difference between a kangaroo and a wallaby except to say that the first is larger than the second. An arbitrary rule is that a kangaroo has hindfeet more than 10 in. long.

The red is found all over Australia. The great grey lives mainly in eastern Australia but there are three races of it, formerly regarded as species: the grey kangaroo or western forester of the southwest; that on Kangaroo Island off Yorke Peninsula, South Australia; and the Tasmanian kangaroo or forester. The wallaroo or euro lives among rocks especially in coastal areas. It has shorter and more stockily built hindlegs than the red or the great grey.

Leaps and bounds

When feeding, and so moving slowly, kangaroos balance themselves on their small forelegs and strong tail and swing the large hindlegs forward. They then bring their arms and tail up to complete the second stage of the movement. When travelling fast, only the two hindfeet are used with the tail held almost horizontally as a balancer. They clear obstacles in the same way, with leaps of up to 26 ft long. Usually the leap does not carry them more than 5 ft off the ground but there are reports of these large kangaroos clearing fences up to 9 ft. Their top speed is always a matter for dispute. They seem to be capable of 25 mph over a 300yd stretch but some people claim a higher speed for them.

Eating down the grass

Kangaroos feed mainly by night resting during the heat of the day. The red kangaroo, because it eats grass, has become a serious competitor with sheep, important in Australia's economy. By creating grasslands man has helped the kangaroo increase in numbers. In turn the kangaroo tends to outgraze the sheep, for which the pastures were grown, not only through its increased numbers but by its manner of feeding. Sheep have teeth (incisors) in only the lower-front jaw, with a dental pad in the upper jaw. Kangaroos have front teeth in both lower and upper jaw which means they crop grass more closely than sheep. At times, it is reported, they also dig out the grass roots. They can go without water for long periods, which suggests they were originally animals of desert or semi-desert, but where water is supplied for sheep kangaroos will, if not kept out, take the greater share.

Kangaroos set a problem

Enemies of the larger kangaroos are few now that the Tasmanian wolf has been banished. The introduced dingo still claims its victims but that is shot at sight. The loss of natural enemies, the creation of wide areas of grassland and the kangaroo being

A place in the sun: a red kangaroo group whiles away a lazy sociable afternoon. The powerful hindlegs and long tails can be clearly seen.

able to breed throughout most of the year, has created a problem, especially for sheep graziers, in Australia. Fencing in the pastures, often thousands of acres in extent, is costly – over £200 a mile – and kangaroos have a trick of squeezing under the fence at any weak spot. So kangaroos are shot. In one year, on nine sheep properties totalling 1 540 000 acres, 140 000 kangaroos were shot and it would have needed double this number of kills to keep the properties clear of them. Another problem is that kangaroos often bound across roads at night and collide with cars causing costly damage and endangering those in the cars.

Bean-sized baby

The manner in which baby kangaroos are born and reach the pouch had been in dispute for well over a century. In 1959-60 all doubts were set at rest when the birth process of the red kangaroo was filmed at Adelaide University. About 33 days after mating the female red kangaroo begins to clean her pouch, holding it open with the forepaws and licking the inside. She then takes up the 'birth position' sitting on the base of her tail with the hindlegs extended forwards and her tail passed forward between them. She then licks the opening of her birth canal or cloaca. The newborn kangaroo, ¾in. long, appears headfirst and grasps its mother's fur with the claws on its forefeet. Its hindlegs are at this time very small. In 3 minutes it has dragged itself

to the pouch, entered it and seized one of the four teats in its mouth. The birth is the same for the great grey except that the female stands, with her tail straight out behind her. The baby kangaroo, born at an early stage of development, weighs $\frac{1}{35}$ oz at birth. It remains in the pouch for 8 months, by which time it weighs nearly 10 lb. It continues to be suckled for nearly 6 months after it has left the pouch and can run about, putting its head in to grasp a teat. Meanwhile, another baby has probably been born and is in the pouch. The red kangaroo has lived for 16 years in captivity.

Overlooking the obvious

The truth about kangaroo birth took a long time to be established. In 1629 Francois Pelsaert, a Dutch sea captain, wrecked on the Abrolhos Islands off southwest Australia, was the first to discover the baby in the pouch of a female wallaby. He thought it was born in the pouch. This is what the Aborigines also believed. In 1830 Alexander Collie, a ship's surgeon on a sloop lying in Cockburn Sound, Western Australia, investigated the birth and showed that the baby was born in the usual manner and made its way unaided into the pouch. From then on various suggestions were put forward: that the mother lifted the newborn baby with her forepaws or her lips and placed it in the pouch, or that the baby was budded off from the teat. In 1883 Sir Richard Owen, distinguished anatomist,

Full steam ahead: a shallow water sprint shows the versatility of bounding movement.

came down heavily on the side of those who said the mother placed the baby in her pouch holding it in her lips, yet in 1882 the Hon L Hope had shown Collie to be correct. In 1913 Mr A Goerling wrote a letter to the Perth *Western Mail* describing how he had watched the baby make its way to the pouch with no help from the mother. It was not until 1923, however, that this view was generally accepted, when Dr WT Hornaday, Director of the New York Zoological Gardens, watched and described the birth. Finally, in 1959-60, the whole process of birth was filmed by GB Sharman, JC Merchant, Phyllis Pilton and Meredith Clark, at Adelaide University, setting the matter at rest for all time. It seems so obvious to us now!

class	**Mammalia**
order	**Marsupialia**
family	**Macropodidae**
genus & species	*Macropus giganteus* great grey kangaroo *M. robustus* rock kangaroo or wallaroo *Megaleia rufa* red kangaroo

Koala

The koala is probably Australia's favourite animal. It is known affectionately as the Australian teddy bear although there are a dozen names to choose from. At various times it has been called bangaroo, koolewong, narnagoon, buidelbeer, native bear, karbor, cullawine, colo, koala wombat and New Holland sloth! The last two have an especial interest. For a long time it was believed the koala was most nearly related to the wombat and was placed in a family on its own, the Phascolarctidae, near that of the wombat. Now it is placed in the Phalangeridae with the opossums. In habits the koala recalls the slow loris and the sloth, two very different animals which also move in a lethargic way.

The koala is like a small bear, 2 ft high, up to 33 lb weight, with tufted ears, small eyes with a vertical slit pupil and a prominent beak-like snout. Tailless except for a very short rounded stump, it has a thick ash-grey fur with a tinge of brown on the upper parts, yellowish white on the hindquarters and white on the under parts. It has cheek pouches for storing food and the brood pouch of the female opens backwards. All four feet are grasping. On the front feet the first two of the five toes are opposed to the rest and the first toe on the hindfoot is opposed. Also on the hindfoot the second and third toes are joined in a common skin.

Ace tree-climbers

The koala is essentially tree-living, only occasionally descending to lick earth—apparently to aid digestion—or to shuffle slowly to another tree. If forced to the ground its main concern is to reach another tree and climb it, scrambling up even smooth trunks to the swaying topmost branches where it clings with the powerful grip of all four feet. Although its legs are short they are strong and there are sharp claws on the toes. When climbing a trunk its forelegs reach out at an angle of 45° while the hindlegs are directly under the body. It climbs in a series of jumps of 4—5 in. at a time. During the day it sleeps curled up in a tree-fork. It never enters hollows in trees. Koalas are inoffensive although they have harsh grating voices, said to be like a hand-saw cutting through a thin board; it has been claimed that they have the loudest Australian voice, other than the flying phalanger.

▽ A koala squatting up a telegraph pole on Phillip Island, off eastern Australia.

▷ *Year-old koala who will soon leave mother.*

Fussy feeders

At night the koala climbs to the topmost branches to find its only food: the tender shoots of eucalyptus, 12 species of which are eaten. A koala is said to smell strongly of eucalyptus. Bernhard Grzimek, well-known German zoologist and ethologist, has spoken of koalas as smelling like cough lozenges. Their feeding is, however, more restricted than this. Different races of koala eat only certain species of gum tree. Koalas on the east coast of Australia feed only on the spotted gum and the tallow wood, in Victoria only the red gum. Even then they cannot use all the leaves on a chosen gum. At certain times the older leaves, sometimes the young leaves at the tips of the branches, release prussic acid – a deadly poison – when chewed. So, as more and more gum trees have been felled, koalas have become increasingly hemmed in, prisoners of their specialised diet. One of the difficulties of saving the koala by having special reserves is to supply enough trees for them of the right kind. Koalas are said to eat mistletoe and box leaves as well, and a koala in captivity was persuaded to eat bread and milk, but without gum leaves they cannot survive.

Get off my back!

Another drawback to preserving the koala is that it is a slow breeder. Usually the animal is solitary or lives in small groups. At breeding time a boss male forms a small harem which he guards. The gestation period is 25–35 days and there is normally only one young at a birth, $\frac{3}{4}$ in. long and $\frac{1}{5}$ oz weight. It is fully furred at 6 months but continues to stay with the mother for another 6 months after leaving the pouch, riding pick-a-back on her, which has led to many endearing photographs. On weaning it obtains nourishment by eating partially digested food that has passed through the mother's digestive tract. The young koala is sexually mature at 4 years, and the longest lived koala was 20 years old when it died.

Pitiless persecution

Until less than a century ago there were millions of koalas, especially in eastern Australia. Now they are numbered in thousands. In 1887–89 and again in 1900–1903 epidemics swept through them, killing large numbers. This was at a time when it was a favourite 'sport' to shoot these sitting targets, often taking several shots to finish one animal which meanwhile cried piteously, like a human baby, a fact that caused Australian naturalists to condemn the sport as the most callous. At all times koalas are a prey to forest fires as well as to land clearance for human settlement. Moreover a market was developed for their pelts, their fur being thick and able to withstand hard usage. In 1908 nearly 58 000 koala pelts were marketed in Sydney alone. In 1920–21 a total of 205 679 were marketed and in 1924 over two million were exported. By this time public opinion was being aroused and before long efforts were being made to protect the surviving populations and to establish sanctuaries for them and ensure their future.

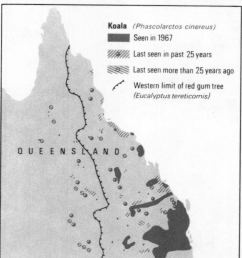

Koala *(Phascolarctos cinereus)*
◼ Seen in 1967
▨ Last seen in past 25 years
▧ Last seen more than 25 years ago
⌇ Western limit of red gum tree
(Eucalyptus tereticornis)

QUEENSLAND

Curious cuddly: favourite of millions, the koala is the Australian teddy bear. It spends most of its time shuffling about its eucalyptus tree-top home. The baby above has climbed onto its mother's back from a downward opening pouch. At a year it will be ready to leave its mother and find its own gum tree. Numbers have seriously decreased in the last 100 years mainly due to fires destroying their gum trees and from persecution by man. From a 1967 survey in Queensland the present-day distribution was established in that state (left).

class	**Mammalia**
order	**Marsupialia**
family	**Phalangeridae**
genus & species	*Phascolarctos cinereus koala*

Shrew

Shrews are the smallest mammals, and for their size probably the most belligerent. Their ancestors are probably among the first true mammals on the earth.

The 170 species are distributed over the world apart from Australasia and the polar regions. They are divided into red-toothed and white-toothed shrews. The red-toothed shrews include the common shrew of Europe and Asia, 4 in. long including a 1½in. tail, and the water shrew, nearly 7 in. long with a 3in. tail. The 34 North American shrews are also red-toothed and they include the common or masked shrew, the pygmy shrew, and the water shrew, all three species being much the same size as their European counterparts.

Of the remaining North American shrews mention can be made of the short-tailed shrew, reputed to have a poisonous bite, the smoky shrew whose tail swells in the breeding season, and the least, little, or lesser short-tailed shrew, 'the furry mite with a mighty fury' (E Laurence Palmer).

Red-toothed shrews are similar in appearance and in habits. They are mouse-like but with small ears and eyes and a tapering snout with many long bristles. The fur is greyish to dark brown on the back and dirty white on the belly.

Nose to the ground: the common shrew is always on the move, searching for insects with its long snout.

Three-hourly rhythm

Shrews live solitary lives in tunnels in grass, among leaf litter or in surface tunnels, where they are seldom seen and are only revealed by their high-pitched squeaks. There is reason to believe that shrews also use ultrasonics for echo-location but not to the high degree found in bats. The common and pygmy shrews, and probably all the other species, have a 3-hourly rhythm of alternately feeding and resting, but are active for a longer proportion of each of the 3 hours during the night. Shrews are also relatively short-lived. In the common shrew and most red-toothed shrews, 15 months represents extreme old age.

There are many legends about shrews. One English legend is that a shrew cannot cross a human path and live, and many people have reported seeing a shrew tottering towards them and dropping at their feet. Such a shrew may have been extremely old, so that it dropped dead in its tracks. Another possibility is that the shrew died of 'cold starvation'.

Vicious food circle

The smaller the animal the greater its surface area in proportion to its bulk, and the more readily it loses heat by radiation. This can only be replaced by food, so a very small animal must move restlessly, searching for food to make good the loss of heat—and the loss of energy in searching for food. One result is that it cannot go without food for long periods, hence the 3-hourly rhythm. A

shrew deprived of food for 2 or 3 hours will die, and the lower the temperature the shorter the period of fasting it can endure. Most reports of shrews seen dropping dead relate to the early morning. This is the time, especially in autumn, when cold starvation is most likely to occur.

Death from shock?

The susceptibility to cold starvation led to another misunderstanding, that shrews were especially prone to death from shock. Naturalists of the late 19th and early 20th centuries reported shrews dying if a gun were fired near them, and even if a blown-up paper bag were burst near them. In fact, shrews are tough and will survive all manner of misadventures so long as they are well fed. When suffering from cold starvation, however, to the point where they are moribund, almost anything will kill them.

Another wrong idea

Shrews are basically insect-eaters but they will eat any animal small enough for them to overpower, such as snails and worms. They will also eat carrion. But they do need some cereal, and this was discovered by Australian zoologist Peter Crowcroft, when keeping them in captivity. He found they remained healthy if given a little cereal or seed each day. It is often said shrews eat more than their own weight of food a day. A more exact estimate puts it at three-quarters their own weight.

High death rate

From spring to autumn each mature female has at least two litters of 4–8 young after a gestation of uncertain length which may be between 13 and 21 days. A newborn shrew weighs $\frac{1}{100}$ oz. Its eyes open at 18–21 days and it is weaned 2 days later. There is probably a heavy infant mortality, in spite of the musk gland in each flank of most shrews which emits a foul odour. Domestic cats, for example, will kill shrews but do not eat them, presumably finding them unpalatable. Birds of prey will eat them, however, especially various owl species, and so will foxes and weasels.

Singing contests

There has long been the idea that shrews are not only savage, ready to use their teeth when handled, but also are extremely quarrelsome among themselves. Naturalists have reported seeing two shrews apparently locked in mortal combat and squeaking furiously. Crowcroft, who made a special study of European shrews, and careful observation of them in captivity, has put a different light on this. He found that if two shrews meet they go towards each other until their whiskers touch, then they squeak. As a rule one of them, usually the intruder will retreat. If it does not do so both rear up onto their haunches, still squeaking. If at this stage neither gives way, they throw themselves onto their backs squeaking even more and wriggling about. Then it usually happens that the muzzle of one comes in contact with the tail of the other and it seizes it with its teeth. As the two shrews continue to wriggle, almost inevitably the second shrew finds the other's tail, seizes it, and the two continue wriggling and squirming apparently in close embrace. Seldom do they hurt each other, or if they do the injuries are not severe. Because food is so vital to them they may become overcrowded and these 'singing contests' are the best way to keep the population evenly spaced over the ground to ensure a maximum food supply for all.

class	**Mammalia**
order	**Insectivora**
family	**Soricidae**
genera & species	**Blarina brevicauda** short-tailed shrew **Cryptotis parva** least shrew **Microsorex hoyi** N. American pygmy shrew **Sorex araneus** European common shrew **S. fumeus** smoky shrew **S. minutus** European pygmy shrew others

Vampire bat

The vampire bat of fact is totally unlike the vampire of fiction except that it feeds on blood. In one way it is worse than the fictional vampire—it is a carrier of rabies, a disease feared the world over. True vampires, of tropical and subtropical America, feed only on the fresh blood of mammals and birds. Unlike the man-sized vampires of fable, they are only $2\frac{1}{2}$–$3\frac{1}{2}$ in. long with a forearm of 2–$2\frac{1}{2}$ in. The weight of an adult varies in the different species from $\frac{1}{2}$ to $1\frac{3}{4}$ oz. Their fur is various shades of brown. They have no tail. The ears are small and the muzzle short and conical without a true noseleaf. Instead there are naked pads on the snout with U-shaped grooves at the tip, which may be sensory. The upper incisor teeth are large and razor-edged, well adapted for gently opening a small wound to take

blood. The grooved, muscular tongue fits over a V-shaped notch in the lower lip, so forming a tube through which the blood is sucked. The stomach is also adapted for liquid feeding, the forward end being drawn out into a long tube. The saliva contains substances that prevent the blood from clotting.

There are three genera, each with a single species. The common vampire bat, the most numerous and widespread of the three, is distinguished by its pointed ears, longer thumb with a basal pad and its naked interfemoral membrane. It has only 20 teeth. It ranges from northern Mexico southward to central Chile, central Argentina and Uruguay. It is now one of the most common and widespread mammals in eastern Mexico.

The second species, the white-winged vampire, is much less numerous. The edges of its wings and part of the wing membrane are white. It has a peculiar

△ *Cutting closeup: the bloodstained mouth and shear-like teeth of a common vampire.*

short thumb about $\frac{1}{8}$th as long as the third finger, and has a single pad underneath. It is the only bat known to have 22 permanent teeth. The white-winged vampire is mainly confined to the tropical regions of South America from Venezuela and the Guianas to Peru and Brazil, but it has also been found on Trinidad and in Mexico.

The hairy-legged vampire, smaller than the common species, is not well known. It has shorter, rounded ears, a short thumb without a basal pad and softer fur. Its interfemoral membrane is well-furred. It has 26 teeth and is unique among bats in having a fan-shaped, seven-lobed outer lower incisor tooth which resembles the lower incisor in the order Dermoptera, the gliding lemurs. This species is found in eastern and southern Mexico, Central America, and southwards to Brazil.

393

Victims attacked while asleep

During the day vampire bats roost in caves, old mines, hollow trees, crevices in rocks and in old buildings. Colonies of the common vampire may number as many as 2 000 but the average is about 100. The sexes roost together and they may share the caves with other species of bats. They are very agile and can walk rapidly on their feet and thumbs either on the ground or up the vertical sides of caves. Shortly after dark the bats leave their roosts with a slow noiseless flight, usually only 3 ft above the ground. The bats attack their victims while they sleep, sometimes alighting near them, crawling up to them, looking rather like large spiders. They make a quick shallow bite with their sharp teeth in a place where there is no hair or feathers. They cut away only a very small piece of skin, making a shallow wound from which they suck the blood without a sound, so the victim does not wake. Unlike other bats they do not cling with their claws but rest lightly on their thumbs and small foot pads, so lightly that even a man is unlikely to be wakened by the visit of a vampire. The common vampire bat in particular can drink such large quantities of blood that it is barely able to fly for some time afterwards.

The common vampire attacks only large mammals such as horses, cattle and occasionally man. Cattle are generally bitten on the neck or leg and a human on the big toe. The white-winged vampire, so far as is known, attacks only birds, biting the neck or ankle, and the hairy-legged vampire appears to prey mainly on birds such as chickens, but it is possible it may also attack some mammals.

In captivity vampire bats have been kept alive on blood defibrinated to prevent clotting. One survived for 13 years in a laboratory in Panama.

Echolocation in vampires

Like all bats, vampires find their way about and detect their prey by echolocation. Since their source of food is large and relatively stationary they do not have the same difficulty in finding their prey as bats that feed on fast-moving insects, or even those that catch fish. Like the fruit-eating bats, which also feed on stationary food, their echolocation is by pulses having only $\frac{1}{1000}$th of the sound energy of those used by bats feeding on insects or fish. It is noteworthy that vampires very seldom attack dogs, presumably because they have more sensitive hearing than larger mammals such as cattle and are able to detect the bat's higher sound frequencies.

Babies left at home

Little or nothing is known of the breeding habits of the white-winged and hairy-legged vampire bats. The common vampire gives birth to a single young after a gestation of 90–120 days. They breed throughout the year and it is possible there is more than one birth a year. The young are not carried about by the mother, as in most other bats, but are left in the roost while she is out foraging.

◁ *Disturbed while sleeping: common vampires prefer retreats of almost complete darkness.*

Desperate measures

The real danger of vampire bats lies not so much in their feeding on the blood of domestic animals and man, although this is bad enough, but in the transmission of disease resulting from the bites and risk of secondary infections. Vampires can transmit rabies which may be fatal in cattle or even in man. They may also transmit the disease to other species of bats and they may die of it themselves. In Mexico alone it is necessary to inoculate thousands of head of cattle each year against the disease. The disease is always fatal to uninoculated cattle.

Various control methods have been tried in the past, including dynamiting the caves where the bats roost and the use of flame-throwers and poison gas. These have been found to be largely ineffective and also highly destructive to other harmless species of bats. The only solution to the problem seems to lie in biological control, including sterilisation, habitat management and the use of selective chemical attractants and repellents. A research centre has now been set up in Mexico City for the ecological study of vampire bats and for research into biological methods of control.

class	**Mammalia**
order	**Chiroptera**
family	**Desmodontidáe**
genera & species	***Desmodus rotundus*** *common vampire bat* ***Diaemus youngi*** *white-winged vampire bat* ***Diphylla ecaudata*** *hairy-legged vampire bat*

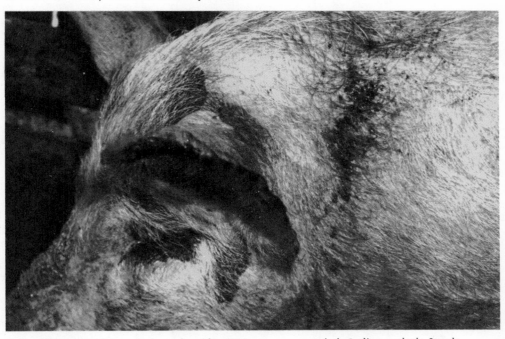

△ *Fresh bites on a pig's neck are grisly evidence of a common vampire's feeding methods. It only feeds on large animals, and because horses and cattle provide such a large supply of easily accessible blood, stockrearing in many tropical areas has proved uneconomical.* ▽ *The culprit on all fours.*

Chimpanzee

One of the great apes and the nearest in intelligence to man, the chimpanzee is one of the most studied and popular of animals. Scientists have examined its mental capacities and sent it into space in anticipation of man. To the general public, the chimpanzee is the familiar clown of circus acts and tea parties at the zoo. Yet despite all our knowledge of the chimpanzee's capabilities in the laboratory, it is only recently that its habits in the wild have been studied, and these are proving to be more remarkable than its antics in captivity.

Chimpanzees need little description. Being apes and not monkeys, they have no tail. Their arms are longer than their legs and they normally run on all fours, but they can walk upright, with toes turned outwards. When erect they stand 3—5 ft high. The hair is long and coarse, black except for a white patch near the rump. The face, ears, hands and feet are naked and, except for the black face, flesh coloured.

Forest families

The single species of chimpanzee lives in the tropical rain forests of Africa, roughly from the Niger basin to Angola. They are at home in the trees, making nests of branches and vines each night to sleep in, but they often come down to the ground to search for food. Whereas their normal gait on the ground is all fours, they will run on three legs, leaving one free to hold food, or on their hind legs, in an amusing waddling gait, when carrying an armful of food.

Chimpanzees live in small parties, occasionally numbering up to 40, but the bonds between the members of a party are weak. There is no fixed social structure like that found in baboon troops. A chimpanzee party is constantly varying in size as members leave to wander off in the forests by themselves or return from such a wandering. The only constant unit of social life is a mother with her young. She may have two or three of different ages with her at any time because they stay with her for several years. The usual size of a group is from 3—6, but numbers increase as chimpanzees gather at a source of plentiful and tasty food, or if a female comes on heat when the males will gather round her for several days.

Within a party, the males are arranged in a social order, the inferior ones respecting the superior ones. Dominance is related to age; a chimpanzee gradually rises in social position from the time he is physically mature and leaves the protection of his mother. The status of a male seems to be partly determined by noisy displays, charging about waving branches or rocks or drumming the feet on the plank-like buttresses of the forest trees. This behaviour is sometimes sparked off by frustration brought on by seeing more dominant males enjoying food without sharing it. Yet the chimpanzees recognize the right of owner-

The gamut of emotions

△ *'I'm content'—relaxed and normal.*

△ *'Hello'—the greeting pout.*

△ *'I'm happy' smile, showing bottom teeth only.*
▽ *Tantrum, showing top and bottom teeth.*

ship sufficiently to prevent a dominant male from wresting food from one of his inferiors.

First aid and affection

When chimpanzees meet after having been apart they greet each other in a very human way, by touching each other or even clasping hands and kissing. The arrival of a dominant male is the signal for the rest to hurry over and pay their respects to him. The members of a party also spend a considerable amount of time grooming each other, and themselves. Mothers carefully go through the fur of their babies for any foreign particles, spending more and more time on the task as the babies grow older. Dirt, burrs, dried skin and ticks are plucked off and splinters may be removed by pinching them out with forefingers or lips. Such mutual help may lead to further first aid. A captive female was once seen to approach her male companion, whimpering. She sat down while the other chimpanzee sat opposite her and, holding her head steady with one hand, pulled the lower lid of one eye down with the other. After a short inspection he removed a speck of grit from her eye with his finger, to her evident relief.

Hunting for meat

About 7 hours a day may be spent feeding either up trees or on the ground. The chimpanzees investigate any source likely to produce food. Crevices in logs are searched for insects and nests are robbed of eggs and chicks, but their usual food consists of fruits, leaves and roots. Ripening fruit crops, of bananas, pawpaws or wild figs, are a special attraction to them and they are sometimes a nuisance when they attack plantations. A big male chimpanzee can eat over 50 bananas at one sitting.

Until recently it was thought that the only flesh eaten by chimpanzees was that of insects and occasionally birds and small rodents. They have now been found to hunt larger animals, some individuals apparently being particularly fond of meat. Young bushbucks and bushpigs have been seen caught by chimpanzees, as well as colobus monkeys and young baboons. Jane Goodall, the British naturalist who spent several years in Africa studying chimpanzees in the wild, has given a very graphic description of a chimpanzee catching a young baboon and killing it by holding its back legs and smashing its head against the ground.

Obedient children

Chimpanzees are promiscuous. When a female comes on heat the males gather round her, bounding and leaping through the branches. All of them mate with her, no matter what their social standing. She remains on heat for several days, then the males lose interest.

A single baby—twins are rare—is born after about 230 days. If it is the female's first baby, she does not at first seem to know what to do with it, but by a combination of instinct, knowledge gained from having seen other babies, and learning, she soon starts to care for it. For 2 years the baby will be completely dependent on her. At first she carries it to her breast, but as it grows larger it rides pick-a-back.

The standard of baby care shown by

Top: Young chimps, Primrose (left) and Peter.
Right: Chimpanzees are the best tool-users apart from man, using natural objects to gather food, crack nuts, and drive off enemies.

Chimpanzee *(Pan troglodytes)*

female chimpanzees varies considerably. Some are ideal mothers, caring for their babies zealously and caressing and kissing them. Others are over-attentive, and the babies are 'spoilt'; and yet others neglect their children. The standard of care and education, however, is on the whole exemplary. The babies are not usually bullied or spoiled, yet they obey the parents' orders instantly. When they leave their mother's back they have considerable freedom, and can climb over dominant males without fear.

The babies are carried for varying periods. Sometimes they are still riding on their mothers when 4 years old. By this time the mother will have another baby and the elder one has to fend more for itself, but chimpanzees have been seen hand feeding young that are 6 or 7 years old.

Tools for chimpanzees

Man is sometimes called the toolmaker to distinguish him from other animals. It is difficult to decide when our ancestors became human-like rather than ape-like,

and toolmaking is one factor used as a line of contrast. Upright gait and speech are others, but it is difficult to make rigid pronouncements about features that must have evolved gradually.

Tools can be regarded as extensions of the body used to help with certain tasks. Few animals are known to use tools, but the real difference that separates man and the rest of the animal world is that he not only uses a variety of tools, he makes them, fashioning natural objects to suit his purpose. In this way, opening a nut with a stone is tool using, but shaping the stone into an axe is toolmaking.

Chimpanzees are the best tool-users apart from man. In captivity, they have been seen to throw stones and brandish clubs when put in a cage near a leopard and they are mentally well equipped to work out how to use tools, which are used by some other animals more or less instinctively. Chimpanzees have solved such problems as fitting two sticks together or balancing boxes on top of each other to get at otherwise inaccessible bananas.

The observations by Jane Goodall and others on wild chimpanzees have shown that they also use a variety of tools. The most common use is to extract honey, ants or termites from nests. Sticks 2—3 ft long are picked off the ground or broken from branches and pushed into nests, then withdrawn, and the honey or insects licked off. Stones are used to crack nuts, or as missiles to drive humans or baboons away from the chimpanzees' food. The stones, which sometimes weigh several pounds, are thrown, overarm, not very accurately but definitely aimed. Another material used for tools is leaves. Chimpanzees have been seen plucking leaves, chewing them up, and using the resultant mass as a sponge. Water, in a natural bowl in a tree, was soaked up into the sponge and squeezed out into the chimpanzee's mouth. Whole leaves have also been used for wiping sticky lips and hands after eating bananas.

The variety of tools used by the chimpanzees is made more interesting because they actually make some of their implements. To make a suitable rod to extract insects, the chimpanzees will strip the leaves off a twig or tear shreds off a grass stem to make it narrower. These are clear signs of modifying natural material for a specific use, as is the chewing of leaves to make a sponge. So man is not the only toolmaker, merely better at it than his relatives.

A final point arises from these observations on wild chimpanzees. Babies were seen to play with tools discarded by their elders after having watched them being used. At first their efforts at imitation were clumsy but by 3 years of age they were using them competently. Here is the beginning of a culture in which individuals learn skills passed on from generation to generation.

class	**Mammalia**
order	**Primates**
family	**Pongidae**
genus & species	***Pan troglodytes***

△ △ *Chimpanzee first-aid: incredible instance of male removing grit from his mate's eye.*
△ *A mother suckles her baby. Chimpanzees show great affection to their young, and discipline is good without the need for bullying.*

Growing old. Youngsters (above) stay with their mother for 5 years but they are 10 or 12 before they are mature and they may live to 40.

Orang utan

The orang utan is one of our more interesting relatives. It occupies an intermediate place within the Hominoidea, the superfamily that comprises the apes and man, as it is less closely related to man than the gorilla or chimpanzee, but more man-like than the gibbon.

The big male orang stands 4½ ft high when upright, and may weigh as much as a man. Females stand only 3 ft 10 in. at the most, and weigh half as much as the male. The arms are 1½ times as long as the legs, both hands and feet are long and narrow and suited for grasping, and the thumb and great toe are very short since they would only 'get in the way' of the hook-like function of the hand. The skin is coarse and dark grey, and the hair, which is reddish, is sparse, so the skin can be seen through it in many places. The male develops large cheek-flanges of unknown function, and grows a beard or moustache, the rest of the face being virtually hairless. There is a great deal of variation in facial appearance; orangs are as individual and instantly recognisable as human beings. Both sexes have a laryngeal pouch, which in the male can be quite large, giving it a flabby appearance on the neck and chest. The forehead is high and rounded, and the jaws are prominent. Youngsters have a blue tinge to the face.

Orang utans are found on Borneo and Sumatra. There are slight differences between the two races, and these are more marked in the male. The Borneo race is maroon-tinted, and the male looks really grotesque, with enormous cheek-flanges and great dewlaps formed by the laryngeal sac. The Sumatran race is slimmer and lighter-coloured, and males can look quite startlingly human, with only small flanges and sac, a long narrow face, and a long gingery moustache.

Old man of the woods

The orang utan is strictly a tropical forest animal. It generally lives in low-lying, even swampy forests, but is also found at 6 000 ft on mountains in Borneo. Here, at any rate, most individuals are entirely arboreal. They swing from branch to branch by their arms, though they may use their feet as well, or walk upright along a branch, steadying themselves with their hands round the branch above. It is reported by the Dyaks of Borneo that big old males become too heavy to live in the trees, so they spend most of their time on the ground.

When they are on the ground, orangs move quadrupedally, with the feet bent inwards and clenched, and the hands either clenched or flat on the ground. This contrasts with the gorilla and chimpanzee, which live mainly on the ground and 'knuckle-walk', with their feet flat on the ground and their hands supported on their knuckles. In captivity, orangs easily learn—or discover for themselves—how to walk erect, but because the leg muscles are insufficiently developed to do this easily, the knee is kept locked and the leg straight.

Anti-social 'burping'

At night the orang utan makes a nest, between 30 and 70 ft above the ground. There is often a kind of sheltering roof over this nest, to protect the orang from the rain—a structure which is not found in nests made by chimps or gorillas. The nest is otherwise much more sketchily made than that of chimps or gorillas. It takes only 5 minutes to make and the orang usually moves on and makes a new nest at its next night's stopping place. Sometimes the same one is used again and the previous night's nest may be used for a daytime nap.

Unlike gorillas and chimpanzees, orang utans seem to have no large social groupings. A female with her infant often travels with other such females for a while, forming something like a smaller version of the chimpanzee's 'nursery group'. A male may join this group, but adult males live alone most of the time. Adolescents of both sexes tend to travel around in groups of twos or threes. It is possible that male orangs, like gibbon families, may be territorial, spacing themselves vocally. The laryngeal sac is filled with air, making the animal swell up terrifyingly, and the air is then released to produce what has been described as a 'loud, two-tone booming burp'. They communicate within a group by making a smacking sound with their lips every few seconds. The most terrifying sound which an orang makes is a roar. This begins on a high note and the tone gets deeper and deeper as the laryngeal sac fills with air. Roaring is heard at night and before dawn, and orangs are said

▽ *An aggressive orang utan burps defiantly.*

to make the same noise when wounded. The Dyaks report that male orangs fight and scars are quite common.

There is no special birth season, food being available all the year round in the Indonesian rain forest. Gestation lasts 9 months. The young orang weighs only $3\frac{1}{2}$–4 lb at birth, and is sparsely covered with hairs on the back and head. At first it clings to its mother's fur, usually slung on her hip, but when it is a little older, it wanders about on its own, sometimes walking along the branch behind its mother, clinging to her rump hairs. At about 5 years or so, orangs seem to leave their mothers and form adolescent bands.

Source of contention

Man is the principal enemy of the orang utan. Orangs love the juicy, evil-smelling durian fruit, and so do human beings, so this is often a source of contention. An orang will react to a human intruder by making a great deal of the smacking sound, and breaking off branches, keeping up a continuous shower of them which is often annoying enough to drive the humans away. A Dyak recently reported that he was attacked for no reason by a huge male orang

that he came upon unexpectedly on the ground. It has few other enemies. There are no tigers in Borneo—Dyaks claim to have exterminated them about 1 000 years ago—and in Sumatra there are only a few. Leopards are unknown on both islands.

Zoos are a danger

The orang's distribution has been steadily declining. Its ancestors' remains have been found in 14 million-year-old deposits in the Siwalik Hills, Punjab, India. In the Pleistocene, 500 000 years ago, the orang was found as far north as China, and as far south as Java. Today it occurs all over Borneo—the largest and least populated of the East Indian islands—and in the north of Sumatra. It seems that deforestation and heavy human populations have affected its distribution very adversely and there are now fears that it may become extinct altogether in the wild. One reason for its decline is its slow breeding rate. A female breeds every fourth year or so, and usually not until the previous young has left her. It is possible that the average female may bear only three or four young in her life.

The biggest threat, however, to the orang's survival is, sad to say, the zoo trade.

Every zoo wants a young ape to display to its visitors, and orangs are the easiest to obtain. Many unscrupulous private zoos, especially in the United States, have paid high prices for baby orangs, and there has been quite a lucrative trade in them in Southeast Asia. Baby orangs are obtained by shooting their mothers. The dealer does not make much effort to ensure the captive's welfare as he probably bought it from the hunter at a low fee, so many youngsters die. For every one orang that reaches a zoo alive, ten orangs have probably died. It is now illegal in Singapore to possess orangs, and smugglers are penalised, but other ports in Southeast Asia are still open for this trade. There is now a list of animals in danger of extinction which, under an international convention, cannot normally be imported into the countries, including the United States, which signed the convention. They can only be imported under special licence, usually for research purposes. This may have some effect on the situation. The deforestation problem, however, remains.

In 1963 Barbara Harrisson, working with her husband, Tom, then Government Ethnologist and Curator of Sarawak Museum, estimated that only 2 000 wild

◁ *A mature orang utan.*

▽ *Brotherly love.* △ *The old man of the woods. A male orang with his large cheek flanges.*

orangs remained in Sabah, 1 000 in Kalimantan (Indonesian Borneo), 700 in Sarawak and 1 000 in Sumatra. Of these, only the Sabah population seems to be anything like adequately protected. In 1964 another estimate put the Sumatra population at only 100. Tom and Barbara Harrisson undertook a programme in Sarawak of reintroducing into the wild, young orangs which had been illegally bought by people. This has met with a certain amount of success. There are about 300 in zoos all over the world and breeding has been achieved several times. Most zoos that breed them now keep the Bornean and Sumatran races separate, which will help to save the Sumatran race.

class	**Mammalia**
order	**Primates**
family	**Pongidae**
genus & species	***Pongo pygmaeus pygmaeus*** *Bornean orang utan* ***P. p. abeli*** *Sumatran orang utan*

Sloth

Sloths are bizarre mammals that spend nearly all their lives hanging upside down. With the anteaters and armadillos, these three South American groups belong to the order Edentata which means without teeth. The anteaters are the only edentates wholly without teeth but sloths have teeth in the cheeks. There are nine on each side and they grow throughout life. Their bodies show some remarkable adaptations for an upside down life in the trees. Sloths hang by means of long curved claws like meat hooks and their hands and feet have lost all other functions, the fingers and toes being united in a common fold of skin. The arms are longer than the legs and the pelvis is small. The back muscles which are well developed in other animals are weak in sloths. The head can turn through 270° so that it can be held almost the right way up while the rest of the body is upside down. The hair lies in the opposite direction to that of other mammals, from belly to back, so rain water still runs off it. The individual hairs are grooved and are usually infested by single-celled algae which make sloths look green.

The seven species of sloth are divided into two-toed and three-toed sloths. The three-toed sloths are about 2 ft long with a short stump-like tail. The two-toed sloths are a little larger but lack a tail. Sloths live in forests, the three-toed sloths from Honduras to northern Argentina and two-toed sloths from Venezuela to Brazil.

Slow-motion animals

As is usual for nocturnal animals living in the forests of South America, very little is known about their habits. Indeed sloths appear to have very few habits for they live in slow motion. Their movements along the branches are so slow that it is often said that a sloth may spend all its life on one tree. They eat, sleep, mate, give birth and nurse their young upside down, although they do not hang from branches all the time, as they will sit in the fork of a tree. They sleep with the head on the chest between the arms, looking very inconspicuous.

Sloths occasionally come to the ground, presumably to reach another tree when they cannot travel overhead by branches and creepers. They are just able to stand on their feet but they cannot walk on them. They move by sprawling on their bellies and dragging themselves forward with their hands. They can, however, swim well.

Despite their sluggish habits sloths can defend themselves well by slashing with their claws and by biting. It is often suggested that this is sufficient defence against their main enemies, jaguars and ocelots, but it is difficult to imagine a nimble cat being unable to outmanoeuvre a sloth. The sloths may benefit more as regards their enemies, from their camouflage of green algae and their sluggish habits which often make them look like a mass of dead leaves.

△ *Just hanging around: a two-toed sloth picks its leisurely path through the tree canopy. All but a small fraction of a sloth's life is spent upside down; it eats, sleeps, mates and gives birth in this position, relying on formidable claws and a close resemblance to a bundle of leaves for defence.*
▽ *Earthbound ignominy: ill-adapted for anything but hanging, a three-toed sloth heaves and grovels its way to the next tree.*

Plant eaters

Sloths eat mainly leaves and shoots with some fruit, which they may hook towards their mouths with their claws. Their stomachs are complex like those of ruminants such as cattle and sheep.

One baby

A single baby is born at the beginning of the dry season after a gestation of 17—26 weeks. It immediately hooks itself into the fur of its mother's breast and stays there until old enough to leave. Sloths have lived for 11 years in captivity.

Strange lodger

If a crop of green algae is not enough, sloth's fur harbours another guest—moths rather like a clothes moth. Three species of pyralid moth have been found on the two species of sloth. They are about ⅓ in. long with flattened bodies and can run agilely through the dense mat of hair. This makes them difficult to collect, especially as the collector has to avoid the sloth's attempts to defend itself. No one has been able to find out why the moths live in sloths' hair. They do not feed there, nor have their eggs or caterpillars been found in the fur. The caterpillars may live a normal life on plants where the eggs were laid by the adults on forays from their host.

class	**Mammalia**
order	**Edentata**
family	**Bradypodidae**
genus & species	***Choloepus didactylus*** *two-toed sloth* ***Bradypus tridactylus*** *three-toed sloth, others*

▽ *Look, no hands: a young two-toed sloth* **Choloepus hoffmanni** *giving a clear illustration of the 'backward' growth of hair, necessary for adequate insulation and waterproofing of the animal.*

▽ *Individual sloth hair showing the one-celled algae, which make sloths look green.*

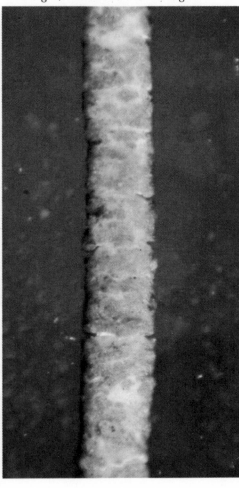

Sloth

◼ 2-toed
(Choloepus didactylus)

▨ 3-toed
(Bradypus tridactylus)

403

Pangolin

Pangolins have sometimes been called animated pine cones because the hair on their backs has been converted into large overlapping brown scales covering the head, back, tail and legs. The underside of the body is, however, soft and hairy. The pangolin's body is long, with a long tail.

Its snout is pointed, with a small mouth at the end and with toothless jaws. Its long tongue can be thrust out for nearly a foot. The pangolin has small eyes and hidden ears. Its legs are short and the five toes on each foot have stout claws used in digging. In Africa there are four species of pangolin, or scaly anteater as it is sometimes called, and three in southern Asia.

The large African pangolin of equatorial Africa is 5 ft or more long as is the giant pangolin. Other African species are the black-bellied or long-tailed pangolin and the small-scaled tree pangolin, from West Africa to Uganda, both 3 ft total length. The largest Asiatic species is the Indian pangolin, 3½ ft long. The Chinese pangolin, of Nepal, southern China, Hainan and Formosa, and the Malayan pangolin are both under 3 ft.

Ground dwellers and tree climbers

Most of these strange scaly beasts climb trees, using their sharp claws and their tail, either wrapping the tail around a branch and sometimes hanging by it, or using it as a support by pressing it against the trunk of a tree. The giant and Indian pangolins both live on the ground, however, the latter sometimes climbing trees for safety when chased. All pangolins are active mainly at night, the ground-living forms resting in burrows dug by other animals, the tree dwellers resting in cavities in the trunks. When on the ground they walk on the sides of their forefeet, or on their knuckles, with their long claws turned inwards. They will sometimes walk on their hindlegs with their body raised semi-erect, their tail raised above the ground as a counterpoise.

Hot meals

This attitude, with the tail supporting the erect or semi-erect body, is also used when a pangolin is tearing open a termites' nest with its long front claws and exploring the galleries of the nests with its long tongue. The tongue is sticky and is flicked in and out to carry the termites into the mouth. Ants are also eaten: adults, pupae, larvae, and eggs. The tough skin of the head protects the pangolin from attacks by soldier termites or the stings of ants. The nostrils and ear openings can be closed and the eyes are protected by thick lids. Ants crawling onto the body are shaken off, and those swallowed are soon ground by the thick muscular walls of the stomach and by the small pebbles that the pangolin swallows. Tree-climbing pangolins eat mainly tree ants. A pangolin drinks by rapidly darting its tongue out and in.

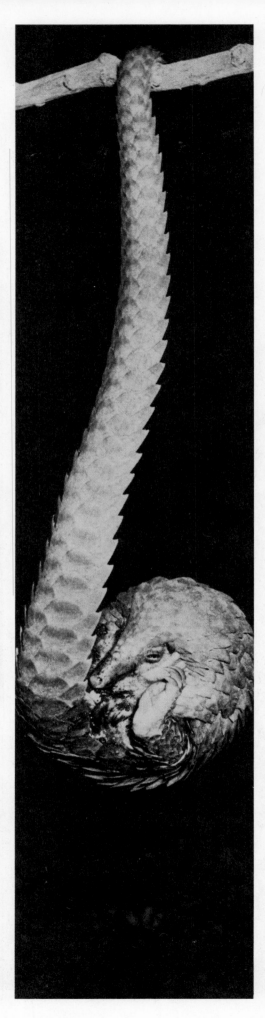

Pangolins do not usually survive long in captivity, a few weeks at most, and post mortem examinations have shown their digestive organs to be heavily parasitized. One lived over 4 years in the New York Zoological Park on finely ground raw beef, cooked cereal, evaporated milk, ant's eggs, with occasional raw egg, cod-liver oil and vitamin concentrate. But it seems likely that termites and ants are essential to them.

Babies ride pick-a-back

Very little is known about the breeding habits of pangolins since they fail to breed in captivity. They have one young, rarely two, in the wild, probably every year. The scales do not harden until the second day after birth. Later the baby rides on the mother clinging to her tail.

Ant-bathing

The main enemy of pangolins is probably man. Animals, such as leopards, sometimes examine them but are, it seems, put off by their scales. They are killed locally for their flesh and their scales are used for ornaments and charms, as well as for their supposed medicinal value. In Africa boys are sent into the burrow to put a rope round a pangolin's tail, to drag it out. Its defence is to roll up but even a light touch on a pangolin's body makes it snap its sharp-edged scales flat and this may act as a deterrent. Some pangolins, possibly all, can give off an obnoxious fluid from glands under their tail. They are said sometimes to hiss when molested.

There is a story that pangolins allow ants to crawl under their scales, then snap the scales down to kill them, afterwards eating the dead ants. The probable explanation is that the scales are snapped down because the observer touches the pangolin, or makes a movement that alarms it. That they do take an ant bath seems likely. There are local beliefs that a pangolin will lie in an ants' nest, allowing the insects to crawl over it, and under its scales onto the soft skin beneath. There are reports about a variety of animals taking ant baths. It is presumed they get satisfaction from the formic acid stimulating the skin. Cecil S Webb, an animal collector, was of the opinion that a pangolin's skin absorbed this acid and it was essential to the animal's health. He suggested this was one reason why they failed to survive in captivity.

An animal puzzle

Pangolin skins brought back from Africa and Asia were known to the Romans and also to the scientists of the 16th century and later. All were puzzled by them, as were the peoples in whose countries they lived. Arabs called the pangolin *abu-khirfa*, 'father of cattle', the Indians named it *bajur-kit*, 'jungle fish', the Chinese name was

◁ *It's easy when you have the equipment! A small-scaled pangolin hangs by its prehensile tail.*
▷△ *Small-scaled youngster grips to mother's tail while she is curled up asleep.*
▷ *Pangolins are quite widespread but not very numerous in any part of their range.*
▷▷ *The pangolin gets its name from its habit of rolling itself into a ball.*

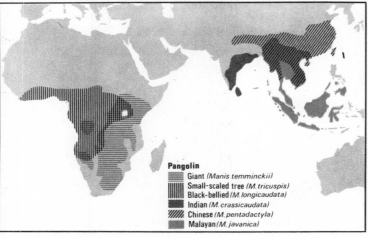

Pangolin
- Giant (*Manis temminckii*)
- Small-scaled tree (*M. tricuspis*)
- Black-bellied (*M. longicaudata*)
- Indian (*M. crassicaudata*)
- Chinese (*M. pentadactyla*)
- Malayan (*M. javanica*)

lungli, 'dragon carp', and the Romans called it an earth-crocodile. The name 'pangolin' is from the Malay *peng-goling*, the roller, from its habit of rolling into a ball. Pangolin skins puzzled the scholars of Europe until early 19th century when Baron Cuvier decided it was a mammal.

class	**Mammalia**
order	**Pholidota**
family	**Manidae**
genus & species	**Manis crassicaudata** Indian. **M. javanica** Malayan **M. longicaudata** black-bellied **M. pentadactyla** Chinese **M. temminckii** giant **M. tricuspis** small-scaled tree

◁ *A black-bellied pangolin illustrates its common description—'animated pine cone'.*
◁ ▽ *Ants swarm over the scales of a giant pangolin intent on eating all it can.*

▽ *A long elastic tongue protruded from the toothless mouth of a large African pangolin seeks out ants and termites on which it feeds.*

Jack rabbit

The jack rabbits of the western United States are hares belonging to the genus **Lepus** – they are close relatives of the brown hare, the varying hare and the snowshoe rabbit. The white-tailed jack rabbit, also known as the plains or prairie hare, has a brownish coat in the summer which changes to white in the winter. Only the 6in. black-tipped ears and 4in. white tail remain unchanged all the year round. This jack rabbit, which weighs up to 10 lb, lives in the prairies of the northwest, but to the south lives the smaller black-tailed or jackass hare. The latter name is derived from the 8in. black-tipped ears. The coat is sandy except for the black upper surface of the tail. It does not turn white in winter. This species lives in the

arid country from Oregon to Mexico and eastwards to Texas. There is also a small population in Florida which has come from imported jack rabbits, used in training greyhounds, that have gone wild.

The remaining jack rabbits, the two species of antelope or white-sided jack rabbits, live in restricted areas of Arizona and New Mexico.

Safety in bounding leaps

Like all hares, jack rabbits live on the surface of the ground and do not burrow. The exception is the white-tailed jack rabbit which in winter burrows under the snow for warmth and also gains protection against predators such as owls. Otherwise jack rabbits escape detection by crouching among the sparse vegetation of the prairies and semi-desert countryside. They lie up in shade during the day and come out in the evening. Each jack rabbit has several forms, hollows in the ground shaded and con-

Hare of the plain and prairie: the jack rabbit of the western United States has two obvious adaptations for grassland life – very long ears, useful for detecting predators at a distance, and long hind legs with which it runs up to 45 mph in a series of bounding leaps.

cealed by plants, within its home range. If flushed, jack rabbits will run extremely fast, sometimes reaching 45 mph in a series of 20ft springing bounds like animated rubber balls. Every so often they leap up 4 or 5 ft to clear the surrounding vegetation and look out for enemies.

Water from cacti

Jack rabbits feed mainly on grass and plants such as sagebrush or snakeweed, and often become serious pests where their numbers build up. To protect crops and to save the grazing for domestic stock, hunts are organised or poisoned bait put down. In the arid parts of their range, when the grass has dried up, jack rabbits survive on mes-

407

quite and cacti. They can get all the water they need from cacti providing they do not lose too much moisture in keeping cool. To eat a prickly cactus a jack rabbit carefully chews around a spiny area and pulls out the loosened section. Then it puts its head into the hole and eats the moist, fleshy pulp which it finds inside.

Born in the open

The length of the breeding season varies according to the range of the jack rabbit, being shorter in the north. At the onset of breeding jack rabbits indulge in the typical mad antics of hares. The males chase to and fro and fight each other. They rear up, sometimes growling, and batter each other with their forepaws. They also bite each other, tearing out tufts of fur or even flesh and occasionally violent kicks are delivered with the hindlegs. A carefully-aimed kick can wound the recipient severely; otherwise the fight continues until one of the combatants turns tail and flees.

The baby jack rabbits are born in open nests concealed by brush or grass and lined with fur which the female pulls from her body. The litters are usually of three or four young but there may be as few as one or as many as eight. The babies weigh 2—6 oz and can stand and walk a few steps immediately after birth, but they do not leave the nest for about 4 weeks.

Precarious heat balance

Large ears are a characteristic of desert animals, such as bat-eared and fennec foxes, and it is usually supposed that as well as improving the animal's hearing they act as radiators for keeping the body cool. There is, however, a drawback to this idea. If heat can be lost from the ears it can also be absorbed. The problem has now been resolved because it has been realised that a clear sky has a low radiant temperature and acts as a heat sink. In the semi-arid home of the black-tailed jack rabbit a clear, blue sky may have a temperature of 10—15°C/50—59°F to which heat can be radiated from the jack rabbit's ears that have a temperature of 38°C/100°F. Only a slight difference in temperature is needed for radiation to take place and the large difference between ears and sky allows efficient heat transfer.

Jack rabbits rely on radiation to keep them cool, for, as we have seen, they do not get enough water to be able to use evaporation as a means of cooling. In hot weather jack rabbits make use of every bit of shade and in their forms the ground temperature is lower than the air or body temperature and so acts as another heat sink.

The heat balance of a jack rabbit is, however, very precarious. On a hot day it is possible for two men easily to run down a jack rabbit. By continually flushing it and keeping it in the open the jack rabbit soon collapses from heat exhaustion and is soon ready for the pot!

class	**Mammalia**
order	**Lagomorpha**
family	**Leporidae**
genus & species	*Lepus californicus* *black-tailed jack rabbit* **L. townsendi** *white-tailed jack rabbit* *others*

◁▽ *On the look-out. White-tailed jack rabbit crouches by sparse vegetation of the prairies.*
▽ *Black-tailed portrait. Named jackass hare, after its 8in. black-tipped ears, this jack rabbit does not change to white in winter as does the white-tailed jack rabbit.*

Beaver

The beaver is the second largest rodent, exceeded in size only by the capybara. Stout-bodied, with a dark brown fur, it is up to $3\frac{1}{2}$ ft long including 1 ft of broad scaly tail, and it may weigh between 30 and 75 lb. Its muzzle is blunt, ears small, and it has five toes on each foot. Those on the front feet are strongly clawed, used for digging, manipulating food and carrying. The hind feet are webbed, with two split claws for grooming the fur and spreading waterproofing oil. The body oil, as well as the dense underfur and the heavy outer coat of guard hairs, not only act as waterproofing but also as insulation against the cold. When a beaver submerges, its nostrils and ears are closed by valves, and it can remain under-water for 15 minutes. The tail is used for steering and sometimes for propulsion through the water. It also forms a tripod with the hind legs when the beaver stands up to gnaw trees or when carrying, with the fore feet, mud or stones for building.

There are two species of beaver, both so alike in appearance and habits that we are fully justified in speaking merely of the beaver. The first, the European beaver, must at one time have been very abundant throughout Europe, even in England, where its bones may still be found. On the Continent of Europe it is still present in small numbers in Scandinavia, along rivers in European Russia, in the Elbe and Rhône valleys, and, where given protection, it shows signs of increasing numbers.

The Canadian beaver formerly enjoyed a wide range across the North American continent, from northern Canada south to beyond the US—Mexico border. Today, in severely depleted numbers, its range extends from Canada into some parts of the northern US.

Habits

Beavers live in loose colonies, each made up of a family unit of up to 12, including the parents, which mate for life. Their home may be in a burrow in a bank, with an underwater entrance or in a lodge in a 'beaver pond', a pool made by damming a river until it overflows. The lodge is built of sticks and mud, often against a clump of young trees, with underwater entrances, a central chamber which is above water level and a ventilating chimney connecting the chamber with the top of the lodge. Secondary dams are built upstream of the lodge, with usually one secondary dam downstream of the main dam. Young trees are felled, cut up and carried to the site, and, if necessary, canals are dug to float logs to the pond.

Intelligence of beavers

Many people are convinced that beavers are unusually intelligent, largely because their dams are such fine examples of engineering works. The structure of the

△ *Beaver in the Canadian autumn. Its tail makes a tripod with the back legs so it can sit up and gnaw tree tunks.*

▽ *A beaver lodge. It is made of sticks and mud, in a pond, which is made by the beavers damming a stream so it overflows.*

Beaver swimming. It can dive instantly if danger threatens, simply by depressing its rudder-like tail, here stretched out behind. When submerged its nostrils and ears are closed by valves and it can stay underwater for 15 minutes.

beaver brain, however, gives no indication of any greater mental capacity than is found in other rodents. Moreover, some of a beaver's actions which appear to be the result of a high order of reasoning can be shown to be due to instinct, the result of an inborn pattern of behaviour.

The lodge is a conical pile of branches and sticks 2–6 ft long, compacted with mud and stones, the upper half of which projects above the surface of the water. From an engineering standpoint it could hardly be improved. It has a central chamber just above water level, one or more escape tunnels leading from the chamber to below-water exits, well-insulated walls and a vertical chimney or ventilating shaft for regulating the temperature inside and to give air-conditioning. The evidence gained from dissecting a lodge suggests that it is built by laying sticks more or less horizontally to construct a pile, with an admixture of mud which stops short a foot or so from the top of the pile. Then the beavers chew their way in, to make the entrance tunnels and the central chamber. The absence of mud packing from the top of the pile means that spaces between the sticks serve for ventilation. In other words, there is no more intelligence required than any other rodent uses to dig in the ground.

The dams are text-book examples of engineering, and beaver dams give way no more frequently than do man-made dams.

One reason for this is that a beaver dam is resilient, subject to immediate repair, is under constant surveillance and is supported by subsidiary dams. All the actions used in its construction can, however, be shown to be the result of a succession of instinctive actions, just as are those that result in the building of a bird's nest.

It is often said that beavers not only show skill in felling trees but use intelligence, by dropping the trees so that they fall towards the nearest water. This is not the case. Moreover, beavers are not uncommonly killed by the trees they fell falling on them.

Beavers often do other stupid things. The classic example is of a small lake in New York that was created by an artificial barrier of stones and cement litter. This was occupied by a family of beavers who were seen to 'repair' the dam with branches and mud although it was fully effective without these. Moreover, although the level of the pond was, so far as could be seen, satisfactory for their needs, the beavers built a subsidiary dam upstream of the pond, the only result of which was to flood the adjacent land to no purpose.

Everything considered, the achievements of beavers are more a tribute to the effectiveness of evolution in developing inherited behaviour patterns than a sign of unusual intelligence. There is, however, one qualification to be made. Young beavers stay with the parents for 2 years. During that time

they must learn a great deal by following the example of the adults. It may be justifiable, therefore, to speak in terms of a cultural inheritance, and this alone would give an appearance of a greater intelligence.

Further evidence for the theory of innate behaviour can be added. Until a few years ago, beavers in the Rhone valley were hunted and they had long taken to burrowing in the river banks. Then they were protected by law, and shortly afterwards they began once more to build lodges and dams. A beaver may live for 20 years, but here they were reverting to a former pattern of behaviour after centuries of suppression due to persecution, using techniques they could not have learned. Only great intelligence, or a very strong instinct, could have brought about this behaviour.

Aspen and willow as food

Beavers eat bark, mainly of aspen and willow, from the smaller branches cut when building. Twigs and branches are stored around the base of the lodge. These have always been regarded as for the winter use of all members of the colony. Recent research has shown that the bulk of these are eaten by youngsters; older beavers live on their fat and eat little during winter.

Life history

Beavers, which are monogamous, mate in January to February. Gestation is 65–128 days and in April, May or early June two to eight kits, sometimes more, are born, with a coat of soft fur and eyes open. At birth each weighs about 1 lb and is 15 in. long including 3½ in. of tail. At one month, each will find and eat solid food, but weaning is not complete until 6 weeks old. Young remain with parents for 2 years, becoming sexually mature at 2—3 years.

Enemies

As with all rodents, beavers are preyed upon by any carnivores of approximately their own weight or more. In this instance the enemies include wolverine, lynx, coyote, wolf, bobcat, puma and bear. A beaver's alarm signal when a predator is in sight is to bring the tail over the back then smack it down with such force on the water that the sound can be heard up to ½ mile away.

Decline of the European beaver

Beavers were once common in Switzerland, as shown by the place names Biberach, Bibersee, Biberstein and Bibermukle (biber is German for beaver). Their extermination was due partly to their valuable fur, but more particularly to slaughter for their glandular secretion used to mark their territories. This, known as castoreum, enjoyed a vogue as a cure-all in the 16th and 17th centuries, with a resulting insensate slaughter of the luckless animals. Analysis has shown castoreum to contain salicylic acid, one of the ingredients of aspirin.

The former presence of beavers in the British Isles, too, is commemorated in many place-names, such as Beverley, Beverege, Bevercotes, Beverstone and Beversbrook in England, and Losleathan in Scotland and Llostlydan in Wales, both meaning broadtail. The animal seems to have still been plentiful in Britain up to the mid-16th century. The value of its fur can be gauged from prices fixed by the Welsh prince, Howel Dha, in the 10th century, at 120 pence a skin as compared with 24 pence for a marten pelt and 18 pence for otter, wolf and fox. This undoubtedly led to the animal's extermination, and in France to its almost complete elimination except in the Rhône Valley. In the 16th century, Henry IV of France, impressed by the demand for beaver pelts for hats, trimmings, fur linings and leather for shoes, sought to increase the economic strength of his country by sending men to Nova Scotia and New-

foundland. In due course the British gained this resource, largely through the Hudson Bay Company, and it was the search for more and more furs, particularly beaver, that led to Canada being opened up.

Profit versus protection

In America, with the arrival of the early settlers, the beaver was recognised as a valuable source of both meat and fur. Trade was soon established with the Indians, who wisely killed only mature animals, so that their hunting could have done little to impair the number of beavers. The brisk fur trade with England that sprang up roused the old spirit of avarice, and before long white trappers joined their efforts with those of the Indians—and killed indiscriminately.

In about 150 years the beaver had been exterminated in the coastal regions of the Eastern States, and seriously reduced elsewhere. The story is, however, patchy, for in some spots their numbers remained relatively unimpaired. Also, beavers in deep rivers were less easy to catch than those in, say, mountain streams. As the North American continent was more and more opened up, so the trade continued unabated, with similar results to those seen in the Eastern States, but on a wider scale.

The Hudson Bay Trading Company was formed in 1670 and such was the growth of its beaver trade that between 1853 and 1877 it marketed nearly 3 million beaver pelts. This steady drain brought about a serious depletion which has been rectified to some extent by official conservation measures.

Beavers were not always killed for profit. At times the animal became a nuisance,

either through its inroads on timber, in settled areas, or when it took a liking to the stalks of corn. In places, too, it became a menace to river banks. Nevertheless, it was early recognised that only harm could result from its total elimination. As early as 1866, it became protected by law in the State of Maine, with the result that by the early years of the present century it had increased so much in numbers that some control had to be imposed to protect plantations.

Since that time, both in the USA and in Canada, with increasing speed to the present day, there have been many efforts made at conservation, either by individual landowners, by public bodies, or by Government action, State or Federal. In some cases the reason behind it has been no more than a desire to preserve an interesting animal. In others it is due to a realisation that the work of beavers contributes to the conservation of water in the land and to the preservation of trout streams. It has been found that it is possible, by the intelligent use of closed seasons, limiting the numbers of pelts taken and having them taken only under licence, not only to bring about increased beaver populations locally, but to derive revenue from the surplus. Consequently, there has been considerable reintroductions to re-stock areas where they had been exterminated.

The conservation of water may be summed up in the following quotation from an American water company's report: 'On almost all the mountain streams they (the beaver) should be protected and encouraged. A series of beaver ponds and dams along the headwaters of a mountain stream would hold back large quantities of mountain water during the dangerous flood season and equalise the flow of the streams so that during the driest seasons the water supply would be greatly increased in the valleys. Beaver-ponds not only hold water but distribute it through the surrounding soil for long distances, acting as enormous sponges as well as reservoirs. A series of ponds also increases the fishing capacity and furnishes a safe retreat for the smaller trout and protection from their enemies.'

The beaver was on the way to extinction in Europe and America in the 19th century, but has since been rigorously protected and the populations are increasing. They have been so successful in some places that control is necessary.

Beaver
Castor fiber, Europe
Castor canadensis

Fear and flight having failed to rescue this beaver, caught away from the relative safety of its pool, it must now turn and fight for its life against the hungry hunting coyote.

class	**Mammalia**
order	**Rodentia**
family	**Castoridae**
genus & species	***Castor fiber*** *European beaver* ***C. canadensis*** *Canadian beaver*

411

Deer mouse

Deer mice are American, very similar to the European long-tailed fieldmouse, both in appearance and in habits, but the two belong to different families. There are about 20 species, varying in colour from sandy or grey to dark brown. Some are almost white and others nearly black, but in general those living in woods are darkish, and those living in open or arid country are pale. The underparts and feet are white, hence the alternative name of white-footed mouse. A deer mouse measures 5—15 in. from nose to tip of tail, the tail varying from 1½—8 in. in different species.

They are found over most of North America, from Alaska and Labrador southwards, and one species extends into South America, reaching the extreme north of Colombia. They inhabit many kinds of country from swamps and forests to arid, almost desert, country, but each species usually has only a limited habitat and consequently is found only in a relatively small part of the total deer mouse range.

Meal among the toadstools: a deer mouse strikes a Disneylike pose while taking a snack.

Overlapping territories

Deer mice are nocturnal, coming out during the day only if they are very hungry, or if there is a cover of snow that allows them to forage under its shelter. During the evening they can be heard trilling or buzzing, a noise quite unlike the squeaks of other mice, and in some parts of the United States this has led to their being called vesper mice. They also drum with the front feet when excited.

Each deer mouse has a home range which it covers regularly in search of food. The extent of the range varies considerably and depends on the amount of food available. In the grasslands of south Michigan the average size of the ranges of male deer mice is ⅔ of an acre, while those of the females are slightly smaller. The home range of a mammal is not strictly comparable with the territory of a bird. Only a few birds keep a territory all through the year, but more important, a mammal does not defend its range so vigorously. The borders of neighbouring ranges overlap, sometimes considerably, and the ranges of two females may be almost identical, but it is only the inner parts of the territory around the nest that will be defended vigorously.

Within its range, a deer mouse may have several refuges in abandoned burrows or birds' nests, under logs or in crevices. Sometimes a deer mouse will come indoors and make its nest in an attic or storage room. Each nest is used for a short time, being abandoned when it becomes soiled, for deer mice limit hygiene to cleaning their fur.

Burrows with a bolt hole

The nest is an untidy mass of grass and leaves, lined with moss, fine grass or feathers. Sometimes the deer mice make their own burrows. The Oldfield mouse, a species of deer mouse living in Alabama and Florida, makes a burrow leading down to a nest which is 1 ft underground. Then from the other side another burrow leads up again but stops just short of the surface. This presumably serves as a bolt hole in case a snake or other narrow-bodied enemy finds its way in. A traditional way of catching these mice is to push a pliable switch or wand down the hole, twiddle it about until it can be pushed up the escape burrow, and catch the mouse as it breaks out.

Are they a pest?

Seeds and berries are the main food of deer mice but they also eat many insects such as beetles, moths and grasshoppers, which are chased and bitten or beaten to death. Insect larvae, snails and slugs are devoured, and deer mice also eat carrion such as dead birds and mammals, and they will gnaw cast antlers.

Deer mice are something of a problem in plantations or on farms, where they eat seeds of new-sown crops, which they smell out and dig up. But even when abundant, they are not as much of a pest as meadow voles and other small rodents. To even the score, deer mice are helpful because they eat chafer grubs that damage the roots of young trees.

Hanging on to mother

In spring the males search for mates, perhaps finding females whose ranges overlap theirs. At first their advances are repulsed but the males eventually move into the females' nests, staying there for a few days only but sometimes, it is thought, forming permanent pairs.

The female gives birth to a litter of 1—9 young after 3 or 4 weeks. At birth the young mice are blind, deaf, and apart from their whiskers, naked. They hang firmly to their mother's teats and she can walk around with them trailing behind. If the nest is disturbed she will drag them in this manner to a new site. Any baby that does fall off is picked up and carried in its mother's mouth.

Litters of deer mice can be found from spring to autumn but more are born in spring and autumn than during the summer, and if the winter is mild, breeding will continue through it. Females begin breeding at 7 weeks, only a few weeks after leaving their mothers, and have up to 4 litters a year.

Many nocturnal enemies

Most deer mice live less than two years, and many never reach maturity but provide food for the many predators that hunt at night. Foxes, weasels, coyotes, bobcats, owls and snakes, all feed on deer mice, and even shrews will occasionally eat them.

Racial 'segregation'

Although similar, the 20 different deer mice can easily be told apart by the specialist in classification, and, one must presume, by the mice themselves. Otherwise they would mix and interbreed and their differences would disappear, especially when different kinds live in the same habitat. Experiments by an American scientist using a Rocky Mountain deer mouse and a Florida deer mouse, which are closely related, showed how the deer mice are segregated.

Special cages were made, each with two side compartments. In preparation for the experiment a Rocky Mountain mouse was put in one compartment and a Florida mouse in the other, and this was repeated for all the cages. After these had remained long enough to impart their smell to the compartments they were taken out. Now, into each cage were put either a Rocky Mountain mouse or a Florida mouse, and these naturally made full use of the available space, including wandering into each compartment. By timing the period each mouse spent in each of the two side compartments of its cage the scientist found that in all cases the test mouse was very obviously drawn to that compartment which carried the smell of its own species. This almost certainly is how mice of the same species, even when sharing a habitat with another species, would be drawn together to breed, for it was noticed that males reacted particularly strongly to the smell of females of their own species on heat. So although it may sometimes appear that there are mixed populations of deer mice, the different species are really living separately.

There was, however, one difference between the Rocky Mountain mice and the Florida mice: the latter were much more likely to spend time in compartments smelling of Rocky Mountain mice. The reason for this seems to be that in Florida there is only one species of deer mouse, and discrimination is no longer necessary; but in the west there are many species and if their strains are to be kept pure, they must be able to distinguish between their own fellows and those of closely related species.

class	**Mammalia**
order	**Rodentia**
family	**Cricetidae**
genus & species	*Peromyscus maniculatus* *others*

Deer mouse cleaning and drying its fur—its only hygienic habit.

Pocket gopher

The name of these small hamster-like animals is derived from the two external furlined cheek pouches, which run from face to shoulder. They are used for carrying food and are turned inside out when they need cleaning.

*There are 30 species of pocket gophers which vary considerably in size, with a body length from 3½ to 13 in. and tails from 1½ to 5½ in. The coat is usually thick and smooth, lighter and thinner on the underside. Pocket gophers living in hot lowland areas have shorter coarser fur. The fur colour varies from almost black through all shades of brown to off-white. Albinos are not uncommon. **Macrogeomys** and **Zygogeomys** have characteristic white patches.*

The body is adapted for burrowing. The skull is large and angular, the body thickset and tapering towards the tail. Ears and eyes are small, the latter being kept moist with a thick fluid to keep the eyeball free from dirt. The legs are short and powerful, especially the forelegs, which have long digging claws. The tail is almost naked and is very sensitive to touch. By arching the tail to raise the tip just off the ground, a pocket gopher can feel its way as it moves rapidly backwards in its burrow.

All pocket gophers have long curving upper incisors, behind which the lips close to prevent earth entering the mouth while they are burrowing.

Peculiar to North America, pocket gophers are found from western Canada south to Panama. They do not travel far and are found in localised areas, often restricted to valleys by mountain barriers.

The solitary burrower

These solitary rodents spend almost their entire life underground, only very occasionally coming to the surface to collect food. Each gopher lives within its own system of burrows and they only come together at mating times. Young pocket gophers can sometimes be found above ground after leaving their parents, and in drought or

after floods adult pocket gophers may be driven out to look for new homes.

The individual burrows are often extensive and are marked by fan shaped mounds of earth around the entrances. These are carefully blocked with earth as protection against predators and to maintain suitable temperature and humidity. There are two types of tunnels: long, shallow ones, used mainly for getting food, and deep ones, used for shelter, with separate chambers for food storage, nesting and latrines. A great assortment of other animals use inhabited and abandoned gopher burrows.

Pocket gophers dig with their strong foreclaws, the curved incisors being used for loosening hard earth and rocks. The incisors are growing continually so replacing the worn surfaces. They may grow as much as 20 in. in one year.

Pocket gophers do not hibernate but may remain relatively inactive for long periods. Evidence of their winter activity is strikingly apparent when the snows melt in high pastures, revealing gopher burrows within the snow lined with earth, and left behind as a mass of criss-crossing 'cores' showing that the animals have burrowed at several levels. The tunnels are up to 40 ft long and 2–3 in. diameter.

Underground vegetarian

The staple diet of pocket gophers is tubers, bulbs and roots of plants which can be found and eaten in the security of the burrow. Occasionally at night, or on overcast days, pocket gophers surface in search of food, but more often plants are seen disappearing in jerks as, from the safety of its burrow, a pocket gopher pulls them down. In agricultural regions, crops often suffer badly as gophers favour sweet-potatoes, sugar cane, peas and fruit. Gophers never seem to drink, probably getting enough moisture from their plant food.

Little is known about the breeding and courtship of gophers, but if the soil and food conditions are suitable their numbers increase rapidly. A female may have one or more litters a year and the number of offspring varies considerably from 2 to 11. The newborn young, weighing about $\frac{1}{12}$ oz, are blind and almost hairless. In most species they leave their mother at about 2 months to make their own burrow network. They are sexually mature within 3 months.

Strong foreclaws (left) dig burrows, marked by fan-shaped mounds of earth at entrance (above).

Safe underground

The best protection a pocket gopher has against its enemies is its underground way of life, but in fights with its own kind it is protected by the loose skin and thick hair around the head. Predators, such as coyotes, badgers and skunks, sometimes succeed in digging pocket gophers out and if they have to come above ground for any length of time owls and hawks make short work of them. Athough snakes and weasels hunt pocket gophers down their burrows, man is by far their worst enemy.

Pocket gophers can be very destructive, eating crops, burrowing through dykes and contributing to soil erosion. But on the credit side they do sterling work improving the soil by loosening, aerating and mixing it with organic matter. They also conserve water since, after a heavy snowfall, the melted water sinks deep into the earth through the maze of gopher tunnels instead of flowing straight into the nearest stream.

All manner of snares, traps, sling shots and spears are used to eliminate the pocket gophers and in Mexico the *tucero*, whose official job is to hunt pocket gophers, is a respected member of the village society.

Slim, tapering bodies

To allow manoeuvrability in tunnels a tapering body is essential, and burrowing animals generally have narrow hips. On the other hand, broad hips are an asset in giving birth. In virgin pocket gophers the pelvis is very narrow, with fused pelvic bones as in other mammals, leaving too small a gap for the passage of offspring during birth. Examination after birth shows, however, an enlarged opening which just allows an easy birth. Much of the bone of the pelvic region had been dissolved away through the action of hormones secreted during pregnancy.

class	**Mammalia**
order	**Rodentia**
family	**Geomyidae**
genera	*Geomys, Thomomys Pappogeomys, Cratogeomys Orthogeomys, Heterogeomys Macrogeomys, Zygogeomys*

Porcupine

The tree porcupines of North and South America are very different from the porcupines of the Old World. To begin with, they live mainly in trees and their hindfeet are adapted for climbing. Some species also have a prehensile tail. The best known, the Canadian or North American porcupine, is up to 3½ ft long, of which 1 ft is tail, and has an average weight of 15 lb although large males may weigh up to 40 lb. It is heavy and clumsily built with a small head, short legs and a short, stout, spiny tail. The hindfoot has a well-developed great toe and very long, powerful claws to help the animal climb. The long fur on the upper parts is brownish-black, sprinkled with long white hairs that conceal the short, barbed spines, which are yellowish-white tipped with black.

The South American tree porcupines, of which the Brazilian tree porcupine is typical, differ from the North American species in having a long, prehensile tail, the tip of which is hairless and by having only four toes on the hindfeet with a broad fleshy pad, opposable to the toes, used rather like a thumb in gripping branches when the animal is climbing. It is of lighter build with short, closely set spines, sometimes concealed by long hairs.

The Canadian porcupine inhabits most of the timbered areas of Alaska, Canada and the United States (except the south-eastern quarter), south to the extreme north of Mexico. South American porcupines extend from Mexico through Central America to Colombia, Venezuela, Brazil, Bolivia, Peru and Ecuador in South America.

△ Long fur conceals the porcupine's spines.
▽ North American porcupine revealing its arsenal of over 20 000 sharp-tipped quills.

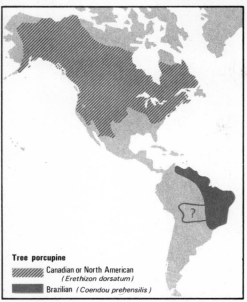

Tree porcupine

▨ Canadian or North American
(*Erethizon dorsatum*)

▰ Brazilian (*Coendou prehensilis*)

◁ *Picking a precarious path, a South American porcupine* Coendou *sp. seeks its typically rodent diet of bark, stems and leaves.*

No hibernation

All the tree porcupines live in wooded areas, the North American species preferring woods of conifers, junipers and poplars. Although clumsily built they can climb well and they will also swim. They lie up during the day among rocks or in hollow trees and feed mainly at dusk and at dawn. They are usually solitary but occasionally several Canadian tree porcupines may shelter together in the same den, especially in winter. They do not hibernate but they take to dens during bad weather.

Salt addicts

The Canadian tree porcupine varies its food with the seasons. In spring it eats the flowers and catkins of the willow, maple and poplar. Later it turns to the new leaves of aspen and larch. In summer it feeds more on herbaceous plants and in winter on evergreens like the hemlock and pine. Its principal food in winter, however, is bark and the porcupines do much damage by ring-barking trees. The young red firs of the Sierra Nevada in California are occasionally destroyed by tree porcupines. When the weather is bad and the snow deep an animal may live in one tree and not leave it until all the bark above the snow-line has been stripped. Tree porcupines also have a strong liking for sweet corn and a few of these animals can completely ravage a field of it.

A more peculiar taste is the porcupine's craving for salt. Handles of farm implements which have been touched by hands moistened with sweat, leaving a trace of salt, will be gnawed. So will gloves, boots, and saddles; even the steering wheel of a car has been gnawed away. The porcupine will also gnaw bones and antlers dropped by deer. But its crowning achievement is to gnaw glass bottles thrown away by campers, presumably for the salt in the glass.

The South American tree porcupines also eat the bark and leaves of trees and tender stems but in addition they eat fruit such as bananas, and occasionally corn.

Well-developed babies

The Canadian tree porcupines mate in the fall or early winter. During courtship the male rubs noses with the female and often urinates over her. Generally a single young is born after a gestation period of 210–217 days. The young are very well-developed at birth; their eyes are open and they are born with long black hair and short soft quills. They weigh about 20 oz and can climb trees when 2 days old. They are weaned in 10 days, and become sexually mature in their second year.

Little is known of the breeding habits of the South American tree porcupines. There is usually a single young at a birth, born from February to May. The young of the Brazilian tree porcupine are comparatively large at birth and are covered with long, reddish hair. Their backs are covered with short spines, which are flexible at birth.

Few natural enemies

Few animals prey on the porcupine because of its spines, but the wolverine, puma and fisher marten will attack the North American species. A tree porcupine is said never to attack an enemy. If cornered, however, it will erect its quills and turn its back on its adversary, striking out repeatedly with its tail. A porcupine does not shoot its quills but they are so lightly attached that when they enter the skin of the enemy they become detached from the porcupine.

Skulls identify species

The crested porcupine is the best known species in the Old World family Hystricidae. Not all the porcupines in that family have such prominent quills as the crested porcupine. One *Trichys lipura* living in Borneo, for example, lacks true quills. It has only short, flat, weak spines and its long tail has a brush of bristles on the end. At first sight it appears not to be a porcupine at all. The same thing can be said of some of the family Erethizontidae. Since the crested and the Canadian porcupines look so alike, the question arises: What is the essential difference between the Old World porcupines and the New World porcupines? The fact that they are widely separated geographically is not important. Both families agree in having species that show a varying tendency to grow quills among the bristly coat, and both families contain a diversity of species. Therefore, those who classify these rodents have to look for something more stable upon which to separate them. They find this in the skull. Any Old World porcupine, whatever it may have in the way of quills, has a very rounded skull which has quite obviously a different shape from that of the New World porcupines.

class	**Mammalia**
order	**Rodentia**
family	**Erethizontidae**
genera & species	*Erethizon dorsatum* Canadian or North American porcupine *Coendou prehensilis* Brazilian tree porcupine, others

Black bear

There are five species of black bear, each placed in a separate genus. All are smaller than the brown bears, and all are sufficiently similar for one of them, the one most studied, to serve as a type for the other four. This is the American black bear which originally inhabited practically all the wooded areas of North America from Central Mexico northwards. Its numbers are much reduced now and it has been eliminated from much of its former range, but in national parks its numbers are increasing and elsewhere it survives close to human settlement. Up to 5 ft long with a 4½ in. tail, and weighing 200–500 lb, it has shorter fur, shorter claws and shorter hind feet than the brown bears. The species also shows a number of colour phases: black, chocolate brown, cinnamon brown, blue-black and white with buff on the head and in the middle of the back. This last is most common in British Columbia, where it has been known as Kermode's bear. These different colour phases may occur in the same litter.

△ *Twin cubs being escorted by their mother. They stay with her until at least 6 months old.*

Friendly habits

Black bears are good tree climbers, powerful, quick to react, harmless to people except when provoked, cornered or injured—or through sheer friendliness. In national parks, where they are familiar with human beings and come begging food, visitors to the parks must keep to the protection of cars to avoid inadvertent injury from the bears' claws. Black bears are solitary except during the breeding season, the two partners separating after mating, to wander far in search of food. The American black bear sleeps through the winter—not hibernation in the usual sense—after laying in fat by heavy autumn feeding. It does not feed during the winter although it may leave its den, a hollow tree or similar shelter, for brief excursions during mild spells. When startled, the adult gives a 'woof', otherwise it is silent. The cubs, when distressed, utter shrill howls.

Mixed diet

Insects, berries and fruits, eggs and young of ground-nesting birds, rodents and carrion form its main foods, but young of deer and pronghorn are killed and eaten. Porcupines are killed, the bear flipping them over with its paw and attacking the soft under-belly, often to its own detriment from the quills. Black bears have been found dead with quills embedded in the mouth. Sometimes a black bear may turn cattle-killer.

Enemies

Old or sickly adults are occasionally killed by pumas and wintering bears may be attacked by wolves.

Life history

The breeding month is June and the gestation period is 100 to 210 days. Usually there are two or three cubs in a litter, exceptionally four, rarely five, born in January and February. At birth the 8 in., 9–12 oz cubs are blind, toothless and naked except for scanty dark hair. The mother continues to sleep for two months after the birth, having roused herself sufficiently to bite through the umbilical cords. The cubs alternately suck and sleep during these two months. They stay with the mother for at least six months, and she mates only every other year.

The original Teddy Bear

In 1902, Theodore (Teddy) Roosevelt, who was a keen naturalist as well as President of the United States, captured a black bear cub on a hunting trip, which he adopted as a pet. Morris Michton, a Brooklyn doll manufacturer, used this bear as model for the first Teddy Bear, so named with the President's permission. The popularity of the Teddy Bear as a toy was immediate and world-wide. The black bear, as already stated, is such a favourite in American national parks that they take liberties with visitors. In European zoos a prime favourite with visitors is the Himalayan black bear. Such general favouritism owes much to the human-like qualities of the bears.

We tend to favour in animals, qualities which reflect our own, as with birds that talk or animals that stand erect such as penguins, owls and bears. In man the bipedal stance is habitual; in bears it is but occasional, the usual way of walking being on all-fours. That does not invalidate the comparison, and the effect of the bears' ability to stand erect at times is reinforced by the way they will sit upright, as if on a chair, and also by the characteristic way a bear will wave a fore-paw (or hand) when soliciting food. Another trait which enables us to see ourselves in bears is their way of lying prone, on their backs.

Bears also appear to be intelligent. Whether they are more intelligent than their near relatives, the cats and dogs, has never been adequately tested. At least we know that the cubs stay with the mother for six months, often longer, and some may stay with her until her next cubs are born. A long period of parental care allows for learning by example and a longer period for experience with security. And if bears are by nature solitary they can, if circumstances compel them, as in bear-pits in zoos, live together with little discord, showing they are, like us, fundamentally friendly.

Yet in spite of the comparisons that can be drawn between bears and ourselves, and in spite of our fondness for Teddy Bears, the fact remains that the American black bear, like all other bears, has long been a target for the hunter's gun—and not only the hunter's. In 1953, 700 black bears were killed in British Columbia to provide bearskins, the ceremonial headwear, for the Brigade of Guards, for the coronation of Queen Elizabeth II. An American writer drily remarked: 'Fortunately for the black bear Great Britain's coronations are infrequent . . .'

class	**Mammalia**
order	**Carnivora**
family	**Ursidae**
genus & species	***Euarctos americanus*** *American black bear*

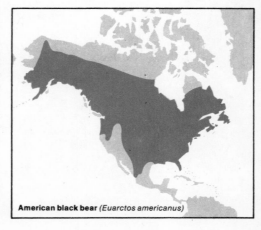

American black bear (*Euarctos americanus*)

418

Returning to their earth after a hunt: North American red fox and two cubs. Night hunting is a way of teaching the cubs how to fend for themselves.

Red fox

It is usually assumed that, but for its careful preservation by the various 'hunts', the red fox would have become extinct long ago in the British Isles except in the wildest and most remote corners. For centuries it has been persecuted outside the hunt areas because of its alleged poultry-killing habits and even today the killing of a fox is still looked on with approval. Yet, in spite of all this, the fox has survived and at times is unusually numerous.

The head and body of the red fox measure just over 2 ft with a 16in. tail, but there are records which greatly exceed these measurements, especially in Scotland. A well grown fox stands only about 14 in. at the shoulder. The dog-fox and vixen are alike except that the vixen is slightly smaller and has a narrower face as she lacks the cheek ruffs of the male. The fur is sandy russet or red-brown above and white on the underparts. The backs of the ears are black, as are the fronts of the legs, but these may be brown, and can change from one colour to the other with the moult. The colours may vary, however, not only between one individual and another, but in the same individual from season to season. The foxes (Tods) of Scotland, although of the same species, usually have greyer fur than the English fox. When fully haired the tail is known as a brush. The tip (or tag) is white but may be black. Weights vary considerably but on average a dog-fox weighs 15 lb, a vixen 12 lb.

The sharp-pointed muzzle, the erect ears and quick movements of the eye with its elliptical pupil combine to give the fox an alert, cunning appearance, so many stories
of its astuteness have been invented in the past. At the moult, in July and August, foxes lose their characteristic appearance and look thin-bodied, long-legged and slender of tail.*

*The red fox ranges over Europe and over Asia as far south as central India, as well as northwest Africa. It is found throughout the British Isles, except for Orkney, Shetland and all Scottish islands, but not Skye. In central Asia it lives up to 14 000 ft above sea-level. The North American red fox **Vulpes fulva** is very like the Old World red fox in build and habits. There are several mutants, the cross fox is red with a black band across the shoulders, and the silver fox has a lustrous black coat with white tips to the guard hairs.*

Tree-climbing foxes

The red fox's traditional cunning is a reflection of its adaptability. It prefers wooded or bushy areas but is found in a variety of habitats. Many foxes today are even found living in urban areas or even near large towns, where they probably live off rats and mice and scavenge in dustbins. Although the fox lives mainly on the ground there are many instances of it climbing trees. Usually this occurs when a tree is leaning or when there is a trailing bough that has broken and is hanging down to the ground, up which the fox can clamber. There is one recorded instance, however, of a fox having its sleeping nest at the top of a bole of an elm, 14 ft from the ground, with no branches between it and the ground. Foxes are largely nocturnal, but they can often be seen during the day. Except at the breeding season the dog-fox and vixen lead solitary lives. Most of the day is spent in an 'earth' which is more of a cavity in the ground than a burrow. They may make this themselves or use a badger's set or rabbit burrow.

Foxes use a great variety of calls, the most familiar being the barking of both the dog-fox and the vixen in winter and the screaming of the vixen, generally during the breeding season. It has now been established that, contrary to common opinion, the dog-fox may also scream sometimes.

Poultry killer?

A great deal has been written about the fox prowling round farms looking for an opportunity to kill an unguarded fowl. Certainly foxes will take poultry and they will take lambs, but these habits tend to be local. A vixen that has taken to killing poultry will teach her cubs to do the same. But not all foxes are habitual poultry stealers and there have been instances of foxes repeatedly visiting poultry farms or private gardens containing a few poultry and never molesting them.

More solid information about their food comes from a Ministry of Agriculture investigation of the stomach contents of dead foxes. This showed that, now that rabbits are scarce, the chief items of food are rats, mice and bank voles. Hedgehogs, squirrels, voles, frogs, even snails and beetles are, however, also eaten, as well as a great deal of vegetable matter. Birds such as partridges and pheasants will also be taken. A fox will soon discover offal or carrion, even if buried 2 ft in the earth. Foxes also visit dustbins and a feature of the many foxes now living in towns is that they have turned scavenger. Railway marshalling yards also have their foxes, probably feeding on food thrown out from restaurant cars or on rats living on this food.

Teaching the cubs

Mating takes place from late December to February. The gestation period is 51–52 days. About April the vixen produces her single litter for the year, usually of four cubs. They are blind until 10 days old, and remain in the earth until nearly a month old, the vixen staying close beside them, while the dog plays a large part in supplying the food. When about a month old the cubs come out in the evening and can be seen playing as a group with the parents outside the earth. This continues for several weeks.

After the cubs are weaned it has been noted, in semi-captivity, that the dog-fox continues to bring food for them and the cubs will take the food from his mouth themselves, or the vixen may take it and the cubs take it from her mouth. The cubs have to jump up to reach the parent's mouth and all the time the parent is moving its head, from side to side or up and down. In this way the cubs are being exercised so developing their limbs, and also learning to co-ordinate movements and senses. During this time the dog plays a great deal with them, more so than the vixen.

Later the vixen takes them hunting at night, so they learn from her example how to fend for themselves. The cubs leave their parents when about 2 months old, reach adult size 6 months after birth, and become sexually mature in their first winter.

'Charming'

Foxes are credited with resorting to a particular stratagem, called 'charming', to attain their end. A story is usually told of a fox which, seeing a party of rabbits feeding and knowing that they will bolt to their holes on its approach, starts rolling about at a safe distance to attract their attention. Then like a kitten it begins chasing its tail, while the rabbits gaze, apparently spell-bound, at the performance. The fox continues without a pause, as though oblivious to the presence of spectators, but all the time it is contriving to get nearer, until a sudden straightening of the body enables it to grab the nearest rabbit in its jaws.

There are too many authentic accounts of foxes charming to leave much doubt about the matter. From these, a more likely explanation evolves: foxes are naturally playful. Like some other mammals they will, without obvious cause, suddenly behave as if they have taken leave of their senses, bounding about, bucking, somersaulting, and so on. Rabbits and birds on seeing these antics are drawn to watch out of curiosity. If the fox is hungry then the spectators suffer. It is possible that a fox playing in this way and finding birds and rabbits attracted to it, might use this tactic again, deliberately. Such learning by experience would not be beyond a fox's intelligence, but there is much to be said for the view that charming, as such, is not primarily a deliberate stratagem.

class	**Mammalia**
order	**Carnivora**
family	**Canidae**
genus & species	*Vulpes vulpes* *European red fox*

▷ *With ears pricked, wary eyes glinting from its mask, the red fox with its magnificent brush is a very wily, sometimes vicious, and yet most handsome animal.*

420

Giant Panda

*This black and white bear-like carnivore has leapt from obscurity to worldwide fame in less than a century. Also called the panda and, by the Chinese, **beishung**, the white bear, it was first made known to the western world in 1869, by the French missionary, Père David.*

The giant panda is stockily built, with a 6 ft long body and a mere stump of a tail and weighs 300 lb. Its thick, dense fur is white except for the black legs and ears, black round the eyes and on the shoulders. There are 5 clawed toes on each foot and each forefoot has a small pad which acts as a thumb for grasping. The cheek teeth are broad and the skull is deep with prominent ridges for the attachment of strong muscles needed in chewing fibrous shoots. It lives in the cold damp bamboo forests on the hillsides of eastern Tibet and Szechwan in southwest China.

Habits unknown . . .

Giant pandas are solitary animals except in the breeding season. They live mainly on the ground but will climb trees when pursued by dogs. They are active all the year. Little more is known of the habits in the wild of this secretive animal which lives in inaccessible country. When live giant pandas were first taken to zoos it was thought they lived solely on bamboo shoots. Later it was learned that during the 10—12 hours a day they spend feeding they eat other plants, such as grasses, gentians, irises and crocuses, and also some animal food. This last includes small rodents, small birds and fishes flipped out of water with their paws.

Breeding unknown . . .

Little is known about the giant panda's breeding habits in spite of attempts to induce a mating between An-an, the male giant panda belonging to the Moscow zoo, and Chi-chi, the female in the London zoo. In 1966 Chi-chi was taken to Moscow but no mating took place, and An-an was brought to London in 1968 with no more success. It is believed that giant pandas mate in spring, and that probably one or two cubs are born in the following January, each cub weighing 3 lb at birth. Several cubs have been born in Chinese zoos. On September 9, 1963, a male cub Ming-ming was born to Li-li and Pi-pi in Peking zoo, and a female cub, Ling-ling, was born on September 4, 1964, to the same parents. A third cub Hua-hua, a male, was born to Chiao-chiao on October 10, 1965.

Bad treatment

In 1869 Père Armand David of the Lazarist Missionary Society, and an experienced naturalist, came upon the skin of an animal

Chinese mother love. Although breeding has not been achieved in the western world, despite the efforts of the Moscow zoo and London zoo to breed An-An and Chi-Chi, there are more than a dozen giant pandas in Chinese zoos, and they have been bred successfully.

in a Chinese farmhouse in Szechwan which he did not recognise. He sent it to Paris and later sent more skins. Not until 1937, however, was the first live giant panda seen outside China. Theodore and Kermit Roosevelt had shot one in the 1920's and in 1936 two other Americans, Ruth and William Harkness, with the animal collector Tangier Smith, captured several. They quarrelled, presumably over the spoils, and all the giant pandas died except one, which Ruth Harkness delivered to the Chicago zoo where it was named Su-lin. Another, given the name Mei-mei, reached the same zoo in 1938. In December the same year a young female, Ming, aged 7 months and two young males, Tang and Sung, reached the London zoo. The two males died before the female reached maturity, and she died in December 1944. In May 1946, the government of the Szechwan Province presented a male, Lien-ho, to the London zoo and he lived until 1950. By 1967 there were a score of giant pandas in various zoos, 16 or more

in Chinese zoos, An-an in Moscow and Chi-chi in London.

Although the species is now protected it was formerly hunted by the local Chinese, and the history of western animal collectors does nothing to offset this. The story of Chi-chi gives point to this. In 1957, Heini Demmer, then living in Nairobi, was commissioned by an American zoo to negotiate the exchange of a collection of East African animals for a giant panda. He reached Peking zoo with his cargo, was given the choice of one of three giant pandas, chose Chi-chi, the youngest, and took charge of her on May 5 1958. Chi-chi had been captured by a Chinese team of collectors on July 5 1957, and was reckoned then to be 6 months old. She had been taken to Peking zoo and cared for night and day by a Chinese girl. By the time Demmer had taken charge of Chi-chi the United States had broken off diplomatic relations with the Chinese People's Republic, so she became automatically a banned import.

Bamboo shoots are not the sole food of giant pandas

Demmer took her on a tour of European zoos during the summer of 1958, reaching the London zoo on September 26.

After such treatment perhaps it is not surprising she refused to be mated! She died on July 21 1972.

London Zoo now has two 3 year-old pandas, Ching-Ching and Chia-Chia, which were presented to Mr Heath during his visit to Peking. Mr Nixon was similarly honoured on his visit there in 1973. In 1974 Tokyo had two pandas, and Korea and Paris owned one each.

class	**Mammalia**
order	**Carnivora**
family	**Procyonidae**
genus & species	***Ailuropoda melanoleuca***

Raccoon

Commonly known as 'coons', raccoons are one of the most familiar North American animals, if only in folklore and stories. Their adaptability has allowed them to withstand drastic changes in the countryside while their intelligence, cleanliness and appealing looks have combined to make them popular. Their head and body length is 16—24 in. with a tail of 8—16 in. and they weigh up to 45 lb. Their fur is grey to black with black rings on the tail and a distinctive black 'burglar mask' over their eyes. Their feet have long toes and the front paws are almost hand-like and very dexterous.

Raccoons are relatives of pandas, kinkajous and coatis. There are seven species, the best known ranges from Canada to Central America. The crab-eating raccoon lives in southern Costa Rica, Panama and the northern regions of South America. The other species are found on islands.

Adaptable coons

Raccoons originally lived in woods and brushy country, usually near water, but as the woods have been cut down they have adapted to life in open country. They are solitary, each one living in a home range of about 4 acres, with a den in a hollow tree or in a rock crevice. They come out more at night, and are good climbers and swimmers. In the northern part of their range raccoons grow a thick coat and sleep through cold spells. The raccoons of southern USA and southwards, are active throughout the year. Where trees have been cut down raccoons move into fox burrows or barns and they have been known to spread into towns, even to the middle of cities where they live in attics and sheds and raid garbage bins for food.

Raiding garbage bins is one of the raccoon's less popular traits. Apart from the mess, the bins are sometimes carried away bodily. There are stories of ropes securing the bins being untied, rather than bitten through. This is evidence of the raccoon's extreme dexterity. They use their hands almost as skilfully as monkeys; experiments have shown that their sense of touch is very well developed.

Varied diet

Raccoons eat a very wide variety of both plant and animal food. It is the ability to take so many kinds of food that is probably the secret of the raccoon's success and of its ability to survive changes in the countryside. Raccoons are primarily carnivores; earthworms, insects, frogs and other small creatures are included in their diet, and raccoons also search in swamps and streams for crayfish and along the shore for shellfish. The eggs and chicks of birds, both ground and tree nesters, are eaten and raccoons are sometimes pests on poultry

Appealing look from large bundle of fur – a raccoon up a tree.

farms and in waterfowl breeding grounds. They are also pests on agricultural land because they invade fields of corn, ripping off the ears and scattering them half-eaten. Fruits, berries and nuts are also eaten.

Irresponsible fathers

Raccoons mate in January or February, each male mating with several females then leaving them to raise the family. The young, usually 3 or 4 in a litter, are born from April to June, after 60—70 days gestation. They weigh 2½ oz at birth and are clad in a coat of fuzzy fur, already bearing the characteristic black mask. Their eyes open in 18 days and at about 10 weeks they emerge from the nest for short trips with their mother. The trips get longer as the young learn to forage for themselves but they stay with their mother until about one year old. Raccoons live as long as 13 years.

Coon currency

Raccoons are a match for most predators and when hunted with dogs the raccoon may come off best, especially if it can lure the hound into water and drown it. Raccoons have always been trapped and hunted in large numbers by Indians and Europeans, both for their hard-wearing fur and because of their attacks on crops. Their fur was the main cause for killing them and even in the 17th century efforts were made by imposing taxes and bans to prevent too many raccoon pelts from being exported. At one time the skins were used as currency and when the frontiersmen of Tennessee set up the State of Franklin, the secretary to the governor received 500 coonskins a year while each member of the assembly drew three a day. Nowadays coonskin is not valuable unless there is a sudden fashion as there was for coonskin hats following the film on Davy Crockett, King of the Wild Frontier.

Why so fastidious?

In the *Systema Naturae* Linnaeus called the raccoon *Ursus* (later *Procyon*) *lotor,* or the 'washing bear'. In other languages the raccoon is similarly named *ratons laveur, ositos lavadores* and *Waschbaren.* Their names testify to the strange habit raccoons have of appearing to wash their food before eating it. This apparently hygienic behaviour has become part of the raccoon folklore and only recently have proper attempts been made to explain it.

Some books state that raccoons always wash their food, others say that the habit may be more common in captive animals, yet there are no authentic reports of food washing in the wild. Naturalists who have studied raccoons deny ever seeing this take place. Food washing must, therefore, be an unnatural habit of captive raccoons.

The first scientific study of food washing was made by Malcolm Lyall-Watson at London Zoo. First, he showed that raccoons do not really wash their food but immerse it, manipulate it, then retrieve it. He suggested that the habit should, therefore, be called dousing.

Lyall-Watson gave a large variety of foods to a number of raccoons. Animal food was doused more often than plant, yet earthworms, the only food that needed cleaning, were doused least of all. In another series of experiments it was shown that the shape, smell and size of food objects governed dousing to some extent, but most important was the distance of the food from water. The nearer the water, the more likely is food to be doused.

The conclusion drawn by Lyall-Watson explains why dousing only occurs in captivity. In the wild, raccoons feed on food found on land and food found in water. In captivity all their food is on land, so they 'go through the motions' of foraging in water by taking their food to water, dropping it then searching for it in an action that has for so long been described as washing. Similar behaviour is seen in captive cats. When presented with dead animals, they often throw them about and pounce on them, 'pretending' to hunt them.

Raccoon
North American *(Procyon lotor)*
Crab-Eating *(P.cancrivorus)*

class	**Mammalia**
order	**Carnivora**
family	**Procyonidae**
genus & species	*Procyon lotor* North American raccoon *P. cancrivorus* crab-eating raccoon others

▽ *An unsuspecting raccoon enjoys the shallow waters, unaware of the threatened danger of a puma waiting for the moment to pounce.*

Otter

The various species of otter are all much alike in appearance and habits. They are long-bodied, short-legged mammals, with a stout tail thickened at the root and tapering towards the tip. There is a pair of scent-glands under the tail. The head is flattened with a broad muzzle and numerous bristling whiskers. The ears are small and almost hidden in the fur. The sleek, dark brown fur consists of a close fawn underfur which is waterproof and an outer layer of long stiff guard hairs, which are grey at their bases and brown at their tips. The throat is whitish and the under-parts pale brown. Each foot has five toes, bearing claws in most species, the forefeet are small, the hindfeet large and webbed.

The common or European otter ranges across Europe and parts of Asia, to Japan and the Kurile Islands. It is 4 ft long, including the tail, but may reach 5½ ft, and weighs up to 25 lb. The bitch is smaller than the dog otter. The Canadian otter, of Canada and the United States, is very similar to the European but has an average larger size. It is sometimes spoken of as the river otter, to distinguish it from the sea otter, a markedly different animal. The small-clawed otter, of India and southeast Asia, is much smaller than the European species but the clawless otter of western and southern Africa is larger and is a marsh dweller, feeding on frogs and molluscs. The giant Brazilian otter is the largest of all the otters. It reaches 6½ ft in length, and has a tail that is flattened from side to side.

Solitary and elusive

Except during the mating season otters are solitary, extremely elusive and secretive, and always alert for any sign of disturbance.

They will submerge in a flash, leaving few ripples or, when on land, they will disappear among vegetation. Their ability to merge into their background on land is helped by the 'boneless' contortions of the body and the changing shades of colour in the coat which is aided by the movements and changes in the guard hairs. For example, the coat can readily pass from looking sleek and smooth to looking, when damp, spiny and almost porcupine-like.

Otters do not hibernate. They will fish under ice with periodic visits to a breathing hole. It has been said that otters will use a trick known in aquatic insects; that is, to come up under ice and breathe out, allowing the 'bubble' to take in oxygen from the air trapped in the ice and lose carbon dioxide to the ice and water, then inhale the re-vitalised 'bubble'. This has not yet been proved, however.

▽ *Prenuptial affectionate play. Usually solitary, otters are sociable in the mating season.*

Master-swimmers

At the surface an otter swims characteristically showing three humps each separated by 5−8 in. of water. The humps are the head, the humped back and the end of the tail curved above the water line. When drifting with the current only the head may be in view. Occasionally an otter may swim with the forelegs held against the flanks, the hindlegs moving so rapidly as to be a blur. When this is done at the surface there is a small area of foam around the hindquarters, with a wake rising in a series of hump-like waves. It will also use this method when submerged, although more commonly it swims with all four legs drawn into the body which, with the tail, is wriggled sinuously, as in an eel. Leaping from the water and plunging in again, in the manner of a dolphin, is another way in which an otter can gain speed in pursuit of a large fish. Underwater it will often progress in a similar, but smoother undulating manner.

An otter shows its skill better in its ability to manoeuvre. It will roll at the surface, or when submerged, pivotting on its long axis, using flicks of the tail to give momentum. It can turn at speed in half its own length, using tail and hindquarters as a rudder, or it may swim round and round in tight circles, creating a vortex that brings mud up from the bottom. This last tactic is used to drag small fishes up that have taken refuge under an overhanging bank.

When an otter surfaces it stretches its neck and turns its flattened, almost reptilian head from side-to-side reconnoitring before swimming at the surface or coming out on land.

Otters are nomads, fishing a river or lake then moving on to take their next meal elsewhere. They are said at times to cover up to 16 miles overland in a night. Certainly the European and Canadian otters are met at times far from the nearest water. Overland they move by humping the back. A favourite trick is to take a couple of bounds then slide on the belly for 4−5 ft. On a steep slope the glide may take them 40−50 ft. On a muddy or snow-covered slope the glide becomes tobogganing, otters often retracing their steps to slide repeatedly down the slope in a form of play.

Otters live in rivers and lakes, especially small rivers running to the sea or to large lakes. They particularly like those free of weed and undisturbed by human beings. In times of scarcity otters will move to the coast and are then spoken of as 'sea-otters', not to be confused with the real sea otters.

Eels and crayfish favoured

The European otter has a varied diet of fish, small invertebrates, particularly crayfish and freshwater mussels, birds, small mammals, frogs and some vegetable matter. The main fish food seems to be eels and slow-moving fishes but salmon and trout are also eaten.

Otter families play sea-serpents

Mating takes place in water, at any time of the year, with a peak in spring and early summer. After a gestation of about 61 days 2 or 3 cubs, exceptionally 4 or 5, are born, blind and toothless, with a silky coat of dark hair. There is uncertainty about when the

△ *A backflip from a European otter. This photo caught an otter leaping playfully into the water for the pure joy of living.*

△ *The African clawless otter has only a small connecting web at the base of the toes.*

eyes open, the only reliable record being 35 days after birth. The cubs stay in the nest for the first 8 weeks and do not leave their mother until just before she mates again.

Young otters swim naturally, as is shown by cubs hand-reared in isolation. The indications are, however, that the mother must coax them, or push them, into the water for their first swim. In the early days of taking to water a cub will sometimes climb onto the mother's back, but normally the cubs swim behind their mother. On rare occasions two or more family parties will swim one behind the other. When this does happen a line of humps is seen, and as the leading otter periodically raises her head to take a look around the procession resembles the traditional picture of the sea-serpent.

Otters as lake monsters

It has been said that any schoolboy knows an otter when he sees one. This is so only as long as the otter runs true to form, but otters are quick-change artists and highly deceptive. Sir Herbert Maxwell has recorded how, at the turn of the century, four gentlemen crossing Loch Arkaig in a steam pinnace saw a 'monster' rise from the depths almost under the bows of their boat, create a tremendous flurry of water at the surface, then dive again out of sight. All were puzzled as to its identity, but when the stalker, a Highlander, present with them in the boat, was questioned later, he was in

no doubt that the 'monster' was an otter.

The monster of Loch Morar, near Loch Arkaig, is traditionally 'like an overturned boat towing three overturned dinghies', which could serve as a reasonable description of a bitch otter followed by her three cubs. The ogo-pogo of Canada is believed to be founded on otters swimming in line, and at least one lake monster in Kenya was proved to be a line of otters.

When President Theodore Roosevelt was big game hunting in 1911 he was out in a boat on Lake Naivasha, in Kenya, when the three humps of the local monster appeared. Roosevelt fired once, two humps disappeared, the third stayed on the surface. The skin of the otter was sent to the American Museum of Natural History in New York.

class	**Mammalia**
order	**Carnivora**
family	**Mustelidae**
genera & species	***Amblonyx cinerea*** *Indian small-clawed otter* ***Aonyx capensis*** *clawless otter* ***Lutra canadensis*** *Canadian otter* ***L. lutra*** *European otter* ***Pteronura brasiliensis*** *giant Brazilian otter* *others*

Tiger

One of the largest of the 'big cats', the tiger's sinuous grace, splendid carriage and distinctive colouring make it one of the most magnificent of all animals. A large male averages 9 ft—9 ft 3 in. in length including a 3ft tail. It stands 3 ft or more at the shoulder and weighs 400—500 lb. Females are a foot or so less in length and weigh about 100 lb less. The various races of tigers vary considerably in size from the small Bali Island tiger to the outsized tiger found in Manchuria which may reach 12 ft in total length. The ground colour of the coat is fawn to rufous red, becoming progressively darker southwards through the animal's range, the Balinese tiger being the darkest. The underparts are white. There have been rare cases of white tigers in India. The coat is overlaid with black to blackish-brown transverse stripes, and these contrasting colours provide an excellent camouflage in forest regions.

In cold climates such as Siberia and Manchuria, tigers have thick, shaggy coats which become shorter and denser in the warmer climates. The hair round the face is longer than on the rest of the body, forming a distinct ruff in adult males.

From its original home in Siberia, the tiger spread across almost the whole of Eurasia during the Ice Ages. Today it is found only in Asia where a number of geographical races are recognised, including those of Siberia, Manchuria, Iran, India, China, Sumatra, Java and Bali. The races differ only in size, colour and markings.

▷ *Solitary splendour: tiger caught by flash.*
▷▷ *Transport solution: a helpless tiger cub is carried in the same way as a domestic kitten.*

Solitary prowler

Although its original home was in the snowy wastes of Siberia the tiger's natural preference is for thick cover. It has, however, become adapted to life in rocky mountainous regions, the reed beds of the Caspian, and the dense steaming jungles of Malaya and islands such as Java and Bali. It cannot, however, tolerate excessive heat and during the heat of the day it will lie up in long grass, caves, ruined buildings, or even in swamps or shallow water.

The tiger is an excellent swimmer and in times of flood has been known to swim from one island to another in search of food. Unlike most members of the cat family it is not a good climber and seldom takes to the trees, but there is a record of a tiger taking a single leap of 18 ft from the ground to pull a man off a tree. Its hearing is very good and is the sense most used in stalking prey. It does not appear able to see unmoving animals, even at a short distance.

The tiger has a variety of calls ranging from a loud 'whoof' of surprise or resentment to a full-throated roar when disturbed or about to launch an attack.

Strength widens choice of prey

A tiger preys on deer, antelope, wild pig and smaller animals such as monkeys and porcupines. It will take fish and turtles in times of flood and locusts in a swarm. It occasionally attacks larger animals such as wild bull buffaloes, springing on their backs and breaking their necks. When food is short it may steal cattle, and an old or injured tiger too weak to hunt may attack humans. Game is, however, its natural food and it is interesting that tigers have completely deserted some forested areas of India where game animals have disappeared even though there were still plenty of wandering cattle about.

A tiger stalks using stealth for the first part of its hunt, finally attacking with a rush at its victim, grasping a shoulder with one paw and then seizing the throat. It then presses upwards, often breaking the neck in the process. After a kill it withdraws to a secluded spot, preferably under cover, taking its prey with it. If it cannot do this, or hide its kill near its lying-up place, it is forced to have a hurried meal and leave the rest of the carcase to the hyaenas and vultures and other carrion eaters.

Small striped cubs

Only while the tigress is in season do male and female tigers come together; according to some authorities, this could be for less than two weeks. During this time a tiger will not allow another male near him and will fight, sometimes to the death, over possession of the female. In India the mating season is variable, but in Malaya it is from November to March and in Manchuria it is during December. A female starts to breed at about 3 years of age and then has a litter every third year, or sometimes sooner. After a gestation of 105 – 113 days, 3 – 4 cubs are born, occasionally as many as 6. The mortality among cubs is high and usually no more than two survive to adulthood. They are born blind and helpless, weighing only 2 – 3 lb, but they have their parents' distinctive striped pattern from the beginning. The cubs grow rapidly; their eyes open after 14 days and they are weaned at 6 weeks. At 7 months they can kill for themselves, but stay with their mother until 2 years old, during which time she trains them in hunting. They are fully grown at 3 years.

Man the hunter

Although the tiger has few natural enemies it has been hunted by man from very early times, at first by the local people and later for sport. In India especially, the coming of the British and the introduction of firearms was disastrous to the tiger and it is estimated that in 1877 alone 1 579 tigers were shot in British India. Today the reduction of game animals and the reduction of its natural habitat is further diminishing its numbers, and as a result six of the eight races of tiger are listed as being in danger of extinction.

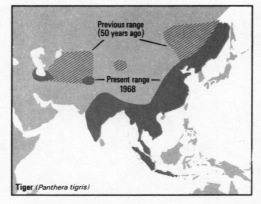

Tiger (Panthera tigris)

△ *Reflected glory: unlike many of the cat family, tigers often take to the water and are strong swimmers. In times of flood they have been known to feed on fish and turtles and to swim in search of stranded prey. They cannot bear excessive heat and will sometimes sit in shallow water in an attempt to keep cool.*

Not normally dangerous

Tigers have a respect and fear for man which is difficult to explain. Even if harassed by curious humans or sportsmen a tiger will not normally react until its patience is well-nigh exhausted. Normally a man can walk in a tiger's habitat without fear or hindrance and there have been several instances of a tiger approaching a man while sitting quietly near his camp and passing by, doing no harm even though it was obvious that it had seen him. Men have been followed for many miles by tigers and have come to no harm; they were probably being escorted off the territory. It is only when its normal hunting routine is disturbed that it becomes really dangerous. It may then become a man-eater, especially when shot at indiscriminately, incapacitating it rather than killing it. A wounded tiger left to its fate, without the strength to hunt, will resort to man-eating or cattle killing, out of necessity, as it will when injured by natural mishap. One of the commonest causes of injury is damage by porcupine quills. If the quills enter the paws or lower limbs the tiger cannot pull down and kill natural prey or cattle. Occasionally the quills may even penetrate the tiger's jaw and the animal starves to death. Old age may also cause a tiger to attack cattle or humans. Once a tiger has turned man-eater or cattle-killer, for whatever reason, every man's hand is against it. Whole villages will turn out and not rest until it is killed, even in areas where the tiger is protected by law.

class	**Mammalia**
order	**Carnivora**
family	**Felidae**
genus & species	*Panthera tigris tiger*

Lion

Lions were once common throughout southern Europe and southern Asia eastwards to northern and central India and over the whole of Africa. The last lion died in Europe between 80—100 AD. By 1884 the only lions left in India were in the Gir forest where only a dozen were left, and they were probably extinct elsewhere in southern Asia, for example, in Iran and Iraq, soon after that date. Since the beginning of this century the Gir lions have been protected and a few years ago they were estimated to number 300. A census taken in 1968, however, puts the figure at about 170. Lions have been wiped out in northern Africa, and in southern Africa, outside the Kruger Park.

The total length of a lion may be up to 9 ft of which 3 ft is tail, the height at the shoulder is $3\frac{1}{2}$ ft and the weight up to 550 lb. The lioness is smaller. The coat is tawny; the mane of the male is tawny to black, dense or thin, and maneless lions occur in some districts. The mane grows on the head, neck and shoulders and may extend to the belly.

▷Shady business: lioness evades the heat.
▷▷An aspiring lion claims a higher position.
▽Pride of the bush: lionesses with their cubs.

Prides and the hunting urge

Lions live in open country with scrub, spreading trees or reedbeds. The only sociable member of the cat family, they live in groups known as prides of up to 20, exceptionally 30, made up of one or more mature lions and a number of lionesses with juveniles or cubs. Members of a pride will co-operate in hunting, to stalk or ambush prey, and they combine for defence. The roar is usually not used when hunting although lions have been heard to roar and to give a grunting roar to keep in touch when stalking. A lion is capable of speeds of up to 40 mph but only in short bursts. It can make standing jumps of up to 12 ft high and leaps of 40 ft. Lions will not normally climb trees but lionesses may jump onto low branches to sun themselves and they as well as lions will sometimes climb trees to reach a kill cached in a fork by a leopard. There is one record of a lioness chasing a leopard, apparently with the intent to kill it, into a tree, but she was foiled by the leopard going into the slender top branches which failed to bear the lioness's weight.

Not wholly carnivorous

Although strongly carnivorous lions take fallen fruit at times. Normally, in addition to the protein, fat, carbohydrate and mineral salts, lions get their vitamins from the entrails of the herbivores they kill. Typically, lions first eat the entrails and hindquarters working forward to the head. In captivity, lions flourish best and breed successfully when vitamins are added to a raw meat diet. Although lionesses often make the kill the lions eat first (hence, 'the lion's share') the lionesses coming next and the cubs last. In general, antelopes and zebra form the bulk of lions' kills but almost anything animal will be taken, from cane rats to elephant, hippopotamus, giraffe, buffalo and even ostrich.

A survey in the Kruger Park showed that in order of numbers killed the prey-species were: wildebeest, impala, zebra, waterbuck, kudu, giraffe, buffalo. A later survey showed a preference descending through waterbuck, wildebeest, kudu, giraffe, sable, tsessebe, zebra, buffalo, reedbuck, impala. When age or injury prevents a lion catching agile prey it may turn to porcupines and smaller rodents, to sheep

▽ *Violence afoot: hampered by the water around them, a pair of paddling lions make the opening moves of a soggy trial of strength.*

and goats, or turn man-killer, taking children and women more particularly. Man-eating can become a habit, however; once a small group of lions at Tsavo held up the building of the Uganda railway through their attacks on the labourers. Dogs may be killed but not eaten.

Exaggerated story of strength

A favourite story is of a lion entering a compound, killing a cow and jumping with it over the stockade. R Hewitt Ivy argues in *African Wild Life* for June 1960 that this is impossible. His explanation is that lions visiting a cattle compound do not all go inside. Possibly one leaps the fence, makes a kill and drags it under the fence to those waiting outside. Should the cattle panic and one leap the fence it will be pulled down by the rest of the pride outside and there eaten.

The lion hunts in silence and it is the lioness that most often kills the prey. The usual method of killing is to leap at the prey and break the neck with the front paws. Alternatively a lion may seize it by the throat with its teeth or throttle it with the forepaws, on the throat or nostrils. Another method is to leap at the hindquarters and pull the prey down. A lion will kill a hippopotamus by scoring its flesh with the claws in a running battle. Lions will kill and eat a crocodile and will also eat carrion, especially if it is fresh, and lion will eat dead lion. An old story tells of the lion's habit of lashing itself into a fury with a spur on the end of its tail, in order to drive itself to attack. Some lions do have what appears to be a claw at the tip of the tail. But this is only the last one or two vertebrae in the tail out of place, due to injury.

Natural control of populations

Lions begin to breed at 2 years but reach their prime at 5 years. The males are polygamous. There is a good deal of roaring before and during mating, and fights with intruding males may take place. Gestation is 105—112 days, the number of cubs in a litter is 2—5, born blind and with a spotted coat. The eyes open at 6 days, weaning is at 3 months after which the lioness teaches the cubs to hunt, which they can do for themselves at a year old. There is a high death rate among cubs because they feed last, so suffering from a diet deficiency, especially of vitamins. This serves as a natural check

▽ *On firmer ground. The skirmish begins as one lion lumbers up onto his rear legs and lunges at his equally cumbersome opponent.*

on numbers. Should numbers fall unduly in a district—as when lions are hunted by man or culled in national parks—prey is more easily killed and there is more food to spare. Lionesses will then kill for their cubs and then the cubs eat first. This richer diet makes for a high survival rate among the cubs, so restoring the balance in the population number.

Dangers for the King of Beasts

There are no natural enemies as such, apart from man, but lions are prone to casualties, especially the young and inexperienced. A zebra stallion may lash out and kick a lion in the teeth, after which the lion may have to hunt small game. The sable antelope is more than a match for a single lion and other antelopes have sometimes impaled lions on their horns. A herd of buffalo may trample a lion or toss it from one set of horns to another until it is dead, although two lions will overcome one large buffalo. One female giraffe attacked a lioness trying to kill her calf. Using hoofs of fore and hindlegs, as well as beating the lioness with her neck, she severely mauled her—and chased the lioness away over a distance of 100 yards. This is a better performance than a rhinoceros can manage. A lion will kill rhino up to three-quarters grown.

class	**Mammalia**
order	**Carnivora**
family	**Felidae**
genus & species	*Panthera leo* *lion*

△▷ *Plan of campaign: lion's strategy observed in Kruger Park. Detecting wildbeest, 16 lions deliberated and split into three parties.*
▷ *Drink up! One lioness remains on watch.*
▽▷ *Lioness casually accepts a mother's duty.*
▽ *An affectionate nudge from mother.*

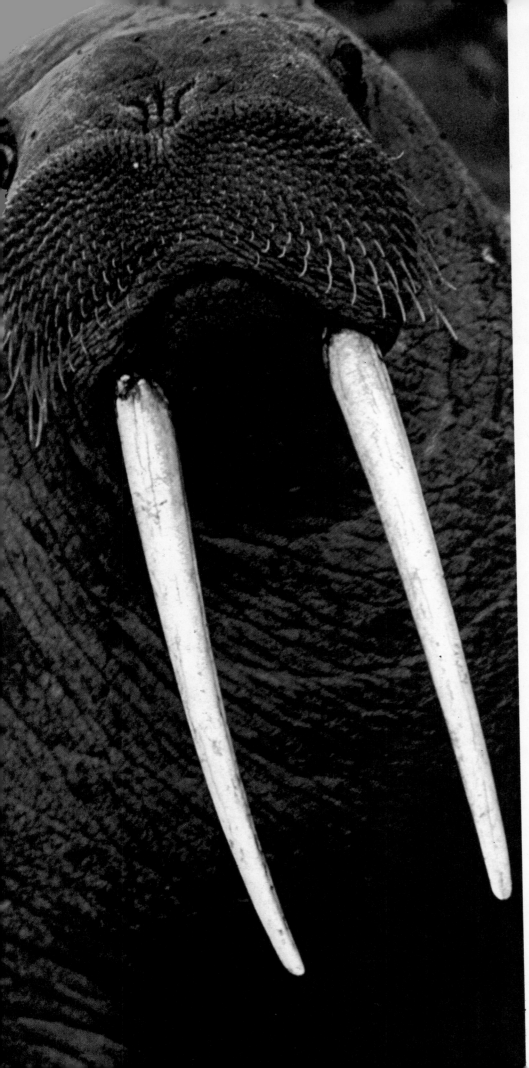

Walrus

Although hunted since the time of the Vikings, almost to the point of extinction, the walrus has survived and today, with strict conservation measures, some herds are very slowly recovering their numbers. The two subspecies, the Pacific walrus and the Atlantic walrus, differ in only minor details. The Pacific bulls average 11—11½ ft long and weigh a little over 2 000 lb but they can reach 13¾ ft and weigh up to 3 700 lb when carrying maximum blubber. The Atlantic bulls average 10 ft long and up to 1 650 lb in weight but may reach 12 ft and weigh 2 800 lb. The cows of both subspecies are smaller, 8½—9½ ft and 1 250 lb, but large Pacific cows may reach almost 12½ ft and a weight of 1 750 lb.

The walrus is heavily built, adult bulls carrying sometimes 900 lb of blubber in winter. The head and muzzle are broad and the neck short, the muzzle being deeper in the Pacific walrus. The cheek teeth are few and of simple structure but the upper canines are elongated to form large ivory tusks, which may reach 3 ft in length and are even longer in the Pacific subspecies. The nostrils in the Pacific subspecies are placed higher on the head. The moustachial bristles are very conspicuous, especially at the corners of the mouth where they may reach a length of 4 or 5 in. The foreflippers are strong and oar-like, being about a quarter the length of the body. The hindflippers are about 6 in. shorter, very broad, but with little real power in them.

The walrus's skin is tough, wrinkled and covered with short hair, reddish-brown or pink in bulls and brown in the cows. The hair becomes scanty after middle age and old males may be almost hairless, with their hide thrown into deep folds.

The Pacific walrus lives mainly in the waters adjacent to Alaska and the Chukchi Sea in the USSR. The Alaskan herds migrate south in the autumn into the Bering Sea and Bristol Bay to escape the encroaching Arctic ice, moving north-wards again in spring when it breaks up.

The Atlantic walrus is sparsely dis-tributed from northern Arctic Canada eastward to western Greenland, with small isolated groups on the east Greenland coast, Spitzbergen, Franz Josef Land and the Barents and Kara Seas. They migrate southward for the winter.

Walruses also inhabit the Laptev Sea near Russia and do not migrate in the winter. It is thought that this herd may be a race midway between the Atlantic and Pacific subspecies.

◁ A long-in-the-tooth bull walrus of the Pacific subspecies. The elongated upper canine teeth are put to a variety of uses, among them defence and digging for clams.

◁ *Playful pups: young walruses nuzzle each other with their sensitive moustaches.*

Tooth-walking bulls

Walruses associate in family herds of cows, calves and young bulls of up to 100 individuals. Except in the breeding season the adult bulls usually form separate herds. They live mainly in shallow coastal waters, sheltering on isolated rocky coasts and islands or congregating on ice floes. Since their persecution by man, however, walruses have learnt to avoid land as much as possible and to keep to the ice floes, sometimes far out to sea. They are normally timid but are readily aroused to belligerence in the face of danger. There seems to be intense devotion to the young, and the killing of a young one will rouse the mother to a fighting fury, quickly joined by the rest.

Walruses can move overland as fast as a man can run and because of their formidable tusks hunters, having roused a herd, have often been hard put to it to keep them at bay. Walruses have even been known to spear the sides of a boat with their tusks or to hook them over the gunwales.

As well as using them as weapons of offence and defence the walrus makes good use of its large tusks for digging food out of the mud and for keeping breathing holes open in the ice. It also uses them as grapnels for hauling itself out onto the ice, heaving up to bring the foreflippers onto the ice. The horny casing of bare hard skin on the palms of the flippers prevents the walrus from slipping. The walrus also uses its tusks for hauling itself along on the ice—indeed the family name Odobenidae means 'those that walk with their teeth'.

Walruses sunbathe and sleep packed close together on the ice floes with their tusks resting on each other's bodies. If the water is not too rough, adult walruses can also sleep vertically in the water by inflating the airsacs under their throats.

Monstrous swine

The walrus was associated in the Middle Ages with a variety of sea monsters. Named the whale-elephant in the 13th century it also became the model for the original sea-horse and sea-cow. In addition it was described as 'a monstrous swine . . . which by means of its teeth climbs to the top of cliffs as up a ladder and then rolls from the summit down into the sea again.'

Clam grubbers

The walrus's diet consists principally of clams, which it grubs out of the mud with its tusks, and sea snails. It will also take mussels and cockles. The snout bristles help in detecting the shellfish. Clams are swallowed whole and no shells have ever been found in the stomach of a walrus, although it is not known how they are disposed of. A walrus also swallows a quantity of pebbles and stones, possibly for helping to crush the food in its stomach. Walruses usually dive for their food in shallow water of about 180 ft or less but occasionally they go down to 300 ft. Probably they deal with pressure problems at such depths by reducing the rate of blood flow as seals do.

Occasionally a walrus, usually an adult bull, will turn carnivorous and feed on whale carcases or it may kill small ringed or bearded seals. Having sampled flesh it may continue to eat it in preference to shellfish.

Hitch-hiking pup

Most matings take place from late April to early June and after a gestation of just over a year one pup is born, every alternate year. Birth takes place on an ice floe. The new-born pup is 4 ft long with a coat of short silver grey hair and weighs 100—150 lb. It is able to swim immediately, although not very expertly, and follows its mother in the water. After a week or two it can swim and dive well. Even so, it usually rides on its mother's back for some time after birth, gripping with its flippers. After a month or two the silver grey hair is replaced by a sparser dark brown coat of stiff hairs. The cow nurses the pup for 18 months to two years but they remain together for several months after weaning. The pups grow quickly, males becoming sexually mature at about 5—6 years, the females at about 4—5 years.

Killed in the rush

Killer whales and polar bears attack walruses but not often, the polar bear particularly being wary of attacking an adult bull even when he is ashore and therefore more vulnerable. Panic when killer whales are near may, however, cause high mortality. In 1936 a large herd was attacked by killer whales and driven ashore on St Lawrence Island. They hauled out onto the beach in such panic that they piled up on each other and 200 of them are said to have been smothered or crushed to death.

Slaughter by man

Walruses have been hunted by man from early times. The Eskimo and Chukchee have always depended on the annual kill to supply all their major needs, including meat, blubber, oil, clothing, boat coverings and sled harnesses. Even today they are largely dependent on it. The annual killings by the local people, however, had no very marked effect on the numbers of the herds. It was the coming of commercially-minded Europeans to the Arctic that started the real extermination. From the 15th century onwards they used the walrus's habit of hauling out on the beaches in massed herds to massacre large numbers in the space of a few hours. After 1861, when whales had become scarce, whalers from New England started harpooning walruses. Then they started using rifles and the Eskimos followed suit. More walruses could be killed but large numbers of carcases fell into the water and could not be recovered. An even greater wastage has been that caused by ivory hunters, who kill for the tusks and discard the rest of the carcase.

By the 1930's the world population of walruses had been reduced to less than 100 000 and strict conservation measures have now been enforced. The Pacific walrus now seems safe from extinction but the Atlantic walrus is still in danger.

class	**Mammalia**
order	**Pinnipedia**
family	**Odobenidae**
genus	***Odobenus rosmarus divergens*** *Pacific walrus* **O. r. rosmarus** *Atlantic walrus*

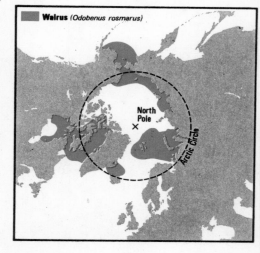

Aardvark

African mammal with a bulky body, 6 ft long including a 2 ft tail, and standing 2 ft high at the shoulder. Its tough grey skin is so sparsely covered with hair that it often appears naked except for areas on the legs and hind quarters. The head is long and narrow, the ears donkey-like; the snout bears a round pig-like muzzle and a small mouth. The tail tapers from a broad root. The feet have very strong claws— four on the front feet and five on the hind feet. The name is the Afrikaans for 'earth-pig'.

△ *The aardvark's nose is guarded by a fringe of bristles and it can also close its nostrils, as a protection against termites.*

▽ *Aardvark at home in African scrub close to a termites' nest where it has been feeding on these soft-bodied insects.*

Distribution and habits

The aardvark has powerful limbs and sharp claws so it can burrow into earth at high speed. This it does if disturbed away from its accustomed burrow. There are records of it digging faster than a team of men with spades. When digging, an aardvark rests on its hind legs and tail and pushes the soil back under its body with its powerful fore feet, dispersing it with the hind legs.

The normal burrow, usually occupied by a lone aardvark, is 3—4 yd long, with a sleeping chamber at the end, big enough to allow the animal to turn round. Each animal has several burrows, some of them miles apart. Abandoned ones may be taken over by warthogs and other creatures.

Years can be spent in Africa without seeing an aardvark, although it is found throughout Africa south of the Sahara, except in dense forest. Little is known of its habits as it is nocturnal and secretive, though it may go long distances for food, unlike other burrowing animals.

Termite feeder

The aardvark's principal food is termites. With its powerful claws it can rip through the wall of termite nests that are difficult for a man to break down even with a pick.

Its method is to tear a small hole in the wall with its claws; at this disturbance the termites swarm, and the aardvark then inserts its slender 18 in. tongue into the hole and picks the insects out. It is protected from their attacks by very tough skin and the ability to close its nostrils—further guarded by a palisade of stiff bristles.

As well as tearing open nests, the aardvark will seek out termites in rotten wood or while they are on the march. It also eats other soft-bodied insects and some fruit, but—unlike the somewhat similar pangolin (see page 404), which has a muscular, gizzard-like stomach filled with grit for crushing hard-bodied insects—it cannot deal with true ants.

Breeding cycle

The single young (twins happen occasionally) is born in midsummer in its mother's burrow, emerging after two weeks to accompany her on feeding trips. For the next few months it moves with her from burrow to burrow, and at six months is able to dig its own.

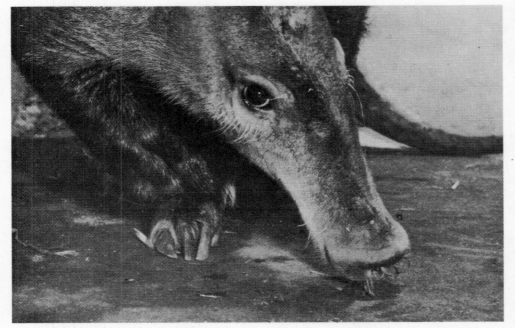

Digs to escape enemies

The aardvark's main enemies are man, hunting dogs, pythons, lions, cheetahs and leopards, and also the honey badger or ratel, while warthogs will eat the young. When suspicious it sits up kangaroo-like on its hind quarters, supported by its tail, the better to detect danger. If the danger is imminent it runs to its burrow or digs a new one; if cornered, it fights back by striking with the tail or feet, even rolling on its back to strike with all four feet together.

On one occasion, when an aardvark had been killed by a lion, the ground was torn up in all directions, suggesting that the termite-eater had given the carnivore a tough struggle for its meal. However, flight and—above all—superb digging ability are the aardvark's first lines of defence for, as with other animals with acute senses like moles and shrews, even a moderate blow on the head is fatal.

The last of its line

One of the most remarkable things about the aardvark is the difficulty zoologists have had in finding it a place in the scientific classification of animals. At first it was placed in the order Edentata (the toothless ones) along with the armadillos and sloths, simply because of its lack of front teeth (incisors and canines). Now it is placed by itself in the order Tubulidentata (the tube-toothed) so called because of the fine tubes radiating through each tooth. These teeth are in themselves very remarkable, for they have no roots or enamel.

So the aardvark is out on an evolutionary limb, a species all on its own with no close living relatives. Or perhaps we should say rather that it is on an evolutionary dead stump, the last of its line.

What is more, although fossil aardvarks have been found—but very few of them—in North America, Asia, Europe and Africa, they give us no real clue to the aardvark's ancestry or its connections with other animals.

class	**Mammalia**
order	**Tubulidentata** *sole representative*
family	**Orycteropidae**
genus & species	*Orycteropus afer*

◁ *The claws of the aardvark are so powerful that it can easily rip through the wall of a termite nest which is so hard it is difficult for a man to break down even with a pick-axe.*

The termites are so disturbed by having their nest opened that they swarm about and the aardvark then puts its pig-like muzzle into the nest to eat them.

It has an 18 in. long, slender, sticky tongue with which it captures and eats the swarming termites that make up the main food of aardvarks.

▷ *A day-old aardvark. It depends on its mother for six months until it can dig its own burrow. The aardvark's snout and round, pig-like muzzle earn it the Afrikaans name for 'earth-pig'.*

Disturbed away from its burrow, the aardvark can escape its enemies by digging at incredible speed. It forces the soil back with its fore feet and kicks it away with its strong hind legs, 'so fast that it can outstrip a team of six men with spades'.

Elephant

The elephant is the largest living land animal and there are two species, the African and the Indian. During fairly recent geological times elephants of many species making up six families ranged over the world except for Australia and Antarctica. The African elephant, the larger of the two surviving species, is up to $11\frac{1}{2}$ ft high and weighs up to 6 tons.

Elephants have a massive body, large head, short neck and stout pillar-like legs. The feet are short and broad with an elastic pad on the sole and hoof-like nails, five on each foot except for the hind foot of the African elephant, which has three. The bones of the skeleton are large, and instead of marrow cavities they are filled with spongy bone. The outstanding feature of elephants is that the snout is remarkably long, forming a flexible trunk with the nostrils at the tip. The trunk is used for carrying food and water to the mouth, for spraying water over the body in bathing or spraying dust in dust-bathing, and for lifting objects, as well as being used for smelling. The single incisor teeth on either side of the upper jaw are elongated and form tusks.

The main differences between the two living species are the larger ears and tusks of the African, its sloping forehead and hollow back, and two 'lips' at the end of the trunk compared with one lip in the Indian elephant.

The African elephant is found in most parts of Africa south of the Sahara, in savannah, bush, forest, river valley or semi-desert. It lives in herds of bulls and cows, each herd being led by an elderly cow, while the older bulls live solitary and join the herd only to mate. The Indian elephant is also native to Sri Lanka, Burma, Thailand, Malaya and Sumatra, living in dense forests. More correctly it should be called Asiatic, not Indian, but the use of 'Indian elephant' is now too deeply rooted for change. The social structure of its herds is much the same as in the African species.

Keeping its skin in condition

Elephants are sometimes grouped with rhinoceroses and hippopotamuses under the loose heading of pachyderms (thickskins). In all the skin is thick and only sparsely haired, and all need to keep the skin in condition by wallowing. An elephant will bathe in water, almost completely submerging itself and will also spray water over itself with its trunk. It indulges in dust baths, too, and if water is scarce it will wallow in mud. The African elephant at least is adept at finding water in times of drought, boring holes in the ground using one of its tusks as a large awl. The requirements of the two species differ because the Indian elephant keeps mainly to dense shade. This also influences other aspects of their behaviour. The African elephant, for example, must seek what shade it can from the midday sun and cool its body by waving its large ears. The enormous surface these present allows for loss of body heat, which is helped by waving the ears back and forth. The Indian elephant, with much

△ *Family group—the youngsters stay with the adults until their teens.*

◁ *Feeding time. At birth the baby is 3 ft high and weighs some 200 lb. It uses its mouth when suckling from the mother's nipples, situated between the cow's forelegs.*

▷ *Largest land animals alive today—African elephants feeding and drinking on the river bank. Their vegetarian diet includes grass, foliage and branches of trees and fruit. The mobile trunk is used to gather and carry food to the mouth.*

smaller ears, keeps itself to dense shade.

Asleep on their feet

A vexed question of long standing is how elephants sleep. Both species can sleep standing, or lying on one side. To lie down an elephant uses similar movements to a horse, but it does what no horse will do: it will sometimes use a pillow of vegetation pulled together on which to rest its head. When standing asleep an elephant breathes at the normal rate. Lying down it breathes at half this rate. When 17 elephants were kept under observation it was found they usually slept for 5 hours each night, in two equal periods. Of this 20 minutes were slept standing, the rest lying down.

Dangers of over-population

The diet is entirely vegetarian and includes grass, foliage and branches of trees and fruit. The trunk is used to gather these and convey them to the mouth. African elephants, living where bushes and trees are scattered, will use the forehead to push over small trees to get at the top foliage. When an area becomes over-populated the loss of trees can be serious. In national parks in Africa the populations of elephants, under protection, tend to increase so much that their ranks have to be thinned out by selective shooting, usually spoken of as culling, to prevent destruction of the habitat. Otherwise all the elephants in the area would be in danger from starvation.

Under free conditions elephant herds trek from one area to another, often seasonally in search of particular fruits. Long distances may then be covered, and this relieves the strain on the vegetation, which can regenerate in their absence.

The molars of elephants have broad crushing surfaces for chewing fibrous vegetation. The wear on them is considerable. Every elephant in its lifetime, assuming it dies of old age (70 years in the Indian, 50 years in the African elephant) has 7 teeth in each half of both upper and lower jaws, exclusive of the tusks. The first are 4 milk teeth which are soon shed. After that a succession of 6 teeth moves down each half of both jaws on a conveyor-belt principle. The first is in use alone but as its surface is getting worn down the next tooth behind it is moving forward, to push out the worn stump and take its place. When the last teeth have come forward and been worn down the elephant must die from starvation, if nothing else.

Purring from the stomach

For a long time big-game hunters and naturalists were perplexed by one feature of elephant behaviour: their tummy-rumblings. Nobody was surprised that these abdominal noises should be so loud and persistent, in view of the enormous quantities of food the huge pachyderms must eat. What puzzled people was that the elephants could apparently control the noises, stopping suddenly when someone approached. Within the last few years it has been discovered that these noises have nothing to do with digestion. When elephants are out of sight of each other they keep up this sort of purring. When danger approaches one of them, it becomes silent. The sudden silence alerts the rest of the herd, which also grows silent. Only when danger has passed is the purring resumed, by which the elephants tell each other that all is well.

Trumpet Voluntary

Apart from these sounds elephants will 'trumpet'. The sound is as startling and as loud, if less pure in tone, as that from the brass wind instrument. In paintings of elephants made in the Middle Ages, or even later, the trunk was always given a trumpet-shaped end, the artists being influenced by travellers' stories of the elephants' trumpeting.

Elephant 'midwives'

Mating is preceded by affectionate play, especially with the bull and the cow entwining trunks or caressing each other's head or shoulders with the trunk. The gestation period is 515—760 days, mostly about 22 months. The single baby—twins are rare —is about 3 ft high and weighs about 200 lb. On several occasions hunters or naturalists have seen a cow elephant retire into a thicket accompanied by another cow. Some time later the two come out again accompanied by a baby. Nobody knows whether the second cow acts as midwife or merely

◁ *Woe betide those who ignore this warning notice.*
▷ *Dressed up for a reception at Bahawalpur, West Pakistan, an Indian elephant looks very decorative. It is distinguished from its larger African relative by its smaller ears, arched back, domed forehead and smoother trunk which has only one 'finger' or lobe at its end compared with the African's two (below). In general, the Indian elephant appears to be an animal of jungle or bush country, although it is found in grassland areas.*
▽ *Enjoying a dustbath, an elephant uses its hose-like trunk to snort dirt over its body.*

stands guard while the calf is being born. The baby is able to walk soon after birth and can keep up with the herd in two days.

Hefty train-stoppers

Such large and powerful animals have few enemies. In India a tiger may kill a baby and in Africa the large predators, such as the lion, may do the same. The power of an elephant in defence can be gauged by the several stories told of a bull elephant meeting a train on a railway and charging the engine head on. In all reports it is stated how the engine driver drew the train to a halt and the elephant charged the engine repeatedly, doing itself great injury yet persisting in the attack. Another feature of elephant defence is the close co-operation between members of a herd. Hunters have reported seeing a shot elephant being helped away by two others ranged either side of it, keeping it upright on its feet. On one occasion the herd combined to drag the carcase of one of their fellows throughout the night, in an abortive attempt at rescue. In 1951, in the Johannesburg *Star,* Major JF Cumming was reported as having seen some elephants dig a grave to bury a dead comrade!

Do they fear mice?

In contrast with the elephant's comparative freedom from large enemies is the long-standing belief that elephants are afraid of mice. Lupton, in his *A Thousand Notable Things,* published in 1595, wrote: 'Elephants of all other beasts do chiefly hate the mouse.' The idea still persists, helped no doubt by such stories as that of the elephant in a zoo found dead from a haemorrhage and with a mouse jammed in its trunk.

In 1938 Francis G Benedict and Robert C Lee, American zoologists, tested zoo elephants with rats and mice in their hay, and by putting rats and mice in the elephants' house. The pachyderms showed no concern even when the rodents ran over their feet or climbed on their trunks. White mice were also put in the elephants' enclosure, again without result. There was, however, one moment when a rat ran over a piece of paper lying on the ground. The unfamiliar noise of rustling paper set the nearest elephant trumpeting and before long all the others were joining in the chorus.

class	**Mammalia**
order	**Proboscidea**
family	**Elephantidae**
genera & species	***Elephas indicus*** *Indian elephant* ***Loxodonta africana*** *African elephant*

△ *Bulls contest for the cow who appears to be rather uninterested in the combat.*
▽ *African elephants were thought to be untameable but the Belgians succeeded at the turn of the century by training immature ones for work using kindness and patience rather than brutality.*

Zebra

Zebras are distinguished from horses and asses by the stripes on their bodies. Their mane is neat and upright. The tail is tufted as in asses, but the hard wart-like knobs known as 'chestnuts', are found on the forelegs only, and not on the hindlegs as in horses. There are differences from both the horse and the ass in the skull and teeth. Three species of zebra live in Africa today. The commonest and best-known is Burchell's zebra, which extends from Zululand in the southeast, and from Etosha Pan in southwest Africa, north as far as southern Somalia and southern Sudan. In this species the stripes reach under the belly, and on the flanks they broaden and bend backwards towards the rump, forming a Y-shaped 'saddle' pattern. Although the races in the southern and northern parts of the range look quite different, the differences are only clinal. That is, there are gradual changes from south to north, but they all belong to one species. In the southernmost race, the 'true' Burchell's zebra, now extinct but once living in the Orange Free State and neighbouring areas, the ground colour was yellowish rather than white; the legs were white and unstriped; the stripes often did not reach under the belly; and between the broad main stripes of the hindquarters and neck were lighter, smudge-grey alternating stripes commonly known as 'shadow-stripes'.

Further north a race known as Chapman's zebra is still found. It has a lighter ground colour than the true Burchell's, the stripes reach further down the legs—usually to below the knees—and the shadow-stripes are still present. All zebras still living from Zululand north to the Zambezi are referred to as members of this race; but at Etosha Pan there are some zebras that have almost no leg stripes and closely resemble 'true' Burchell's.

North of the Zambezi is the East African race, known as Grant's zebra. Its ground colour is white, the stripes continue all the way down to the hoofs and there are rarely any shadow-stripes. Grant's zebra is smaller than the southern races, about 50 in. high, weighs 500—600 lb, and has a smaller

mane. In the northern districts the mane has disappeared altogether. Maneless zebras occur in southern Sudan, the Karamoja district of Uganda and the Juba valley of Somalia.

South and southwest of the Burchell's zebras' range lives the mountain zebra, about the same size as Burchell's but with a prominent dewlap halfway between the jaw angle and the forelegs. Its stripes always stop short of the white belly. Its ground colour is whitish and, although the stripes on the flanks bend back to the rump, as in Burchell's, the vertical bands continue as well, giving a 'grid iron' effect. The southern race, the stockily built, broad-banded Cape mountain zebra, is nearly extinct, preserved only on a few private

properties. The race in southwest Africa, Hartmann's zebra, is still fairly common. It is larger and longer-limbed than the Cape mountain zebra, with narrower stripes and a buff ground colour.

The third species is Grévy's zebra, from Somalia, eastern Ethiopia and northern Kenya, a very striking, tall zebra. The belly is white and unstriped, and there are no stripes on the hindquarters, except the dorsal stripe which bisects it. On the haunches the stripes from the flanks, rump and hindlegs seem to bend towards each other and join up.

▽ At the waterhole: a herd of southeast African Burchell's zebra. This race generally has striped legs and a paler ground colour than the now extinct true Burchell's zebra.

Belligerent stallions

Burchell's zebras are strongly gregarious. Groups of 1–6 mares with their foals keep together under the leadership of a stallion, who protects them and also wards off other stallions. Sometimes, for no apparent reason, the male simply disappears and another one takes his place. The surplus stallions live singly, or in bachelor groups of up to 15 members. Burchell's zebras are rather tame, not showing as much fear of man as the gnu with which they associate. When alarmed they utter their barking alarm call, a hoarse 'kwa-ha, kwa-ha', ending with a whinny. Then the herd wheels off, following the gnu. When cornered, however, the herd stallion puts up a stiff resistance, kicking and biting.

Mountain zebras, said to be more savage than Burchell's, live in herds of up to six, although sometimes they assemble in large numbers where food is plentiful. They seem to have regular paths over the rugged hills and move along them in single file. The call of the mountain zebra has been described as a low, snuffling whinny, quite different from that of the Burchell's.

Although in Grévy's zebra there are family groups as well as bachelor herds, the biggest and strongest stallions, weighing up to 1 000 lb, are solitary, each occupying a territory of about a mile in diameter.

Slow breeding rate

A newborn foal has brown stripes and is short-bodied and high-legged like the foal of a domestic horse. It is born after a gestation of 370 days. It weighs 66–77 lb and stands about 33 in. high. The mares come into season again a few days after foaling, but only 15% are fertilised a second time; usually a mare has one foal every three years. They reach sexual maturity at a little over 1 year, but do not seem to be fertile before about 2 years. Young males leave the herd between 1 and 3 years and join the bachelor herd. At 5 or 6 years many of them attempt to kidnap young females and if successful a new one-male herd is formed. The unsuccessful ones remain in the bachelor herd, or become solitary. Zebras live about as long as horses.

Lions beware

Man still hunts the zebra for meat but in protected areas, at least, very little of this continues. The zebra, with the gnu, is the lion's favourite prey. Because zebras are potentially dangerous, the lion must make a swift kill and young lions have been routed by zebra stallions that turned on them. Astley Maberley, the wildlife artist and writer, tells the story of an African poacher who was killed and fearfully mangled by an irate troop of Burchell's zebras after he had killed a foal.

(1) Linear line-up: a row of Grévy's zebra, large, handsomely-marked animals recognised by the huge ears and narrowly-spaced stripes.
(2) Topi antelope and Grant's zebra — a species having stripes that reach below the knees. The odd-looking animal on the left of the picture is a rare melanistic form of Grant's zebra.
(3) Grant's zebra spar in the dust of Ngorongoro crater. Zebra stallions are aggressive not only to males of the same species but also to predators, including man.

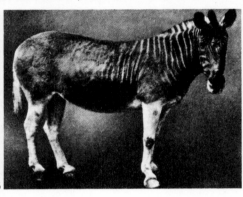

The lost quagga

A fourth species of zebra, the quagga, was extremely common in South Africa 150 years ago. It has since been completely exterminated. Most closely resembling Burchell's zebra, the quagga was distinctly striped brown and off-white on the head and neck only. Along the flanks the stripes gradually faded out to a plain brown, sometimes extending to just behind the shoulders, sometimes reaching the haunches. The legs and belly were white. Its barking, high-pitched cry, after which it was named, was rather like that of the Burchell's zebra.

The early explorers, around 1750–1800, met quaggas as far southwest as the Swellendam and Ceres districts, a short way inland from Cape Town. The Boer farmers did not appreciate quaggas except as food for their Hottentot servants. Their method of hunting was to take a train of wagons out onto the veldt and blaze away at everything within sight. Then large numbers of carcasses would be loaded onto the wagons, and the rest of the dead and dying animals were simply left to rot. It is no wonder that today Cape Province is virtually denuded of wild game. When Cape Province was emptied, the trekkers to the Orange Free State repeated the process there. By 1820 the quaggas' range was already severely curtailed; they were almost gone even from the broad plains of the Great Fish River, which had been named 'Quagga's Flats' from the vast numbers of them roaming there. A few lingered for another 20 years or so in the far east of Cape Province and in the Orange Free State, the last wild ones being shot near Aberdeen, CP, in 1858, and near Kingwilliamstown in 1861. Strange to say, no one realised that they were even endangered. Zoos looking for replacements for their quaggas that had died were quite shocked to be told, 'But there aren't any more'.

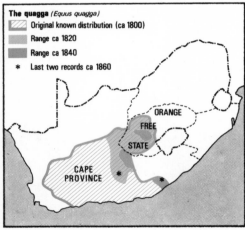

The quagga (Equus quagga)
- ⬚ Original known distribution (ca 1800)
- ▨ Range ca 1820
- ▨ Range ca 1840
- ＊ Last two records ca 1860

ORANGE FREE STATE

CAPE PROVINCE

class	**Mammalia**
order	**Perissodactyla**
family	**Equidae**
genus & species	***Equus burchelli burchelli*** *true Burchell's zebra or bontequagga* ***E. b. antiquorum*** *Chapman's or southeast African Burchell's* ***E. b. boehmi*** *Grant's or East African Burchell's* ***E. b. borensis*** *maneless zebra* ***E. grevyi*** *Grévy's zebra* ***E. quagga*** *quagga* ***E. zebra zebra*** *Cape mountain zebra* ***E. z. hartmannae*** *Hartmann's mountain zebra*

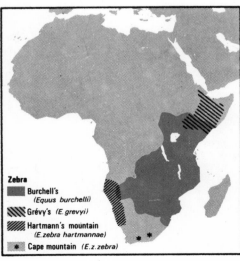

Zebra
- ■ Burchell's (Equus burchelli)
- ▨ Grévy's (E. grevyi)
- ▨ Hartmann's mountain (E. zebra hartmannae)
- ＊ Cape mountain (E.z. zebra)

(4) '. . . along a mountain track' — Hartmann's mountain zebra, a race of the Cape mountain zebra described in 1898, has a large dewlap between chin and forelegs and stripes that end short of the belly. The stripes form a 'gridiron' effect on the rump.
(5) Nearly extinct: less than 200 Cape mountain zebra live in specially protected areas of high tableland in western Cape province.
(6) Extinct: the quagga was hunted in large numbers by early white settlers to South Africa.

Hippopotamus

Distantly related to the pigs, the hippopotamus rivals the great Indian rhinoceros as the second largest living land animal. Up to 14 ft long and 4 ft 10 in. at the shoulder it weighs up to 4 tons. The enormous body is supported on short pillar-like legs, each with four toes ending in hoof-like nails, placed well apart. A hippo trail in swamps shows as two deep ruts made by the feet with a dip in the middle made by the belly. The eyes are raised on top of the large flattish head, the ears are small and the nostrils slit-like and high up on the muzzle. The body is hairless except for sparse bristles on the muzzle, inside the ears and on the tip of the short tail. There is a thick layer of fat under the skin and there are pores in the skin which give out an oily pink fluid, known as pink sweat. This lubricates the skin. The mouth is armed with large canine tusks; these average 2½ ft long but may be over 5 ft long including the long root embedded in the gums.

Once numerous in rivers throughout Africa, the hippopotamus is now extinct north of Khartoum and south of the Zambezi river, except for some that are found in a few protected areas such as the Kruger National Park.

The pygmy hippopotamus, a separate species, lives in Liberia, Sierra Leone and parts of southern Nigeria in forest streams. It is 5 ft long, 2 ft 8 in. at the shoulder and weighs up to 600 lb. Its head is smaller in proportion to the body, and it lives singly or in pairs.

Rulebook of the river-horse

The name means literally river-horse and the hippopotamus spends most of its time in water, but comes on land to feed, mainly at night. It can remain submerged for up to 4½ minutes and spends the day basking lethargically on a sandbar, or lazing in the water with little more than ears, eyes and nostrils showing above water, at most with its back and upper part of the head exposed. Where heavily persecuted, hippopotamuses keep to reed beds. Each group, sometimes spoken of as a school, numbers around 20—100 and its territory is made up of a central crèche occupied by females and juveniles with separate areas, known as refuges, around its perimeter each occupied by an adult male. The crèche is on a sandbar in midstream or on a raised bank of the river or lake. Special paths lead from the males' refuges to the feeding grounds, each male marking his own path with his dung. The females have their own paths but are less exclusive.

The organisation of the territories is preserved by rules of behaviour which, in some of their aspects, resemble rules of committees. Outside the breeding season a female may pay a social call on a male and he may return this, but on the female's terms. He must enter the crèche with no sign of aggression and should one of the females rise on her feet he must lie down. Only when she lies down again may he rise. A male failing to observe these rules will be driven out by the adult females attacking him *en masse.*

Matriarch hippos

It was long thought that a hippopotamus school was led by the oldest male. It is in fact a matriarchy. For example, young males, on leaving the crèche, are forced to take up

a refuge beyond the ring of refuges lying on the perimeter of the crèche. From there each must win his way to an inner refuge, which entitles him to mate with one of the females, by fighting. Should a young male be over-persecuted by the senior males he can re-enter the crèche for sanctuary, protected by the combined weight of the females.

The characteristic yawning has nothing to do with sleep. It is an aggressive gesture, a preliminary challenge to fight. Combats are vigorous, the two contestants rearing up out of the water, enormous mouths wide open, seeking to deliver slashing cuts with the long tusks. Frightful gashes are inflicted and a wounded hippo falling back into water screams with pain, but the wounds quickly heal. The aim of the fighting is for one hippo to break a foreleg of his opponent. This is fatal because the animal can no longer walk on land to feed.

Nightly wanderings

Hippos feed mostly at night, coming on land to eat mainly grass. During one night an individual may wander anything up to 20 miles but usually does not venture far from water. Hippos have been known to wander through the outskirts of large towns at times, and two surprised just before dawn by a motorist entering Nairobi showed him they could run at 30 mph.

Babies in nursery school

When in season the female goes out to choose her mate and he must treat her with deference as she enters his refuge. The baby is born 210—255 days later. It is 3 ft long, 1½ ft high and 60 lb weight. Birth may take place in water but normally it is on land, the mother preparing a bed of trampled reeds. The baby can walk, run or swim 5 minutes after birth. Outside the crèche

A trio of hippos in single file moves ponderously through a mixed throng of cormorants, pelicans and gulls, with a hippo youngster in the lead.

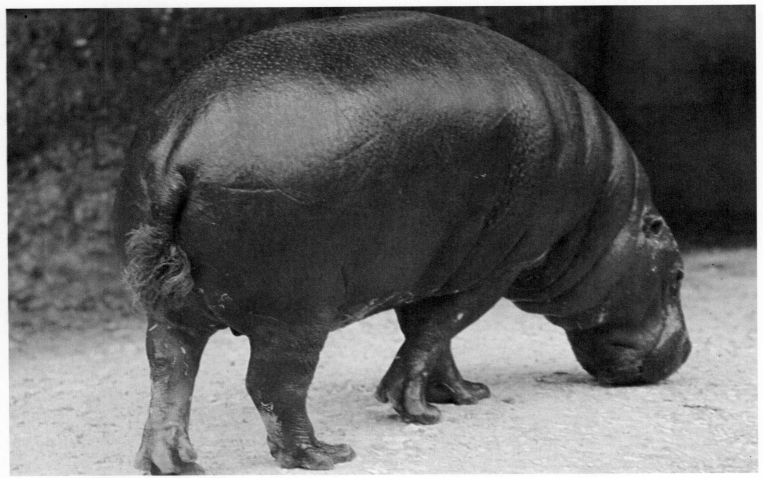

A mournful-looking pygmy hippo **Choeropsis liberiensis,** *from West Africa. Its well-oiled look is due to the secretion of a clear, viscous material through its skin pores. When frightened, the pygmy hippo prefers to head for the undergrowth, whereas the big hippos invariably seek safety in water.*

the organisation of the school is dependent on fighting and the females educate the young accordingly. This is one of the few instances of deliberate teaching in the animal kingdom. In a short while after its birth the baby hippo is taken on land for walks, not along the usual paths used when going to pasture but in a random promenade. The youngster must walk level with the mother's neck presumably so she can keep an eye on it. If the mother quickens her pace, the baby must do the same. If she stops, it must stop. In water the baby must swim level with her shoulder. On land the lighter female is more agile than the male, so she can defend her baby without difficulty. In the water the larger male, with his longer tusks, has the advantage, so the baby must be where the mother can quickly interpose her own body to protect her offspring from an aggressive male. Later, when she takes it to pasture, the baby must walk at heel, and if she has more than one youngster with her, which can happen because her offspring stay with her for several years, they walk behind her in order of precedence, the elder bringing up the rear.

Obedience, or else . . .

The youngsters must show strict obedience, and the penalty for failing to do so is punishment, the mother lashing the erring youngster with her head, often rolling it over and over. She may even slash it with her tusks. The punishment continues until the

youngster cowers in submission, when the mother licks and caresses it.

Babysitting was not invented by the human race: hippos brought it to a fine art long ago. If a female leaves the crèche for feeding or mating she places her youngster in charge of another female, who may already have several others under her supervision. The way for this is made easy, for hippo mothers with young of similar age tend to keep together in the crèche.

The young hippos play with others of similar age, the young females together playing a form of hide-and-seek or rolling over in the water with stiff legs. The young males play together but they indulge in mock fights in addition to the other games.

Few enemies for the hippo

Hippos have few enemies apart from man, the most important being the lion which may occasionally spring on the back of a hippo on land, raking its hide with its claws. But even this is rare.

The wanderlust hippo

Many animals sometimes wander well inland for no obvious reason. Huberta was a famous hippopotamus that wandered a thousand miles. She left St Lucia Bay, in Zululand, in 1928 and wandered on and on until in 1931 she reached Cape Province. Each day she stopped to wallow in a river or lake, and her passage was noted in the local newspapers all along her route, so her

journey is fully documented. Throughout that time she never came into contact with another hippo. Huberta became almost a pet of the people of South Africa and a law was passed to protect her. She was finally shot, however, by a trigger-happy person in April 1931, and was then found to be a male. So it will never be known how much farther Hubert might have wandered.

class	**Mammalia**
order	**Artiodactyla**
family	**Hippopotamidae**
genera & species	***Hippopotamus amphibius*** ***Choeropsis liberiensis*** *pygmy hippo*

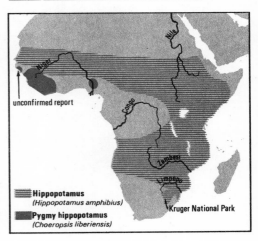

unconfirmed report

Hippopotamus
(Hippopotamus amphibius)
Pygmy hippopotamus
(Choeropsis liberiensis)

Kruger National Park

Camel

There are two species of camel: the Arabian or one-humped and the Bactrian or two-humped. The first is not known as a wild animal, though the second survives in the wild in the Gobi desert. A dromedary is a special breed of the one-humped camel, used for riding, although the name is commonly but wrongly used to denote the Arabian camel as a whole.

Camels have long legs and a long neck, coarse hair and tufted tails. Their feet have two toes united by a tough web, with nails and tough padded soles. The length of head, neck and body is up to 10 ft, the tail is 1½ ft long, height at the shoulder is up to 6 ft, and the weight is up to 1100 lb.

Habits

The wild camels of the Gobi desert are active by day, associating in groups of half-a-dozen, made up of one male and the rest females. They are extremely shy and make off at first sight of an intruder, moving with a characteristic swaying stride, due to the

One-humped camels drinking at a water-hole in the desert. Having taken their fill of water, camels can survive for several days in the desert without drinking, or for several weeks if they have access to succulent desert plants. Water is drawn from the body tissues to maintain the fluid in the blood.

fore and hind legs on each side moving together. Their shyness may be partly due to persecution in former times.

It is often said that a camel cannot swim. Reports suggest they do not readily take to water, but they have been seen swimming.

Adaptations to desert life

Everything about a camel, both its external features and its physiology, show it to be adapted to life in deserts. Its eyes have long lashes which protect them from wind-blown sand. The nostrils are muscular so they can be readily closed, or partly closed to keep out sand. The form of the body, with the long neck and long legs, provides a large surface area relative to the volume of the body, which allows for easy loss of heat.

The camel's physiology shows other adaptations which provide protection from over-heating, and help it to withstand desiccation and to indulge in physical exertion with a minimum of feeding and drinking. These characteristics are often seen in stories of journeys made across waterless deserts. Many of these are exaggerated, but even those that are true are remarkable enough. There is one instance of a march through Somalia of 8 days without water and in Northern Australia a journey of 537 miles was made, using camels which were without a drink for 34 days. Most of the camels in this second journey died, but a few that were able to graze dew-wetted vegetation survived.

Most desert journeys are made in winter, however, and during that season even a man

can go without drinking if he feeds largely on juicy fruits and vegetables. Knut Schmidt-Nielsen tested camels in the desert winter and found that even on a completely dry diet, camels could go several weeks without drinking, although they lost water steadily through their skin and their breath as well as in the urine and faeces. Normally, however, a camel feeds on desert plants with a high water content.

Do camels store water?

There are many stories of travellers in the desert killing a camel and drinking the water contained in its stomach. From these arose the myth, which has not yet been completely killed, that a camel stores water in its stomach. Pliny (AD 23-79), the Roman naturalist, first set it on record. Buffon (1707-1788) and Cuvier (1769-1832), celebrated French scientists, accepted it. Owen (1804-1892) and Lyddeker (1849-1915), British anatomists and zoologists, supported it.

In 1801 George Shaw, British zoologist, wrote of a camel having four stomachs with a fifth bag which serves as a reservoir for water. Everard Home, the Scottish surgeon, dissected a camel and in 1806 published his celebrated drawing of alleged water pockets in the first two compartments of the stomach, a drawing which has many times been reproduced in books, and which has served to bolster the story. It was not until the researches of Schmidt-Nielsen and his team, working in the Sahara in 1953-4, that the full story emerged. In the living camel, these pockets are filled with an evil-smelling soup,

the liquefied masticated food, which might be drunk, so saving his life, by a man crazy for water—but not otherwise.

Another of the camel's achievements which served to support the story is its ability to drink 27 gallons of water, or more, in 10 minutes. It will do so only to replenish the body supply after intense desiccation. In those 10 minutes a camel will pass from an emaciated animal, showing its ribs, to a normal condition. This is something few other animals can do. But the water does not stay in the stomach; it passes into the tissues, and a camel after a long drink looks swollen.

A camel can lose water equal to 25% of its body weight and show no signs of distress. A man losing 12% of his body water is in dire distress because this water is drawn from his tissues and his blood. The blood becomes thick and sticky, so that the heart has greater difficulty in pumping. A camel loses water from its tissues but not from the blood, so there is no strain on the heart, and an emaciated camel is capable of the same physical exertion as normal. The mechanism for this is not known. The only obvious difference between the blood of a camel and any other mammal is that its red corpuscles are oval instead of being discoid.

The camel's hump

The hump contains a store of fat and it has often been argued that this can be converted to water, and therefore the hump is a water reserve. The hump of the Arabian camel may contain as much as 100 lb of fat, each pound of which can yield 1·1 lb of water, or over 13 gallons for a 100 lb hump. To convert this, however, extra oxygen is needed, and it has been calculated that the breathing needed to get this extra oxygen would itself lead to the loss of more than 13 gallons of water as vapour in the breath. The fat stored in the hump is broken down to supply energy, releasing water which is lost. The hump is thus really a reserve of energy.

Other physiological advantages possessed by a camel are that in summer it excretes less urine and, more important, it sweats little. The highest daytime temperature is 40°C/105°F but during the night it drops to 34°C/93°F. A man's temperature remains constant at just under 39°C/100°F and as soon as the day starts to warm up he begins to feel the heat. A camel starts with a temperature of 34°C/93°F at dawn and does not heat up to 40°C/105°F until nearly midday. A camel's coat provides insulation against the heat of the day and it keeps the animal warm during the cold desert nights.

With all these advantages, camels should be even-tempered, but everyone agrees that they are bad-tempered to a degree. One writer has described them as stupid, unwilling, recalcitrant, obnoxious, untrustworthy and openly vicious, with an ability to bite destructively. There is a traditional joke that there are no wild camels, nor any tame ones.

The power of the bite is linked with the camel's unusual dentition. At birth it has six incisors in both upper and lower jaws, a canine on each side, then a premolar followed by a gap before the cheek teeth are reached. As the young camel grows, it quickly loses all but the outside incisors of the six in the upper jaw and these take on a similar shape to the canines. So in making a slashing bite a camel has, in effect, double the fang capacity of a dog.

Breeding

A baby camel is a miniature of its parents, apart from its incisors, its soft fleece, lack of knee pads and hump. There is a single calf, exceptionally two, born 370—440 days after conception. Its only call is a soft *baa*. It can walk freely at the end of the first day but is not fully independent until 4 years old, and becomes sexually mature at 5 years. Maximum recorded life is 50 years.

Origins of the camel

Camels originated in North America, where many fossils have been found of camels, small and large, with short necks or long, as in the giraffe-like camels. The smallest was the size of a hare, the largest stood 15 ft at the shoulder. As the species multiplied there was one migration southwards into South America and another northwestwards, and then across the land-bridge where the Bering Straits now are, into Asia. As the numerous species died out, over the last 45 million years, the survivors remained as the S. American llamas and Asiatic camels.

A few species reached eastern Europe and died out. None reached Africa. Until 6 000 years or more ago there was only the one species in Asia, the two-humped Bactrian camel. The date is impossible to fix with

In a sandstorm the long lashes protect the camel's eyes, and its nostrils can readily be closed to keep the sand out.

Camels have been used as pack animals since early times, and can carry a load of about 400 lb for long distances.

certainty, as is the date when the one-humped camel came into existence, but the evidence suggests that it is a domesticated form derived from the Bactrian camel. Both readily interbreed, and the offspring usually have two humps, the hind hump smaller than that in front.

Surprisingly, the first record of a one-humped camel is on pottery from the sixth dynasty of Ancient Egypt (about 3500 BC) for the camel was not known in the Nile Valley until 3 000 years later. Its representation on the pottery may have been inspired by a wandering camel train from Asia Minor. Meanwhile, on Assyrian monuments

dated 1115–1102 BC, and from then onwards, the camel appears quite often, and when the Queen of Sheba visited King Solomon in Jerusalem, in 955 BC, she brought with her draught camels. The name seems to be from the Semitic *gamal* or *hamal*, meaning 'carrying a burden'.

The one-humped camel was presumably selectively bred from domesticated two-humped camels, in Central Asia, by peoples who left no records. It is also suggested that the nickname 'ship of the desert' is derived from 'animal brought in a ship from the desert' by mis-translation—a reference to the Assyrian habit of naming an animal

according to the place from which it came. Presumably this would mean camels were brought by ship across the Persian Gulf.

Feral camels

Today the Bactrian camel is confined to Asia but most of the 3 million Arabian camels are on African soil. Some have, however, been introduced into countries far from Africa or Asia. In 1622 some were taken to Tuscany where a herd still lives on the sandy plains near Pisa. On the plains of the Guadalquivir are feral camels taken to Spain by the Moors earlier still. Camels were taken to South America in the 16th century

◁ *Camel herd of an Arabian caravan. A miniature from a manuscript of about the 12th century illustrates the work of the poet Harari. (Cairo)*

▷ *Camels develop leathery callosities on their knees and other joints through kneeling down for loading.*

452

by the Spanish conquistadors but these have died out. Others were taken to Virginia in 1701, and there was a second importation into the United States in 1856. The survivors from these were still running wild in the deserts of Arizona and Nevada in 1915. Camels were taken to Northern Australia, and there also they have reverted to the wild.

For a long time text books reiterated that no camels are now known in the wild state, although they had been mentioned in Chinese literature since the 5th century, and Marco Polo wrote about them. Then, in 1879, Nikolai Przewalski reported wild two-humped camels still living around Lake Lob, southeast of the Gobi desert. The local people told him they had been numerous a few decades prior to his visit but that they hunted them for their hides and flesh. There were reports also of camels in the Gobi, but nobody was prepared to say whether these were truly wild or merely feral camels. In 1945, the Soviet zoologist AG Bannikov rediscovered them and in 1955 a Mongolian film unit secured several shots of them.

These Gobi camels are two-humped but the humps are small. They are swift, with long slender legs, small feet and no knee pads. Their coat is short, the ears smaller than in the domesticated camels, and the coat is a brownish-red.

The Mongolian film shows the Gobi camel to be different from the typical Bactrian and Arabian camels, and it would be not unreasonable to conclude that it represents the ancestral stock from which the other two were domesticated.

class	**Mammalia**
order	**Artiodactyla**
suborder	**Tylopoda**
family	**Camelidae**
genus & species	*Camelus dromedarius* 1-humped camel *Camelus bactrianus* 2-humped camel

△ *The camel draws water from the well while his keeper sleeps peacefully.*

▽ *Dromedaries are the riding strain of the one-humped camel, and can travel 100 miles in a day*

453

Reindeer

Some scientists regard the reindeer of Northern Europe and the caribou of North America as varieties of one species. The reindeer, of arctic Europe and Asia, are now domesticated or at least semi-domesticated. They are up to 43 in. at the shoulder, and a good bull may weigh 224 lb. Reindeer are perhaps the tamest of all domesticated animals, and it is said that even a child can manage a herd of them. The domestication of the reindeer is thought to have begun in the 5th century when they were used as decoys for hunting wild reindeer. The hunter, with four or five tame beasts on ropes, and himself in the middle, would approach a wild herd without alarming them, and then loose his arrows at short range. One tribe in Siberia is known to have used tame hinds in the rutting season to attract wild stags, which were then shot. In time, the tame hinds produced enough fawns to build up herds, and the domestication of the reindeer gradually came about in this way.

Reindeer are all profit

Reindeer are to the Lapps and the northern tribes of the USSR what cattle were to early man farther south. They provide everything he needs. The hide makes a soft leather used for clothing and a variety of other purposes, such as cushions and curtains. Reindeer give milk, cheese and flesh. Their sinews can be used for sewing boots or for covering a canoe, and their bones for needles. The stretched bowel makes a window covering or bag for minced meat.

Reindeer are used as pack animals or for drawing sleighs, and are most economical animals to keep as they can withstand exposure and so need no stabling, and they can forage for themselves, digging down through the snow for the spongy lichen known as reindeer moss. Today, however, the use of reindeer products is declining in favour of manufactured goods or preserved foods especially where towns are accessible.

Man the parasite

The reindeer is a nomad like the people who domesticated it. One valuable quality of the reindeer is its ability to find its way in a snowstorm, and this and its nomadism, together with its many other uses, has made some scientists speak of man's social parasitism on the reindeer. In the association between the animal and the human, the animal gains little besides protection from enemies—an advantage largely offset by man killing some of them for food. Otherwise the advantages are all with the human.

The reindeer's achievements as a draught animal are greater than those of horse or dog over uneven or frozen ground. A reindeer will pull 300 lb at an average of 8 mph, and while a daily journey averages 25—35 miles, up to 75—100 miles a day have been recorded. In an annual race in Sweden

▷ *Reindeer, the cattle of the Scandinavian Arctic, provide all the Lapps' requirements.*

two reindeer pulled a sledge and driver 5 miles in 14½ minutes. At a reindeer festival held on Christmas day on the Kola peninsula a mile course has been covered in 2½ minutes. At Nome in Alaska in an annual race a 10-mile course was invariably covered in under half an hour.

Why reindeer cows have antlers

Because reindeer are domesticated it has been possible to experiment on some aspects of their behaviour. For example, why do female reindeer have antlers, the only deer apart from caribou to do so? A possible answer lies in an experiment carried out in 1962-3 by Yngve Espmark of the University of Stockholm. A group of 16 reindeer were marked and kept in an enclosure, and at the same time observations were made on free-ranging reindeer. The social hierarchy—usually called the peck-order—changes during the course of a season, but generally speaking the larger the antlers the higher the male is in the social order. During the rut the mature bulls, with their large antlers, are the bosses. After the rut the males shed

their antlers before the females, and then the females become boss. Moreover, each calf shares its mother's rank. The importance of the antlers was tested by cutting off the antlers of some of the males, who then dropped in the social ranking. One male was castrated and from what is known in other species he should have fallen to a very subordinate rank. He did not and all the circumstances suggest that an old male, experienced in fighting and in holding his rank, has learned to 'know his own strength', which may explain how stags without antlers hold their own.

During the winter the calf stays with its mother and feeds from the 'crater' she makes in the snow. If she had no antlers there is a fair chance both might be driven from the crater by other members of the herd looking for an easy meal, and the calf would starve.

Epic arctic journey

Reindeer once took part in an historic drive across Arctic Canada. In the 1890's a herd of 171 was taken into Alaska from Siberia to save the Eskimos from starvation. These

flourished and increased in numbers, but many mistakes were made, such as poor herding, and by the mid 1940's the number had dropped to 120 000, from a peak of nearly a million 10 years previously. In 1929 the Canadian government introduced reindeer into its Northwestern

◁ *Man and his beasts; or beasts and their man?*
Many think the reindeer domesticated the Lapps.
◁ ▽ *Reindeer keep their heads above water.*
▽ *Reindeer crocodile. A Lapp leads the way.*
▽ ▽ *Reindeer camp. They do not need stabling.*

Territory to build up an industry for the Eskimos there. A herd of 3 400 left Kotzebue Sound in Alaska under the supervision of a Lapp, Andrew Bahr, who delivered 2 370 animals at the Mackenzie River delta 5 years later. The journey was made across unknown territory and included crossing a mountain range, fording one river after another and by-passing lakes. Wolves harried the flanks of the herd, taking a continual toll. Plagues of mosquitoes in summer sometimes held the herd up as did the blizzards in winter, for the journey was made

well within the Arctic Circle. On arrival less than 20% of the original herd remained, the rest having been born on the journey.

class	**Mammalia**
order	**Artiodactyla**
family	**Cervidae**
genus & species	***Rangifer tarandus*** *reindeer*

Giraffe

Tallest animal in the world, the giraffe is remarkable for its long legs and long neck. An old bull may be 18 ft to the top of his head. Females are smaller. The head tapers to mobile hairy lips, the tongue is extensile and the eyes are large. There are 2—5 horns, bony knobs covered with skin, including one pair on the forehead, a boss in front, and, in some races, a small pair farther back. The shoulders are high and the back slopes down to a long tufted tail. The coat is boldly spotted and irregularly blotched chestnut, dark brown or liver-coloured on a pale buff ground, giving the effect of a network of light-coloured lines. A number of species and races have been recognised in the past, differing mainly in details of colour and number of horns, but the current view is that all belong to one species. The number of races recognised, however, varies between 8 and 13 species depending on the authority.

The present-day range of the giraffe is the dry savannah and semi-desert of Africa south of the Sahara although it was formerly more widespread. Its range today is from Sudan and Somalia south to South Africa and westwards to northern Nigeria. In many parts of its former range it has been wiped out for its hide.

A leisurely anarchy

Giraffes live in herds with a fairly casual social structure. It seems that males live in groups in forested zones, the old males often solitary, and the females and young live apart from them in more open country. Males visit these herds mainly for mating.

Giraffes do not move about much, and tend to walk at a leisurely pace unless disturbed. When walking slowly the legs move in much the same way as those of a horse. That is, the right hindleg touches the ground just after the right foreleg leaves it, and a little later the left legs make the same movement. The body is therefore supported on three legs most of the time while walking. As the pace quickens to a gallop the giraffe's leg movements change to the legs on each side moving forward together, the two right hoofs hitting the ground together followed by the two left legs moving together.

The long neck not only allows a giraffe to browse high foliage, the eyes set on top of the high head form a sort of watch-tower to look out for enemies. In addition, the long neck and heavy head assist movement by acting as a counterpoise. When resting crouched, with legs folded under the body the neck may be held erect or, if sleeping, the giraffe lays its neck along its back. To rise, the forelegs are half-unfolded, the neck being swung back to take the weight off the forequarters. Then it is swung forwards to take the weight off the hindlegs, for them to be unfolded. By repeated movements of this kind the animal finally gets to its feet.

Necking parties

The habit of 'necking' has been something of a puzzle. Two giraffes stand side-by-side and belabour each other with their heads, swinging their long necks slowly and forcibly. Only rarely does any injury result, and the necking seems to be a ritualised fighting, to establish dominance, and confined exclusively, or nearly so, to the male herds.

Not so dumb

One long-standing puzzle concerns the voice. For a long time everyone accepted the idea that giraffes are mute—yet they have an unusually large voice-box. During the last 25 years it has been found that a young giraffe will bleat like the calf of domestic cattle, that the adult female makes a sound like 'wa-ray' and that adult bulls, and sometimes cows, will make a husky grunt or cough. Nevertheless, there are many zoo-keepers who have never heard a giraffe utter a call and there is still the puzzle why there should be such a large voice-box when so little use is made of it. Some zoologists have suggested the giraffe may use ultra-sonics.

Controlled blood pressure

In feeding, leaves are grasped with the long tongue and mobile lips. Trees and bushes tend to become hourglass-shaped from giraffes browsing all round at a particular level. Acacia is the main source of food but many others are browsed, giraffes showing definite preferences for some species of trees or bushes over others.

Giraffes drink regularly when water is available but can go long periods without drinking. They straddle the front legs widely to bring the head down to water, or else straddle them slightly and then bend them at the knees. Another long-standing puzzle concerns the blood pressure in the head, some zoologists maintaining a giraffe must lower and raise its head slowly to prevent a rush of blood to the head. In fact, the blood vessels have valves, reservoirs of blood in the head and alternative routes for the blood, and so there is no upset from changes in the level of the head, no matter how quickly the giraffe moves.

Casual mothers

Mating and calving appear to take place all the year, with peak periods which may vary from one region to another. The gestation period is 420—468 days, the single calf being able to walk within an hour of birth, when it is 6 ft to the top of the head and weighs 117 lb. Reports vary about the suckling which is said to continue for 9 months, but in one study the calves were browsing at the age of one week and were not seen suckling after that. The bond between mother and infant is, in any case, a loose one. Giraffe milk has a high fat content and the young grow fast. Captive giraffes often live for over 20 years.

Defensive hoofs

Giraffes have few enemies. A lion may take a young calf or several lions may combine to kill an adult. Even these events are rare because the long legs and heavy hoofs can be used to deadly effect, striking down at an attacker.

Symbol of friendliness

Rock engravings of giraffes have been found over the whole of Africa and some of the most imposing are at Fezzan in the middle of what is now the Sahara desert. The animal must have lingered on in North Africa until 500 B.C. Some of the engravings are life size, or even larger, and many depict the trap used to capture giraffes, while others show typical features of its behaviour, including the necking. The engravings also show ostriches, dibatag, and gerenuk. Giraffes were also figured on the slate palettes, used for grinding malachite and haematite for eye-shadows, the cosmetics used by ladies of rank in Ancient Egypt. The last giraffe depicted in Egyptian antiquities is on the tomb of Rameses the Great, 1225 BC.

There are references to the animal in Greek and Roman writings and a few pictures survive from the Roman era, but from then until the 7th or 8th century AD the principal records are in Arabic literature. The description given by Zakariya al-Qaswini in his 13th-century *Marvels of Creation* reflects the accepted view, that 'the giraffe is produced by the camel mare, the male hyaena and the wild cow'. The giraffe was taken to India by the Arabs, and from there to China, the first arriving in 1414 in the Imperial Zoological Garden in Peking. To the Chinese it symbolised gentleness and peace and the Arabs adopted this symbolism, so a gift of a giraffe became a sign of peace and friendliness between rulers.

In medieval Europe, and until the end of the 18th century, knowledge of the giraffe was based on descriptions in Greek and Roman writings and on hearsay accounts. It was at best a legendary beast.

class	**Mammalia**
order	**Artiodactyla**
family	**Giraffidae**
genus & species	***Giraffa camelopardalis***

▷ *Dappled freaks of the African veld: a group of giraffes rear their extraordinary necks against the skyline of a pale sunset. Wiped out for its hide in many parts of its range, the present day distribution of the giraffe is much reduced. A number of races are recognised within the single species.*

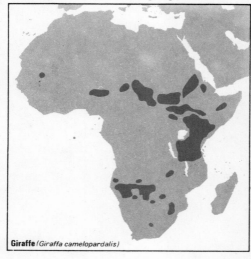

Giraffe *(Giraffa camelopardalis)*

Impala

The impala is one of the most graceful of the antelopes. About 30—40 in. high, weighing 140—160 lb, it is chestnut brown with a lighter brown area on the flanks and a sharply defined white belly. The male has lyre-shaped, ribbed horns, 20—30 in. long, which make one spiral turn; the female is hornless. The neck and limbs are slender and delicate. The impala occupies a rather isolated position in the family Bovidae. In the past there have been divided opinions on whether it was more nearly related to the gazelles or to the reedbuck. Recently Alan Gentry has suggested, on a study of the skull, teeth and horn-cores, that the impala is more nearly related to the hartebeest and gnu.

Taking to cover

Impala inhabit a wide area of East and South Africa. They seem to like being near water and they avoid open country, being more usually found where there are low trees and tall shrubs, without much ground cover, in scrub and thornbush country especially. Their distribution is patchy because they do not venture much into either overgrown or open land. So, although abundant in most of the Kruger National Park, they are absent from much of its northern end.

△ Poise in triplicate: a female impala trio nose down in their local river. Impala seldom stray far from water, and will not venture into arid surroundings or bushy thickets.

According to its suitability for the impala, an area may have a density of anything from seven to over 200 per square mile; the usual figure is 50—70. Concentrations are highest in the dry season, as with most African ungulates; this also happens to be the time of the rut. In the wet season, impala are more scattered, and occupy small home ranges; but they may wander as much as 15 miles for water.

Impala both graze and browse, but in most areas they eat mainly grass.

460

Born when the grass sprouts

The rut takes place in the beginning of the dry season. The lambs are born, one to each ewe, after a gestation of 180—210 days, early in the wet season when there is most food for them.

In Rhodesia, the first lambs are dropped in early December and the peak of lambing is from December 15 to January 1. Two-year-old ewes, breeding for the first time, give birth later in the season than older ones. The young grow rapidly—in young males the horns begin to sprout in late February—and are usually weaned before the next rut, at which time they may form separate bands. In the rut nearly all ewes breed, at least 97% of the older ones, and 85% of the two-year-olds.

The rut begins when the males set up their territories in late May or early June. Surplus rams attach themselves to small groups of ewes, and the yearlings form small bands by themselves. The ewes live in herds the year round. At the end of the lambing season these may number (including lambs) as much as 100. At Fort Tuli, Rhodesia, herds of 200—300 have been counted. These large herds stay together from January to May, and only a few males associate with them; then in May they break into smaller groups, which pass through the rams' territories and are covered by them. After the rut, the ram groups reform but groups of mixed sex and age predominate. By December, the groups are reduced in size to ten or less; the ewes become secretive, separating off for a while to give birth.

The main predator is probably the leopard. Existing populations of impala are often subject to poaching, but this does not severely affect their numbers.

△ *The roving eye: a handsome male runs a casual glance over the scrubland.*

▽ *Poetry in motion: female in full flight.*

Switchback fugitives

Impala rams become quite aggressive in the rutting season, especially when setting up territories. At this time, fighting and chasing are common. The rams, once the territories are set up, leave their bases to drink at the waterholes, which are a no-man's-land. But the most conspicuous piece of impala behaviour is their alarm reaction. When disturbed, the whole group indulge in a magnificent display of leaping. They jump forward, straight up or with side turns, as much as 10 ft into the air, up and down, round and in all directions. What is the function of this behaviour? It has been suggested that in reality its purpose is to confuse a predator, such as a big cat who is trying to single out one animal from the group it is attacking. The leaping impala, helped by their contrasting colours, seem to be wholly successful in preventing this, and completely confuse the attacker.

A number of animals show this sort of behaviour when alarmed by a predator. Instead of putting as much ground between themselves and their adversary they jink to and fro to cause confusion. The jinking of hares is an example that readily comes to mind and it has been suggested that continually changing direction prevents an enemy from cutting off its prey.

class	**Mammalia**
order	**Artiodactyla**
family	**Bovidae**
genus & species	*Aepyceros melampus*

Bottlenose dolphin

Also often known as the common porpoise, this is the animal that in the last 20 years has become a star per-former in the seaquaria of the United States. It is up to 12 ft long, weighs as much as 440 lb and is black above and white underneath, with a bulbous head and a marked snout. The forehead of the male is more protruding than that of the female. The moderate-sized flippers taper to a point and the fin in the middle of the back has a sharply-pointed apex directed backwards, making the hinder margin concave. It has 20—22 conical teeth in each half of both upper and lower jaw. Although as well suited to life in the water as any fish it is in fact a mammal like whales or, for that matter, man, giving birth to fully-developed young which are suckled on milk. The bottlenose is the commonest cetacean (family name of the whales) off the Atlantic coast of North America, from Florida to Maine. It occurs in the Bay of Biscay and Mediterranean also. It occasionally ranges to Britain, and is also found off West Africa, south to Dakar.

Cooperative schools

Bottlenose dolphins live in schools contain-ing individuals of both sexes and all ages. Apparently there is no leader, but males in the school observe a 'peck order' based on size. When food is plentiful the schools may be large, breaking into smaller schools when it is scarce. The dolphins pack together at times of danger. They also assist an injured member of the school by one ranging either side of it and, pushing their heads under its flippers, raising it to the surface to breathe. In schools they keep in touch by sounds.

They sleep by night and are active by day, although each feeding session is followed by an hour's doze. Females sleep at the surface with only the blowhole exposed and this periodically opens and closes, as it does in stranded dolphins, by reflex action. The males sleep a foot below the surface, periodi-cally rising to breathe.

The main swimming action is in the tail, with its horizontal flukes. This, the flexible part of the animal, is used with an up-and-down movement in swimming, quite unlike that of fishes, with only an occasional side-ways movement. The flippers help in steer-ing and balance. The dorsal fin also aids stability, but it is the lungs placed high up in the body that are chiefly responsible for keeping a dolphin balanced.

The depths to which bottle-nosed dol-phins can dive has to be deduced from the remains of fishes in their stomachs. These show they go down for food to at least 70 ft, and they can stay submerged for up to 15 minutes. Their lung capacity is half as much again as that of a land animal and in addi-tion they fill their lungs to capacity. Land animals, including ourselves, use only about half the lung capacity and change only 10—15% of the air in the lungs with each breath. A dolphin changes up to 90%.

Tame dolphin leaping some 30 ft into the air to take fish accurately, which proves that its small eyes are still quite useful out of water.

Well equipped for marine life

Since a dolphin's lungs are compressed when diving, air would be squeezed into the bronchial tubes, where no gaseous exchange would take place, unless this were prevented by valves. There are 25–40 of these in the bronchial tubes of the bottlenose dolphin and they act as a series of taps controlling the pressure in the lungs according to whether the animal is diving, swimming on the level or rising to the surface.

At the surface the pulse of the bottlenose dolphin is 110 a minute. When submerged it drops to 50 a minute and starts to increase as the animal nears the surface. The drop is related to the way the blood circulation is shut off so that the oxygen supply goes mainly to essential organs, notably the heart and brain. This extends the time of sub-mergence by reducing the frequency with which visits need be made to the surface to breathe.

Whales and dolphins have an insulating layer of blubber, but they have no sweat glands and they cannot pant, so other means are needed to lose excess body heat. The tail flukes and the flippers are always warmer to the touch than the rest of the body and their temperature is not only higher than that of other parts of the body but varies through a greater range. They also have a much thinner layer of blubber. It is assumed therefore that these parts lose heat to the surrounding water. In brief, whales and dolphins keep cool through their flukes and flippers.

A dolphin's eyesight is not particularly good. Yet the animal can move its eyelids, shut its eyes, even wink. At one time it was thought the eyes were of little value and were quite useless out of water. This last seems proved wrong by the way dolphins in seaquaria will leap out of water and accur-ately snatch fish from the attendant's hand. Moreover, the visual fields of left and right eyes overlap, so presumably they have partially stereoscopic vision. The sense of smell is, however, either non-existent or almost wholly so.

Hearing is the main sense, apart from taste and touch. This is acute and is especi-ally sensitive to high tones. It is probably second only to the hearing of bats. A dol-phin is sensitive to the pulses of an echo-sounder or asdic and will respond to fre-quencies as high as 120 kilocycles or beyond, whereas we can hear 30 kilocycles at the most. At sea it has been noticed that bottle-nose dolphins will avoid a boat that has been used for hunting them but will not be disturbed by other boats. The assump-tion is that they can recognize individual boats by the sounds they make.

Feeding

Fish form one of the main items in the diet but a fair amount of cuttlefish is eaten, the dolphin spitting out the chalky cuttlebone and swallowing only the soft parts. Shrimps also are eaten. In captivity a bottlenose will eat 22 lb of fish a day, yielding 237 calories per pound of its body weight, compared with the 116 calories/lb taken by man.

Life history

Bottlenose dolphins become sexually mature

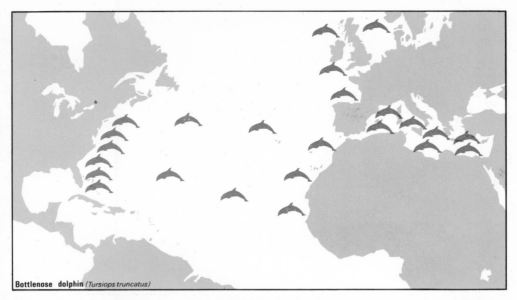
Bottlenose dolphin (Tursiops truncatus)

△△ Bottlenose dolphin jaws are well armed with teeth that help it catch its mainly cuttlefish food.
△ Baby dolphin with its mother. As with most mammals it stays with its mother for some time and is suckled on milk, being weaned after 5 months or more. Note the blowhole or nostril on top of the head.

at 5–6 years. The breeding season extends from spring to summer. The gestation period is 11–12 months, births taking place mainly from March to May. The baby is born tail-first and as soon as free it rises to the surface to take a breath, often assisted by the mother usually using her snout to lift it gently up. Just prior to the birth the cow slows down and at the moment of birth she is accompanied by two other cows. These swim one either side of her, their role being protective, especially against sharks, who may be attracted to the spot by the smell of blood lost during the birth process. Weaning may take place between 6–18 months; reports vary considerably.

For the first 2 weeks the calf stays close beside the mother, being able to swim rapidly soon after birth. Then it begins to move away, even to chase fish, although quite ineffectively. However, it readily dashes back to its mother's side or to its 'aunt', the latter being another female that attaches herself to the mother and shares in the care of the calf. The aunt is the only one the mother allows near her offspring.

The calf is born with the teeth still embedded in the gums. These begin to erupt in the first weeks of life but the calf makes little attempt to chew until 5 months old and some take much longer before they attempt to swallow solid food. Even then there may be difficulties and in captivity a calf at about this time has been seen to bring up its first meal, the mother then massaging its belly with her snout.

Suckling is under water. The mother's nipples are small and each lies in a groove on the abdomen. The mother slows down to feed her calf which comes in behind her and lies slightly to one side, taking a nipple between its tongue and the palate. The mother then, by muscular pressure on the mammary glands, squirts the milk into its mouth. Should the calf let go the nipple the milk continues to squirt out. The baby bottlenose must come to the surface to breathe every half minute, so suckling must be rapid. In this species it consists of one to nine sucks, each lasting a few seconds. For the first 2 weeks the calf is suckled about twice an hour, night and day, but by 6 months it is down to six feeds a day.

Can dolphins talk?

It is not all that time ago that it was generally believed that whales, porpoises and dolphins were more or less mute, although the whalers themselves held very definite views to the contrary. It was not until after World War II, when bottlenose dolphins were being first kept in captivity in the large seaquaria, first in Florida and later in California and elsewhere, that it began to be realized fully that they have a wide vocabulary of sounds. Then, a few years ago, came the startling suggestion that these cetaceans might be capable of imitating human speech, even perhaps of being able to talk to people, in a sort of Donald Duck language in which words are 'gabbled' in a very high pitch. These high hopes do not seem to have been realised, but apart from this much has been learned about the noises they make.

One thing that has long been known is that air can be released from the blowhole while the animal is still submerged. This can be seen, by direct observation, emerging as a stream of bubbles. It can be used to produce sounds, and part of the mechanism for it is the many small pouches around the exit from the blowhole which act as safety valves, preventing any inrush of water.

It has been known for some time that some cetaceans are attracted over long distances by the cries of their fellows in distress. Conversely, people have been calling the animals to them by using whistles emitting sounds similar to their calls. Pliny, the Roman naturalist of the first century AD, knew of this, and in modern times the people on the Black Sea coasts have continued to do this. Sir Arthur Grimble also left us an account of what he called porpoise calling in South Pacific Islands. He described how local peoples in this area would call the porpoises from a distance to the shore. These items indicate an acute sense of hearing in dolphins and porpoises and a potentiality for communication by sounds on their part.

Underwater microphones as well as more direct observations in the various seaquaria have established that these cetaceans use a wide range of sounds. These have been variously described as whistles, squawks, clicks, creaks, quacks and blats, singing notes and wailings. It has been found that two dolphins which have been companions will, if separated, call to each other, and that a calf separated from its mother will call to her. Dolphins trained to leap out of water for food have been heard to make sounds at their attendants.

These are, however, only the sounds audible to our ears, which can deal only with the lower frequencies. Much of dolphin language is in the ultrasonic range, and if they are able to understand what we are saying, as one investigator has somewhat unconvincingly suggested, they could be using their own vocalizations to call us by rude names without our knowing it!

It has often been said that if whales cried out in pain we might be less ready to slaughter them. Scattered reports suggest that in fact they do precisely this. Freshly captured bottlenose dolphins placed in the tanks in Florida's Marineland have been heard through the thick plate glass windows to cry with shrill notes of discomfort and alarm. At sea similar distress calls have been heard from injured or wounded whales, porpoises and dolphins.

class	**Mammalia**
order	**Cetacea**
family	**Delphinidae**
genus & species	*Tursiops truncatus*

Bottlenose dolphins leaping out of the water in formation. This demonstrates the powerful swimming action of the tail with its horizontal fluke unlike a fish's tailfin which is vertical. It also shows their sociability.

Dolphins try to find each other by echo-locating 'clicks'. Then they talk in 'whistles' with a few 'grunts' and 'cracks'. Their sounds were analysed in 1965 when TG Lang and HAP Smith of the US Naval Ordnance Test Station put two newly captured bottlenose dolphins, Doris and Dash, in separate tanks linked by a two-way hydrophone system so the experimenters could tap their conversations. The first 4 of a total of 16 two-minute periods shown here indicate how the animals conversed when they were linked by phone and how sporadic noises were made when the line was 'dead'.

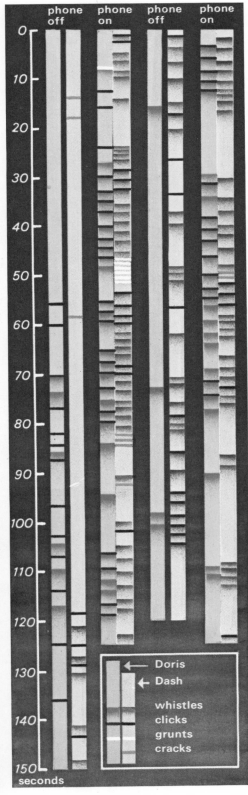

465

Killer whale

The killer whale is closely related to the false killer whale and also the pilot whale. It has a very bad reputation for ferocity which is probably unjustified. Killer whales are small for whales, the females growing up to a maximum of about 15 ft, but an old male may be as long as 30 ft. They are one of the few whales in which there is a marked difference in size between the sexes, the sperm whale being another example. The colour is very striking and distinctive, both sexes having similar markings, which are black on the back and white on the underside. Occasionally the white is some-what yellowish. The chin is white and there is a characteristic white oval patch just above and behind the eye. There is a small whitish patch just behind the dorsal fin which varies quite considerably in shape and hue in different animals. The white on the underside sweeps up towards the tail and the flanks are white between the dorsal fin and the tail. The flippers, which are broad and rounded, are black all over, but the underside of the tail flukes are white. The dorsal fin is very conspicuous, usually about 2 ft high, but in the old males it may be 6 ft. The oldest males also have very long flippers, up to $\frac{1}{5}$ the animal's total length, the average length of the flipper in juvenile males and adult females being $\frac{1}{9}$ only.

Killer whales are found in all seas but are particularly numerous in the Arctic and Antarctic where there is abundant food to satisfy their voracious appetite. They are not uncommon around the British Isles, where a number have been stranded, mainly on the north and east coasts. These strandings take place in most months of the year. A larger number than usual were stranded on British coasts during the last war, mostly on the North Sea coast, probably due in part at least to anti-submarine activities.

Killer whale showing off its strength and beauty. Despite their reputation for ferocity, killer whales kept in oceanaria have been unaggressive and many are hand-tame.

△ *Running at the surface with blowhole open,
a killer whale in relaxed mood.*

▽ *Affectionate play between a pair of killers.
Sensory pits can be seen on the head.*

Living in packs

Killer whales hunt together in packs made
up of both sexes. They are inquisitive and
appear to take a close interest in anything
likely to be edible. Nothing is known about
their movements in the oceans or how much,
if at all, the populations in different oceans
mix. In the Antarctic they are often seen
around whaling factory ships and probably
they tend to follow the ships around as they
offer an easy source of food. Otherwise very
little is known about their habits.

Ruthless hunters

The killer whale is a voracious feeder and
will take anything that swims in the sea.
Included in its diet are whales, dolphins,
seals, penguins, fish and squid. It will attack
even the larger blue whales and quite often
killers will hunt in packs numbering from
two or three up to as many as 40 or more.
When attacking a large whale they are said
to work as a team. First one or two will
seize the tail flukes to stop the whale thrashing about and slow it down, then others will
attack the head and try to bite the lips.
Gradually the whale becomes exhausted and
its tongue lolls from its mouth—to be immediately seized by the killers. At this
point all is over for the whale: the tongue
is rapidly removed and the killers take their
fill, seeming to favour a meal from around
the head of their monster victim.

Apart from attacking fully-grown and
healthy whales, killers have earned the hate
of whalers because they often take the
tongues from whales that have been har-
pooned and are lying alongside the factory
ship waiting to be processed. They will even
take the tongue from whales being towed by
the catcher boat, and in an effort to stop
this looting a man may be posted with a
rifle to deter the killers. If he should injure
a killer all the others in the pack turn on
it and it very soon becomes their next meal.

Killer whales also eat seals and porpoises,
and there are a number of records of complete seals found in a killer's stomach. The
greatest number recorded is the remains of
13 porpoises and 14 seals that were taken
from the stomach of one killer whale, while
another contained remains of 32 seals. Off
the Pribilof Islands in the Bering Sea, killer
whales are often seen lying in wait for the
young fur seal pups swimming out into the
open sea for the first time. The number of
seals actually taken by killers is not certain
but it is likely that large numbers of pups
must meet their end in this way before they
reach the age of one year.

In the Antarctic, penguins form an important part of the killer whale diet. On
many occasions killer whales have been seen
swimming underneath ice floes, either singly
or sometimes several at a time, and then
coming up quickly under the floe either to
tip it or break it up, thereby causing the
penguins to fall into the water and into the
waiting jaws of the killers.

Once killer whales were seen cruising
close to an island where there was a colony
of grey seals. As the killers came close in
the seals hurried ashore in spite of a couple
of people standing nearby. The certain
danger from killer whales was more important to the seals than possible danger
from man. It is said that when killer whales

467

attack grey whales, these become so terrified that they just float on their backs unable to make any effort to escape.

Seven-footer calves

Very little is known about the breeding habits of the whale. They are thought to produce their young towards the end of the year, in November and December after a 16-month gestation. This is supported by examination of some of the stranded whales washed up on the beach and found to be pregnant. The calf at birth is about 7 ft long. The females suckle the young in the same way as other whales, but how long this lasts is not known.

No enemies

The killer whale probably has no real enemies. A few are killed by man, usually irate whalers. They are not a very valuable catch to a whaler although some Russian whaling fleets do catch a few, usually if there is nothing else worth shooting.

Chased by killers

The most famous story of killer whales is that told by Herbert Ponting who was the official photographer to the British *Terra Nova* Antarctic expedition led by Captain Scott in 1911. While the ship's cargo was being unloaded onto the ice some killer whales appeared nearby. Ponting went to take some photographs carrying the bulky photographic apparatus of those days over the floes. As he went across the ice the killers thrust up alongside and then followed him as he crossed the floes, tipping them from beneath. Ponting just managed to get to the safety of the fast ice in front of the killers—a lucky escape.

Ponting's experience must have been terrifying, yet it is often found that a reputation for ferocity is unfounded. Divers who have met killer whales have not been molested and several killer whales have been kept in oceanaria. All have been un-aggressive or even hand-tame. One story tells of a fisherman of Long Island, New York, who threw a harpoon at a killer whale. The whale pulled free and followed the boat and its terrified occupants to shallow water, but it made no attempt to harm them despite such severe provocation.

class	**Mammalia**
order	**Cetacea**
family	**Delphinidae**
genus & species	*Orcinus orca* *killer whale*

◁ *Flukes aloft, a killer sounds with a minimum of splash—a tribute to its streamlining.*

△ *A killer pack surges round the edges of encroaching ice.* ▽ *Killer curiosity.*

*Grey whale **Eschrichtius glaucus**.*

Grey whale

At one time the Californian grey whale lived in the Atlantic Ocean, for its remains have been found in reclaimed land in the Zuider Zee. Now it is confined to the North Pacific where there are populations on both sides of that ocean.

It is a rather unusual whale, having points in common with both the rorqual (family Balaenopteridae) and right whales (family Balaenidae). It is about the size of the right whales, reaching 45 ft long and 20 tons in weight. The flukes of the tail are proportionally longer and more delicate than those of right whales, but more stubby than those of rorquals. The dorsal fin is replaced by 8−10 small humps along the tail just in front of the flukes. On the throat the grey whale has 2−3, rarely 4, grooves extending a short distance as compared with the 40−100 grooves extending to the belly in rorquals and the complete absence of grooves in right whales.

As the name implies, the grey whale is usually dark slate-grey but it may sometimes be blackish. It is lighter on the belly than on the back, as is usual in marine animals. Many grey whales have crescent-shaped marks or patches on the skin, especially on the back. These are caused either by lampreys or by barnacles.

Sluggish swimmers

Grey whales are very slow, usually swimming at 2−3 knots with bursts of 6−7 knots when alarmed, compared with 20 knots of a fin whale. As they also come very close inshore this makes them very vulnerable to hunters. In early spring the grey whales migrate down the west coast of North America. In 1840 there were estimated to be around 25 000 grey whales but soon after this there was very intense hunting all along the coast. By 1875 it was unusual to see more than 50 migrating whales at a time, although they used to be seen by the thousand. While the whales were in the Arctic Ocean they

were hunted by Eskimos; in the Bay of Vancouver and around the Queen Charlotte Islands they were attacked by Indians from canoes, and farther south the Yankee whalers chased them in sailing boats.

Dog food or tourist bait?

By 1936 the world population was thought to be as low as 100−200. Then the governments of America, Japan and Russia came to an agreement on the future of the grey whale and declared it a protected species. This protection, together with the animal's fairly high rate of reproduction, has resulted in a gradual build-up of the population and it is now thought that they number between 5 and 10 thousand. But the grey whale's future is still dubious: it has recently been reported that the Mexican government is planning to kill grey whales when they migrate south to Mexican water, the idea being to use the carcasses as dog food. This is a short-sighted plan: far more could be made out of tourism, for each year thousands of tourists gather on the west coast to watch the grey whales come down from the Bering Sea to give birth to their calves in the shallow and sheltered coastal waters of California and Mexico.

Straining out their food

Like the rarer blue whale the grey whales collect their food by means of rows of baleen plates in their mouths. Various crustaceans and molluscs floating in the sea are eaten in this manner.

Swimming south to breed

The migration of the grey whale is one of the better known aspects of its behaviour. They spend the summer months in the far north, principally in the Bering Sea, where they live in mixed herds. As summer draws to a close they swim slowly southwards and come in close to the coast, particularly so when they approach California where they can be seen swimming only a mile or so offshore. Here the herds segregate; the females stay together and led by an older cow come really close into the bays and lagoons where they get shelter from the weather to give birth to the calves. These are usually born at about the end of January, measuring

about 15 ft in length and weighing around 1 500 lb. Normally only a single calf is produced but twin births have been recorded, the calves suckling for about 9−10 months. As spring approaches the migration is reversed. The males, who have been waiting in deeper water, join the females with their newborn calves and the herds make their way back to the northern oceans to feed again in the colder waters where food is more abundant.

Chivalrous males

It has sometimes been noticed that grey whales show a one-sided faithfulness. If a female is injured or gets into difficulties one or more males may go to her aid, either to keep her at the surface where she can breathe, or to defend her from the attacks of killer whales. But if a male gets into similar difficulties, the females have been seen swimming away from the scene of trouble!

After man, killer whales are the greatest danger to grey whales. It is said that when a small school of grey whales are attacked by a large group of killers they may become so terrified by the attacks that they just float at the surface, belly uppermost, paralysed by fear and making themselves extremely vulnerable to further attack. The grey whales' habit of coming close inshore during the breeding season probably keeps them fairly clear of the attacks of killer whales who prefer deeper water. Sometimes grey whales have come so close inshore that they have practically run aground, and on one occasion a grey whale was seen playing about in the surf like a seal. They have also been found stranded at low tide, apparently without ill effect as they just floated off again at the next high water. This is most unusual since, for almost every other species of whale, stranding means death.

class	**Mammalia**
order	**Cetacea**
family	**Eschrichtidae**
genus	***Eschrichtius glaucus***
& species	*grey whale*

Index

This book is adapted from 'Purnell's Encyclopedia of Animal Life', published in the United States under the title of 'International Wild Life'. It has been produced by Phoebus Publishing Company in cooperation with Octopus Books Limited.
AFA: F G H Allen; E H Herbert, Geoffrey Kinns, A C Wheeler; J Allan Cash; Heather Angel; Toni Angermayer; R Apfelbach; Atlas: Drogesco; Australian News and Information Bureau; M E Bacchus; Barnabys; Bavaria: Sune Berkeman, W Harstrick, Helmut Heinpel, B Leidmann, W Rohdich, H W Silvester, A Sycholt; S Beaufoy; S Bisserôt; R Boardman; K Boldt; Michael Boorer; British Antarctic Survey; British Museum, Natural History; Alice Brown; Fred Bruemmer; Ralph Buchsbaum; Kent Burgess; Jane Burton; Robert Burton; H R Bustard; Colin Butler; N A Callow; Camera Press; Carolina Biological Supply Co; James Carr; Centre de Documentation du CNRS; A Christiansen; John Clegg; F Collet; Dolly Connelly; J A L Cooke; Gene Cox; Micro-colour Int.; Ben Cropp; Gerald Cubitt; Cyr Colour Agency; Peter David; W T Davidson; R B Davies; T Dennett; Colin Doeg; G T Dunger; Herman Eisenbeiss; André Fatras; Douglas Faulkner; Forestry, Fish & Game Commission, USA; Harry & Claudy Frauca; J B Free; Carl Gans; G S Giacomelli; John Goddard; E Grave; Hans Gundel; W D Haacke; H Hansen; R A Harris & K R Duff; Bruce Hayward; Robert C Hermes; Peter Hill; M J Hirons; E S Hobson; W Hoflinger; E O Hoppe; Eric Hosking; Chris Howell-Jones; David Hughes; G E Hyde; Jacana: Brosset, A R Devez, J & M Fievel, Gerard, P Summ, B Tollu, J P Varin, P & C Vasselet, J Vasserot, Bel G Vienne, A Visage; Roy Jarris; Michael Johns; Palle Johnsen; Peter Johnson; Keystone; G E Kirkpatrick; E F Kilian; H Klingel; A B Klots; A Kress; H V Lacey; Yves Lanceau; Leonard Lee Rue III; Henning Lender; D B Lewis; E Lindsey; H A E Lucas; Wolfgang Lummer; Michael Lyster; Kendall McDonald; Malcolm McGregor; Steve McGutcheon; Mansell; Aldo Margiocco; Marineland, Florida, USA; John Markham; Meston; Walter Miles; Carl Mills; Lorus & Margery Milne; G Mundey; N Myers; Natural History Museum; K B Newman; NHPA: Andrew Anderson, F Baillie, Anthony Bannister, F Blackburn, Joe Blossom, N A Callow, J M Clayton, Stephen Dalton, E Elkan, C McDermot, W J C Murray, Hugh Newman, Brian O'Donnell, Graham Pizzey, Gordon F Woods; Okapia; Oxford Scientific Films; Ram Panjabi; Klaus Paysan; B Pengilley; Photographic Library of Australia; Photo Library Inc; Photo Res: Des Bartlett, Jane Burton, Bob Campbell, C Ciapanna, Jack Dermid, Peter Jackson, Russ Kinne, N Myers, R T Peterson, D C Pike, Masood Quarishy, Dick Robinson, H W Silvester, Vincent Serventy, James Simon, Tomanek, Simon Trevor, Howard E Uible, Joe Van Wormer; Graham Pizzey; Joyce Pope; Popperfoto; Roebild; Root/Okapia; G Puppell; Walter Scheilhauer; Friedel Schox; Philippa Scott; Gunter Senfft; M Severn; Shell Photograph; H Shrempp; E Slater; M F Soper; South African Tourist Corporation: A J Southward; Helmut Stellrucht; W M Stephens; John Tashjian at Arizona Sonard Desert Museum, Fort Worth Zoo, San Diego Zoo, Steinhart Aquarium, Tacoma Aquarium, Vancouver Aquarium; Ron Taylor; Ronald Thompson; Sally Anne Thompson; Time Life Inc; William Vandivert; John Visser; J J Ward; P Ward; John Warham; Constance P Warner; A N Warren; Birgit Webb; We-Ha; Alison Wilson; D P Wilson; M A Wilson; Gene Wolfsheimer; John Norris Wood; Zoological Society, London.